American Heritage® and the eagle logo are registered trademarks of Forbes Inc. Their use is pursuant to a license agreement with Forbes Inc.

Words included in this book that are known to have current trademark registrations are shown with initial capital and are also identified as trademarks. No investigation has been made of common-law trademark rights in any word, because such investigation is impracticable. The inclusion of any word in this book is not, however, an expression of the Publisher's opinion as to whether or not it is subject to proprietary rights. Indeed, no word in this book is to be regarded as affecting the validity of any trademark.

Copyright © 2001 by Houghton Mifflin Company.
All rights reserved.

No part of this work may be reproduced or transmitted in any form or by any means, electronic or mechanical, including photocopying and recording, or by any information storage or retrieval system without the prior written permission of Houghton Mifflin Company unless such copying is expressly permitted by federal copyright law. Address inquiries to Reference Permissions, Houghton Mifflin Company, 222 Berkeley Street, Boston MA 02116.

Visit our website: www.houghtonmifflinbooks.com

ISBN 0-618-13216-3

Manufactured in the United States of America

STAFF/PERSONAL

Editors/Redacción
Priscila Baldoví, Evelyn Boria Rivera, Helen Bronk, Wade A. Ostrowski, David Pritchard, Hanna Schonthal

Production/Producción
Christopher Granniss, Christopher Leonesio

GUIDE

Alphabetical order of entries reflects international rules of alphabetization. Therefore, *ch* and *ll* are no longer considered separate letters of the Spanish alphabet. However, it is convenient to think of *ch* and *ll* as unique for the purposes of pronunciation (see Spanish Pronunciation Guide, next column).

Irregular verbs are referenced to the Spanish Verb Table (p. 2) with a boldface section number (e.g., **dar §12**). The number corresponds to the appropriate model verb in the Table.

Common idioms and phrases are listed as run-on entries at the appropriate part of speech. The first run-on is introduced by a solid square (■). Additional run-ons follow in alphabetical order and are separated by bold bullets (•). Idioms involving the plural usage of the entry word are introduced by a solid square followed by the plural label (■ *pl*).

GUÍA

Todos los vocablos están escritos en orden alfabético. Los vocablos compuestos escritos en forma abierta (**air conditioner**), con guión (**father-in-law**) o en forma sólida (**businesswoman**) están escritos como si fueran sólidos.

Verbos irregulares se indican con una estrella después del vocablo (p.e., **give***). El pretérito y el participio pasivo de estos verbos aparecen en la lista de Verbos Irregulares del Inglés (p. 2).

Modismos y locuciones de interés general aparecen en la parte de la oración a la que corresponden, precedidos por un cuadrado en negrilla (■), y separados en forma alfabética por el símbolo (•). Las locuciones que se usan en su forma plural se indican con un cuadrado en negrilla seguido por el rótulo plural (■ *pl*).

ABBREVIATIONS/ABREVIATURAS

adj	adjective/adjetivo	*indef*	indefinite/indefinido
adv	adverb/adverbio	*interj*	interjection/interjección
art	article/artículo	*intr*	intransitive/intransitivo
aux	auxiliary	JER.	jerga
COLL.	colloquial	*m, mpl*	masculine (plural)
conj	conjunction/conjunción	*pron*	pronoun/pronombre
contr	contraction/contracción	*reflex*	reflexive
def	definite/definido	*s, ssg, spl*	sustantivo (singular, plural)
f, fpl	feminine (plural)	SL.	slang
FAM.	familiar	*tr*	transitive/transitivo
FIG.	figurative		

(Other abbreviations, such as COMPUT. for "computers," are considered self-evident. / Otras abreviaturas, como COMPUT. para "computadoras," se consideran evidentes.)

SPANISH

Letter	Spanish Example	English Example	
a	pata	father	
b	boca	bib	At the beginning of a word
	rabo		Between vowels, closer to *v*
c	calco	cat	Before *a, o, u*, like *k*
	cedro	cedar	Before *e, i* like *s*; in much of Spain pronounced like *th* of *thick*
(ch)	chiste	church	
d	dar	die	At the beginning of a word
	cada		Between vowels, like *th* of *rather*
e	leche	café	
f	fácil	fat	
g	gente		Before *e, i*, like *h* of *ha!*
	guerra	guide	With *u* before *e, i*, a hard *g*
	gato	got	Before *a, o, u*, a hard *g*
h	honor		Always silent
i	silla	machine	
j	jugo		Like *h* in *ha!*
k	kilo	kite	
l	listo	list	
(ll)	llama		In Spain, like *lli* of *million*; elsewhere like Spanish consonant *y* (see below)
m	mamá	mum	
n	nona	none	
ñ	año		Like *ny* of *canyon*
o	solo	so	
p	papa	pipe	
q	quita	raquet	
r	caro		Like *dd* of *ladder*
(rr)	carro		Strongly trilled
s	soso	sass	
t	tonto	tight	
u	luto	lute	
	agüero	anguish	
v	vino		Identical to initial Spanish *b*
	lava		Identical to intervocalic Spanish *b*
w	wat		Pronounced either like English *v* or *w*
x	éxito	exit	Exception: in the words "México" and "mexicano" *x* is like Spanish *j*
	mixto		Before a consonant, may be pronounced *s*
y	y		Like *i* of *machine*
	yeso	yes	In River Plate, like *s* of *vision*
z	zona		Like *s* in *sass*; in much of Spain, like *th* of *thick*

GUÍA PARA LA PRONUNCIACIÓN INGLESA

letra	ejemplos y/o sonidos aproximados
a	pat (entre la *a* y la *e*); pay, mate (rey); care, hair (parecido a *ea* en *brea*, con la *r*); father (año); caught, paw (corre); swat (la)
b	bib (boca)
c	cat (casa); piece (sapo); church (chico); pick (casa)
d	deed, milled (dar); judge (entre la *y* inicial y la *ch*)
e	pet, feather (el); bee, me (mil); dear, mere (entre *ía* en *día* e *íe* en *fíe*, con la *r*); term (parecido a una *e* que tira a la *o*, con la *r*); few (ciudad)
f	fife (fama)
g	gag (gato); rough (fama)
h	hat (joya)
i	pit (entre la *i* y la *e*); piece (mil); pie, mice (aire); pier (entre *ía* en *día* e *íe* en *fíe*, con la *r*); firm (parecido a una *e* que tira a la *o*, con la *r*)
j	jump, major (entre la *y* inicial y la *ch*)
k	kid, make (casa)
l	lid, needle (luz)
m	mime (muy)
n	no, line, sudden (no); thing (inglés)
o	pot (la); toe, go, boat (solo); for (corre); noise, boy (oigo); took (parecido a la *u* en *yogur*, más breve); boot (uno); out, cow (auto); rough (parecido a una *o* que tira a la *a*)
p	pipe (pan); phase (fama)
q	quick (cuan); pique (casa)
r	roar (una *ere* con la lengua curvada hacia atrás)
s	saw, pass (sapo); ship, dish (una *che* suavizada, más como la *ese*); vision, pleasure (parecido a la *ll* de Argentina)
t	time, mate, stopped (tu); thin, path (parecido a la *ce* de Castilla); this, bathe (cada)
u	cut (parecido a una *o* que tira a la *a*); use (ciudad); urge (parecido a una *e* que tira a la *o*, con la *r*); suit (uno)
v	valve (una *efe* sonora)
w	with (cual); which (juez)
x	box, taxi (taxi); xylem (mismo)
y	yes (yo); by (aire)
z	zebra (mismo)

SPANISH VERB TABLE

The following list shows model conjugations for regular verbs and the most common irregular verbs. The tenses shown include the present indicative, imperfect, and preterit tenses and the past participle. Only tenses in which an irregular conjugation occurs are presented. Irregular forms are printed in bold type. Irregular verbs are referenced to the Table by means of section numbers; thus **despedir** §32 follows the model conjugations given at §32 PEDIR in the Table.

§01 REGULAR VERBS

-AR Verbs: AMAR	-ER Verbs: VENDER	-IR Verbs: PARTIR
Present		
AM -o	VEND -o	PART-o
-as	-es	-es
-a	-e	-e
-amos	-emos	-imos
-áis	-éis	-ís
-an	-en	-en
Imperfect		
AM -aba	VEND -ía	PART-ía
-abas	-ías	-ías
-aba	-ía	-ía
-ábamos	-íamos	-íamos
-abais	-íais	-íais
-aban	-ían	-ían
Preterit		
AM -é	VEND -í	PART-í
-aste	-iste	-iste
-ó	-ió	-ió
-amos	-imos	-imos
-asteis	-isteis	-isteis
-aron	-ieron	-ieron
Past Participle		
amado	vendido	partido

IRREGULAR VERBS

§02 ALZAR Pret. **alcé**, alzaste, etc.
§03 ANDAR Pret. **anduve, anduviste, anduvo, anduvimos, anduvisteis, anduvieron**
§04 AVERGONZAR Pres. **avergüenzo, avergüenzas, avergüenza**, avergonzamos, avergonzáis, **avergüenzan** Pret. **avergoncé**, avergonzaste, etc.
§05 AVERIGUAR Pret. **averigüé**, averiguaste, etc.
§06 CABER Pres. **quepo**, cabes, etc. Pret. **cupe, cupiste, cupo, cupimos, cupisteis, cupieron**
§07 CAER Pres. **caigo**, caes, etc. Pret. **caí, caíste, cayó, caímos, caísteis, cayeron** Past Part. **caído**
§08 COLGAR Pres. **cuelgo, cuelgas, cuelga**, colgamos, colgáis, **cuelgan** Pret. **colgué**, colgaste, etc.
§09 CONOCER Pres. **conozco**, conoces, etc.
§10 CONSTRUIR Pres. **construyo, construyes, construye**, construimos, construís, **construyen** Pret. construí, construiste, **construyó**, construimos, construisteis, **construyeron**
§11 CONTAR Pres. **cuento, cuentas, cuenta**, contamos, contáis, **cuentan**
§12 DAR Pres. **doy**, das, etc. Pret. **di, diste, dio, dimos, disteis, dieron**
§13 DECIR Pres. **digo, dices, dice**, decimos, decís, **dicen** Past Part. **dicho**
§14 DEDUCIR Pres. **deduzco**, deduces, etc. Pret. **deduje, dedujiste, dedujo, dedujimos, dedujisteis, dedujeron**
§15 DISTINGUIR Pres. **distingo**, distingues, etc.
§16 DORMIR Pres. **duermo, duermes, duerme**, dormimos, dormís, **duermen** Pret. dormí, dormiste, **durmió**, dormimos, dormisteis, **durmieron**
§17 EMPEZAR Pres. **empiezo, empiezas, empieza**, empezamos, empezáis, **empiezan** Pret. **empecé**, empezaste, etc.
§18 ENVIAR Pres. **envío, envías, envía**, enviamos, enviáis, **envían**
§19 ERIGIR Pres. **erijo**, eriges, etc.
§20 ESCOGER Pres. **escojo**, escoges, etc.
§21 ESTAR Pres. **estoy, estás, está**, estamos, estáis, **están** Pret. **estuve, estuviste, estuvo, estuvimos, estuvisteis, estuvieron**
§22 FORZAR Pres. **fuerzo, fuerzas, fuerza**, forzamos, forzáis, **fuerzan** Pret. **forcé**, forzaste, etc.
§23 HABER Pres. **he, has, ha, hemos**, habéis, **han** Pret. **hube, hubiste, hubo, hubimos, hubisteis, hubieron**
§24 HACER Pres. **hago**, haces, etc. Pret. **hice, hiciste, hizo, hicimos, hicisteis, hicieron** Past Part. **hecho**
§25 IR Pres. **voy, vas, va, vamos, vais, van** Imp. **iba**, etc. Pret. **fui, fuiste, fue, fuimos, fuisteis, fueron**
§26 JUGAR Pres. **juego, juegas, juega**, jugamos, jugáis, **juegan** Pret. **jugué**, jugaste, etc.
§27 LEER Pret. **leí, leiste, leyó, leímos, leísteis, leyeron**
§28 LUCIR Pres. **luzco**, luces, etc.
§29 OÍR Pres. **oigo, oyes, oye, oímos**, oís, **oyen** Pret. **oí, oíste, oyó, oímos, oísteis, oyeron** Past Part. **oído**
§30 OLER Pres. **huelo, hueles, huele**, olemos, oléis, **huelen**
§31 PAGAR Pres. **pagué**, pagas, etc.
§32 PEDIR Pres. **pido, pides, pide**, pedimos, pedís, **piden** Pret. pedí, pediste, **pidió**, pedimos, pedisteis, **pidieron**
§33 PENSAR Pres. **pienso, piensas, piensa**, pensamos, pensáis, **piensan**
§34 PERDER Pres. **pierdo, pierdes, pierde**, perdemos, perdéis, **pierden**
§35 PLEGAR Pres. **pliego, pliegas, pliega**, plegamos, plegáis, **pliegan** Pret. **plegué**, plegaste, etc.
§36 PODER Pres. **puedo, puedes, puede**, podemos, podéis, **pueden** Pret. **pude, pudiste, pudo, pudimos, pudisteis, pudieron**
§37 PONER Pres. **pongo**, pones, etc. Pret. **puse, pusiste, puso, pusimos, pusisteis, pusieron** Past Part. **puesto**
§38 QUERER Pres. **quiero, quieres, quiere**, queremos, queréis, **quieren** Pret. **quise, quisiste, quiso, quisimos, quisisteis, quisieron**
§39 REÍR Pres. **río, ríes, ríe, reímos**, reís, **ríen** Pret. **reí, reíste, rió, reímos, reísteis, rieron** Past Part. **reído**
§40 SABER Pres. **sé**, sabes, etc. Pret. **supe, supiste, supo, supimos, supisteis, supieron**
§41 SALIR Pres. **salgo**, sales, etc.
§42 SEGUIR Pres. **sigo, sigues, sigue**, seguimos, seguís, **siguen** Pret. seguí, seguiste, **siguió**, seguimos, seguisteis, **siguieron**
§43 SENTIR Pres. **siento, sientes, siente**, sentimos, sentís, **sienten** Pret. sentí, sentiste, **sintió**, sentimos, sentisteis, **sintieron**
§44 SER Pres. **soy, eres, es, somos, sois, son** Imp. **era**, etc. Pret. **fui, fuiste, fue, fuimos, fuisteis, fueron**
§45 SITUAR Pres. **sitúo, sitúas, sitúa**, situamos, situáis, **sitúan**
§46 TENER Pres. **tengo, tienes, tiene**, tenemos, tenéis, **tienen** Pret. **tuve, tuviste, tuvo, tuvimos, tuvisteis, tuvieron**
§47 TOCAR Pret. **toqué**, tocaste, etc.
§48 TORCER Pres. **tuerzo, tuerces, tuerce**, torcemos, torcéis, **tuercen**
§49 TRAER Pres. **traigo**, traes, etc. Pret. **traje, trajiste, trajo, trajimos, trajisteis, trajeron** Past Part. **traído**
§50 VALER Pres. **valgo**, vales, etc.
§51 VENCER Pres. **venzo**, vences, etc.
§52 VENIR Pres. **vengo, vienes, viene**, venimos, venís, **vienen** Pret. **vine, viniste, vino, vinimos, vinisteis, vinieron**
§53 VER Pres. **veo**, ves, etc. Imp. **veía**, etc. Pret. **vi**, viste, **vio**, vimos, visteis, vieron Past Part. **visto**
§54 VOLVER Pres. **vuelvo, vuelves, vuelve**, volvemos, volvéis, **vuelven**
§55 IRREGULAR PAST PARTICIPLES
The following verbs are regular except for their past participles: abrir **abierto**; cubrir **cubierto**; escribir **escrito**; freír **frito**; imprimir **impreso**; romper **roto**

VERBOS IRREGULARES DEL INGLÉS

La siguiente lista de verbos da el infinitivo, el pretérito y el participio pasivo de los verbos irregulares del inglés.

abide	abided *o* abode, abided *o* abode
arise	arose, arisen
awake	awoke, awaked
be	was, been
bear	bore, born *o* borne
beat	beat, beaten *o* beat
begin	began, begun
bend	bent, bent
bet	bet *o* betted, bet *o* betted
bid	bade *o* bid, bidden *o* bid
bind	bound, bound
bite	bit, bitten
bleed	bled, bled
blend	blended *o* blent, blended *o* blent
bless	blessed *o* blest, blessed *o* blessed
blow	blew, blown
break	broke, broken
breed	bred, bred
bring	brought, brought
build	built, built
burn	burned *o* burnt, burned *o* burnt
buy	bought, bought
cast	cast, cast
catch	caught, caught
choose	chose, chosen
cling	clung, clung
come	came, come
cost	cost, cost
creep	crept, crept
crow	crowed *o* crew, crowed
curse	cursed *o* curst, cursed *o* curst
cut	cut, cut
deal	dealt, dealt
dig	dug, dug
dive	dived *o* dove, dived
do	did, done
draw	drew, drawn
dream	dreamed *o* dreamt, dreamed *o* dreamt
drink	drank, drunk
drive	drove, driven
dwell	dwelled *o* dwelt, dwelled *o* dwelt
eat	ate, eaten
fall	fell, fallen
feed	fed, fed
feel	felt, felt
fight	fought, fought
find	found, found
flee	fled, fled
fling	flung, flung
fly	flew, flown
freeze	froze, frozen
get	got, got *o* gotten
give	gave, given
go	went, gone
grind	ground, ground
grow	grew, grown
hang	hung, hung
have	had, had
hear	heard, heard
hide	hid, hidden *o* hid
hit	hit, hit
hold	held, held
hurt	hurt, hurt
keep	kept, kept
kneel	knelt *o* kneeled, knelt *o* kneeled
knit	knit *o* knitted, knit *o* knitted
know	knew, known
lay	laid, laid
lead	led, led
lean	leaned *o* leant, leaned *o* leant
leap	leaped *o* leapt, leaped *o* leapt
learn	learned *o* learnt, learned *o* learnt
leave	left, left
lend	lent, lent
let	let, let
lie	lay, lain
light	lighted *o* lit, lighted *o* lit
lose	lost, lost
make	made, made
mean	meant, meant
meet	met, met
mow	mowed, mowed *o* mown
pay	paid, paid
prove	proved, proved *o* proven
put	put, put
quit	quit *o* quitted, quit *o* quitted
read	read, read
rid	rid *o* ridded, rid *o* ridded
ride	rode, ridden
ring	rang, rung
rise	rose, risen
run	ran, run
saw	sawed, sawed *o* sawn
say	said, said
see	saw, seen
seek	sought, sought
sell	sold, sold
send	sent, sent
set	set, set
sew	sewed, sewn *o* sewed
shake	shook, shaken
shave	shaved, shaved *o* shaven
shed	shed, shed
shine	shone *o* shined, shone *o* shined
shoe	shod, shod *o* shodden
shoot	shot, shot
show	showed, shown *o* showed
shrink	shrank *o* shrunk, shrunk *o* shrunken
shut	shut, shut
sing	sang, sung
sink	sank *o* sunk, sunk
sit	sat, sat
slay	slew, slain
sleep	slept, slept
slide	slid, slid
sling	slung, slung
slit	slit, slit
smell	smelled *o* smelt, smelled *o* smelt
sow	sowed, sown *o* sowed
speak	spoke, spoken
speed	sped *o* speeded, sped *o* speeded
spend	spent, spent
spill	spilled *o* spilt, spilled *o* spilt
spin	spun, spun
spit	spat *o* spit, spat *o* spit
split	split, split
spoil	spoiled *o* spoilt, spoiled *o* spoilt
spread	spread, spread
spring	sprang *o* sprung, sprung
stand	stood, stood
steal	stole, stolen
stick	stuck, stuck
sting	stung, stung
stink	stank *o* stunk, stunk
strew	strewed, strewed *o* strewn
stride	strode, stridden
strike	struck, struck *o* stricken
string	strung, strung
strive	strove *o* strived, striven *o* strived
swear	swore, sworn
sweat	sweat *o* sweated, sweat *o* sweated
sweep	swept, swept
swell	swelled, swelled *o* swollen
swim	swam, swum
swing	swung, swung
take	took, taken
teach	taught, taught
tear	tore, torn
tell	told, told
think	thought, thought
thrive	throve *o* thrived, thrived *o* thriven
throw	threw, thrown
thrust	thrust, thrust
tread	trod, trodden *o* trod
wake	woke *o* waked, waked *o* woken
wear	wore, worn
weave	wove *o* weaved, woven *o* weaved
weep	wept, wept
wet	wet *o* wetted, wet *o* wetted
win	won, won
wind	wound, wound
wrap	wrapt *o* wrapped, wrapt *o* wrapped
wring	wrung, wrung
write	wrote, written

Spanish/English
A

a ➤ *prep* to, into • **a las dos** at two o'clock • **a pie** on foot • **a poco** after a while • **a 3 de Mayo** on May 3 • **mirar al sur** look to the south • **voy a la tienda** I'm going to the store • **llegó a Lima** she arrived in Lima.

abad ➤ *m* abbot.

abadesa ➤ *f* abbess.

abadía ➤ *f* abbey.

abajo ➤ *adv* down; (*en casa*) downstairs; (*posición*) below, underneath ■ **hacia a.** downwards.

abandonar ➤ *tr* to abandon, desert; (*desertar*) to leave; (*renunciar*) to give up ➤ *reflex* (*entregarse a*) to abandon oneself to; (*descuidarse*) to become slovenly.

abandono ➤ *m* abandonment; (*descuido*) neglect; (*desenfrenamiento*) abandon.

abanico ➤ *m* fan.

abaratar ➤ *tr* to reduce (prices).

abarcar §47 ➤ *tr* (*contener*) to include, cover; (*abrazar*) to embrace; (*divisar*) to take in.

abarrotado, a ➤ *adj* full, crowded.

abarrotar ➤ *tr* (*llenar*) to fill up; (*exceso*) to overstock.

abarrotes ➤ *mpl* AMER. (*comestibles*) groceries.

abastecedor, a ➤ *mf* supplier.

abastecer §09 ➤ *tr* to supply, provide (*de* with).

abastecimiento ➤ *m* (*provisión*) supply; (*aprovisionamiento*) supplying.

abasto ➤ *m* supplying ■ *pl* supplies, provisions.

abatido, a ➤ *adj* despondent.

abatir ➤ *tr* (*derribar*) to knock down, demolish; (*desanimar*) to depress.

abdicar §47 ➤ *tr & intr* to abdicate.

abdomen ➤ *m* abdomen.

abdominal ➤ *adj* abdominal.

abecedario ➤ *m* alphabet.

abedul ➤ *m* birch.

abeja ➤ *f* bee.

abejorro ➤ *m* bumblebee; (*pesado*) pest.

abertura ➤ *f* opening; (*hendidura*) crack; PHOTOG. aperture.

abeto ➤ *m* fir.

abierto, a ➤ *adj* open; (*raso*) open, clear; (*franco*) candid; (*sincero*) sincere.

abigarrado, a ➤ *adj* variegated, multicolored.

abismal ➤ *adj* abysmal.

abismo ➤ *m* abyss.

abjurar ➤ *tr* to abjure, renounce.

ablandamiento ➤ *m* softening.

ablandar ➤ *tr* to soften; (*suavizar*) to mollify; (*mitigar*) to mitigate ➤ *intr* (*la nieve*) to thaw ➤ *reflex* to soften.

abnegación ➤ *f* abnegation.

abnegar §35 ➤ *tr* to abnegate, renounce ➤ *reflex* to deny oneself.

abofetear ➤ *tr* to slap.

abogacía ➤ *f* law (profession).

abogado, a ➤ *mf* lawyer, attorney.

abolengo ➤ *m* ancestry, lineage; (*patrimonio*) inheritance.

abolición ➤ *f* abolition, repeal.

abolicionista ➤ *mf* abolitionist.

abolir ➤ *tr* to abolish, repeal.

abolladura ➤ *f* dent.

abollar ➤ *tr* to dent.

abominable ➤ *adj* abominable, detestable.

abominar ➤ *tr* to detest.

abonado, a ➤ *mf* subscriber, season ticket holder; (*viajero*) commuter.

abonar ➤ *tr* to vouch for, guarantee; AGR. to fertilize; (*pagar*) to pay ➤ *reflex* to subscribe.

abono ➤ *m* fertilizer; (*billete*) subscription; AMER. payment, installment.

abordar ➤ *tr* MARIT. to board; (*acercar*) to approach; (*emprender*) to tackle (a problem) ➤ *intr* MARIT. to dock.

aborigen ➤ *adj & mf* aboriginal.

aborrecer §09 ➤ *tr* to hate, abhor.

aborrecimiento ➤ *m* hatred, loathing.

abortar ➤ *tr & intr* to abort.

aborto ➤ *m* abortion.

abotonar ➤ *tr & reflex* to button (up) ➤ *intr* to bud.

abovedado ➤ *m* ARCHIT. vaulting.

abrasar ➤ *tr* (*quemar*) to burn; (*calentar*) to overheat. ➤ *intr & reflex* to burn up.

abrazar §02 ➤ *tr* to embrace, hug;

(*adoptar*) to adopt ➤ *reflex* to embrace (each other).

abrazo ➤ *m* embrace, hug.

abrelatas ➤ *m* can opener.

abrevadero ➤ *m* watering hole *or* trough.

abreviado, a ➤ *adj* brief, short; (*libros*) abridged.

abreviar ➤ *tr* (*reducir*) to abbreviate; (*libros*) to abridge; (*acelerar*) to shorten, hasten.

abreviatura ➤ *f* abbreviation; (*compendio*) compendium, résumé.

abrigar §31 ➤ *tr* (*proteger*) to shelter; (*cubrir*) to keep warm; (*sospechas*) to harbor ➤ *reflex* to wrap oneself up.

abrigo ➤ *m* (*protección*) shelter, cover; (*sobretodo*) overcoat.

abril ➤ *m* April.

abrir §55 ➤ *tr* to open; (*desplegar*) to spread out; (*empezar*) to begin; (*encabezar*) to lead, head.

abrochar ➤ *tr* (*con botones*) to button (up); (*con broches*) to fasten.

abrogar §31 ➤ *tr* to abrogate, repeal.

abrojo ➤ *m* thistle.

abrumador, a ➤ *adj* overwhelming.

abrumar ➤ *tr* to overwhelm, oppress ➤ *reflex* to become foggy.

abrupto, a ➤ *adj* abrupt; (*escarpado*) craggy.

absceso ➤ *m* abscess.

absolución ➤ *f* absolution.

absoluto, a ➤ *adj* absolute; (*sin mezcla*) pure (alcohol) ■ **en a.** absolutely not, not at all • **lo a.** the absolute ➤ *f* (*proposición*) absolute.

absolver §54 ➤ *tr* to absolve; LAW to acquit.

absorbente ➤ *adj* absorbent; FIG. absorbing.

absorber ➤ *tr* to absorb ➤ *reflex* to become absorbed *or* engrossed.

absorción ➤ *f* absorption.

abstemio, a ➤ *adj* abstemious, teetotaling ➤ *mf* teetotaler, non-drinker.

abstención ➤ *f* abstention.

abstenerse §46 ➤ *reflex* to abstain.

abstinencia ➤ *f* abstinence.

abstracto, a ➤ *adj & m* abstract.

abstraer §49 ➤ *tr* to abstract ➤ *reflex* to become withdrawn *or* lost in thought.

abstraído, a ➤ *adj* (*distraído*) absorbed; (*retirado*) withdrawn.

absurdidad ➤ *f* absurdity.

absurdo, a ➤ *adj* absurd, ridiculous ➤ *m* absurdity.

abuela ➤ *f* grandmother.

abuelo ➤ *m* grandfather ■ *pl* grandparents.

abultado, a ➤ *adj* large, bulky.

abultar ➤ *tr* (*engrosar*) to enlarge; (*hinchar*) to swell ➤ *intr* to be bulky.

abundancia ➤ *f* abundance.

abundante ➤ *adj* abundant, plentiful.

abundar ➤ *intr* to abound.

aburrido, a ➤ *adj* (*cansado*) bored; (*tedioso*) boring.

aburrir ➤ *tr* to bore ➤ *reflex* to become bored.

abusador, a ➤ *adj* AMER. abusive ➤ *mf* abuser.

abusar ➤ *intr* to go too far, exceed ■ **a. de** to abuse, misuse.

abuso ➤ *m* abuse, excess ■ **a. de alcohol** alcohol abuse • **a. sexual** sexual abuse.

acá ➤ *adv* here, over here ■ **a. y allá** here and there, everywhere • **más a.** closer.

acabado, a ➤ *adj* finished; (*perfecto*) complete, consummate ➤ *m* finish.

acabar ➤ *tr* to finish, complete; (*perfeccionar*) to put the finishing touches on; (*consumir*) to use up ➤ *intr* to end, stop ■ **a. de** to have just • **a. por** to end up ➤ *reflex* to end, terminate • **¡se acabó!** that's the end of that! • **se me acabó el tiempo** I ran out of time.

academia ➤ *f* academy.

académico, a ➤ *adj* academic ➤ *mf* academician.

acallar ➤ *tr* to hush, quiet.

acalorado, a ➤ *adj* heated, warm; (*enardecido*) heated, animated.

acalorar ➤ *tr* to warm up ➤ *reflex* to heat up; (*irritarse*) to get excited.

acampanado, a ➤ *adj* bell-shaped.

acampar ➤ *tr, intr, & reflex* to camp.

acantilado, a ➤ *adj* steep ➤ *m* cliff.

acaparar ➤ *tr* (*acumular*) to stockpile, hoard; (*monopolizar*) to monopolize.

acápite ➤ *m* S. AMER. (*párrafo*) paragraph; (*subtítulo*) subheading.

acariciar ➤ *tr* to caress; (*abrigar*) to

cherish.

acarrear ➤ *tr* to cart, transport.

acaso ➤ *m* chance ➤ *adv* perhaps, maybe ■ **por si a.** just in case.

acatamiento ➤ *m* respect, reverence.

acatar ➤ *tr* (*respetar*) to respect; (*obedecer*) to observe, comply with.

acatarrarse ➤ *reflex* to catch a cold.

acaudalado, a ➤ *adj* wealthy, rich.

acceder ➤ *intr* to agree; (*al trono*) to accede.

acceso ➤ *m* (*entrada*) access, entry; (*accesibilidad*) accessibility.

accesorio, a ➤ *adj & m* accessory.

accidentado, a ➤ *adj* rough, uneven.

accidental ➤ *adj* accidental.

accidente ➤ *m* accident; (*del terreno*) roughness, unevenness ■ **por a.** by chance.

acción ➤ *f* action; (*hecho*) act, deed; (*efecto*) effect; (*judicial*) legal action, lawsuit; COM. share (of stock).

accionar ➤ *tr* to work, operate.

accionista ➤ *mf* shareholder, stockholder.

acechar ➤ *tr* to watch, spy on.

acecho ➤ *m* watching, spying.

aceitar ➤ *tr* to oil, lubricate.

aceite ➤ *m* oil ■ **a. vegetal** vegetable oil.

aceituna ➤ *f* olive.

acelerador ➤ *m* accelerator.

acelerar ➤ *tr* to speed up ➤ *intr* to hurry; (*motores*) to race.

acento ➤ *m* accent; (*signo*) accent mark; (*tono*) tone.

acentuar §45 ➤ *tr* to accent; (*hacer resaltar*) to accentuate ➤ *reflex* to stand out.

acepción ➤ *f* meaning.

aceptar ➤ *tr* to accept; (*admitir*) to believe in; (*aprobar*) to approve of.

acequia ➤ *f* irrigation ditch.

acera ➤ *f* sidewalk.

acerca de ➤ *prep* about, concerning.

acercar §47 ➤ *tr* to bring near ➤ *reflex* to approach, draw near.

acero ➤ *m* steel; (*arma*) blade, sword.

acérrimo, a ➤ *adj* staunch, stalwart.

acertado, a ➤ *adj* correct, accurate.

acertar §33 ➤ *tr* (*adivinar*) to guess correctly; (*encontrar*) to find, hit upon ➤ *intr* (*tener razón*) to hit the mark, be correct.

acertijo ➤ *m* riddle.

acetato ➤ *m* acetate.

acetona ➤ *f* acetone.

achacar §47 ➤ *tr* to attribute, to impute.

achaque ➤ *m* ailment, illness.

achicar §47 ➤ *tr* (*disminuir*) to reduce; (*humillar*) to humiliate; (*ropa*) to take in.

acicalado, a ➤ *adj* spruced up.

acicalar ➤ *tr & reflex* to dress or spruce up.

acidez ➤ *f* acidity.

ácido, a ➤ *adj* acid; (*agrio*) sour, tart ➤ *m* acid.

acierto ➤ *m* (*logro*) good shot, hit; (*éxito*) success; (*cordura*) good sense; (*habilidad*) skill.

aclaración ➤ *f* clarification.

aclarar ➤ *tr* to clarify; (*explicar*) to explain; (*aguar*) to thin; (*enjuagar*) to rinse ➤ *intr* (*clarear*) to clear up.

aclimatar ➤ *tr* to acclimatize, acclimate.

acné ➤ *f* acne.

acobardar ➤ *tr* to intimidate ➤ *reflex* to become intimidated.

acogedor, a ➤ *adj* (*cordial*) welcoming; (*cómodo*) inviting, cozy.

acoger §20 ➤ *tr* (*dar bienvenida*) to welcome; (*amparar*) to shelter ➤ *reflex* to take refuge ■ **a. a** to resort to.

acogida ➤ *f* reception, welcome.

acolchado, a ➤ *adj* padded, quilted ➤ *m* (*relleno*) padding; ARG. bedspread.

acometer ➤ *tr* to attack; (*intentar*) to undertake; (*dominar*) to overcome.

acometida ➤ *f* attack, assault.

acomodado, a ➤ *adj* (*rico*) well-off.

acomodador, a ➤ *mf* usher.

acomodar ➤ *tr* (*arreglar*) to arrange; (*adaptar*) to adapt; (*colocar*) to accommodate ➤ *intr* to suit ➤ *reflex* AMER. to set oneself up.

acomodo ➤ *m* (*alojamiento*) lodgings.

acompañamiento ➤ *m* accompaniment; (*comitiva*) retinue.

acompañante, a ➤ *adj* accompanying ➤ *mf* companion; MUS. accompanist.

acompañar ➤ *tr* to accompany; (*agre-*

gar) to enclose ■ **a. en el sentimiento** to express one's condolences.

acondicionado, a ➤ *adj* conditioned ■ **aire a.** air-conditioning.

acondicionador ➤ *m* conditioner ■ **a. de aire** air conditioner.

acondicionar ➤ *tr* (*disponer*) to prepare; (*reparar*) to repair; (*el aire*) to air-condition.

aconsejar ➤ *tr* to advise, counsel.

acontecer §09 ➤ *intr* to happen, occur.

acontecimiento ➤ *m* event, occurrence.

acopiar ➤ *tr* to gather, collect.

acordado, a ➤ *adj* agreed (upon).

acordar §11 ➤ *tr* (*concordar*) to agree; (*decidir*) to decide; AMER. to grant ➤ *intr* to go together ➤ *reflex* (*recordar*) to remember; (*convenir*) to agree.

acorde ➤ *adj* in agreement ➤ *m* chord.

acordeón ➤ *m* accordion.

acorralar ➤ *tr* (*encerrar*) to pen; (*atrapar*) to corner.

acortar ➤ *tr* to shorten ➤ *reflex* to become shorter.

acosar ➤ *tr* (*perseguir*) to harass.

acostado, a ➤ *adj* in bed, lying down.

acostar §11 ➤ *tr* to put to bed ➤ *reflex* to go to bed.

acostumbrado, a ➤ *adj* accustomed *or* used (*a* to); (*habitual*) customary.

acostumbrar ➤ *tr & reflex* to accustom (oneself) ➤ *intr* to get accustomed.

acotar ➤ *tr* (*anotar*) to annotate; (*notar*) to remark; (*admitir*) to admit.

acre[1] ➤ *m* acre.

acre[2] ➤ *adj* acrid.

acrecentar §33 ➤ *tr* (*aumentar*) to increase; (*avanzar*) to promote.

acreditado, a ➤ *adj* accredited; (*ilustre*) reputable.

acreditar ➤ *tr* (*embajador*) to accredit; (*asegurar*) guarantee, vouch for.

acreedor, a ➤ *mf* creditor.

acribillar ➤ *tr* (*agujerear*) to riddle (*a* with); (*molestar*) to hound.

acrílico, a ➤ *adj & mf* acrylic.

acróbata ➤ *mf* acrobat.

acta ➤ *f* (*informe*) record; (*minutas*) minutes.

actitud ➤ *f* attitude.

activar ➤ *tr* to activate; (*acelerar*) to expedite.

actividad ➤ *f* activity.

activo, a ➤ *adj* active ➤ *m* COM. assets.

acto ➤ *m* act; (*acción*) action.

actor ➤ *m* actor.

actriz ➤ *f* actress.

actuación ➤ *f* performance; (*acción*) action.

actual ➤ *adj* present-day, current.

actualidad ➤ *f* present (time); current situation ■ **en la a.** nowadays ➤ *pl* news, current events.

actualizar §02 ➤ *tr* to modernize, update; COMPUT. to upgrade.

actualmente ➤ *adv* at present, nowadays.

actuar §45 ➤ *tr* to act.

acuarela ➤ *f* water color.

acuario ➤ *m* aquarium.

acuático, a ➤ *adj* aquatic.

acudir ➤ *intr* (*presentarse*) to go, come.

acueducto ➤ *m* aqueduct.

acuerdo ➤ *m* (*convenio*) agreement, accord ■ **de a. con** in agreement *or* accordance with.

acumular ➤ *tr* to accumulate, gather.

acunar ➤ *tr* to rock, cradle.

acuñar ➤ *tr* (*monedas*) to coin, mint.

acupuntura ➤ *f* acupuncture.

acurrucarse §47 ➤ *reflex* to curl up.

acusación ➤ *f* accusation, charge.

acusado, a ➤ *adj & mf* accused.

acusar ➤ *tr* to accuse.

acústico, a ➤ *adj* acoustic(al) ➤ *f* acoustics.

adaptar ➤ *tr & reflex* to adapt (oneself).

adecuado, a ➤ *adj* (*apropiado*) appropriate, suitable; (*suficiente*) adequate, sufficient.

adelantado, a ➤ *adj* (*precoz*) precocious, advanced; (*reloj*) fast ■ **por a.** in advance.

adelantar ➤ *tr* to advance, move forward; (*acelerar*) to speed up; (*aventajar*) to surpass; AUTO. to overtake, pass ➤ *intr* to advance; (*relojes*) to be fast; FIG. (*progresar*) to make progress ➤ *reflex* ■ **a. a** to get ahead of.

adelante ➤ *adv* forward, ahead ■ **¡a.!** come in! • **de aquí en a.** from now on • **más a.** farther on.

adelanto ➤ *m (de paga)* advance; *(progreso)* progress.

adelgazar §02 ➤ *intr* to lose weight, become slim.

ademán ➤ *m* gesture.

además ➤ *adv* besides, in addition.

adentro ➤ *adv* within, inside.

adherir §43 ➤ *intr & reflex (pegarse)* to stick, adhere.

adhesivo, a ➤ *adj & m* adhesive.

adición ➤ *f* addition; AMER. bill, check.

adicional ➤ *adj* additional, added.

adicto, a ➤ *adj* addicted; *(dedicado)* fond, attached ➤ *mf* addict; *(partidario)* follower.

adiestrado, a ➤ *adj* trained.

adiestrar ➤ *tr (instruir)* to train, coach; *(guiar)* to guide, lead.

adinerado, a ➤ *adj* wealthy, affluent.

adiós ➤ *interj & m* goodbye.

aditivo, a ➤ *adj & m* additive.

adivinanza ➤ *f* riddle, puzzle.

adivinar ➤ *tr* to predict; *(conjeturar)* to guess; *(resolver)* to solve.

adivino, a ➤ *mf* fortuneteller.

adjetivo, a ➤ *adj* adjectival ➤ *m* adjective.

adjudicar §47 ➤ *tr* to award ➤ *reflex* to appropriate (for oneself).

adjunto, a ➤ *adj* attached, enclosed; *(persona)* assistant, adjunct ➤ *mf* associate.

administración ➤ *f* administration, management.

administrador, a ➤ *mf* administrator, manager.

administrar ➤ *tr (dirigir)* to manage; *(conferir)* to administer.

administrativo, a ➤ *adj* administrative.

admiración ➤ *f* admiration; *(sorpresa)* surprise, wonder.

admirar ➤ *tr* to admire ➤ *reflex* to marvel at.

admisión ➤ *f* admission.

admitir ➤ *tr* to admit.

adobar ➤ *tr (aderezar)* to marinate; *(preservar)* to pickle.

adobe ➤ *m* adobe.

adobo ➤ *m* marinade, seasoning.

adolecer §09 ➤ *intr* to fall ill.

adolescencia ➤ *f* adolescence, youth.

adolescente ➤ *adj & mf* adolescent, youth.

adonde ➤ *conj* where.

adónde ➤ *adv* where ■ **¿a. vas?** where are you going?

adopción ➤ *f* adoption.

adoptar ➤ *tr* to adopt.

adoptivo, a ➤ *adj* adoptive, adopted.

adoquinado ➤ *m* pavement.

adoración ➤ *f* adoration, worship.

adorar ➤ *tr & intr* to adore, worship.

adormecer §09 ➤ *tr* to put to sleep ➤ *reflex* to doze off, get sleepy.

adormecido, a ➤ *adj* sleepy, drowsy; *(un miembro)* numb, asleep.

adornar ➤ *tr* to adorn; CUL. to garnish.

adorno ➤ *m* adornment, decoration.

adquirir ➤ *tr* to acquire, buy.

adquisición ➤ *f* acquisition, purchase.

adrede ➤ *adv* on purpose, deliberately.

aduana ➤ *f* customs.

aduanero, a ➤ *adj* customs ➤ *m* customs officer.

aducir §14 ➤ *tr* to adduce, cite.

adueñarse ➤ *reflex* to take over, take possession (*de* of).

adulteración ➤ *f* adulteration.

adulterar ➤ *tr* to adulterate ➤ *intr* to commit adultery.

adúltero, a ➤ *mf* adulterer.

adulto, a ➤ *adj & mf* adult.

adverbio ➤ *m* adverb.

adversario, a ➤ *mf* adversary, opponent.

adversidad ➤ *f* adversity, misfortune.

adverso, a ➤ *adj (desfavorable)* adverse.

advertencia ➤ *f (admonición)* warning; *(consejo)* advice; *(noticia)* notice.

advertir §43 ➤ *tr (fijar)* to notice; *(avisar)* to warn; *(aconsejar)* to advise.

adyacente ➤ *adj* adjacent.

aéreo, a ➤ *adj* air, aerial.

aerodinámico, a ➤ *adj* aerodynamic(al) ➤ *f* aerodynamics.

aeródromo ➤ *m* airdrome, aerodrome (G.B.).

aerolínea ➤ *f* airline.

aeromozo, a ➤ *mf* flight attendant.

aeronáutico, a ➤ *adj* aeronautic(al) ➤ *f* aeronautics.

aeropuerto ➤ *m* airport.

afable ➤ *adj* affable, genial.

afamado, a ➤ *adj* famous, renowned.

afán ➤ *m (fervor)* eagerness, zeal; *(anhelo)* urge.

afectación ➤ *f* affectation.

afectado, a ➤ *adj* affected; *(fingido)* feigned.

afectar ➤ *tr* to affect ➤ *reflex (impresionarse)* to be moved *or* affected.

afecto, a ➤ *adj* fond (*a* of).

afectuoso, a ➤ *adj* affectionate, loving.

afeitar ➤ *tr & reflex* to shave (oneself).

afeminado, a ➤ *adj* effeminate.

aferrar §33 ➤ *tr* to grasp ➤ *reflex* to cling (*a* to); *(insistir)* to persist (*a* in).

afianzar §02 ➤ *tr (garantizar)* to guarantee; *(asegurar)* to secure.

afición ➤ *f* inclination, liking (*a* for).

aficionado, a ➤ *adj* fond (*a* of); *(novicio)* amateur ➤ *mf* fan, enthusiast; *(novicio)* amateur.

afilado, a ➤ *adj* sharp.

afilador ➤ *m* sharpener.

afilar ➤ *tr* to sharpen.

afín ➤ *adj (próximo)* adjacent; *(parecido)* similar.

afinar ➤ *tr* to refine; MUS. to tune ➤ *intr* to be in tune.

afinidad ➤ *f* affinity.

afirmación ➤ *f* affirmation.

afirmar ➤ *tr* to affirm; *(afianzar)* to secure ➤ *reflex* to steady oneself.

afirmativo, a ➤ *adj & f* affirmative.

afligido, a ➤ *adj* distressed; *(por la muerte)* bereaved.

afligir §19 ➤ *tr* to trouble, distress ➤ *reflex* to be troubled *or* distressed (*con, de, por* by).

aflojar ➤ *tr* to loosen, slacken ➤ *intr (disminuir)* to diminish; *(decaer)* to grow lax, slack.

afluencia ➤ *f* flow; *(de gente)* crowding; *(abundancia)* affluence.

afluir §10 ➤ *intr (manar)* to flow; *(acudir)* to flock.

afónico, a ➤ *adj* hoarse.

afortunado, a ➤ *adj* fortunate, lucky.

afrenta ➤ *f* affront.

afrentar ➤ *tr* to affront.

África ➤ *f* Africa.

africano, a ➤ *mf* African.

afrontar ➤ *tr* to face (up to), confront.

afuera ➤ *adv* out, outside ➤ *fpl* outskirts.

agacharse ➤ *reflex* to crouch, squat.

agalla ➤ *f (de pez)* gill ■ *pl* COLL. guts, courage.

agarradera ➤ *f* AMER. handle, holder.

agarrar ➤ *tr (asir)* to grab, grasp; *(enfermedad)* to catch.

agasajar ➤ *tr* to entertain; *(regalar)* to lavish gifts on.

agasajo ➤ *m* entertainment; *(regalo)* present.

agencia ➤ *f* agency; *(oficina)* bureau.

agenda ➤ *f* notebook.

agente ➤ *mf* agent ■ **a. de bolsa** stockbroker, broker • **a. de policía** police officer.

ágil ➤ *adj* agile, nimble.

agilidad ➤ *f* agility, nimbleness.

agitación ➤ *f* agitation; *(alboroto)* excitement.

agitar ➤ *tr* to shake; *(alborotar)* to excite ➤ *reflex* to wave, flutter; *(perturbarse)* to be agitated; MARIT. to get rough *or* choppy.

agobiado, a ➤ *adj* bent over, stooped; *(fatigado)* exhausted, weary.

agobiar ➤ *tr (cargar)* to weigh down; *(cansar)* to weary; *(deprimir)* to depress.

agobio ➤ *m (carga)* burden; *(fatiga)* fatigue.

agonía ➤ *f* agony, anguish.

agonizar §02 ➤ *intr* to be at death's door; FIG. to be in agony.

agosto ➤ *m* August.

agotado, a ➤ *adj* exhausted; *(libros)* out-of-print; COM. sold-out.

agotador, a ➤ *adj* exhausting, tiring.

agotar ➤ *tr* to exhaust ➤ *reflex* to be used up; *(cansarse)* to be exhausted; *(libros)* to be out of print.

agraciar ➤ *tr* to embellish; *(favorecer)* to grace; *(premiar)* to award.

agradable ➤ *adj* agreeable, pleasant.

agradar ➤ *tr & intr* to please.

agradecer §09 ➤ *tr* to thank.

agradecido, a ➤ *adj* grateful, thankful ➤ *mf* grateful person.

agradecimiento ➤ *m* gratitude, thanks.

agrandar ➤ *tr* to enlarge; *(exagerar)* to exaggerate.

agrario, a ➤ *adj* agrarian, agricultural.

agravar ➤ *tr & reflex* to worsen.

agraviar ➤ *tr* to offend; *(perjudicar)* to harm ➤ *reflex* to take offense.

agravio ➤ *m* offense; *(perjuicio)* injury.

agredir ➤ *tr* to attack, assault.

agregar §31 ➤ *tr* to add, attach.

agriar ➤ *tr* to (make) sour ➤ *reflex* to become sour.

agrícola *or* **agricultor, a** ➤ *adj* agricultural, farming ➤ *mf* agriculturist, farmer.

agricultura ➤ *f* agriculture, farming.

agridulce ➤ *adj* bittersweet.

agrietar ➤ *tr & reflex* to crack, split.

agrio, a ➤ *adj* sour; *(áspero)* rude, disagreeable ➤ *m* sourness, acidity.

agrupación ➤ *f (grupo)* group; *(asociación)* association, union.

agrupar ➤ *tr & reflex* to group, cluster (together).

agua ➤ *f* water; *(lluvia)* rain ■ **a. abajo, arriba** downstream, upstream • **a. corriente** running water • **a. oxigenada** hydrogen peroxide.

aguacate ➤ *m* avocado.

aguacero ➤ *m* downpour.

aguanieve ➤ *f* sleet.

aguantar ➤ *tr* to endure, tolerate; *(sostener)* to hold up ➤ *reflex* to contain oneself.

aguar §05 ➤ *tr* to water down.

aguardar ➤ *tr* to wait for, await ➤ *intr* to wait.

aguarrás ➤ *m* turpentine.

agudeza ➤ *f* sharpness; *(ingenio)* wit.

agudo, a ➤ *adj* sharp; *(chillón)* shrill; MUS. high-pitched; GEOM., GRAM. acute.

agüero ➤ *m* prediction; *(señal)* omen.

aguijar ➤ *tr* to goad.

aguijón ➤ *m* sting; BOT. thorn.

águila ➤ *f* eagle.

aguja ➤ *f* needle; *(del reloj)* hand; ARCHIT. steeple ■ **a. de gancho** crochet hook.

agujerear ➤ *tr* to pierce, perforate.

agujero ➤ *m* hole.

aguzar §02 ➤ *tr* to sharpen ■ **a. las orejas** *or* **los oídos** to prick up one's ears.

ahí ➤ *adv* there ■ **a. no más** right over there • **de a. que** hence • **por a.** thereabouts.

ahijado, a ➤ *mf* godchild ➤ *m* godson ➤ *f* goddaughter.

ahínco ➤ *m* eagerness, zeal.

ahogado, a ➤ *adj* stifling ➤ *mf* drowned person.

ahogar §31 ➤ *tr* to drown; *(sofocar)* to choke; *(oprimir)* to oppress ➤ *reflex* to drown; *(sentir sofocación)* to choke.

ahondar ➤ *tr* to go deeper into ➤ *intr* to go deep.

ahora ➤ *adv* now; *(pronto)* soon; *(hace poco)* just now, a few moments ago ■ **a. bien** *or* **pues** well, now then • **a. mismo** right now • **por a.** for the time being.

ahorcar §47 ➤ *tr & reflex* to hang (oneself).

ahorrar ➤ *tr* to save.

ahorro ➤ *m* saving ■ *pl* savings.

ahuecar §47 ➤ *tr* to hollow out; *(mullir)* to fluff up; *(la voz)* to make deep.

ahumar ➤ *tr* CUL. to smoke, cure.

ahuyentar ➤ *tr* to drive *or* scare away.

airado, a ➤ *adj* angry, irate.

aire ➤ *m* air; *(viento)* wind; *(apariencia)* appearance; *(gracia)* grace; MUS. air, tune ■ **a. acondicionado** air conditioning • **al a. libre** in the open air • **en el a.** RAD., TELEV. on the air.

airear ➤ *tr* to ventilate, aerate.

aislado, a ➤ *adj* isolated; ELEC. insulated.

aislar ➤ *tr* to isolate; ELEC. to insulate.

ajar ➤ *tr* to crumple, wrinkle ➤ *reflex* to get crumpled *or* wrinkled.

ajedrez ➤ *m* chess; *(piezas)* chess set.

ajeno, a ➤ *adj* another's, someone else's; *(libre)* free, devoid; *(impropio)* inappropriate.

ajetreo ➤ *m* bustle, rush.

ají ➤ *m* red *or* green pepper.

ajo ➤ *m* garlic; *(diente)* garlic clove.

ajuar ➤ *m* trousseau.

ajustado, a ➤ *adj* tight.

ajustar ➤ *tr* to adjust, adapt; *(modificar)* to alter; *(reconciliar)* to reconcile; *(apretar)* to tighten.

ajuste ➤ *m* adjustment; *(modificación)* alteration, fitting.

ala ➤ *f* wing; *(del sombrero)* brim; *(de la hélice)* blade.

alabar ➤ *tr* to praise, laud ➤ *reflex* to boast, brag.

alambrado ➤ *m* wire fence.

alambre ➤ *m* wire ■ **a. de púas** barbed wire.

alameda ➤ *f* poplar grove; *(paseo)* boulevard.

álamo ➤ *m* poplar.

alardear ➤ *intr* to boast, brag.

alargar §31 ➤ *tr* to lengthen; *(extender)* to extend, prolong; *(estirar)* to stretch (out).

alarido ➤ *m* yell, howl.

alarma ➤ *f* alarm ■ **dar la a.** to sound the alarm.

alarmar ➤ *tr* to alarm; *(asustar)* to scare.

alba ➤ *f* dawn, daybreak; RELIG. alb.

albañil ➤ *mf* bricklayer, mason.

albañilería ➤ *f* masonry.

albaricoque ➤ *m* apricot.

alberca ➤ *f (tanque)* reservoir, tank; MEX. swimming pool.

albergar §31 ➤ *tr* to lodge, house.

albergue ➤ *m (alojamiento)* lodging; *(refugio)* shelter, refuge.

albóndiga ➤ *f* meatball.

albornoz ➤ *m (capa)* burnoose; *(bata)* bathrobe.

alborotado, a ➤ *adj (agitado)* excited; *(ruidoso)* rowdy; *(atolondrado)* rash; *(el mar)* rough.

alborotar ➤ *tr (agitar)* to agitate; *(incitar)* to incite; *(excitar)* to excite ➤ *intr* to make a racket.

alboroto ➤ *m* uproar; *(ruido)* racket.

alborozar §02 ➤ *tr* to delight ➤ *reflex* to be elated, rejoice.

alcachofa ➤ *f* artichoke.

alcalde ➤ *m* mayor.

alcaldía ➤ *f* mayor's office.

alcalino, a ➤ *adj* alkaline.

alcance ➤ *m (distancia)* reach; *(extensión)* range, scope ■ **al a.** accessible, within reach (*de* to, of).

alcantarilla ➤ *f (cloaca)* sewer, drain.

alcanzar §02 ➤ *tr* to reach (up to); *(tomar)* to catch; *(conseguir)* to attain; *(comprender)* to grasp; *(igualar)* to catch up with.

alcaparra ➤ *f* caper.

alcázar ➤ *m* castle, fortress.

alce ➤ *m* elk, moose.

alcoba ➤ *f* bedroom.

alcohol ➤ *m* alcohol.

alcohólico, a ➤ *adj & mf* alcoholic.

alcornoque ➤ *m* cork oak.

aldea ➤ *f* village, hamlet.

alegación ➤ *f* allegation.

alegar §31 ➤ *tr* to allege.

alegoría ➤ *f* allegory.

alegórico, a ➤ *adj* allegorical.

alegrar ➤ *tr* to cheer; *(avivar)* to enliven ➤ *reflex* to rejoice, be happy.

alegre ➤ *adj* happy, glad; *(disposición)* cheerful; *(color)* bright; FIG. tipsy, high.

alegría ➤ *f* happiness, joy.

alejado, a ➤ *adj* distant, remote.

alejar ➤ *tr* to put farther away ➤ *reflex* to move away, withdraw.

alentador, a ➤ *adj* encouraging.

alentar §33 ➤ *intr* to breathe ➤ *tr* to encourage, inspire.

alergia ➤ *f* allergy.

alérgico, a ➤ *adj* allergic.

alero ➤ *m* eaves.

alerta ➤ *adv* on the alert ➤ *m* alert, warning.

alertar ➤ *tr* to alert, warn.

aleta ➤ *f (de pez)* fin; *(hélice)* blade.

alfabético, a ➤ *adj* alphabetical.

alfabeto ➤ *m* alphabet ■ **a. Morse** Morse code.

alfarería ➤ *f* pottery.

alfarero, a ➤ *mf* potter, ceramist.

alférez ➤ *mf* second lieutenant.

alfil ➤ *m* bishop (in chess).

alfiler ➤ *m* pin ■ **a. de gancho** AMER. safety pin.

alfombra ➤ *f* carpet; *(tapete)* rug, mat.

alfombrar ➤ *tr* to carpet.

alfombrilla ➤ *f* rug, mat, pad ■ **a. de ratón** mouse pad.

alforja ➤ *f* knapsack; *(provisión)* supplies.

alforza ➤ *f* pleat, tuck.

alga ➤ *f* alga, seaweed.

algarabía ➤ *f* uproar, din.

álgebra ➤ *f* algebra.

algo ➤ *pron* something; *(in questions, negatives)* anything; *(cantidad)* some ■ **¿hay a. para mí?** is there anything for me?

algodón ➤ *m* cotton.
alguacil ➤ *m* sheriff.
alguien ➤ *pron* someone, somebody; *(in questions, negatives)* anyone, anybody ■ **¿has visto a a.?** have you seen anyone?
algún ➤ *adj contr of* **alguno.**
alguno, a ➤ *adj* some; *(in questions, negatives)* any ■ **no tengo duda a.** I don't have any doubt ➤ *pron* someone ■ *pl* some.
alhaja ➤ *f* jewel, gem.
aliado, a ➤ *adj* allied ➤ *mf* ally.
alianza ➤ *f* alliance.
aliar §18 ➤ *tr* to ally, join.
alicates ➤ *mpl* pliers, pincers.
aliciente ➤ *m* incentive.
alienar ➤ *tr* to alienate.
aliento ➤ *m* breath; *(valor)* courage.
aligerar ➤ *tr* to lighten; *(acelerar)* to quicken.
alimentación ➤ *f* feeding; *(comida)* food.
alimentar ➤ *tr* to feed, nourish.
alimento ➤ *m* food, nourishment ■ *pl* alimony, support.
alinear ➤ *tr & reflex* to align, line up.
aliñar ➤ *tr* to straighten, tidy; CUL. to season.
alisar ➤ *tr* to smooth; *(el pelo)* to slick.
alistar ➤ *tr* to list ➤ *reflex* MIL. to enlist.
aliviar ➤ *tr* to alleviate, ease; *(aligerar)* to lighten ➤ *reflex* to get better.
alivio ➤ *m* alleviation; *(cese)* relief.
allá ➤ *adv* there, over there; *(en tiempo remoto)* way back ■ **más a.** farther • **más a. de** beyond • **por a.** over there.
allanamiento ➤ *m* raid.
allanar ➤ *tr (nivelar)* to flatten; *(invadir)* to raid; *(superar)* to overcome.
allegado, a ➤ *mf (pariente)* relative, relation; *(partidario)* supporter.
allegar §31 ➤ *tr* to place near, gather ➤ *reflex* to approach.
allí ➤ *adv* there ■ **por a.** *(sitio)* over there; *(camino)* that way.
alma ➤ *f* soul.
almacén ➤ *m* store, shop; *(depósito)* warehouse.
almacenamiento ➤ *m* storage.
almacenar ➤ *tr* to store, warehouse.
almanaque ➤ *m* calendar, almanac.
almeja ➤ *f* clam.
almendra ➤ *f* almond.
almendrado, a ➤ *adj* almond-shaped ➤ *m (pasta)* almond paste; *(macarrón)* macaroon.
almendro ➤ *m* almond tree.
almíbar ➤ *m* syrup.
almidón ➤ *m* starch.
almidonar ➤ *tr* to starch.
almirante ➤ *mf* admiral.
almohada ➤ *f* pillow.
almohadilla ➤ *f* small cushion.
almorranas ➤ *fpl* hemorrhoids, piles.
almorzar §22 ➤ *intr* to lunch, eat lunch.
almuerzo ➤ *m* lunch.
alojamiento ➤ *m* lodging(s); *(vivienda)* housing.
alojar ➤ *tr* to lodge; *(albergar)* to house ➤ *reflex* to lodge.
alondra ➤ *f* lark.
alpargata ➤ *f* espadrille.
alpinista ➤ *mf* mountain climber.
alpiste ➤ *m* birdseed; COLL. alcohol.
alquilar ➤ *tr* to rent, lease; *(personas)* to hire ■ **se alquila** to let, for hire.
alquiler ➤ *m* renting, hiring; *(renta)* rent ■ **de a.** for hire, for rent.
alquitrán ➤ *m* tar, pitch.
alrededor ➤ *adv (en torno)* around; *(cerca)* about ➤ *mpl (cercanías)* surroundings; *(afueras)* outskirts.
altanería ➤ *f* arrogance, haughtiness.
altanero, a ➤ *adj (pájaro)* high-flying; FIG. arrogant.
altavoz ➤ *m* loudspeaker.
alteración ➤ *f* alteration; *(alboroto)* disturbance; *(disputa)* altercation.
alterar ➤ *tr* to alter; *(perturbar)* to upset; *(enfadar)* to annoy ➤ *reflex (perturbarse)* to get upset.
alternar ➤ *tr & intr* to alternate ■ **a. con** to mix *or* socialize with.
alternativa ➤ *f* alternative, choice.
alternativo, a *or* **alterno, a** ➤ *adj* alternating, alternate.
alteza ➤ *f* Highness; *(altura)* height.
altiplanicie ➤ *f or* **altiplano** ➤ *m* high plateau, altiplano.
altitud ➤ *f* altitude, height.
altivo, a ➤ *adj* haughty, proud.
alto, a ➤ *adj* high; *(estatura)* tall; *(piso)* upper; *(voz)* loud ■ **a. costura** haute couture • **altas horas** late hours ➤ *m* height, elevation; MUS. alto; MIL. halt ■ **de lo a.** from on high, from above ■ *pl* AMER. upper floors ➤ *f* MED. discharge; *(ingreso)* entry ■ **dar de a.** MIL. to admit; MED. to discharge ➤ *adv (arriba)* up high, above; *(en voz fuerte)* aloud ➤ *interj* halt!, stop!
altoparlante ➤ *m* loudspeaker.
altura ➤ *f* height; *(altitud)* altitude ■ *pl* the heavens • **a estas a.** at this point.
alubia ➤ *f* French *or* kidney bean.
alud ➤ *m* avalanche.
aludido, a ➤ *adj* abovementioned.
aludir ➤ *intr* to allude, refer (*a* to).
alumbrado, a ➤ *adj* lighted, lit ➤ *m* lighting.
alumbrar ➤ *tr* to light (up), illuminate ➤ *intr* to give light; *(dar a luz)* to give birth.
aluminio ➤ *m* aluminum.
alumno, a ➤ *mf* pupil, student.
alusión ➤ *f* allusion.
alza ➤ *f* rise, increase ■ **en a.** on the rise.
alzamiento ➤ *m* POL. uprising.
alzar §02 ➤ *tr* to raise, lift (up); *(recoger)* to gather ➤ *reflex* to rise, get up; POL. to rebel.
ama ➤ *f (señora)* lady of the house, mistress; *(dueña)* proprietor ■ **a. de casa** housewife.
amabilidad ➤ *f* kindness.
amable ➤ *adj* kind.
amado, a ➤ *adj & mf* beloved, dear (one).
amaestrar ➤ *tr* to train.
amainar ➤ *tr* MARIT. to lower ➤ *intr* to die down, let up.
amamantar ➤ *tr* to suckle, nurse.
amanecer §09 ➤ *intr* to dawn ➤ *m* dawn ■ **al a.** at dawn.
amanerado, a ➤ *adj* mannered, affected.
amante ➤ *adj* fond, loving ➤ *mf* lover.
amapola ➤ *f* poppy.
amar ➤ *tr* to love.
amargado, a ➤ *adj* bitter, embittered.
amargar §31 ➤ *tr* to make bitter ➤ *intr & reflex* to become embittered.
amargo, a ➤ *adj* bitter.
amargura ➤ *f* bitterness.
amarillo, a ➤ *adj & m* yellow.
amarrar ➤ *tr* to tie (up), fasten; MARIT. to moor.
amateur ➤ *adj & mf* amateur.
amatista ➤ *f* MIN. amethyst.
amazona ➤ *f* MYTH. Amazon.
Amazonas ➤ *m* Amazon (River).
ambar ➤ *m* amber ■ **a. gris** ambergris.
ambición ➤ *f* ambition.
ambiente ➤ *adj* surrounding, ambient ■ **el medio a.** the environment ➤ *m* METEOROL., FIG. atmosphere.
ambigüedad ➤ *f* ambiguity.
ambiguo, a ➤ *adj* ambiguous.
ámbito ➤ *m* boundary, limit.
ambos, as ➤ *adj & indef pron* both.
ambulancia ➤ *f* ambulance.
ambulante ➤ *adj* traveling, itinerant.
ambular ➤ *intr* to stroll, amble.
amenaza ➤ *f* threat, menace.
amenazador, a *or* **amenazante** ➤ *adj* threatening.
amenazar §02 ➤ *tr & intr* to threaten.
amenidad ➤ *f* amenity, pleasantness.
ameno, a ➤ *adj* pleasant, agreeable.
América ➤ *f* America ■ **A. del Norte, del Sur** North America, South America.
americano, a ➤ *adj & mf* American; *(norteamericano)* North American.
ametralladora ➤ *f* machine gun.
amianto ➤ *m* asbestos.
amigable ➤ *adj* amicable.
amígdala ➤ *f* tonsil.
amigdalitis ➤ *f* tonsilitis.
amigo, a ➤ *mf* friend ■ **a. íntimo** *or* **del alma** close friend ➤ *adj* friendly; FIG. fond of.
aminorar ➤ *tr* to reduce, diminish.
amistad ➤ *f* friendship ■ *pl* friends, acquaintances.
amistoso, a ➤ *adj* amicable, friendly.
amnistía ➤ *f* amnesty.
amo ➤ *m* master; *(dueño)* owner, proprietor.
amoldar ➤ *tr* to mold, model; FIG. to adapt.
amonestación ➤ *f* reprimand; *(advertencia)* warning.
amonestar ➤ *tr* to reprimand; *(advertir)* to warn.
amoniaco *or* **amoníaco** ➤ *m (gas)* ammonia.
amontonar ➤ *tr* to heap *or* pile (up); *(acumular)* to accumulate, gather.
amor ➤ *m* love; *(afecto)* affection; *(querido)* darling, beloved ■ **a. propio** pride.
amorío ➤ *m* fling, love affair.
amortiguador, a ➤ *adj (de golpes)* cushioning; *(de ruidos)* muffling ➤ *m* AUTO. shock absorber; *(parachoques)* bumper ■ **a. de luz** dimmer.
amortiguar §05 ➤ *tr (golpes)* to absorb; *(ruidos)* to muffle; *(luces)* to dim.
amortización ➤ *f* LAW amortization.
amortizar §02 ➤ *tr (un bono)* to redeem; *(una deuda)* to pay off.
amparar ➤ *tr* to protect ➤ *reflex* to protect oneself; *(acogerse)* to seek protection.
amparo ➤ *m* protection; *(defensa)* aid.
ampliar §18 ➤ *tr* to expand; *(aumentar)* to increase; *(ensanchar)* to widen; PHOTOG. to enlarge.
amplificación ➤ *f* amplification, magnification; PHOTOG. enlargement.
amplificador, a ➤ *adj* amplifying ➤ *m* ELEC., RAD. amplifier.
amplificar §47 ➤ *tr* to amplify; *(con microscopio)* to magnify; PHOTOG. to enlarge.
amplio, a ➤ *adj (espacioso)* spacious, roomy; *(extenso)* ample, broad; *(ancho)* full, wide.
amplitud ➤ *f (anchura)* fullness; *(extensión)* extent.
ampolla ➤ *f* blister.
amueblar ➤ *tr* to furnish.
amurallado, a ➤ *adj* walled.
anales ➤ *mpl* annals.
analfabeto, a ➤ *adj & mf* illiterate.
analgésico, a ➤ *adj & m* analgesic.
análisis ➤ *m* analysis ■ **a. de sangre** blood test.
analista ➤ *mf* analyst; *(historiador)* annalist.
analizar §02 ➤ *tr* to analyze, examine.
ananá(s) ➤ *m* pineapple.
anaquel ➤ *m* shelf.
anaranjado, a ➤ *adj & m (color)* orange.
anarquía ➤ *f* anarchy.
anarquista ➤ *mf* anarchist ➤ *adj* anarchistic.
anatomía ➤ *f* anatomy.
anca ➤ *f* rump, buttock.
ancho, a ➤ *adj* wide, broad; *(holgado)* loose, full ■ **de a.** wide ➤ *m* width, breadth ■ **a sus anchas** as one pleases.
anchoa ➤ *f* anchovy.
anchura ➤ *f* width, breadth; *(amplitud)* fullness.
anciano, a ➤ *adj* old, elderly ➤ *m* old *or* elderly man ➤ *f* old *or* elderly woman.
ancla ➤ *f* anchor.
anclar ➤ *intr* to anchor, drop anchor.
andamio ➤ *m* scaffold; *(tablado)* platform.
andar[1] §03 ➤ *intr* to walk; *(marchar)* to go, move ■ **¡anda!** get going!
andar[2] ➤ *m* pace, gait.
andén ➤ *m* station *or* railway platform.
andinista ➤ *mf* mountain climber.
andrajoso, a ➤ *adj* tattered, ragged.
anécdota ➤ *f* anecdote.
anejo, a ➤ *adj* attached, annexed.
anexar ➤ *tr* to join; *(documentos)* to enclose.
anexo, a ➤ *adj* joined; *(documento)* enclosed ➤ *m (suplemento)* annex.
anfitrión, ona ➤ *m* host ➤ *f* hostess.
ángel ➤ *m* angel ■ **a. de la guardia** guardian angel.
angélico, a *or* **angelical** ➤ *adj* angelic(al).
angosto, a ➤ *adj* narrow, tight.
anguila ➤ *f* eel.
ángulo ➤ *m* angle; *(esquina)* corner, angle ■ **de á. ancho** PHOTOG. wide-angle • **en á.** at an angle.
angustia ➤ *f* anguish.
angustiar ➤ *tr* to (cause) anguish.
anhelar ➤ *intr* to yearn, long; *(jadear)* to gasp, pant ■ **a. regresar** to long to return ➤ *tr* to yearn *or* long for.
anhelo ➤ *m* yearning, longing.
anillo ➤ *m* ring.
ánima ➤ *f* soul, spirit.
animación ➤ *f* animation.
animado, a ➤ *adj* animated, lively; *(movido)* motivated; ZOOL. animate.
animal ➤ *adj & m* animal.
animar ➤ *tr* to animate; *(avivar)* to enliven; *(alentar)* to encourage.
ánimo ➤ *m* spirit; *(energía)* energy, vitality ■ **¡a.!** courage!
anís ➤ *m* anise; *(licor)* anisette.
aniversario, a ➤ *adj & m* anniversary.
ano ➤ *m* anus.
anoche ➤ *adv* last night, yesterday evening.
anochecer §09 ➤ *intr* to get dark ➤ *m* nightfall, dusk.
anomalía ➤ *f* anomaly.
anómalo, a ➤ *adj* anomalous.
anonadar ➤ *tr* to overwhelm, dishearten.
anónimo, a ➤ *adj* anonymous.
anormal ➤ *adj* abnormal.
anotación ➤ *f* annotation.
anotar ➤ *tr (poner notas)* to annotate; *(apuntar)* to make note of.
ansia ➤ *f (inquietud)* anxiety; *(angustia)* anguish; *(anhelo)* yearning.
ansiar §18 ➤ *tr* to yearn *or* long for.
ansiedad ➤ *f* anxiety.
ansioso, a ➤ *adj (preocupado)* anxious; *(deseoso)* eager.
antagonista ➤ *adj* antagonist, antagonistic ➤ *mf* antagonist, rival.
antaño ➤ *adv* in days gone by.
ante[1] ➤ *m* ZOOL. elk.
ante[2] ➤ *prep (delante de)* before, in front of; *(considerando)* in view of, regarding.
anteanoche ➤ *adv* the night before last.
anteayer ➤ *adv* the day before yesterday.
antebrazo ➤ *m* forearm.
antecedente ➤ *adj* preceding ➤ *m* antecedent ■ *pl* background.
antecesor, a ➤ *adj* former ➤ *mf* predecessor; *(antepasado)* ancestor.
antedicho, a ➤ *adj* aforesaid, aforementioned.
antelación ➤ *f* ■ **con a.** in advance • **con a.** prior to.
antemano ➤ *adv* ■ **de a.** in advance.
antena ➤ *f* antenna.
anteojos ➤ *mpl (lentes)* glasses, eyeglasses; *(anteojeras)* blinders; INDUS., SPORT. goggles.
antepasado, a ➤ *adj* before last ➤ *mf* ancestor.
antepecho ➤ *m (baranda)* rail, railing.
anteponer §37 ➤ *tr* to put before.
anterior ➤ *adj* previous, before (*a* to); ANAT. front.
anterioridad ➤ *f* ■ **con a.** beforehand, in advance • **con a. a** prior to.
antes ➤ *adj & adv* before; *(antiguamente)* previously, formerly; *(más bien)* rather, sooner ■ **a. de** before, prior to • **a. de ayer** the day before yesterday • **a. que** before; *(en vez de)* rather than ➤ *conj* rather, on the contrary.
antesala ➤ *f* anteroom, vestibule.
antibiótico, a ➤ *adj & m* antibiotic.
anticipación ➤ *f* anticipation ■ **con a.** in advance.
anticipado, a ➤ *adj* advance, advanced ■ **por a.** in advance.
anticipar ➤ *tr (fecha)* to advance, move forward; S. AMER. to anticipate ➤ *reflex* to be *or* arrive early.
anticonceptivo, a ➤ *adj & m* contraceptive.
anticuado, a ➤ *adj* antiquated; *(pasado de moda)* old-fashioned.
anticuario, a ➤ *adj* antiquarian ➤ *m* antique dealer.
antídoto ➤ *m* antidote.
antifaz ➤ *m* mask.
antigüedad ➤ *f (vejez)* old age; *(época)* ancient times; *(en el empleo)* seniority ■ *pl* antiques.
antiguo, a ➤ *adj (viejo)* ancient, old; *(anterior)* former ■ **a la a.** in the old-fashioned way ➤ *m* old-timer ■ **los antiguos** the ancients.
antílope ➤ *m* antelope.
antipático, a ➤ *adj* disagreeable, unpleasant.
antiséptico, a ➤ *adj & m* antiseptic.
antisocial ➤ *adj* antisocial.
antítesis ➤ *f* antithesis.
antojarse ➤ *reflex (gustar)* to fancy, feel like; *(parecer)* to seem.
antojo ➤ *m (capricho)* whim; *(de comida)* craving; *(lunar)* birthmark.
antorcha ➤ *f* torch; FIG. guide.
antropología ➤ *f* anthropology.
antropólogo, a ➤ *mf* anthropologist.
anual ➤ *adj* annual, yearly.
anualidad ➤ *f* annual payment.
anuario ➤ *m* yearbook, annual.

anublar ➤ *tr* to cloud.
anudar ➤ *tr (hacer nudos)* to tie in knots; *(atar)* to tie together.
anulación ➤ *f* annulment, nullification.
anular ➤ *tr* to annul; *(desautorizar)* to remove from power.
anunciar ➤ *tr* to announce; COM. to advertise.
anuncio ➤ *m* announcement; *(cartel)* poster; *(señal)* sign; COM. advertisement.
anzuelo ➤ *m* fishhook; FIG. lure.
añadidura ➤ *f* addition.
añadir ➤ *tr* to add; *(aumentar)* to increase.
añejo, a ➤ *adj* aged, mature.
añicos ➤ *mpl* bits, pieces
añil ➤ *m* BOT. indigo; *(para lavado)* bluing.
año ➤ *m* year ■ **a. bisiesto** leap year • **tener . . . años** to be . . . years old.
añoranza ➤ *f* nostalgia.
añorar ➤ *tr & intr* to long, yearn (for).
apacentar §33 ➤ *tr & reflex* to graze, pasture.
apacible ➤ *adj* calm, gentle.
apaciguar §05 ➤ *tr* to appease.
apadrinar ➤ *tr* to sponsor; *(apoyar)* to support; *(a un niño)* to be godfather to.
apagado, a ➤ *adj (fuego, luz)* out; *(apocado)* shy; *(color)* dull, subdued.
apagar §31 ➤ *tr (fuego)* to put out; *(luz)* to turn out; *(cal)* to slake; *(ruido)* to silence; *(color)* to tone down.
apagón ➤ *m* blackout, power failure.
apalear ➤ *tr* to thrash; AGR. to winnow.
aparador ➤ *m (armario)* sideboard, cupboard; *(taller)* studio; *(escaparate)* window.
aparato ➤ *m* apparatus, device ■ **a. de televisión** television set.
aparcamiento ➤ *m* parking lot, garage.
aparcar §47 ➤ *tr & intr* to park.
aparear ➤ *tr* to match up, pair off.
aparecer §09 ➤ *intr & reflex* to appear.
aparejado, a ➤ *adj* apt, fit.
aparejar ➤ *tr* to prepare, make ready; *(los caballos)* to harness ➤ *reflex* to get ready.
aparejo ➤ *m* preparation; *(equipo)* gear, equipment; *(arreo)* harness; PAINT. priming.
aparentar ➤ *tr (fingir)* to pretend; *(parecer)* to seem.
aparición ➤ *f* appearance; *(fantasma)* apparition, specter.
apariencia ➤ *f* appearance ■ **en a.** apparently.
apartado, a ➤ *adj* remote, isolated ➤ *m (casilla postal)* post office box; *(párrafo)* paragraph, section.
apartamento ➤ *m* apartment, flat (G.B.).
apartar ➤ *tr* to separate; *(llevar aparte)* to take aside; *(alejar)* to put aside ➤ *reflex* to withdraw, move away.
aparte ➤ *adv (por separado)* apart, separate; *(a un lado)* aside, to one side.
apasionado, a ➤ *adj* enthusiastic, intense.
apasionante ➤ *adj* exciting, thrilling.
apatía ➤ *f* apathy, indifference.
apeadero ➤ *m (poyo)* mounting block; *(fonda)* inn; RAIL. way station.
apear ➤ *tr* to dismount ➤ *reflex (de un vehículo)* to get out of.
apegarse §31 ➤ *reflex* to become attached *or* fond (*a* to, of).
apego ➤ *m* attachment, fondness.
apelación ➤ *f* LAW appeal; *(recurso)* recourse.
apelar ➤ *intr* LAW to appeal.
apellidar ➤ *tr* to call, name ➤ *reflex* to be called *or* named.
apellido ➤ *m* last name, surname ■ **a. de soltera** maiden name.
apenar ➤ *tr* to grieve, pain ➤ *reflex* to be grieved *or* pained.
apenas ➤ *adv* scarcely, hardly.
apéndice ➤ *m* appendage; ANAT. appendix.
apendicitis ➤ *f* appendicitis.
apercibir ➤ *tr (disponer)* to make ready; *(advertir)* to warn ➤ *reflex* to prepare oneself.
aperitivo ➤ *m* CUL. apéritif, appetizer.
apertura ➤ *f* opening.
apestar ➤ *tr (contaminar)* to infect (with the plague) ➤ *intr* to stink.
apetecer §09 ➤ *tr* to feel like, desire.
apetito ➤ *m* appetite ■ **abrir, dar** *or* **despertar el a.** to whet one's appetite.

ápice ➤ *m (cima)* apex, top, pinnacle; FIG. *(nonada)* iota, whit ■ **no ceder un a.** not to give an inch.
apicultor, a ➤ *mf* beekeeper.
apilar ➤ *tr* to pile *or* heap.
apiñar ➤ *tr & reflex* to cram, jam.
apio ➤ *m* celery.
apisonadora ➤ *f* steamroller.
apisonar ➤ *tr (tierra)* to pack down; *(carretera)* to steamroller.
aplacar §47 ➤ *tr* to appease, placate.
aplanar ➤ *tr* to level, flatten.
aplastar ➤ *tr (estrujar)* to crush; *(vencer)* to overwhelm.
aplaudir ➤ *tr* to applaud.
aplauso ➤ *m* applause, clapping.
aplazamiento ➤ *m* postponement.
aplazar §02 ➤ *tr* to postpone, put off.
aplicable ➤ *adj* applicable.
aplicado, a ➤ *adj* diligent.
aplicar §47 ➤ *tr* to apply.
aplomo ➤ *m* aplomb; *(verticalidad)* vertical alignment.
apodar ➤ *tr* to nickname.
apoderado, a ➤ *adj* empowered, authorized ➤ *mf (poderhabiente)* attorney, proxy; *(empresario)* manager, agent.
apoderar ➤ *tr* to grant power of attorney to ➤ *reflex* ■ **a. de** to take possession of.
apodo ➤ *m* nickname.
apogeo ➤ *m* apogee.
aporrear ➤ *tr (golpear)* to beat; *(instrumento)* to bang on; *(insistir)* to harp on.
aportar ➤ *tr (traer)* to bring; *(contribuir)* to contribute.
aporte ➤ *m* AMER. contribution, donation.
aposentar ➤ *tr & reflex* to lodge.
aposento ➤ *m (habitación)* room; *(hospedaje)* lodging, quarters.
apostar §11 ➤ *tr (jugar)* to wager; *(colocar)* to post, station.
apóstol ➤ *m* apostle.
apóstrofo ➤ *m* GRAM. apostrophe.
apoyar ➤ *tr* to lean, rest; *(ayudar)* to aid, support ➤ *intr* to lean, rest ➤ *reflex* ■ **a. en** to rest on, lean against; FIG. to rely on.
apoyo ➤ *m* support.
apreciación ➤ *f (valorización)* appraisal; *(aprecio)* appreciation.
apreciar ➤ *tr* COM. to appraise, assess; *(estimar)* to appreciate, esteem.
aprecio ➤ *m* COM. appraisal, valuation; *(estima)* esteem.
aprehender ➤ *tr* to apprehend, arrest; *(confiscar)* to seize.
apremiante ➤ *adj* pressing, urgent.
apremiar ➤ *tr (acelerar)* to press; *(oprimir)* to oppress; LAW to compel.
apremio ➤ *m* urgency; LAW judicial order.
aprender ➤ *tr* to learn (*a* to).
aprendiz, a ➤ *mf* apprentice.
aprendizaje ➤ *m* apprenticeship.
aprensión ➤ *f (miedo)* apprehension; *(sospecha)* suspicion.
aprensivo, a ➤ *adj* apprehensive.
apresar ➤ *tr* to capture; ZOOL. to grasp.
aprestar ➤ *tr (preparar)* to make ready.
apresto ➤ *m* preparation.
apresurar ➤ *tr* to hurry, hasten ➤ *reflex* to hurry, make haste (*a, por* to).
apretado, a ➤ *adj (comprimido)* cramped, tight.
apretar §33 ➤ *tr (nudo)* to tighten; *(tecla, pedal)* to press *(estrujar)* to squeeze; *(comprimir)* to compress ■ **a. la mano** to shake hands.
apretón ➤ *m* grip, squeeze ■ **a. de manos** handshake.
aprieto ➤ *m* jam, fix.
aprisa ➤ *adv* quickly, swiftly.
aprobado, a ➤ *adj* approved ➤ *m* passing grade.
aprobar §11 ➤ *tr (consentir)* to approve of; *(examen)* to pass.
apropiación ➤ *f* appropriation.
apropiado, a ➤ *adj* appropriate, suitable.
apropiar ➤ *tr* AMER., FIN. to earmark ➤ *reflex* to take possession (*de* of).
aprovechamiento ➤ *m* use, utilization.
aprovechar ➤ *intr* to be useful ➤ *tr* to make good use of ➤ *reflex* ■ **a. de** to take advantage of.
aproximación ➤ *f (proximidad)* nearness; *(estimación)* approximation.
aproximadamente ➤ *adv* approximately.

aproximar ➤ *tr* to bring near ➤ *reflex* to draw near.
aptitud ➤ *f* aptitude ■ *pl* gift, talent.
apto, a ➤ *adj (hábil)* able, competent; *(conveniente)* apt, fit.
apuntalar ➤ *tr* to prop up, shore up.
apuntar ➤ *tr (arma)* to aim, point; *(señalar)* to point to *or* at, indicate; *(tomar nota)* to make a note of; THEAT. to prompt.
apunte ➤ *m (nota)* note, notation; THEAT. *(persona)* prompter; *(señal)* cue.
apuñalar ➤ *tr* to stab, knife.
apurado, a ➤ *adj* AMER. in a hurry.
apurar ➤ *tr* AMER. to hurry, press; *(purificar)* to refine; *(agotar)* to use *or* finish up; *(enfadar)* to annoy.
apuro ➤ *m* hurry.
aquejar ➤ *tr* to afflict, distress.
aquel, lla ➤ *adj* that ■ **aquella mujer** that woman (over there) ■ *pl* those • **aquellos zapatos** those shoes.
aquél, lla ➤ *pron* that one (over there); *(el primero)* the former ■ *pl* those • **dame aquellos** give me those.
aquello ➤ *pron* that, that matter ■ **a. de** that business about.
aquí ➤ *adv (en este lugar)* here; *(ahora)* now; *(entonces)* then, at that point ■ **por a.** *(alrededor)* around here; *(por este lado)* this way.
aquietar ➤ *tr* to calm, soothe ➤ *reflex* to calm down, become calm.
arada ➤ *f* plowing; *(tierra)* plowed land.
arado ➤ *m* plow; *(acción)* plowing.
arancel ➤ *m* tariff, duty.
araña ➤ *f* spider.
arañar ➤ *tr (rasgar)* to scratch, scrape.
arañazo ➤ *m* scratch.
arar ➤ *tr* to plow.
arbitraje ➤ *m* arbitration; COM. arbitrage.
arbitrar ➤ *tr* to arbitrate; SPORT. to referee ➤ *reflex* to get along, manage.
arbitrario, a ➤ *adj* arbitrary.
árbitro, a ➤ *mf* arbitrator; SPORT. referee, umpire.
árbol ➤ *m* tree.
arbolado, a ➤ *adj* wooded ➤ *m* grove.
arboleda ➤ *f* grove, wood.
arbusto ➤ *m* bush, shrub.
arca ➤ *f (cofre)* chest.
arcada ➤ *f* ARCHIT. arcade; *(de un puente)* span, arch ■ *pl* retching, heaves.
arcaico, a ➤ *adj* archaic, old-fashioned.
arce ➤ *m* maple (tree).
archipiélago ➤ *m* archipelago.
archivador, a ➤ *mf* filing clerk ➤ *m* filing cabinet.
archivar ➤ *tr* to file, put into a file.
archivo ➤ *m* archives; *(de oficina)* files; COMPUT. file.
arcilla ➤ *f* clay.
arco ➤ *m* GEOM. arc; ARCHIT., ANAT. arch; ARM., MUS. bow ■ **a. iris** rainbow.
arder ➤ *intr* to burn.
ardid ➤ *m* ruse, scheme.
ardiente ➤ *adj* burning, ardent.
ardilla ➤ *f* squirrel ■ **a. listada** chipmunk, ground squirrel.
ardor ➤ *m* heat; FIG. zeal.
arduo, a ➤ *adj* arduous, difficult.
área ➤ *f* area.
arena ➤ *f* sand; *(redondel)* ring; *(campo de batalla)* battlefield ■ **arenas movedizas** quicksand.
arenal ➤ *m* sandy ground; *(arenas movedizas)* quicksand.
arenga ➤ *f* harangue; FIG. sermon.
arenisco, a ➤ *adj* sandy ➤ *f* sandstone.
arenoso, a ➤ *adj* sandy.
arenque ➤ *m* herring.
arete ➤ *m (aro)* hoop, ring; *(pendiente)* earring.
argamasa ➤ *f* mortar, plaster.
argentino, a ➤ *adj & mf* Argentine, Argentinian.
argentinismo ➤ *m* Argentine word *or* expression.
argolla ➤ *f* ring; S. AMER. wedding ring.
argot ➤ *m* slang, jargon.
argüir ➤ *intr* to argue ➤ *tr (deducir)* to deduce; *(probar)* to prove.
argumento ➤ *m (razonamiento)* line of reasoning; *(trama)* plot; *(sumario)* summary.
aria ➤ *f* aria.
aridez ➤ *f* aridity, aridness.
árido, a ➤ *adj* arid, dry.
arisco, a ➤ *adj* unfriendly.
aristocracia ➤ *f* aristocracy.

aristócrata ➤ *mf* aristocrat.
aristocrático, a ➤ *adj* aristocratic.
aritmética ➤ *f* arithmetic.
arma ➤ *f* weapon, arm ■ **a. de fuego** firearm.
armadura ➤ *f* MIL. armor; *(armazón)* frame, framework.
armamento ➤ *m* armament; *(armas)* weapons.
armar ➤ *tr (dar armas)* to arm; *(aprestar)* to prime; *(montar)* to assemble; FIG. to create.
armario ➤ *m* closet, wardrobe.
armazón ➤ *m or f* framework, frame.
armería ➤ *f* military museum.
armisticio ➤ *m* armistice.
armonía ➤ *f* harmony.
armónico, a ➤ *adj & m* harmonic ➤ *f* harmonica.
armonioso, a ➤ *adj* harmonious.
armonizar §02 ➤ *tr & intr* to harmonize.
aro ➤ *m* hoop, ring.
aroma ➤ *m* aroma, scent; *(del vino)* bouquet.
aromático, a ➤ *adj* aromatic.
aromatizar §02 ➤ *tr* to perfume; CUL. to flavor.
arpa ➤ *f* harp.
arpía ➤ *f* harpy.
arpón ➤ *m* harpoon; ARCHIT. clamp.
arqueada ➤ *f* MUS. bowing.
arquear ➤ *tr (curvar)* to curve; MARIT. to gauge.
arqueo ➤ *m (acción)* curve; COM. audit ■ **a. bruto** MARIT. gross tonnage.
arqueología ➤ *f* archaeology.
arqueólogo, a ➤ *mf* archaeologist.
arquitecto, a ➤ *mf* architect.
arquitectura ➤ *f* architecture.
arraigar §31 ➤ *intr* BOT. to take root.
arrancar §47 ➤ *tr (de raíz)* to pull up; *(con violencia)* to pull *or* yank out.
arranque ➤ *m (acción)* uprooting; *(toma)* seizure; *(arrebato)* outburst; AUTO. starter.
arrasar ➤ *tr* to level.
arrastrar ➤ *tr* to pull, drag; *(los pies)* to drag, shuffle.
arrastre ➤ *m* dragging.
arrebatado, a ➤ *adj (impetuoso)* impetuous; *(sonrojado)* flushed.
arrebatar ➤ *tr (arrancar)* to snatch; FIG. *(conmover)* to move, stir.
arrebato ➤ *m (arranque)* fit, seizure; *(furor)* rage.
arrecife ➤ *m* reef.
arreglado, a ➤ *adj* orderly, neat.
arreglar ➤ *tr (ordenar)* to put in order; *(acomodar)* to tidy up; *(reparar)* to repair; MUS. to arrange.
arreglo ➤ *m* arrangement; *(orden)* order; *(compostura)* repair.
arremeter ➤ *tr* to attack.
arrendador, a ➤ *mf (propietario)* landlord; *(inquilino)* tenant.
arrendamiento ➤ *m (acción)* rental; *(alquiler)* rent.
arrendar §33 ➤ *tr* to rent.
arrendatario, a ➤ *adj* renting ➤ *mf* tenant.
arrepentimiento ➤ *m* repentance.
arrepentirse §43 ➤ *reflex* to repent; FIG. to regret.
arrestar ➤ *tr* to arrest, detain.
arresto ➤ *m* arrest; *(reclusión)* imprisonment; *(audacia)* boldness.
arriar §18 ➤ *tr* MARIT. to lower; *(aflojar)* to slacken.
arriba ➤ *adv* above; *(en casa)* upstairs ■ **de a.** from above ■ **de a. abajo** from top to bottom; *(desde el principio al fin)* from beginning to end • **para a.** upwards, up.
arribar ➤ *intr* to arrive ■ **a. a** to manage to.
arriesgado, a ➤ *adj (peligroso)* risky; *(audaz)* daring.
arriesgar §31 ➤ *tr* to risk, venture.
arrimar ➤ *tr* to bring *or* draw near.
arrinconar ➤ *tr* to put in a corner, put aside; *(perseguir)* to corner.
arrobamiento ➤ *m* ecstasy, rapture.
arrobar ➤ *tr* to enrapture ➤ *reflex (extasiarse)* to be enraptured.
arrodillar ➤ *tr* to make (someone) kneel ➤ *reflex* to kneel (down).
arrogancia ➤ *f* arrogance.
arrogante ➤ *adj* arrogant.
arrojar ➤ *tr* to hurl, fling; *(emitir)* to emit; *(vomitar)* to throw up.
arrojo ➤ *m (atrevimiento)* boldness;

(resolución) resoluteness.
arrollar ➤ *tr (envolver)* to roll up; *(llevar)* to sweep *or* carry away.
arropar ➤ *tr (cubrir)* to wrap with clothes; *(acostar)* to tuck in (to bed).
arroyo ➤ *m* brook; *(cuneta)* gutter.
arroz ➤ *m* rice ▪ **a. con leche** rice pudding.
arruga ➤ *f (en la piel)* wrinkle; *(en la ropa)* crease; GEOL. fold.
arrugado, a ➤ *adj* wrinkled.
arrugar §31 ➤ *tr* to wrinkle; *(hacer arrugas)* to crease; *(papel)* to crumple.
arruinar ➤ *tr* to ruin; FIG. to destroy.
arrullar ➤ *tr* to coo; *(adormecer)* to lull to sleep.
arsénico ➤ *m* arsenic.
arte ➤ *m or f* art; *(habilidad)* art, skill ▪ **bellas artes** fine arts.
arteria ➤ *f* artery.
artesanía ➤ *f (habilidad)* craftsmanship; *(producto)* crafts.
artesano, a ➤ *mf* artisan, craftsman ➤ *f* craftswoman.
ártico, a ➤ *adj & m* Arctic.
articulación ➤ *f* ANAT., MECH. joint; *(pronunciación)* enunciation.
articular[1] ➤ *adj* ANAT. articular, of the joints.
articular[2] ➤ *tr (palabra)* to enunciate.
artículo ➤ *m* article; *(cosa)* item, thing; *(escrito)* essay.
artificial ➤ *adj* artificial.
artificio ➤ *m (habilidad)* ability; *(aparato)* device; *(ardid)* trick.
artillería ➤ *f* artillery.
artilugio ➤ *m (aparato)* contraption; *(trampa)* gimmick.
artimaña ➤ *f (trampa)* trick; *(astucia)* cunning.
artista ➤ *mf* artist; *(actor, actriz)* actor, actress.
artístico, a ➤ *adj* artistic.
artritis ➤ *f* MED. arthritis.
arzobispo ➤ *m* archbishop.
as ➤ *m* ace.
asa ➤ *f* handle.
asado ➤ *m (carne)* roasted meat; AMER. barbecued meat; *(comida)* cookout, barbecue.
asalariado, a ➤ *adj* salaried ➤ *mf* salaried worker.
asaltar ➤ *tr (atacar)* to assault; *(sobrevenir)* to overtake.
asalto ➤ *m (ataque)* assault; *(en el boxeo)* round.
asamblea ➤ *f (reunión)* meeting; *(congreso)* conference.
asar ➤ *tr* to roast ▪ **a. al horno** to bake • **a. a la parrilla** to broil.
ascendencia ➤ *f* ancestry.
ascender §34 ➤ *intr* to rise; *(de categoría)* to be promoted.
ascendiente ➤ *adj* ascending.
ascensión ➤ *f* ascension, rise.
ascenso ➤ *m (adelanto)* promotion; *(subida)* ascent, rise.
ascensor ➤ *m* elevator, lift (G.B.).
ascético, a ➤ *adj* ascetic ➤ *f* asceticism.
asco ➤ *m* disgust, revulsion.
ascua ➤ *f* ember.
aseado, a ➤ *adj (limpio)* clean; *(ordenado)* neat, tidy.
asear ➤ *tr (lavar)* to wash; *(limpiar)* to clean; *(ordenar)* to tidy (up).
asedio ➤ *m* siege.
asegurado, a ➤ *adj* insured ➤ *mf* insured (person), policyholder.
asegurar ➤ *tr (afirmar)* to secure; *(garantizar)* to guarantee; *(tranquilizar)* to assure; COM. to insure.
asentado, a ➤ *adj (juicioso)* judicious; *(estable)* stable.
asentar §33 ➤ *tr (anotar)* to record; *(fundar)* to found; *(colocar)* to place; *(afirmar)* to affirm; *(aplanar)* to level.
asentir §43 ➤ *intr* to assent, agree.
aseo ➤ *m (limpieza)* cleanliness; *(orden)* neatness, tidiness.
asequible ➤ *adj (accesible)* accessible; *(posible)* feasible.
aserradero ➤ *m* sawmill.
aserrar §33 ➤ *tr* to saw.
aserrín ➤ *m* sawdust.
asesinar ➤ *tr* to murder; POL. to assassinate.
asesinato ➤ *m* murder; POL. assassination.
asesino, a ➤ *mf* murderer; POL. assassin.
asesor, a ➤ *adj* advising, advisory ➤ *mf* adviser, counselor.
asesorar ➤ *tr* to advise ➤ *reflex* to seek advice.
asestar ➤ *tr (arma)* to aim; *(golpe)* to deal.
aseverar ➤ *tr* to assert.
asfalto ➤ *m* asphalt.
asfixiar ➤ *tr* to asphyxiate ➤ *reflex* to suffocate.
así ➤ *adv (de esta manera)* so, this way; *(de esa manera)* that way, like that; *(tanto)* so, in such a way ▪ **a. a.** so-so, fair • **a. como** as soon as ➤ *conj (en consecuencia)* therefore, thus; *(aunque)* even if, even though ➤ *adj* such.
Asia ➤ *f* Asia.
asiático, a ➤ *adj & mf* Asian.
asiduo, a ➤ *adj* assiduous.
asiento ➤ *m* seat; *(silla)* chair; *(sitio)* site.
asignación ➤ *f (distribución)* allotment; *(cita)* appointment.
asignar ➤ *tr (señalar)* to assign; *(nombrar)* to appoint.
asignatura ➤ *f* EDUC. subject, course ▪ **aprobar una a.** to pass a course.
asilo ➤ *m* asylum; *(refugio)* shelter.
asimilar ➤ *tr* to assimilate.
asimismo ➤ *adj (igualmente)* likewise, in like manner; *(también)* also, too.
asir ➤ *tr & intr* to grasp.
asistencia ➤ *f (concurrencia)* attendance; *(ayuda)* aid.
asistente, a ➤ *adj* assisting ➤ *mf (ayudante)* assistant.
asistir ➤ *intr* to attend ➤ *tr (acompañar)* to accompany; *(ayudar)* to aid; *(cuidar)* to nurse.
asma ➤ *f* asthma.
asno ➤ *m* donkey; FIG. jackass.
asociación ➤ *f* association ▪ **a. gremial** trade union • **a. sindical** labor union.
asociado, a ➤ *adj* associated ➤ *mf* associate.
asociar ➤ *tr (ligar)* to connect; *(combinar)* to combine ➤ *reflex* to become partners.
asolador, a ➤ *adj* ravaging.
asolar §11 ➤ *tr* to ravage.
asomar ➤ *intr* to appear ➤ *tr* to show ➤ *reflex* to appear; *(de una ventana)* to look *or* lean out.
asombrar ➤ *tr* to amaze, astonish ➤ *reflex* to be amazed *or* astonished.
asombro ➤ *m* amazement; *(maravilla)* marvel.
asombroso, a ➤ *adj* amazing, astonishing.
aspa ➤ *f (cruz)* X-shaped cross; *(devanadera)* spool; *(de molinos)* blade.
aspecto ➤ *m* aspect.
aspereza ➤ *f (escabrosidad)* ruggedness; *(brusquedad)* gruffness.
áspero, a ➤ *adj (rugoso)* rough; *(escabroso)* rugged; *(brusco)* gruff.
aspiradora ➤ *f* vacuum cleaner.
aspirina ➤ *f* aspirin.
asquear ➤ *tr* to disgust ➤ *intr* to be disgusting.
asqueroso, a ➤ *adj (repugnante)* repulsive; *(sucio)* filthy.
asta ➤ *f (lanza)* spear; *(de lanza)* shaft; *(de bandera)* flagpole; *(cuerno)* horn, antler.
asterisco ➤ *m* asterisk.
asteroide ➤ *m* asteroid ➤ *adj* asteroidal.
astilla ➤ *f* splinter ▪ **hacer astillas** to splinter.
astringente ➤ *adj & m* astringent.
astringir §19 ➤ *tr* to contract.
astro ➤ *m* star.
astrólogo, a ➤ *mf* astrologist ➤ *adj* astrological.
astronauta ➤ *mf* astronaut.
astronomía ➤ *f* astronomy.
astrónomo, a ➤ *mf* astronomer.
astucia ➤ *f* astuteness; *(ardid)* trick.
astuto, a ➤ *adj (listo)* astute, clever; *(mañoso)* crafty, shrewd.
asumir ➤ *tr* to assume, take on.
asunción ➤ *f* assumption.
asunto ➤ *m (tópico)* topic; *(tema)* subject matter; *(argumento)* plot.
asustadizo, a ➤ *adj* easily frightened, skittish.
asustar ➤ *tr* to frighten, scare ➤ *reflex* to be frightened *or* scared *(de, por, con* by).
atacar §47 ➤ *tr* to attack.
atajo ➤ *m* short cut.
ataque ➤ *m* attack ▪ **a. aéreo** air raid.
atar ➤ *tr* to tie, fasten.
atascadero ➤ *m* bog.
atascamiento ➤ *m* obstruction.
atascar §47 ➤ *tr (obstruir)* to clog; *(impedir)* to hamper.
atasco ➤ *m* obstruction; FIG. obstacle.
ataúd ➤ *m* coffin, casket.
ataviar §18 ➤ *tr* to adorn, deck out.
atemorizar §02 ➤ *tr* to frighten.
atención ➤ *f* attention ▪ **llamar la a.** *(atraer)* to catch the eye • **prestar a.** to pay attention ▪ *pl* courtesies.
atender §34 ➤ *tr (hacer caso de)* to pay attention to; COM. to wait on ➤ *intr* to pay attention.
atentado ➤ *m* crime; *(ataque)* attempt.
atento, a ➤ *adj (observador)* attentive; *(cortés)* considerate ▪ **a.** a in view of.
aterrar ➤ *tr* to terrify.
aterrizaje ➤ *m* landing.
aterrizar §02 ➤ *intr* to land.
aterrorizador, a ➤ *adj* terrifying.
aterrorizar §02 ➤ *tr* to terrorize.
ático ➤ *m* attic.
atizar §02 ➤ *tr (el fuego)* to poke, stir.
atlas ➤ *m* atlas.
atleta ➤ *mf* athlete.
atlético, a ➤ *adj* athletic.
atmósfera ➤ *f* atmosphere.
atolondrado, a ➤ *adj* reckless.
atómico, a ➤ *adj* atomic.
atomizador ➤ *m* atomizer, sprayer.
átomo ➤ *m* atom.
atónito, a ➤ *adj* astonished, amazed.
atontar ➤ *tr (embrutecer)* to stun; *(aturdir)* to confuse.
atormentar ➤ *tr* to torment; *(torturar)* to torture ➤ *reflex* to worry.
atornillar ➤ *tr* to screw in *or* on.
atracadero ➤ *m* pier, dock.
atracar §47 ➤ *tr (asaltar)* to hold up; COLL. *(hartar)* to stuff, cram ➤ *intr* MARIT. to dock ➤ *reflex* to stuff *or* gorge oneself.
atracción ➤ *f* attraction.
atraco ➤ *m* holdup, robbery.
atractivo, a ➤ *adj* attractive.
atraer §49 ➤ *tr* to attract, draw.
atragantarse ➤ *reflex* COLL. to get tongue-tied ▪ **a. con** to choke on.
atrancar §47 ➤ *tr (cerrar)* to bolt ➤ *reflex* to get stuck.
atranco *or* **atranque** ➤ *m* obstruction; FIG. jam.
atrapar ➤ *tr* COLL. to catch, trap.
atrás ➤ *adv* back, behind; *(antes)* back, ago ▪ **¡a.!** get back! • **dar marcha a.** AUTO. to back up • **ir hacia a.** to go backward.
atrasado, a ➤ *adj (reloj)* slow; *(persona)* late; *(país)* underdeveloped.
atrasar ➤ *tr* to delay; *(reloj)* to set back ➤ *intr* to be slow ➤ *reflex* to be late.
atraso ➤ *m* delay; *(retraso)* tardiness ▪ *pl* arrears.
atravesar §33 ➤ *tr (pasar)* to cross (over); *(traspasar)* to pierce ➤ *reflex (obstruir)* to block.
atreverse ➤ *reflex* to dare (*a* to).
atrevido, a ➤ *adj (osado)* bold; *(descarado)* impudent.
atribuir ➤ *tr* to credit; *(imputar)* to grant.
atributo ➤ *m* attribute.
atrio ➤ *m (patio)* atrium; *(entrada)* vestibule.
atrocidad ➤ *f* atrocity; FIG. enormity.
atrofiado, a ➤ *adj* atrophied, atrophic.
atropellar ➤ *tr (derribar)* to run over; *(agraviar)* to bully; *(hacer precipitadamente)* to rush through.
atropello ➤ *m* assault; FIG. abuse.
atroz ➤ *adj* atrocious; FIG. enormous.
atuendo ➤ *m* attire.
atún ➤ *m* tuna (fish).
aturdido, a ➤ *adj (estupefacto)* stunned; *(turbado)* confused.
aturdir ➤ *tr (atontar)* to stun; *(turbar)* to confuse.
audacia ➤ *f* audacity.
audaz ➤ *adj* audacious.
audición ➤ *f (facultad)* hearing; *(programa)* program; THEAT. audition.
audiencia ➤ *f* audience.
audífono ➤ *m* hearing aid; *(auricular)* earphone.
audiovisual ➤ *adj* audio-visual.
auditorio, a ➤ *m (público)* audience; *(sala)* auditorium.
auge ➤ *m (apogeo)* peak; COM. boom, expansion; ASTRON. apogee.
augurio ➤ *m* augury, omen.
aula ➤ *f* classroom, lecture hall.
aullido *or* **aúllo** ➤ *m* howl, wail ▪ **dar aullidos** to howl, wail.
aumentar ➤ *tr* to increase; RAD. to amplify; *(salario)* to raise ➤ *intr* to increase.
aumento ➤ *m* increase; RAD. amplification; *(de sueldo)* raise.
aun ➤ *adv* even ▪ **a. así** even so.
aún ➤ *adv* still, yet ▪ **a. no** not yet • **más a.** furthermore.
aunque ➤ *conj (si bien)* although, even though; *(a pesar de)* even if.
aureola ➤ *f* RELIG. halo; ASTRON. aureole.
auricular ➤ *m* TELEC. earpiece ▪ *pl* earphones.
aurora ➤ *f* dawn.
ausencia ➤ *f* absence.
ausentarse ➤ *reflex (alejarse)* to leave.
ausente ➤ *adj* absent ➤ *mf* absentee.
austero, a ➤ *adj* austere.
austral ➤ *adj* austral, southern.
Australia ➤ *f* Australia.
australiano, a ➤ *adj & mf* Australian.
auténtico, a ➤ *adj* authentic, genuine.
auto[1] ➤ *m* LAW judicial decree *or* ruling; ▪ *pl* LAW case file.
auto[2] ➤ *m* COLL. car, auto.
autobiografía ➤ *f* autobiography.
autobiográfico, a ➤ *adj* autobiographical.
autobús ➤ *m* bus.
autoedición ➤ *f* desktop publishing.
autógrafo ➤ *m* autograph.
automático, a ➤ *adj* automatic.
automóvil ➤ *m* automobile, car.
automovilista ➤ *mf* driver, motorist.
autonomía ➤ *f* autonomy.
autopista ➤ *f* expressway, superhighway.
autopsia ➤ *f* autopsy.
autor, a ➤ *mf* author, writer.
autoridad ➤ *f* authority; *(oficial)* official.
autoritario, a ➤ *adj* authoritarian.
autorizado, a ➤ *adj* authorized.
autorizar §02 ➤ *tr* to authorize.
autorretrato ➤ *m* self-portrait.
auto-stop ➤ *m* hitchhiking ▪ **hacer a.** to hitchhike.
autosuficiencia ➤ *f* self-sufficiency.
auxiliar[1] ➤ *adj* auxiliary ➤ *mf (subalterno)* assistant ➤ *m* GRAM. auxiliary.
auxiliar[2] ➤ *tr* to assist, aid.
auxilio ➤ *m* assistance, aid ▪ **primeros auxilios** first aid.
avalancha ➤ *f* avalanche.
avance[1] ➤ *m* advance.
avance[2] ➤ *m* preview.
avanzado, a ➤ *adj* advanced.
avanzar §02 ➤ *tr* to advance.
avaricia ➤ *f* avarice, greed.
avaro, a ➤ *adj (tacaño)* miserly; *(codicioso)* greedy ➤ *mf (tacaño)* miser.
ave ➤ *f* bird.
avellano, a ➤ *adj* hazel ➤ *m* hazel (tree) ➤ *f* hazelnut.
avena ➤ *f* oat, oats.
avenida ➤ *f* avenue.
avenirse §52 ➤ *reflex* to come to an agreement.
aventajar ➤ *tr (superar)* to surpass; *(ganar)* to beat; *(llevar ventaja)* to be ahead of.
aventura ➤ *f* adventure; *(riesgo)* risk.
aventurarse ➤ *reflex* to take a risk.
aventurero, a ➤ *adj* adventurous ➤ *m* adventurer ➤ *f* adventuress.
avergonzar §04 ➤ *tr* to shame ➤ *reflex* to be ashamed (*de* to, *por* of).
avería ➤ *f (rotura)* breakdown.
averiar §18 ➤ *tr (estropear)* to damage ➤ *reflex* to become damaged; *(descomponerse)* to break (down).
averiguar §05 ➤ *tr* to find out, ascertain; *(investigar)* to investigate; *(verificar)* to verify.
avestruz ➤ *m* ostrich.
aviación ➤ *f* aviation; MIL. air force.
aviador, a ➤ *mf* pilot, aviator.
avidez ➤ *f* avidity; *(codicia)* greed.
ávido, a ➤ *adj* avid, eager; *(codicioso)* greedy.
avinagrado, a ➤ *adj* sour.
avión ➤ *m* airplane, plane ▪ **por a.** by air mail.
avioneta ➤ *f* light airplane.
avisar ➤ *tr (informar)* to inform; *(advertir)* to warn.
aviso ➤ *m (notificación)* notice; *(advertencia)* warning.
avispa ➤ *f* wasp.
avivar ➤ *tr (un fuego)* to stoke; *(encender)* to arouse ➤ *intr & reflex* to revive, liven up.
axila ➤ *f* BOT. axil; ANAT. axilla, armpit.
¡ay! ➤ *interj* oh!; *(dolor)* ow!, ouch!

ayer ➤ *adv* yesterday; *(en el pasado)* formerly, in the past ➤ *m* yesterday, past.
ayuda ➤ *f (auxilio)* help, aid.
ayudante, a ➤ *mf* assistant, aide.
ayudar ➤ *tr* to help, aid.
ayunar ➤ *intr* to fast.
ayuno ➤ *m* fast ■ **en a.** *(sin comer)* fasting ➤ *m* fast, fasting.
ayuntamiento ➤ *m (corporación)* city council; *(edificio)* city hall.
azada ➤ *f* hoe.
azafata ➤ *f* AVIA. flight attendant.
azafrán ➤ *m* saffron.
azahar ➤ *f* orange, lemon, *or* citron blossom.
azar ➤ *m (casualidad)* chance ■ **al a.** at random • **por a.** by chance.
azorar ➤ *tr* to confuse ➤ *reflex* to become confused *or* bewildered.
azotaina ➤ *f* COLL. flogging.
azotar ➤ *tr* to flog; FIG. to beat upon.
azote ➤ *m* spanking.
azotea ➤ *f (tejado)* terraced roof.
azúcar ➤ *m or f* sugar.
azucarado, a ➤ *adj* sweet.
azucarera ➤ *f* sugar bowl.
azucena ➤ *f* white lily.
azul ➤ *adj & m* blue ■ **a. celeste** sky blue • **a. marino** navy blue • **a. turquí** indigo.
azulejo ➤ *m* glazed tile.

B

baba ➤ *f* spittle.
babero ➤ *m* bib.
babor ➤ *m* MARIT. port.
baboso, a ➤ *adj* drooling; C. AMER. foolish ➤ *mf* drooler ➤ *f* ZOOL. slug.
bacalao ➤ *m* codfish.
bache ➤ *m* pothole; AER. air pocket.
bachillerato ➤ *m* studies required to enter a university, equivalent to a high school diploma.
bacteria ➤ *f* bacterium.
bahía ➤ *f* bay.
bailador, a ➤ *mf* dancer.
bailar ➤ *intr* to dance.
bailarín, ina ➤ *mf* dancer ➤ *m* ballet dancer ➤ *f* ballerina.
baile ➤ *m* dance.
baja ➤ *f* drop; MIL. loss ■ **dar de b.** to expel; MIL. *(un soldado)* to discharge.
bajada ➤ *f* drop; *(camino)* sloped path.
bajamar ➤ *f* low tide.
bajar ➤ *intr* to descend; *(apearse)* to get off; *(disminuir)* to drop ➤ *tr* to lower; *(llevar abajo)* to bring *or* take down; *(ir abajo)* to go down; COMPUT. to download.
bajo ➤ *m (voz)* bass ■ *pl (piso)* ground floor ➤ *adv (abajo)* below; *(en voz baja)* low ➤ *prep* under, beneath.
bajo, a ➤ *adj* low; *(persona)* short; *(inclinado)* downcast; *(poco vivo)* pale.
bajón ➤ *m* drop, slump; MUS. bassoon.
bala ➤ *f* bullet; *(de cañón)* cannonball; *(de carabina)* shot; *(fardo)* bale.
balada ➤ *f* ballad(e).
balance ➤ *m* balance ■ **b. comercial** balance of trade • **b. pendiente** balance due.
balanza ➤ *f* scales ■ **b. comercial** *or* **mercantil** ECON. balance of trade.
balazo ➤ *m (golpe)* shot; *(herida)* bullet wound.
balbucir ➤ *intr* to stammer.
balcón ➤ *m* balcony.
balde[1] ➤ *m* pail ■ **como un b. de agua fría** like a ton of bricks.
balde[2] ➤ *adv* ■ **de b.** *(gratuitamente)* free; *(sin motivo)* without reason • **en b.** in vain.
baldosa ➤ *f* floor tile.
balín ➤ *m* pellet, shot ■ *pl* buckshot.
ballena ➤ *f* whale; *(de un corsé)* stay.
ballet ➤ *m* ballet.
balneario, a ➤ *adj* bathing ➤ *m* spa.
balón ➤ *m* soccer ball, football (G.B.).
baloncesto ➤ *m* basketball.
balonmano ➤ *m* handball.
balonvolea ➤ *m* volleyball.
balota ➤ *f* ballot.
balsa ➤ *f (charca)* pool; *(embarcación)* raft.
bálsamo ➤ *m* balsam.
bambú ➤ *m* bamboo.
banana ➤ *f* banana.
banca ➤ *f* bench; COM. banking.
bancarrota ➤ *f* bankruptcy.
banco ➤ *m* bench; COM. bank ■ **b. de ahorros** savings bank • **b. de arena** sandbar • **b. de datos** data bank • **b. de nieve** snowbank.
banda[1] ➤ *f (faja)* band; *(cinta)* ribbon ■ **b. sonora** *or* **de sonido** soundtrack • **b. transportadora** conveyor belt.
banda[2] ➤ *f* MIL. troop, band; *(pandilla)* gang; MUS. band.
bandada ➤ *f* group; *(de aves)* flock.
bandeja ➤ *f* tray.
bandera ➤ *f* flag.
banderín ➤ *m* pennant.
bandido ➤ *m* bandit; COLL. rascal.
bandolero ➤ *m* bandit.
banjo ➤ *m* banjo.
banquero, a ➤ *mf* banker.
banqueta ➤ *f* stool; *(para los pies)* footstool.
banquete ➤ *m* banquet.
bañador, a ➤ *adj* bathing ➤ *mf* AMER. bather ➤ *m* bathing suit.
bañar ➤ *tr* to bathe ➤ *reflex* to bathe, take a bath.
bañera ➤ *f* bathtub.
bañista ➤ *mf* swimmer.
baño ➤ *m (ducha)* bath; *(bañera)* bathtub; *(cuarto de baño)* bathroom ■ **b. de María** double boiler ■ *pl* spa.
baptisterio ➤ *m* baptistry.
bar ➤ *m* barroom, bar.
baraja ➤ *f* deck (of cards).
baranda ➤ *f* banister; *(de billar)* cushion.
barandilla ➤ *f* banister, handrail.
baratija ➤ *f* trinket, bauble ■ *pl* junk.
barato, a ➤ *adj & adv* cheap(ly), inexpensive(ly).
barba ➤ *f (barbilla)* chin; *(pelo)* beard.
barbacoa ➤ *f* barbecue; AMER. makeshift cot.
barbaridad ➤ *f* barbarity; *(necedad)* foolish act, nonsense.
barbería ➤ *f* barbershop.
barbero ➤ *m* barber.
barbilla ➤ *f* chin.
barbudo, a ➤ *adj* heavily bearded.
barca ➤ *f* small boat.
barcaza ➤ *f* launch.
barco ➤ *m* boat, ship ■ **b. de carga** freighter.
barítono ➤ *m* baritone.
barlovento ➤ *m* windward.
barniz ➤ *m* varnish, lacquer.
barómetro ➤ *m* barometer.
barquillo ➤ *m* CUL. rolled wafer; *(helado)* ice-cream cone.
barra ➤ *f* bar; *(barandilla)* railing; *(mostrador)* counter; *(de arena)* sandbar ■ **b. de tareas** COMPUT. taskbar.
barraca ➤ *f* hut, cabin; AMER. warehouse.
barranco ➤ *m or* **barranca** ➤ *f* ravine, gorge.
barrendero, a ➤ *mf* street sweeper.
barreno ➤ *m (instrumento)* large drill, auger; MIN. blasting hole.
barrer ➤ *tr* to sweep.
barrera ➤ *f* barrier ■ **b. de peaje** tollgate.
barricada ➤ *f* barricade, barrier.
barriga ➤ *f* abdomen, stomach, belly.
barril ➤ *m* barrel, keg; *(jarro)* jug.
barrio ➤ *m* neighborhood ■ **barrios bajos** slums.
barro ➤ *m (lodo)* mud; *(arcilla)* clay.
barroco, a ➤ *adj* baroque; *(extravagante)* ornate, elaborate.
bártulos ➤ *mpl* household goods, belongings.
barullo ➤ *m* COLL. racket, rowdiness.
basar ➤ *tr* to base, support ➤ *reflex* to be based.
base ➤ *f* base; FIG. basis, foundation.
básico, a ➤ *adj* basic.
bastante ➤ *adj* enough, sufficient ➤ *adv* enough, sufficiently; *(muy)* rather, quite.
bastar ➤ *intr* to be enough, suffice ■ **¡basta!** that's enough of that! ➤ *reflex* to be self-sufficient.
bastidor ➤ *m* frame, framework; THEAT. wing; AUTO. chassis ■ **entre bastidores** FIG. behind the scenes; THEAT. off-stage.
basto, a ➤ *adj* coarse, rough ➤ *m (albarda)* packsaddle ➤ *f* SEW. basting.
bastón ➤ *m* cane, walking stick.
basura ➤ *f* garbage, trash.
basurero ➤ *m* garbage collector; *(cubo)* garbage *or* trash can; *(basural)* dump.
bata ➤ *f* housecoat, robe; *(de trabajo)* frock, smock.
batalla ➤ *f* battle.
batallón ➤ *m* battalion.
batata ➤ *f* sweet potato, yam.
bate ➤ *m* SPORT. bat.
bateador, a ➤ *mf* SPORT. batter, hitter.
batear ➤ *tr* SPORT. to bat, hit.
batería ➤ *f* battery; MUS. drums, percussion ■ **b. de cocina** kitchen utensils.
batido ➤ *m (bebida)* shake.
batidora ➤ *f* CUL. whisk; ELEC. blender.
batir ➤ *tr* to beat, hit; *(revolver)* to beat, mix; *(agitar)* to beat, flap.
batuta ➤ *f* MUS. baton.
baúl ➤ *m* trunk; *(cofre)* coffer, chest.
bautismo ➤ *m* baptism, christening.
bautisterio ➤ *m* baptistry, baptistery.
bautizar §02 ➤ *tr* to baptize, christen.
bautizo ➤ *m* baptism, christening.
bazar ➤ *m* bazaar, marketplace.
bazo ➤ *m* ANAT. spleen.
beato, a ➤ *adj (beatificado)* beatified; *(piadoso)* pious.
bebé ➤ *m* baby.
beber ➤ *tr* to drink.
bebida ➤ *f* drink, beverage.
beca ➤ *f* grant, scholarship.
becario, a ➤ *mf* scholarship student.
becerro, a ➤ *m* yearling bull.
bechamel ➤ *f* white *or* béchamel sauce.
bedel ➤ *m* EDUC. proctor.
béisbol ➤ *m* baseball.
belén ➤ *m* crèche, nativity scene.
bélico, a ➤ *adj* bellicose, warlike.
belleza ➤ *f* beauty.
bello, a ➤ *adj* beautiful, lovely.
bellota ➤ *f* acorn.
bemol ➤ *m & adj* MUS. flat.
bencina ➤ *f* benzine.
bendecir ➤ *tr* to bless.
bendición ➤ *f* blessing.
bendito, a ➤ *adj* blessed.
beneficencia ➤ *f* welfare, public assistance.
beneficiar ➤ *tr* to benefit ➤ *intr* to be of benefit ➤ *reflex* to profit (*de* by, from).
beneficiario, a ➤ *mf* beneficiary.
beneficio ➤ *m* benefit, advantage; *(ganancia)* profit, gain.
beneficioso, a ➤ *adj* beneficial.
benéfico, a ➤ *adj* beneficent, charitable.
benevolencia ➤ *f* benevolence.
benigno, a ➤ *adj* benign.
berenjena ➤ *f* eggplant.
bermuda ➤ *f* Bermuda grass ■ *pl* Bermuda shorts.
berrinche ➤ *m* COLL. rage, tantrum.
berro ➤ *m* watercress.
besar ➤ *tr* to kiss.
beso ➤ *m* kiss.
bestia ➤ *f* beast.
besugo ➤ *m* sea bream; COLL. idiot.
betún ➤ *m* shoe polish.
biberón ➤ *m* baby bottle.
biblia ➤ *f* Bible.
bibliografía ➤ *f* bibliography.
biblioteca ➤ *f* library; AMER. bookcase.
bicarbonato ➤ *m* bicarbonate ■ **b. de sodio** *or* **de sosa** CUL. baking soda.
bicentenario ➤ *m* bicentennial.
bíceps ➤ *m* biceps.
bicho ➤ *m* bug, insect.
bicicleta ➤ *f* bicycle.
bien ➤ *m* good, goodness; *(provecho)* good, benefit ■ **hacer (el) b.** to do good ■ *pl* property, goods • **b. inmuebles** *or* **raíces** real estate ➤ *adv* well; *(justamente)* right, correctly; *(de buena gana)* willingly; *(sin dificultad)* easily; *(bastante)* very; *(sí)* okay ■ **más b.** rather • **o b.** or else, otherwise • **por b.** willingly • **pues b.** then, well now • **y b.** well then.
bienestar ➤ *m* well-being, comfort.
bienvenida ➤ *f* welcome, greetings.
bife ➤ *m* AMER. steak, beefsteak.
bifocal ➤ *adj* bifocal.
biftec ➤ *m* steak, beefsteak.
bifurcación ➤ *f* bifurcation, branch; *(de un camino)* fork; RAIL. junction.
bigote ➤ *m* mustache ■ *pl* whiskers.
bilateral ➤ *adj* bilateral.
bilingüe ➤ *adj* bilingual.
bilis ➤ *f* bile.
billar ➤ *m* billiards.
billete ➤ *m* ticket; *(papel moneda)* bill.
billetera ➤ *f* wallet, billfold.
billón ➤ *m* $[10^{12}]$ trillion (U.S.), billion (G.B.).
bimotor ➤ *adj & m* AVIA. twin-engine (plane).
binario, a ➤ *adj* binary.
binocular ➤ *adj* binocular.
biografía ➤ *f* biography.
biología ➤ *f* biology.
biológico, a ➤ *adj* biologic(al).
biólogo, a ➤ *mf* biologist.
biombo ➤ *m* folding screen.
biopsia ➤ *f* biopsy.
biosfera ➤ *f* biosphere.
birlocha ➤ *f* kite (toy).
birrete ➤ *m* RELIG. biretta; *(bonete)* cap.
bisabuelo, a ➤ *mf* great-grandparent.
bisagra ➤ *f* hinge.
bisiesto ➤ *adj & m* leap (year).
bisnieto, a ➤ *mf* great-grandchild.
bisonte ➤ *m* bison.
bisté *or* **bistec** ➤ *m* beefsteak.
bisutería ➤ *f* costume jewelry.
bitio ➤ *m* COMPUT. bit.
bizantino, a ➤ *adj & mf* Byzantine.
bizco, a ➤ *adj & mf* cross-eyed.
bizcocho ➤ *m* sponge cake.
biznieto, a ➤ *m* var. of **bisnieto.**
blanco, a ➤ *adj* white; *(claro)* fair, light ➤ *mf* white (person) ➤ *m* white; *(tiro)* target; *(centro)* center; *(espacio)* blank space, blank ■ **dar en el b.** to hit the nail on the head.
blando, a ➤ *adj* soft; *(tierno)* tender.
blanquear ➤ *tr* to whiten; *(dar cal)* to whitewash; *(ropa)* to bleach.
blasfemia ➤ *f* blasphemy.
blasón ➤ *m* heraldry; *(escudo)* coat of arms.
blindado, a ➤ *adj* armored, armor-plated.
bloc ➤ *m* writing pad *or* tablet.
bloque ➤ *m* block; *(grupo)* bloc, coalition; *(papel)* pad, notepad.
bloquear ➤ *tr* MIL. to blockade; *(impedir)* to block, obstruct; *(obstruir)* to jam.
blusa ➤ *f* blouse.
blusón ➤ *m* loose blouse, smock.
boa ➤ *f* ZOOL. boa (constrictor).
bobada ➤ *f* foolish act *or* remark.
bobina ➤ *f* spool, reel; SEW. bobbin.
bobo, a ➤ *adj* silly, foolish ➤ *mf* fool.
boca ➤ *f* mouth; ZOOL. pincer ■ **b. abajo, arriba** face down, up • **¡cállate la b.!** COLL. be quiet!, shut up!
bocacalle ➤ *f* intersection.
bocadillo ➤ *m* sandwich.
bocado ➤ *m* mouthful, bite.
bocanada ➤ *f* swallow, swig; *(de humo)* puff; *(de aire)* gust, rush.
boceto ➤ *m* sketch, draft.
bocha ➤ *f* wooden ball.
bochinche ➤ *m* COLL. uproar, commotion.
bochorno ➤ *m (vergüenza)* embarrassment, shame; *(calor)* suffocating heat.
bocina ➤ *f* horn; MARIT. foghorn.
boda ➤ *f* wedding, marriage.
bodega ➤ *f* wine cellar; *(taberna)* tavern, bar; AMER. grocery store.
bodegón ➤ *m (taberna)* tavern, bar; ARTS still life.
bofetada ➤ *f* slap; *(afrenta)* insult.
bohemio, a ➤ *adj & mf* bohemian.
bohío ➤ *m* AMER. hut, shack.
boicotear ➤ *tr* to boycott.
boina ➤ *f* beret, cap.
boite ➤ *f* nightclub.
bola ➤ *f* ball; *(canica)* marble; *(mentira)* lie, fib ■ **b. de nieve** snowball.
bolera ➤ *f* bowling alley.
bolero ➤ *m* MUS. bolero.
boletería ➤ *f* AMER. ticket *or* box office.
boletín ➤ *m* bulletin.
boleto ➤ *m* AMER. ticket.
bolígrafo ➤ *m* ballpoint pen.
boliviano, a ➤ *adj* Bolivian ➤ *mf* Bolivian ➤ *m* BOL., FIN. boliviano.
bolívar ➤ *m* VEN., FIN. bolivar.
bollo ➤ *m* bun, roll; *(hueco)* dent.
bolos ➤ *mpl* bowling, ninepins.
bolsa ➤ *f (saco)* sack, bag; FIN. stock market ■ **b. de comercio** commodity exchange.
bolsillo ➤ *m* pocket; *(dinero)* purse, money.
bolso ➤ *m* purse, pocketbook.
bomba ➤ *f* MIL. bomb, shell; TECH. pump; *(sorpresa)* bombshell, stunning news ■ **pasarlo b.** to have a ball.
bombardear ➤ *tr* to bombard, bomb.
bombardeo ➤ *m* bombardment.
bombero, a ➤ *mf* fireman, firefighter.
bombilla ➤ *f* light bulb.
bombo ➤ *m* bass drum.
bombón ➤ *m* bonbon, chocolate.
bonachón, ona ➤ *adj & mf* COLL. good-natured (person).
bondad ➤ *f* goodness, kindness.
bondadoso, a ➤ *adj* good, kind.
boniato ➤ *m* sweet potato.
bonito, a ➤ *adj (lindo)* pretty, nice-looking ➤ *m* tuna, bonito.
bono ➤ *m (vale)* voucher; COM. *(fianza)*

bond.
boquera ➤ *f* lip sore, mouth ulcer.
boquerón ➤ *m* anchovy.
boquete ➤ *m (agujero)* hole.
boquiabierto, a ➤ *adj* open-mouthed, gaping; *(atónito)* amazed, astonished.
boquilla ➤ *f* MUS. mouthpiece; *(del cigarillo)* cigarette holder; *(filtro)* filter tip.
borbotear ➤ *intr* to boil, bubble.
bordado ➤ *m* embroidery.
bordar ➤ *tr* to embroider.
borde ➤ *m* border, edge; *(canto)* brim, rim.
bordear ➤ *tr* to border; *(ir por el borde)* to skirt, go around.
bordillo ➤ *m* curb.
boreal ➤ *adj* boreal, northern.
borgoña ➤ *m* Burgundy (wine).
borla ➤ *f* tassel.
borrachera ➤ *f (ebriedad)* drunkenness; *(parranda)* binge, spree.
borracho, a ➤ *adj* drunk; CUL. rum-soaked ➤ *mf* drunk, drunkard.
borrador ➤ *m (escrito)* rough draft; *(papel)* scratch pad; *(de borrar)* eraser.
borrar ➤ *tr* to erase.
borrasca ➤ *f* storm, tempest.
borrego, a ➤ *mf* lamb.
borrico ➤ *m* ass, donkey.
borroso, a ➤ *adj* blurred, fuzzy.
bosque ➤ *m* woods, forest; FIG. confusion.
bosquejo ➤ *m* sketch, outline, draft.
bostezar §02 ➤ *intr* to yawn.
bostezo ➤ *m* yawn.
bota ➤ *f* boot; *(odre)* wineskin; *(tonel)* wooden cask.
botánico, a ➤ *adj* botanical ➤ *mf* botanist ➤ *f* botany.
botar ➤ *tr* to fling, hurl; AMER. *(tirar)* to throw away; *(malgastar)* to waste, squander ➤ *intr* to bounce.
bote ➤ *m (brinco)* prance; *(rebote)* bounce; *(pote)* pot, jar; *(lata)* tin can; *(barco)* rowboat.
botella ➤ *f* bottle.
botica ➤ *f* pharmacy, drugstore.
botijo ➤ *m* earthenware jug.
botín ➤ *m* booty, spoils.
botiquín ➤ *m* medicine chest *or* cabinet; *(estuche)* first-aid kit.
botón ➤ *m* button.
botones ➤ *mpl* bellboy, bellhop.
bóveda ➤ *f* vault; *(techo)* dome, cupola; *(cripta)* crypt ■ **b. celeste firmament**, heavens.
boxeador, a ➤ *mf* boxer.
boxeo ➤ *m* boxing.
boya ➤ *f* buoy.
bozal ➤ *m* muzzle.
bracero ➤ *m* laborer, worker.
braga ➤ *f (pañal)* diapers ■ *pl (calzón femenino)* panties.
bragueta ➤ *f* fly (of pants).
brasa ➤ *f* live *or* hot coal.
brasero ➤ *m* brazier.
brasileño, a ➤ *adj & mf* Brazilian.
bravo, a ➤ *adj* brave, valiant; *(feroz)* ferocious, wild; *(enojado)* angry, furious ■ **¡b.!** bravo!, well done!
brazada ➤ *f* breaststroke.
brazalete ➤ *m* bracelet.
brazo ➤ *m* arm ■ *pl (jornaleros)* hands, laborers.
brecha ➤ *f* gap, opening.
brécol ➤ *m* broccoli.
breve ➤ *adj* brief, short ■ **en b.** *(pronto)* shortly, soon.
bribón, ona ➤ *adj & mf (pícaro)* roguish (person).
bridge ➤ *m (naipes)* bridge; DENT. bridge, bridgework.
brigada ➤ *f* brigade; *(división)* squad, unit; *(equipo)* gang, team.
brillante ➤ *adj* brilliant.
brillar ➤ *intr* to shine.
brillo ➤ *m (lustre)* brilliance, shine; *(gloria)* distinction, glory ■ **dar** *or* **sacar b. a** to shine.
brincar §47 ➤ *intr* to jump, leap about.
brindar ➤ *intr* to toast, drink a toast.
brindis ➤ *m* toast.
brío ➤ *m* strength, vigor; *(garbo)* grace, charm.
brisa ➤ *f* breeze, light wind.
británico, a ➤ *adj & mf* British (person).
brocado, a ➤ *adj & m* brocade.
brocha ➤ *f* paintbrush; *(de afeitar)* shaving brush.
broche ➤ *m* clasp, hook and eye; *(prendedor)* brooch.
bróculi ➤ *m* broccoli.
broma ➤ *f* joke, prank; *(diversión)* fun, jest ■ **b. pesada** practical joke, prank • **ni en b.** not on your life.
bromear ➤ *intr* to joke, jest.
bronce ➤ *m* bronze.
bronceado, a ➤ *adj (tostado)* tanned ➤ *m (piel tostada)* suntan.
bronceador ➤ *m* suntan lotion.
broncear ➤ *tr (piel)* to tan, suntan ➤ *reflex* to get a tan, suntan.
bronquitis ➤ *f* bronchitis.
brotar ➤ *intr* BOT. to bud, sprout; *(agua)* to spring, flow; *(estallar)* to break out, spring up.
bruja ➤ *f* witch, sorceress.
brújula ➤ *f* compass; *(norma)* standard, norm.
bruma ➤ *f* fog, mist.
bruñido, a ➤ *adj* burnished, polished.
brusco, a ➤ *adj* brusque.
brutalidad ➤ *f* brutality; *(incapacidad)* stupidity, foolishness; *(gran cantidad)* loads, slew.
bruto, a ➤ *adj* brutish, boorish; *(necio)* stupid, ignorant; *(diamante)* rough, uncut; COM. gross.
bucear ➤ *intr* to swim under water.
buceo ➤ *m* underwater swimming; *(exploración)* exploration, searching.
bucólico, a ➤ *adj* bucolic, pastoral.
buen ➤ *adj contr of* **bueno.**
bueno, a ➤ *adj* good; *(bondadoso)* kind, benevolent; *(útil)* fit, appropriate; *(sano)* well, healthy; *(bonachón)* innocent, naive ■ **buenas noches, tardes** good night, afternoon • **buenos días** good morning ➤ *adv* all right, okay ➤ *m* ■ **lo b.** (the) good.
buey ➤ *m* ox, bullock.
búfalo, a ➤ *mf (buey salvaje)* buffalo; *(bisonte)* bison.
bufanda ➤ *f* scarf, muffler.
bufete ➤ *m* lawyer's office.
buhardilla ➤ *f (ventana)* dormer; *(desván)* attic, garret.
búho ➤ *m* horned owl; *(recluso)* hermit.
buitre ➤ *m* vulture, buzzard.
bujía ➤ *f (vela)* candle; ELEC. spark plug.
bulbo ➤ *m* bulb.
bullicio ➤ *m* bustle, hubbub.
bullicioso, a ➤ *adj* bustling.
bulto ➤ *m (forma)* form, shape; *(fardo)* package, bundle; MED. swelling, lump.
buñuelo ➤ *m* fried dough, fritter.
buque ➤ *m* ship, vessel.
burbuja ➤ *f* bubble.
burdel ➤ *m* brothel.
burguesía ➤ *f* bourgeoisie, middle class.
burla ➤ *f* jeer, taunt.
burlarse ➤ *reflex* to make fun, joke ■ **b. de** to make fun of, ridicule.
burocracia ➤ *f* bureaucracy.
burra ➤ *f* donkey, jenny; COLL. *(ignorante)* dunce.
burro ➤ *m* donkey, jackass; *(ignorante)* dunce.
bursátil ➤ *adj* stock, stock market.
busca ➤ *f* search ■ **ir en** *or* **a la b. de** to go in search of.
buscador, a ➤ *mf* searcher ➤ *m* COMPUT. search engine.
buscar §47 ➤ *tr* to search *or* look for, seek.
búsqueda ➤ *f* search.
busto ➤ *m* ANAT. chest, bust; SCULP. bust.
butaca ➤ *f* armchair, easy chair; THEAT. orchestra *or* box seat.
butano ➤ *m* butane.
buzo ➤ *m* (deep-sea) diver; *(prenda)* overalls, jumpsuit.
buzón ➤ *m* mailbox, letter box.

C

cabalgar §31 ➤ *intr* to ride horseback.
caballa ➤ *f* mackerel.
caballería ➤ *f (animal)* mount, steed; MIL. cavalry.
caballeriza ➤ *f* stable; *(criados)* stablehands.
caballero ➤ *m* knight; *(señor)* gentleman ■ **armar c. a** to knight.
caballete ➤ *m* easel.
caballo ➤ *m* horse; *(en ajedrez)* knight ■ **a c.** on horseback • **c. de montar** *or* **de silla** saddle horse • **montar a c.** to go horseback riding ■ *pl* horsepower.
cabaña ➤ *f* hut, cabin.
cabaret ➤ *m* night club, cabaret.
cabecera ➤ *f (lugar principal)* head; *(de una cama)* headboard ■ **médico de c.** attending physician.
cabecilla ➤ *mf* ringleader.
cabellera ➤ *f* head of hair.
cabello ➤ *m* hair.
caber §06 ➤ *intr (tener lugar)* to fit; *(corresponder)* to fall to; *(ser posible)* to be possible ■ **cabe decir one might say** • **no cabe duda** there is no doubt • **no cabe más** FIG. that's the limit.
cabeza ➤ *f* head; *(jefe)* chief ■ **a la c. de** at the head of; *(en control)* in charge of • **subirse a la c.** to go to one's head.
cabida ➤ *f* capacity.
cabildo ➤ *m* town council.
cabina ➤ *f* booth.
cable ➤ *m* cable.
cablevisión ➤ *f* cable television.
cabo ➤ *m* end; *(pedazo)* stub, bit; GEOG. cape; MARIT. cable; MIL. corporal ■ **al c. de** at the end of • **atar cabos** to put two and two together • **llevar a c.** to carry out.
cabra ➤ *f* goat.
cabritilla ➤ *f* lambskin, kid.
cacahuete ➤ *m* peanut.
cacao ➤ *m* cacao; CUL. cocoa.
cacatúa ➤ *f* cockatoo.
cacería ➤ *f (caza)* hunting; *(partida)* hunting party.
cacerola ➤ *f* casserole, pot.
cachalote ➤ *m* sperm whale.
cacharro ➤ *m (vasija)* crock; COLL. *(trasto)* piece of junk; *(máquina)* wreck; *(coche)* jalopy ■ *pl* junk.
cachemira ➤ *f* cashmere.
cachete ➤ *m (mejilla)* cheek; *(cachetada)* slap.
cachivache ➤ *m* piece of junk.
cacho ➤ *m (pedazo)* piece.
cachorro, a ➤ *mf (perro)* puppy; *(de otros mamíferos)* cub.
cacique ➤ *mf* COLL. *(jefe)* political boss; *(déspota)* tyrant.
caco ➤ *m* burglar.
cactus *or* **cacto** ➤ *m* cactus.
cada ➤ *adj* each, every ■ **c. cual** *or* **uno** each one, everyone • **¿c. cuánto?** how often? • **c. vez más** more and more • **c. vez menos** less and less • **c. vez peor** worse and worse • **c. vez que** whenever.
cadáver ➤ *m* corpse, cadaver.
cadena ➤ *f* chain ■ **c. de emisoras** network • **c. de montañas** mountain range • **c. perpetua** life imprisonment.
cadera ➤ *f* hip, hip joint.
caducar §47 ➤ *intr* to lapse, expire.
caducidad ➤ *f* expiration.
caer §07 ➤ *intr* to fall; *(derrumbarse)* to fall down, collapse; *(los precios)* to drop; *(el sol)* to set; *(comprender)* to see; COMPUT. to crash ■ **al c. la noche** at nightfall • **c. bien** *(prenda)* to suit; *(persona)* to make a good impression on; *(alimento)* to agree with • **c. mal** *(prenda)* to fit poorly; *(persona)* to displease; *(alimento)* to upset one's stomach ➤ *reflex* to fall; *(de las manos)* to drop, fall.
café ➤ *m* coffee; *(cafetería)* café.
cafetal ➤ *m* coffee plantation.
cafetera ➤ *f* CUL. coffeepot ■ **c. de filtro** percolator.
cafetería ➤ *f* coffee shop, café.
caída ➤ *f* fall; *(de la temperatura)* drop; *(tumbo)* tumble; *(ruina)* downfall.
caimán ➤ *m* alligator.
cairel ➤ *m* hairpiece; *(fleco)* fringe.
caja ➤ *f* box; *(de madera)* chest; *(ataúd)* coffin; *(ventanilla)* cashier's window ■ **c. de ahorros** savings bank • **c. de cambios** *or* **velocidades** AUTO. transmission • **c. de fusibles** ELEC. fuse box • **c. de seguridad** safe-deposit box • **c. fuerte** safe.
cajero, a ➤ *mf* teller, cashier ■ **c. automático** automated teller machine.
cajón ➤ *m (caja grande)* case; *(gaveta)* drawer.
cal ➤ *f* MIN. lime.
calabaza ➤ *f* squash, pumpkin.
calabozo ➤ *m (cárcel)* underground prison; *(celda)* jail cell.
calamar ➤ *m* squid.
calambre ➤ *m* cramp, spasm.
calamidad ➤ *f* misfortune.
calar ➤ *tr (mojar)* to drench; *(penetrar)* to penetrate ➤ *reflex (mojarse)* to get drenched; *(ponerse)* to put on.
calavera ➤ *f* skull.
calcar §47 ➤ *tr* to trace; FIG. to copy.
calcetín ➤ *m* sock.
calcio ➤ *m* calcium.
calco ➤ *m* tracing; FIG. copy.
calcomanía ➤ *f* decal, transfer.
calculadora ➤ *f* calculator.
calcular ➤ *tr (computar)* to calculate; *(proyectar)* to estimate.
cálculo ➤ *m (proceso)* calculation; *(suposición)* estimate; MED. stone, calculus; MATH. calculus.
caldera ➤ *f* MECH. boiler.
caldero ➤ *m* small caldron.
caldo ➤ *m* broth.
calefacción ➤ *f* heat, heating.
calendario ➤ *m* calendar; *(programa)* schedule.
calentador ➤ *m* heater; *(para agua)* water heater.
calentar §33 ➤ *tr* to warm *or* heat (up); ➤ *reflex* to warm oneself up.
calentura ➤ *f* fever.
calidad ➤ *f* quality.
cálido, a ➤ *adj* warm.
cal(e)idoscopio ➤ *m* kaleidoscope.
caliente ➤ *adj* hot, warm; FIG. heated.
calificar §47 ➤ *tr* EDUC. to grade.
calificativo ➤ *m* qualifier.
caligrafía ➤ *f* calligraphy.
cáliz ➤ *m* chalice.
callar ➤ *intr* to be *or* become silent ➤ *tr (silenciar)* to silence, hush ➤ *reflex (guardar silencio)* to be quiet *or* silent; *(quedarse callado)* to keep quiet ■ **¡cállate!** be quiet!
calle ➤ *f* street.
callejón ➤ *m* alley ■ **c. sin salida** blind alley.
callo ➤ *m* corn ■ *pl* tripe.
callosidad ➤ *f* callosity, callus.
calmante ➤ *adj & m* sedative.
calmar ➤ *tr* to soothe, calm (down) ➤ *intr* to calm (down), abate ➤ *reflex* to calm down.
calma ➤ *f* calm ■ **con c.** calmly.
caló ➤ *m* Gypsy dialect; *(jerga)* slang.
calor ➤ *m* warmth, heat ■ **hacer c.** *(tiempo)* to be hot *or* warm • **tener c.** *(persona)* to be hot *or* warm.
caloría ➤ *f* calorie.
calumnia ➤ *f* calumny, slander.
caluroso, a ➤ *adj* warm, hot; FIG. warm, enthusiastic.
calvario ➤ *m* calvary; RELIG. Calvary.
calvo, a ➤ *adj* bald ➤ *mf* bald person ➤ *f* bald spot.
calzada ➤ *f* highway, road.
calzado ➤ *m* footwear.
calzador ➤ *m* shoehorn.
calzar §02 ➤ *tr* to put (shoes) on; *(rueda)* to wedge ■ **¿qué número calza?** what size shoe do you take? ➤ *reflex* to put on shoes.
calzón ➤ *m or* **calzones** ➤ *mpl* pants, trousers.
calzoncillos ➤ *mpl* underwear, boxers.
cama ➤ *f* bed ■ **c. gemela** twin bed • **c. matrimonial** double bed.
cámara ➤ *f (sala)* hall; *(junta)* chamber; AUTO. inner tube; PHOTOG. camera ■ **c. cinematográfica** movie camera • **c. lenta** slow motion.
camarada ➤ *mf* comrade.
camarero, a ➤ *mf* waiter, waitress.
camarín ➤ *m* THEAT. dressing room.
camarón ➤ *m* shrimp, prawn.
camarote ➤ *m* MARIT. cabin, berth.
cambiar ➤ *tr* to change; *(alterar)* to alter; *(reemplazar)* to replace; COM. to exchange, change ➤ *intr* to change ■ **c. de casa** to move • **c. de color** to change color • **c. de ropa** to change clothes ➤ *reflex* to change.
cambio ➤ *m* change; *(alteración)* alteration; COM. rate of exchange ■ **a c. de** in exchange for • **c. automático** automatic transmission • **c. de marchas** *or* **velocidades** gearshift • **casa de c.** foreign exchange office.
camello ➤ *m* camel.
camerino ➤ *m* THEAT. dressing room.
camilla ➤ *f* MED. stretcher.
caminar ➤ *intr & tr* to walk.
caminata ➤ *f* walk, hike.
camino ➤ *m* road; *(senda)* path, trail; *(vía)* route ■ **abrir c.** to make way • **a medio c.** halfway • **c. a** towards • **en c.** on the way • **en c. de** FIG. on the way to.
camión ➤ *m* truck, lorry (G.B.); MEX. bus ■ **c. de bomberos** fire engine • **c. de mudanzas** moving van.
camionero, a ➤ *mf* truck driver.
camioneta ➤ *f* van.
camisa ➤ *f* shirt ■ **c. de fuerza** strait-jacket • **en mangas de c.** in shirt-

sleeves.

camiseta ➤ *f* T-shirt; *(ropa interior)* undershirt; SPORT. jersey.

camisón ➤ *m* nightgown.

camote AMER. ➤ *m* sweet potato.

campamento ➤ *m* camp ■ **c. de verano** summer camp.

campana ➤ *f* bell.

campanada ➤ *f* stroke, ring (of a bell).

campanario ➤ *m* bell tower, belfry.

campanilla ➤ *f* hand bell; *(timbre)* doorbell.

campaña ➤ *f* *(llanura)* plain; MIL., POL. campaign ■ **hacer c.** to campaign • **tienda de c.** tent.

campeón, ona ➤ *mf* champion.

campeonato ➤ *m* championship.

campesino, a ➤ *adj* rustic ➤ *mf* peasant.

campo ➤ *m* country, countryside; *(plantío)* field; MIL., SPORT. field ■ **a c. traviesa** cross-country • **casa de c.** country house • **c. de golf** golf course.

camposanto ➤ *m* cemetery, graveyard.

camuflar ➤ *tr* to camouflage.

can ➤ *m* dog.

cana ➤ *f* gray hair.

canadiense ➤ *adj & mf* Canadian.

canal ➤ *m* canal; *(estrecho)* strait, channel; *(de puerto)* navigation channel; TELEV. channel.

canalización ➤ *f* ELEC. wiring.

canalla COLL. ➤ *m* scoundrel ➤ *f* riffraff.

canalón ➤ *m* gutter, drainpipe.

canapé ➤ *m* sofa; CUL. canapé.

canastilla ➤ *f* small basket; *(de bebé)* layette.

canasto ➤ *m* basket.

cancelar ➤ *tr* to cancel; *(saldar)* to pay off.

cáncer ➤ *m* cancer.

canceroso, a ➤ *adj* cancerous.

cancha ➤ *f* playing field; *(de tenis)* court; AMER. open ground.

canciller ➤ *mf* chancellor.

canción ➤ *f* song ■ **c. de cuna** lullaby.

candado ➤ *m* padlock.

candela ➤ *f* candle.

candelabro ➤ *m* candelabrum.

candidato, a ➤ *mf* candidate.

candidatura ➤ *f* candidacy.

candoroso, a ➤ *adj* frank, candid; *(ingenuo)* naive.

canela ➤ *f* cinnamon.

canelones ➤ *mpl* canneloni (pasta).

cangrejo ➤ *m* crab ■ **c. de río** crayfish.

canguro ➤ *m* kangaroo.

caníbal ➤ *adj* cannibalistic ➤ *mf* cannibal.

canica ➤ *f* marble ■ *pl* (game of) marbles.

canícula ➤ *f* dog days, midsummer heat.

canoa ➤ *f* canoe; *(bote)* rowboat.

canoso, a ➤ *adj* gray-haired.

cansado, a ➤ *adj* *(fatigado)* tired; *(agotado)* worn-out.

cansancio ➤ *m* tiredness ■ **muerto de c.** dog-tired.

cansar ➤ *tr* to tire, make tired; *(aburrir)* to bore; *(fastidiar)* to annoy ■ **c. la vista** to strain one's eyes ➤ *reflex* to become *or* get tired ➤ *intr* to be tiring; *(aburrir)* to be boring.

cantante ➤ *mf* singer, vocalist.

cantar ➤ *tr & intr* to sing.

cántaro ➤ *m* jug ■ **llover a cántaros** COLL. to rain cats and dogs.

cantera ➤ *f* quarry, pit.

cántico ➤ *m* canticle; FIG. song.

cantidad ➤ *f* quantity; *(suma)* sum.

cantimplora ➤ *f* canteen.

canto[1] ➤ *m* song; *(arte)* singing.

canto[2] ➤ *m* *(extremo)* edge; *(borde)* border ■ **de c.** on end, on edge.

canturrear ➤ *intr* COLL. to sing softly.

caña ➤ *f* reed; *(de azúcar)* cane; *(tallo)* stalk ■ **c. de pescar** fishing rod.

cañaveral ➤ *m* cane thicket; *(plantación)* sugar-cane plantation.

cañería ➤ *f* pipe; *(tubería)* pipeline.

caño ➤ *m* pipe, tube.

cañón ➤ *m* MIL. cannon; ARM. barrel; GEOG. canyon, gorge.

cañonazo ➤ *m* cannon shot.

caoba ➤ *f* mahogany.

caos ➤ *m* chaos.

caótico, a ➤ *adj* chaotic.

capa ➤ *f* *(manto)* cape; *(de pintura)* coat; *(cubierta)* covering; GEOL. layer.

capacidad ➤ *f* capacity.

caparazón ➤ *m* shell, carapace.

capataz ➤ *mf* foreman/woman.

capaz ➤ *adj* capable.

capilla ➤ *f* chapel.

capital ➤ *adj* capital; *(esencial)* vital ➤ *m* FIN. capital; *(el que produce intereses)* principal ➤ *f* capital, capital city.

capitalista ➤ *adj & mf* capitalist.

capitán, ana ➤ *m* captain.

capitel ➤ *m* capital (of a column).

capitolio ➤ *m* capitol.

capitulación ➤ *f* capitulation.

capítulo ➤ *m* chapter; *(reunión)* assembly.

capó ➤ *m* AUTO. hood, bonnet (G.B.).

capote ➤ *m* cape ■ **c. de montar** riding cape.

capricho ➤ *m* whim; *(antojo)* fancy.

caprichoso, a ➤ *adj* whimsical; *(inconstante)* fickle.

cápsula ➤ *f* capsule.

captar ➤ *tr* to attract, win.

captura ➤ *f* capture.

capturar ➤ *tr* to capture.

capucha ➤ *f* hood.

capullo ➤ *m* *(brote)* bud; *(de larva)* cocoon ■ **c. de rosa** rosebud.

caqui ➤ *m* BOT. persimmon; *(tela y color)* khaki.

cara ➤ *f* face; *(superficie)* surface; *(frente)* front; *(aspecto)* appearance ■ **hacer c. a** to confront.

caracol ➤ *m* snail; *(espiral)* spiral.

caracola ➤ *f* conch.

carácter ➤ *m* character; *(índole)* nature; *(rasgo)* trait.

característico, a ➤ *adj & f* characteristic.

caracterizar §02 ➤ *tr* to characterize; THEAT. to portray (a role) expressively.

¡caramba! ➤ *interj* *(asombro)* good heavens!; *(enfado)* damn it!

carámbano ➤ *m* icicle.

caramelo ➤ *m* caramel; *(dulce)* candy.

caravana ➤ *f* caravan.

carbón ➤ *m* coal; *(de leña)* charcoal; *(lápiz)* carbon pencil.

carboncillo ➤ *m* ARTS charcoal pencil.

carbono ➤ *m* carbon.

carburador ➤ *m* carburetor.

carburante ➤ *m* fuel.

carcajada ➤ *f* loud laughter ■ **reír a carcajadas** to split one's sides laughing.

cárcel ➤ *f* *(prisión)* jail; TECH. clamp.

carcelero, a ➤ *mf* jailer ➤ *adj* jail.

cardenal ➤ *m* RELIG., ORNITH. cardinal; COLL. *(mancha)* bruise, welt.

cardiaco, a *or* **cardíaco, a** ➤ *adj* cardiac ■ **ataque c.** heart attack.

cardinal ➤ *adj* cardinal.

cardiograma ➤ *m* electrocardiogram.

cardiólogo, a ➤ *mf* cardiologist.

cardo ➤ *m* thistle.

cardume(n) ➤ *m* school (of fish).

carecer §09 ➤ *intr* ■ **c. de** to lack.

carencia ➤ *f* lack; MED. deficiency.

carente ➤ *adj* lacking (in), devoid of.

carestía ➤ *f* scarcity.

careta ➤ *f* mask ■ **c. antigás** gas mask.

carey ➤ *m* sea turtle; *(caparazón)* tortoiseshell.

carga ➤ *f* load; *(acción)* loading; *(flete)* cargo; *(peso)* burden; ELEC. charge ■ **llevar la c. de** to be responsible for.

cargado, a ➤ *adj* laden; *(sabor)* strong; *(atmósfera)* heavy; ELEC. charged ■ **c. de años** old, ancient • **c. de espaldas** round-shouldered.

cargamento ➤ *m* load, cargo.

cargar §31 ➤ *tr* to load; *(llenar)* to fill; *(imputar)* to ascribe; *(con obligaciones)* to burden; *(con impuestos)* to impose; COLL. *(importunar)* to pester; ELEC., MIL. to charge; COM. to debit; AMER. to carry ■ **c. en cuenta** COM. to charge to one's account ➤ *intr* to load ■ **c. con** to carry; FIG. to shoulder ➤ *reflex* COLL. *(molestarse)* to become annoyed; METEOROL. to cloud over.

cargo ➤ *m* *(peso)* load; *(dignidad)* position; *(acusación)* charge; COM. debit ■ **a c. de** in charge of • **hacerse c. de** to take charge of.

caribe *or* **caribeño, a** ➤ *adj* Caribbean.

caricatura ➤ *f* caricature.

caricia ➤ *f* caress ■ **hacer caricias a** to caress, fondle.

caridad ➤ *f* charity.

caries ➤ *f* MED. caries, decay.

cariño ➤ *m* affection; *(amor)* love.

cariñoso, a ➤ *adj* affectionate, loving.

caritativo, a ➤ *adj* charitable.

carnaval ➤ *m* carnival.

carne ➤ *f* flesh; CUL. meat; BOT. pulp ■ **c. asada al horno** roast (of meat) • **c. asada a la parrilla** broiled meat • **c. de gallina** COLL. goose bumps. • **c. picada** chopped meat, ground meat.

carnero ➤ *m* sheep; *(macho)* ram; CUL. mutton.

carnet *or* **carné** ➤ *m* card.

carnicería ➤ *f* butcher shop; FIG. carnage, butchery.

carnicero, a ➤ *mf* butcher.

caro, a ➤ *adj* *(costoso)* expensive; *(amado)* dear ➤ *adv* at a high price.

carpa ➤ *f* AMER. tent; *(toldo)* awning.

carpeta ➤ *f* folder.

carpintería ➤ *f* *(oficio)* carpentry; *(taller)* carpenter shop.

carpintero, a ➤ *mf* carpenter ➤ *m* ORNITH. woodpecker.

carraspear ➤ *intr* to clear one's throat.

carraspeo ➤ *m* hoarseness.

carrera ➤ *f* race; *(pista)* racetrack; *(profesión)* career; *(hilera)* row; ARCHIT. beam **c. a pie** footrace • **c. de relevos** relay race ■ *pl* races.

carrete ➤ *m* *(bobina)* bobbin; *(de la caña de pescar)* reel.

carretera ➤ *f* highway, road ■ **c. de circunvalación** bypass • **c. de cuatro vías** four-lane highway • **c. de vía libre** expressway.

carretilla ➤ *f* *(carro pequeño)* cart; *(de una rueda)* wheelbarrow.

carril *(de tránsito)* lane; RAIL. rail.

carrillo ➤ *m* jowl ■ **comer a dos carrillos** to stuff oneself.

carrito ➤ *m* cart ■ **c. de compras** shopping cart.

carro ➤ *m* *(vehículo)* cart; AMER. *(automóvil)* car; *(de máquina)* carriage ■ **c. blindado** armored car.

carrocería ➤ *f* AUTO. body.

carruaje ➤ *m* carriage.

carrusel ➤ *m* carousel, merry-go-round.

carta ➤ *f* letter; *(naipe)* playing card; *(de derechos)* charter; *(documento)* document ■ **a la c.** a la carte • **c. aérea** airmail letter.

cartel ➤ *m* poster, bill; FIN. cartel.

cartelera ➤ *f* billboard; *(de un periódico)* entertainment section.

cartera ➤ *f* *(de hombre)* billfold, wallet; *(de mujer)* pocketbook; *(portadocumentos)* briefcase; *(de bolsillo)* pocket flap; *(ministerio)* cabinet post.

cartero, a ➤ *mf* mail carrier.

cartón ➤ *m* *(papel)* cardboard; *(caja)* cardboard box; *(de cigarrillos)* carton.

cartucho ➤ *m* *(cono)* paper cone; *(bolsa)* paper bag.

cartulina ➤ *f* pasteboard.

casa ➤ *f* house; *(residencia)* home; COM. firm ■ **c. de la moneda** mint • **c. editorial** publishing house • **en c.** at home • **estar de c.** to be casually dressed.

casado, a ➤ *adj & mf* married (person) ■ **recién casados** newlyweds.

casamiento ➤ *m* marriage, wedding.

casar ➤ *intr* to marry ➤ *tr* to marry (off) ➤ *reflex* to get married.

cascabel ➤ *m* small bell ■ **serpiente de c.** rattlesnake.

cascada ➤ *f* waterfall.

cascanueces ➤ *m* nutcracker.

cascar §47 ➤ *tr & reflex* to crack.

cáscara ➤ *f* shell; *(de fruta)* skin; *(de queso, fruta)* rind; *(de cereal)* husk.

cascarón ➤ *m* eggshell.

casco ➤ *m* MIL. helmet; *(tonel)* barrel; MARIT. hull; ZOOL. hoof.

caserío ➤ *m* *(pueblo)* hamlet; *(cortijo)* country house *or* estate.

casero, a ➤ *adj* *(de la casa)* domestic; *(de la familia)* family; *(hecho en casa)* homemade; *(hogareño)* home-loving ■ **cocina c.** home cooking ➤ *mf* *(dueño)* owner, landlord ➤ *f* landlady.

caserón ➤ *m* COLL. large ramshackle house.

caseta ➤ *f* cottage; *(casilla)* booth.

casete ➤ *f* cassette, tape cartridge.

casi ➤ *adv* almost, nearly ■ **c. c.** COLL. very nearly • **c. nada** next to nothing • **c. nunca** hardly ever.

casino ➤ *m* casino.

caso ➤ *m* case; *(acontecimiento)* event; *(circunstancia)* circumstance ■ **en c. de** in the event of • **en c. de que** in case • **en todo c.** in any case • **hacer** *or* **venir al c.** COLL. to be relevant • **hacer c. a** to heed • **hacer c. de** to pay attention to.

caspa ➤ *f* dandruff.

castaña ➤ *f* *(fruta)* chestnut.

castañeta ➤ *f* castanet.

castaño, a ➤ *adj* chestnut, brown ➤ *m* *(árbol)* chestnut tree.

castellano ➤ *m* Spanish.

castigar §31 ➤ *tr* to punish; *(mortificar)* to discipline; SPORT. to penalize.

castigo ➤ *m* punishment; *(mortificación)* self-denial; SPORT. penalty.

castillo ➤ *m* castle.

casual ➤ *adj* chance, coincidental.

casualidad ➤ *f* chance ■ **de c.** by chance • **por c.** by any chance.

casualmente ➤ *adv* by chance *or* accident.

cataclismo ➤ *m* cataclysm, upheaval.

catacumbas ➤ *fpl* catacombs.

catador, a ➤ *mf* taster, sampler.

catalogar §31 ➤ *tr* to catalog(ue), list.

catálogo ➤ *m* catalog(ue).

catar ➤ *tr* to sample, taste.

catarata ➤ *f* waterfall; MED. cataract.

catarro ➤ *m* cold, catarrh.

catástrofe ➤ *f* catastrophe.

cátedra ➤ *f* *(rango)* professorship; *(asiento)* professor's chair.

catedral ➤ *f* cathedral.

catedrático, a ➤ *mf* university professor.

categoría ➤ *f* category; *(clase)* type.

católico, a ➤ *adj & mf* Catholic.

catorce ➤ *adj & m* fourteen.

cauce ➤ *m* riverbed; *(acequia)* ditch.

caucho ➤ *m* rubber.

caudal ➤ *adj* ZOOL. caudal; *(río)* deep ➤ *m* *(del río)* volume; *(riqueza)* wealth.

caudillo ➤ *m* leader; AMER. political boss.

causa ➤ *f* cause; *(motivo)* reason; LAW lawsuit.

causante ➤ *adj* causative ➤ *mf* originator.

causar ➤ *tr* to cause; *(ira)* to provoke.

cautela ➤ *f* caution.

cautivar ➤ *tr* *(aprisionar)* to capture; *(fascinar)* to captivate.

cautiverio ➤ *m or* **cautividad** ➤ *f* captivity.

cautivo, a ➤ *adj & mf* captive.

cavar ➤ *tr* to dig.

caverna ➤ *f* cavern, cave.

cavidad ➤ *f* cavity.

cavilar ➤ *intr* to ponder, ruminate.

cayo ➤ *m* MARIT. key, islet.

caza ➤ *f* *(cacería)* hunt; *(animales)* game ■ **ir de c.** to go hunting.

cazador, a ➤ *adj* hunting; ZOOL. predatory ➤ *mf* hunter.

cazar §02 ➤ *tr* to hunt.

cazo ➤ *m* CUL. *(cucharón)* ladle; *(cacerola)* saucepan.

cazuela ➤ *f* casserole; *(guisado)* stew.

cebado, a ➤ *adj* AMER., ZOOL. fattened ➤ *f* BOT. barley.

cebiche ➤ *m* AMER. marinated raw fish.

cebo ➤ *m* *(alimento)* feed; *(detonador)* charge; *(del anzuelo)* bait.

cebolla ➤ *f* onion; *(bulbo)* bulb.

cebra ➤ *f* zebra.

ceder ➤ *tr* to cede; *(transferir)* to transfer; SPORT. to pass ➤ *intr* to cede; *(rendirse)* to yield, give in *or* up; *(disminuirse)* to abate.

cédula ➤ *f* document ■ **c. de identidad** identification card *or* papers.

cegar §35 ➤ *tr* to blind ➤ *reflex* FIG. to be blinded.

ceguera *or* **ceguedad** ➤ *f* blindness.

ceja ➤ *f* eyebrow.

celada ➤ *f* ambush; FIG. trap.

celador, a ➤ *mf* *(en la escuela)* monitor; *(de prisión)* guard.

celda ➤ *f* *(del cárcel, monasterio)* cell.

celebración ➤ *f* celebration; *(aclamación)* praise.

celebrar ➤ *tr* to celebrate; *(alabar)* to praise; *(venerar)* to venerate; *(una reunión)* to hold; *(un acuerdo)* to reach ➤ *reflex* *(cumpleaños)* to be *or* fall on; *(una reunión)* to take place.

célebre ➤ *adj* celebrated, famous.

celebridad ➤ *f* celebrity.

celeste ➤ *adj* sky-blue ■ **cuerpo c.** heavenly body ➤ *m* sky blue.

célibe ➤ *adj & mf* celibate.

celo ➤ *m* *(cuidado)* diligence; *(entusiasmo)* zeal; *(envidia)* jealousy ➤ *pl* jealousy • **dar c.** to make jealous • **tener c.** to be jealous.

celoso, a ➤ *adj* jealous.

célula ➤ *f* BIOL., ELEC., POL. cell.

celular ➤ *adj* cellular ➤ *m* cell phone.

celulitis ➤ *f* cellulitis.
celuloso, a ➤ *adj* cellulous, cellular ➤ *f* cellulose.
cementerio ➤ *m* cemetery.
cemento ➤ *m* cement; *(hormigón)* concrete.
cena ➤ *f* dinner, supper.
cenar ➤ *intr* to have dinner *or* supper.
cenicero ➤ *m* ashtray.
cenit ➤ *m* zenith.
censo ➤ *m* census; *(lista)* roll; *(arrendamiento)* rental ■ **levantar el c.** to take a census.
censura ➤ *f* censure; *(de expresión, arte)* censorship.
censurar ➤ *tr* to censor; *(criticar)* to criticize.
centavo, a ➤ *adj* hundredth ➤ *m* cent.
centellear *or* **centellar** ➤ *intr (fulgurar)* to sparkle; *(destellar)* to twinkle; *(chispear)* to flicker.
centena ➤ *f* (one) hundred.
centenar ➤ *m* (one) hundred.
centenario, a ➤ *adj & m* centennial.
centeno ➤ *m* rye.
centésimo, a ➤ *adj & m* hundredth.
centígrado, a ➤ *adj* centigrade.
centigramo ➤ *m* centigram.
centilitro ➤ *m* centiliter.
centímetro ➤ *m* centimeter.
céntimo, a ➤ *adj* hundredth ➤ *m* cent.
centinela ➤ *mf* sentinel, sentry; FIG. lookout.
centolla ➤ *m* spider crab.
central ➤ *adj* central ➤ *f (oficina)* headquarters; ELEC. power plant ■ **c. de correos** main post office.
centrar ➤ *tr* to center; *(determinar)* to find the center of; *(enfocar)* to focus; FIG. to aim.
céntrico, a ➤ *adj* central, centric.
centro ➤ *m* center; *(medio)* middle; *(núcleo)* core; *(ciudad)* downtown ■ **c. comercial** shopping center.
centroamericano, a ➤ *adj & mf* Central American.
ceño ➤ *m* frown ■ **arrugar** *or* **fruncir el c.** to frown.
cepa ➤ *f (de la vid)* rootstalk; *(vid)* vine.
cepillar ➤ *tr (limpiar)* to brush.
cepillo ➤ *m* brush ■ **c. de dientes** toothbrush • **c. para el pelo** hairbrush.
cera ➤ *f* wax; *(de los oídos)* earwax; *(de lustrar)* polish.
cerámico, a ➤ *adj* ceramic ➤ *f* ceramics.
cerca ➤ *adv* nearby, close by ■ **c. de** *(cercano a)* near, close to; *(alrededor de)* about • **de c.** closely ➤ *f* fence.
cercano, a ➤ *adj (próximo)* close; *(vecino)* neighboring; FIG. impending.
cercar §47 ➤ *tr (con cerca)* to fence in; *(rodear)* to surround; MIL. to besiege.
cerco ➤ *m* circle; *(borde)* edge; *(seto)* hedge; *(cercado)* enclosure.
cerdo ➤ *m* pig ■ **carne de c.** pork.
cereal ➤ *adj & m* cereal ■ *pl* cereals, grain.
cerebro ➤ *m* brain; FIG. brains.
ceremonia ➤ *f* ceremony.
cereza ➤ *f* cherry (fruit).
cerezo ➤ *m* cherry (tree).
cerilla ➤ *f (fósforo)* match.
cero ➤ *m* zero.
cerrado, a ➤ *adj* closed ■ **a puerta c.** behind closed doors.
cerradura ➤ *f* lock.
cerrar §33 ➤ *tr* to close (up), shut; *(con cerrojo)* to bolt; *(paquete, abertura)* to seal (up); *(negocio)* to close down; *(llave)* to turn off; *(camino, acceso)* to block off; *(cuenta bancaria)* to close out ■ **c. con llave** to lock ➤ *intr* to close, shut.
cerro ➤ *m* hill.
cerrojo ➤ *m* bolt, latch.
certamen ➤ *m* contest, competition.
certificado, a ➤ *adj* certified; *(cartas)* registered ➤ *m* certificate.
cervecería ➤ *f (fábrica)* brewery; *(taberna)* bar, pub.
cerveza ➤ *f* beer, ale ■ **c. de barril** draft beer • **c. negra** dark beer.
cesar ➤ *intr* to end, stop ➤ *tr* to fire, dismiss ■ **sin c.** unceasingly.
cese ➤ *m* cessation; *(de un empleado)* dismissal ■ **c. de fuege** cease-fire.
césped ➤ *m* lawn, grass.
cesta ➤ *f* basket.
cesto ➤ *m* basket ■ **c. de** *or* **para papeles** wastepaper basket.
chacra ➤ *f* AMER. farm.
chal ➤ *m* shawl.
chaleco ➤ *m* vest ■ **c. salvavidas** life jacket.
chalet ➤ *m* chalet; *(de playa)* beach house; *(de lujo)* villa.
champán ➤ *m* champagne.
champiñón ➤ *m* mushroom.
champú ➤ *m* shampoo.
chance ➤ *m* chance.
chancleta ➤ *f (zapatilla)* slipper.
chancho ➤ *m* pig, hog.
chantaje ➤ *m* blackmail.
chapa ➤ *f (de metal)* sheet; *(de madera)* panel; *(tapa)* bottletop.
chapado, a ➤ *adj (de metal)* plated; *(de madera)* veneered.
chaparrón ➤ *m* downpour; FIG. shower.
chapotear ➤ *intr* to splash.
chapucería ➤ *f* COLL. sloppy job.
chapuza ➤ *f* COLL. botched job.
chapuzón ➤ *m* dip, swim; *(zambullida)* dive ■ **darse un c.** to go for a swim.
chaqué ➤ *m* morning coat.
chaqueta ➤ *f* jacket ■ **c. de fumar** smoking jacket • **c. salvavidas** life jacket.
chaquetón ➤ *m* overcoat.
charca ➤ *f* pond, pool.
charco ➤ *m* puddle, pool.
charla ➤ *f (conversación)* chat; *(conferencia)* talk ■ **sala de c.** chat room.
charlar ➤ *intr* COLL. *(parlotear)* to chatter; *(hablar)* to chat.
charlatán, ana ➤ *adj (parlanchín)* talkative; *(chismoso)* gossipy ➤ *mf (parlanchín)* chatterbox; *(murmurador)* gossip; *(curandero)* quack.
charol ➤ *m (barniz)* lacquer; *(cuero)* patent leather.
chasco ➤ *m (burla)* trick; *(decepción)* disappointment.
chasis ➤ *m* chassis.
chasquido ➤ *m* crack, snap.
chatarra ➤ *f* scrap iron.
chato, a ➤ *adj (de nariz)* flat-nosed; *(la nariz)* flat.
chauvinista ➤ *adj* chauvinistic ➤ *mf* chauvinist.
chaval, a ➤ *adj* young ➤ *m* youngster, lad ➤ *f* young girl, lass.
cheque ➤ *m* check, cheque (G.B.) ■ **c. de viajero** traveler's check.
chequeo ➤ *m* AMER. inspection, check; MED. checkup.
chic ➤ *adj* chic, stylish.
chicano, a ➤ *adj & mf* Mexican-American, Chicano, Chicana.
chicle ➤ *m (de mascar)* chewing gum; *(gomorresina)* chicle.
chico, a ➤ *adj* small, little ➤ *m* boy ➤ *f* girl.
chícharo ➤ *m* pea.
chicharra ➤ *f* cicada.
chicharrón ➤ *m* fried pork rind.
chichón ➤ *m* bump (on the head).
chiflado, a ➤ *adj* COLL. *(loco)* nuts; *(enamorado)* in love.
chile ➤ *m* AMER. pepper, chili.
chileno, a ➤ *adj & mf* Chilean.
chillar ➤ *intr* to shriek; *(chirriar)* to squeak; *(destacarse)* to be loud.
chillido ➤ *m* shriek; *(chirrido)* squeak.
chillón, ona ➤ *adj* COLL. *(gritón)* shrieking; *(estridente)* loud ➤ *mf* screamer.
chimenea ➤ *f* chimney; *(hogar)* fireplace, hearth.
chincheta ➤ *f* thumbtack.
chiquillada ➤ *f* childish act.
chiquillo, a ➤ *adj* small ➤ *mf* child.
chirriar §18 ➤ *intr (rueda)* to squeak; *(pájaro)* to screech; *(al freír)* to sizzle.
chirrido ➤ *m (ruido)* screeching; COLL. *(grito)* shriek; *(al freír)* sizzle.
chisme ➤ *m (murmuración)* gossip; COLL. *(baratija)* trinket.
chismear ➤ *intr* to gossip.
chismoso, a ➤ *adj* gossipy ➤ *mf* gossipmonger.
chispa ➤ *f or* **chispazo** ➤ *m* spark.
chispear ➤ *intr* to spark; *(lloviznar)* to drizzle; *(brillar)* to be brilliant.
chisporrotear ➤ *intr* to spark, crackle.
chiste ➤ *m* joke.
chistoso, a ➤ *adj* funny.
chivo, a ➤ *mf* ZOOL. kid.
chocante ➤ *adj* offensive.
chocar §47 ➤ *intr (topar)* to crash; *(pelear)* to clash; COLL. *(disgustar)* to offend ■ **c. de frente** to hit head on.
chochear ➤ *intr* to be senile.
chocho, a ➤ *adj (caduco)* senile; COLL. *(lelo)* doting.
chocolate ➤ *adj* chocolate ➤ *m* chocolate; *(bebida)* hot chocolate, cocoa.
chófer *or* **chofer** ➤ *mf* chauffeur.
chopo ➤ *m* black poplar.
choque ➤ *m (colisión)* collision; *(impacto)* impact; *(pelea)* clash.
chorizo ➤ *m* sausage.
chorrear ➤ *intr (fluir)* to gush; *(gotear)* to trickle ➤ *tr (derramar)* to pour.
chorro ➤ *m (de líquido)* spout; *(de luz)* flood ■ **a c.** abundantly.
chubasco ➤ *m* squall, downpour.
chuchería ➤ *f* trinket.
chucho, a ➤ *m* COLL. dog.
chuleta ➤ *f (carne)* cutlet.
chupado, a ➤ *adj* COLL. emaciated.
chupar ➤ *tr* to suck; *(absorber)* to soak up.
chupete ➤ *m (de niños)* pacifier.
churrasco ➤ *m* AMER. grilled *or* broiled steak.
churrete ➤ *m* stain.
churro ➤ *m* CUL. fritter.
ciático, a ➤ *adj* sciatic ➤ *f* sciatica.
ciberespacio ➤ *m* cyberspace.
cibernética ➤ *f* cybernetics.
cicatriz ➤ *f* scar.
cicatrizar §02 ➤ *tr & intr* to heal.
ciclista ➤ *adj* cycling ➤ *mf* cyclist.
ciclo ➤ *m* cycle.
ciclomotor ➤ *m* moped, motorbike.
ciclón ➤ *m* cyclone.
ciego, a ➤ *adj & mf* blind (person) ■ *pl* **a ciegas** blindly • **andar a ciegas** to grope one's way.
cielo ➤ *m* sky; *(paraíso)* heaven ■ **c. raso** ceiling.
ciempiés ➤ *m* centipede.
cien ➤ *adj contr of* **ciento.**
ciénaga ➤ *f* swamp, marsh.
ciencia ➤ *f* science; *(erudición)* knowledge ■ **a** *or* **de c. cierto** for certain.
cieno ➤ *m* muck.
científico, a ➤ *adj* scientific ➤ *mf* scientist.
ciento ➤ *adj & m* one hundred, a hundred ■ **c. por c.** one hundred per cent • **por c.** per cent.
cierre ➤ *m (acción)* closing; *(clausura)* shut down ■ **c. patronal** R.P. lockout.
cierto, a ➤ *adj* certain; *(determinado)* definite; *(verdadero)* true; *(alguno)* some ➤ *adv* certainly ■ **lo c. es que** the fact is that • **por c.** *(a propósito)* incidentally; *(ciertamente)* certainly.
ciervo ➤ *m* deer, stag.
cifra ➤ *f (número)* digit; *(cantidad)* quantity; *(total)* sum (total).
cigarra ➤ *f* cicada.
cigarrillo ➤ *m* cigarette.
cigarro ➤ *m* cigar.
cigüeña ➤ *f* stork.
cilantro ➤ *m* coriander.
cilindro ➤ *m* cylinder; *(rodillo)* roller.
cima ➤ *f* summit; FIG. pinnacle.
cimiento ➤ *mpl* CONSTR. foundation; FIG. basis.
cincel ➤ *m* chisel.
cinco ➤ *adj & m* five ■ **las c.** five o'clock.
cincuenta ➤ *adj & m* fifty.
cine ➤ *m* cinema; PHOTOG., TECH. cinematography; COLL. *(espectáculo)* movies; *(teatro)* movie theater.
cínico, a ➤ *adj* cynical ➤ *mf* cynic.
cinta ➤ *f* ribbon; *(película)* film ■ **c. adhesiva** adhesive tape • **c. magnetofónica** recording tape • **c. métrica** tape measure.
cintura ➤ *f* waist, waistline.
cinturón ➤ *m* belt ■ **c. de seguridad** seat *or* safety belt.
ciprés ➤ *m* cypress.
circo ➤ *m* circus; GEOL. cirque.
circuito ➤ *m* circuit ■ **corto c.** short circuit.
circulación ➤ *f* circulation; *(transmisión)* dissemination; *(tráfico)* traffic.
circular[1] ➤ *adj* circular ➤ *f* circular, flier.
circular[2] ➤ *intr & tr* to circulate.
círculo ➤ *m* circle; *(circunferencia)* circumference.
circuncisión ➤ *f* circumcision.
circunferencia ➤ *f* circumference.
circunflejo, a ➤ *adj & m* circumflex.
circunstancia ➤ *f* circumstance.
cirio ➤ *m* church candle.
ciruela ➤ *f* plum ■ **c. pasa** prune.
ciruelo ➤ *m* plum tree.
cirugía ➤ *f* surgery ■ **c. plástica** *or* **estética** plastic *or* cosmetic surgery.
cirujano, a ➤ *mf* surgeon.
cisne ➤ *m* swan; R.P. powder puff.
cisterna ➤ *f* cistern, reservoir.
cita ➤ *f (entrevista)* appointment; meeting; *(con novio, amigo)* date; *(referencia)* quote.
citar ➤ *tr* to cite; LAW to summon.
cítrico, a ➤ *adj* citric; BOT. citrus ➤ *mpl* citrus fruits.
ciudad ➤ *f* city.
ciudadanía ➤ *f* citizenship.
ciudadano, a ➤ *adj* civic, city ➤ *mf* citizen.
ciudadela ➤ *f* citadel, fortress.
cívico, a ➤ *adj* civic.
civil ➤ *adj* civil ➤ *mf* civilian.
civilización ➤ *f* civilization.
civilizado, a ➤ *adj* civilized, refined.
civismo ➤ *m* civic-mindedness.
clamoroso, a ➤ *adj* clamorous.
clan ➤ *m* clan.
clandestino, a ➤ *adj* clandestine.
claraboya ➤ *f* skylight.
clarear ➤ *tr & intr* to dawn.
clarete ➤ *adj & m* claret (wine).
claridad ➤ *f* clarity; *(luz)* brightness; *(nitidez)* clearness ■ **con c.** clearly.
clarinete ➤ *m* clarinet; *(músico)* clarinetist.
claro, a ➤ *adj* clear; *(luminoso)* bright; *(aguado)* thin ■ **verde c.** light green ➤ *adv* plainly ■ **¡c.!** *or* **¡c. que sí!** of course!, sure! ➤ *m (espacio)* clearing ■ **c. de luna** moonlight • **poner** *or* **sacar en c.** to clarify, explain ➤ *f* white (of egg).
claroscuro ➤ *m* chiaroscuro.
clase ➤ *f* class; *(lección)* lesson; *(aula)* classroom ■ **c. turista** coach • **toda c. de** all kinds of.
clásico, a ➤ *adj* classic, classical ➤ *mf* classic author ➤ *m (obra)* classic.
clasificación ➤ *f* classification.
clasificar §47 ➤ *tr* to classify; *(archivar)* to file ➤ *reflex* SPORT. to qualify.
claustro ➤ *m* cloister; EDUC. faculty.
cláusula ➤ *f* clause.
clausura ➤ *f (abadía)* cloister; *(estado)* monastic life; *(conclusión)* closing ceremony; AMER. *(cierre)* closing; EDUC. commencement.
clavar ➤ *tr* to nail; *(hincar)* to drive.
clave ➤ *f (cifra)* code; *(esencia)* key; *(acceso)* password.
clavel ➤ *m* carnation.
clavícula ➤ *f* clavicle, collarbone.
clavo ➤ *m* nail; BOT. clove ■ **dar en el c.** COLL. to hit the nail on the head.
clemencia ➤ *f* clemency.
clérigo ➤ *m* clergyman.
clero ➤ *m* clergy.
cliché ➤ *m* cliché; PHOTO. negative.
cliente ➤ *mf* client, customer.
clima ➤ *m* climate.
climatizar §02 ➤ *tr* to air-condition.
clínica ➤ *f* private hospital.
cloaca ➤ *f* sewer.
cloro ➤ *m* chlorine.
cloroformo ➤ *m* chloroform.
club ➤ *m* club.
coacción ➤ *f* coercion; LAW duress.
coalición ➤ *f* coalition.
coartada ➤ *f* alibi.
cobarde ➤ *adj* cowardly ➤ *mf* coward.
cobertizo ➤ *m (protección)* shelter; *(barraca)* shed; AUTO. carport.
cobertor ➤ *m (colcha)* bedspread; *(de plumas)* comforter; *(manta)* blanket.
cobija ➤ *f* blanket.
cobijar ➤ *tr* to cover (up).
cobra ➤ *f* cobra.
cobrador, a ➤ *mf (recaudador)* bill *or* tax collector; *(perro)* retriever.
cobrar ➤ *tr (recibir)* to collect; *(recuperar)* to retrieve; *(precios)* to charge; *(un cheque)* to cash.
cobre ➤ *m* copper; AMER. cent.
cobro ➤ *m* collection, collecting; *(de un cheque)* cashing.
cocaína ➤ *f* cocaine.
cocción ➤ *f* cooking; *(hervor)* boiling; *(en un horno)* baking.
cocer §48 ➤ *tr* to cook; *(hervir)* to boil; *(en un horno)* to bake ➤ *intr* to boil.
coche ➤ *m* car *(carruaje)* carriage ■ **c. cama** sleeper, sleeping car.
cochino, a ➤ *mf* pig; COLL. *(persona)* swine ➤ *adj* filthy; COLL. *(ruin)* rotten.
cocina ➤ *f (cuarto)* kitchen; *(aparato)* stove, range; *(estilo)* cuisine.
cocinar ➤ *tr & intr* to cook.
cocinero, a ➤ *mf* cook, chef.
coco ➤ *m* coconut.
cocodrilo ➤ *m* crocodile.
cocotero ➤ *m* coconut palm.

cóctel ➤ *m* (*bebida*) cocktail; (*reunión*) cocktail party.

codazo ➤ *m* jab, poke (with one's elbow) ■ dar un c. to jab, poke.

codicia ➤ *f* greed.

codicioso, a ➤ *adj & mf* greedy (person).

código ➤ *m* code ■ c. postal zip code.

codo ➤ *m* elbow ■ *pl* hablar por los c. to be a chatterbox.

coetáneo, a ➤ *adj & mf* contemporary.

coexistir ➤ *intr* to coexist.

cofre ➤ *m* (*arca*) chest; (*caja*) box.

coger §20 ➤ *tr* to grab, grasp; (*recoger*) to gather up; (*sorprender*) to catch by surprise; (*enfermedad*) to catch; (*entender*) to understand.

cogote ➤ *m* back of the neck.

cohabitar ➤ *intr* to live together, cohabit.

coherente ➤ *adj* coherent.

cohete ➤ *m* rocket.

cohibir ➤ *tr* (*inhibir*) to inhibit ➤ *reflex* to be or feel inhibited.

coincidencia ➤ *f* coincidence.

coincidir ➤ *intr* to coincide; (*concordar*) to agree.

cojear ➤ *intr* to limp; (*una mesa*) to wobble.

cojera ➤ *f* limp, lameness.

cojín ➤ *m* cushion.

cojinete MECH. bearing.

cojo, a ➤ *adj & mf* lame (person).

col ➤ *f* cabbage ■ c. de Bruselas Brussels sprouts • c. rizada kale.

cola¹ ➤ *f* tail; (*de vestido*) train; (*fila*) line, queue (G.B.); (*parte final*) rear ■ a la c. last • c. de caballo BOT. horsetail; (*pelo*) ponytail • hacer c. to line up.

cola² ➤ *f* glue, gum.

colaboración ➤ *f* collaboration.

colaborador, a ➤ *adj* collaborating; LIT. contributing ➤ *mf* collaborator; LIT. contributor.

colaborar ➤ *intr* to collaborate; LIT. to contribute.

colada ➤ *f* whitening.

colador ➤ *m* strainer; RELIG. collator.

colapso ➤ *m* collapse ■ c. nervioso nervous breakdown.

colar §11 ➤ *tr* to strain; COLL. to pass or foist (off) ➤ *reflex* to sneak in.

colcha ➤ *f* bedspread.

colchón ➤ *m* mattress.

colchoneta ➤ *f* light mattress.

colección ➤ *f* collection; LIT. anthology.

coleccionar ➤ *tr* to collect.

colectivo, a ➤ *adj* collective; (*mutuo*) joint ➤ *m* GRAM. collective (noun); ARG., BOL., PERU small bus.

colega ➤ *mf* colleague, associate.

colegial ➤ *adj* school.

colegial, a ➤ *mf* schoolboy, schoolgirl.

colegio ➤ *m* (*primario*) elementary school; (*secundario*) high school; (*asociación*) college, association.

cólera ➤ *f* choler; FIG. anger ■ dar c. to infuriate ➤ *m* MED. cholera.

colesterol ➤ *m* cholesterol.

colgante ➤ *adj* hanging ➤ *m* pendant.

colgar §08 ➤ *tr* to hang (up) ➤ *intr* to hang; (*caer*) to hang down; COMPUT. to crash.

colibrí ➤ *m* hummingbird.

cólico, a ➤ *adj* colonic ➤ *m* colic.

coliflor ➤ *f* cauliflower.

colina ➤ *f* hill.

colirio ➤ *m* eyewash.

coliseo ➤ *m* coliseum, colosseum.

colisión ➤ *f* collision; FIG. conflict.

collado ➤ *m* (*cerro*) hill; (*entre montañas*) mountain pass.

collar ➤ *m* (*adorno*) necklace; (*de animal*) collar.

colmado, a ➤ *adj* (*lleno*) full, filled; (*cucharada*) heaping.

colmena ➤ *f* beehive, hive.

colmillo ➤ *m* canine tooth, eyetooth; ZOOL. (*del elefante*) tusk; (*del perro*) fang.

colmo ➤ *m* (*exceso*) overflow; (*cumbre*) height; (*límite*) limit.

colocación ➤ *f* (*acción*) placing; (*lugar*) place; (*empleo*) position.

colocar §47 ➤ *tr* to place, position; (*dinero*) to invest.

colombiano, a ➤ *adj & mf* Colombian.

colonia ➤ *f* colony; (*perfume*) cologne.

colonial ➤ *adj* colonial.

colonizar §02 ➤ *tr* to colonize, settle.

coloquio ➤ *m* (*conversación*) talk; (*conferencia*) seminar.

color ➤ *m* color; (*aspecto*) aspect ■ a c.

in color • de c. colored ■ *pl* ponerse de mil c. COLL. to flush.

colorado, a ➤ *adj* red ■ ponerse c. to blush ➤ *m* red.

colorante ➤ *adj* coloring ➤ *m* colorant.

colorear ➤ *tr* to color.

colorete ➤ *m* rouge.

colorido ➤ *m* (*acción*) coloring; (*colores*) coloration; (*color*) color.

columna ➤ *f* column, pillar ■ c. vertebral spine, spinal column.

columpio ➤ *m* swing.

coma¹ ➤ *f* comma.

coma² ➤ *m* MED. coma.

comadrona ➤ *f* midwife.

comandancia ➤ *f* headquarters.

comandante ➤ *mf* commanding officer, commander; (*grado*) major ■ c. en jefe or general commander-in-chief.

comarca ➤ *f* region, district.

combate ➤ *m* combat ■ ganar por fuera de c. SPORT. to win by a knockout.

combatir ➤ *intr* to battle ➤ *tr* (*luchar contra*) to fight.

combinación ➤ *f* combination; (*prenda*) slip.

combinar ➤ *tr* to combine; (*arreglar*) to arrange, work out.

combustible ➤ *adj* combustible ➤ *m* fuel ■ c. fósil fossil fuel.

comedia ➤ *f* comedy.

comedor ➤ *m* dining room ■ coche c. dining car.

comentador, a ➤ *mf* commentator.

comentar ➤ *tr* to comment on.

comentario ➤ *m* commentary ■ sin c. no comment.

comenzar §17 ➤ *tr & intr* to begin, start ■ c. a to begin to • c. con to begin with • c. por to begin with or by.

comer ➤ *tr & intr* to eat ■ dar de c. to feed ➤ *reflex* to eat up; FIG. to squander.

comercial ➤ *adj* commercial ■ centro c. shopping center.

comerciante ➤ *mf* merchant.

comerciar ➤ *intr* to trade, deal.

comercio ➤ *m* (*negocio*) business; (*tienda*) store.

comestible ➤ *adj* edible ➤ *m* foodstuff ■ *pl* groceries.

cometa ➤ *m* comet ➤ *f* (*juguete*) kite.

cometer ➤ *tr* (*un crimen*) to commit; (*un error*) to make.

comezón ➤ *f* itch.

cómico, a ➤ *adj* comical, funny ➤ *m* comic actor ➤ *f* comic actress.

comida ➤ *f* (*almuerzo, cena*) food, meal; (*almuerzo*) lunch.

comienzo ➤ *m* beginning, start ■ dar c. to begin, start.

comillas ➤ *fpl* quotation marks ■ entre c. in quotes.

comisaría ➤ *f* police station.

comisión ➤ *f* commission; (*encargo*) assignment.

comité ➤ *m* committee.

comitiva ➤ *f* retinue, party.

como ➤ *adv* as; (*de tal modo*) like; (*casi*) about, approximately ■ c. quiera que no matter how • c. sea one way or the other ➤ *conj* (*puesto que*) as, since; (*si*) if; (*así que*) as; (*por ejemplo*) such as, like ■ así c. as soon as • c. que or si as if.

cómo ➤ *adv* (*en qué condiciones*) how; (*por qué*) why, how come ■ ¿a c.? how much? • ■¡c. no! AMER. of course!

cómoda ➤ *f* chest of drawers, bureau.

comodidad ➤ *f* (*confort*) comfortableness; (*conveniencia*) convenience.

cómodo, a ➤ *adj* (*confortable*) comfortable; (*útil*) convenient.

compacto, a ➤ *adj* (*apretado*) compact; (*denso*) tight.

compadecer §09 ➤ *tr & reflex* to sympathize (with), feel sorry (for).

compañero, a ➤ *mf* companion ■ c. de clase classmate • c. de cuarto roommate.

compañía ➤ *f* company.

comparación ➤ *f* comparison; LIT. simile ■ en c. con in comparison with or to • sin c. beyond compare.

comparar ➤ *tr* (*relacionar*) to compare; (*cotejar*) to collate, check.

compartim(i)ento ➤ *m* compartment.

compartir ➤ *tr* to share.

compás ➤ *m* compass; MUS. rhythm.

compasión ➤ *f* compassion, pity.

compatible ➤ *adj* compatible.

compatriota ➤ *mf* compatriot.

compensación ➤ *f* compensation.

compensar ➤ *tr* to compensate; (*recompensar*) to indemnify.

competencia ➤ *f* competition; (*rivalidad*) rivalry; (*aptitud*) competence.

competición ➤ *f* competition; (*rivalidad*) rivalry.

competir §32 ➤ *intr* to compete.

compinche ➤ *mf* COLL. pal, chum; (*cómplice*) accomplice.

complacer ➤ *tr* to please, gratify ➤ *reflex* c. en or de to delight in, take pleasure in.

complejo, a ➤ *adj & m* complex.

complemento ➤ *m* complement; GRAM. object.

completar ➤ *tr* to complete; (*acabar*) to finish.

completo, a ➤ *adj* complete; (*acabado*) finished; (*lleno*) full ■ por c. completely.

complicado, a ➤ *adj* complicated.

complicar §47 ➤ *tr* to complicate; (*embrollar*) to entangle ➤ *reflex* to become complicated.

cómplice ➤ *mf* accomplice.

complot ➤ *m* plot; (*intriga*) scheme.

componer §37 ➤ *tr* to compose; (*reparar*) to fix ➤ *intr* to compose ➤ *reflex* to be made up (de of).

comportamiento ➤ *m* behavior, conduct.

comportar ➤ *reflex* to behave ■ c. mal to misbehave.

composición ➤ *f* composition.

compra ➤ *f* (*acción*) purchasing; (*adquisición*) purchase ➤ *pl* hacer c. to shop • ir de c. to go shopping.

comprar ➤ *tr* to buy, purchase.

comprender ➤ *tr* to understand; (*contener*) to include.

comprensible ➤ *adj* comprehensible.

comprensión ➤ *f* understanding.

comprensivo, a ➤ *adj* comprehensive.

compresión ➤ *f* compression.

comprimir ➤ *tr* to compress.

comprobante ➤ *m* proof; COM. voucher ■ c. de venta sales slip.

comprobar §11 ➤ *tr* (*cotejar*) to check; (*verificar*) to verify.

comprometer ➤ *tr* (*poner en peligro*) to endanger; (*poner en apuros*) to compromise; (*salud*) to impair ➤ *reflex* (*obligarse*) to commit oneself; (*ponerse en peligro*) to compromise oneself; (*novios*) to get engaged.

compromiso ➤ *m* obligation; (*apuro*) jam; (*convenio*) agreement; (*novios*) engagement.

computadora ➤ *f* computer ■ c. portátil laptop computer.

computar ➤ *tr* to compute, calculate.

común ➤ *adj* common; (*usual*) customary, usual; (*compartido*) shared, joint; (*vulgar*) common, vulgar; FIN. common, public ■ por lo c. generally.

comunicación ➤ *f* communication; TELEC. connection ■ medios de c. mass media.

comunicar §47 ➤ *tr* to communicate; (*transmitir*) to transmit ➤ *intr* (*tener paso*) to adjoin ➤ *reflex* to communicate; (*tener paso*) to be connected.

comunidad ➤ *f* community.

comunión ➤ *f* communion; (*comunicación*) fellowship.

con ➤ *prep* with ■ c. que so then • c. tal (de) que provided that • c. todo nevertheless.

concebir §32 ➤ *tr* to imagine, conceive of; (*comprender*) to understand ➤ *intr* to conceive, become pregnant.

conceder ➤ *tr* (*otorgar*) to grant; (*admitir*) to concede.

concejal, a ➤ *mf* (*town*) councilor ➤ *m* councilman ➤ *f* councilwoman.

concentración ➤ *f* concentration.

concentrar ➤ *tr & reflex* to concentrate.

concepción ➤ *f* conception.

concepto ➤ *m* concept, idea ■ bajo ningun c. under no circumstances • en or por c. de as, by way of.

concertar §33 ➤ *tr* to arrange, coordinate.

concesionario, a ➤ *adj* concessionary ➤ *mf* concessionaire, licensee.

concha ➤ *f* ZOOL. shell; (*molusco*) shellfish, mollusk; (*carey*) tortoise shell.

conciencia ➤ *f* conscience; (*integridad*) conscientiousness; (*conocimiento*) consciousness ■ a c. conscientiously • en c. in good conscience.

concienzudo, a ➤ *adj* conscientious.

concierto ➤ *m* concert; (*ajuste*) agree-

ment; MUS. harmony; (*obra*) concerto.

concluir §10 ➤ *tr* to conclude, finish; (*deducir*) to deduce ➤ *intr* to finish, end.

conclusión ➤ *f* conclusion, end; (*deducción*) deduction; (*decisión*) decision.

concretar ➤ *tr* to summarize; (*precisar*) to specify ➤ *reflex* to limit oneself.

concreto, a ➤ *adj* concrete ■ en c. in short ➤ *m* AMER. concrete.

concurrencia ➤ *f* audience, crowd; (*simultaneidad*) concurrence.

concurrido, a ➤ *adj* (*animado*) busy, crowded; (*popular*) well-attended; (*frecuentado*) frequented.

concursante ➤ *mf* competitor, contestant.

concurso ➤ *m* competition, contest ■ c. hípico horse show.

condado ➤ *m* (*dignidad*) earldom; (*territorio*) county.

condena ➤ *f* LAW (*juicio*) sentence.

condenar ➤ *tr* to condemn, sentence; (*declarar culpable*) to convict.

condensación ➤ *f* condensation.

condensar ➤ *tr* (*reducir*) to condense; (*abreviar*) to shorten.

condición ➤ *f* condition; (*estado*) state ■ a c. de que on the condition that ■ *pl* (*circunstancias*) circumstances • c. convenidas COM. terms agreed upon • estar en c. de to be fit for.

condimento ➤ *m* condiment, seasoning.

condominio ➤ *m* condominium.

condón ➤ *m* condom.

conducir §14 ➤ *tr* (*guiar*) to lead; AUTO. to drive ➤ *intr* to lead; AUTO. to drive.

conducta ➤ *f* conduct.

conducto ➤ *m* conduit.

conductor, a ➤ *mf* AUTO. driver.

conectado, a ➤ *adj* connected; COMPUT. on-line.

conectar ➤ *tr* to connect; (*enchufar*) to plug in ➤ *reflex* COMPUT. to log in or on.

conejo ➤ *m* rabbit.

conexión ➤ *f* connection.

confección ➤ *f* manufacture; (*ropa hecha*) ready-to-wear clothing.

conferencia ➤ *f* conference; (*discurso*) lecture.

confesar §33 ➤ *tr* to confess; (*admitir*) to admit ➤ *reflex* to confess.

confesión ➤ *f* confession.

confianza ➤ *f* confidence; (*seguridad*) self-confidence; (*familiaridad*) closeness ■ de c. (*confiable*) reliable • tener c. con alguien to be on close terms with someone.

confiar §18 ➤ *intr* to trust, feel confident; (*contar con*) to count, rely (en on) ➤ *tr* (*encargar*) to entrust; (*un secreto*) to confide ➤ *reflex* to trust.

confidencial ➤ *adj* confidential.

confirmar ➤ *tr* to confirm; (*corroborar*) to endorse.

confiscar §47 ➤ *tr* to confiscate.

confitería ➤ *f* candy store.

confitura ➤ *f* CUL. jam, preserve.

conflicto ➤ *m* conflict; (*lucha*) struggle.

confluir §10 ➤ *intr* to converge.

conformar ➤ *tr* (*adaptar*) to conform, adapt ➤ *intr* to agree (con, en with, on) ➤ *reflex* to resign oneself.

conforme ➤ *adj* ■ c. a consistent with • c. con resigned to • c. en in agreement on ➤ *adv* as soon as ■ c. a in accordance with.

confort ➤ *m* comfort.

confortable ➤ *adj* comfortable.

confrontación ➤ *f* confrontation.

confrontar ➤ *tr* to confront.

confundido, a ➤ *adj* confused.

confundir ➤ *tr* to confuse; (*desconcertar*) to perplex ➤ *reflex* to be or get mixed up; (*en una multitud*) to mingle.

confusión ➤ *f* confusion.

confuso, a ➤ *adj* jumbled, mixed up.

congelador ➤ *m* freezer.

congelar ➤ *tr* to freeze ➤ *reflex* to become frozen.

congestión ➤ *f* congestion.

congoja ➤ *f* anguish; (*pena*) grief.

congreso ➤ *m* congress, meeting; POL. Congress (of the United States).

conjugación ➤ *f* conjugation.

conjugar §31 GRAM. to conjugate.

conjunción ➤ *f* conjunction.

conjunto ➤ *m* whole; (*agregado*) collection; (*vestido*) outfit; (*de muebles*) suite (of furniture); MECH. unit; MUS. band ■ en c. altogether.

conmemoración ➤ *f* commemoration.
conmigo ➤ *pron* with me.
conmoción ➤ *f* commotion; *(sacudimiento)* shock; *(tumulto)* upheaval ■ c. cerebral concussion.
conmovedor, a ➤ *adj* moving, touching.
conmover §54 ➤ *tr (emocionar)* to move, touch; *(sacudir)* to shake ➤ *reflex* to be moved *or* touched.
conmutar ➤ *tr* to trade; LAW to commute.
cono ➤ *m* cone.
conocedor, a ➤ *adj* knowledgeable, informed ➤ *mf* connoisseur.
conocer §09 ➤ *tr* to know, be acquainted with; *(tener contacto)* to meet; *(reconocer)* to recognize; *(un tema)* to know about ■ **c. de nombre** to know by name • **c. de vista** to know by sight.
conocido, a ➤ *adj* well-known, famous ➤ *mf* acquaintance.
conocimiento ➤ *m* knowledge; *(entendimiento)* understanding; MED. consciousness.
conquista ➤ *f* conquest.
conquistador, a ➤ *adj* conquering ➤ *mf* conqueror.
conquistar ➤ *tr* to conquer; *(conseguir)* to win.
consagrar ➤ *tr* to consecrate ➤ *reflex* to devote *or* dedicate oneself (*a* to).
consciente ➤ *adj (enterado)* aware; MED. conscious.
consecuencia ➤ *f* consequence; *(deducción)* deduction ■ **a** *or* **como c. de** as a result *or* consequence of • **en c.** accordingly • **por c.** consequently, therefore.
consecutivo, a ➤ *adj* consecutive.
conseguir §42 ➤ *tr* to obtain; *(llegar a hacer)* to attain; *(lograr)* to manage.
consejero, a ➤ *mf (guía)* counselor; *(de un consejo)* councilor.
consejo ➤ *m* advice; POL. council ■ **c. de ministros** cabinet.
consenso ➤ *m* consensus.
consentido, a ➤ *adj* spoiled, pampered.
consentimiento ➤ *m* consent.
consentir §43 ➤ *tr (autorizar)* to consent to; *(permitir)* to allow ■ **c. a** *or* **con** to be indulgent with.
conserje ➤ *mf (custodio)* concierge; *(portero)* porter.
conserjería ➤ *f* concierge's office; *(de un hotel)* reception desk.
conserva ➤ *f (confitura)* jam, preserve; *(alimentos)* preserved food ■ **conservas alimenticias** canned goods • **en c.** canned.
conservador, a conservative; *(prudente)* prudent ➤ *mf* conservative.
conservar ➤ *tr* to conserve; *(preservar)* preserve; *(guardar)* to keep; *(cuidar)* to keep up; CUL. to can ➤ *reflex (permanecer)* to survive; *(cuidarse)* to take care of oneself; *(guardar para sí)* to keep for oneself; CUL. to keep, stay fresh.
conservatorio ➤ *m* conservatory.
considerado, a ➤ *adj (respetuoso)* considerate; *(respetado)* respected.
considerar ➤ *tr* to consider; *(reflexionar)* to take into consideration; *(estimar)* to regard.
consigna ➤ *f (slogan)* watchword; *(depósito)* checkroom.
consignar ➤ *tr* to consign.
consigo ➤ *pron* with him, her, them, you.
consiguiente ➤ *adj* consequent, resulting ■ **por c.** consequently, therefore.
consistente ➤ *adj* consistent.
consistir ➤ *intr* to consist (*en* of, in).
consola ➤ *f* console table; COMPUT. workstation.
consolar §11 ➤ *tr & reflex* to console (oneself).
consomé ➤ *m* consommé.
consonante ➤ *adj & f* consonant.
consorcio ➤ *m* consortium.
consorte ➤ *mf* consort.
conspiración ➤ *f* conspiracy.
conspirar ➤ *intr* to conspire.
constante ➤ *adj* constant; *(perseverante)* persevering ➤ *f* constant.
constar ➤ *intr (ser cierto)* to be clear *or* evident; *(quedar registrado)* to be on record; *(consistir)* to consist (*de* of) ■ **que conste que** let it be clearly known that.
constatar ➤ *tr* to verify, confirm.
constelación ➤ *f* constellation.
consternar ➤ *tr* to consternate ➤ *reflex* to be dismayed.
constipado, a ➤ *adj* congested, stopped up ➤ *m* MED. cold, head cold.
constitución ➤ *f* constitution.
constituir §10 ➤ *tr* to constitute ➤ *reflex* to be established.
construcción ➤ *f* construction; *(edificio)* building.
constructor, a ➤ *mf* builder.
construir §10 ➤ *tr* to construct, build.
consuelo ➤ *m* consolation, solace.
cónsul ➤ *mf* consul.
consulado ➤ *m* consulate.
consulta ➤ *f* consultation; *(opinión)* opinion, advice.
consultar ➤ *intr* to consult, discuss (*con* with) ➤ *tr* to consult.
consultorio ➤ *m (oficina)* office; MED. doctor's office.
consumidor, a ➤ *adj & mf* consumer.
consumir ➤ *tr* to consume; *(gastar)* use up; *(destruir)* to destroy ➤ *reflex* to be consumed *or* used (up).
consumo ➤ *m* consumption ■ **bienes de c.** consumer goods.
contabilidad ➤ *f (teneduría de libros)* bookkeeping; *(profesión)* accounting.
contable ➤ *adj* countable.
contacto ➤ *m* contact ■ **lentes** *or* **lentillas de c.** contact lenses • **ponerse en c.** to get in touch.
contado, a ➤ *adj* rare ■ **al c.** (in) cash.
contador, a ➤ *mf (de libros)* accountant; TECH. meter.
contagiar ➤ *tr* MED. to contaminate; FIG. to corrupt ➤ *reflex* MED. to become infected.
contagioso, a ➤ *adj* contagious, catching.
contaminación ➤ *f* contamination; *(del aire, agua)* pollution.
contar §11 ➤ *tr* to count; *(referir)* to tell, relate ➤ *intr* to count ■ **c. con** *(confiar)* to count *or* rely on.
contemplar ➤ *tr & intr* to contemplate.
contemporáneo, a ➤ *adj & mf* contemporary.
contender §34 ➤ *intr* to contend; *(competir)* to compete; *(disputar)* to dispute.
contendiente ➤ *mf* contender, competitor.
contener §46 ➤ *tr* to contain; *(impedir)* to hold back ➤ *reflex* to control oneself.
contenido, a ➤ *adj* contained, controlled ➤ *m* content(s).
contentar ➤ *tr* to content, satisfy ➤ *reflex* to be content.
contento, a ➤ *adj* happy, pleased; *(satisfecho)* satisfied, content ➤ *m* happiness; *(satisfacción)* contentment.
contestación ➤ *f* answer.
contestar ➤ *tr* to answer.
contienda ➤ *f (pelea)* battle; *(disputa)* argument.
contigo ➤ *pron* with you.
contiguo, a ➤ *adj* contiguous, adjacent.
continente ➤ *adj & m* continent.
continuación ➤ *f* continuation ■ **a c.** next, following.
continuar §45 ➤ *tr* to continue, keep on ➤ *intr* to continue, go on (*con* with).
continuo, a ➤ *adj* continuous; *(constante)* constant.
contra ➤ *prep* against ■ **en c. de** against ➤ *m* ■ **el pro y el c.** the pros and cons.
contrabando ➤ *m (mercancía)* contraband; *(acción)* smuggling.
contracción ➤ *f* contraction.
contracepción ➤ *f* contraception.
contraceptivo, a ➤ *adj & m* contraceptive.
contradecir ➤ *tr* to contradict ➤ *reflex* to contradict oneself.
contradicción ➤ *f* contradiction.
contraer §49 ➤ *tr* to contract; *(enfermedad)* to catch • **c. matrimonio** to get married.
contrapeso ➤ *m* counterbalance.
contraproducente ➤ *adj* counterproductive.
contrariedad ➤ *f (obstáculo)* obstacle; *(desazón)* annoyance; *(contratiempo)* setback; *(percance)* mishap.
contrario, a ➤ *adj* opposite; *(adverso)* adverse ■ **al c.** to the contrary • **al c. de** contrary to • **todo lo c.** quite the opposite ➤ *mf* opponent, adversary ➤ *f* ■ **llevar la c.** COLL. to contradict.
contrarrestar ➤ *tr* to counteract, offset; *(resistir)* to resist, oppose.
contrastar ➤ *intr* to contrast, differ ➤ *tr* to verify.
contraste ➤ *m* contrast.
contratar ➤ *tr* to contract for; *(emplear)* to hire.
contratiempo ➤ *m* setback; MUS. syncopation.
contratista ➤ *mf* contractor ■ **c. de obras** building contractor.
contrato ➤ *m* contract.
contribución ➤ *f* contribution; *(impuesto)* tax.
contribuidor, a ➤ *adj* contributory, contributing ➤ *mf* contributor.
contribuir §10 ➤ *tr & intr* to contribute.
contribuyente ➤ *mf* contributor; *(que paga impuestos)* taxpayer.
contrincante ➤ *mf* rival, opponent.
control ➤ *m* control; *(inspección)* check; *(lugar)* checkpoint.
controlador, a ➤ *mf* controller; COMPUT. driver ■ **c. aéreo** air-traffic controller.
controlar ➤ *tr* to control; *(inspeccionar)* to inspect; *(comprobar)* to check; COM. to audit.
controversia ➤ *f* controversy, dispute.
contusión ➤ *f* bruise, contusion.
convalecencia ➤ *f* convalescence.
convalidar ➤ *tr* to confirm, ratify.
convencer §51 ➤ *tr* to convince ➤ *reflex* to be *or* become convinced.
convenido ➤ *adv* agreed.
conveniencia ➤ *f* convenience.
conveniente ➤ *adj* convenient; *(oportuno)* suitable.
convenio ➤ *m* agreement; *(pacto)* pact.
convenir §52 ➤ *intr (acordar)* to concur; *(corresponder)* to be fitting; *(venir bien)* to suit.
convento ➤ *m* convent; *(monasterio)* monastery.
conversación ➤ *f* conversation.
conversar ➤ *intr* to converse, talk.
conversión ➤ *f* conversion.
convertible ➤ *adj* convertible ➤ *m* AUTO. convertible.
convertir §43 ➤ *tr (cambiar)* to change, turn ➤ *reflex* to convert, be converted ■ **c. en** to turn into.
convicción ➤ *f* conviction.
convidado, a ➤ *adj* invited ➤ *mf* guest.
convidar ➤ *tr* to invite.
convite ➤ *m (invitación)* invitation; *(banquete)* banquet, feast.
convivencia ➤ *f* living together; *(coexistencia)* coexistence.
convivir ➤ *intr* to live together.
convocar §47 ➤ *tr* to convoke, summon.
convocatoria ➤ *f* summons, notice.
convulsión ➤ *f* convulsion; FIG. upheaval; GEOL. *(temblor)* tremor.
conyugal ➤ *adj* conjugal, connubial.
cónyuge ➤ *mf* spouse ■ *pl* husband and wife.
coñac ➤ *m* cognac, brandy.
cooperación ➤ *f* cooperation.
cooperar ➤ *intr* to cooperate.
cooperativo, a ➤ *adj & f* cooperative.
coordenada ➤ *f* MATH. coordinate.
coordinación ➤ *f* coordination.
coordinar ➤ *tr* to coordinate.
copa ➤ *f* glass, goblet; *(trago)* drink; *(de árbol)* treetop; *(de sombrero)* crown; SPORT. cup ■ **tomarse una c.** to have a drink *or* cocktail.
copia ➤ *f* copy; *(duplicado)* duplicate.
copiadora ➤ *f* photocopier.
copiar ➤ *tr* to copy.
copla ➤ *f* ballad; *(estrofa)* stanza.
copo ➤ *m (de nieve)* snowflake.
coquetear ➤ *intr* to flirt.
coqueto, a ➤ *adj* flirtatious; *(agradable)* charming.
coraje ➤ *m (valor)* courage; *(ira)* anger.
coral[1] ➤ *m* coral.
coral[2] ➤ *adj* choral ➤ *m* chorale.
corazón ➤ *m* heart ■ **de c.** sincerely.
corbata ➤ *f* tie, necktie.
corcho ➤ *m* cork; *(de la pesca)* float.
cordel ➤ *m* cord, thin rope.
cordero ➤ *m* lamb; *(piel)* lambskin.
cordial ➤ *adj* cordial, warm.
cordón ➤ *m (cuerda)* cord; *(cinta)* cordon; *(de zapatos)* shoelace.
cornada ➤ *f (golpe)* butt (with a horn); *(herida)* goring.
corneta ➤ *f* bugle; MIL. cornet.
cornisa ➤ *f* cornice.
coro ➤ *m* chorus, choir ■ **a c.** in unison.
corona ➤ *f* crown; *(de laureles)* wreath; *(aureola)* halo; ASTRON. corona.
coronación ➤ *f* crowning, coronation.
coronel ➤ *mf* colonel.
coronilla ➤ *f* ANAT. crown ■ **estar hasta la c.** COLL. to be fed up.
corporación ➤ *f* corporation.
corral ➤ *m* corral; *(redil)* pen.
correa ➤ *f (de cuero)* strap; *(cinturón)* belt; TECH. belt.
corrección ➤ *f* correction; *(modificación)* adjustment; *(urbanidad)* propriety.
corredizo, a ➤ *adj (puerta)* sliding; *(nudo)* slip, running.
corredor, a ➤ *adj* running ➤ *mf* runner ➤ *m (pasillo)* corridor; COM. agent.
corregir ➤ *tr* to correct; *(castigar)* to punish ➤ *reflex* to mend one's ways.
correo ➤ *m* mail; *(buzón)* mailbox; *(oficina)* post office ■ **c. aéreo** air mail • **c. basura** COMPUT. junk mail, spam • **c. de voz** voice mail • **c. electrónico** COMPUT. e-mail • **echar al c.** to mail • **por c.** by mail ■ *pl (servicio)* mail service; *(oficina)* post office.
correr ➤ *intr* to run; *(en una carrera)* to race; *(aguas)* to flow; *(viento)* to blow; *(camino)* to run; *(horas)* to pass; *(rumor)* to circulate ➤ *tr* to race; *(riesgo)* to run; *(cortinas)* to draw; *(cerrojo)* to slide; *(aventuras)* to meet with ➤ *reflex (deslizarse)* to slide; *(moverse)* to slide over.
correspondencia ➤ *f* correspondence, mail.
corresponder ➤ *intr* to correspond, match; *(reciprocar)* to return; *(tocar)* to be one's turn; *(pertenecer)* to belong ➤ *reflex (escribir)* to correspond.
correspondiente ➤ *adj* corresponding ➤ *mf* correspondent.
corresponsal ➤ *adj & mf* correspondent.
corrida ➤ *f* race, run ■ **c. de toros** bullfight.
corriente ➤ *adj* running; *(actual)* current; *(usual)* usual; *(ordinario)* ordinary; *(moderno)* up-to-date ■ **poner al c.** to bring up-to-date • **tener al c.** to keep informed ➤ *f* current ■ **c. alterna, directa** alternating, direct current.
corro ➤ *m* circle, ring.
corromper ➤ *tr* to corrupt; *(pudrir)* to decay.
corrupción ➤ *f* corruption.
cortacésped ➤ *m* lawnmower.
cortacircuitos ➤ *m* circuit breaker.
cortado, a ➤ *adj (estilo)* disjointed; COLL. *(sin palabras)* speechless ➤ *m* coffee with milk.
cortar ➤ *tr* to cut; *(recortar)* to trim; *(carne, aves)* to carve; *(un árbol)* to cut down, fell; *(atravesar)* to cut through; *(omitir)* to cut out; *(interrumpir)* to cut off ➤ *reflex* to become flustered; *(la piel)* to chap; *(la leche)* to curdle.
cortaúñas ➤ *m* nail clipper.
corte[1] ➤ *m* cutting; *(filo)* (cutting) edge; SEW. cutting (out); *(estilo)* cut ■ **c. de pelo** haircut • **c. y confección** dressmaking.
corte[2] ➤ *f* (royal) court.
cortés ➤ *adj* courteous, polite.
cortesía ➤ *f* courtesy.
corteza ➤ *f (de árbol)* bark; *(del pan)* crust; *(de queso, tocino)* rind.
cortijo ➤ *m* farm, grange.
cortina ➤ *f* curtain.
corto, a ➤ *adj* short; *(breve)* brief; *(escaso)* short.
cortocircuito ➤ *m* short circuit.
cosa ➤ *f* thing; *(asunto)* business ■ **como si tal c.** COLL. as if such a thing had never happened • **no es gran c.** it's nothing great **¿ que c.?** COLL. what did you say?
cosecha ➤ *f* harvest; *(temporada)* harvest time; FIG. crop.
cosechar ➤ *tr* to harvest; *(frutas, flores)* to pick ➤ *intr* to harvest.
coser ➤ *tr* to sew.
cosmético, a ➤ *adj & m* cosmetic.
cosmonauta ➤ *mf* cosmonaut.
cosmos ➤ *m* cosmos, universe.
cosquillas ➤ *fpl* ticklishness ■ **hacer c.** to tickle.
costa ➤ *f (costo)* cost; *(orilla)* shore.
costado ➤ *m* side, flank.
costar §11 ➤ *intr* to cost ■ **c. barato** to be cheap *or* inexpensive • **c. caro** to be

expensive • c. trabajo to take a lot to • me cuesta creerlo I find it hard to believe.
costarriqueño, a ➤ *adj & mf* Costa Rican.
coste ➤ *m* cost.
costear ➤ *tr* to finance; MARIT. to coast.
costero, a ➤ *adj* coastal ➤ *f* shore.
costilla ➤ *f* ANAT. rib; *(chuleta)* cutlet, chop.
costo ➤ *m* cost.
costra ➤ *f* crust; MED. scab.
costumbre ➤ *f* custom; *(hábito)* habit ■ de c. usual, usually.
costura ➤ *f* needlework; *(unión)* seam ■ alta c. high fashion.
costurera ➤ *f* seamstress.
costurero ➤ *m* sewing basket.
cotidiano, a ➤ *adj* daily, everyday.
cotización ➤ *f* COM. quotation, price.
cotizar §02 ➤ *tr* COM. to quote, price.
coto ➤ *m* *(terreno)* reserved area; *(mojón)* boundary marker ■ c. de caza game preserve.
coz ➤ *f* backward kick; ARM. recoil; *(culata)* butt ■ dar *or* pegar coces to kick.
cráneo ➤ *m* cranium, skull.
cráter ➤ *m* crater.
creación ➤ *f* creation.
crear ➤ *tr* to create.
crecer §09 ➤ *intr* to grow; *(un río)* to swell; *(la luna)* to wax.
crecimiento ➤ *m* *(acción)* growth; *(aumento)* increase.
credencial ➤ *adj* accrediting ➤ *f* credential.
crédito ➤ *m* COM. credit; *(asenso)* credence ■ abrir *or* dar c. a to give *or* extend credit to • a c. on credit.
creer §27 ➤ *tr* to believe; *(imaginar)* to think ■ c. que sí to think so ➤ *intr* to believe ■ ver es c. seeing is believing ➤ *reflex* to consider *or* regard oneself.
crema ➤ *f* cream; *(natillas)* custard.
cremallera ➤ *f* zipper.
crematorio, a ➤ *adj & m* crematory.
cremoso, a ➤ *adj* creamy.
crepé ➤ *m* *(tela fina)* crepe, crêpe.
crepúsculo ➤ *m* twilight.
cresta ➤ *f* crest; *(cima)* summit ■ c. de gallo cockscomb.
cría ➤ *f* raising; *(animal)* offspring; *(camada)* litter.
criado, a ➤ *adj* bred, brought up ➤ *m* servant ➤ *f* maid.
crianza ➤ *f* nurturing; ZOOL. raising.
criar §18 ➤ *tr* *(nutrir)* to nurse; *(animales)* to raise; *(niños)* to bring up.
criatura ➤ *f* *(niño)* infant; *(cosa creada)* creature.
criba ➤ *f* screen, sieve.
crimen ➤ *m* crime; FIG. shame.
criminal ➤ *adj & mf* criminal.
crin ➤ *f* horsehair.
crío ➤ *m* COLL. *(de pecho)* infant; *(niño)* kid.
criollo, a ➤ *adj & mf* native, Creole.
crisis ➤ *f* crisis; *(escasez)* shortage ■ c. nerviosa nervous breakdown.
cristal ➤ *m* crystal; *(vidrio)* glass.
cristiano, a ➤ *adj & mf* Christian.
criterio ➤ *m* *(regla)* criterion; *(juicio)* judgment; *(opinión)* opinion.
crítico, a ➤ *adj* critical; *(crucial)* crucial ➤ *mf* critic ➤ *f* criticism.
cromosoma ➤ *m* chromosome.
crónico, a ➤ *adj* chronic ➤ *f* *(historia)* chronicle; *(artículo)* article.
cronología ➤ *f* chronology.
cronológico, a ➤ *adj* chronologic(al).
cronómetro ➤ *m* chronometer.
croqueta ➤ *f* CUL. croquette.
croquis ➤ *m* sketch.
cruce ➤ *m* *(acción)* crossing; *(punto)* intersection.
crucero ➤ *m* cruise; ARCHIT. transept; MIL. cruiser.
crucifijo ➤ *m* crucifix.
crucigrama ➤ *m* crossword puzzle.
crudo, a ➤ *adj* raw; *(verde)* green; *(petróleo)* crude; *(clima)* harsh ➤ *m* crude oil.
cruel ➤ *adj* cruel.
crueldad ➤ *f* cruelty.
crujir ➤ *intr* *(hoja, tela)* to rustle; *(puerta, madera)* to creak; *(huesos)* to crack; *(grava)* to crunch.
cruz ➤ *f* cross; *(reverso)* tails.
cruzado, a ➤ *adj* crossed; BIOL., ZOOL. hybrid.
cruzar §02 ➤ *tr* to cross ➤ *reflex* to cross one another; *(pasarse)* to pass ■ c. de brazos to do nothing.
cuaderno ➤ *m* notebook.
cuadra ➤ *f* stable; *(de casas)* block.
cuadrado, a ➤ *adj & m* square.
cuadrícula ➤ *f* grid.
cuadrilla ➤ *f* *(de obreros)* crew; *(de malhechores)* gang; TAUR. team assisting a bullfighter.
cuadro ➤ *m* square; ARTS painting.
cual ➤ *rel pron* ■ al c. *(persona)* to whom; *(cosa)* to which • el c. *(persona)* who; *(cosa)* which • por lo c. whereby, because of which.
cuál ➤ *adj* which ➤ *rel pron* which (one) ➤ *indef pron* some ➤ *adv* how.
cualidad ➤ *f* quality, characteristic.
cualquier ➤ *adj contr of* **cualquiera.**
cualquiera ➤ *adj* (just) any, any ordinary ➤ *indef pron* any(one), anybody ■ un (hombre) c. a nobody ➤ *rel pron* *(persona)* whoever; *(cosa)* whatever; *(nadie)* nobody.
cuán ➤ *adv* how ■ c. tonto how silly.
cuando ➤ *adv* when, since ■ de c. en c. from time to time ➤ *conj* when; *(aunque)* although, even if; *(puesto que)* since; *(si)* if ■ c. quiera whenever ➤ *prep* *(durante)* at the time of ■ c. niño as a child.
cuándo ➤ *adv* when ■ ¿c. llegó el tren? when did the train arrive?
cuanto[1] ➤ *m* PHYS. quantum.
cuanto[2] ➤ *adv* as much as; *(todo el tiempo que)* as long as ■ c. antes as soon as possible • c. más even more so • en c. as soon as • en c. a as to, as for.
cuánto ➤ *adv* how ■ ¡c. me alegro! how happy I am! • ¡c. cuesta la carne! how expensive beef is!
cuanto, a ➤ *adj* as much as ■ c. más. . . (tanto) más the more . . . the more • c. menos the less • cuantos as many • unos cuantos a few, some ➤ *pron* all that, everything, as much as ■ unos cuantos some, a few.
cuánto, a ➤ *adj* how much ■ ¿cada c. tiempo? how often? • cuántos, cuántas how many ➤ *pron* how much ■ cuántos, cuántas how many.
cuarenta ➤ *adj & m* forty.
cuartel ➤ *m* MIL. barracks.
cuarto, a ➤ *adj* fourth ➤ *m* *(habitación)* room; *(cantidad)* fourth, quarter ■ c. de baño bathroom.
cuatro ➤ *adj & m* four ■ las c. four o'clock.
cuatrocientos, as ➤ *adj & m* four hundred.
cuba ➤ *f* *(tonel)* cask; *(tina)* vat.
cubano, a ➤ *adj & mf* Cuban.
cubierto, a ➤ *m* *(comida)* meal (at a fixed price) ➤ *f* cover; MARIT. deck ■ bajo c. under cover.
cubo ➤ *m* cube; *(balde)* bucket; *(tina)* vat; *(de rueda)* hub.
cubrir §55 ➤ *tr* to cover (up); *(esconder)* to conceal ➤ *reflex* to cover oneself.
cucaracha ➤ *f* cockroach.
cuchara ➤ *f* spoon ■ c. sopera *or* de sopa soupspoon, tablespoon.
cucharada ➤ *f* spoonful.
cucharón ➤ *m* ladle; TECH. scoop.
cuchichear ➤ *intr* to whisper.
cuchilla ➤ *f* *(cuchillo)* knife; *(hoja)* blade; *(de afeitar)* razor blade.
cuchillo ➤ *m* knife.
cuco ➤ *m* cuckoo.
cuello ➤ *m* neck ■ c. alto turtleneck.
cuenca ➤ *f* valley; *(hoya)* river basin.
cuenco ➤ *m* earthenware bowl.
cuenta ➤ *f* *(de restaurante)* check; *(bolita)* bead; COM. account; *(explicación)* account; *(cargo)* responsibility ■ c. bancaria *or* de banco bank account • c. corriente checking account • c. de ahorros savings account • darse c. de to realize • perder la c. de to lose track of • trabajar por su c. to be self-employed ■ *pl* accounts ■ llevar las c. to keep the books • pedir c. a to call to account.
cuentagotas ➤ *m* eyedropper.
cuentakilómetros ➤ *m* odometer.
cuento ➤ *m* story, tale; LIT. short story ■ c. de hadas fairy tale.
cuerda ➤ *f* *(cordón)* cord, string; *(del reloj)* watch spring; MUS. string ■ dar c. a un reloj to wind a watch ■ *pl* c. vocales ANAT. vocal cords.
cuerdo, a ➤ *adj & mf* sane, sensible (person).
cuerno ➤ *m* ZOOL., MUS. horn.
cuero ➤ *m* *(piel)* hide; *(de zapatos)* leather ■ c. charolado patent leather • en cueros naked.
cuerpo ➤ *m* body; *(torso)* torso; *(figura)* figure ■ c. celeste heavenly body • c. diplomático diplomatic corps.
cuervo ➤ *m* crow, raven.
cuesta ➤ *f* slope, hill ■ c. abajo downhill • c. arriba uphill.
cuestión ➤ *f* *(asunto)* question, matter; *(duda)* dispute.
cuestionario ➤ *m* *(encuesta)* questionnaire; *(examen)* test questions.
cueva ➤ *f* cave.
cuidado ➤ *m* care; *(cautela)* caution; *(miedo)* concern ■ con c. carefully • c. con beware of • tener c. to be careful.
cuidadoso, a ➤ *adj* careful, cautious.
cuidar ➤ *tr & intr* ■ c. (de) to take care of ➤ *reflex* to take care of oneself ■ c. de *(preocuparse)* to care about; *(protegerse)* to be careful about.
culebra ➤ *f* snake.
culpa ➤ *f* blame, guilt; *(falta)* fault ■ por c. de through the fault of • echar la c. a uno to blame someone • tener la c. to be to blame.
culpabilidad ➤ *f* guilt.
culpable ➤ *adj* guilty; *(acusado)* accused ■ confesarse c. to plead guilty • declarar c. to find guilty ➤ *mf* culprit.
cultivar ➤ *tr* to cultivate.
cultivo ➤ *m* cultivation; *(cosecha)* crop.
culto, a ➤ *adj* *(civilizado)* cultured; *(instruido)* learned ➤ *m* *(secta)* cult; *(homenaje)* worship; *(rito)* ritual.
cultura ➤ *f* culture.
cumbre ➤ *m* summit; FIG. pinnacle.
cumpleaños ➤ *m* birthday.
cumplir ➤ *tr* *(llevar a cabo)* to carry out; *(la palabra)* to keep; *(la ley)* to obey ■ hoy cumple diez años today she is ten years old ➤ *intr* ■ c. con *(promesa)* to fulfill; *(obligaciones)* to fulfill one's obligations to ➤ *reflex* *(realizarse)* to be fulfilled; COM. to fall due.
cuna ➤ *f* cradle; *(lugar de nacimiento)* birthplace ■ canción de c. lullaby.
cuneta ➤ *f* *(de un foso)* ditch; *(de una calle)* gutter.
cuñado, a ➤ *mf* brother/sister-in-law.
cuota ➤ *f* quota, share; *(pago)* fee, dues ■ c. de admisión admission fee.
cupón ➤ *m* coupon.
cúpula ➤ *f* dome, cupola.
cura[1] ➤ *m* RELIG. priest.
cura[2] ➤ *f* MED. cure.
curar ➤ *intr* ■ c. de MED. to recover from ➤ *tr* MED. to cure; *(tratar)* to treat; FIG. to soothe.
curiosidad ➤ *f* curiosity; *(cosa)* curio.
curioso, a ➤ *adj* curious; *(limpio)* neat; *(cuidadoso)* careful; *(excepcional)* odd ➤ *mf* curious person; *(entremetido)* busybody.
curriculum vitae ➤ *m* resumé.
cursar ➤ *tr* *(estudiar)* to study; *(dar curso a)* to attend to.
cursi ➤ *adj* *(presumido)* pretentious; *(de mal gusto)* tasteless.
cursillo ➤ *m* *(curso)* short course; *(conferencias)* series of lectures.
curso ➤ *m* course; FIN. circulation ■ c. acelerado crash course • tener c. legal to be legal tender.
cursor ➤ *m* cursor.
curtir ➤ *tr* *(adobar)* to tan ➤ *reflex* to become weather-beaten.
curva ➤ *f* curve; *(recodo)* curve, bend ■ c. cerrada sharp curve.
custodia ➤ *f* custody; *(cuidado)* care.
custodiar ➤ *tr* to take care of; *(vigilar)* to watch over; *(proteger)* to protect.
cutícula ➤ *f* cuticle.
cutis ➤ *m* skin, complexion.
cuyo, a ➤ *rel pron* whose; *(personas)* of whom; *(cosas)* of which.

D

dado, a ➤ *adj* given ➤ *m* die ■ *pl* dice.
dalia ➤ *f* dahlia.
dama ➤ *f* lady; *(de la reina)* lady-in-waiting ■ *pl* checkers, draughts (G.B.).
damnificado, a ➤ *adj* damaged ➤ *mf* victim.
danza ➤ *f* dance.
danzarín, ina ➤ *mf* dancer.
daño ➤ *m* damage, harm ■ hacer d. to be painful; *(perjudicar)* to harm, injure.
dar §12 ➤ *tr* to give; *(conferir)* to grant; *(proponer)* to propose, offer; *(sacrificar)* to give up; *(repartir)* to deal; *(producir)* to produce, bear; *(soltar)* to give off, emit; *(imponer)* to impose; *(sonar)* to strike; THEAT. to show; *(comunicar)* to express, convey ■ d. a luz to give birth • darle ganas de to feel like, have a mind to • d. gusto a to please, make happy • d. una vuelta, paseo to take a stroll ➤ *intr* *(ocurrir)* to arise, occur ■ d. a to overlook, face • ¡dale! (¡apúrate!) hurry up!; (¡adelante!) keep it up! • d. con *(encontrar)* to find, hit on; *(encontrarse)* to meet, run into; *(chocar)* to hit • d. igual *or* lo mismo to be all the same ➤ *reflex* to give oneself up, surrender; *(suceder)* to arise, occur ■ d. cuenta de to realize • d. las manos *or* la mano to shake hands • d. por to consider oneself • d. prisa to hurry.
dardo ➤ *m* dart, arrow.
data ➤ *f* date; COM. data, items.
datar ➤ *tr* to date; COM. to enter, credit ➤ *intr* to date, begin.
dato ➤ *m* fact, datum; *(documento)* document ■ *pl* data, information.
de ➤ *prep* of, from ■ a las tres de la tarde at three in the afternoon • de rodillas on one's knees • hablar de to talk about • lejos de aquí far from here • los ojos del niño the child's eyes • más de diez more than ten • soy de Chile I'm from Chile • tiritar del frío to shiver with cold.
debajo ➤ *adv* underneath, below ■ (por) d. de under, underneath, beneath.
debate ➤ *m* debate, discussion.
debatir ➤ *tr* to debate, discuss; *(combatir)* to fight, struggle.
debe ➤ *m* COM. debit.
deber[1] ➤ *tr* to owe; *(hay que)* to ought to ■ d. de to be probable ➤ *reflex* to be due to.
deber[2] ➤ *m* duty, obligation; *(faena)* chore; *(deuda)* debt ■ *pl* AMER. homework.
debidamente ➤ *adv* properly, duly.
debido, a ➤ *adj* due; *(apropiado)* fitting.
débil ➤ *adj* weak.
debilidad ➤ *f* weakness.
debutar ➤ *intr* to begin; THEAT. to debut.
década ➤ *f* decade.
decadencia ➤ *f* decadence, decline.
decaimiento ➤ *m* decadence, decline; *(debilidad)* weakness; *(desaliento)* discouragement.
decano ➤ *mf* EDUC. dean.
decatlón ➤ *m* decathlon.
decena ➤ *f* group of ten; MUS. tenth.
decente ➤ *adj* decent.
decepción ➤ *f* deception; *(desengaño)* disenchantment, disappointment.
decidido, a ➤ *adj* determined, resolute.
decidir ➤ *tr, intr & reflex* to decide.
decimal ➤ *adj & m* decimal.
décimo, a ➤ *adj & m* tenth.
decir §13 ➤ *tr* to say; *(relatar)* to tell; *(hablar)* to speak; *(nombrar)* to call, name ■ es d. that is (to say) • ¡no me digas! you don't say!, really! • querer d. to mean.
decisión ➤ *f* decision; *(firmeza)* determination; LAW verdict, ruling.
decisivo, a ➤ *adj* decisive, conclusive.
declamar ➤ *tr & intr* to declaim, recite.
declaración ➤ *f* declaration, statement; LAW deposition; *(de cartas)* bid, call.
declaradamente ➤ *adv* manifestly, openly.
declarante ➤ *adj* declaring ➤ *mf* LAW declarant, witness.
declarar ➤ *tr & intr* to declare.
decoración ➤ *f* decoration; THEAT. scenery.
decorar ➤ *tr* to decorate; *(memorizar)* to memorize, learn by heart.
decorativo, a ➤ *adj* decorative.
decreto ➤ *m* decree, order.
dedal ➤ *m* thimble.
dedicar §47 ➤ *tr & reflex* to dedicate (oneself).
dedo ➤ *m* finger; *(del pie)* toe; *(porción)* bit, smidgen ■ d. meñique little finger, pinky • d. pulgar *or* gordo thumb; *(del pie)* big toe.
deducir §14 ➤ *tr* to deduce, conclude; *(rebajar)* to deduct, subtract.
defecar §47 ➤ *tr & intr* to defecate.
defecto ➤ *m* defect, flaw; *(falta)* absence, lack ■ ser por d. COMPUT. to default.
defectuoso, a ➤ *adj* defective, faulty.

defender §34 ➤ *tr* to defend ➤ *intr & reflex* to defend *or* protect oneself; *(arreglárselas)* to manage, get by.
defensa ➤ *f* defense ▪ **d. propia** *or* **legítima** self-defense.
defensivo, a ➤ *adj* defensive ➤ *m* defense, safeguard ➤ *f* defensive.
deficiente ➤ *adj* deficient, lacking.
definición ➤ *f* definition; *(determinación)* determination, decision.
definir ➤ *tr* to define; *(determinar)* to determine, decide.
definitivamente ➤ *adv* definitely.
deformar ➤ *tr* to deform ➤ *reflex* to be *or* become deformed.
defraudar ➤ *tr* to defraud, cheat.
degenerado, a ➤ *adj & mf* degenerate.
degradante ➤ *adj* degrading, debasing.
degustación ➤ *f* tasting, sampling.
dejar ➤ *tr* to leave; *(consentir)* to let, allow; *(desamparar)* to abandon, desert ▪ **¡deja!** *or* **¡déjalo!** never mind! • **d. caer** to drop, let go of ➤ *intr* ▪ **d. de** to stop, leave off ➤ *reflex (descuidarse)* to let oneself go, become sloppy.
del ➤ *contr of* **de** *and* **el.**
delantal ➤ *m* apron.
delante ➤ *adv (con prioridad)* in front, ahead; *(enfrente)* facing, opposite ▪ **d. de** in front of.
delatar ➤ *tr* to denounce, inform on; *(revelar)* to reveal, expose.
delegación ➤ *f* delegation; *(oficina)* office, branch.
delegado, a ➤ *mf* delegate.
deletrear ➤ *tr (pronunciar)* to spell (out); *(descifrar)* to decipher.
delfín ➤ *m* dolphin.
delgado, a ➤ *adj (esbelto)* slender, slim; *(flaco)* thin ▪ **ponerse d.** to lose weight.
deliberado, a ➤ *adj* deliberate, intentional.
delicadeza ➤ *f* delicacy; *(discreción)* tact.
delicado, a ➤ *adj* delicate; *(quebradizo)* fragile.
delicioso, a ➤ *adj (agradable)* delightful; *(sabroso)* delicious.
delincuente ➤ *adj & mf* delinquent.
delirar ➤ *intr* to be delirious.
delirio ➤ *m* delirium; *(manía)* mania, frenzy.
delito ➤ *m* offense, crime.
demanda ➤ *f* demand; *(petición)* appeal, request; *(pregunta)* question, inquiry; *(empresa)* enterprise; *(empeño)* perseverance; ELEC. load; LAW *(escrito)* writ; *(acción)* lawsuit.
demandar ➤ *tr (pedir)* to request, ask for; LAW to sue, file suit against.
demás ➤ *adj* other, rest of the ▪ **lo d.** the rest • **por d.** *(en demasía)* excessively, too much; *(inútilmente)* in vain • **por lo d.** otherwise, other than that.
demasiado, a ➤ *adj* too much *or* many ➤ *adv* too, too much.
demencia ➤ *f* dementia.
democracia ➤ *f* democracy.
demócrata ➤ *mf* democrat.
democrático, a ➤ *adj* democratic.
demográfico, a ➤ *adj* demographic.
demoler §54 ➤ *tr* to demolish, destroy.
demonio ➤ *m* demon, devil.
demora ➤ *f* delay, wait.
demorar ➤ *tr* to delay, hold up ➤ *intr* to linger, stay ➤ *reflex* to take a long time, delay.
demostrar §11 ➤ *tr* to demonstrate, show.
denegar §35 ➤ *tr (rechazar)* to refuse, reject; *(negar)* to deny.
denigrar ➤ *tr* to denigrate, disparage.
denominación ➤ *f* denomination.
denominador ➤ *m* denominator.
denominar ➤ *tr* to denominate, name.
denotar ➤ *tr* to denote.
densidad ➤ *f* density.
denso, a ➤ *adj* dense, thick; *(sólido)* heavy, solid; *(oscuro)* dark, black.
dentadura ➤ *f* (set of) teeth.
dental ➤ *adj* dental.
dentífrico ➤ *m* toothpaste.
dentista ➤ *mf* dentist.
dentro ➤ *adv* inside, within; *(de un edificio)* inside, indoors ▪ **d. de poco** shortly, soon • **por d.** inwardly, (on the) inside.
denuncia ➤ *f* accusation, denunciation; *(declaración)* declaration, report.
denunciar ➤ *tr* to accuse, denounce; *(pronosticar)* to foretell; *(declarar)* to declare, announce.
departamento ➤ *m* department, section; *(distrito)* province, district; *(compartimiento)* compartment; *(piso)* apartment, flat (G.B.).
depender ➤ *intr* to depend *(de* on).
dependiente, a ➤ *adj* dependent ➤ *mf (empleado)* employee; *(de tienda)* clerk, salesperson.
depilar ➤ *tr* to depilate.
deponer §37 ➤ *tr (apartar)* to lay *or* put aside; *(privar)* to depose; LAW to testify, provide testimony for.
deportar ➤ *tr* to deport, exile.
deporte ➤ *m* sport.
deportista ➤ *adj* sporting, sporty; COLL. *(aficionado)* fond of sports ➤ *mf* sports fan, sportsman/woman.
deportivo, a ➤ *adj* sporting, sports; *(aficionado)* fond of sports.
depositar ➤ *tr* to deposit; *(encomendar)* to place ➤ *reflex* to settle.
depósito ➤ *m* deposit; *(almacén)* warehouse; *(cisterna)* cistern, tank; MIL. depot, dump.
depresión ➤ *f* depression.
deprimente ➤ *adj* depressing.
deprimir ➤ *tr* to depress ➤ *reflex* to get depressed.
derecho, a ➤ *adj* right, right-hand; *(vertical)* upright, straight ➤ *f (lado derecho)* right *or* right-hand side; *(diestra)* right hand; POL. right, right wing ▪ **a la d.** to *or* on the right ➤ *m* right; LAW. privilege ▪ **de d.** LAW de jure, by right • **tener d. a** to have a right to ▪ *pl (impuestos)* duties, taxes; *(honorarios)* fees, charges • **d. de autor** royalties ➤ *adv* straight, right ▪ **todo d.** straight ahead.
derivación ➤ *f* derivation; ELEC. *(pérdida)* loss of current; *(circuito)* bypass, shunt.
derivar ➤ *tr* to derive ➤ *intr* to derive, be derived.
dermatología ➤ *f* dermatology.
dermatólogo, a ➤ *mf* dermatologist.
derramar ➤ *tr* to spill, pour out; *(sangre)* to shed; *(diseminar)* to spread, scatter ➤ *reflex* to overflow, spill over.
derretir §32 ➤ *tr* to dissolve; *(hielo)* to melt ➤ *reflex* to fall madly in love.
derribar ➤ *tr* to knock down; *(subvertir)* to overthrow, topple.
derrocar §47 ➤ *tr* to throw down; *(arruinar)* to demolish; *(subvertir)* to overthrow.
derrochar ➤ *tr* to squander, waste.
derroche ➤ *m* squandering, waste.
derrota ➤ *f* defeat, rout.
derrotar ➤ *tr* to defeat, beat.
derruir §10 ➤ *tr* to knock down, demolish.
derrumbar ➤ *tr (despeñar)* to hurl down; *(demoler)* to knock down, demolish ➤ *reflex (caerse)* to collapse, fall; AMER. to fail.
desabrigar §31 ➤ *tr* to uncover, expose.
desabrochar ➤ *tr* to undo, unfasten.
desacertado, a ➤ *adj* mistaken.
desacierto ➤ *m* error, mistake.
desacreditar ➤ *tr* to discredit, disgrace.
desactivar ➤ *tr* to deactivate.
desacuerdo ➤ *m* disagreement; *(error)* error, mistake; *(olvido)* forgetfulness.
desafiar §18 ➤ *tr* to challenge, dare; *(competir)* to oppose, compete with.
desafinar ➤ *intr* MUS. to be out of tune.
desafío ➤ *m* challenge, defiance.
desafortunado, a ➤ *adj* unfortunate.
desagradable ➤ *adj* disagreeable.
desagradar ➤ *tr* to displease, offend.
desagradecido, a ➤ *adj & mf* ungrateful (person).
desagrado ➤ *m* displeasure, discontent.
desagüe ➤ *m* drainage; *(desaguadero)* drain.
desahogado, a ➤ *adj (descarado)* brazen, fresh; *(despejado)* clear, open; *(espacioso)* roomy, spacious; *(acomodado)* relaxing, easy.
desahogar §31 ➤ *tr* to alleviate, ease; *(dar rienda suelta)* to vent ➤ *reflex* to let off steam; *(confiarse)* to confide; *(descansar)* to relax, take it easy.
desahogo ➤ *m* relief, alleviation; *(descanso)* rest, respite; *(expansión)* space, room; *(libertad)* freedom; *(comodidad)* comfort, ease.
desahuciar ➤ *tr* to remove all hope from; *(un inquilino)* to evict.
desaire ➤ *m (falta de gracia)* gracelessness; *(desprecio)* slight, snub.
desajuste ➤ *m* maladjustment; *(avería)* breakdown, failure.
desalentar §33 ➤ *tr* to leave breathless; *(desanimar)* to discourage ➤ *reflex* to become discouraged.
desaliento ➤ *m* discouragement.
desaliñado, a ➤ *adj* slovenly, untidy.
desaliño ➤ *m (descompostura)* slovenliness, untidiness.
desalmado, a ➤ *adj* heartless, cruel.
desalojar ➤ *tr* to remove, expel; *(desplazar)* to dislodge, displace; *(abandonar)* to abandon, evacuate ➤ *intr* to leave.
desangrar ➤ *tr* to bleed (a patient) ➤ *reflex* to bleed profusely.
desanimado, a ➤ *adj* downhearted; *(poco animado)* dull, lifeless.
desanimar ➤ *tr* to discourage, depress ➤ *reflex* to become discouraged.
desánimo ➤ *m* discouragement, dejection.
desapacible ➤ *adj* unpleasant, disagreeable.
desaparecer §09 ➤ *tr* to make disappear ➤ *intr & reflex* to disappear.
desaparición ➤ *f* disappearance, vanishing.
desarmar ➤ *tr, intr & reflex* to disarm.
desarme ➤ *m* disarmament; *(desmontaje)* dismantling.
desarraigado, a ➤ *adj* uprooted, rootless.
desarreglar ➤ *tr* to make untidy, mess (up); *(quebrar)* to break ➤ *reflex* to break (down).
desarrollado, a ➤ *adj* developed.
desarrollar ➤ *tr & reflex* to unroll, unfold; *(extender)* to develop, expand.
desarrollo ➤ *m* unrolling, unfolding; *(extensión)* development, expansion.
desarticular ➤ *tr (desmontar)* to disassemble, take apart.
desasir ➤ *tr* to release, let go ➤ *reflex* to yield, give up.
desasosiego ➤ *m* uneasiness, restlessness.
desastre ➤ *m* disaster, catastrophe.
desatar ➤ *tr* to untie, undo; *(soltar)* to unleash, let go; *(aclarar)* to unravel, solve ➤ *reflex* to come untied *or* undone; *(soltarse)* to break loose.
desatino ➤ *m* nonsense, foolishness.
desatrancar §47 ➤ *tr (la puerta)* to unbolt; *(desatrampar)* to clear, unblock.
desautorizar §02 ➤ *tr* to deprive of authority; *(desmentir)* to deny; *(prohibir)* to prohibit.
desavenencia ➤ *f* discord, enmity.
desayunar ➤ *intr & reflex* to have breakfast, breakfast.
desayuno ➤ *m* breakfast.
desbarajuste ➤ *m* confusion, disorder.
desbaratar ➤ *tr* to ruin, wreck; *(malgastar)* to squander, waste ➤ *intr* to talk *or* act wildly.
desbordamiento ➤ *m* overflowing, running over; *(de cólera)* outburst.
desbordar ➤ *intr & reflex (derramarse)* to overflow, run over; *(rebosar)* to burst *or* brim with.
descabellado, a ➤ *adj* wild, crazy.
descafeinado, a ➤ *adj & m* decaffeinated (coffee).
descalabrar ➤ *tr* to injure, wound ➤ *reflex* to injure one's head.
descalabro ➤ *m* setback; MIL. defeat.
descalificar §47 ➤ *tr* to disqualify.
descalzar §02 ➤ *tr* to take off ➤ *reflex* to take off one's shoes.
descalzo, a ➤ *adj* barefoot(ed), shoeless; *(pobre)* destitute, poor.
descampado, a ➤ *adj* open, clear ➤ *m* open field.
descansado, a ➤ *adj (tranquilo)* restful, tranquil; *(refrescado)* rested, relaxed.
descansar ➤ *intr* to rest, take a rest; *(calmarse)* to relax ➤ *tr* to rest, give rest to; *(apoyar)* to rest *or* lean (something) on ➤ *reflex* to rest, take a rest.
descanso ➤ *m* rest; *(alivio)* relief; *(período)* break; SPORT. half time; THEAT. intermission.
descapotable ➤ *adj & m* AUTO. convertible.
descarado, a ➤ *adj & mf* shameless (person).
descarga ➤ *f* unloading; ARM. discharge, firing; ELEC. discharge.
descargar §31 ➤ *tr* to unload; *(disparar)* to discharge, shoot; ELEC. to discharge; *(liberar)* to release, free; *(aliviar)* to ease, relieve; COMPUT. to download ➤ *intr* to flow, empty ➤ *reflex (dimitir)* to resign, quit; *(eximirse)* to unburden oneself; *(exonerarse)* to clear oneself.
descargo ➤ *m* unloading; COM. entry; *(excusa)* excuse; *(dispensa)* release.
descaro ➤ *m* shamelessness.
descarriar §18 ➤ *tr* to misdirect, send the wrong way; *(apartar de la razón)* to lead astray ➤ *reflex* to stray, get lost.
descarrilamiento ➤ *m* RAIL. derailment; *(descarrío)* act of going astray.
descarrilar ➤ *intr* to jump the track; *(una persona)* to get off the track.
descartar ➤ *tr* to discard, put aside ➤ *reflex* to discard ▪ **d. de** to excuse oneself from.
descendencia ➤ *f (hijos)* descendants, offspring; *(linaje)* descent, origin.
descender §34 ➤ *intr* to descend, go down; *(proceder)* to be descended from; *(un líquido)* to run *or* flow down; *(de nivel)* to drop, fall ➤ *tr (bajar)* to descend, go down; *(bajar una cosa)* to lower, bring down.
descendiente ➤ *adj* descending ➤ *mf* descendant, offspring.
descenso ➤ *m* descent, going down; *(de nivel)* fall, drop.
descifrar ➤ *tr* to decipher, decode.
descolgar §08 ➤ *tr (quitar)* to take down; *(bajar)* to let down; *(teléfono)* to pick up ➤ *reflex* to come down; *(presentarse)* to show up, drop in.
descolorido, a ➤ *adj* discolored; *(pálido)* pallid, colorless.
descomponer §37 ➤ *tr (desordenar)* to disarrange, mess up; *(podrir)* to decompose; MECH. to break; *(trastornar)* to upset, disturb ➤ *reflex (corromperse)* to decompose; MECH. to break down; *(indisponerse)* to feel sick; *(irritarse)* to get upset.
descomposición ➤ *f* decomposition, decay; *(desarreglo)* disorder, disarrangement.
descompuesto, a ➤ *adj* decomposed; *(desarreglado)* messy; MECH. out of order, broken; *(perturbado)* upset.
descomunal ➤ *adj (enorme)* enormous, huge; *(extraordinario)* extraordinary.
desconcertante ➤ *adj* disconcerting.
desconcertar §33 ➤ *tr* to disconcert, upset; *(desordenar)* to disarrange, disrupt; MED. to dislocate ➤ *reflex* to be disconcerted; *(desavenirse)* to fall out, disagree; *(descomedirse)* to go off the deep end; MED. to become dislocated.
desconectar ➤ *tr* to disconnect ➤ *reflex* to become disconnected; COMPUT. to log out *or* off.
desconfiado, a ➤ *adj & mf* distrustful, suspicious (person).
desconfianza ➤ *f* distrust, mistrust.
desconfiar §18 ➤ *intr* to distrust, mistrust.
descongelar ➤ *tr* to thaw, defrost.
desconocer §09 ➤ *tr* not to know; *(no reconocer)* not to recognize; *(negar)* to deny, disavow; *(desentenderse)* to ignore.
desconocido, a ➤ *adj* unknown; *(extraño)* strange, unfamiliar ➤ *mf (extraño)* stranger.
desconsolado, a ➤ *adj* disconsolate.
desconsuelo ➤ *m* grief, distress.
descontar §11 ➤ *tr (quitar)* to deduct; *(rebajar)* to discount; *(dar por cierto)* to take for granted.
descontento, a ➤ *adj* discontented, dissatisfied ➤ *m* discontent, dissatisfaction.
descorchar ➤ *tr* to uncork.
descorrer ➤ *tr (cortinas)* to draw back, open ➤ *intr & reflex* to flow.
descortesía ➤ *f* discourtesy, rudeness.
descoser ➤ *tr* SEW. to unstitch, rip ➤ *reflex* SEW. to come unstitched, rip.
descosido, a ➤ *adj* SEW. unstitched, ripped; *(indiscreto)* indiscreet, talkative.
descrédito ➤ *m* discredit, disrepute.
describir §55 ➤ *tr* to describe; *(trazar)* to trace, describe.
descripción ➤ *f* description.
descubierto, a ➤ *adj* uncovered, exposed; *(yermo)* bare, barren; *(sin sombrero)* bareheaded ▪ **al d.** COM. short; FIG. openly, in the open • **estar en d.** COM. to be overdrawn ➤ *m* COM. deficit, shortage.

descubrimiento ➤ *m* discovery; *(revelación)* disclosure, revelation.

descubrir §55 ➤ *tr* to discover; *(revelar)* to reveal, uncover.

descuento ➤ *m* discount, reduction.

descuidado, a ➤ *adj (negligente)* careless; *(desaliñado)* untidy, slovenly; *(abandonado)* neglected ➤ *mf* careless person; *(desaliñado)* slob.

descuidar ➤ *tr* to neglect, forget ➤ *reflex* to be careless; *(desaliñarse)* to neglect oneself, be sloppy.

descuido ➤ *m* carelessness, neglect; *(desaliño)* untidiness.

desde ➤ *prep* from, since ▪ **d. hace un año** for a year • **d. luego** of course • **d. que** since.

desdén ➤ *m* disdain, scorn.

desdeñar ➤ *tr* to disdain, scorn ➤ *reflex* to be disdainful ▪ **d.** de not to deign to.

desdichado, a ➤ *adj (desgraciado)* unfortunate, pitiful; *(infeliz)* unhappy, wretched ➤ *mf* wretch.

desdoblar ➤ *tr* to unfold, spread out; *(separar)* to split, break down.

desear ➤ *tr* to wish, desire.

desechar ➤ *tr* to reject, decline; *(apartar)* to get rid of.

desembarcar §47 ➤ *tr* to disembark, unload ➤ *intr* to disembark, go ashore.

desembarco ➤ *m* landing, disembarkation.

desembarque ➤ *m (de mercancías)* debarkation, unloading; *(de pasajeros)* landing.

desembocadura ➤ *f* outlet.

desembocar §47 ➤ *intr (río)* to flow, run; *(calle)* to lead to, run.

desempaquetar ➤ *tr* to unpack, unwrap.

desempatar ➤ *tr* to break a tie between.

desempeñar ➤ *tr (rescatar)* to recover, redeem; *(pagar)* to get out of debt; *(cumplir)* to fulfill, carry out; *(sacar de apuro)* to get (someone) out of trouble; THEAT. to play (a part).

desempeño ➤ *m (rescate)* redemption, redeeming; *(de deudas)* freeing from debt; *(cumplimiento)* fulfillment; THEAT. performance.

desempleado, a ➤ *adj & mf* unemployed (person).

desempleo ➤ *m* unemployment.

desencadenamiento ➤ *m* unchaining; *(de sucesos)* unfolding.

desencadenar ➤ *tr* to unchain, unfetter; *(incitar)* to start, incite ➤ *reflex* to break loose.

desencanto ➤ *m* disenchantment.

desenchufar ➤ *tr* to unplug, disconnect.

desenclavijar ➤ *tr* to disconnect, loosen.

desenfadado, a ➤ *adj* confident, self-assured; *(despreocupado)* carefree, uninhibited.

desenfado ➤ *m* confidence, self-assurance; *(facilidad)* ease, naturalness.

desenfreno ➤ *m* wantonness, licentiousness.

desenganchar ➤ *tr* to unhook, unfasten.

desengañar ➤ *tr* to disillusion ➤ *reflex* to become disillusioned.

desengaño ➤ *m* disillusionment; *(comprensión)* enlightenment.

desengrasar ➤ *tr* to remove the grease from ➤ *intr* to lose weight.

desenlace ➤ *m* untying, unfastening; LIT. denouement, ending; *(resultado)* result, outcome.

desenmascarar ➤ *tr* to unmask, expose.

desenredar ➤ *tr* to disentangle, unravel; *(poner en orden)* to put in order, straighten out ➤ *reflex* to extricate oneself.

desenrollar ➤ *tr* to unroll, unwind.

desentenderse §34 ➤ *reflex* to pretend not to know ▪ **d.** de to have nothing to do with.

desentrañar ➤ *tr* to eviscerate; *(solucionar)* to get to the bottom of ➤ *reflex* to give one's all.

desenvolver §54 ➤ *tr* to unroll, unwrap; *(aclarar)* to unravel, disentangle ➤ *reflex* to come unrolled *or* unwrapped.

desenvuelto, a ➤ *adj (confiado)* natural, confident; *(elocuente)* eloquent; *(desvergonzado)* forward, brazen.

deseo ➤ *m* desire, wish.

desequilibrado, a ➤ *adj & mf* unbalanced (person).

desequilibrio ➤ *m* imbalance.

desértico, a ➤ *adj* desert-like, barren.

desesperación ➤ *f* despair, desperation.

desesperado, a ➤ *adj & mf* hopeless, desperate (person).

desesperar ➤ *tr* to drive to despair, discourage; *(irritar)* to exasperate ➤ *intr & reflex* to lose hope, despair.

desfachatez ➤ *f* cheek, nerve.

desfallecer §09 ➤ *tr* to weaken ➤ *intr* to faint.

desfallecido, a ➤ *adj* faint, dizzy.

desfavorable ➤ *adj* unfavorable, adverse.

desfigurar ➤ *tr (afear)* to disfigure; *(deformar)* to deform, misshape; *(desvirtuar)* to distort, misrepresent.

desfiladero ➤ *m* defile, narrow pass.

desfilar ➤ *intr* to parade, march.

desfile ➤ *m* march, procession; MIL. parade.

desganado, a ➤ *adj* without appetite, not hungry; *(sin entusiasmo)* unenthusiastic.

desgastar ➤ *tr* to wear down; *(debilitar)* to weaken ➤ *reflex* to become weak.

desgaste ➤ *m* erosion; *(daño)* damage, wear; *(debilitación)* weakening, debilitation.

desgracia ➤ *f* misfortune, adversity; *(accidente)* mishap, setback; *(pérdida de favor)* disgrace, disfavor; *(desagrado)* displeasure ▪ **por d.** unfortunately.

desgraciadamente ➤ *adv* unfortunately.

desgraciado, a ➤ *adj & mf* unfortunate (person); *(infeliz)* unhappy (person); *(desagradable)* unpleasant (person); *(sinvergüenza)* despicable (person).

desgravar ➤ *tr* to reduce taxes *or* duties.

deshabitado, a ➤ *adj* uninhabited.

deshacer §24 ➤ *tr* to undo; *(destruir)* to destroy, ruin; *(dividir)* to cut up; *(desarmar)* to take apart; *(disolver)* to melt, dissolve; *(desconcertar)* to break; *(desempacar)* to unpack ➤ *reflex (descomponerse)* to fall apart, break; *(desaparecer)* to vanish; *(extenuarse)* to weaken ▪ **d.** de to get rid of.

deshecho, a ➤ *adj* undone; *(cansado)* tired, worn out.

deshidratar ➤ *tr* to dehydrate ➤ *reflex* to become dehydrated.

deshonesto, a ➤ *adj* dishonest; *(indecente)* indecent, improper.

deshora ➤ *f* inconvenient time.

deshuesar ➤ *tr (carne)* to debone; *(fruta)* to remove the pit from.

desierto, a ➤ *adj* deserted, uninhabited; *(desolado)* desolate, bleak ➤ *m* desert.

designar ➤ *tr* to design, plan; *(nombrar)* to designate, appoint; *(señalar)* to point out.

desigual ➤ *adj* unequal; *(quebrado)* uneven; *(diferente)* different.

desigualdad ➤ *f* inequality, disparity; *(aspereza)* roughness, ruggedness.

desilusión ➤ *f* disillusionment.

desilusionar ➤ *tr* to disillusion ➤ *reflex* to become disillusioned.

desinfectante ➤ *adj & m* disinfectant.

desinfectar ➤ *tr* to disinfect.

desinflamar ➤ *tr* to reduce inflammation in.

desinflar ➤ *tr* to deflate, let air out of.

desintegrar ➤ *tr* to disintegrate; PHYS. to split.

desinteresado, a ➤ *adj* disinterested, impartial; *(generoso)* altruistic, unselfish.

desistir ➤ *intr* to desist *(de* from*)*; *(de un derecho)* to waive a right.

deslenguado, a ➤ *adj* foul-mouthed, coarse.

deslizar §02 ➤ *tr & intr* to slide, slip ➤ *reflex (resbalarse)* to slide; *(caerse)* to slip (and fall).

deslumbrante *or* **deslumbrador, a** ➤ *adj (brillante)* dazzling, brilliant; *(asombrante)* overwhelming.

deslumbrar ➤ *tr (cegar)* to dazzle, blind; *(confundir)* to overwhelm, bewilder.

desmandar ➤ *tr* to countermand ➤ *reflex* to go too far, get out of hand.

desmantelar ➤ *tr (derribar)* to knock down, dismantle; *(una casa)* to vacate, abandon.

desmayarse ➤ *reflex* to faint, swoon.

desmayo ➤ *m (síncope)* faint, swoon; *(desánimo)* downheartedness; BOT. weeping willow.

desmejorar ➤ *tr* to impair, damage ➤ *intr & reflex* to deteriorate, get worse.

desmemoriado, a ➤ *adj & mf* forgetful, absent-minded (person).

desmentida ➤ *f (negación)* denial; *(contradicción)* contradiction.

desmentir §43 ➤ *tr* to contradict; *(refutar)* to refute, disprove.

desmenuzar §02 ➤ *tr* to crumble, break into pieces; *(examinar)* to scrutinize.

desmesurado, a ➤ *adj (desmedido)* excessive, inordinate; *(sin límite)* boundless, limitless.

desmontar ➤ *tr* dismantle, disassemble; *(árboles)* to fell, cut down; *(terreno)* to level ➤ *intr & reflex* to dismount.

desmoralizar §02 ➤ *tr* to demoralize; *(corromper)* to corrupt.

desnatar ➤ *tr* to skim the cream off.

desnivel ➤ *m* unevenness; *(depresión)* depression, drop; *(diferencia)* difference, disparity.

desnudar ➤ *tr* to strip, undress; *(descubrir)* to lay bare, uncover ➤ *reflex* to strip.

desnudo, a ➤ *adj* undressed; *(en cueros)* naked, nude; *(despojado)* stripped, bare ➤ *m* ARTS nude.

desnutrición ➤ *f* malnutrition.

desobedecer §09 ➤ *tr* to disobey.

desobediencia ➤ *f* disobedience.

desobediente ➤ *adj & mf* disobedient (person).

desodorante ➤ *adj* deodorizing ➤ *m* deodorant.

desolación ➤ *f* desolation.

desolar §11 ➤ *tr* to desolate ➤ *reflex* to be grieved, be distressed.

desorden ➤ *m* disorder, disarray; *(lío)* muddle, mess; *(conducta)* unruliness.

desordenado, a ➤ *adj* disorderly; *(falta de aseo)* slovenly, untidy.

desordenar ➤ *tr* to disorder; *(causar confusión)* to throw into confusion; *(desasear)* to make messy ➤ *reflex* to become disorderly.

desorientar ➤ *tr* to disorient; *(confundir)* to confuse ➤ *reflex* to be disoriented; *(confundirse)* to become confused.

despabilado, a ➤ *adj (despierto)* alert, wide-awake; *(listo)* clever, sharp.

despachar ➤ *tr* to complete, conclude; *(resolver)* to resolve, settle; *(enviar)* to dispatch, send; *(despedir)* to fire, dismiss ➤ *intr (darse prisa)* to hurry up; *(hablar)* to speak one's mind; COM. to do business ➤ *reflex* AMER. *(darse prisa)* to hurry up ▪ **d.** de to get rid of.

despacho ➤ *m* dispatch; *(oficina)* office, bureau.

despacio ➤ *adv* slow, slowly; AMER. in a low voice, quietly.

desparramar ➤ *tr* to spread; *(derramar)* to spill, splash ➤ *reflex* to scatter, spread.

despavorido, a ➤ *adj* terrified, afraid.

despectivo, a ➤ *adj* disparaging, pejorative.

despedida ➤ *f (adiós)* goodbye, farewell; *(despacho)* dismissal, firing.

despedir §32 ➤ *tr (decir adiós)* to say goodbye; *(despachar)* to dismiss, fire ➤ *reflex* to say goodbye *(de* to*)*.

despegable ➤ *adj* detachable.

despegar §31 ➤ *tr* to unstick; *(separar)* to detach; *(quitar)* to remove ➤ *intr* AVIA. to take off ➤ *reflex* to become unglued; *(separarse)* to become detached.

despegue ➤ *m* takeoff.

despeinar ➤ *tr* to mess, tousle (a hairdo).

despejar ➤ *tr* to clear up, sort out ➤ *reflex* METEOROL. to clear up; *(divertirse)* to enjoy oneself.

despensa ➤ *f* larder, pantry; *(provisiones)* provisions, supplies; *(oficio)* stewardship.

despeñar ➤ *tr* to hurl, throw ➤ *reflex (precipitarse)* to hurl *or* throw oneself; *(entregarse)* to give oneself up.

desperdiciar ➤ *tr* to waste, squander; *(no aprovecharse de)* not to take advantage of, miss.

desperdicio ➤ *m* waste, squandering; *(residuo)* waste, remains.

desperezarse §02 ➤ *reflex* to stretch.

desperfecto ➤ *m* flaw, blemish; *(deterioro)* wear and tear.

despertador, a ➤ *adj* awakening, arousing ➤ *m* alarm clock; *(aviso)* warning.

despertar §33 ➤ *tr* to wake up ➤ *intr* to wake up, awaken; *(ser más listo)* to wise up ➤ *reflex* to wake up, awaken.

despiadado, a ➤ *adj* pitiless, merciless.

despido ➤ *m* dismissal, firing.

despierto, a ➤ *adj* awake; *(despabilado)* alert, wide-awake; *(listo)* clever.

despilfarrar ➤ *tr* to squander, waste ➤ *reflex* to squander a fortune.

despistado, a ➤ *adj & mf* absent-minded (person).

despistar ➤ *tr* to lead astray ➤ *reflex* to be disoriented, lose one's bearings.

desplazamiento ➤ *m* displacement.

desplazar §02 ➤ *tr* to displace; *(trasladar)* to move, shift.

desplegar §35 ➤ *tr* to unfold, spread out; *(aclarar)* to explain; *(mostrar)* to display, show ➤ *reflex* to unfold, spread out.

despliegue ➤ *m* display, show.

despojar ➤ *tr* to deprive, dispossess; *(quitar)* to strip; *(robar)* to rob ➤ *reflex (renunciar)* to give up, relinquish.

desposarse ➤ *reflex (persona)* to get engaged *or* married *(con* to*)*; *(pareja)* to get engaged *or* to marry.

déspota ➤ *mf* despot, tyrant.

despreciar ➤ *tr* to disdain, scorn.

desprecio ➤ *m* disdain, scorn; *(desaire)* slight, snub.

desprender ➤ *tr* to unfasten, detach; *(soltar)* to loosen; *(emitir)* to emit, give off ➤ *reflex* to become detached; *(ser emitido)* to issue, emanate ▪ **d.** de to give up, part with.

despreocupado, a ➤ *adj* unconcerned, nonchalant.

desprestigiar ➤ *tr* to ruin (someone's) reputation; *(desacreditar)* to discredit, disparage.

desprevenido, a ➤ *adj* unprepared, off guard.

después ➤ *adv (más tarde)* afterward, later; *(entonces)* next, then ▪ **d. de (que)** after.

destacar §47 ➤ *tr* to emphasize, highlight; MIL. to detail, assign ➤ *intr & reflex* to stand out, be outstanding.

destapar ➤ *tr* to open, uncover; *(una botella)* to uncork, uncap.

destartalado, a ➤ *adj* ramshackle, dilapidated.

destello ➤ *m* flash (of light); *(centelleo)* sparkle, glitter ▪ *pl* signs, indications.

desteñir ➤ *tr & intr* to fade, discolor.

destilar ➤ *tr* to distill.

destilería ➤ *f* distillery.

destinar ➤ *tr* to destine, intend; *(asignar)* to assign, appoint ➤ *reflex* to intend to go into.

destino ➤ *m* destiny, fate; *(destinación)* destination; *(empleo)* job, position.

destituir §10 ➤ *tr (revocar)* to dismiss; *(privar)* to deprive.

destornillador ➤ *m* screwdriver.

destreza ➤ *f* skill, dexterity.

destrozar §02 ➤ *tr* to smash, break into pieces; *(arruinar)* to destroy.

destrucción ➤ *f* destruction.

destruir §10 ➤ *tr* to destroy, ruin.

desuso ➤ *m* disuse, obsolescence.

desvalijar ➤ *tr* to rob, plunder.

desván ➤ *m* attic, garret.

desvanecer §09 ➤ *tr* to make vanish *or* disappear ➤ *reflex (desmayarse)* to become dizzy, faint.

desvarío ➤ *m* delirium, madness; *(disparate)* raving, nonsense; *(capricho)* whim.

desvelar ➤ *tr & reflex* to stay awake, go without sleep.

desventaja ➤ *f* disadvantage, drawback.

desventura ➤ *f* misfortune, bad luck.

desvergonzado, a ➤ *adj & mf* impudent, shameless (person).

desvestir §32 ➤ *tr & reflex* to undress.

desviar §18 ➤ *tr* to divert, deflect ➤ *reflex* to turn off; *(hacer un rodeo)* to take a detour; *(apartarse)* to deviate.

desvío ➤ *m* detour, diversion.

detallar ➤ *tr* to detail; *(especificar)* to specify, itemize.

detalle ➤ *m* detail; *(gesto)* gesture, kind thought.

detallista ➤ *adj* retail ➤ *mf* COM.

retailer; *(considerado)* thoughtful person.

detectar ➤ *tr* to detect.

detective ➤ *mf* detective.

detector, a ➤ *m* detector ■ **d. de metales** metal detector ➤ *adj* detecting.

detener §46 ➤ *tr* to stop, halt; *(retrasar)* to delay, detain; *(arrestar)* to arrest ➤ *reflex* to stop; *(retardarse)* to linger.

detenido, a ➤ *adj (preso)* detained, in custody ➤ *mf* person under arrest.

detergente ➤ *adj & m* detergent.

deterioración ➤ *f* deterioration.

deteriorar ➤ *tr* to deteriorate; *(estropear)* to damage, spoil; *(desgastar)* to wear (out) ➤ *reflex (dañarse)* to damage, harm; *(desgastarse)* to wear out.

determinado, a ➤ *adj* determined, resolute; *(preciso)* specific, particular.

determinar ➤ *tr* to determine; *(convencer)* to convince, decide ➤ *reflex* to decide, make up one's mind.

detestar ➤ *tr* to detest, hate.

detrás ➤ *adv* behind ■ **d. de** behind, in back of • **por d.** behind one's back.

deuda ➤ *f* debt.

deudo, a ➤ *mf* relative.

deudor, a ➤ *adj* debit; *(que debe)* indebted ➤ *mf* debtor.

devaluación ➤ *f* devaluation.

devaluar §45 ➤ *tr* to devaluate.

devastar ➤ *tr* to devastate, destroy.

devoción ➤ *f* devotion; *(piedad)* piety.

devolución ➤ *f* return; *(restauración)* restoration; COM. refund.

devolver §54 ➤ *tr* to return, give back; *(restaurar)* to restore; COM. to refund ➤ *reflex* AMER. to return.

devorar ➤ *tr* to devour, eat up.

devoto, a ➤ *adj* devout, pious; *(aficionado)* devoted ➤ *mf* devout person; *(aficionado)* devotee, enthusiast.

día ➤ *m* day; *(no noche)* daytime, daylight ■ **al d.** per day, a day; *(al corriente)* up to date • **al otro d.** on the following day, the next day • **de d.** by day • **d. de fiesta** holiday • **hoy (en) d.** nowadays, these days ■ *pl* **¡buenos d.!** good morning • **ocho d.** a week • **quince d.** two weeks, fortnight • **todos los d.** every day, daily.

diabético, a ➤ *adj & mf* diabetic.

diablo ➤ *m* devil, demon.

diafragma ➤ *m* diaphragm.

diagnosis ➤ *f* diagnosis.

diagonal ➤ *adj & f* diagonal.

diálogo ➤ *m* dialogue.

diamante ➤ *m* diamond.

diámetro ➤ *m* diameter.

diapositiva ➤ *f* slide, transparency.

diariamente ➤ *adv* daily, every day.

diario, a ➤ *adj* daily ➤ *m* daily (paper); *(relación)* diary, journal ➤ *adv* daily ■ **a d.** daily, every day • **de d.** *(diariamente)* daily, every day; *(ordinario)* everyday.

diarrea ➤ *f* diarrhea.

dibujante ➤ *adj* drawing, sketching ➤ *mf* drawer, sketcher; *(de dibujos animados)* cartoonist; TECH. draftsman.

dibujar ➤ *tr* to draw; *(describir)* to describe, depict.

dibujo ➤ *m* drawing, sketch ■ *pl* **d. animados** cartoons.

dicción ➤ *f* diction.

diccionario ➤ *m* dictionary.

dicha ➤ *f* happiness; *(suerte)* good fortune ■ **a** *o* **por d.** fortunately, happily.

dicho, a ➤ *adj* said, aforementioned ■ **d. y hecho** no sooner said than done • **mejor d.** rather, more accurately ➤ *m (refrán)* saying, proverb ■ *pl* marriage vows.

dichoso, a ➤ *adj (feliz)* happy, contented; *(afortunado)* lucky, fortunate.

diciembre ➤ *m* December.

dictador, a ➤ *mf* dictator.

dictar ➤ *tr* to dictate; *(sentencia)* to pronounce; AMER. *(una clase)* to give, teach.

didáctico, a ➤ *adj* didactic.

diecinueve ➤ *adj & m* nineteen.

dieciocho ➤ *adj & m* eighteen.

dieciséis ➤ *adj & m* sixteen.

diecisiete ➤ *adj & m* seventeen.

diente ➤ *m* tooth; ZOOL. fang; *(de un tenedor)* prong; BOT. clove ■ **d. de león** dandelion.

diestro, a ➤ *adj* deft, dexterous; *(derecho)* right ➤ *f* right hand.

dieta ➤ *f* diet.

dietético, a ➤ *adj* dietetic, dietary ➤ *mf* dietician.

diez ➤ *adj & m* ten ■ **las d.** ten o'clock.

diferencia ➤ *f* difference ■ **a d. de** unlike.

diferenciar ➤ *tr* to differentiate, distinguish ➤ *intr* to differ.

diferente ➤ *adj* different ■ **diferentes** various, several ➤ *adv* differently.

difícil ➤ *adj* difficult.

dificultad ➤ *f* difficulty, obstacle.

difundir ➤ *tr* to diffuse; *(derramar)* to spread, scatter ➤ *reflex* to spread out.

difunto, a ➤ *adj* deceased, dead ➤ *mf* dead person; *(cadáver)* corpse.

difusión ➤ *f* diffusion; *(radio)* broadcasting.

difuso, a ➤ *adj* diffuse; *(ancho)* wide, extended; *(vago)* vague, hazy.

digerir ➤ *tr* to digest.

digestión ➤ *f* digestion.

digital ➤ *adj* digital.

dígito ➤ *m* digit.

dignidad ➤ *f* dignity; *(rango)* rank.

digno, a ➤ *adj* worthy; *(apropiado)* proper, fitting; *(mesurado)* dignified.

dilatar ➤ *tr* to dilate, expand; *(retrasar)* to delay; *(propagar)* to spread ➤ *reflex* to dilate, expand.

dilema ➤ *m* dilemma.

diligencia ➤ *f* diligence; *(prisa)* speed, briskness; *(recado)* errand, task; LAW proceeding.

diluir §10 ➤ *tr* to dilute; *(disolver)* to dissolve.

diluviar ➤ *intr* to pour down, rain hard.

dimensión ➤ *f* dimension.

diminutivo, a ➤ *adj & m* diminutive.

diminuto, a ➤ *adj* diminutive, little.

dimisión ➤ *f* resignation (from office).

dinámico, a ➤ *adj* dynamic ➤ *f* dynamics.

dinamita ➤ *f* dynamite.

dinamo *or* **dínamo** ➤ *f* dynamo.

dinero ➤ *m* money; *(caudal)* wealth, fortune.

dinosaurio ➤ *m* dinosaur.

dios ➤ *m* god ■ **D.** God • **¡D. mío!** my God!, oh my! • **por D.** for God's sake.

diploma ➤ *m* diploma, certificate.

diplomacia ➤ *f* diplomacy.

diplomado, a ➤ *adj* having a diploma ➤ *mf* graduate.

diplomático, a ➤ *adj* diplomatic ➤ *mf* diplomat ➤ *f* diplomacy.

diptongo ➤ *m* diphthong.

dique ➤ *m* dike, sea wall; *(restricción)* check, restriction.

dirección ➤ *f* direction; *(junta)* board of directors; *(cargo)* directorship; *(señas)* address; AUTO., TECH. steering ■ **d. general** headquarters.

directo, a ➤ *adj* direct; *(derecho)* straight ➤ *f* AUTO. high gear.

director, a ➤ *adj* directing ➤ *mf* director; *(de escuela)* principal; MUS. conductor.

dirigir §19 ➤ *tr* to direct; *(administrar)* to manage; *(una carta)* to address; *(guiar)* to guide; AUTO. to drive, steer; MUS. to conduct ➤ *reflex* to go, make one's way; *(hablar)* to address, speak.

discapacitado, a ➤ *adj & mf* disabled, handicapped (person).

disciplina ➤ *f* discipline; *(doctrina)* doctrine.

discípulo, a ➤ *mf* disciple; *(alumno)* student.

disco ➤ *m* disk, disc; *(para escuchar)* record; *(para el tránsito)* traffic signal; SPORT. discus; COMPUT. diskette ■ **d. compacto** compact disk • **d. rígido** *or* **duro** COMPUT. hard disk.

discoteca ➤ *f* discotheque.

discreción ➤ *f* discretion, tact.

discrepancia ➤ *f* discrepancy.

discreto, a ➤ *adj* discreet; *(ingenioso)* witty, clever; MATH., PHYS. discrete.

disculpa ➤ *f (por una ofensa)* apology; *(excusa)* excuse.

disculpar ➤ *tr* to excuse, pardon ➤ *reflex* to apologize *(con* to; *de, por* for).

discurrir ➤ *intr* to roam; *(reflexionar)* to reflect; *(hablar)* to discourse; *(fluir)* to flow, run.

discurso ➤ *m* speech, discourse; *(facultad)* reasoning; *(transcurso)* passage, course.

discusión ➤ *f* discussion; *(disputa)* dispute, argument.

discutir ➤ *tr* to discuss, debate ➤ *intr (debatir)* to discuss, talk about; *(disputar)* to argue.

diseñar ➤ *tr* to design; *(dibujar)* to draw, sketch.

diseño ➤ *m* design; *(dibujo)* drawing, sketch.

disfraz ➤ *m* disguise; *(máscara)* mask.

disfrazar §02 ➤ *tr & reflex* to disguise (oneself).

disfrutar ➤ *tr (gozar)* to enjoy; *(aprovechar)* to make the most of ➤ *intr* to enjoy oneself ■ **d. de** to enjoy.

disgustado, a ➤ *adj* annoyed, displeased.

disgustar ➤ *tr* to annoy, displease ➤ *reflex (desagradarse)* to be annoyed *or* displeased; *(desazonarse)* to fall out.

disgusto ➤ *m (desagrado)* annoyance, displeasure; *(contienda)* quarrel, disagreement.

disimular ➤ *tr* to conceal, hide; *(fingir)* to feign, pretend.

disipar ➤ *tr* to dissipate; *(derrochar)* to squander, waste; *(una duda)* to dispel ➤ *reflex (desaparecer)* to disappear, vanish; *(dispersarse)* to scatter.

dislocar §47 ➤ *tr & reflex* to dislocate.

disminuir §10 ➤ *tr, intr & reflex* to diminish.

disolver §54 ➤ *tr & reflex* to dissolve.

disparar ➤ *tr* to fire, shoot; *(echar)* to throw, hurl ➤ *intr* to fire, shoot; *(disparatar)* to act foolishly ➤ *reflex (una arma)* to go off, fire.

disparate ➤ *m* absurd *or* nonsensical thing ■ *pl* nonsense.

dispensar ➤ *tr* to dispense, give out; *(eximir)* to exempt; *(perdonar)* to forgive, excuse.

dispensario ➤ *m* dispensary, clinic.

dispersar ➤ *tr & reflex* to disperse, scatter; *(dividir)* to divide.

disponer §37 ➤ *tr* to arrange, place; *(preparar)* to prepare ➤ *intr* ■ **d. de** *(poseer)* to have at one's disposal; *(utilizar)* to make use of; *(deshacerse de)* to dispose of ➤ *reflex* to prepare, get ready.

disponible ➤ *adj* available, on hand.

disposición ➤ *f* disposition; *(posesión)* disposal; LAW *(precepto)* provision; *(orden)* decree, order ■ **estar en d. de** to be ready to • **última d.** last will and testament ■ *pl* measures.

dispositivo ➤ *m* device, mechanism.

disputa ➤ *f* dispute.

disquete ➤ *m* diskette, floppy disk.

distancia ➤ *f* distance; *(diferencia)* difference ■ **a (la) d.** at *or* from a distance • **a larga d.** long-distance.

distante ➤ *adj* distant.

distinguido, a ➤ *adj* distinguished.

distinguir §15 ➤ *tr* to distinguish; *(preferir)* to favor; *(honrar)* to pay tribute to, honor ➤ *intr* to distinguish, discriminate ➤ *reflex (ser distinto)* to be distinguished, differ; *(sobresalir)* to distinguish oneself, excel.

distinto, a ➤ *adj (diferente)* distinct, different; *(claro)* distinct.

distracción ➤ *f* distraction; *(error)* slip, oversight.

distraer §49 ➤ *tr* to distract; *(entretener)* to amuse, entertain ➤ *intr* to be entertaining ➤ *reflex (entretenerse)* to amuse oneself; *(descuidarse)* to be distracted.

distraído, a ➤ *adj (divertido)* entertaining; *(desatento)* absent-minded.

distribuidor, a ➤ *adj* distributing, distributive ➤ *mf* distributor.

distribuir §10 ➤ *tr* to distribute.

distrito ➤ *m* district, zone.

disturbar ➤ *tr* to disturb.

disturbio ➤ *m* disturbance, trouble.

disuadir ➤ *tr* to dissuade, discourage.

diván ➤ *m* divan, couch.

diverso, a ➤ *adj* diverse ■ *pl* several, various.

divertido, a ➤ *adj* amusing, entertaining.

divertir §43 ➤ *tr* to amuse, entertain; *(distraer)* to divert, distract ➤ *reflex* to amuse oneself, have a good time; *(distraerse)* to be distracted.

dividendo ➤ *m* dividend.

dividir ➤ *tr* to divide ➤ *reflex* to divide; *(separarse)* to separate.

divisa ➤ *f* emblem, insignia; COM. currency.

divisar ➤ *tr* to discern, make out.

división ➤ *f* division.

divisor, a ➤ *adj* dividing ➤ *m* divider; MATH. divisor, denominator.

divorciado, a ➤ *adj* divorced ➤ *m* divorcé ➤ *f* divorcée.

divorciar ➤ *tr* to divorce; *(separar)* to separate, divide ➤ *reflex* to divorce, get divorced.

divorcio ➤ *m* divorce; *(separación)* separation, division.

divulgar §31 ➤ *tr* to divulge, disclose; *(popularizar)* to popularize ➤ *reflex* to be divulged.

dobladillo ➤ *m* hem.

dobladura ➤ *f* fold, crease.

doblar ➤ *tr* to double; *(encorvar)* to bend; CINEM. to dub ■ **d. la esquina** to turn the corner.

doble ➤ *adj* double; *(grueso)* thick, heavy; *(disimulado)* two-faced ➤ *m* double; *(pliegue)* fold, crease; *(copia)* copy ■ **al d.** doubly ➤ *mf (actor)* double, stand-in ➤ *adv* doubly.

doce ➤ *adj & m* twelve ■ **las d.** twelve o'clock.

docena ➤ *f* dozen.

docente ➤ *adj* teaching, educational.

dócil ➤ *adj* docile; *(dúctil)* ductile.

doctor, a ➤ *mf* doctor; *(maestro)* teacher, professor.

doctorado ➤ *m* doctorate.

documentación ➤ *f* documentation.

documental ➤ *adj & m* documentary.

documento ➤ *m* document; *(prueba)* proof, evidence ■ **d. justificativo** voucher, certificate.

dólar ➤ *m* dollar.

doler §54 ➤ *intr* to hurt ➤ *reflex* to repent; *(sentir)* to regret; *(compadecerse)* to sympathize, be sorry.

dolor ➤ *m* pain, ache; *(congoja)* sorrow, distress; *(arrepentimiento)* regret.

domar ➤ *tr* to tame, domesticate; *(vencer)* to subdue, master.

doméstico, a ➤ *adj* domestic ➤ *mf* domestic, household servant.

domicilio ➤ *m* domicile, residence ■ **d. social** head office, corporate headquarters.

dominar ➤ *tr* to dominate; *(someter)* to subdue, control; *(saber a fondo)* to know well, master ➤ *intr* to dominate, stand out ➤ *reflex* to control *or* restrain oneself.

domingo ➤ *m* Sunday.

dominicano, a ➤ *adj & mf* Dominican.

dominio ➤ *m* dominion, domain; *(superioridad)* dominance; *(maestría)* mastery, command.

dominó ➤ *m* dominoes.

don[1] ➤ *m (regalo)* gift, present; *(gracia)* gift, talent, knack.

don[2] ➤ *m* Don (title of respect used before a man's first name).

donar ➤ *tr* to donate, give.

donativo ➤ *m* donation, gift.

donde ➤ *adv* where ■ **d.** no otherwise • **en d.** in which • **por d.** whereby ➤ *prep* S. AMER. to *or* at the house of.

dónde ➤ *adv* when ■ **¿a d.?** where? • **¿de d.?** from where? • **¿por d.?** why?

dondequiera ➤ *adv* anywhere ■ **d. que** wherever • **por d.** everywhere, all over the place.

doña ➤ *f* Mrs., Madame (title of respect used before a woman's first name).

dorado, a ➤ *adj* golden; *(cubierto de oro)* gilt, gilded ➤ *m* gilding.

dormilón, ona ➤ *adj* sleepy ➤ *mf* sleepyhead ➤ *f* easy chair.

dormir §16 ➤ *intr* to sleep ➤ *reflex* to fall asleep ➤ *tr* to put to sleep ■ **d. la siesta** to take a nap.

dormitorio ➤ *m* bedroom; *(residencia)* dormitory.

dorso ➤ *m* back.

dos ➤ *adj & m* two ■ **las d.** two o'clock • **los** *or* **las d.** both.

doscientos, as ➤ *adj & m* two hundred.

dosis ➤ *f* dose; FIG. portion, quantity.

dragón ➤ *m* dragon; BOT. snapdragon; MIL. dragoon.

drama ➤ *m* drama.

dramático, a ➤ *adj* dramatic ➤ *mf* dramatist, playwright; *(actor)* actor ➤ *f* actress; *(arte dramático)* drama.

drástico, a ➤ *adj* drastic.

droga ➤ *f* drug.

drogadicto, a ➤ *mf* drug addict.

drogar §31 ➤ *tr* to drug, dope.

droguería ➤ *f* drugstore, pharmacy; *(comercio)* drug trade.

ducha ➤ *f (baño)* shower; MED. douche.

duda ➤ *f* doubt, uncertainty ■ **no cabe** *or* **no hay d.** (there is) no doubt •

poner en d. to question, doubt.

dudar ➤ *tr & intr* to doubt.

dueña ➤ *f* owner; *(ama)* landlady.

dueño ➤ *m* owner; *(amo)* landlord.

dulce ➤ *adj* sweet; *(dúctil)* soft, ductile; *(agua)* fresh ➤ *m* candy, sweet.

duna ➤ *f* dune.

duodécimo, a ➤ *adj & m* twelfth.

duplicar §47 ➤ *tr* to duplicate, copy; *(doblar)* to double.

duración ➤ *f* duration.

durante ➤ *prep* during.

durar ➤ *intr* to last, endure; *(quedar)* to remain.

durazno ➤ *m* peach.

dureza ➤ *f* hardness; *(dificultad)* difficulty; *(severidad)* severity, *(obstinación)* obstinacy, stubbornness.

duro, a ➤ *adj* hard; *(fuerte)* tough, strong; *(resistente)* resistant, resilient; *(obstinado)* stubborn, obstinate; *(áspero)* harsh ➤ *adv* hard.

E

e ➤ *conj* and (before *i-* and *hi-*).

ebanista ➤ *mf* cabinetmaker, woodworker.

ébano ➤ *m* ebony.

echar ➤ *tr* to throw, cast, toss; *(expulsar)* to expel; *(empleado)* to fire; *(desechar)* to throw out *or* away; *(emitir)* to emit, give off; *(verter)* to pour; *(añadir)* to add, put in; BOT. to sprout; *(aplicar)* to apply; *(imponer)* to impose, give; LAW to condemn, sentence; *(llave)* to turn; *(cerrojo)* to shoot; *(publicar)* to publish; *(drama)* to put on, present; *(discurso)* to give, deliver; *(presentar)* to bring, present ■ **e. a perder** to spoil, ruin • **e. de menos** to miss ➤ *intr* to grow, sprout ■ **e. por** *(una carrera)* to choose, go into; *(ir)* to go ➤ *reflex* to throw oneself; *(tenderse)* to lie down, stretch out ■ **e. a** to begin, start.

echarpe ➤ *m* stole, shawl.

eclesiástico, a ➤ *adj & m* ecclesiastic.

eclipse ➤ *m* eclipse.

eco ➤ *m* echo ■ **tener e.** to catch on, be popular.

ecología ➤ *f* ecology.

economía ➤ *f* economy; *(ciencia)* economics; *(parsimonia)* thrift, frugality.

económico, a ➤ *adj* economic(al).

economista ➤ *mf* economist.

economizar §02 ➤ *tr* to economize on.

ecosistema ➤ *m* ecosystem.

ecuación ➤ *f* equation.

ecuador ➤ *m* equator.

ecuánime ➤ *adj* even-tempered, levelheaded.

ecuatorial ➤ *adj* equatorial.

ecuatoriano, a ➤ *adj & mf* Ecuadorian.

ecuestre ➤ *adj* equestrian.

edad ➤ *f* age; *(período)* time; *(época)* era, epoch ■ **E. Media** Middle Ages • **mayor de e.** of age • **menor de e.** underage • **¿qué e. tienes?** how old are you?

edición ➤ *f* publication; *(conjunto de libros o periódicos)* edition; *(conjunto de revistas)* issue.

edicto ➤ *m* edict, proclamation.

edificio ➤ *m* building, edifice; FIG. structure, fabric.

editar ➤ *tr* to publish.

editor, a ➤ *adj* publishing ➤ *mf* publisher; *(redactor)* editor.

editorial ➤ *adj* publishing ➤ *m* editorial ➤ *f* publishing house.

educación ➤ *f* education, training.

educado, a ➤ *adj* educated, trained; *(cortés)* well-mannered, polite.

educar §47 ➤ *tr* to educate, teach; *(criar)* to raise, bring up; *(desarrollar)* to develop, train.

efectivamente ➤ *adv* really, in fact; *(por supuesto)* indeed, certainly.

efectivo, a ➤ *adj* effective; *(verdadero)* real, actual; *(permanente)* permanent ➤ *m* (hard) cash ■ **en e.** in cash.

efecto ➤ *m* effect, result; *(fin)* end, purpose; *(impresión)* impression, impact; *(rotación)* spin ■ **en e.** *(efectivamente)* in effect, in fact; *(en conclusión)* indeed, precisely • **efectos de resultado** *or* **de residuo** COMPUT. output • **e. útil** MECH. output • **tener e.** *(efectuarse)* to take effect; *(ocurrir)* to take place ■ *pl* effects, property; *(mercancía)* goods, merchandise; FIN. bills, securities.

efectuar §45 ➤ *tr* to effect, bring about ➤ *reflex* to take effect.

eficacia ➤ *f* efficacy, effectiveness.

eficaz ➤ *adj* efficacious, effective.

eficiente ➤ *adj* efficient, effective.

efusivo, a ➤ *adj* effusive.

egoísta ➤ *adj & mf* egoistic (person).

egresar ➤ *intr* AMER. to graduate.

eje ➤ *m* axis; FIG. crux, main point; MECH., TECH. shaft, axle.

ejecutar ➤ *tr* to execute; COMPUT. *(un programa)* to run.

ejecutivo, a ➤ *adj & mf* executive.

ejemplar ➤ *adj* exemplary ➤ *m* example; PRINT. copy; *(número)* number, issue; SCI. specimen.

ejemplo ➤ *m* example ■ **por e.** for example, for instance.

ejercer §51 ➤ *tr* to exercise; *(una profesión)* to practice.

ejercicio ➤ *m* exercise; *(desempeño)* practice; *(prueba)* examination ■ **e. económico** fiscal year.

ejercitar ➤ *tr (una profesión)* to practice; *(adiestrar)* to train, drill ➤ *reflex* to train, drill.

ejército ➤ *m* MIL. army; FIG. army, flock.

el ➤ *def art* the ➤ *pron* the one ■ **el que** the one that; *(él)* he who.

él ➤ *pron* he, him, it ■ **de él** his • **él mismo** he himself • **para él** for him ■ *pl* **ellos** they, them • **de ellos** theirs • **ellos mismos** they themselves.

elaborar ➤ *tr (fabricar)* to manufacture; *(crear)* to make, create; *(preparar)* to prepare, work out.

elasticidad ➤ *f* elasticity.

elástico, a ➤ *adj* elastic; *(flexible)* flexible ➤ *m* elastic, rubber band ■ *pl* suspenders.

elección ➤ *f* election; *(selección)* selection, choice.

electorado ➤ *m* electorate.

electricidad ➤ *f* electricity.

electricista ➤ *adj* electrical ➤ *mf* electrician.

eléctrico, a ➤ *adj* electric(al); FIG. lightning-fast.

electrocutar ➤ *tr* to electrocute.

electrónico, a ➤ *adj* electronic ➤ *f* electronics.

elefante, a ➤ *mf* elephant.

elegancia ➤ *f* elegance, polish.

elegante ➤ *adj* elegant, stylish.

elegir ➤ *tr* to choose, select; POL. to elect.

elemental ➤ *adj* elemental; *(obvio)* elementary, obvious; *(fundamental)* fundamental, essential.

elemento ➤ *m* element; *(miembro)* member; ELEC. cell ■ *pl* rudiments, basic principles; *(recursos)* resources, means; *(lluvia, etc.)* elements.

elevación ➤ *f* elevation; *(construcción)* erection, building; FIG. promotion; *(enajenamiento)* rapture, ecstasy; MATH. raising.

elevado, a ➤ *adj* tall, high; *(sublime)* elevated, lofty.

elevador ➤ *m* AMER. elevator.

elevar ➤ *tr* to elevate; *(ennoblecer)* to ennoble; MATH. to raise.

eliminar ➤ *tr* to eliminate.

ella ➤ *pron* she, her, it ■ **de e.** hers • **e. misma** she herself • **para e.** for her ■ *pl* **ellas** they, them • **de ellas** theirs • **ellas mismas** they themselves.

ello ➤ *pron* it.

ellos, ellas ➤ *pron* they, them.

elocuente ➤ *adj* eloquent.

elogiar ➤ *tr* to eulogize, praise.

eludir ➤ *tr* to elude, avoid.

embajada ➤ *f* embassy; *(cargo)* ambassadorship.

embajador, a ➤ *mf* ambassador.

embalaje ➤ *m* packing, crating; *(materia)* packing material.

embalar ➤ *tr* to pack, crate; *(motor)* to rev ➤ *intr* to race, sprint.

embalse ➤ *m* dam.

embarazada ➤ *adj* pregnant ➤ *f* pregnant woman.

embarazo ➤ *m (preñez)* pregnancy; *(dificultad)* difficulty.

embarazoso, a ➤ *adj* troublesome.

embarcación ➤ *f* boat, vessel; *(embarco)* embarkation; *(viaje)* voyage.

embarcadero ➤ *m* pier; *(muelle)* wharf, dock; AMER. loading platform.

embarcar §47 ➤ *tr* to embark; *(poner a bordo)* to load, ship aboard ➤ *reflex* to embark; *(enredarse)* to get involved in, engage in.

embarque ➤ *m* loading, shipment.

embestir §32 ➤ *tr & intr* to attack.

emblema ➤ *m* emblem, symbol.

émbolo ➤ *m* piston.

embolsar ➤ *tr* to pocket, collect.

emborrachar ➤ *tr* to intoxicate; *(adormecer)* to make drowsy ➤ *reflex* to get drunk.

emboscada ➤ *f* ambush.

embotellamiento ➤ *m* bottling; *(de la circulación)* traffic jam, bottleneck.

embotellar ➤ *tr* to bottle; *(obstruir)* to jam, block.

embrague ➤ *m* AUTO. clutch.

embriagar §31 ➤ *tr* to intoxicate ➤ *reflex* to get drunk.

embrollar ➤ *tr* to confuse, embroil.

embrollo ➤ *m* confusion, tangle; *(embuste)* trick, fraud.

embrujo ➤ *m* spell, charm.

embudo ➤ *m* funnel; *(trampa)* trick, fraud.

embuste ➤ *m* hoax, fraud; *(mentira)* lie.

embustero, a ➤ *adj* lying, deceitful ➤ *mf* liar, cheat.

embutido ➤ *m* ARTS inlay, marquetry; CUL. sausage.

emergencia ➤ *f (surgimiento)* emergence; *(accidente)* emergency.

emigrante ➤ *adj* emigrating, migrating ➤ *mf* emigrant, émigré.

emigrar ➤ *intr* to emigrate; ZOOL. to migrate.

emisión ➤ *f* emission; TELEC. transmission, broadcast; COM. issuance, issue.

emisor, a ➤ *adj* TELEC. broadcasting; COM. issuing ➤ *mf* issuer ➤ *m* TELEC. *(aparato)* transmitter ➤ *f (estación)* broadcasting station.

emitir ➤ *tr* to emit; *(poner en circulación)* to issue; *(expresar)* to utter ➤ *intr* to broadcast, transmit.

emoción ➤ *f* emotion, feeling.

emocionante ➤ *adj* moving, thrilling.

emocionar ➤ *tr* to move, affect ➤ *reflex* to be moved *or* affected.

empacar §47 ➤ *tr & intr* to pack.

empacho ➤ *m* indigestion.

empalmar ➤ *tr (unir)* to connect, join ➤ *intr & reflex* to meet, join.

empalme ➤ *m* join, joint; RAIL., AUTO. junction; PHOTOG. splice.

empanada ➤ *f* CUL. turnover.

empañar ➤ *tr (con pañales)* to diaper, swaddle; *(obscurecer)* to blur, mist.

empapar ➤ *tr* to soak; *(absorber)* to absorb, soak up ➤ *reflex* to get soaked.

empapelar ➤ *tr* to wrap in paper; *(forrar)* to paper, wallpaper.

empaquetar ➤ *tr* to pack, wrap.

empaste ➤ *m (de diente)* filling; *(de libros)* bookbinding.

empatar ➤ *tr* to tie, equal; *(estorbar)* to impede, hold up ➤ *intr* to tie, be equal ➤ *reflex* to result in a tie *or* draw.

empate ➤ *m* tie, draw; AMER. *(estorbo)* obstacle; *(unión)* joint, connection.

empedrado, a ➤ *adj* dappled, spotted ➤ *m* cobblestones.

empeine ➤ *m (del vientre)* groin; *(del pie)* instep; MED. impetigo.

empeñar ➤ *tr* to pawn ➤ *reflex (entramparse)* to go into debt; *(insistir)* to insist, persist ■ **e. en** to be bent on *or* determined to.

empeño ➤ *m* pawn, pledge; *(constancia)* insistence, tenacity.

empeorar ➤ *tr* to make worse ➤ *intr & reflex* to worsen, deteriorate.

emperador ➤ *m* emperor.

emperatriz ➤ *f* empress.

empezar §17 ➤ *tr & intr* to begin (*a* to, *por* by) ■ **al e.** at the beginning *or* start • **para e.** to begin with, first.

empleado, a ➤ *mf* employee.

emplear ➤ *tr* to employ; *(invertir)* to invest ➤ *reflex* to get a job, become employed.

empleo ➤ *m* job, occupation; *(uso)* use.

emplomar ➤ *tr (diente)* to fill.

empobrecer §09 ➤ *tr* to impoverish ➤ *intr & reflex* to become poor *or* impoverished.

empobrecimiento ➤ *m* impoverishment.

emporio ➤ *m* emporium, market; *(lugar famoso)* capital, center; AMER. department store.

emprendedor, a ➤ *adj* enterprising.

emprender ➤ *tr* to begin, set about ■ **emprenderla con** to quarrel with.

empresa ➤ *f* enterprise; *(sociedad)* company, firm; *(dirección)* management.

empresarial ➤ *adj* managerial, management.

empresario, a ➤ *mf* manager, director.

empujar ➤ *tr* to push.

empujón ➤ *m* push, shove.

emulsión ➤ *f* emulsion.

en ➤ *prep* in, into ■ **en aquel momento** at that time • **en avión** by plane • **en la mesa** on the table • **estar en casa** to be at home.

enaguas ➤ *fpl* petticoat, underskirt.

enamorado, a ➤ *adj* enamored, in love (*de* with, of) ➤ *mf* lover.

enamorarse ➤ *reflex* to fall in love (*de* with); *(aficionarse)* to become enamored (*de* of).

enano, a ➤ *adj* small, minute ➤ *mf* dwarf.

enarbolar ➤ *tr* to raise, hoist.

encabezamiento ➤ *m* caption, headline; *(de una carta)* heading; *(registro)* census list.

encabezar §02 ➤ *tr* to head.

encajar ➤ *tr* to fit, insert; *(forzar)* to force ➤ *intr* to fit (well) ➤ *reflex* to squeeze in.

encaje ➤ *m* lace; *(inserción)* insertion, fit.

encallar ➤ *intr* MARIT. to run aground.

encaminar ➤ *tr* to direct, guide ➤ *reflex* to make for, set out for.

encantado, a ➤ *adj* delighted, charmed; *(casa)* haunted.

encantador, a ➤ *adj* enchanting, charming ➤ *mf* charmer ➤ *m* sorcerer ➤ *f* sorceress.

encantar ➤ *tr* to enchant, charm; *(hechizar)* to bewitch, cast a spell on.

encanto ➤ *m* enchantment, bewitchment; *(magia)* magic ■ *pl* charms.

encapricharse ➤ *reflex* to take it into one's head, take a fancy (*por, con* to).

encaramar ➤ *tr (levantar)* to lift, raise ➤ *reflex* to climb up; AMER. to blush.

encarar ➤ *intr, tr & reflex* to face, confront.

encarcelar ➤ *tr* to incarcerate, imprison; CARP. to clamp.

encargado, a ➤ *adj* in charge ➤ *mf* person in charge.

encargar §31 ➤ *tr* to put in charge; *(pedir)* to advise; *(ordenar)* to order ➤ *reflex* to take charge.

encargo ➤ *m* errand, task; *(trabajo)* assignment, job; *(empleo)* post.

encariñarse ➤ *reflex* to become fond (*con* of).

encarnado, a ➤ *adj & m* red.

encarnar ➤ *tr* to personify, embody.

encauzar §02 ➤ *tr* to channel, direct.

encender §34 ➤ *tr* to light; *(incendiar)* to set on fire; *(luz)* to turn on ➤ *reflex* to catch on fire.

encendido, a ➤ *adj* lit, switched on; *(hecho ascua)* red, red-hot ➤ *m* AUTO. ignition.

encerado, a ➤ *adj (pulido)* waxed, polished ➤ *m (pizarra)* blackboard.

encerrar §33 ➤ *tr* to enclose, confine; *(incluir)* to hold, contain; *(implicar)* to involve, entail ➤ *reflex* to go into seclusion.

enchufar ➤ *tr* ELEC. to connect, plug in; *(acoplar tubos)* to fit together, couple.

enchufe ➤ *m* ELEC., TECH. connection; *(hembra)* socket; *(macho)* plug.

encía ➤ *f* ANAT. gum, gingiva.

enciclopedia ➤ *f* encyclop(a)edia.

encima ➤ *adv (sobre)* on top; *(además)* in addition, besides ■ **e. de** above • **por e.** superficially • **por e. de** in spite of.

encinta ➤ *adj* pregnant.

encintar ➤ *tr* to adorn with ribbon.

enclenque ➤ *adj & mf* weak, sickly (person).

encoger §20 ➤ *tr* to contract, draw in; *(reducir)* to shrink ➤ *intr & reflex* to contract; *(reducirse)* to shrink ■ **e. de hombros** to shrug one's shoulders.

encolar ➤ *tr* to glue, stick.

encolerizar §02 ➤ *tr* to anger, enrage ➤ *reflex* to become angry *or* enraged.

encono ➤ *m* rancor, ill will.

encontrar §11 ➤ *tr* to find; *(topar)* to meet, encounter ➤ *intr* to meet ➤ *reflex* to meet; *(estar)* to be, be located; *(sentirse)* to find oneself ■ **e. con** to meet, run into.

encrucijada ➤ *f* crossroads, intersection.

encuadernar ➤ *tr* to bind.
encubrir §55 ➤ *tr* to hide, conceal.
encuentro ➤ *m* meeting, encounter; SPORT. match, game.
encuesta ➤ *f* investigation, inquiry; *(sondeo)* survey, poll.
endeble ➤ *adj* weak, flimsy.
endémico, a ➤ *adj* endemic.
enderezar §02 ➤ *tr* to straighten; *(poner vertical)* to set *or* stand up straight; *(enmendar)* to correct, rectify.
endeudarse ➤ *reflex* to fall into debt; FIG. to become indebted.
endiablado, a ➤ *adj* diabolical; *(feísimo)* hideous, repulsive.
endibia ➤ *f* endive.
endosar ➤ *tr (un cheque)* to endorse; *(encajar)* to palm off.
endovenoso, a ➤ *adj* intravenous.
endulzar §02 ➤ *tr* to sweeten; *(suavizar)* to soften, ease.
endurecer §09 ➤ *tr & reflex* to harden; *(robustecer)* to toughen (up).
enemigo, a ➤ *mf* enemy, adversary ➤ *f* enmity.
enemistar ➤ *tr* to antagonize ➤ *reflex* to become enemies.
energía ➤ *f* energy; *(vigor)* vitality, vigor; *(eficacia)* efficacy, effectiveness; *(ánimo)* spirit.
enérgico, a ➤ *adj* energetic.
enero ➤ *m* January.
enfadar ➤ *tr* to anger, annoy ➤ *reflex* to get angry *or* annoyed.
enfado ➤ *m* annoyance, anger.
énfasis ➤ *m* emphasis.
enfermar ➤ *intr* to get sick, become sick ➤ *tr* to make ill; *(debilitar)* to weaken.
enfermedad ➤ *f* illness, sickness.
enfermería ➤ *f* infirmary.
enfermero, a ➤ *mf* nurse.
enfermizo, a ➤ *adj* sickly, unhealthy.
enfermo, a ➤ *adj & mf* sick (person).
enfocar §47 ➤ *tr* to focus.
enfrentar ➤ *tr* to bring *or* put face to face ➤ *intr* to face ➤ *reflex* to confront, face.
enfrente ➤ *adv* facing, opposite; *(delante)* in front.
enfriar §18 ➤ *tr & intr* to cool ➤ *reflex* to be cold; MED. to catch a cold.
enfurecer §09 ➤ *tr* to madden, infuriate ➤ *reflex* to become furious, lose one's temper.
enganchar ➤ *tr* to hook; *(colgar)* to hang (up); FIG. to persuade; MIL. to recruit ➤ *reflex* to get caught up; MIL. to enlist.
engañar ➤ *tr* to deceive, trick ➤ *intr* to be deceptive *or* misleading ➤ *reflex* to deceive oneself; *(equivocarse)* to be wrong.
engaño ➤ *m (equivocación)* error, mistake; *(trampa)* deception, trick.
engañoso, a ➤ *adj* deceptive, tricky; *(deshonesto)* dishonest, deceitful; *(mentiroso)* misleading, wrong.
engastar ➤ *tr* JEWEL. to set, mount.
engendrar ➤ *tr* to engender.
englobar ➤ *tr* to include, comprise.
engordar ➤ *tr* to fatten ➤ *intr* to get fat.
engorro ➤ *m* obstacle, impediment.
engranaje ➤ *m* MECH. gear; *(acción)* meshing; COLL. connection, link.
engrasar ➤ *tr* to grease; *(aceitar)* to oil.
engreído, a ➤ *adj* conceited, arrogant; AMER. spoiled.
engrudo ➤ *m* paste.
engullir ➤ *tr* to gulp down, gobble.
enhorabuena ➤ *f* congratulations.
enigma ➤ *m* enigma, riddle.
enjabonar ➤ *tr* to soap, wash with soap; *(adular)* to flatter; *(reprender)* to scold.
enjambre ➤ *m* swarm.
enjaular ➤ *tr* to cage, put in a cage.
enjuagar §31 ➤ *tr & reflex* to rinse.
enjugar §31 ➤ *tr* to dry ➤ *reflex* to wipe, dry ■ **e. las lágrimas** to dry one's tears.
enjuiciar ➤ *tr (juzgar)* to judge; *(sujetar a juicio)* to indict, prosecute.
enlace ➤ *m* connection, link; *(casamiento)* marriage, matrimony; COMPUT. hyperlink, link.
enlazar §02 ➤ *tr* to lace, interlace; *(trabar)* to link, connect ➤ *intr* RAIL. to connect.
enloquecer §09 ➤ *tr* to drive mad *or* insane; *(excitar)* to excite, drive crazy ➤ *intr & reflex* to go insane.
enmarañar ➤ *tr* to entangle, snarl; *(confundir)* to muddle, confuse ➤ *reflex* to become tangled.
enmarcar §47 ➤ *tr* to frame.
enmascarado, a ➤ *adj & mf* masked (person).
enmascarar ➤ *tr* to mask; *(disfrazar)* to conceal, disguise.
enmendar §33 ➤ *tr* to correct, amend.
enmienda ➤ *f* amendment; *(reparo)* reparation, compensation.
enmohecer §09 ➤ *tr & reflex* to make moldy; *(metales)* to rust.
enmudecer §09 ➤ *tr* to silence, hush ➤ *intr* to be silent, keep quiet.
ennegrecer §09 ➤ *tr* to blacken *or* darken ➤ *reflex* to turn black *or* dark.
enojar ➤ *tr* to anger, make angry ➤ *reflex* to get angry.
enojoso, a ➤ *adj* bothersome, annoying.
enorgullecer §09 ➤ *tr* to make proud ➤ *reflex* to be proud.
enorme ➤ *adj* enormous, huge.
enrarecer §09 ➤ *intr & reflex* to become rare *or* scarce.
enredadera ➤ *adj* climbing, trailing ➤ *f* climbing plant, creeper.
enredar ➤ *tr* to tangle up, snarl; *(embrollar)* to confuse; *(comprometer)* to involve ➤ *intr* to get into mischief ➤ *reflex* to get tangled up; *(complicarse)* to become confused; *(comprometerse)* to become involved.
enriquecer §09 ➤ *tr* to enrich, make wealthy ➤ *intr & reflex* to get rich.
enrojecer §09 ➤ *intr* to blush, turn red.
enrollar ➤ *tr* to roll *or* wind up ➤ *intr* COMPUT. to scroll ➤ *reflex* to be rolled *or* wound up; COLL. to get involved.
enroscar §47 ➤ *tr* to coil, twist; *(atornillar)* to screw in.
ensalada ➤ *f* salad; FIG. hodgepodge.
ensanchar ➤ *tr* to widen, expand ➤ *intr & reflex* to get conceited; *(engrandecerse)* to expand.
ensanche ➤ *m* extension, expansion; *(barrio)* suburban development.
ensangrentar §33 ➤ *tr* to stain with blood ➤ *reflex* to become bloodstained; FIG. to become furious.
ensayar ➤ *tr* to test, try out; THEAT. to rehearse, practice; *(adiestrar)* to train, teach; *(intentar)* to try *or* attempt ➤ *reflex* to practice, rehearse.
ensayo ➤ *m* test, trial; *(ejercicio)* exercise, practice; *(intento)* attempt; LIT. essay; METAL. assay; THEAT. rehearsal.
enseguida ➤ *adv* immediately, at once.
ensenada ➤ *f* cove, inlet.
enseñanza ➤ *f* teaching; *(instrucción)* training; *(educación)* education; *(lección)* lesson.
enseñar ➤ *tr* to teach; *(indicar)* to indicate, point out; *(mostrar)* to show.
enseres ➤ *mpl* ■ **e. domésticos** household goods.
ensimismarse ➤ *reflex* to be absorbed in thought; AMER. to become vain.
ensombrecerse §09 ➤ *reflex* to darken, get dark; FIG. to become sad *or* gloomy.
ensordecedor, a ➤ *adj* deafening.
ensuciar ➤ *tr* to dirty, soil; *(estropear)* to make a mess of, mess up ➤ *reflex* to become dirty *or* soiled.
ensueño ➤ *m* dream; *(fantasía)* fantasy, illusion.
entablar ➤ *tr* to board (up); *(empezar)* to begin, start; LAW to bring, file ■ **e. amistad** to become friends.
ente ➤ *m* entity, being; COM. firm, company.
entender §34 ➤ *tr* to understand, comprehend; *(creer)* to believe, think ➤ *intr* ■ **e. en** *or* **de** to be good at • **e. mal** to misunderstand ➤ *reflex* to be understood; *(interpretarse)* to be meant; *(ponerse de acuerdo)* to come to an agreement; *(llevarse bien)* to get along; *(tener relaciones amorosas)* to have an affair ➤ *m* opinion.
entendimiento ➤ *m* understanding, comprehension; *(juicio)* judgment, sense.
enterar ➤ *tr* to inform, make aware ➤ *reflex* to find out, become aware.
entereza ➤ *f* integrity, uprightness.
enternecer §09 ➤ *tr* to soften, make tender ➤ *reflex (conmoverse)* to be touched *or* moved.
entero, a ➤ *adj* entire, complete; MATH. whole ■ **por e.** entirely, completely.
enterrar §33 ➤ *tr* to bury.
entidad ➤ *f* entity; *(organización)* organization.
entierro ➤ *m* burial; *(funerales)* funeral; *(sepulcro)* tomb, grave.
entonar ➤ *tr* to intone; MED. to tone up.
entonces ➤ *adv (en aquel momento)* then, at that time; *(en tal caso)* then, in that case ■ **desde e.** since then, from then on • **en aquel e.** *or* **por e.** around that time • **hasta e.** till then.
entornar ➤ *tr* to half-close, leave ajar.
entorpecer §09 ➤ *tr* to make torpid *or* slow; FIG. to dull, deaden.
entrada ➤ *f* entry, entrance; *(vestíbulo)* vestibule, entrance hall; *(ingreso)* admission; *(desembolso)* deposit, down payment; CUL. entrée; COMPUT., ELEC., input.
entrañable ➤ *adj* intimate, close; *(querido)* beloved, dear.
entrar ➤ *intr* to enter, come in; *(ser admitido)* to be admitted; *(ingresar)* to join; *(encajar)* to go, fit; *(desaguar)* to flow; *(formar parte)* to be part; *(ser contado)* to be counted; *(emplearse)* to go, be used; *(empezar)* to begin; COMPUT. to log in *or* on ■ **e. en** to enter, go in ➤ *tr (meter)* to bring *or* put inside; COMPUT. to input.
entre ➤ *prep* between; *(en el número de)* among ■ **e. tanto** meanwhile.
entreabierto, a ➤ *adj* half-open, ajar.
entrecejo ➤ *m* ANAT. space between the eyebrows; *(ceño)* frown.
entrega ➤ *f* delivery; *(rendición)* handing over.
entregar §31 ➤ *tr (dar)* to deliver; *(poner en manos)* to hand over *or* in ➤ *reflex (rendirse)* to surrender, submit.
entrelazar §02 ➤ *tr* to interlace, interweave.
entremés ➤ *m* appetizer.
entremeter ➤ *tr* to insert, put *or* place in between ➤ *reflex (injerirse)* to meddle, interfere.
entremetido, a ➤ *adj* meddlesome, interfering ➤ *mf* meddler, busybody.
entrenador, a ➤ *mf* trainer, coach.
entrenamiento ➤ *m* training, coaching.
entrenar ➤ *tr & reflex* to train.
entresuelo ➤ *m* mezzanine.
entretanto ➤ *adv* meanwhile, in the meantime ➤ *m* meantime, meanwhile.
entretener §46 ➤ *tr* to entertain, amuse; *(detener)* to detain, delay ➤ *reflex (detenerse)* to dally, dawdle; *(divertirse)* to be entertained *or* amused.
entretenido, a ➤ *adj* amusing, entertaining.
entretenimiento ➤ *m* amusement, entertainment; *(detenimiento)* detainment, delay.
entretiempo ➤ *m* between-season.
entrevista ➤ *f* meeting, conference; JOURN. interview.
entrevistar ➤ *tr* to interview ➤ *reflex* to hold an interview *or* a meeting.
entristecer §09 ➤ *tr* to sadden, grieve ➤ *reflex* to become sad *or* grieved.
entumecer §09 ➤ *tr* to (make) numb ➤ *reflex* to go *or* become numb; *(hincharse)* to swell.
enturbiar ➤ *tr* to cloud ➤ *reflex* to become clouded *or* cloudy.
entusiasmar ➤ *tr* to enthuse ➤ *reflex* to become enthusiastic.
entusiasmo ➤ *m* enthusiasm.
enumerar ➤ *tr* to enumerate.
envasar ➤ *tr* to pack, package; *(embotellar)* to bottle.
envase ➤ *m* packing, packaging; *(paquete)* package; *(botella)* bottle.
envejecer §09 ➤ *tr* to age, make old ➤ *intr & reflex* to grow old, age.
envenenar ➤ *tr* to poison.
envergadura ➤ *f* wingspan, wingspread; FIG. importance, significance.
enviar §18 ➤ *tr* to send, dispatch; *(transmitir)* to convey, transmit.
envidia ➤ *f* envy.
envidiar ➤ *tr* to envy, be envious of.
envidioso, a ➤ *adj & mf* envious (person).
envío ➤ *m* dispatch; *(paquete)* package; *(dinero)* remittance; *(mercancías)* shipment, consignment.
envoltorio ➤ *m* bundle; *(cubierta)* wrapper.
envolver §54 ➤ *tr (cubrir)* to envelop, cover; *(empaquetar)* to pack, wrap up.
enyesar ➤ *tr* to plaster; MED. to set in plaster, put a cast on.
epidemia ➤ *f* epidemic.
epilepsia ➤ *f* epilepsy.
episodio ➤ *m* episode.
época ➤ *f* epoch, era; *(período)* time, period; GEOL. age ■ **en aquella é.** at that time.
equilibrio ➤ *m* equilibrium.
equilibrista ➤ *mf* tightrope walker.
equipaje ➤ *m* luggage, baggage; MARIT. crew.
equipar ➤ *tr* to equip, outfit.
equipo ➤ *m (acción)* outfitting; *(equipamiento)* equipment, gear; SPORT. team; *(de trabajadores)* shift, crew.
equitación ➤ *f* riding, equitation.
equitativo, a ➤ *adj* equitable, fair.
equivalente ➤ *adj & m* equivalent.
equivocación ➤ *f* error, mistake.
equivocado, a ➤ *adj* wrong, mistaken.
equivocar §47 ➤ *tr* to mistake ➤ *intr* to equivocate, lie ➤ *reflex* to be mistaken.
equívoco, a ➤ *adj* equivocal, ambiguous ➤ *m* ambiguity; *(malentendido)* misunderstanding.
era ➤ *f* era, age; *(período)* period, time.
erguir ➤ *tr* to raise, lift up ➤ *reflex* to straighten up.
erigir §19 ➤ *tr* to erect, build; *(fundar)* to found, establish.
erizar §02 ➤ *tr* to make stand on end, set on end ➤ *reflex* to stand on end.
erosión ➤ *f* erosion.
erradicar §47 ➤ *tr* to eradicate.
errante ➤ *adj* errant, wandering.
errar ➤ *tr* to miss; *(faltar)* to fail (someone) ➤ *intr* to wander, roam; *(equivocarse)* to make a mistake.
errata ➤ *f* erratum.
erróneo, a ➤ *adj* erroneous, mistaken.
error ➤ *m* error, mistake.
eructar ➤ *intr* to burp, belch.
eructo ➤ *m* burp, belch.
erudito, a ➤ *adj & mf* erudite.
erupción ➤ *f* eruption.
esbelto, a ➤ *adj* slender, svelte.
escabeche ➤ *m (adobo)* marinade; *(pescado)* marinated fish salad.
escabullirse ➤ *reflex* to escape.
escala ➤ *f* scale; *(escalera de mano)* ladder; MARIT. port of call, AVIA. stop.
escalar ➤ *tr* to scale, climb ➤ *intr* MIL., POL. to escalate.
escaldar ➤ *tr* to scald, burn.
escalera ➤ *f* stairs, staircase; *(escalerilla)* ladder; *(de naipes)* straight ■ **e. mecánica** *or* **automática** escalator.
escalerilla ➤ *f* stepladder.
escalfar ➤ *tr* to poach.
escalofrío ➤ *m (de miedo)* shiver, shudder; *(de fiebre)* chill, shiver.
escalón ➤ *m* step, stair.
escalonar ➤ *tr (colocar)* to space out; *(horas)* to stagger; AGR. to terrace.
escama ➤ *f* scale.
escamotear ➤ *tr* to make disappear; COLL. *(robar)* to steal.
escampar ➤ *tr & intr* to clear (up).
escandalizar §02 ➤ *tr* to scandalize, shock ➤ *reflex* to be shocked.
escándalo ➤ *m* scandal ■ **armar un e.** to make a scene.
escanear ➤ *tr* COMPUT. *(foto)* to scan.
escáner ➤ *m* COMPUT. scanner.
escapada ➤ *f* escape, flight.
escapar ➤ *intr & reflex* to escape.
escaparate ➤ *m* shop *or* display window; AMER. *(ropero)* wardrobe, closet.
escape ➤ *m* escape, flight; AUTO. exhaust (pipe).
escarabajo ➤ *m* scarab, black beetle.
escarbadientes ➤ *m* toothpick.
escarbar ➤ *tr (rascar)* to scrape, scratch; *(los dientes)* to pick.
escarcha ➤ *f* frost.
escarlata ➤ *adj & f* scarlet.
escarlatina ➤ *f* scarlet fever.
escarmentar §33 ➤ *tr* to chastise, teach a lesson to ➤ *intr* to learn one's lesson.
escarmiento ➤ *m (aviso)* warning, lesson; *(castigo)* punishment.
escarola ➤ *f* escarole.
escarpado, a ➤ *adj (pendiente)* steep, sheer; *(escabroso)* craggy, rugged.
escasear ➤ *intr* to become *or* be scarce.
escasez ➤ *f* scarcity, lack.
escaso, a ➤ *adj* scarce, limited.
escena ➤ *f* scene; THEAT. stage ■ **poner en e.** to stage, present.
escenario ➤ *m* stage, scene.
escéptico, a ➤ *adj* skeptical ➤ *mf* skeptic.
esclarecer §09 ➤ *tr* to illuminate, light

up; *(elucidar)* to clarify.
esclavo, a ➤ *adj* enslaved ➤ *mf* slave.
esclusa ➤ *f* lock, sluice; *(compuerta)* floodgate.
escoba ➤ *f* broom.
escocer §48 ➤ *intr* to sting, smart.
escoger §20 ➤ *tr* to choose, select.
escolar ➤ *adj* scholastic, school ➤ *mf* pupil, student.
escolta ➤ *f* escort.
escoltar ➤ *tr* to escort.
escollo ➤ *m* reef, rock; FIG. stumbling block.
escombro ➤ *m* rubble, debris; MIN. slag.
esconder ➤ *tr & reflex* to hide, conceal.
escondidas ➤ *fpl* ■ **a e.** secretly, covertly.
escondite ➤ *m* hiding place; *(juego)* hide-and-seek.
escondrijo ➤ *m* hiding place.
escopeta ➤ *f* shotgun, rifle.
escorpión ➤ *m* scorpion.
escote ➤ *m* neck, neckline.
escotilla ➤ *f* hatch(way).
escozor ➤ *m* smarting; *(pena)* grief, sorrow.
escribir §55 ➤ *tr & intr* to write ■ **e. a máquina** to type.
escrito, a ➤ *adj* written ➤ *m* document, writing ■ **por e.** in writing.
escritor, a ➤ *mf* writer.
escritorio ➤ *m* desk; *(despacho)* office, study.
escritura ➤ *f* writing; *(sistema de signos)* script; LAW document.
escrúpulo ➤ *m* scruple.
escrupuloso, a ➤ *adj* scrupulous.
escrutinio ➤ *m* scrutiny, examination.
escuadra ➤ *f* carpenter's square; MIL. squad, squadron.
escuálido, a ➤ *adj* squalid, filthy.
escuchar ➤ *tr* to listen to.
escudo ➤ *m* shield; HER. coat of arms, escutcheon.
escuela ➤ *f* school ■ **e. primaria, secundaria** elementary, high school.
escueto, a ➤ *adj* concise, direct; *(libre)* free, unencumbered.
escultor, a ➤ *mf* sculptor.
escultura ➤ *f* sculpture, carving.
escupir ➤ *tr* to spit; COLL. *(pagar)* to cough up, fork over *or* out; *(confesar)* to spill, give ➤ *intr* to spit.
escurridizo, a ➤ *adj* slippery.
escurridor ➤ *m* colander.
escurrir ➤ *tr* to drain; *(hacer que chorrea)* to wring (out) ➤ *intr* to drip, trickle; *(deslizar)* to slip, slide ➤ *reflex* to slip out, escape.
ese, esa ➤ *adj* that ■ *pl* those.
ése, ésa ➤ *pron* that one; *(el primero)* the former; *(allí)* there ■ *pl* those.
esencia ➤ *f* essence ■ **quinta e.** quintessence.
esencial ➤ *adj* essential.
esfera ➤ *f* sphere; *(del reloj)* dial, face.
esforzar §22 ➤ *tr* to strengthen; *(dar ánimo)* to encourage ➤ *reflex* to strive.
esfuerzo ➤ *m* effort, exertion.
esfumarse ➤ *reflex* to disappear, vanish.
esguince ➤ *m* sprain, twist.
eslabón ➤ *m* link.
esmalte ➤ *m* enamel.
esmeralda ➤ *f* emerald.
esmerarse ➤ *reflex* to be painstaking, take great care.
esmoquin ➤ *m* dinner jacket, tuxedo.
esnob ➤ *mf* snob.
eso ➤ *pron* that ■ **a e. de** about, around • **e. es** that's it • **e. mismo** exactly, the same • **por e.** therefore, that's why.
espacial ➤ *adj* spatial; *(del espacio)* space ■ **nave e.** spaceship.
espacio ➤ *m* space.
espacioso, a ➤ *adj* spacious, roomy; *(lento)* slow, deliberate.
espada ➤ *f* sword; *(naipe)* spade ■ **entre la e. y la pared** between a rock and a hard place.
espagueti ➤ *m* spaghetti.
espalda ➤ *f* back ■ **dar** *or* **volver la e.** to turn one's back ■ *pl* back ■ **de e.** from behind.
espantapájaros ➤ *m* scarecrow.
espantar ➤ *tr* to frighten, scare ➤ *reflex* to be frightened *or* scared.
espantoso, a ➤ *adj* frightening, scary.
español, a ➤ *adj* Spanish ➤ *m* *(idioma)* Spanish ➤ *mf* Spaniard.
esparadrapo ➤ *m* adhesive tape.
esparcir ➤ *tr* to scatter, spread ➤ *reflex* to scatter, be scattered.
espárrago ➤ *m* asparagus.
espátula ➤ *f* CUL. spatula; ORNITH. spoonbill.
especia ➤ *f* spice.
especial ➤ *adj* special ■ **en e.** especially.
especialidad ➤ *f* specialty.
especialista ➤ *adj & mf* specialist.
especializar §02 ➤ *tr, intr & reflex* to specialize.
especialmente ➤ *adv* especially.
especie ➤ *f* species; *(tipo)* type, kind; *(asunto)* matter, affair.
especificar §47 ➤ *tr* to specify.
específico, a ➤ *adj & m* specific.
espectacular ➤ *adj* spectacular.
espectáculo, ➤ *m* spectacle.
espectador, a ➤ *mf* spectator, onlooker.
espectro ➤ *m* PHYS. spectrum; *(fantasma)* ghost, spook; *(horror)* specter.
especulación ➤ *f* speculation.
especulador, a ➤ *mf* speculator.
espejismo ➤ *m* mirage.
espejo ➤ *m* mirror; *(modelo)* model, example.
espeluznante ➤ *adj* COLL. hair-raising.
espera ➤ *f* wait; LAW respite.
esperanza ➤ *f* hope.
esperar ➤ *tr* to hope (for); *(aguardar)* to wait for; *(confiar en)* to expect; *(ser inminente)* to await ➤ *intr* to wait.
esperma ➤ *f* sperm, semen.
espesar ➤ *tr* to thicken ➤ *reflex* to grow *or* become thicker.
espeso, a ➤ *adj* thick; *(sucio)* dirty, unkempt.
espesor ➤ *m* thickness; *(densidad)* density.
espía ➤ *mf* spy ➤ *f* MARIT. warping.
espiar §18 ➤ *tr & intr* to spy (on).
espiga ➤ *f* BOT. spike, ear; CARP. tenon; *(clavija)* peg, pin.
espigado, a ➤ *adj* spiky.
espina ➤ *f* thorn; *(de pez)* fishbone; ANAT. spine; *(pesar)* grief, sorrow.
espinaca ➤ *f* spinach.
espinazo ➤ *m* ANAT. spine, backbone; ARCHIT. keystone.
espinilla ➤ *f* shinbone; *(granillo)* blackhead.
espionaje ➤ *m* espionage, spying.
espiral ➤ *adj* spiral, winding ➤ *m* balance spring, hairspring; MED. coil ➤ *f* spiral.
espirar ➤ *tr & intr* to exhale, breathe out.
espíritu ➤ *m* spirit; *(alma)* soul ■ **e. de cuerpo** esprit de corps.
espiritual ➤ *adj & m* spiritual.
espléndido, a ➤ *adj* splendid; *(generoso)* generous.
esplendor ➤ *m* splendor.
esponja ➤ *f* sponge.
esponjoso, a ➤ *adj* spongy.
espontáneo, a ➤ *adj* spontaneous.
esposa ➤ *f* wife, spouse ■ *pl* handcuffs.
esposar ➤ *tr* to handcuff.
esposo ➤ *m* husband, spouse.
espuela ➤ *f* spur.
espuma ➤ *f* foam; *(de un líquido)* froth, spume; *(de jabón)* lather.
espumoso, a ➤ *adj* frothy, foamy.
esqueleto ➤ *m* skeleton.
esquema ➤ *m* scheme, outline.
esquemático, a ➤ *adj* schematic.
esquí ➤ *m* ski; *(deporte)* skiing.
esquiador, a ➤ *mf* skier.
esquiar §18 ➤ *intr* to ski.
esquina ➤ *f* corner ■ **a la vuelta de la e.** just around the corner • **doblar la e.** to turn the corner.
esquivar ➤ *tr* to avoid, evade; *(un golpe)* to dodge ➤ *reflex* to withdraw, shy away.
estabilidad ➤ *f* stability.
estabilizar §02 ➤ *tr* to stabilize, make stable.
estable ➤ *adj* stable.
establecedor, a ➤ *adj* establishing, founding ➤ *mf* establisher, founder.
establecer §09 ➤ *tr* to establish, found ➤ *reflex* to establish oneself.
establecimiento ➤ *m* establishment.
establo ➤ *m* stable.
estaca ➤ *f* stake, post; CARP. spike, nail.
estación ➤ *f* *(estado)* position; *(tiempo)* season; RAIL., TELEC. station.
estacionamiento ➤ *m* stationing, positioning; AUTO. parking place *or* space.
estacionar ➤ *tr* to station, place; AUTO. to park ➤ *reflex* to park.
estacionario, a ➤ *adj* stationary.
estadio ➤ *m* stadium; *(fase)* phase, stage.
estadista ➤ *mf* statesman/woman; *(estadístico)* statistician.
estado ➤ *m* state; *(condición)* condition ■ **e. civil** marital status.
estafa ➤ *f* swindle, hoax.
estafar ➤ *tr* to swindle, cheat.
estafeta ➤ *f* mail, post; *(de correo)* post office.
estalactita ➤ *f* stalactite.
estalagmita ➤ *f* stalagmite.
estallar ➤ *intr* to burst, explode; *(sobrevenir)* to break out.
estallido ➤ *m* explosion; FIG. outbreak, outburst.
estampado, a ➤ *adj* TEX. stamped ➤ *m* printing, engraving.
estampilla ➤ *f* stamp, seal; AMER. postage stamp.
estancar §47 ➤ *tr* to dam up, stem ➤ *reflex* to stagnate.
estancia ➤ *f* *(mansión)* country house, estate; *(estadía)* stay; AMER. ranch.
estanque ➤ *m* *(charca)* pond, pool; *(depósito)* tank, reservoir.
estante ➤ *m* shelving, shelf.
estantería ➤ *f* shelving, shelves.
estaño ➤ *m* tin.
estar §21 ➤ *intr* to be ■ **¿cómo estás?** how are you? • **e. bien, mal** to be well, ill • **e. de más** to be superfluous • **e. en** *(entender)* to understand; *(consistir en)* to depend on • **e. para** to be about to • **e. por** *(favorecer)* to be for, be in favor of • **e. por irse** to be about to go.
estatal ➤ *adj* state, of the state.
estatua ➤ *f* statue; COLL. cold fish.
estatura ➤ *f* stature.
estatuto ➤ *m* statute, law; *(regla)* rule.
este ➤ *adj* eastern, easterly ➤ *m* east.
este, a ➤ *adj* this ■ *pl* these.
éste, a ➤ *pron* this one; *(el segundo)* the latter; *(aquí)* here ■ *pl* these.
estela ➤ *f* AVIA. trail; MARIT. wake.
estepa ➤ *f* steppe.
estera ➤ *f* matting.
estéreo ➤ *adj & f* stereo.
estereofónico, a ➤ *adj* stereophonic, stereo.
estereotipo ➤ *m* stereotype.
estéril ➤ *adj* sterile, infertile.
esterlina ➤ *adj* sterling.
esternón ➤ *m* sternum, breastbone.
estero ➤ *m* estuary; AMER. *(pantano)* marsh, swamp.
estético, a ➤ *adj* aesthetic ➤ *m* aesthetic, aesthete ➤ *f* aesthetics.
estilar ➤ *intr & reflex* to be customary; *(estar de moda)* to be in fashion.
estilo ➤ *m* style ■ **por el e.** like that.
estilográfica ➤ *f* fountain pen.
estima ➤ *f* esteem, respect.
estimación ➤ *f* esteem, respect; COM. appraisal, valuation.
estimar ➤ *tr* to esteem, hold in esteem; COM. to appraise; *(juzgar)* to consider, deem ➤ *reflex* to be esteemed.
estimulante ➤ *adj* stimulating ➤ *m* stimulant.
estimular ➤ *tr* to stimulate; *(incitar)* to urge on; *(la curiosidad)* to arouse.
estímulo ➤ *m* stimulus.
estío ➤ *m* summer.
estirar ➤ *tr* to stretch; *(extender)* to extend ➤ *reflex* to stretch oneself.
estival ➤ *adj* summer.
esto ➤ *pron* this; *(asunto)* this business *or* matter ■ **por e.** for this reason.
estocada ➤ *f* thrust, stab.
estofado, a ➤ *adj* stewed; *(acolchado)* quilted ➤ *m* stew; SEW. quilting.
estómago ➤ *m* stomach.
estorbar ➤ *tr* to obstruct, block; *(dificultar)* to hinder, hamper.
estorbo ➤ *m* obstruction, obstacle; *(molestia)* bother, annoyance.
estornudar ➤ *intr* to sneeze.
estornudo ➤ *m* sneeze.
estragón ➤ *m* tarragon.
estrangular ➤ *tr* to strangle.
estratagema ➤ *f* stratagem.
estratégico, a ➤ *adj* strategic.
estraza ➤ *f* rag.
estrechamiento ➤ *m* narrowing, tightening.
estrechar ➤ *tr* *(reducir)* to narrow; *(apretar)* to tighten; *(sisar)* to take in ■ **e. la mano a** to shake hands with ➤ *reflex* to narrow; *(apretarse)* to tighten; *(ceñirse)* to squeeze together; *(amistarse)* to become close.
estrechez ➤ *f* narrowness; *(pobreza)* poverty, need; *(austeridad)* austerity ■ *pl* *(apuros)* dire straits.
estrecho, a ➤ *adj* narrow; *(apretado)* tight; *(íntimo)* close, intimate; *(rígido)* rigid, severe ➤ *m* strait, channel.
estrella ➤ *f* star; *(asterisco)* asterisk ■ **e. de mar** starfish.
estrellar ➤ *tr & reflex* COLL. *(romper)* to smash, crash.
estremecer §09 ➤ *tr* to shake; FIG. to shock, disturb ➤ *reflex* to shake, tremble.
estrenar ➤ *tr* to use *or* wear for the first time; CINEM., THEAT. to première, open ➤ *reflex* to première, debut.
estreno ➤ *m* opening, debut; CINEM., THEAT. première.
estreñimiento ➤ *m* constipation.
estrépito ➤ *m* uproar, din.
estribillo ➤ *m* POET. refrain; MUS. chorus.
estribo ➤ *m* stirrup; *(de carruaje)* footboard ■ **perder los estribos** to lose one's head.
estribor ➤ *m* starboard.
estricto, a ➤ *adj* strict.
estropajo ➤ *m* dishcloth, rag.
estropear ➤ *tr* to damage, ruin; *(maltratar)* to mistreat, mishandle.
estructura ➤ *f* structure.
estruendo ➤ *m* clamor, uproar.
estrujar ➤ *tr* to squeeze, crush.
estuche ➤ *m* case, box; *(vaina)* sheath.
estudiante ➤ *mf* student, pupil.
estudiar ➤ *tr & intr* to study.
estudio ➤ *m* study; *(cuarto)* study, studio.
estudioso, a ➤ *adj & mf* studious (person).
estufa ➤ *f* stove, heater.
estupefaciente ➤ *adj* stupefying, astonishing ➤ *m* narcotic, stupefacient.
estupefacto, a ➤ *adj* stupefied, astonished.
estupendo, a ➤ *adj* stupendous, tremendous.
estupidez ➤ *f* stupidity, idiocy.
estúpido, a ➤ *adj* stupid, dumb ➤ *mf* idiot, dumbbell.
etapa ➤ *f* phase, stage.
etcétera ➤ *adv* et cetera.
eternidad ➤ *f* eternity.
eterno, a ➤ *adj* eternal.
ético, a ➤ *adj* ethical, moral ➤ *mf* moralist ➤ *f* ethics.
etiqueta ➤ *f* etiquette, ceremony; *(rótulo)* tag, label ■ **de e.** formal.
étnico, a ➤ *adj* ethnic.
eucalipto ➤ *m* eucalyptus.
eufórico, a ➤ *adj* euphoric, jubilant.
Europa ➤ *f* Europe.
europeo, a ➤ *adj & mf* European.
eutanasia ➤ *f* euthanasia.
evacuación ➤ *f* evacuation.
evacuar ➤ *tr* to evacuate.
evadir ➤ *tr* to evade, avoid ➤ *reflex* to escape, sneak away.
evaluar §45 ➤ *tr* to evaluate, assess.
evangelio ➤ *m* gospel.
evaporación ➤ *f* evaporation.
evaporar ➤ *tr & reflex* to evaporate.
evasión ➤ *f* escape; *(evasiva)* evasion.
evasivo, a ➤ *adj* evasive ➤ *f* evasion.
evento ➤ *m* chance event, contingency.
eventual ➤ *adj* unexpected, incidental.
evidencia ➤ *f* proof, evidence.
evidente ➤ *adj* evident, clear.
evitar ➤ *tr* to avoid.
evolución ➤ *f* evolution.
evolucionar ➤ *intr* to evolve.
exacerbar ➤ *tr* to exacerbate, aggravate.
exactitud ➤ *f* exactitude, exactness; *(puntualidad)* punctuality.
exacto, a ➤ *adj* exact, precise; *(puntual)* punctual.
exageración ➤ *f* exaggeration.
exagerado, a ➤ *adj* exaggerated.
exagerar ➤ *tr* to exaggerate.
exaltar ➤ *tr* to exalt, glorify ➤ *reflex* to get worked up.
examen ➤ *m* examination, test; *(interrogación)* interrogation.
examinar ➤ *tr* to examine ➤ *reflex* to take an exam.
exasperar ➤ *tr* to exasperate ➤ *reflex* to become exasperated.
excavación ➤ *f* excavation.
excavar ➤ *tr* to excavate, dig.
excedente ➤ *adj* excessive; *(sobrante)* excess, surplus ➤ *m* excess, surplus.
exceder ➤ *tr* to exceed, surpass ➤ *reflex* *(sobrepasarse)* to go too far.
excelencia ➤ *f* excellence.
excelente ➤ *adj* excellent.
excéntrico, a ➤ *adj* eccentric.
excepción ➤ *f* exception ■ **a** *or* **con e. de**

except for.
excepcional ➤ *adj* exceptional.
excepto ➤ *prep* except, excepting.
exceptuar §45 ➤ *tr* to exclude, exempt ➤ *reflex* to be excluded *or* exempted.
excesivo, a ➤ *adj* excessive.
exceso ➤ *m* excess; COM. surplus.
excitación ➤ *f* excitement.
excitante ➤ *adj* stimulating ➤ *m* stimulant.
excitar ➤ *tr* to excite ➤ *reflex* to become excited.
exclamación ➤ *f* exclamation; *(signo ortográfico)* exclamation point.
exclamar ➤ *intr* to exclaim.
excluir §10 ➤ *tr* to exclude; *(expulsar)* to throw out, expel.
exclusive ➤ *adv* exclusively; *(no incluyendo)* exclusive of, not including.
exclusivo, a ➤ *adj* exclusive ➤ *f (repulsa)* rejection; *(privilegio)* exclusive *or* sole right.
excursión ➤ *f* excursion.
excursionista ➤ *mf* sightseer.
excusa ➤ *f* excuse ■ **a e.** secretly.
excusar ➤ *tr* to excuse ➤ *reflex* to excuse oneself ■ **e. de** to refuse.
exento, a ➤ *adj* exempt, free.
exhalar ➤ *tr* to exhale.
exhaustivo, a ➤ *adj* exhaustive.
exhausto, a ➤ *adj* exhausted.
exhibición ➤ *f* exhibition, exhibit.
exhibir ➤ *tr* to exhibit, display ➤ *reflex* to show up, to show oneself.
exigencia ➤ *f* exigency, demand.
exigente ➤ *adj* demanding.
exigir §19 ➤ *tr* to demand, require.
exil(i)ado, a ➤ *adj* exiled, in exile ➤ *mf* exile.
exil(i)ar ➤ *tr* to exile, banish.
exilio ➤ *m* exile, banishment.
existencia ➤ *f* existence ■ *pl* stock, goods.
existente ➤ *adj* existent; COM. in stock.
existir ➤ *intr* to exist, be in existence.
éxito ➤ *m* success; *(resultado)* result, outcome ■ **tener é.** to be successful.
exitoso, a ➤ *adj* AMER. successful.
éxodo ➤ *m* exodus.
exorbitante ➤ *adj* exorbitant, excessive.
exótico, a ➤ *adj* exotic.
expandir ➤ *tr & reflex* to expand.
expansión ➤ *f* expansion; *(recreo)* relaxation, recreation; *(franqueza)* expansiveness.
expectación ➤ *f* expectation.
expectativo, a ➤ *adj* expectant, hopeful ➤ *f* expectation, anticipation.
expedición ➤ *f* expedition; *(prontitud)* speed, dispatch; COM. shipping, shipment.
expediente ➤ *adj* expedient ➤ *m* expedient; *(archivo)* file, dossier, record.
expedir §32 ➤ *tr (enviar)* to send, ship; *(despachar)* to expedite, dispatch; *(dictar)* to issue.
expensas ➤ *fpl* expenses, costs.
experiencia ➤ *f* experience; CHEM., PHYS. experiment.
experimentado, a ➤ *adj* experienced.
experimental ➤ *adj* experimental.
experimentar ➤ *tr* to try out, test; *(sentir en sí)* to experience, undergo.
experimento ➤ *m* experiment.
experto, a ➤ *adj & mf* expert.
expirar ➤ *intr* to expire.
explanada ➤ *f* esplanade.
explicación ➤ *f* explanation.
explicar §47 ➤ *tr* to explain; *(enseñar)* to teach ➤ *reflex* to explain oneself; *(comprender)* to understand.
exploración ➤ *f* exploration.
explorador, a ➤ *adj* exploratory ➤ *mf* explorer ➤ *m* COMPUT. browser.
explorar ➤ *tr & intr* to explore.
explosión ➤ *f* explosion.
explosivo, a ➤ *adj & mf* explosive.
explotación ➤ *f* exploitation; *(operación)* running; *(cultivo)* cultivation.
explotar ➤ *tr* to exploit; *(operar)* to run, operate; *(cultivar)* to cultivate ➤ *intr* to go off, explode.
exponer §37 ➤ *tr* to expose; *(explicar)* to propound, explain; *(exhibir)* to exhibit ➤ *reflex* to expose oneself.
exportación ➤ *f* exportation; *(mercancías)* exports; *(artículo)* export.
exportador, a ➤ *adj* exporting ➤ *mf* exporter.
exportar ➤ *tr & intr* to export.
exposición ➤ *f* exhibition, show; *(explicación)* explanation; *(orientación)* exposure.
expresamente ➤ *adv* clearly, explicitly; *(de propósito)* specifically.
expresar ➤ *tr & reflex* to express (oneself).
expresión ➤ *f* expression.
expreso, a ➤ *adj* express ➤ *m (tren)* express train; *(correo)* express mail.
exprimidor ➤ *m* squeezer, juicer.
exprimir ➤ *tr* to squeeze.
expulsar ➤ *tr* to expel, drive out.
exquisito, a ➤ *adj* exquisite.
extender §34 ➤ *tr* to extend, enlarge; *(desdoblar)* to spread out, spread ➤ *reflex* to stretch, extend.
extensión ➤ *f* extension; *(amplitud)* expanse, stretch; *(dimensión)* extent.
extenso, a ➤ *adj* extensive, ample, vast.
extenuado, a ➤ *adj* debilitated, weakened.
extenuar §45 ➤ *tr* to debilitate, weaken.
exterior ➤ *adj* exterior, outer; *(extranjero)* foreign ➤ *m* exterior, outside.
exterminar ➤ *tr* to exterminate.
externo, a ➤ *adj* external, outward.
extinguir §15 ➤ *tr* to extinguish, put out ➤ *reflex* to fade, go out.
extinto, a ➤ *adj* extinguished; *(desaparecido)* extinct.
extorsión ➤ *f* extortion; *(molestia)* harm, trouble.
extorsionar ➤ *tr* to extort.
extra ➤ *adj* extra ➤ *prep* ■ **e. de** COLL. besides, in addition to ➤ *mf* CINEM., THEAT. extra ➤ *m* gratuity; *(gasto)* extra charge.
extracto ➤ *m* extract; *(compendio)* summary.
extraer §49 ➤ *tr* to extract.
extranjero, a ➤ *adj* alien, foreign ➤ *mf* foreigner, alien ➤ *m* abroad.
extrañar ➤ *tr* to find strange, not to be used to; AMER. to miss ➤ *reflex* to be surprised *or* astonished.
extraño, a ➤ *adj* foreign, alien; *(raro)* strange, odd; *(que no tiene que ver)* extraneous ➤ *mf* foreigner.
extraoficial ➤ *adj* unofficial.
extraordinario, a ➤ *adj* extraordinary ➤ *m (correo urgente)* special delivery; *(periódico)* special edition.
extravagancia ➤ *f* extravagance.
extravagante ➤ *adj* extravagant ➤ *mf* eccentric.
extraviar §18 ➤ *tr (desviar)* to lead astray, misguide; *(perder)* to misplace, lose ➤ *reflex* to get lost.
extremidad ➤ *f (punta)* end, tip; *(parte extrema)* extremity ■ *pl* extremities.
extremo, a ➤ *adj (último)* last, ultimate; *(intenso)* extreme, greatest, utmost; *(distante)* farthest ➤ *m* extreme.
extrovertido, a ➤ *adj* extroverted, extraverted ➤ *mf* extrovert, extravert.
exuberancia ➤ *f* exuberance, abundance.

F

fábrica ➤ *f* factory, plant.
fabricación ➤ *f* manufacture.
fabricante ➤ *mf* manufacturer.
fabricar §47 ➤ *tr* to manufacture, make.
fábula ➤ *f* fable; *(invención)* lie, fiction.
fabuloso, a ➤ *adj* fabled, imaginary; *(extraordinario)* fabulous.
facción ➤ *f* faction, party ■ *pl (rasgo)* features, facial features.
fácil ➤ *adj* easy; *(probable)* likely, probable; *(dócil)* easygoing ➤ *adv* easily.
facilidad ➤ *f* facility, ease ■ *pl* terms.
facilitar ➤ *tr* to facilitate, make easy; *(proporcionar)* to supply, furnish.
facsímile ➤ *m* facsimile.
factoría ➤ *f* AMER. plant, factory.
factura ➤ *f* COM. invoice, bill.
facturación ➤ *f* billing, invoicing.
facturar ➤ *tr* to invoice, bill.
facultad ➤ *f* faculty; *(derecho)* power, right; *(licencia)* license, permission; EDUC. school, college, faculty.
faena ➤ *f* task, chore; *(mental)* mental task; COLL. *(trastada)* dirty trick.
faisán ➤ *m* pheasant.
faja ➤ *f (corsé)* girdle, corset; ;*(tira de papel)* wrapper; AMER. belt, waistband.
fajo ➤ *m* bundle, sheaf; *(de billetes)* wad, roll.
falda ➤ *f* skirt; *(ala de sombrero)* brim, flap; *(de un monte)* foot; *(regazo)* lap.
falla ➤ *f* defect, fault; GEOG., MIN. fault.
fallar ➤ *tr* to fail, disappoint ➤ *intr* to fail; COMPUT. to crash.
fallecer §09➤ *intr* to die, expire.
fallo ➤ *m (sentencia)* ruling, judgment; *(falta)* error, fault ■ **f. de sistema** COMPUT. crash.
falsificar §47 ➤ *tr* to falsify; *(copiar)* to counterfeit, forge.
falso, a ➤ *adj* false; *(falsificado)* counterfeit, fake.
falta ➤ *f* lack, shortage; *(ausencia)* absence; *(defecto)* flaw; *(infracción)* misdemeanor; *(culpa)* fault; *(error)* error ■ **a f. de** for want of • **hacer f.** *(faltar)* to need, be lacking; *(ser necesario)* to be necessary • **sin f.** without fail.
faltar ➤ *intr (hacer falta)* to be lacking; *(estar ausente)* to be missing (*de* from); *(no responder)* to fail to function; *(ofender)* to insult ■ **f. a** *(la clase)* to miss, be absent from; *(un deber)* to fail in; *(una promesa)* to break • **f. mucho para** to be a long way off • **faltan diez minutos para las ocho** it is ten minutes to eight • **f. poco para** not to be long before • **nos falta dinero** we need money.
fama ➤ *f* fame, reputation.
familia ➤ *f* family.
familiar ➤ *adj (relativo a la familia)* familial, family; *(llano)* casual; *(conocido)* familiar ➤ *mf* family member; *(amigo íntimo)* intimate friend.
famoso, a ➤ *adj* famous; COLL. excellent.
fanático, a ➤ *adj* fanatic(al) ➤ *mf* fanatic; *(entusiasta)* fan.
fango ➤ *m* mud, mire.
fantasía ➤ *f* fantasy ■ **de f.** fancy.
fantasma ➤ *m* ghost, apparition; *(visión)* vision, illusion; *(persona seria)* stuffed shirt.
fantástico, a ➤ *adj* fantastic.
fardo ➤ *m* large bundle *or* parcel.
farmacéutico, a ➤ *adj* pharmaceutical ➤ *mf* pharmacist, druggist.
farmacia ➤ *f* pharmacy.
faro ➤ *m (torre)* lighthouse; *(señal)* beacon; AUTO. headlight.
farol ➤ *m* lantern; *(luz pública)* street lamp.
farola ➤ *f (farol)* streetlight, street lamp; *(faro)* beacon.
fascinación ➤ *f* fascination.
fascinante ➤ *adj* fascinating.
fascinar ➤ *tr* to fascinate; *(engañar)* to deceive.
fascista ➤ *adj & mf* fascist, Fascist.
fase ➤ *f* phase; TECH. stage.
fastidiar ➤ *tr* to annoy; *(cansar)* to tire, bore ➤ *reflex* to get annoyed.
fast(u)oso, a ➤ *adj* lavish, splendid.
fatal ➤ *adj* fatal; *(funesto)* unfortunate.
fatiga ➤ *f* fatigue.
fatigar §31 ➤ *tr* to fatigue; *(molestar)* to annoy ➤ *reflex* to get tired.
fauna ➤ *f* fauna, animal life.
favor ➤ *m* favor; *(amparo)* protection ■ **a f. de** in favor of, in behalf of • **de f.** complimentary, free • **por f.** please.
favorable ➤ *adj* favorable.
favorecer §09 ➤ *tr* to favor, support ➤ *reflex* to help one another ■ **f. de** to avail oneself of.
favorito, a ➤ *adj & mf* favorite.
fe ➤ *f* faith; *(creencia)* credence; *(confianza)* trust, confidence.
fealdad ➤ *f* ugliness, foulness.
febrero ➤ *m* February.
fecha ➤ *f* date ■ **hasta la f.** so far, to date.
fechar ➤ *tr* to date.
federal ➤ *adj & mf* federal.
felicidad ➤ *f* felicity, happiness; *(suerte feliz)* good luck ■ *pl (enhorabuena)* congratulations; *(deseos amistosos)* best *or* warm wishes.
felicitar ➤ *tr* to congratulate.
feliz ➤ *adj* happy; *(acertado)* felicitous, apt; *(oportuno)* lucky.
felpa ➤ *f* plush.
felpudo, a ➤ *adj* plush, velvety ➤ *m* mat.
femenino, a ➤ *adj & m* feminine.
feminista ➤ *adj & mf* feminist.
fémur ➤ *m* femur, thighbone.
fenomenal ➤ *adj* phenomenal.
fenómeno ➤ *m* phenomenon.
feo, a ➤ *adj* ugly ➤ *adv* AMER. awful.
féretro ➤ *m (ataúd)* coffin; *(andas)* bier.
feria ➤ *f (mercado)* market; *(exposición)* fair; *(día de fiesta)* holiday.
fermentar ➤ *tr & intr* to ferment.
ferocidad ➤ *f* ferocity.
feroz ➤ *adj* ferocious, fierce.
ferretería ➤ *f* foundry; *(comercio)* hardware store; *(quincalla)* hardware.
ferrocarril ➤ *m* railroad, railway.
ferroviario, a ➤ *adj* railroad.
fértil ➤ *adj* fertile.
fertilidad ➤ *f* fertility.
fertilizante ➤ *adj* fertilizing ➤ *m* fertilizer.
fertilizar §02 ➤ *tr* to fertilize.
festejar ➤ *tr* to entertain; *(celebrar)* to celebrate.
festejo ➤ *m* entertainment, feast; AMER. celebration, party.
festín ➤ *m* banquet, feast.
festival ➤ *m* festival.
festivo, a ➤ *adj* festive; *(agudo)* witty, humorous.
feto ➤ *m* fetus.
fiable ➤ *adj* reliable, dependable.
fiador, a ➤ *mf* guarantor.
fiambre ➤ *adj* CUL. (served) cold ➤ *m* cold cut.
fianza ➤ *f* guaranty; *(depósito)* deposit.
fibra ➤ *f* fiber; *(de madera)* grain; MIN. vein.
ficción ➤ *f* fiction.
ficha ➤ *f (en los juegos)* counter, chip; *(dominó)* domino; *(disco de metal)* token; *(tarjeta)* index card.
fichar ➤ *tr* to keep on an index card; *(en bares, restaurantes)* to keep on a tab; *(en fábricas)* to punch (a clock) in *or* out; *(en dominó)* to play.
fichero ➤ *m* file (cabinet); COMPUT. file.
ficticio, a ➤ *adj* fictitious.
fidelidad ➤ *f* fidelity; *(exactitud)* accuracy.
fideo ➤ *m* noodle.
fiebre ➤ *f* fever.
fiel ➤ *adj* faithful, loyal; *(exacto)* exact, accurate; *(honrado)* trustworthy.
fieltro ➤ *m* felt; *(sombrero)* felt hat.
fierro AMER. ➤ *m* brand, mark ■ *pl* tools.
fiesta ➤ *f* party, celebration; *(feriado)* holiday; RELIG. feast, holy day.
figura ➤ *f* figure; *(actor)* character; *(mudanza)* dance step; MUS. note.
figurar ➤ *tr* to represent, depict; *(fingir)* to feign, simulate ➤ *intr* to figure, take part ➤ *reflex* to imagine, figure ■ **¡figúrate!** just imagine!
fijador, a ➤ *adj* fixative ➤ *m (para el pelo)* hair spray; PHOTOG. fixative.
fijamente ➤ *adv* firmly, assuredly; *(atentamente)* fixedly, steadfastly.
fijar ➤ *tr* to fix, fasten; *(establecer)* to establish ➤ *reflex* to settle, become fixed; *(atender)* to pay attention ■ **¡fíjate!** just imagine!
fijo, a ➤ *adj* fixed; *(permanente)* permanent; *(estable)* stable, steady; *(de colores)* fast, indelible ➤ *f (bisagra)* large hinge; CONSTR. trowel.
fila ➤ *f (hilera)* file; *(cola)* line, queue (G.B.); *(línea)* row, tier; MIL. rank.
filántropo, a ➤ *mf* philanthropist.
filarmónico, a ➤ *adj* philharmonic.
filete ➤ *m* CUL. fillet; TECH. thread.
filial ➤ *adj* filial; COM. subsidiary, branch ➤ *f* COM. *(sucursal)* branch (office); *(subdivisión)* subsidiary.
film *or* **filme** ➤ *m* film, movie.
filmar ➤ *tr* to film, shoot.
filo ➤ *m* (cutting) edge ■ **al f. de la medianoche** at the stroke of midnight • **dar (un) f.** *(afilar)* to sharpen.
filosofía ➤ *f* philosophy.
filósofo, a ➤ *adj* philosophic(al) ➤ *mf* philosopher.
filtración ➤ *f* filtration.
filtrar ➤ *tr & intr* to filter ➤ *reflex (pasarse)* to filter, pass through; *(disminuirse)* to dwindle.
filtro ➤ *m* filter.
fin ➤ *m* end; *(meta)* aim ■ **a f. de** in order to • **a f. de cuentas** in the final analysis • **a f. de que** so that • **a fines de** at the end of • **al** *or* **por f.** at last, finally • **al f. y al cabo** after all, when all is said and done • **en f.** finally; *(en resumen)* in short • **f. de semana** weekend.
final ➤ *adj* final, last ➤ *m (fin)* end, ending; MUS. finale ➤ *f* SPORT. final ■ **al f.** in *or* at the end.
finalizar §02 ➤ *tr* to finish, conclude ➤ *intr* to (come to an) end.
financiación ➤ *f or* **financiamiento** ➤ *m* financing.
financiar ➤ *tr* to finance.
financiero, a ➤ *adj* financial ➤ *mf* financier.

finca ➤ *f* property, real estate; AMER. farm.
fingir §19 ➤ *tr* to pretend, feign.
fino, a ➤ *adj* fine; *(precioso)* precious; *(cortés)* refined, elegant; *(delicado)* delicate.
firma ➤ *f* signature; *(acción)* signing; COM. firm, company.
firmamento ➤ *m* firmament, heavens.
firmar ➤ *tr & reflex* to sign.
firme ➤ *adj* firm; *(constante)* steadfast, staunch ➤ *m* foundation, bed ➤ *adv* firmly, steadily.
firmeza ➤ *f* firmness.
fiscal ➤ *adj* fiscal ➤ *mf (tesorero)* treasurer; *(abogado)* district attorney.
fisco ➤ *m* public treasury.
físico, a ➤ *adj* physical ➤ *mf* physicist ➤ *m* physique; *(apariencia)* looks, appearance ➤ *f* physics.
fisiología ➤ *f* physiology.
fisioterapia ➤ *f* physiotherapy.
flaco, a ➤ *adj* thin, lean; *(sin fuerza)* weak.
flamenco, a ➤ *adj* flamenco ➤ *m* ORNITH. flamingo.
flan ➤ *m* flan, caramel custard.
flanco ➤ *m* side, flank.
flaquear ➤ *intr* to weaken.
flauta ➤ *f* flute ➤ *mf* flautist, flutist.
fleco ➤ *m* fringe; *(borde desgastado)* frayed edge; *(flequillo)* bangs.
flecha ➤ *f* arrow.
flechazo ➤ *m* arrow shot *or* wound.
flema ➤ *f* phlegm.
flemático, a ➤ *adj* phlegmatic(al).
flequillo ➤ *m* bangs.
fletar ➤ *tr (alquilar)* to charter; *(embarcar)* to load; AMER. to hire, rent.
flexible ➤ *adj* flexible ➤ *m* electric cord.
flexión ➤ *f* flexion; GRAM. inflection.
flirtear ➤ *intr* to flirt.
flojera ➤ *f* laziness, carelessness.
flojo, a ➤ *adj (suelto)* loose, slack; *(débil)* weak; *(holgazán)* lazy, shiftless ➤ *mf* idler, loafer.
flor ➤ *f* flower ■ **en f.** in bloom.
flora ➤ *f* flora.
florecer §09 ➤ *intr* to flower, bloom; *(prosperar)* to flourish.
florero ➤ *m* (flower) vase.
flota ➤ *f* fleet; AER. squadron.
flotador, a ➤ *adj* floating, buoyant ➤ *m* float; MARIT. outrigger.
flotar ➤ *intr* to float.
flote ➤ *m* ■ **a f.** afloat.
flotilla ➤ *f* flotilla.
fluctuar §45 ➤ *intr* to fluctuate; *(dudar)* to vacillate, waver.
fluido, a ➤ *adj* fluid; *(inseguro)* in flux ➤ *m* fluid; ELEC. current.
fluir §10 ➤ *intr* to flow; *(brotar)* to gush, stream.
flujo ➤ *m* flow, flux.
flúor ➤ *m* fluorine.
fluorescente ➤ *adj* fluorescent.
fluvial ➤ *adj* fluvial, river.
fobia ➤ *f* phobia.
foca ➤ *f* seal.
foco ➤ *m* focus; *(fuente)* source; *(reflector)* spotlight.
fogata ➤ *f* bonfire.
fogón ➤ *m* stove, range; AMER. bonfire.
folio ➤ *m* page, leaf.
folklórico, a ➤ *adj* folk, folkloric.
follaje ➤ *m* foliage.
folletín ➤ *m* serial.
folleto ➤ *m* pamphlet, brochure.
fomentar ➤ *tr* to foment, stir up; *(promover)* to promote, foster.
fomento ➤ *m* promotion, development.
fonda ➤ *f (posada)* inn; *(restaurante)* restaurant; AMER. tavern, bar.
fondear ➤ *tr* to sound, fathom; *(examinar)* to investigate, probe ➤ *intr* MARIT. to drop anchor.
fondo ➤ *m (base)* bottom; *(hondura)* depth, bed; *(parte más lejos)* rear, back; *(campo)* background; *(residuo)* residue; *(lo principal)* essence; *(reserva)* store, reservoir ■ **a f.** completely, thoroughly • **echar a f.** to sink • **irse a f.** to sink, founder • **sin f.** bottomless ■ *pl* funds, capital • **f. disponibles** ready cash.
fonético, a ➤ *adj* phonetic ➤ *f* phonetics.
forastero, a ➤ *adj* foreign, alien ➤ *mf* stranger, outsider.
forcejar ➤ *intr* to struggle, resist.
forcejeo ➤ *m* struggle, struggling.
forense ➤ *adj* forensic.
forestal ➤ *adj* forest, of a forest.
forjar ➤ *tr* to forge, hammer; *(fabricar)* to make, form.
forma ➤ *f* form; *(dimensiones)* shape; *(silueta)* figure, outline; *(molde)* mold, pattern; *(documento)* form, questionnaire; *(manera)* way, method ■ **de f. que** so that, in such a way that.
formación ➤ *f* formation; *(educación)* upbringing, training.
formal ➤ *adj* formal.
formalidad ➤ *f* formality.
formalizar §02 ➤ *tr* to formalize.
formar ➤ *tr* to form; *(moldear)* to shape; *(criar)* to bring up, rear ➤ *intr* MIL. to fall in ➤ *reflex* to take form; *(desarrollarse)* to develop.
formatear ➤ *tr* to format.
formato ➤ *m* format; *(tamaño)* size.
formidable ➤ *adj* formidable.
fórmula ➤ *f* formula; MED. prescription; CUL. recipe.
formular ➤ *tr* to formulate ➤ *adj* formulaic.
formulario ➤ *m* form, blank.
forrar ➤ *tr (coser)* to line; *(cubrir)* to cover ➤ *reflex* AMER., COLL. to get rich.
forro ➤ *m* lining; *(cubierta)* cover, covering.
fortalecer §09 ➤ *tr* to fortify.
fortaleza ➤ *f (vigor)* strength, vigor; *(virtud)* fortitude; *(fortín)* fortress.
fortificar §09 ➤ *tr* to fortify.
fortuna ➤ *f* fortune ■ **por f.** fortunately.
forzado, a ➤ *adj* forced.
forzar §22 ➤ *tr* to force; *(capturar)* to take by force.
forzoso, a ➤ *adj* unavoidable, inevitable.
fosa ➤ *f* grave, tomb ■ **fosas nasales** nostrils.
fósforo ➤ *m* phosphorus; *(cerilla)* match.
fósil ➤ *m* fossil ➤ *adj* fossil, fossilized; COLL. *(antiguo)* old, outdated.
fosilizarse §02 ➤ *reflex* to fossilize.
foso ➤ *m* pit, ditch; THEAT. pit; MIL. moat.
foto ➤ *f* photo, picture ■ **sacar fotos** to take pictures.
fotocopia ➤ *f* photocopy.
fotocopiar ➤ *tr* to photocopy.
fotografía ➤ *f* photography; *(retrato)* photograph, picture; *(taller)* photography studio.
fotografiar §18 ➤ *tr* to photograph.
fotógrafo, a ➤ *mf* photographer.
frac ➤ *m* tails, formal coat.
fracasar ➤ *intr* to fail.
fracaso ➤ *m* failure.
fracción ➤ *f* fraction.
fraccionar ➤ *tr* to divide, break (into parts); CHEM. to fractionate.
fractura ➤ *f* fracture, break.
fragancia ➤ *f* fragrance, perfume.
frágil ➤ *adj* fragile; *(fugaz)* fleeting.
fragmento ➤ *m* fragment; *(trozo)* passage, excerpt.
fraile ➤ *m* friar, monk.
frambuesa ➤ *f* raspberry.
franco, a ➤ *adj* frank; *(liberal)* generous; *(exento)* exempt ➤ *m* FIN. franc.
franela ➤ *f* TEX. flannel; AMER. undershirt.
franja ➤ *f* fringe, border; *(banda)* strip, band.
franqueza ➤ *f* frankness, candor; *(exención)* freedom, exemption; *(generosidad)* generosity.
frasco ➤ *m* small bottle; *(redoma)* flask, vial.
frase ➤ *f* sentence, phrase ■ **f. hecha** set expression.
fraterno, a ➤ *adj* fraternal.
fraude ➤ *m* fraud.
frazada ➤ *f* blanket.
frecuencia ➤ *f* frequency.
frecuentar ➤ *tr* to frequent.
frecuente ➤ *adj* frequent; *(común)* common, habitual.
fregadero ➤ *m* kitchen sink.
fregar §35 ➤ *tr* to scour, scrub; *(lavar)* to wash; AMER., COLL. to annoy ➤ *reflex* AMER. to become annoyed.
fregón, ona ➤ *adj* AMER. annoying ➤ *mf* AMER. pest, annoyance ➤ *f* mop.
freír §39 ➤ *tr* to fry.
frenar ➤ *tr* to brake, apply the brake to; *(hábito, vicio)* to curb, check.
frenazo ➤ *m* sudden braking.
frenético, a ➤ *adj* frenetic, frenzied; *(colérico)* mad, furious.
freno ➤ *m* EQUIT. bit; MECH. brake.
frente ➤ *f* forehead, brow; *(rostro)* face ➤ *m* front; *(fachada)* face, façade; MIL., METEOROL. front ■ **al** *or* **en f.** in front, opposite • **al f. de** at the head of, in charge of • **f. a** facing, opposite.
fresa ➤ *adj & f* strawberry.
fresco, a ➤ *adj* cool; *(nuevo)* fresh; *(descarado)* fresh, impudent ➤ *m* cool, coolness; *(aire)* fresh air; ARTS fresco.
frescura ➤ *f* freshness, coolness; *(chanza)* fresh remark.
friamente ➤ *adv* coldly, coolly.
fricción ➤ *f* friction; *(masaje)* massage.
frígido, a ➤ *adj* frigid.
frigorífico ➤ *m* refrigerator.
fríjol *or* **frijol** ➤ *m* bean.
frío, a ➤ *adj* cold; *(sin gracia)* insipid ➤ *m* cold, coldness ■ **hacer f.** *(tiempo)* to be cold • **tener f.** *(persona)* to be cold.
friolero, a ➤ *adj* sensitive to the cold ➤ *f* trifle, bauble.
frívolo, a ➤ *adj* frivolous.
frontera ➤ *f* border, frontier.
frontón ➤ *m* handball court; ARCHIT. pediment, gable.
frotar ➤ *tr & reflex* to rub (together).
fruncir ➤ *tr* SEW. to gather; *(labios)* to purse; *(frente)* to wrinkle.
frustrado, a ➤ *adj* frustrated, thwarted.
frustrar ➤ *tr* to frustrate, thwart ➤ *reflex (fracasar)* to fail, come to nothing; *(privarse)* to be frustrated.
fruta ➤ *f* fruit; FIG., COLL. fruit, result.
frutería ➤ *f* fruit store *or* stand.
fruto ➤ *m* fruit.
fuego ➤ *m* fire; *(llama)* flame, heat; *(hogar)* hearth, home; *(fósforo)* light ■ **a f. lento** little by little; CUL. on a low flame • **fuegos artificiales** fireworks.
fuente ➤ *f (manantial)* spring; *(aparato)* fountain, water fountain; *(plato)* platter, serving dish; *(origen)* source, origin.
fuera ➤ *adv* outside, out ■ **¡f.!** get out! • **f. de** outside of; *(además de)* besides, except for • **f. de que** aside from the fact that • **f. de sí** beside oneself • **por f.** on the outside.
fuerte ➤ *adj* strong; *(fortificado)* fortified; *(intenso)* powerful, forceful; *(con voz alta)* loud ➤ *m* fort, fortress; *(talento)* forte, strong point ➤ *adv* hard; *(en voz alta)* loudly.
fuerza ➤ *f* force, strength; *(poder)* power ■ **a f. de** by dint of • **a la f.** *or* **por f.** by force, forcibly; *(forzosamente)* necessarily.
fuga ➤ *f* flight, escape; *(ardor)* ardor; *(escape)* leak, leakage; MUS. fugue.
fugarse §31 ➤ *reflex* to flee, run away; *(salirse)* to leak (out).
fulgir §19 ➤ *intr* to shine, sparkle.
fumador, a ➤ *adj* smoking ➤ *mf* smoker.
fumar ➤ *intr & tr* to smoke.
funcionar ➤ *intr* to work, run.
funcionario, a ➤ *mf* civil servant, official.
funda ➤ *f* cover, case.
fundación ➤ *f* foundation.
fundamental ➤ *adj* fundamental.
fundar ➤ *tr* to found, establish; *(apoyar)* to base, rest ➤ *reflex* FIG. to be founded *or* based.
fundir ➤ *tr* METAL. to melt, smelt; *(moldear)* to cast, mold; *(bombilla)* to burn out ➤ *reflex* to merge, fuse; AMER. to go bankrupt.
funeral ➤ *adj & m* funeral.
furgoneta ➤ *f* van, truck.
furia ➤ *f* fury.
furioso, a ➤ *adj* furious; *(grande)* tremendous.
furor ➤ *m* fury, rage.
furtivo, a ➤ *adj* furtive, stealthy.
fusible ➤ *adj* fusible ➤ *m* fuse.
fusil ➤ *m* rifle, gun.
fusilar ➤ *tr* to shoot.
fusión ➤ *f* melting, fusion; COM. merger.
fusionar ➤ *intr* to merge.
fútbol *or* **futbol** ➤ *m* soccer, football (G.B.) ■ **f. americano** football.
futbolista ➤ *mf* soccer player, footballer (G.B.).
futuro, a ➤ *adj & m* future ➤ *m* future.

G

gabán ➤ *m* overcoat, topcoat.
gabardina ➤ *f* gabardine; *(sobretodo)* raincoat.
gabinete ➤ *m (cuarto)* study, office; *(laboratorio)* laboratory; POL. cabinet.
gacho, a ➤ *adj (inclinado)* bowed, bent; *(flojo)* drooping, floppy ➤ *f* mush, paste ■ *pl* porridge.
gafas ➤ *fpl* (eye)glasses ■ **g. de esquí, seguridad** ski, safety goggles.
gaita ➤ *f* MUS. bagpipe; *(organillo)* hurdy-gurdy.
gajo ➤ *m (de naranja)* section.
gala ➤ *f (vestido)* full dress; *(gracia)* elegance; *(regalos)* wedding gifts.
galán ➤ *m* handsome man; *(pretendiente)* suitor; THEAT. leading man.
galante ➤ *adj* gallant; *(amatorio)* flirtatious.
galápago ➤ *m* ZOOL. freshwater tortoise; METAL. ingot; EQUIT. English saddle.
galardón ➤ *m* award, prize.
galardonar ➤ *tr* to award.
galería ➤ *f* gallery.
gallardía ➤ *f* elegance, grace.
gallardo, a ➤ *adj* elegant, graceful.
galleta ➤ *f* cookie, biscuit (G.B.); *(salada)* cracker.
gallina ➤ *f* hen, chicken.
gallinero ➤ *m* chicken coop, henhouse.
gallo ➤ *m* cock, rooster.
galón ➤ *m* gallon.
galopar *or* **galopear** ➤ *intr* to gallop.
galope ➤ *m* gallop.
gama ➤ *f* gamut.
gamba ➤ *f* prawn.
gamuza ➤ *f* chamois.
gana ➤ *f (deseo)* desire, longing; *(apetito)* appetite ■ **darle ganas** *or* **darle la g. de** to feel like • **de buena, mala g.** willingly, unwillingly ■ *pl* **tener g. de** to want to, feel like.
ganado ➤ *m* livestock; AMER. cattle.
ganador, a ➤ *adj* winning, victorious ➤ *mf* winner.
ganancia ➤ *f* profit, gain.
ganar ➤ *tr (lograr)* to gain; *(llevarse)* to win, get; *(recibir)* to earn.
ganchillo ➤ *m (aguja)* crochet needle; *(labor)* crochet.
gancho ➤ *m* hook; AMER. hairpin.
ganga ➤ *f* bargain.
ganso, a ➤ *m* gander ➤ *f* goose.
garabato ➤ *m (gancho)* hook; *(letra)* scribble, scrawl.
garaje ➤ *m* garage.
garantía ➤ *f* guarantee.
garantizar §02 ➤ *tr* to guarantee.
garbanzo ➤ *m* chickpea.
garfio ➤ *m* grappling iron, grapple.
garganta ➤ *f* throat; *(del pie)* instep; *(desfiladero)* gorge.
garra ➤ *f* claw, talon.
garrafa ➤ *f* carafe, decanter.
garrapata ➤ *f* tick, mite; *(caballo)* nag.
garrotazo ➤ *m* blow.
garrote ➤ *m (palo)* club; *(tormento)* garrote.
garza ➤ *f* heron.
gas ➤ *m* gas.
gasa ➤ *f* gauze; *(de luto)* crepe.
gasolina ➤ *f* gasoline, gas.
gasolinera ➤ *f* gas station.
gastar ➤ *tr (pagar)* to spend; *(consumir)* to consume, exhaust; *(echar a perder)* to wear out; *(malgastar)* to waste ➤ *intr* to spend ➤ *reflex (consumirse)* to be used up, to wear out.
gasto ➤ *m* expenditure, expense.
gastronomía ➤ *f* gastronomy.
gatear ➤ *intr* to walk on all fours.
gatillo ➤ *m* trigger.
gato, a ➤ *mf* cat ➤ *m* TECH., ELEC. jack ■ **a gatas** on all fours.
gaucho, a ➤ *adj & m* gaucho.
gaveta ➤ *f* drawer.
gavilla ➤ *f (cereales)* sheaf of grain; *(gente)* gang, band.
gaviota ➤ *f* seagull, gull.
gaznate ➤ *m* throat, windpipe.
gazpacho ➤ *m* gazpacho.
géiser ➤ *m* geyser.
gelatina ➤ *f* gelatin.
gemelo, a ➤ *adj & mf* twin ■ *mpl (anteojos)* binoculars; *(de camisa)* cuff links • **g. de teatro** opera glasses.
gemido ➤ *m* moan, groan.
gemir §32 ➤ *intr* to moan, groan.
gen *or* **gene** ➤ *m* gene.
generación ➤ *f* generation.
general ➤ *adj* general ■ **en g.** *or* **por lo g.**

generally, in general ➤ *mf* general.
generalizar §02 ➤ *tr* to generalize.
generar ➤ *tr* to generate, produce.
género ➤ *m* type, kind; AMER. fabric, material; BIOL. genus.
generosidad ➤ *f* generosity.
generoso, a ➤ *adj* generous.
genético, a ➤ *adj* genetic ➤ *f* genetics.
genial ➤ *adj* brilliant, inspired.
genio ➤ *m (carácter)* temperament, disposition; *(talento)* genius ■ **de mal g.** bad-tempered.
gente ➤ *f* people; *(nación)* folk.
gentío ➤ *m* crowd, mob.
gentuza ➤ *f* riffraff, rabble.
genuino, a ➤ *adj* genuine.
geografía ➤ *f* geography.
geología ➤ *f* geology.
geometría ➤ *f* geometry.
geranio ➤ *m* geranium.
gerencia ➤ *f* management.
gerente ➤ *mf* manager, director.
germen ➤ *m* germ.
gerundio ➤ *m* GRAM. *(del español)* present participle; *(del latín)* gerund.
gestación ➤ *f* gestation.
gesticular ➤ *intr* to gesture, gesticulate; *(hacer muecas)* to grimace, make faces.
gestión ➤ *f (dirección)* administration, management; *(trámite)* step, measure.
gesto ➤ *m* gesture, gesticulation.
giganta ➤ *f* giant, giantess.
gigante ➤ *adj* giant, gigantic ➤ *m* giant.
gigantesco, a ➤ *adj* gigantic, huge.
gimnasia ➤ *f* gymnastics.
gimnasio ➤ *m* gymnasium, gym.
gimnasta ➤ *mf* gymnast.
gimnástica ➤ *f* gymnastics.
ginecólogo, a ➤ *mf* gynecologist.
gira ➤ *f* trip, outing; *(viaje)* tour.
girar ➤ *intr (dar vueltas)* to revolve, rotate; *(alrededor de un eje)* to gyrate; *(torcer)* to turn; COM. to draw.
girasol ➤ *m* BOT. sunflower.
giratorio, a ➤ *adj* turning, rotating.
giro ➤ *m* turn; *(frase)* turn of phrase; COM. draft ■ **g. postal** money order.
gitano, a ➤ *adj & mf* Gypsy.
glaciar ➤ *m* glacier ➤ *adj* glacial.
glándula ➤ *f* gland.
glicerina ➤ *f* glycerine.
global ➤ *adj* global; COM. total.
globo ➤ *m* globe; *(de goma)* balloon.
gloria ➤ *f* glory; *(honor)* fame; *(cielo)* heaven.
glorieta ➤ *f* plaza, square; *(cenador)* arbor.
glosario ➤ *m* glossary.
glotón, ona ➤ *adj* gluttonous ➤ *mf* glutton.
glucosa ➤ *f* glucose.
gobernación ➤ *f* government ■ **Ministerio de la G.** Ministry of the Interior.
gobernador, a ➤ *mf* governor.
gobernante ➤ *adj* ruling, governing ➤ *mf* ruler, leader.
gobernar §33 ➤ *tr* to govern.
gobierno ➤ *m* government.
gol ➤ *m* goal ■ **marcar** *or* **meter un g.** to make *or* score a goal.
golf ➤ *m* golf ■ **campo de g.** golf course.
golfo ➤ *m* GEOG. gulf; *(bahía)* bay.
golfo, a ➤ *mf* urchin.
golondrina ➤ *f* swallow.
golosina ➤ *f* sweet, delicacy.
goloso, a ➤ *mf* sweet-toothed.
golpe ➤ *m* blow, hit; *(sacudida)* bump; COMPUT. hit ■ **de g.** suddenly • **g. de estado** coup d'état.
golpear ➤ *tr & intr* to beat, strike.
goma ➤ *f (caucho)* rubber; *(pegamento)* glue; *(elástico)* rubber band ■ **g. de borrar** eraser.
góndola ➤ *f* gondola.
gordo, a ➤ *adj (obeso)* fat, plump; *(abultado)* big; *(graso)* fatty, greasy.
gordura ➤ *f (grasa)* fat, grease; *(corpulencia)* obesity, fatness.
gorila ➤ *m* gorilla.
gorjear ➤ *intr* to warble, trill.
gorjeo ➤ *m* warble, trill.
gorra ➤ *f* cap; *(de bebé)* bonnet.
gorrear ➤ *intr* AMER. to freeload.
gorrión ➤ *m* sparrow.
gorro ➤ *m* cap; *(de niños)* bonnet.
gota ➤ *f* drop; MED. gout ■ **g. a g.** bit by bit, little by little.
gotear ➤ *intr* to drip, trickle.
goteo ➤ *m* dripping, trickling.
gotera ➤ *f* leak.
gótico, a ➤ *adj & mf* Gothic.
gozar §02 ➤ *tr & intr* to enjoy, take pleasure in.
gozne ➤ *m* hinge.
grabación ➤ *f* recording.
grabado ➤ *m (arte, obra)* engraving; *(ilustración)* print, illustration ■ **g. en madera** woodcut.
grabador, a ➤ *mf* engraver ➤ *f* tape recorder ■ **g. de video** VCR.
grabar ➤ *tr* to engrave; *(registrar sonidos)* to record, tape; COMPUT. to save.
gracia ➤ *f (donaire)* charm, grace; *(agudeza)* witty remark, joke ■ **tener g.** to be funny ■ *pl* thank you, thanks • **dar g.** to give thanks.
gracioso, a ➤ *adj (encantador)* charming; *(divertido)* amusing, funny.
grada ➤ *f* step, stair; *(asientos)* tier.
grado ➤ *m (calidad)* grade, quality; *(nivel)* degree; *(título académico)* degree, academic title.
graduación ➤ *f* graduation.
graduado, a ➤ *mf* graduate.
gradual ➤ *adj* gradual.
graduar §45 ➤ *tr & reflex* to graduate.
gráfico, a ➤ *adj* graphic ➤ *m o f* graph, chart ■ *mpl* graphics.
gragea ➤ *f* sugar-coated pill.
gramática ➤ *f* grammar.
gramo ➤ *m* gram, gramme (G.B.).
gran ➤ *adj contr of* **grande**.
granada ➤ *f* pomegranate; MIL. grenade, shell.
granate ➤ *adj* maroon ➤ *m* garnet.
grande ➤ *adj* large, big; *(considerable)* great ■ **en g.** on a grand scale.
granel ➤ *m* ■ **a g.** in bulk, loose.
granero ➤ *m* granary.
granito ➤ *m* granite; MED. small pimple.
granizada ➤ *f* hailstorm.
granizado ➤ *m* iced drink.
granizo ➤ *m* hail.
granja ➤ *f* farm.
granjero, a ➤ *mf* farmer.
grano ➤ *m (semilla)* grain, seed; *(fruto)* grain, cereal; MED. pimple.
granuja ➤ *m* COLL. *(pícaro)* rogue, scoundrel; *(pilluelo)* street urchin.
grapa ➤ *f (para los papeles)* staple.
grapadora ➤ *f* stapler.
grasiento, a ➤ *adj* greasy.
graso, a ➤ *adj* fatty, greasy.
gratis ➤ *adv* gratis, free.
gratitud ➤ *f* gratitude.
gratuito, a ➤ *adj* free (of charge).
grava ➤ *f* gravel.
gravar ➤ *tr* to levy, impose.
grave ➤ *adj (serio)* grave, serious; *(bajo)* deep, low.
gravedad ➤ *f* gravity, seriousness; PHYS. gravity.
gremio ➤ *m (sindicato)* union, trade union; *(asociación)* association, society; HIST. guild.
greña ➤ *f* shock *or* mop of hair.
greñudo, a ➤ *adj* disheveled.
gresca ➤ *f* uproar, hubbub.
grey ➤ *f (rebaño)* flock, herd; *(fieles)* congregation.
grieta ➤ *f* crack, crevice.
grifo ➤ *m* tap, spigot.
grillete ➤ *m* fetter, shackle.
grillo ➤ *m* cricket.
gringo, a ➤ *adj* foreign; *(de E.U.)* Yankee ➤ *mf* foreigner; *(de E.U.)* Yankee.
gripe ➤ *f* grippe, flu.
gris ➤ *adj* gray.
grisáceo, a ➤ *adj* grayish.
gritar ➤ *intr* to shout, scream.
grito ➤ *m* shout, scream.
grosella ➤ *f* currant ■ **g. silvestre** gooseberry.
grosería ➤ *f (tosquedad)* coarseness; *(indecencia)* vulgarity.
grosero, a ➤ *adj* coarse, crude.
grosor ➤ *m* thickness.
grotesco, a ➤ *adj* grotesque.
grúa ➤ *f (máquina)* crane, derrick; *(camión de auxilio)* tow truck.
grueso, a ➤ *adj (corpulento)* stout, fat; *(de grosor)* thick ➤ *m (espesor)* thickness; *(parte principal)* bulk.
grumo ➤ *m (de líquido)* lump.
gruñido ➤ *m* grunt; *(de un perro)* growl.
gruñir ➤ *intr* to grunt; *(un perro)* to growl; *(refunfuñar)* to grumble.
gruñón, ona ➤ *adj* COLL. grouchy, grumpy.
grupo ➤ *m* group.
gruta ➤ *f* grotto, cavern.
guaba ➤ *f* guava.
guacho, a ➤ *adj* S. AMER. orphaned.
guagua ➤ *f* S. AMER. baby; CARIB. bus.
guante ➤ *m* glove.
guantera ➤ *f* glove compartment.
guapo, a ➤ *adj* good-looking, attractive.
guarda ➤ *mf* guard, custodian.
guardabarros ➤ *mpl* fender, mudguard.
guardabosque(s) ➤ *mf* forest ranger.
guardacostas ➤ *m* coast guard cutter.
guardaespaldas ➤ *mf* bodyguard.
guardameta ➤ *mf* goalkeeper, goalie.
guardar ➤ *tr (proteger)* to protect; *(animales)* to keep, tend; *(conservar)* to save, put away; COMPUT. to save.
guardarropa ➤ *m* cloakroom, checkroom; *(ropero)* wardrobe, closet.
guardería ➤ *f* daycare center, nursery.
guardia ➤ *f (tropas)* guard; *(defensa)* defense, protection ➤ *mf (centinela)* guard; *(policía)* policeman/woman.
guardián, ana ➤ *mf* guardian, custodian; *(vigilante)* watchman.
guardilla ➤ *f* attic, garret.
guasa ➤ *f* joke, jest.
guatemalteco, a ➤ *adj & mf* Guatemalan.
guayaba ➤ *f* BOT. guava; *(jalea)* guava jelly.
guayabera ➤ *f* AMER. lightweight shirt.
guerra ➤ *f* war; *(ciencia)* warfare ■ **hacer la g.** to wage war • **Primera, Segunda Guerra Mundial** First, Second World War.
guerrero, a ➤ *adj* warring, fighting ➤ *mf* warrior, fighter.
guerrilla ➤ *f* MIL. guerrilla warfare; *(partida)* band of guerrillas.
guerrillero, a ➤ *mf* guerilla.
guía ➤ *mf* guide; *(consejero)* adviser; *(libro)* guide, directory.
guiar §18 ➤ *tr* to guide, lead; *(conducir)* to drive.
guijarro ➤ *m* pebble.
guinda ➤ *f* sour cherry.
guindilla ➤ *f* red pepper.
guiñar ➤ *tr* to wink.
guiño ➤ *m* wink.
guión ➤ *m* CINEM., THEAT. script; GRAM. hyphen.
guirnalda ➤ *f* garland, wreath.
guisado ➤ *m* stew.
guisante ➤ *m* pea.
guisar ➤ *tr* to cook; *(estofar)* to stew.
guiso ➤ *m* stew; *(plato)* cooked dish.
guita ➤ *f* twine.
guitarra ➤ *f* guitar.
guitarrista ➤ *mf* guitarist.
gula ➤ *f* gluttony.
gusano ➤ *m* worm; *(oruga)* caterpillar.
gustar ➤ *tr (probar)* to taste, sample; *(experimentar)* to test, try ➤ *intr* to please, be pleasing ■ **me gustan los mariscos** I like seafood • **¿te gustaría conocerla?** would you like to meet her?
gusto ➤ *m* taste; *(sabor)* flavor; *(placer)* pleasure ■ **a g.** comfortable; *(a voluntad)* at will; CUL. to taste • **con mucho g.** with pleasure.
gustoso, a ➤ *adj* tasty, savory.

H

haba ➤ *f* fava bean.
haber[1] ➤ *m* COM. credit ■ *pl* assets, property.
haber[2] §23 ➤ *aux* to have ■ **h. de** to have to, must ➤ *impers* ■ **ha** ago • **hay** there is, there are • **hay que** it is necessary • **no hay de qué** don't mention it, you're welcome • **¿qué hay?** what's up? ➤ *tr (poseer)* to have.
hábil ➤ *adj* capable; *(diestro)* skillful.
habilidad ➤ *f (capacidad)* capability; *(ingeniosidad)* skill.
habitación ➤ *f (cuarto)* room; *(domicilio)* dwelling, residence.
habitante ➤ *mf* inhabitant.
habitar ➤ *tr* to inhabit, live in.
hábito ➤ *m* habit.
habituar §45 ➤ *tr* to habituate ➤ *reflex* to become accustomed (*a* to).
hablador, a ➤ *adj* talkative.
hablar ➤ *intr & tr* to speak, talk ■ **¡ni h!** out of the question!
hacer §24 ➤ *tr* to make; *(efectuar)* to do; *(causar)* to cause ■ **h. cara** *or* **frente a** to face • **h. caso de** *or* **a** to pay attention to • **h. falta** *(faltar)* to be needed; *(echar de menos)* to be missed • **h. saber** to let know • **h. una maleta** to pack a suitcase • **h. una pregunta** to ask a question • **h. una visita** to pay a visit ➤ *impers* ■ **desde hace** for • **hace frío** it is cold • **hace mucho** long ago • **hace poco** a little while ago ➤ *reflex* to become; *(convertirse)* to turn into.
hacha ➤ *f* ax, axe.
hachís ➤ *m* hashish.
hacia ➤ *prep* toward; *(alrededor de)* about, around ■ **h. abajo** downward • **h. acá** here, this way • **h. adelante** forward • **h. arriba** upward • **h. atrás** backward.
hacienda ➤ *f* ranch.
hada ➤ *f* fairy ■ **cuento de hadas** fairy tale.
halagar §31 ➤ *tr* to flatter.
halago ➤ *m* flattery.
halcón ➤ *m* falcon, hawk.
hallar ➤ *tr (por casualidad)* to come across; *(encontrar)* to find; *(averiguar)* to find out ➤ *reflex (encontrarse)* to be, find oneself.
hallazgo ➤ *m* discovery.
hamaca ➤ *f* hammock.
hambre ➤ *f* hunger; *(de una nación)* famine ■ **tener h.** to be hungry.
hamburguesa ➤ *f* hamburger.
harina ➤ *f* flour.
hartar ➤ *tr (saciar el apetito)* to stuff; *(satisfacer)* to satisfy; *(fastidiar)* to annoy; *(cansar)* to tire.
harto, a ➤ *adj (cansado)* fed up ➤ *adv (bastante)* enough; *(muy)* very.
hasta ➤ *prep* until ■ **fueron h. el río** they went as far as the river • **h. la vista** *or* **h. luego** see you, so long • **h. que** until ➤ *adv* even ■ **h. los vecinos lo vieron** even the neighbors saw it.
hebilla ➤ *f* buckle, clasp.
hebra ➤ *f (hilo)* thread; *(fibra)* fiber.
hechicería ➤ *f (brujería)* witchcraft; *(hechizo)* spell.
hechizo ➤ *m (sortilegio)* spell; *(encanto)* charm.
hecho, a ➤ *adj* done; *(ropa)* ready-made ■ **h. y derecho** in every respect ➤ *m (acto)* act, action; *(hazaña)* deed; *(suceso)* event; *(realidad)* fact; *(asunto)* point ■ **de h.** *(en realidad)* as a matter of fact.
hedor ➤ *m* stench, stink.
heladería ➤ *f* ice-cream parlor.
helado, a ➤ *adj* frozen; *(muy frío)* freezing ➤ *m* ice cream; *(sorbete)* sherbet.
helar §33 ➤ *tr & reflex* to freeze.
hélice ➤ *f* helix; AVIA. propeller; ZOOL. snail.
helicóptero ➤ *m* helicopter.
hembra ➤ *f* woman; *(animal)* female.
hemisferio ➤ *m* hemisphere.
hemorragia ➤ *f* hemorrhage.
hendidura ➤ *f* crack.
heno ➤ *m* hay.
hepatitis ➤ *f* hepatitis.
herbolario ➤ *m* herbalist's shop.
heredar ➤ *tr* to inherit.
heredero, a ➤ *m* heir ➤ *f* heiress.
herencia ➤ *f (patrimonio)* inheritance; *(tradición)* heritage; BIOL. heredity.
herido, a ➤ *adj* wounded ➤ *mf (persona)* wounded *or* injured person.
herir §43 ➤ *tr* to wound.
hermanastro, a ➤ *mf* stepbrother/sister.
hermano, a ➤ *m* brother ■ **h. gemelo** twin brother • **primo h.** first cousin ➤ *f* sister ■ **h. gemela** twin sister • **prima h.** first cousin.
hermético, a ➤ *adj* airtight.
hermoso, a ➤ *adj* beautiful.
hermosura ➤ *f* beauty.
héroe ➤ *m* hero.
heroína ➤ *f* heroine; *(droga)* heroin.
herradura ➤ *f* horseshoe.
herramienta ➤ *f* tool.
hervir §43 ➤ *intr* to boil.
heterogéneo, a ➤ *adj* heterogeneous.
híbrido, a ➤ *adj & mf* hybrid.
hidratar ➤ *tr* to hydrate.
hidráulica ➤ *f* hydraulics.
hidroavión ➤ *m* hydroplane.
hidroeléctrico, a ➤ *adj* hydroelectric.
hidrógeno ➤ *m* hydrogen.
hidroplano ➤ *m* MARIT. hydrofoil; AVIA. seaplane.
hiedra ➤ *f* ivy.
hielo ➤ *m* ice.
hiena ➤ *f* hyena.
hierba ➤ *f* grass; *(medicinal)* herb; COLL. marijuana ■ **mala h.** weed.
hierbabuena ➤ *f* mint.
hierro ➤ *m* iron; *(marca)* brand ■ **h. forjado** wrought iron.
hígado ➤ *m* liver.
higiénico, a ➤ *adj* hygienic.
higo ➤ *m* fig.

higuera ➤ *f* fig tree.

hijastro, a ➤ *mf* stepchild, stepson/daughter.

hijo, a ➤ *m* son ➤ *f* daughter ■ *pl* children.

hilera ➤ *f* row, file.

hilo ➤ *m (hebra)* thread; *(tejido)* linen.

himno ➤ *m* hymn ■ **h. nacional** national anthem.

hincapié ➤ *m* planting one's feet ■ **hacer h. en** COLL. to insist on, stress.

hincar §47 ➤ *tr (clavar)* to sink, drive (in) ➤ *reflex* to sink into *or* down.

hincha ➤ *f* grudge ➤ *m* COLL. fan, supporter.

hinchado, a ➤ *adj* swollen.

hinchar ➤ *tr (aumentar)* to swell; *(inflar)* to inflate, blow up ➤ *reflex* MED. to swell.

hinchazón ➤ *f* MED. swelling.

hinojo ➤ *m* fennel.

hiperenlace ➤ *m* hyperlink, link.

hipertensión ➤ *f* hypertension, high blood pressure.

hipertexto ➤ *m* hypertext.

hípico, a ➤ *adj* horse, equine.

hipnosis ➤ *f* hypnosis.

hipnotizar §02 ➤ *tr* to hypnotize.

hipo ➤ *m* hiccup.

hipocresía ➤ *f* hypocrisy.

hipócrita ➤ *adj* hypocritical ➤ *mf* hypocrite.

hipopótamo ➤ *m* hippopotamus.

hipoteca ➤ *f* mortgage.

hipotecar §47 ➤ *tr* to mortgage; *(comprometer)* to compromise.

hipótesis ➤ *f* hypothesis.

hirviente ➤ *adj* boiling.

hispano, a ➤ *adj & mf* Hispanic.

hispanohablante ➤ *adj & mf* Spanish-speaking (person).

histeria ➤ *f* hysteria.

histérico, a ➤ *adj (alterado)* hysteric(al).

historia ➤ *f* history; *(cuento)* story.

historiador, a ➤ *mf* historian.

historial ➤ *m* file, dossier.

histórico, a ➤ *adj* historic(al).

historieta ➤ *f* story, anecdote ■ *pl* **h. ilustradas** *or* **cómicas** comic strips.

hocico ➤ *m* ZOOL. muzzle, snout.

hogar ➤ *m (de una chimenea)* hearth, fireplace; *(casa)* home.

hoguera ➤ *f* bonfire.

hoja ➤ *f* leaf; *(pétalo)* petal; *(de papel)* sheet; *(documento)* form; *(cuchilla)* blade ■ **h. de cálculo** spreadsheet.

hojalata ➤ *f* tin.

hojaldre ➤ *mf* puff pastry.

hojarasca ➤ *f* dead *or* fallen leaves.

hojear ➤ *tr* to skim *or* leaf (through); COMPUT. *(una lista)* to browse.

¡hola! ➤ *interj* hello!, hi!

holgado, a ➤ *adj (ancho)* big, loose; *(vida)* comfortable, well-off.

holgazán, ana ➤ *adj* lazy.

hollín ➤ *m* soot.

hombre ➤ *m* man; *(humanidad)* mankind; *(esposo)* husband ■ **h. de negocios** businessman.

hombrera ➤ *f* shoulder pad.

hombro ➤ *m* shoulder ■ **a hombros** piggyback • **encogerse de hombros** to shrug.

homenaje ➤ *m* homage.

homicidio ➤ *m* homicide.

homogéneo, a ➤ *adj* homogeneous.

homosexual ➤ *adj & mf* homosexual.

hondo, a ➤ *adj* deep.

hondureño, a ➤ *adj & mf* Honduran.

honestidad ➤ *f* honesty.

honesto, a ➤ *adj (honrado)* honest; *(decente)* decent; *(pudoroso)* modest.

hongo ➤ *m* mushroom; MED. fungus; *(sombrero)* derby, bowler (hat).

honor ➤ *m* honor ■ **hacer h. a** to honor.

honorario, a ➤ *adj* honorary ➤ *m* honorarium ■ *pl* fees.

honra ➤ *f* honor, self-respect; *(buena fama)* reputation ■ *pl* last respects.

honradez ➤ *f* honesty, integrity.

honrado, a ➤ *adj* honest, honorable.

honrar ➤ *tr* to honor, respect.

hora ➤ *f* hour; *(momento)* time ■ **a la h.** on time, punctually **¿a qué h.?** at what time?, when? • **a última h.** at the last minute; *(por la noche)* last thing at night • **h. punta** rush hour • **por h.** per hour • **¿qué h. es?** what time is it? ■ *pl* **h. de oficina** office hours.

horario ➤ *m* schedule, timetable.

horca ➤ *f* gallows; AGR. pitchfork.

horcajadas ➤ *adv* ■ **a h.** astride, straddling.

horizontal ➤ *adj & f* horizontal.

horizonte ➤ *m* horizon.

hormiga ➤ *f* ant.

hormigón ➤ *m* concrete.

hormiguero ➤ *m* ENTOM. anthill.

hormona ➤ *f* hormone.

hornada ➤ *f* CUL. batch (of baked goods).

hornear ➤ *intr & tr* to bake.

horno ➤ *m* oven; TECH. furnace; CERAM. kiln ■ **h. microondas** microwave oven.

horóscopo ➤ *m* horoscope.

horquilla ➤ *f* hairpin, hair clip.

horrible ➤ *adj* horrible.

horror ➤ *m* horror; *(temor)* terror.

horrorizar §02 ➤ *tr* to horrify ➤ *reflex* to be horrified.

horroroso, a ➤ *adj* horrid; COLL. *(feo)* hideous; *(muy malo)* terrible.

hortaliza ➤ *f* vegetable.

hortensia ➤ *f* hydrangea.

horticultura ➤ *f* horticulture.

hosco, a ➤ *adj (áspero)* gruff, surly.

hospedaje ➤ *m* lodging.

hospedar ➤ *tr* to lodge, put up ➤ *reflex* to lodge *or* stay (*en* at).

hospicio ➤ *m* orphanage.

hospital ➤ *m* hospital.

hospitalario, a ➤ *adj* hospitable.

hospitalidad ➤ *f* hospitality.

hospitalizar §02 ➤ *tr* to hospitalize.

hostelería ➤ *f* hotel management; *(industria)* hotel business.

hostil ➤ *adj* hostile.

hotel ➤ *m* hotel.

hotelero, a ➤ *adj* hotel ➤ *mf (dueño)* hotelkeeper, hotel owner.

hoy ➤ *adv (en este día)* today; *(en el tiempo presente)* nowadays ■ **de** *or* **desde h. en adelante** from now on • **h. (en) día** nowadays.

hoyo ➤ *m* hole.

hoz ➤ *f* sickle.

hucha ➤ *f (alcancía)* piggy bank; *(arca)* chest; *(ahorros)* savings.

hueco, a ➤ *adj* hollow ➤ *m (cavidad)* hollow; *(espacio)* space.

huelga ➤ *f (paro)* strike ■ **declararse en h.** to go on strike.

huelguista ➤ *mf* striker.

huella ➤ *f (del pie)* footprint; *(de un animal)* track, print ■ **h. digital** *or* **dactilar** fingerprint.

huérfano, a ➤ *adj* orphan(ed) ➤ *mf* orphan.

huerta ➤ *f (sembrado)* large vegetable garden; *(de árboles)* orchard; SP. *(regadío)* irrigated land.

huerto ➤ *m (jardín)* vegetable garden; *(de árboles)* orchard.

hueso ➤ *m* ANAT. bone; BOT. pit, stone.

huésped, a ➤ *mf (invitado)* guest; BIOL. host ➤ *m (invitante)* host ➤ *f* hostess.

huevo ➤ *m* egg ■ **h. duro** hard-boiled egg • **huevos revueltos** scrambled eggs.

huida ➤ *f* escape.

huir §10 ➤ *intr* to escape, run away ■ **h. de** flee from ➤ *reflex* to run away, flee.

hule ➤ *m* rubber; *(tela)* oilcloth.

hulla ➤ *f* coal.

humanidad ➤ *f* humanity; *(género)* mankind.

humanitario, a ➤ *adj* humanitarian.

humano, a ➤ *adj* human; *(benévolo)* humane ➤ *m* human (being).

humear ➤ *intr (echar humo)* to smoke; *(echar vapor)* to steam ➤ *tr* AMER. to fumigate.

humedad ➤ *f* humidity; *(calidad de húmedo)* dampness, moisture.

humedecer §09 ➤ *tr* to humidify; *(mojar)* to dampen, moisten.

húmedo, a ➤ *adj* humid; *(mojado)* damp, moist.

humildad ➤ *f* humility.

humilde ➤ *adj* humble, meek; *(bajo)* lowly; *(de poco monto)* modest, poor.

humillar ➤ *tr (rebajar)* to humble; *(avergonzar)* humiliate.

humo ➤ *m* smoke.

humor ➤ *m* humor; *(talante)* mood, humor; *(agudeza)* humor, wit.

hundimiento ➤ *m (naufragio)* sinking; *(derrumbe)* cave-in; *(ruina)* ruin.

hundir ➤ *tr (sumergir)* to sink; *(clavar)* to plunge ➤ *reflex (sumergirse)* to sink; *(caer)* to fall down, collapse.

huracán ➤ *m* hurricane.

huraño, a ➤ *adj* unsociable.

hurgar §31 ➤ *tr* to poke *or* rummage around in.

hurtar ➤ *tr* to steal.

hurto ➤ *m* theft, robbery.

I

icono ➤ *m* icon.

ida ➤ *f (acción)* going; *(viaje)* trip ■ **i. y vuelta** round trip.

idea ➤ *f* idea; *(concepto)* concept; *(noción)* notion ■ **cambiar de i.** to change one's mind.

ideal ➤ *adj* ideal.

idealista ➤ *adj & mf* idealist.

idear ➤ *tr* to think up, plan.

idéntico, a ➤ *adj* identical.

identidad ➤ *f* identity.

identificación ➤ *f* identification.

identificar §47 ➤ *tr* to identify ➤ *reflex* to identify (oneself) with.

ideología ➤ *f* ideology.

idilio ➤ *m* idyll.

idioma ➤ *m* language, tongue.

idiota ➤ *adj* foolish, idiotic ➤ *mf* idiot, imbecile.

idolatría ➤ *f* idolatry.

ídolo ➤ *m* idol.

idóneo, a ➤ *adj (apto)* capable, apt; *(conveniente)* suitable, fit.

iglesia ➤ *f* church.

ignorancia ➤ *f* ignorance.

ignorante ➤ *adj* ignorant, uneducated ➤ *mf* ignoramus.

ignorar ➤ *tr* to be ignorant of, not to know.

igual ➤ *adj* equal; *(parejo)* even, level ■ **darle a uno i.** to be the same to one ➤ *m* MATH. equal sign ➤ *mf* equal ■ **al i. que** just like • **i. que** the same as.

igualar ➤ *tr* to equalize, make equal ➤ *intr* ■ **i. a** *or* **con** to be equal to.

igualdad ➤ *f* equality.

igualmente ➤ *adv* equally; *(en la misma manera)* the same, likewise.

ilegal ➤ *adj & mf* illegal (person).

ilegible ➤ *adj* illegible.

ilegítimo, a ➤ *adj* illegitimate.

ileso, a ➤ *adj* unhurt, unscathed.

ilícito, a ➤ *adj* illicit.

iluminación ➤ *f* illumination; *(alumbrado)* lighting.

iluminar ➤ *tr* to illuminate; *(alumbrar)* to light.

ilusión ➤ *f* illusion; *(esperanza)* hope ■ **hacerse la i. de que** to imagine that.

ilusionar ➤ *tr* to build up (someone's) hopes; *(engañar)* to deceive ➤ *reflex* to get one's hopes up.

ilustración ➤ *f* illustration; *(grabado)* picture.

ilustrar ➤ *tr* to illustrate.

ilustre ➤ *adj* illustrious, distinguished.

imagen ➤ *f* image.

imaginación ➤ *f* imagination.

imaginar ➤ *tr* to imagine.

imán ➤ *m* magnet.

imbécil ➤ *adj & mf* imbecile.

imitación ➤ *f* imitation.

imitar ➤ *tr* to imitate, mimic.

impacientar ➤ *tr* to make (someone) lose patience ➤ *reflex* to lose one's patience.

impaciente ➤ *adj* impatient, restless.

impacto ➤ *m* impact; *(choque)* shock.

impar ➤ *adj* odd, uneven.

imparcial ➤ *adj* impartial.

impasible ➤ *adj* impassive.

impecable ➤ *adj* impeccable.

impedido, a ➤ *adj & mf* disabled (person).

impedimento ➤ *m* impediment.

impedir §32 ➤ *tr* to prevent, obstruct.

impenetrable ➤ *adj* impenetrable.

imperativo, a ➤ *adj & m* imperative.

imperdible ➤ *m* safety pin.

imperfecto, a ➤ *adj* imperfect.

imperial ➤ *adj* imperial.

imperio ➤ *m* empire; *(autoridad)* authority; *(duración)* reign.

impermeable ➤ *adj* impermeable, waterproof ➤ *m* raincoat, mackintosh (G.B.).

impersonal ➤ *adj* impersonal.

impertinencia ➤ *f* impertinence.

impertinente ➤ *adj* impertinent.

ímpetu ➤ *m* impetus; *(violencia)* violence; *(energía)* energy; *(fogosidad)* impetuosity.

impetuoso, a ➤ *adj* violent; *(fogoso)* impetuous.

implacable ➤ *adj* implacable.

implantar ➤ *tr* to implant.

implicar §47 ➤ *tr* to implicate; *(significar)* to imply, mean ➤ *reflex* to become involved.

implícito, a ➤ *adj* implicit.

implorar ➤ *tr* to implore.

imponente ➤ *adj* imposing.

imponer §37 ➤ *tr (ordenar)* to impose; *(infundir)* to inspire, instill ➤ *reflex* ■ **i. a** to dominate.

importación ➤ *f* import.

importador, a ➤ *mf* importer.

importancia ➤ *f* importance.

importante ➤ *adj* important.

importar ➤ *intr* to be important, matter ➤ *tr* to cost; COM. to import.

importe ➤ *m* amount, cost.

imposibilitar ➤ *tr* to make impossible.

imposible ➤ *adj* impossible.

impostor, a ➤ *mf* impostor.

impotencia ➤ *f* impotence.

imprenta ➤ *f (arte)* printing; *(establecimiento)* printing house.

imprescindible ➤ *adj* indispensable.

impresión ➤ *f* impression; *(edición)* printing; *(obra)* edition.

impresionante ➤ *adj* impressive.

impresionar ➤ *tr* to make an impression on, impress ➤ *reflex* to be moved.

impresionista ➤ *adj & mf* impressionist.

impreso, a ➤ *adj* printed.

impresora ➤ *f* COMPUT. printer.

imprevisible ➤ *adj* unpredictable.

imprevisto, a ➤ *adj* unforeseen, unexpected.

imprimir §55 ➤ *tr* to print.

impropio, a ➤ *adj* inappropriate.

improvisar ➤ *tr* to improvise.

imprudencia ➤ *f* imprudence.

impuesto ➤ *m* tax, duty ■ **i. a las rentas** income tax • **i. a las ventas** sales tax.

impulsar ➤ *tr* to impel, drive.

impulso ➤ *m* impulse.

impureza ➤ *f* impurity.

inacabable ➤ *adj* interminable, endless.

inaccesible ➤ *adj* inaccessible.

inaceptable ➤ *adj* unacceptable.

inactivo, a ➤ *adj* inactive.

inadecuado, a ➤ *adj* unsuitable, inadequate.

inagotable ➤ *adj* inexhaustible, endless.

inaguantable ➤ *adj* unbearable, insufferable.

inalámbrico, a ➤ *adj* wireless.

inanimado, a ➤ *adj* inanimate, lifeless.

inauguración ➤ *f* inauguration.

inaugurar ➤ *tr* to inaugurate, open.

incalculable ➤ *adj* incalculable.

incansable ➤ *adj* untiring, tireless.

incapacitado, a ➤ *adj* incapacitated; *(discapacitado)* disabled, handicapped.

incapacitar ➤ *tr* to incapacitate.

incapaz ➤ *adj* incapable.

incendiar ➤ *tr* to set on fire, set fire to ➤ *reflex* to catch fire.

incendio ➤ *m* fire.

incentivo ➤ *m* incentive.

incertidumbre ➤ *f* uncertainty, doubt.

incinerar ➤ *tr* to incinerate, cremate.

incipiente ➤ *adj* incipient.

incitar ➤ *tr* to incite, instigate.

inclinación ➤ *f* inclination; *(del cuerpo)* bowing; *(pendiente)* slope, slant.

inclinar ➤ *tr (la cabeza)* to bow, lower; *(torcer)* to slant, tilt ➤ *reflex (doblarse)* to bow; *(parecerse)* to resemble; *(estar dispuesto)* to be *or* feel inclined.

incluir §10 ➤ *tr* to include; *(encerrar)* to enclose; *(comprender)* to comprise.

incluso ➤ *adv (inclusivamente)* inclusively; *(aun más)* even.

incógnito, a ➤ *adj* unknown ■ **de i.** incognito ➤ *f* MATH. unknown quantity.

incoherente ➤ *adj* incoherent.

incoloro, a ➤ *adj* colorless.

incombustible ➤ *adj* incombustible, fireproof.

incomible ➤ *adj* inedible.

incomodidad ➤ *f* discomfort; *(molestia)* inconvenience.

incómodo, a ➤ *adj* uncomfortable.

incomparable ➤ *adj* incomparable.

incompatible ➤ *adj* incompatible.

incompetente ➤ *adj* incompetent.

incompleto, a ➤ *adj* incomplete, unfinished.

incomprensible ➤ *adj* incomprehensible.

incomunicado, a ➤ *adj* isolated, cut off; CRIMIN. incommunicado.

inconcebible ➤ *adj* inconceivable.

incondicional ➤ *adj* unconditional.
inconfundible ➤ *adj* unmistakable.
incongruente ➤ *adj* incongruous.
inconsciente ➤ *adj* unconscious; unaware; *(irreflexivo)* thoughtless ➤ *m* unconscious.
inconsecuente ➤ *adj* inconsistent.
inconsistente ➤ *adj* inconsistent.
inconsolable ➤ *adj* inconsolable.
incontable ➤ *adj* countless.
incontrolable ➤ *adj* uncontrollable.
inconveniente ➤ *adj* inconvenient; *(inapropiado)* inappropriate ➤ *m* *(obstáculo)* obstacle; *(objeción)* objection; *(desventaja)* drawback ■ **tener i.** to mind, object.
incorporación ➤ *f* incorporation.
incorporar ➤ *tr* to incorporate ➤ *reflex* to sit up; *(unirse a)* to join.
incorrecto, a ➤ *adj* incorrect.
incorregible ➤ *adj* incorrigible.
incrédulo, a ➤ *adj* incredulous.
increíble ➤ *adj* incredible, unbelievable.
incrementar ➤ *tr* to increase, augment.
inculto, a ➤ *adj* uncultured, uneducated.
incurable ➤ *adj* incurable.
incurrir ➤ *intr* ■ **i. en** *(error, crimen)* to commit; *(deuda, ira)* incur.
indagar §31 ➤ *tr* to investigate, inquire into.
indecente ➤ *adj* indecent.
indecisión ➤ *f* indecision.
indeciso, a ➤ *adj* *(irresoluto)* undecided; *(incierto)* indecisive.
indefenso, a ➤ *adj* defenseless.
indefinido, a ➤ *adj* undefined; *(indeterminado)* indefinite.
indemnización ➤ *f* indemnity.
independencia ➤ *f* independence.
independiente ➤ *adj & mf* independent ➤ *adv* independently.
indescifrable ➤ *adj* undecipherable.
indescriptible ➤ *adj* indescribable.
indeseable ➤ *adj & mf* undesirable.
indeterminado, a ➤ *adj* indeterminate; *(indeciso)* indecisive, irresolute.
indicación ➤ *f* indication; *(señal)* sign; *(sugerencia)* suggestion; *(instrucción)* direction, instruction.
indicador, a ➤ *adj* indicating ➤ *m* indicator.
indicar §47 ➤ *tr* to indicate.
indicativo, a ➤ *adj & m* indicative.
índice ➤ *m* index; *(general)* table of contents; *(de biblioteca)* catalogue; *(dedo)* index finger.
indicio ➤ *m* indication, sign ■ *pl* clues.
indiferencia ➤ *f* indifference.
indiferente ➤ *adj* indifferent.
indígena ➤ *adj & mf* native.
indigestión ➤ *f* indigestion.
indignación ➤ *f* indignation.
indignar ➤ *tr* to anger, infuriate ➤ *reflex* to become indignant.
índigo ➤ *m* indigo.
indio, a ➤ *adj & mf* Indian.
indirecto, a ➤ *adj* indirect ➤ *f* hint.
indiscreto, a ➤ *adj* indiscreet.
indiscutible ➤ *adj* indisputable.
indispensable ➤ *adj* indispensable.
indisponer §37 ➤ *tr* to set against ➤ *reflex* *(enfermarse)* to become indisposed; *(malquistarse)* to fall out.
indisposición ➤ *f* indisposition.
indispuesto, a ➤ *adj* indisposed.
individual ➤ *adj* individual; *(habitación)* single.
individuo, a ➤ *adj & m* individual.
indivisible ➤ *adj* indivisible.
índole ➤ *f* *(naturaleza)* nature, character; *(tipo)* type, kind.
inducir §14 ➤ *tr* to induce.
indudable ➤ *adj* indubitable, certain.
indulgente ➤ *adj* indulgent.
indultar ➤ *tr* *(perdonar)* to pardon; *(exonerar)* to exempt.
indumentaria ➤ *f* clothing, garments.
industria ➤ *f* industry.
industrial ➤ *adj* industrial ➤ *m* industrialist.
industrializar §02 ➤ *tr* to industrialize.
ineficaz ➤ *adj* ineffective, inefficacious.
ineptitud ➤ *f* ineptitude.
inepto, a ➤ *adj & mf* inept (person).
inerte ➤ *adj* inert.
inesperado, a ➤ *adj* unexpected.
inestable ➤ *adj* unstable.
inevitable ➤ *adj* inevitable.
inexacto, a ➤ *adj* inexact, inaccurate.
inexistente ➤ *adj* nonexistent.
inexplicable ➤ *adj* inexplicable.

inexplorado, a ➤ *adj* unexplored.
infalible ➤ *adj* *(inequívoco)* infallible; *(inevitable)* inevitable.
infancia ➤ *f* infancy.
infantería ➤ *f* infantry.
infantil ➤ *adj* infantile; *(aniñado)* childish.
infarto ➤ *m* infarct, infarction.
infección ➤ *f* infection.
infectar ➤ *tr* to infect ➤ *reflex* to become infected.
infeliz ➤ *adj* unhappy; *(desgraciado)* unfortunate; *(miserable)* wretched.
inferior ➤ *adj* *(de abajo)* lower; *(menor)* inferior; *(menos)* less.
infestar ➤ *tr* to infest.
infidelidad ➤ *f* infidelity.
infierno ➤ *m* hell.
infinidad ➤ *f* infinity.
infinitivo, a ➤ *adj & m* infinitive.
infinito, a ➤ *adj & m* infinite.
inflación ➤ *f* inflation.
inflamación ➤ *f* inflammation.
inflamar ➤ *tr* to set on fire; *(las pasiones)* to inflame ➤ *reflex* to catch fire.
inflar ➤ *tr* to inflate.
inflexible ➤ *adj* inflexible, rigid.
influencia ➤ *f* influence.
influir §10 ➤ *intr* to have influence.
información ➤ *f* information; *(datos)* data.
informal ➤ *adj* informal; *(de poco fiar)* unreliable.
informalidad ➤ *f* informality; *(falta de seriedad)* irresponsibility.
informar ➤ *tr* to inform, tell *(de of, sobre about)* ➤ *reflex* to find out.
informática ➤ *f* computer science.
informe ➤ *m* report ■ *pl* information.
infortunio ➤ *m* misfortune, bad luck.
infracción ➤ *f* infraction.
infraestructura ➤ *f* infrastructure.
infringir §19 ➤ *tr* to infringe, violate.
infundir ➤ *tr* to instill, arouse.
infusión ➤ *f* infusion.
ingeniería ➤ *f* engineering.
ingeniero, a ➤ *mf* engineer.
ingenio ➤ *m* *(habilidad)* ingenuity; *(talento)* talent; *(agudeza)* wit.
ingenioso, a ➤ *adj* ingenious.
ingenuo, a ➤ *adj & mf* naive (person).
ingle ➤ *f* groin.
inglés, a ➤ *adj* English ➤ *m* *(idioma)* English ➤ *mf* Englishman/woman.
ingratitud ➤ *f* ingratitude.
ingrato, a ➤ *adj* ungrateful; *(que no satisface)* thankless.
ingrediente ➤ *m* ingredient.
ingresar ➤ *intr* to enter, go in; *(hacerse miembro)* to join ➤ *tr* to deposit.
ingreso ➤ *m* *(acción)* entrance; *(entrada)* entryway; *(de dinero)* income ■ *pl* earnings.
inhabilidad ➤ *f* *(falta de maña)* unskillfulness; *(impedimento)* handicap.
inhalar ➤ *tr* to inhale.
inhumano, a ➤ *adj* inhuman, cruel.
inicial ➤ *adj & f* initial.
iniciar ➤ *tr* to initiate; *(admitir)* to introduce; COMPUT. to boot.
iniciativa ➤ *f* initiative.
inicio ➤ *m* beginning.
injerir §43 ➤ *tr* to insert ➤ *reflex* to interfere, meddle.
injuria ➤ *f* insult; *(daño)* injury.
injuriar ➤ *tr* *(ofender)* to insult; *(dañar)* to injure.
injusticia ➤ *f* injustice.
injustificable ➤ *adj* unjustifiable.
injusto, a ➤ *adj* unjust.
inmaculado, a ➤ *adj* immaculate.
inmaduro, a ➤ *adj* *(fruta)* unripe, green; *(persona)* immature.
inmediato, a ➤ *adj* next to, adjoining ■ **de i.** immediately, at once.
inmenso, a ➤ *adj* immense.
inmigración ➤ *f* immigration.
inmigrante ➤ *adj & mf* immigrant.
inmigrar ➤ *intr* to immigrate.
inminente ➤ *adj* imminent.
inmobiliario, a ➤ *adj* real estate.
inmoral ➤ *adj* immoral.
inmortal ➤ *adj* immortal.
inmóvil ➤ *adj* immobile.
inmovilizar §02 ➤ *tr* to immobilize.
inmueble ➤ *adj* ■ **bienes inmuebles** real estate ➤ *m* building.
inmunización ➤ *f* immunization.
inmunizar §02 ➤ *tr* to immunize.
inmutable ➤ *adj* immutable.
innato, a ➤ *adj* innate.
innecesario, a ➤ *adj* unnecessary.
innegable ➤ *adj* undeniable.

innovación ➤ *f* innovation.
innumerable ➤ *adj* innumerable.
inocencia ➤ *f* innocence.
inocente ➤ *adj & mf* innocent.
inoculación ➤ *f* inoculation.
inolvidable ➤ *adj* unforgettable.
inoportuno, a ➤ *adj* inopportune.
inoxidable ➤ *adj* rustproof ■ **acero i.** stainless steel.
inquietante ➤ *adj* worrying, disturbing.
inquieto, a ➤ *adj* *(intranquilo)* restless; *(desasosegado)* worried, anxious.
inquilino, a ➤ *mf* tenant.
inquisitivo, a ➤ *adj* inquisitive.
insaciable ➤ *adj* insatiable.
insatisfecho, a ➤ *adj* *(deseo)* unsatisfied; *(persona)* dissatisfied.
inscribir §55 ➤ *tr* *(grabar)* to engrave; *(matricular)* to register; *(anotar)* to record ➤ *reflex* to register, enroll.
inscripción ➤ *f* inscription; *(anotación)* record; *(matriculación)* enrollment.
insecticida ➤ *m* insecticide.
insecto ➤ *m* insect.
inseguro, a ➤ *adj* insecure.
insensato, a ➤ *adj* foolish, senseless ➤ *mf* fool, dolt.
insensible ➤ *adj* *(que no siente)* insensible; *(sin compasión)* unfeeling.
inseparable ➤ *adj* inseparable.
insertar ➤ *tr* to insert.
insignia ➤ *f* badge, emblem.
insignificante ➤ *adj* insignificant.
insinuar §45 ➤ *tr* to insinuate ➤ *reflex* to ingratiate oneself.
insistir ➤ *intr* to insist *(en on)*.
insolación ➤ *f* MED. sunstroke.
insolencia ➤ *f* insolence.
insolente ➤ *adj* insolent.
insólito, a ➤ *adj* unusual, uncommon.
insomnio ➤ *m* insomnia, sleeplessness.
insoportable ➤ *adj* unbearable.
inspección ➤ *f* inspection.
inspeccionar ➤ *tr* to inspect, examine.
inspector, a ➤ *mf* inspector.
inspiración ➤ *f* inspiration; *(de aire)* inhalation.
inspirar ➤ *tr* to inhale; *(infundir sentimientos)* to inspire ➤ *reflex* to be inspired *(en by)*.
instalación ➤ *f* installation; *(equipo)* equipment ■ **i. sanitaria** plumbing.
instalar ➤ *tr* to install ➤ *reflex* to establish oneself.
instancia ➤ *f* instance ■ **a i. de** at the request of.
instantáneo, a ➤ *adj* instantaneous.
instante ➤ *m* instant, moment ■ **al i.** immediately.
instaurar ➤ *tr* to establish.
instigar §31 ➤ *tr* to incite.
instintivo, a ➤ *adj* instinctive.
instinto ➤ *m* instinct.
institución ➤ *f* institution.
instituir §10 ➤ *tr* to institute.
instituto ➤ *m* institute; *(escuela)* school.
instrucción ➤ *f* instruction ■ *pl* directions.
instructor, a ➤ *mf* instructor.
instruir §10 ➤ *tr* to instruct, teach.
instrumental ➤ *adj* instrumental ➤ *m* instruments.
instrumento ➤ *m* instrument.
insubordinar ➤ *tr* to incite to rebellion ➤ *reflex* to rebel.
insuficiente ➤ *adj* insufficient.
insulina ➤ *f* insulin.
insultar ➤ *tr* to insult.
insulto ➤ *m* insult.
insurrección ➤ *f* insurrection.
intacto, a ➤ *adj* intact.
integral ➤ *adj & f* integral.
integrar ➤ *tr* to integrate.
integridad ➤ *f* integrity.
íntegro, a ➤ *adj* whole, complete.
intelectual ➤ *adj & mf* intellectual.
inteligencia ➤ *f* intelligence.
inteligente ➤ *adj* intelligent.
inteligible ➤ *adj* intelligible.
intemperie ➤ *f* bad weather ■ **a la i.** outdoors.
intención ➤ *f* intention; *(voluntad)* wish.
intensidad ➤ *f* intensity, strength.
intensificar §47 ➤ *tr* to intensify.
intenso, a ➤ *adj* intense.
intentar ➤ *tr* *(tener intención)* to intend, plan; *(ensayar)* to try, attempt.
intento ➤ *m* *(propósito)* intent; *(tentativa)* attempt, try.
interacción ➤ *f* interaction.

intercambio ➤ *m* exchange.
interceder ➤ *tr* to intercede.
interceptar ➤ *tr* to intercept.
interés ➤ *m* interest ■ *pl* possessions.
interesante ➤ *adj* interesting.
interesar ➤ *tr* to interest ➤ *intr* to be of interest ➤ *reflex* to be or become interested *(en, por in)*.
interferencia ➤ *f* interference.
interior ➤ *adj* interior, inner; *(nacional)* domestic, internal ➤ *m* *(parte interna)* interior, inside.
interjección ➤ *f* interjection.
intermediario, a ➤ *adj* intermediate ➤ *mf* intermediary.
intermedio, a ➤ *adj* intermediate ➤ *m* interval; THEAT. intermission.
interminable ➤ *adj* interminable.
intermitente ➤ *adj* intermittent.
internacional ➤ *adj* international.
internado, a ➤ *adj* institutionalized ➤ *m* boarding school.
internar ➤ *tr* to hospitalize; *(encerrar)* to confine ➤ *reflex* to penetrate.
Internet ➤ *m* Internet.
interno, a ➤ *adj* internal ➤ *mf* boarding student; *(médico)* internist.
interpretación ➤ *f* interpretation.
interpretar ➤ *tr* to interpret; MUS. to perform.
intérprete ➤ *mf* *(traductor)* interpreter; *(cantante)* singer.
interrogación ➤ *f* interrogation; GRAM. question mark.
interrogar §31 ➤ *tr* to interrogate, question.
interrumpir ➤ *tr* to interrupt.
interruptor ➤ *m* ELEC. switch.
intervalo ➤ *m* interval.
intervenir §52 ➤ *intr* to intervene ➤ *tr* *(las cuentas)* to audit.
intestino ➤ *m* intestine.
intimidar ➤ *tr* to intimidate.
íntimo, a ➤ *adj* *(interior)* intimate; *(privado)* private.
intoxicación ➤ *f* intoxication.
intranquilo, a ➤ *adj* uneasy.
intransitivo, a ➤ *adj* intransitive.
intriga ➤ *f* intrigue.
intrigar §31 ➤ *intr & tr* to intrigue.
introducir §14 ➤ *tr* *(insertar)* to insert; *(presentar)* to introduce.
introvertido, a ➤ *adj* introverted ➤ *mf* introvert.
intruso, a ➤ *adj* intrusive, meddlesome ➤ *mf* intruder.
intuición ➤ *f* intuition.
intuir §10 ➤ *tr* to intuit, sense.
inundación ➤ *f* flood.
inundar ➤ *tr* to flood.
inusitado, a ➤ *adj* unusual, uncommon.
inútil ➤ *adj* useless; *(vano)* vain.
inválido, a ➤ *adj* invalid, disabled; *(nulo)* invalid, null ➤ *mf* invalid, disabled person.
invariable ➤ *adj* invariable.
invasión ➤ *f* invasion.
invasor, a ➤ *adj* invading ➤ *mf* invader.
invencible ➤ *adj* invincible.
invención ➤ *f* invention.
inventar ➤ *tr* to invent; *(forjar)* to make up.
inventario ➤ *f* inventory.
invento ➤ *m* invention; *(creación)* creation.
invernadero ➤ *m* greenhouse.
invernar §33 ➤ *intr* to hibernate.
inversión ➤ *f* inversion; FIN. investment.
inverso, a ➤ *adj* inverse, inverted.
invertir §43 ➤ *tr* to invert; COM., FIN. to invest.
investigación ➤ *f* investigation; *(estudio)* research, study.
investigar §31 ➤ *tr* to investigate; *(estudiar)* to research, study.
invierno ➤ *m* winter.
invisible ➤ *adj* invisible.
invitación ➤ *f* invitation.
invitado, a ➤ *mf* guest.
invitar ➤ *tr* to invite.
involuntario, a ➤ *adj* involuntary.
inyección ➤ *f* injection.
ir §25 ➤ *intr* to go; *(moverse)* to move; *(caminar)* to walk; *(viajar)* to travel; *(extenderse)* to extend; *(quedar bien)* to suit, become ■ **¿cómo le va?** how is it going? • **i. de compras** to go shopping • **i. de mal en peor** to go from bad to worse • **i. de paseo** to go for a walk • **i. de viaje** to go on a trip • **¡vaya!** *(sor-*

presa) you don't say! ➤ *reflex* to go away, leave ■ **i. abajo** to topple, collapse • **vámonos** let's go.

ira ➤ *f (cólera)* anger; *(furia)* fury.

irascible ➤ *adj* irascible.

iris ➤ *m* ANAT. iris ■ **arco i.** rainbow.

ironía ➤ *f* irony.

irónico, a ➤ *adj* ironic(al).

irracional ➤ *adj* irrational.

irreal ➤ *adj* unreal.

irregular ➤ *adj* irregular.

irresistible ➤ *adj* irresistible.

irresponsable ➤ *adj* irresponsible.

irritar ➤ *tr* to irritate.

irrumpir ➤ *intr* to burst (*en* into).

isla ➤ *f* island.

islámico, a ➤ *adj* Islamic.

itinerario, a ➤ *adj & m* itinerary.

izquierdo, a ➤ *adj* left ➤ *f (mano)* left hand; *(lado)* left ■ **a la i.** *(dirección)* left, to the left; *(sitio)* on the left • **por la i.** on the left.

J

jabalí ➤ *m* wild boar.

jabón ➤ *m* soap.

jabonera ➤ *f* soap dish.

jacinto ➤ *m* BOT. hyacinth.

jactarse ➤ *reflex* to boast (*de* about).

jadear ➤ *intr* to pant, gasp.

jalea ➤ *f* jelly.

jaleo ➤ *m* riotous fun, uproar.

jamás ➤ *adv (nunca)* never; *(alguna vez)* ever ■ **nunca j.** never again.

jamón ➤ *m* ham ■ **j. serrano** cured ham.

jaque ➤ *m* check ■ **j. mate** checkmate.

jaqueca ➤ *f* migraine headache.

jarabe ➤ *m* syrup.

jardín ➤ *m* garden ■ **j. de infancia** *or* **infantes** kindergarten.

jardinera ➤ *f* flower stand *or* box.

jardinero, a ➤ *mf* gardener.

jarra ➤ *f or* **jarro** ➤ *m* jug, pitcher.

jarrón ➤ *m* urn, vase.

jaula ➤ *f* cage; *(embalaje)* crate; *(para niños)* playpen.

jazmín ➤ *m* jasmine ■ **j. del Cabo** gardenia.

jefatura ➤ *f (dirección)* management; *(oficina)* headquarters.

jefe, a ➤ *mf* boss, chief; *(gerente)* manager; *(líder)* leader.

jején ➤ *m* gnat.

jengibre ➤ *m* ginger.

jerez ➤ *m* sherry.

jerga ➤ *f* jargon; *(galimatías)* gibberish.

jeringa ➤ *f* syringe.

jeroglífico, a ➤ *adj* hieroglyphic ➤ *m* hieroglyph.

jilguero ➤ *m* goldfinch, linnet.

jinete ➤ *mf* horseman/woman.

jira ➤ *f* excursion.

jirafa ➤ *f* giraffe.

jirón ➤ *m* shred, tatter.

jornada ➤ *f* journey, trip; *(día de trabajo)* workday ■ **de media j.** part-time.

jornal ➤ *m* day's wage.

jornalero, a ➤ *mf* day laborer.

jorobado, a ➤ *adj* hunchbacked ➤ *mf* hunchback.

joven ➤ *adj* young, youthful ➤ *mf* young person, youth.

joya ➤ *f* jewel ➤ *pl* jewelry • **j. de fantasía** costume jewelry.

joyería ➤ *f* jewelry store.

joyero, a ➤ *mf* jeweler, jeweller (G.B.) ➤ *m (caja)* jewelry box.

jubilado, a ➤ *adj & mf* retired (person).

jubilar ➤ *tr & reflex* to retire.

judío, a ➤ *adj* Jewish ➤ *mf* Jew ➤ *f* BOT. bean ■ **j. verde** green bean.

juego ➤ *m* play, game; *(deporte)* sport; *(vicio)* gambling; *(en naipes)* hand; *(de loza, cristal)* set ■ **hacer j.** to match • **j. de damas** checkers.

juerga ➤ *f* fun ■ **ir de j.** to live it up.

jueves ➤ *m* Thursday.

juez ➤ *mf* judge ■ **j. de línea** SPORT. linesman.

jugada ➤ *f* play, move.

jugador, a ➤ *mf (en los juegos)* player; *(en el azar)* gambler.

jugar §26 ➤ *intr* to play ➤ *tr* to play; *(apostar)* to wager ➤ *reflex* to risk.

jugo ➤ *m* juice.

juguete ➤ *m* toy.

juicio ➤ *m* judgment; *(opinión)* opinion; LAW *(pleito)* trial.

julio ➤ *m* July.

junco ➤ *m* BOT. rush.

junio ➤ *m* June.

junior ➤ *m* junior.

juntar ➤ *tr (unir)* to join; *(reunir)* to assemble ➤ *reflex (reunirse)* to gather; *(asociarse)* to get together.

junto, a ➤ *adj (cercano)* close ➤ *adv* together ■ **j. a** close to, near • **j. con** along with, together with • **todo j.** at the same time, all together ➤ *f (de personas)* board; *(reunión)* meeting, session; *(unión)* union.

jurado ➤ *m* jury; *(miembro)* juror.

juramento ➤ *m* oath.

jurar ➤ *tr* to swear.

justicia ➤ *f* justice.

justificar §47 ➤ *tr* to justify ➤ *reflex (explicarse)* to explain oneself.

justo, a ➤ *adj* just, fair; *(exacto)* exact, precise; *(apretado)* tight ➤ *mf* just person.

juvenil ➤ *adj* young, youthful.

juventud ➤ *f (edad)* youth.

juzgado ➤ *m (tribunal)* court.

juzgar §31 ➤ *tr* to judge ■ **a j. por** judging by *or* from.

K

karate ➤ *m* karate.

kilo ➤ *m* kilo, kilogram.

kilogramo ➤ *m* kilogram.

kilómetro ➤ *m* kilometer.

kiwi ➤ *m* kiwi.

L

la ➤ *def art* the ➤ *pron* her, you, it.

laberinto ➤ *m* labyrinth.

labio ➤ *m* lip.

labor ➤ *f (trabajo)* work; *(faena)* task, job; *(bordado)* embroidery.

laborable ➤ *adj* work, working.

laboral ➤ *adj (del trabajo)* labor; *(técnico)* technical.

laboratorio ➤ *m* laboratory.

laca ➤ *f* lacquer; *(pelo)* hair spray ■ **l. de uñas** nail polish.

ladear ➤ *tr* to bend, tilt.

ladera ➤ *f* slope.

lado ➤ *m* side ■ **al l.** near, close at hand • **al l. de** beside, next to • **por otro l.** on the other hand • **por un l.** on the one hand.

ladrar ➤ *intr* to bark.

ladrillo ➤ *m* brick.

ladrón, ona ➤ *mf* thief, robber.

lagartija ➤ *f* small lizard.

lagarto ➤ *m* lizard.

lago ➤ *m* lake.

lágrima ➤ *f* tear.

laguna ➤ *f* lagoon.

lamentar ➤ *tr (sentir)* to regret ➤ *reflex* to grieve, lament.

lamer ➤ *tr* to lick.

lámina ➤ *f* lamina, plate.

lámpara ➤ *f* lamp.

lana ➤ *f* wool.

lancha ➤ *f* boat ■ **l. motora** motorboat • **l. salvavidas** lifeboat.

langosta ➤ *f* ENTOM. locust; ZOOL. lobster.

langostino ➤ *m* crayfish.

lanza ➤ *f* lance, spear.

lanzar §02 ➤ *tr (arrojar)* to throw; *(un proyectil)* to launch ➤ *reflex* to throw oneself.

lápiz ➤ *m* pencil ■ **l. de labios** lipstick.

largo, a ➤ *adj* long ■ **a la l.** in the long run • **a lo l.** lengthwise; *(por)* along; *(a través)* throughout ➤ *m* length ■ **tener diez pies de l.** to be ten feet long ➤ *interj* get out! ■ **¡l. de aquí!** get out of here!

las ➤ *def art* the ➤ *pron* them.

láser ➤ *m* laser ■ **rayo l.** laser beam.

lástima ➤ *f* pity ■ **es una l. que** it's a shame that • **¡qué l.!** what a shame!

lata ➤ *f* tin plate; *(envase)* tin can.

lateral ➤ *adj* lateral, side.

latido ➤ *m (del corazón)* beat, throb.

látigo ➤ *m* whip.

latino, a ➤ *adj & mf (latinoamericano)* Latino.

latinoamericano, a ➤ *adj & mf* Latin American.

latir ➤ *intr (el corazón)* to beat, throb.

latitud ➤ *f* GEOG. latitude.

latón ➤ *m* brass.

laurel ➤ *m* laurel, bay.

lava ➤ *f* lava.

lavable ➤ *adj* washable.

lavabo ➤ *m (lavamanos)* sink, wash basin; *(cuarto)* bathroom.

lavado ➤ *m (acción)* washing, wash ■ **l. en seco** dry cleaning.

lavador, a ➤ *mf* washer ➤ *f* washing machine ■ **l. de platos** dishwasher.

lavanda ➤ *f* lavender.

lavandería ➤ *f* laundry, laundromat.

lavaplatos ➤ *m* dishwasher.

lavar ➤ *tr* to wash.

lazo ➤ *m (nudo)* knot.

le ➤ *pron* him, you; to him, her, it, or you; for him, her, it, *or* you; from him, her, it, *or* you.

leal ➤ *adj* loyal, faithful.

lección ➤ *f* lesson.

leche ➤ *f* milk ■ **l. desnatada** skim milk.

lechón ➤ *m* suckling pig.

lechuga ➤ *f* lettuce.

lechuza ➤ *f* owl.

lector, a ➤ *adj* reading ➤ *mf* reader.

lectura ➤ *f (acción)* reading.

leer §27 ➤ *tr* to read.

legal ➤ *adj* legal.

legislación ➤ *f* legislation.

legítimo, a ➤ *adj* legitimate; *(cierto)* genuine.

legumbre ➤ *f* legume; CUL. vegetable.

lejano, a ➤ *adj* distant, remote.

lejía ➤ *f* bleach.

lejos ➤ *adv* far (away) ■ **a lo l.** in the distance, far away • **desde l.** from afar, from a distance • **l. de** far from.

lema ➤ *m* motto.

lencería ➤ *f (ropa blanca)* lingerie; *(géneros)* linen goods.

lengua ➤ *f* tongue; *(idioma)* language.

lenguado ➤ *m* sole, flounder.

lenguaje ➤ *m* language, speech.

lente ➤ *m or f* lens ■ **l. de contacto** contact lens ➤ *pl* eyeglasses, glasses.

lenteja ➤ *f* lentil.

lentilla ➤ *f* contact lens.

lento, a ➤ *adj* slow.

leña ➤ *f* firewood.

leño ➤ *m* log.

león ➤ *m* lion.

leona ➤ *f* lioness.

leopardo ➤ *m* leopard.

leotardo ➤ *m* leotard.

les ➤ *pron* to them *or* you; for them *or* you; from them *or* you.

lesión ➤ *f* lesion, injury.

lesionar ➤ *tr* to wound, injure.

letal ➤ *adj* lethal.

letargo ➤ *m* lethargy.

letra ➤ *f* letter; *(modo de escribir)* handwriting; MUS. lyrics ■ **l. de cambio** bill of exchange • **l. mayúscula** capital letter • **l. minúscula** lower-case letter ■ *pl* letters, learning.

letrero ➤ *m* sign; *(etiqueta)* label.

levadura ➤ *f* yeast ■ **l. de cerveza** brewer's yeast • **l. en polvo** baking powder.

levantamiento ➤ *m (acción)* raising, lifting; *(motín)* uprising.

levantar ➤ *tr* to raise, lift ➤ *reflex* to rise; *(ponerse de pie)* to stand up; *(de la cama)* to get out of bed.

ley ➤ *f* law, statute; *(regla)* rule.

leyenda ➤ *f (fábula)* legend; *(texto)* legend, caption.

liar §18 ➤ *tr (atar)* to tie, bind; *(envolver)* to wrap *(up)* ➤ *reflex (mezclarse)* to be mixed up in.

liberación ➤ *f* liberation.

liberal ➤ *adj* liberal; *(generoso)* generous ➤ *mf* liberal.

liberar ➤ *tr* to free, liberate.

libertad ➤ *f* liberty, freedom.

libra ➤ *f* pound.

librar ➤ *tr (salvar)* to free, deliver; *(eximir)* to exempt, release ➤ *reflex* to avoid, escape.

libre ➤ *adj* free.

librecambio ➤ *m* free trade.

librería ➤ *f (tienda)* bookstore; *(armario)* bookcase, bookshelf.

libreta ➤ *f* notebook.

libro ➤ *m* book ■ **l. de texto** textbook.

licencia ➤ *f* license, permit; *(permiso)* permission.

licenciado, a ➤ *mf* EDUC. university graduate, bachelor; AMER. lawyer.

licenciatura ➤ *f (título)* bachelor's degree; *(estudios)* degree program.

licor ➤ *m* liquor, spirits.

licuadora ➤ *f* mixer, blender.

líder ➤ *mf* leader, chief.

lidia ➤ *f* fight, battle.

lidiar ➤ *tr (torear)* to fight (bulls).

liebre ➤ *f* hare.

liga ➤ *f* league.

ligar §31 ➤ *tr (atar)* to tie, bind; *(unir)* to join.

ligereza ➤ *f (liviandad)* lightness; *(rapidez)* quickness, swiftness.

ligero, a ➤ *adj (leve)* light; *(rápido)* quick, swift; *(ágil)* agile, nimble.

lija ➤ *f* sandpaper.

lijar ➤ *tr* to sand.

lima ➤ *f* file ■ **l. para las uñas** nail file.

limitar ➤ *tr* to limit; *(delimitar)* to delimit; *(restringir)* to restrict ➤ *reflex* to limit oneself.

límite ➤ *m* limit; *(frontera)* boundary ■ **fecha l.** deadline.

limón ➤ *m (fruto)* lemon.

limonada ➤ *f* lemonade.

limonero ➤ *m* lemon tree.

limpiaparabrisas ➤ *m* windshield wiper.

limpiar ➤ *tr* to clean, cleanse.

limpieza ➤ *f (calidad)* cleanliness; *(acción)* cleaning, cleansing.

limpio, a ➤ *adj (sin mancha)* clean, spotless ➤ *adv* fair.

lindar ➤ *intr* to border (on), be adjacent (to).

lindo, a ➤ *adj* pretty, lovely ■ **de lo l.** much, a lot.

línea ➤ *f* line ■ **l. aérea** airline.

lingüístico, a ➤ *adj* linguistic ➤ *f* linguistics.

lino ➤ *m* linen.

linterna ➤ *f* lantern; *(de bolsillo)* flashlight.

lío ➤ *m (bulto)* bundle, package; COLL. *(embrollo)* jam, mess ■ **armar un l.** to make a fuss *or* racket.

liquidación ➤ *f (un negocio)* liquidation; *(venta)* clearance sale.

liquidar ➤ *tr* to sell off, liquidate.

líquido, a ➤ *adj* liquid; *(sin gravamen)* net ➤ *m* liquid.

lirio ➤ *m* iris; *(azucena)* lily.

liso, a ➤ *adj (parejo)* smooth, even; *(llano)* flat.

lista ➤ *f* list; *(raya)* stripe.

listado, a ➤ *adj* striped.

listo, a ➤ *adj (inteligente)* smart, clever; *(preparado)* ready.

litera ➤ *f* MARIT., RAIL. berth, bunk; *(cama)* bunk bed.

literatura ➤ *f* literature.

litigio ➤ *m* lawsuit.

litoral ➤ *adj & m* littoral, coast.

litro ➤ *m* liter.

llaga ➤ *f* wound, sore.

llama ➤ *f* flame ■ **en llamas** in flames.

llamada ➤ *f* call; TELEC. telephone call.

llamar ➤ *tr* to call ■ **l. por teléfono** to telephone, phone ➤ *intr* to ring a doorbell; *(tocar a la puerta)* to knock at the door; *(por teléfono)* to call, telephone ➤ *reflex* to be called *or* named.

llano, a ➤ *adj (liso)* flat, even; *(sencillo)* natural, simple.

llanta ➤ *f (de rueda)* rim; AMER. tire.

llanto ➤ *m* crying, weeping.

llanura ➤ *f* GEOG. plain.

llave ➤ *f* key; *(grifo)* tap, faucet; ELEC. switch; MECH. wrench ■ **l. inglesa** monkey wrench.

llavero ➤ *m* key ring.

llegada ➤ *f* arrival; SPORT. finish.

llegar §31 ➤ *intr (venir)* to arrive ■ **l. a** to arrive at, reach.

llenar ➤ *tr* to fill (up); *(cumplir)* to fulfill, meet ➤ *intr* ASTRON. to be full ➤ *reflex* to fill up.

lleno, a ➤ *adj* full, filled.

llevar ➤ *tr (transportar)* to carry, take; *(vestir)* to wear; *(pasar)* to have spent, have been ➤ *intr* to lead ➤ *reflex (sacar)* to take away, carry off ■ **l. bien, mal** to get along well, badly.

llorar ➤ *intr* to cry, weep.

llover §54 ➤ *intr* to rain.

llovizna ➤ *f* drizzle.

lluvia ➤ *f* rain.

lluvioso, a ➤ *adj* rainy, wet.

lo ➤ *def art* the . . . thing, the . . . part ■ **lo de** the matter of, the business of • **lo que** what, which ➤ *pron* it, him.

lobo, a ➤ *m* wolf ➤ *f* wolf, she-wolf.

local ➤ *adj* local ➤ *m* premises.

localidad ➤ *f (población)* district; *(local)* locale, site; THEAT. seat.

localizar §02 ➤ *tr* to localize; *(encontrar)* to locate.

loción ➤ *f* lotion.

loco, a ➤ *adj* mad, crazy ■ **volverse l.** to go crazy ➤ *mf* crazy person.

locomotora ➤ *f* locomotive.

locura ➤ *f* madness, insanity.

locutor, a ➤ *mf* radio announcer.

lodo ➤ *m* mud.

lógico, a ➤ *adj* logical.

lograr ➤ *tr (obtener)* to get, obtain; *(realizar)* to achieve ➤ *reflex* to succeed, be successful.
lombriz ➤ *f* worm, earthworm.
lomo ➤ *m* ANAT., CUL. loin; ZOOL. back.
longaniza ➤ *f* pork sausage.
longitud ➤ *f* length; GEOG. longitude.
lonja ➤ *f (tira)* slice; COM. *(edificio)* marketplace, exchange.
loro ➤ *m* parrot.
los ➤ *def art* the ➤ *pron* them.
losa ➤ *f* slab, stone.
lote ➤ *m* lot, share.
lotería ➤ *f* lottery ■ **l. casera** bingo.
loza ➤ *f (barro vidriado)* glazed pottery; *(platos)* china.
lubricante ➤ *m* lubricant.
lucha ➤ *f* struggle, conflict; SPORT. wrestling.
luchar ➤ *intr* to fight; SPORT. to wrestle.
lucir §28 ➤ *intr* to shine ➤ *tr* to show off, display ➤ *reflex (vestir bien)* to dress up; *(distinguirse)* to shine.
luego ➤ *adv (después)* then, afterward; *(más tarde)* later, later on ■ **desde l.** of course, naturally • **hasta l.** so long ➤ *conj* therefore.
lugar ➤ *m (sitio)* place ■ **en l. de** instead of • **en primer l.** in the first place, first.
lujo ➤ *m* luxury.
lujuria ➤ *f* lust.
lumbre ➤ *f* fire; FIG. brilliance.
luminoso, a ➤ *adj* luminous.
luna ➤ *f* moon; *(espejo)* mirror ■ **estar en la l.** to be daydreaming • **l. de miel** honeymoon.
lunar ➤ *m* mole, beauty mark.
lunes ➤ *m* Monday.
lupa ➤ *f* magnifying glass.
lustre ➤ *m* luster, shine.
luto ➤ *m* mourning.
luz ➤ *f* light ■ **dar a l.** to give birth • **sacar a l.** *(descubrirse)* to come to light ■ *pl* enlightenment, learning.

M

macarrón ➤ *m* macaroon ■ *pl* macaroni.
maceta ➤ *f* flowerpot.
machacar §47 ➤ *tr* to crush, pound.
machete ➤ *m* machete.
macho ➤ *adj* male; *(viril)* manly, virile ➤ *m (animal)* male; COLL. he-man.
macizo, a ➤ *adj* solid ➤ *m* GEOL. massif.
madeja ➤ *f* skein (of wool); *(pelo)* mop.
madera ➤ *f* wood; *(de construcción)* lumber ■ **de m.** wooden, of wood.
madrastra ➤ *f* stepmother.
madre ➤ *f* mother ■ **¡m. mía!** my goodness! • **m. patria** mother country.
madrina ➤ *f (de bautismo)* godmother; *(de boda)* bridesmaid.
madrugada ➤ *f* dawn ■ **de m.** at daybreak, very early.
madrugador, a ➤ *adj* early-rising ➤ *mf* early riser.
madrugar §31 ➤ *intr* to get up early.
madurar ➤ *tr* AGR to ripen, mature.
maduro, a ➤ *adj* AGR ripe; *(juicioso)* wise; *(entrado en años)* mature.
maestría ➤ *f (habilidad)* mastery, skill; *(título avanzado)* Master's degree.
maestro, a ➤ *adj* masterly ➤ *m (profesor)* teacher; *(artesano)* master; MUS. maestro ➤ *f (profesora)* teacher.
magia ➤ *f* magic.
mágico, a ➤ *adj* magic(al) ➤ *f* magic.
magistrado, a ➤ *mf* magistrate.
magnético, a ➤ *adj* magnetic.
magnetófono ➤ *m* tape recorder.
magnífico, a ➤ *adj* magnificent.
mago ➤ *m* magician, wizard ■ **los Reyes Magos** the Magi.
magullar ➤ *tr* to bruise, batter.
maicena ➤ *f* cornstarch.
maíz ➤ *m* corn, maize.
majestad ➤ *f* majesty.
majo, a ➤ *adj* SP. *(bonito)* pretty, *(simpático)* nice, sweet.
mal[1] ➤ *adj contr of* **malo** ➤ *m (vicio)* evil; *(daño)* harm; *(enfermedad)* illness ■ **hacer m.** to harm, hurt • **m. de mar** seasickness.
mal[2] ➤ *adv (pobremente)* badly; *(difícilmente)* hardly ■ **de m. en peor** from bad to worse • **menos m.** just as well.
malabarista ➤ *mf* juggler.
malcontento, a ➤ *adj* discontented, unhappy ➤ *mf* malcontent.
malcriado, a ➤ *adj* rude, ill-bred.
maldad ➤ *f* wickedness, evil.
maldecido, a ➤ *adj* evil, wicked.
maldecir ➤ *tr* to curse.
maldición ➤ *f* curse, damnation.
maldito, a ➤ *adj* damned.
malecón ➤ *m* sea wall, jetty.
maleducado, a ➤ *adj* bad-mannered.
malentendido ➤ *m* misunderstanding.
malestar ➤ *m* malaise, indisposition; *(inquietud)* uneasiness.
maleta ➤ *f* suitcase ■ **hacer la m.** to pack one's bag.
maletero ➤ *m* station porter; AUTO. trunk.
maletín ➤ *m* small suitcase, briefcase.
maleza ➤ *f* BOT. weeds, underbrush.
malgastar ➤ *tr* to waste, misspend.
malhablado, a ➤ *adj* foul-mouthed, vulgar.
malhechor, a ➤ *mf* wrongdoer.
malhumor ➤ *m* bad temper.
malicia ➤ *f* malice, wickedness.
malicioso, a ➤ *adj* malicious; *(astuto)* sly.
malla ➤ *f (de red)* mesh, netting; AMER. *(traje de baño)* swimsuit.
malo, a ➤ *adj* bad; *(perverso)* evil; *(dañino)* harmful; *(desagradable)* unpleasant; *(enfermo)* sick, ill ■ **a (las) malas** on bad terms • **lo m. es que** the trouble is . . . • **ponerse m.** to become sick • **por las malas** by force.
malpensado, a ➤ *adj & mf* evil-minded *or* malicious (person).
malta ➤ *f* malt.
maltratar ➤ *tr* to mistreat.
mamá ➤ *f* mama, mommy.
mamar ➤ *tr* to suckle, nurse.
mamífero ➤ *m* mammal.
mampara ➤ *f* screen, partition.
manada ➤ *f (hato)* flock, herd; *(de lobos)* pack.
manantial ➤ *m* spring.
mancha ➤ *f* stain, spot.
manchar ➤ *tr* to stain, spot.
manco, a ➤ *adj & mf* one-handed *or* one-armed (person).
mandado ➤ *m (orden)* order; *(encargo)* task, assignment; *(recado)* errand.
mandar ➤ *tr* to order, command; *(enviar)* to send ➤ *intr* to be in charge.
mandarina ➤ *f* mandarin orange, tangerine.
mandato ➤ *m* order, command.
mandíbula ➤ *f* jaw.
mando ➤ *m (autoridad)* authority; *(dirección)* command; MECH. control ■ **estar al m.** to be in command • **tablero de mandos** instrument panel.
manecilla ➤ *f (del reloj)* hand.
manejable ➤ *adj* manageable.
manejar ➤ *tr* to handle; *(empresa)* to run, manage; *(automóvil)* to drive ➤ *reflex* to get *or* move around.
manejo ➤ *m (uso)* handling; *(funcionamiento)* running, operation ■ **instrucciones de m.** directions.
manera ➤ *f* manner; *(modo)* way; *(tipo)* type; *(estilo)* style ■ **de alguna m.** somehow, in some way • **de cualquier m.** anyhow • **de ninguna m.** by no means, in no way • **de otra m.** otherwise • **de tal m.** in such a way • **de todas maneras** at any rate, anyway.
manga ➤ *f* sleeve; *(manguera)* hose.
mango[1] ➤ *m* handle.
mango[2] ➤ *m* mango (tree and fruit).
manguera ➤ *f* garden hose.
maní ➤ *m* peanut.
manía ➤ *f* mania; *(capricho)* craze, fad.
maniático, a ➤ *adj* maniacal ➤ *mf* maniac.
manicomio ➤ *m* mental health facility.
manifestación ➤ *f* manifestation; POL. demonstration.
manifestar §33 ➤ *tr (expresar)* to declare; *(anunciar)* to show, reveal ➤ *intr* to be evident; POL. to demonstrate.
manija ➤ *f* handle.
manilla ➤ *f* bracelet; *(manija)* handle.
manillar ➤ *m* handlebars (of a bicycle).
maniobra ➤ *f* maneuver, stratagem.
manipular ➤ *tr* to manipulate; *(manejar)* to handle.
maniquí ➤ *m* mannequin.
manivela ➤ *f* crank.
manjar ➤ *m* dish.
mano[1] ➤ *f* hand; *(pata)* forefoot, front paw; *(lado)* side ■ **a m.** by hand; *(cerca)* at hand, on hand • **dar la m. a** to shake hands with • **de primera m.** firsthand • **de segunda m.** secondhand • **m. de obra** labor.
manojo ➤ *m* bundle, bunch.
mansión ➤ *f* mansion, residence.
manso, a ➤ *adj* tame.
manta ➤ *f* blanket.
manteca ➤ *f (grasa)* fat; *(de cerdo)* lard; *(de vaca)* butter.
mantel ➤ *m* tablecloth.
mantener §46 ➤ *tr* to maintain, support; *(conservar)* to keep; *(continuar)* to keep up; *(afirmar)* to affirm ➤ *reflex (alimentarse)* to feed oneself; *(sustentarse)* to support oneself.
mantenimiento ➤ *m* maintenance; *(sustento)* sustenance, food.
mantequilla ➤ *f* butter.
manto ➤ *m* cloak.
mantón ➤ *m* shawl.
manual ➤ *adj & m* manual.
manubrio ➤ *m* crank; *(manija)* handle.
manufactura ➤ *f* manufacture.
manufacturar ➤ *tr* to manufacture.
manuscrito ➤ *m* manuscript.
manzana ➤ *f* apple; *(cuadra)* block.
manzano ➤ *m* apple tree.
maña ➤ *f (habilidad)* skill, dexterity; *(astucia)* craftiness, guile.
mañana ➤ *f* morning ■ **a la m. siguiente** the next morning • **ayer por la m.** yesterday morning • **de** *or* **en** *or* **por la m.** in the morning ➤ *adv* tomorrow; *(en el futuro)* in the future ■ **a partir de m.** starting tomorrow, as of tomorrow • **hasta m.** see you tomorrow • **m. por la m.** tomorrow morning • **pasado m.** the day after tomorrow.
mañoso, a ➤ *adj* skillful.
mapa ➤ *m* map, chart.
maquillaje ➤ *m* makeup, cosmetics.
maquillar ➤ *tr* to put makeup on.
máquina ➤ *f* machine; *(cámara)* camera ■ **hecho a m.** machine-made • **m. de escribir** typewriter • **m. de lavar** washing machine • **m. registradora** S. AMER. cash register.
maquinaria ➤ *f (conjunto)* machinery; *(mecanismo)* mechanism.
maquinilla ➤ *f* small machine *or* device ■ **m. de afeitar** safety razor.
mar ➤ *m or f* sea ■ **alta m.** high seas.
maravilla ➤ *f* wonder, marvel.
maravilloso, a ➤ *adj* marvelous, wonderful.
marca ➤ *f* mark; *(tipo)* make, brand; COM. trademark; SPORT. record ■ **m. registrada** (registered) trademark.
marcar §47 ➤ *tr (poner marca)* to mark; *(el pelo)* to set; *(un número de teléfono)* to dial; SPORT. to score.
marcha ➤ *f* march; *(funcionamiento)* operation, running; FIG. progress, course ■ **a toda m.** at full speed • **m. atrás** AUTO. reverse • **poner(se) en m.** to start (off).
marchar ➤ *intr (ir)* to go; *(andar)* to walk; *(progresar)* to go, proceed; MIL. to march ➤ *reflex* to go (away), leave.
marco ➤ *m (cerco)* frame; FIN. mark.
marea ➤ *f* tide ■ **m. alta** high tide • **m. baja** low tide.
marearse ➤ *reflex* to become nauseated *or* seasick.
marejada ➤ *f (del mar)* swell.
mareo ➤ *m* nausea; MARIT. seasickness; *(en vehículos)* motion sickness.
margarina ➤ *f* margarine.
margarita ➤ *f* BOT. daisy.
margen ➤ *m* margin, border; COM. margin.
marginar ➤ *tr* to leave out.
marido ➤ *m* husband, spouse.
marinero ➤ *m* sailor, mariner.
marino, a ➤ *adj* marine ■ **azul m.** navy blue ➤ *m* marine, sailor.
mariposa ➤ *f* butterfly.
marisco ➤ *m* shellfish, crustacean.
marítimo, a ➤ *adj* maritime, sea.
mármol ➤ *m* marble.
marrano, a ➤ *adj* dirty, filthy ➤ *m* ZOOL. pig, hog; COLL. *(sucio)* slob.
marrón ➤ *adj* brown.
martes ➤ *m* Tuesday.
martillo ➤ *m* hammer.
mártir ➤ *mf* martyr.
marzo ➤ *m* March.
más ➤ *adv* more, most ■ **a m. y mejor** a lot, really • **de m.** too much, extra • **durar m.** to last longer • **m. allá** further • **m. bien** rather • **m. de** more than • **m. que** more than; *(sino)* but, except • **ni m. ni menos** no more, no less • **no m.** only, no more • **no m. que** only • **por m. que** no matter how much ➤ *m* plus sign ■ ➤ *prep* plus.
masa ➤ *f* mass; *(volumen)* volume, bulk; *(pasta)* dough.
masaje ➤ *m* massage.
mascar §47 ➤ *tr* to chew.
máscara ➤ *f* mask.
masculino, a ➤ *adj & m* masculine.
masticar §47 ➤ *tr* to chew.
mástil ➤ *m* mast.
mata ➤ *f* bush, shrub.
matador, a ➤ *mf* bullfighter, matador.
matar ➤ *tr* to kill.
mate[1] ➤ *adj (sin brillo)* matte; *(apagado)* dull.
mate[2] ➤ *m (ajedrez)* mate; *(bebida)* S. AMER. maté, tea.
matemática ➤ *fpl* mathematics.
materia ➤ *f* matter; *(material)* material, substance; EDUC. subject ■ **m. prima** raw material.
material ➤ *adj* material ➤ *m* materials.
maternal ➤ *adj* maternal.
maternidad ➤ *f* maternity.
materno, a ➤ *adj* maternal.
matinal ➤ *adj* morning, matinal.
matrícula ➤ *f (inscripción)* registration, matriculation; *(gente matriculada)* roll; AUTO. registration.
matricular ➤ *tr & reflex* to register, matriculate.
matrimonio ➤ *m* marriage, matrimony; COLL. *(marido y mujer)* married couple ■ **fuera del m.** out of wedlock • **m. civil** civil marriage • **partida de m.** marriage certificate.
matrona ➤ *f* midwife.
maullar ➤ *intr* to meow, mew.
máximo, a ➤ *adj* maximum, greatest ➤ *m* maximum ■ **al m.** to the maximum • **como m.** at the most • **hacer el m.** to do one's utmost.
mayo ➤ *m* May.
mayonesa ➤ *f* mayonnaise.
mayor ➤ *adj (más grande)* bigger, larger; *(el más grande)* biggest, largest; *(importante)* greater; *(el más importante)* greatest; *(de más edad)* older, elder; *(entrado en años)* elderly; *(el más viejo)* oldest, eldest; *(adulto)* adult; *(principal)* main ■ **al por m.** COM. wholesale • **m. de edad** of age.
mayoría ➤ *f* majority ■ **en la m. de los casos** in most cases • **m. de edad** legal age.
mayúscula ➤ *f* capital letter.
mazmorra ➤ *f* dungeon.
mazo ➤ *m* mallet; *(manojo)* bunch.
mazorca ➤ *f* ear (of corn).
me ➤ *pron* me; to, for, *or* from me; myself.
mecánico, a ➤ *adj* mechanical ➤ *mf* mechanic ➤ *f* mechanics.
mecanismo ➤ *m* mechanism.
mecedora ➤ *f* rocking chair, rocker.
mecer §51 ➤ *tr & reflex* to rock.
mechón ➤ *m (de pelo)* lock, tuft.
medalla ➤ *f* medal.
media ➤ *f (de mujer)* stocking; *(de hombre)* sock ■ **las dos y m.** half past two ➤ *mpl* the media.
mediador, a ➤ *mf* mediator.
mediano, a ➤ *adj* medium.
medianoche ➤ *f* midnight.
mediante ➤ *adv* through, by means of.
medicamento ➤ *m* medicine, medication.
medicina ➤ *f* medicine.
médico, a ➤ *adj* medical ➤ *mf* doctor, physician.
medida ➤ *f* measure, measurement ■ **a m. que** as, while • **en menor m.** to a lesser extent • **hecho a la m.** made-to-order • **sin m.** in excess.
medieval ➤ *adj* medieval.
medio, a ➤ *adj* half; *(mediano)* middle, medium; *(central)* middle, midway; *(regular)* average ■ **m. hermano, a** half brother, sister • **m. luna** half-moon • **m. pasaje** half fare ➤ *m (centro)* middle, center; *(medida)* measure; *(moderación)* middle ground • **en m. de** in the middle of • **m. ambiente** environment • ➤ *adv* half, partially ■ **a medias** halfway.
mediocre ➤ *adj* mediocre.
mediodía ➤ *m* midday, noon.
medir §32 ➤ *tr* to measure.
meditar ➤ *tr & intr* to meditate.
medula *or* **médula** ➤ *f* marrow.
mejilla ➤ *f* cheek.
mejillón ➤ *m* mussel.
mejor ➤ *adj* better, best ■ **lo m. posible** as well as possible ➤ *adv (más bien)* better; *(antes)* rather ■ **a lo m.** maybe, perhaps • **en el m. de los casos** at best • **m. dicho** rather, more specifically •

tanto m. so much the better.

mejora ➤ *f (adelanto)* improvement, betterment; *(aumento)* increase.

mejorar ➤ *tr* to improve, make better; *(aumentar)* to raise ➤ *intr & reflex* to improve, get better; *(el tiempo)* to clear up.

melancolía ➤ *f* melancholy.

melancólico, a ➤ *adj* melancholy.

melena ➤ *f (cabello)* long hair, mop (of hair); *(de león)* mane.

melifluo, a ➤ *adj* mellifluous.

mellizo, a ➤ *mf & adj* twin.

melocotón ➤ *m* peach.

melodía ➤ *f* melody, tune.

melón ➤ *m* melon; FIG. idiot, fool.

membrana ➤ *f* membrane.

membrillo ➤ *m (fruta)* quince; *(dulce)* quince jam *or* jelly.

memoria ➤ *f* memory; COM. *(informe)* financial report *or* statement ▪ **de m.** by heart • **venir a la m.** to come to mind ▪ *pl (libro)* memoirs.

mención ➤ *f* mention.

mencionar ➤ *tr* to mention.

mendigo, a ➤ *mf* beggar, mendicant.

mendrugo ➤ *m* crust, crumb.

menear ➤ *tr & reflex (mover)* to move; *(agitar)* to shake, wag; *(oscilar)* to sway, swing.

menguar §05 ➤ *intr* to diminish, decrease.

menor ➤ *adj* less, lesser; *(mínimo)* least; *(más joven)* younger; *(el más joven)* youngest ▪ **al por m.** COM. retail • **m. de edad** minor, under age ➤ *mf* minor, juvenile ▪ **tribunal de menores** juvenile court.

menos ➤ *adv* less, least; *(número)* fewer ▪ **al m.** at least • **a m. que** unless • **cada vez m.** less and less • **cuanto m. . . . m.** the less . . . the less • **de m.** short • **echar a alguien de m.** to miss someone • **más o m.** more or less • **lo m.** the least • **m. de** less than • **m. que** less than • **ni más ni m.** exactly • **por lo m.** at least ➤ *m* minus sign ➤ *conj* but, except ➤ *prep* minus.

menosprecio ➤ *m* contempt.

mensaje ➤ *m* message.

mensajero, a ➤ *adj & mf* messenger.

mensual ➤ *adj* monthly.

menta ➤ *f* mint.

mental ➤ *adj* mental.

mente ➤ *f* mind.

mentir §43 ➤ *intr* to lie, tell lies.

mentira ➤ *f* lie, falsehood.

menú ➤ *m* menu, bill of fare.

menudo, a ➤ *adj* small, little ▪ **a m.** often, frequently ➤ *mpl* CUL. giblets.

mercadeo ➤ *m* marketing.

mercado ➤ *m* market; *(sitio)* marketplace.

mercancía ➤ *f (artículo)* piece of merchandise, article; *(existencias)* merchandise, goods.

mercantil ➤ *adj* mercantile, commercial.

merecer §09 ➤ *tr* to deserve ▪ **m. la pena** to be worthwhile, be worth the trouble ➤ *reflex* to be deserving *or* worthy.

merendar §33 ➤ *tr* to snack on ➤ *intr* to have a snack.

meridional ➤ *adj* southern.

merienda ➤ *f* snack.

mérito ➤ *m* merit.

merluza ➤ *f* hake.

mermelada ➤ *f* jam, marmalade.

mes ➤ *m* month ▪ **al** *or* **por m.** by the month.

mesa ➤ *f* table ▪ **poner la m.** to set the table.

meseta ➤ *f* GEOG. plateau.

mesón ➤ *m* inn, tavern.

meta ➤ *f (fin)* goal, objective; *(de carrera)* finish.

metal ➤ *m* metal.

metálico, a ➤ *adj* metallic ➤ *m* cash, currency.

meteorología ➤ *f* meteorology.

meter ➤ *tr* to insert, put (in, inside); *(implicar)* to involve, get into ➤ *reflex (entrar)* to get into, enter; *(entremeterse)* to intervene, butt in; *(enredarse)* to get mixed up in ▪ **m. con** to annoy • **m. en todo** to meddle.

método ➤ *m* method.

métrico, a ➤ *adj* metric ▪ **cinta m.** tape measure.

metro[1] ➤ *m (medida)* meter.

metro[2] ➤ *m* subway.

mexicano, a ➤ *adj & mf* Mexican.

mezcla ➤ *f (acción)* mixing; *(combinación)* mixture, combination.

mezclar ➤ *tr & reflex* to mix, blend.

mezquino, a ➤ *adj (pobre)* poor, wretched; *(avaro)* stingy, miserly.

mezquita ➤ *f* mosque.

mí ➤ *pron* me ▪ **me toca a mí** it's my turn.

mi, mis ➤ *adj* my.

microbio ➤ *m* microbe.

microbús ➤ *m* microbus, minibus.

micrófono ➤ *m* microphone.

microonda ➤ *f* microwave.

microscopio ➤ *m* microscope ▪ **m. electrónico** electron microscope.

miedo ➤ *m (temor)* fear, dread; *(aprensión)* apprehension • **que da** *or* **mete m.** frightening, fearsome • **tener m.** (a *or* de) to be afraid (of), fear • **tener m.** (de) que to be afraid that.

miedoso, a ➤ *adj* fearful.

miel ➤ *f* honey.

miembro ➤ *m* member.

mientras ➤ *adv* ▪ **m. más** the more • **m. tanto** meanwhile, in the meantime ➤ *conj (pero)* while, whereas; *(durante)* while, as long as ▪ **m. que** while.

miércoles ➤ *m* Wednesday ▪ **m. de ceniza** RELIG. Ash Wednesday.

miga ➤ *f* crumb.

mil ➤ *adj* thousand ▪ **m. millones** billion, milliard (G.B.).

milagro ➤ *m* miracle.

milésimo, a ➤ *adj & m* thousandth.

militar ➤ *adj* military ➤ *mf* soldier.

milla ➤ *f* mile.

millar ➤ *m* thousand.

millón ➤ *m* million.

millonario, a ➤ *adj & mf* millionaire.

mimar ➤ *tr* to spoil.

mimbre ➤ *m* wicker.

mina ➤ *f* mine; *(de lápiz)* pencil lead.

minarete ➤ *m* minaret.

mineral ➤ *adj & m* mineral.

minero, a ➤ *adj* mining ➤ *m* miner.

miniatura ➤ *f* miniature.

minicomputadora ➤ *f* minicomputer.

mínimo, a ➤ *adj* minimum, least; *(minucioso)* minimal ➤ *m* minimum.

ministerio ➤ *m* ministry; *(cuerpo de ministros)* cabinet ▪ **M. de Relaciones Exteriores** State Department.

ministro ➤ *mf* minister ▪ **M. de Relaciones Exteriores** Secretary of State • **primer m.** POL. prime minister.

minoría *or* **minoridad** ➤ *f* minority.

minúsculo, a ➤ *adj* minuscule, tiny ➤ *f* small *or* lowercase letter.

minuto ➤ *m* minute ▪ **al m.** at once.

mío, a ➤ *adj* mine, my; *(querido)* my dear ➤ *pron* mine ▪ **lo m.** my affair, my business • **los míos** my people.

miope ➤ *adj* myopic, nearsighted.

mirada ➤ *f (acción)* look, glance; *(apariencia)* look, expression ▪ **echar una m. a** to cast a glance at.

mirar ➤ *tr* to look at; *(observar)* to watch, observe ➤ *intr* to look; *(observar)* to watch; *(dar a)* to look out on, overlook ➤ *reflex* to look at oneself; *(a otro)* to look at one another.

mirasol ➤ *m* sunflower.

misa ➤ *f* Mass.

miserable ➤ *adj (pobre)* poor, wretched; *(tacaño)* stingy, miserly; *(lastimoso)* miserable.

miseria ➤ *f* misery, suffering; *(pobreza)* poverty; *(avaricia)* miserliness.

misión ➤ *f* mission.

misionero, a ➤ *adj & mf* missionary.

mismo, a ➤ *adj (idéntico)* same; *(exacto)* very ▪ **ahora m.** right now • **así m.** *(de esta manera)* in the same way, likewise; *(también)* also • **lo m.** the same thing • **por lo m.** for that (very) reason • **yo m.** I myself.

misterio ➤ *m* mystery.

mitad ➤ *f* half; *(medio)* middle ▪ **a** *or* **en la m. de** in the middle of • **por la m.** in half, in two.

mítico, a ➤ *adj* mythic(al).

mito ➤ *m* myth; *(leyenda)* legend.

mixto, a ➤ *adj* mixed.

mobiliario, a ➤ *m* furniture, furnishings.

mochila ➤ *f* backpack, knapsack.

mocoso, a ➤ *mf* snotty kid, brat.

moda ➤ *f* style, fashion ▪ **a la m.** *or* **de m.** fashionable, in fashion • **desfile de modas** fashion show • **pasado de m.** old-fashioned.

modelo ➤ *adj & m* model ➤ *mf* fashion model.

módem ➤ *m* COMPUT. modem.

moderado, a ➤ *adj & mf* moderate.

modernista ➤ *adj & mf* modernist.

modernizar §02 ➤ *tr* to modernize.

moderno, a ➤ *adj* modern.

modesto, a ➤ *adj* modest.

modificar §47 ➤ *tr* to modify.

modista ➤ *mf* dressmaker.

modo ➤ *m* manner, way ▪ **de m. que** so that • **de ningún m.** by no means • **de todos modos** anyway • **m. de ser** character, way of being ▪ *pl* manners.

moho ➤ *m* mold, mildew.

mohoso, a ➤ *adj* moldy, mildewed.

mojar ➤ *tr* to wet, make wet; *(empapar)* to drench, soak; *(bañar)* to dip ➤ *reflex* to get wet.

molde ➤ *m* mold; *(forma)* pattern, model.

moler §54 ➤ *tr* to grind.

molestar ➤ *tr* to bother, annoy ➤ *reflex* to bother, take the trouble ▪ **no se moleste** don't bother.

molestia ➤ *f (fastidio)* bother, annoyance; *(malestar)* discomfort ▪ **si no es m.** if it isn't too much trouble.

molesto, a ➤ *adj* bothersome, annoying; *(enojado)* bothered, annoyed.

molino ➤ *m* mill ▪ **m. de viento** windmill.

momentáneo, a ➤ *adj* momentary.

momento ➤ *m* moment; *(ocasión)* occasion, time ▪ **a partir de este m.** from this moment (on) • **de un m. a otro** at any moment • **dentro de un m.** in a moment.

monasterio ➤ *m* monastery.

moneda ➤ *f* coin ▪ **m. corriente** currency.

monedero ➤ *m* change purse.

monetario, a ➤ *adj* monetary.

monitor, a ➤ *mf* trainer, coach ➤ *m* COMPUT. monitor.

monja ➤ *f* nun.

monje ➤ *m* monk.

mono, a ➤ *adj* COLL. cute, darling ➤ *mf* monkey.

monopolio ➤ *m* monopoly.

monótono, a ➤ *adj* monotonous.

monstruo ➤ *m* monster.

montaje ➤ *m* assembly, installation.

montaña ➤ *f* mountain ▪ **m. rusa** roller coaster.

montañoso, a ➤ *adj* mountainous.

montar ➤ *intr (subir a caballo)* to mount ▪ **m. a caballo** to ride horseback • **m. en** *(bicicleta)* to ride (a bicycle) ➤ *tr* to mount; *(armar)* to assemble, set up; *(establecer)* to set up.

monte ➤ *m* mount, mountain.

montón ➤ *m* pile, heap.

montura ➤ *f (caballo, etc.)* mount.

monumento ➤ *m* monument.

moño ➤ *m (pelo)* bun, chignon.

morado, a ➤ *adj* purple.

moral ➤ *adj* moral ➤ *f (ética)* morals, ethics; *(ánimo)* morale, spirits.

morcilla ➤ *f* CUL. blood pudding.

mordaz ➤ *adj* mordant.

morder §54 ➤ *tr* to bite.

mordisco ➤ *m* nibble, bite.

moreno, a ➤ *adj (pardo)* brown; *(tostado)* brown-skinned, dark-skinned; *(pelo)* brown ➤ *mf (negro)* Black; *(de pelo castaño)* brunette.

morir §16 ➤ *intr* to die; *(lumbre)* to die, go out ▪ **m. ahogado** to drown • **m. de frío** to freeze to death • **m. de risa** to die laughing ➤ *reflex* to die ▪ **m. de aburrimiento** to be bored to death • **m. por** *(estar loco por)* to be crazy about; *(querer)* to be dying to.

morro ➤ *m* snout, nose.

mortal ➤ *adj* mortal; *(penoso)* dreadful, awful ➤ *m* mortal.

mosca ➤ *f* fly.

mosquito ➤ *m* mosquito.

mostaza ➤ *f* mustard.

mostrar §11 ➤ *tr (enseñar)* to show; *(explicar)* to demonstrate, show; *(indicar)* to point out ➤ *reflex (darse a conocer)* to show oneself.

mote[1] ➤ *m* nickname.

mote[2] ➤ *m* AMER. stewed corn.

motín ➤ *m* insurrection, riot.

motivo ➤ *m* motive, cause.

moto ➤ *f* COLL. moped, motorcycle.

motocicleta ➤ *f* motorcycle.

motociclista ➤ *mf* motorcyclist.

motor, a ➤ *adj* motor ➤ *m* motor, engine ▪ **m. de reacción** *or* **de chorro** jet engine • **m. de vapor** steam engine • **m. diesel** diesel.

motorista ➤ *mf* motorist.

mover §54 ➤ *tr* to move; MECH. to drive, power ➤ *reflex* to move.

movimiento ➤ *m* movement, motion; MECH. motion; COM. activity ▪ **poner en m.** to put in motion.

mozo, a ➤ *adj* young ➤ *m* boy; *(camarero)* waiter; *(en hotel, etc.)* porter ▪ **buen m.** AMER. handsome ➤ *f* girl.

muchacho, a ➤ *mf* child, youngster ➤ *m* boy ➤ *f* girl.

muchedumbre ➤ *f* multitude, crowd.

mucho, a ➤ *adj* much, a lot of ▪ **hace m. frío** it's very cold ▪ *pl* many, a lot of ➤ *pron* a lot ▪ *pl* many ➤ *adv* a lot, much ▪ **hace mucho** for a long time • **m. después** much later • **ni m. menos** not by a long shot • **por m. que** no matter how much • **tener en m.** to hold in high regard.

mudanza ➤ *f (traslado)* move, moving ▪ **estar de m.** to be moving.

mudar ➤ *tr (cambiar)* to change; *(trasladar)* to move ➤ *reflex* to move.

mudo, a ➤ *adj* mute, dumb.

mueble ➤ *m* piece of furniture ▪ *pl* furniture.

muela ➤ *f* ANAT. molar ▪ **m. de juicio** wisdom tooth.

muelle[1] ➤ *m* MECH. spring.

muelle[2] ➤ *m* pier, dock.

muérdago ➤ *m* mistletoe.

muerte ➤ *f* death ▪ **de m.** seriously, fatally.

muerto, a ➤ *adj* dead ▪ **m. de** dying of ➤ *mf* dead person; *(cadáver)* corpse ▪ **hacerse el m.** COLL. to play dead.

muestra ➤ *f (ejemplo)* sample, specimen; *(señal)* sign, indication; *(modelo)* model, guide.

mugre ➤ *f* filth, grime.

mujer ➤ *f* woman; *(esposa)* wife ▪ **m. de la limpieza** cleaning woman • **m. de (su) casa** housewife.

mulato, a ➤ *adj & mf* mulatto.

muleta ➤ *f* crutch; FIG. support.

mulo, a ➤ *mf* mule.

multa ➤ *f* fine; AUTO. parking ticket.

multinacional ➤ *adj* multinational.

múltiple ➤ *adj* multiple.

multiplicación ➤ *f* multiplication.

multiplicar §47 ➤ *tr & reflex* to multiply.

multiprocesador ➤ *adj & m* COMPUT. multiprocessor.

multitud ➤ *f* multitude.

mundial ➤ *adj* world; *(universal)* worldwide ▪ **guerra m.** world war ➤ *m* world championship ▪ **m. de fútbol** world soccer championship.

mundo ➤ *m* world; *(tierra)* earth.

municipalidad ➤ *f* municipality.

municipio ➤ *m (ayuntamiento)* town council; *(pueblo)* township, district.

muñeca ➤ *f* wrist; *(juguete)* doll.

muñeco ➤ *m (juguete)* doll; *(marioneta)* puppet.

muralla ➤ *f* wall, rampart.

murmullo ➤ *m* murmur.

murmurar ➤ *intr* to whisper; *(hojas)* to rustle; *(quejar)* to grumble; COLL. *(chismear)* to gossip.

muro ➤ *m* wall.

músculo ➤ *m* muscle.

museo ➤ *m* museum.

musgo ➤ *m* moss.

musical ➤ *adj & m* musical.

músico, a ➤ *mf* musician.

muslo ➤ *m* thigh; *(de pollo)* drumstick.

mutilar ➤ *tr* to mutilate.

mutuo, a ➤ *adj* mutual.

muy ➤ *adv* very ▪ **m. señor mío** Dear Sir • **ser m. de su casa** COLL. to be a homebody.

N

nabo ➤ *m* turnip.

nácar ➤ *m* nacre, mother-of-pearl.

nacer §09 ➤ *intr* to be born; *(los astros)* to rise; *(brotar)* to rise, start to flow ▪ **al n.** at birth.

nación ➤ *f* nation; *(pueblo)* people.

nacional ➤ *adj* national, domestic.

nacionalidad ➤ *f* nationality.

nada ➤ *pron* nothing, not anything ▪ **antes de n.** first, before anything else • **de n.** you're welcome • **n. de no,** none • **n. menos** no less, nothing less • **ni n.** COLL. or anything ➤ *in* no way, not at all ➤ *f* nothingness, nothing; *(cosa mínima)* the slightest thing.

nadar ➤ *intr* to swim.

nadie ➤ *pron* nobody, no one ➤ *m* a nobody ■ **no ser n.** to be a nobody.
nafta ➤ *f* naphtha; AMER. gasoline.
naipe ➤ *m* card, playing card.
nalga ➤ *f* buttock.
nana ➤ *f* COLL. *(abuela)* granny; *(arrullo)* lullaby; AMER. nanny.
naranja ➤ *f* orange ➤ *m* orange (color).
naranjada ➤ *f* orangeade.
naranjo ➤ *m* orange tree.
nariz ➤ *f* nose.
narrar ➤ *tr* to narrate, relate.
nata ➤ *f* cream.
natación ➤ *f* swimming.
natillas ➤ *fpl* custard.
natural ➤ *adj* natural ■ **al n.** naturally, without adornment.
naturaleza ➤ *f* nature.
naturalidad ➤ *f* naturalness.
naturalizar §02 ➤ *tr* to naturalize, nationalize.
naufragar §31 ➤ *intr* MARIT. to be shipwrecked.
naufragio ➤ *m* MARIT. shipwreck.
náusea ➤ *f* nausea; *(repugnancia)* disgust ■ **dar náuseas** to disgust, nauseate • **sentir náuseas** to feel sick.
navaja ➤ *f* jackknife, penknife ■ **n. de afeitar** razor.
nave ➤ *f* ship, vessel; ARCHIT. nave.
navegación ➤ *f* navigation.
navegador, a ➤ *mf* navigator ➤ *m* COMPUT. browser.
navegar §31 ➤ *intr* to navigate; *(por barco)* to sail; COMPUT. to browse.
Navidad ➤ *f* Christmas, Nativity ■ **¡Feliz N.!** Merry Christmas!
navío ➤ *m* ship, vessel.
neblina ➤ *f* mist, fog.
necesario, a ➤ *adj* necessary; *(esencial)* essential.
necesidad ➤ *f* necessity, need.
necesitar ➤ *tr* to need, want.
necio, a ➤ *adj* ignorant, foolish ➤ *mf* fool, simpleton.
nectarina ➤ *f* nectarine.
negación ➤ *f* negation, denial.
negar §35 ➤ *tr* to deny; *(rehusar)* to refuse ➤ *reflex (rehusar)* to refuse; *(privarse)* to deny oneself.
negativo, a ➤ *adj* negative ➤ *f* negation, denial ➤ *m* PHOTOG. negative.
negligencia ➤ *f* negligence.
negligente ➤ *adj* negligent.
negociación ➤ *f* negotiation.
negociar ➤ *intr (tratar)* to negotiate, discuss; *(comerciar)* to deal, do business *(con, en,* in) ➤ *tr* to negotiate.
negocio ➤ *m (comercio)* business; *(transacción)* transaction, deal; *(utilidad)* profit, return; *(asunto)* affair, concern; R.P. shop, store ■ **persona de negocios** business person • **encargado de negocios** chargé d'affaires.
negro, a ➤ *adj* black; *(oscuro)* dark, black ■ **ponerse n.** to get angry ➤ *mf* Black person; AMER. *(querido)* dear, darling ➤ *m (color)* black.
nene, a ➤ *mf* COLL. baby, infant.
neolítico, a ➤ *adj* Neolithic.
nervio ➤ *m* nerve; *(tendón)* tendon, sinew; BOT. rib, vein.
nervioso, a ➤ *adj* nervous ■ **ponerse n.** to get nervous.
neto, a ➤ *adj* COM. net.
neumático, a ➤ *adj* pneumatic ➤ *m* tire.
neumonía ➤ *f* pneumonia.
neurosis ➤ *f* neurosis.
neurótico, a ➤ *adj & mf* neurotic.
neutral ➤ *adj & mf* neutral.
neutro, a ➤ *adj* neutral.
nevado, a ➤ *adj* snowy, snow-covered; FIG. snow-white ➤ *f* snowfall.
nevar §33 ➤ *intr* to snow.
nevera ➤ *f* refrigerator.
ni ➤ *conj* neither, nor ■ **ni . . . ni** neither . . . nor • **ni me vió** she didn't even see me • **ni que** not even if.
nicaragüense ➤ *adj & mf* Nicaraguan.
nido ➤ *m* nest.
niebla ➤ *f* fog, mist; *(nube)* cloud.
nieto, a ➤ *mf* grandchild, grandson/daughter ■ *pl* grandchildren.
nieve ➤ *f* snow.
ningún ➤ *adj contr of* **ninguno** ■ **de n. modo** in no way.
ninguno, a ➤ *adj* none, no, not any ■ **de n. manera** in no way, by no means • **en n. parte** nowhere ➤ *pron* none, not any; *(nadie)* no one, nobody.
niñero, a ➤ *adj* fond of children ➤ *f* nursemaid, nanny, babysitter.
niño, a ➤ *adj* young ➤ *mf* child ➤ *m* boy ■ **de n.** as a child • **desde n.** from childhood ■ *pl* children ➤ *f* girl; *(del ojo)* pupil (of the eye).
nitrógeno ➤ *m* nitrogen.
nivel ➤ *m* level, height ■ **n. de vida** standard of living • **n. del mar** sea level.
no ➤ *adv* no ■ **¿cómo no?** of course, why not? • **no bebedor** nondrinker • **no bien** no sooner • **no más** no more, only; AMER., COLL. feel free to • **no obstante** nevertheless • **no sea que** in case, lest • **no vengo** I'm not coming ➤ *m* no.
noble ➤ *adj (aristocrático)* noble, aristocratic; *(elevado)* noble, honorable ➤ *mf* nobleman/woman.
noche ➤ *f* night, evening ■ **buenas noches** good evening, good night • **de la n. a la mañana** suddenly, overnight • **de n.** *or* **por la n.** at night, in the evening • **esta n.** tonight.
Nochebuena ➤ *f* Christmas Eve.
noción ➤ *f* notion, idea.
nocturno, a ➤ *adj* nocturnal, nightly; *(triste)* sad, melancholy.
nombrar ➤ *tr* to name, mention by name.
nombre ➤ *m* name; GRAM. noun ■ **de n.** by name • **n. y apellido** full name.
nordeste *or* **noreste** ➤ *m* northeast.
norma ➤ *f (modelo)* norm; *(regla)* rule.
normal ➤ *adj* normal, standard.
normalizar §02 ➤ *tr* to normalize; INDUS. to standardize.
noroeste ➤ *m* northwest.
norte ➤ *adj* northern, northerly ➤ *m* north.
Norteamérica ➤ *f* North America.
norteamericano, a ➤ *adj & mf* North American.
nos ➤ *pron* us; to, for, *or* from us ■ **n. vimos** we saw each other.
nosotros, as ➤ *pron* we, us.
nostalgia ➤ *f* nostalgia, homesickness.
nota ➤ *f* note, notation; *(reparo)* notice, heed; EDUC. grade, mark.
notable ➤ *adj* notable, noteworthy; *(superior)* outstanding, striking.
notar ➤ *tr* to note, point out; *(observar)* to notice ➤ *reflex* to see, notice.
notario, a ➤ *mf* notary, notary public.
noticia ➤ *f* news item ■ *pl* news ■ **n. de última hora** the latest news.
noticiero ➤ *m* news report.
notificar §47 ➤ *tr* to notify, inform.
novato, a ➤ *mf* COLL. beginner, novice.
novecientos, as ➤ *adj & m* nine hundred.
novedad ➤ *f* novelty, innovation; *(cambio)* change; *(noticia)* recent event.
novela ➤ *f* novel ■ **n. policíaca** detective story.
novelista ➤ *mf* novelist.
noveno, a ➤ *adj & m* ninth.
noventa ➤ *adj & m* ninety.
noviembre ➤ *m* November.
novillo, a ➤ *m* young bull ➤ *f* heifer, young cow.
novio, a ➤ *m* boyfriend; *(prometido)* fiancé; *(recién casado)* groom ■ *pl (casados)* newlyweds; *(prometidos)* engaged couple ➤ *f* girlfriend; *(prometida)* fiancée; *(recién casada)* bride.
nube ➤ *f* cloud.
nublado, a ➤ *adj* cloudy, overcast.
nublar ➤ *tr* to cloud, darken ➤ *reflex* to become cloudy *or* overcast.
nuca ➤ *f* nape (of the neck).
nuclear ➤ *adj* nuclear.
núcleo ➤ *m* nucleus; ELEC. core; BOT. kernel, pit; *(esencial)* core, essence.
nudillo ➤ *m* knuckle.
nudista ➤ *mf* nudist.
nudo ➤ *m* knot.
nuera ➤ *f* daughter-in-law.
nuestro, a ➤ *adj* our ➤ *pron* ours, of ours ■ **el n. es rojo** ours is red.
nueve ➤ *adj & m* nine ■ **las n.** nine o'clock.
nuevo, a ➤ *adj* new.
nuez ➤ *f* walnut; ANAT. Adam's apple
numeral ➤ *adj* numeral.
numerar ➤ *tr (foliar)* to number; *(contar)* to count, enumerate.
numérico, a ➤ *adj* numerical.
número ➤ *m* number; *(ejemplar)* issue, copy; *(medida)* size.
numeroso, a ➤ *adj* numerous.
nunca ➤ *adv* never, not ever ■ **más que n.** more than ever • **n. jamás** *or* **n. más** never again.
nutrición ➤ *f* nutrition.
nutrir ➤ *tr* to nourish, feed.
nutritivo, a ➤ *adj* nutritious, nutritive.

Ñ

ñame ➤ *m* yam.
ñoñería *or* **ñoñez** ➤ *f* foolishness, simplemindedness.
ñoño, a ➤ *adj & mf* COLL. *(apocado)* bashful (person); *(soso)* dull (person).

O

o ➤ *conj* or ■ **o . . . o** either . . . or • **o sea** that is to say.
oasis ➤ *m* oasis.
obedecer §09 ➤ *tr* to obey.
obediente ➤ *adj* obedient.
obeso, a ➤ *adj* obese.
obispo ➤ *m* bishop.
objetivo, a ➤ *adj & m* objective.
objeto ➤ *m* object, aim.
oblicuo, a ➤ *adj* oblique, slanting.
obligación ➤ *f* obligation.
obligar §31 ➤ *tr* to oblige, obligate; *(compeler)* to force, compel.
obligatorio, a ➤ *adj* obligatory.
oblongo, a ➤ *adj* oblong.
obra ➤ *f* work; *(acto)* act; *(construcción)* construction site ■ **o. maestra** masterpiece • **obras públicas** public works.
obrar ➤ *tr (madera, etc.)* to work ➤ *intr* to act, proceed.
obrero, a ➤ *adj* working ■ **sindicato o.** labor union ➤ *mf* worker.
obsceno, a ➤ *adj* obscene.
obscuro ➤ *adj var of* **oscuro**.
obsequio ➤ *m* gift, present.
observador, a ➤ *adj* observant ➤ *mf* observer.
observar ➤ *tr* to observe; *(espiar)* to watch; *(notar)* to notice; *(comentar)* to remark.
observatorio ➤ *m* observatory.
obsesión ➤ *f* obsession.
obstáculo ➤ *m* obstacle.
obstante ➤ *adj* ■ **no o.** nevertheless.
obstinado, a ➤ *adj* obstinate.
obstinarse ➤ *reflex* to be *or* become obstinate.
obstruir §10 ➤ *tr* to obstruct.
obtener §46 ➤ *tr* to obtain, get.
obvio, a ➤ *adj* obvious.
ocasión ➤ *f* occasion; *(oportunidad)* opportunity; *(circunstancia)* circumstance ■ **en ocasiones** sometimes.
ocasionar ➤ *tr* to cause.
occidental ➤ *adj* western.
occidente ➤ *m* west, occident.
océano ➤ *m* ocean; FIG. ocean, sea.
ochenta ➤ *adj & m* eighty.
ocho ➤ *adj & m* eight ■ **las o.** eight o'clock.
ocio ➤ *m (inactividad)* idleness, inactivity; *(tiempo libre)* leisure, free time.
octavo, a ➤ *adj & m* eighth.
octubre ➤ *m* October.
oculista ➤ *mf* optometrist.
ocultar ➤ *tr* to hide, conceal *(de* from).
ocupación ➤ *f* occupation.
ocupado, a ➤ *adj (teléfono, línea)* busy; *(territorio)* occupied; *(seat)* taken.
ocupante ➤ *adj* occupying ➤ *mf* occupant.
ocupar ➤ *tr* to occupy; *(emplear)* to employ, give work to ➤ *reflex* to occupy oneself; *(atender a)* to attend, pay attention *(de* to).
ocurrencia ➤ *f* witticism.
ocurrir ➤ *intr* to occur, happen ➤ *reflex* to occur to, strike.
odiar ➤ *tr* to hate, loathe.
odio ➤ *m* hatred, loathing.
odontología ➤ *f* dentistry.
oeste ➤ *adj* western, westerly ➤ *m* west.
ofender ➤ *tr* to offend, insult ➤ *reflex* to take offense.
ofensa ➤ *f* offense.
ofensivo, a ➤ *adj & f* offensive.
oferta ➤ *f* offer; COM. bid.
oficial ➤ *adj* official ➤ *mf* official, officer; *(obrero)* skilled worker.
oficina ➤ *f* office ■ **horas de o.** business hours.
oficinista ➤ *mf* clerk, office worker.
oficio ➤ *m (ocupación)* labor, work; *(artesanía)* trade, craft.
ofrecer §09 ➤ *tr* to offer ➤ *reflex* to offer oneself, volunteer.
ofrecimiento ➤ *m* offer, offering.
oftalmólogo, a ➤ *mf* ophthalmologist.
oído ➤ *m* hearing, sense of hearing; ANAT. ear.
oír §29 ➤ *tr* to hear ■ **¡oye!** *or* **¡oiga!** *(para llamar la atención)* listen!; *(para reprender)* look here!
ojal ➤ *m* buttonhole.
¡ojalá! ➤ *interj* would to God!, if only ■ **o. que . . .** I hope that . . . .
ojeada ➤ *f* glance, glimpse.
ojear ➤ *tr* to look at.
ojera ➤ *f* dark circle (under the eyes).
ojo ➤ *m* eye; *(agujero)* hole; *(de la cerradura)* keyhole ■ **abrir los ojos** to be on the alert • **¡ojo!** look out!
ola ➤ *f* wave.
oleaje ➤ *m (olas)* surf, waves; *(marejada)* swell.
óleo ➤ *m* oil ■ **pintura al ó.** oil painting.
oleoducto ➤ *m* oil pipeline.
oler §30 ➤ *tr* to smell ➤ *intr (tener olor)* to smell ■ **o. a** to smell of *or* like.
olfato ➤ *m* sense of smell.
olímpico, a ➤ *adj* Olympian, Olympic ■ **juegos olímpicos** Olympic Games.
oliva ➤ *adj & f* olive.
olivo ➤ *m* olive tree; *(color)* olive.
olla ➤ *f (vasija)* pot, kettle; *(cocido)* stew ■ **o. de presión** pressure cooker.
olor ➤ *m* smell.
oloroso, a ➤ *adj* perfumed, fragrant.
olvidar ➤ *tr & reflex (no recordar)* to forget; *(dejar)* to leave (behind) ■ **olvidarse de** to forget to.
ombligo ➤ *m* navel.
omisión ➤ *f* omission.
omitir ➤ *tr* to omit.
omóplato ➤ *m* shoulder blade.
once ➤ *adj & m* eleven ■ **las o.** eleven o'clock.
onda ➤ *f* wave.
ondulado, a ➤ *adj* wavy.
ondular ➤ *intr* to wave, undulate.
onza ➤ *f* ounce.
opaco, a ➤ *adj* opaque.
opcional ➤ *adj* optional.
ópera ➤ *f* opera.
operación ➤ *f* operation; FIN. transaction.
operador, a ➤ *adj* operating ➤ *mf* operator.
operar ➤ *intr* to operate; COM. to deal, do business ➤ *tr* to operate on.
opinar ➤ *intr (formar opinión)* to think, have an opinion; *(expresar la opinión)* to express an opinion.
opinión ➤ *f* opinion.
oponerse §37 ➤ *reflex* ■ **o. a** to oppose, object to; *(ser contrario)* to be in opposition to.
oporto ➤ *m* port (wine).
oportunidad ➤ *f* opportunity.
oportuno, a ➤ *adj* opportune, timely.
oposición ➤ *f* opposition.
opresión ➤ *f* oppression.
oprimir ➤ *tr (tiranizar)* to oppress, tyrannize; *(apretar)* to press, squeeze.
optativo, a ➤ *adj* optional.
óptico, a ➤ *adj* optical ➤ *m* optician.
optimista ➤ *adj* optimistic ➤ *mf* optimist.
óptimo, a ➤ *adj* optimal, best.
opuesto, a ➤ *adj (enfrente)* opposite; *(contrario)* opposing, contrary.
opulencia ➤ *f* opulence.
oración ➤ *f* RELIG. prayer; GRAM. *(frase)* sentence; *(cláusula)* clause.
orador, a ➤ *mf* orator.
oral ➤ *adj* oral.
orar ➤ *intr* to pray.
orden ➤ *m (disposición)* order ■ **o. del día** agenda • **poner en o.** to put in order ➤ *f (mandato)* order ■ **a la o. de** at the order of • **a sus ordenes** at your service.
ordenado, a ➤ *adj* orderly, methodical.
ordenador, a ➤ *m or f* computer.
ordenar ➤ *tr* put in order; *(arreglar)* to arrange; *(mandar)* to order.
ordeñar ➤ *tr* to milk.
ordinal ➤ *adj & m* ordinal.
ordinario, a ➤ *adj* ordinary, common.
oreja ➤ *f* ear.
orfanato ➤ *m* orphanage.
orfebrería ➤ *f* gold *or* silver work.
orgánico, a ➤ *adj* organic.
organismo ➤ *m* organism; *(organización)* organization, institution.
organización ➤ *f* organization.
organizar §02 ➤ *tr* to organize ➤ *reflex* to be organized.
órgano ➤ *m* organ.
orgullo ➤ *m (arrogancia)* arrogance, conceit; *(sentimiento legítimo)* pride.
orgulloso, a ➤ *adj* proud.

orientación ➤ *f* orientation; *(colocación)* positioning; *(consejo)* guidance, direction.
oriental ➤ *adj* oriental, eastern ➤ *mf* Oriental.
orientar ➤ *tr* to position; *(un edificio)* to orient; *(encaminar)* to guide.
oriente ➤ *m* east, orient.
orificio ➤ *m* orifice, opening.
origen ➤ *m* origin.
original ➤ *adj & m* original.
orilla ➤ *f (borde)* border, edge; *(del mar)* shore; *(de un río)* bank.
orinar ➤ *intr* to urinate.
orla TEX. border, hem.
ornamento ➤ *m* ornament, adornment; ARCHIT. ornamentation.
oro ➤ *m* gold ■ **chapado de o.** gold-plated.
orquesta ➤ *f* orchestra.
ortodoxo, a ➤ *adj* orthodox.
ortografía ➤ *f* orthography.
ortopédico, a ➤ *adj* orthopedic.
oruga ➤ *f* ENTOM. caterpillar.
os ➤ *pron* you; to, for, *or* from you.
osadía ➤ *f* boldness, audacity.
oscilar ➤ *intr* to oscillate.
oscurecer §09 ➤ *tr* to darken ➤ *intr* to be getting dark ➤ *reflex (nublarse)* to become cloudy *or* overcast.
oscuridad ➤ *f* darkness.
oscuro, a ➤ *adj* dark; *(desconocido)* obscure; *(nebuloso)* cloudy, overcast.
oso ➤ *m* bear ■ **o. gris** grizzly bear.
ostentación ➤ *f* ostentation.
ostra ➤ *f* oyster.
otoño ➤ *m* autumn, fall.
otorgar §31 ➤ *tr* to grant, give.
otro, a ➤ *adj* other, another ■ **o. vez** again • **por o. parte** on the other hand ➤ *pron* another one ■ **unos a otros** each other, one another ■ *pl* others.
ovación ➤ *f* ovation.
oval *or* **ovalado, a** ➤ *adj* oval.
oveja ➤ *f* ewe, female sheep.
ovillo ➤ *m (de hilo)* ball.
ovni ➤ *m* UFO.
oxidar ➤ *tr & reflex* to oxidize, rust.
óxido ➤ *m* oxide.
oxígeno ➤ *m* oxygen.
ozono ➤ *m* ozone.

P

pabellón ➤ *m (banderal)* flag, banner; *(edificio)* pavilion.
paciencia ➤ *f* patience.
paciente ➤ *adj & mf* patient.
pacificar §47 ➤ *tr* to pacify.
pacifista ➤ *adj & mf* pacifist.
pactar ➤ *tr* to agree to ➤ *intr* to come to an agreement, make a pact.
pacto ➤ *m* pact, agreement.
padecer §09 ➤ *tr & intr* to suffer ■ **p. del corazón** to have heart trouble.
padrastro ➤ *m* stepfather; *(pellejo)* hangnail.
padre ➤ *m* father ■ *pl* parents.
padrenuestro ➤ *m* Lord's Prayer.
padrino ➤ *m (de niño)* godfather; *(de boda)* best man ■ *pl* godparents.
padrón ➤ *m* census.
paella ➤ *f* dish of rice with meat or chicken.
paga ➤ *f (acción)* payment; *(sueldo)* wages.
pagar §31 ➤ *tr & intr* to pay; *(recompensar)* to repay ■ **p. a crédito** *or* **a plazos** to pay in installments • **p. por adelantado** to pay in advance.
pagaré ➤ *m* promissory note, IOU.
página ➤ *f* page.
pago ➤ *m (entrega)* payment; *(recompensa)* repayment, recompense.
país ➤ *m* country, nation.
paisaje ➤ *m* landscape.
paja ➤ *f* straw.
pájaro ➤ *m* bird.
pala ➤ *f (herramienta)* shovel, spade; *(del remo)* blade.
palabra ➤ *f* word; *(promesa)* word, promise ■ **bajo p.** on one's word of honor • **cumplir** *or* **mantener su p.** uno to keep one's word.
palabrota ➤ *f* COLL. swearword.
palacio ➤ *m* palace ■ **p. de justicia** courthouse.
paladear ➤ *tr* to savor, relish.
palanca ➤ *f* lever ■ **p. de cambio** gear-shift.
palco ➤ *m* THEAT. box.
paleta ➤ *f* small shovel; *(del pintor)* palette; *(del albañil)* trowel.
palidecer §09 ➤ *intr* to turn pale.
palidez ➤ *f* paleness, pallor.
pálido, a ➤ *adj* pale.
palillo ➤ *m (mondadientes)* toothpick; *(de tambor)* drumstick.
paliza ➤ *f* beating, thrashing.
palma ➤ *f (de la mano)* palm; *(palmera)* palm (tree).
palmada ➤ *f* slap, pat ■ **dar palmadas** to clap.
palmera ➤ *f* palm tree.
palmo ➤ *m* span ■ **p. a p.** little by little, inch by inch.
palo ➤ *m (vara)* stick, pole; *(mango)* stick, handle ■ **palos de golf** golf clubs.
paloma ➤ *f* dove, pigeon.
palomita ➤ *f* popcorn.
palpar ➤ *tr* to touch, feel.
palpitar ➤ *intr* to palpitate.
palurdo, a ➤ *adj* boorish ➤ *mf* boor.
pampa ➤ *f* pampa, plain.
pan ➤ *m* bread ■ **p. integral** whole-wheat bread.
pana ➤ *f* corduroy.
panadería ➤ *f* bakery.
panal ➤ *m* honeycomb.
pandilla ➤ *f* gang, band.
panecillo ➤ *m* roll, bun.
panfleto ➤ *m* pamphlet.
pánico, a ➤ *adj & m* panic.
panorama ➤ *m* panorama.
pantalla ➤ *f* CINEM., COMPUT. screen; *(de lámpara)* lamp shade.
pantalón *or* **pantalones** ➤ *m(pl)* pants ■ **p. corto** shorts • **p. vaquero** jeans.
pantano ➤ *m* marsh.
panteón ➤ *m* pantheon.
pantera ➤ *f* panther.
pantorrilla ➤ *f* ANAT. calf.
pantufla ➤ *f* slipper.
pañal ➤ *m* diaper.
paño ➤ *m (tela)* cloth; *(trapo)* rag.
pañuelo ➤ *m* handkerchief; *(pañoleta)* scarf.
papa[1] ➤ *m* Pope.
papa[2] ➤ *f* AMER. potato.
papá ➤ *m* papa, daddy.
papagayo ➤ *m* parrot.
papaya ➤ *f* papaya.
papel ➤ *m* paper; *(hoja)* piece of paper; THEAT. role ■ **p. de cartas** stationery • **p. de seda** tissue paper • **p. higiénico** toilet paper ■ *pl* papers, documents.
papelería ➤ *f* stationery store.
papera ➤ *pl* mumps.
papilla ➤ *f* soft food, pap.
paquete ➤ *m (bulto)* package; *(caja)* pack, packet.
par ➤ *adj (igual)* equal; MATH. even ➤ *m (dos)* couple; *(zapatos, etc.)* pair; MATH. even number ■ **al p. de** on the same level as • **a pares** *or* **en pares** in pairs, by twos • **de p. en p.** wide.
para ➤ *prep* for, to; *(con el propósito de)* in order to ■ **estoy p. salir** I'm about to leave • **p. mañana** for *or* by tomorrow • **p. que** so that • **¿p. qué?** why?, for what? • **p. siempre** forever • **un cuarto p. las** once a quarter to eleven.
parabrisas ➤ *m* windshield.
paracaídas ➤ *f* parachute.
parachoques ➤ *m* bumper, fender.
paradero ➤ *m* whereabouts.
parado, a ➤ *adj (inmóvil)* stationary; *(detenido)* stopped; *(inactivo)* idle; *(sin empleo)* unemployed; AMER. standing ■ **salir bien, mal p.** to come off well, badly ➤ *f* stop; *(suspensión)* halt ■ **p. de taxis** taxi stand.
parador ➤ *m* inn, roadhouse.
paraguas ➤ *m* umbrella.
paraguayo, a ➤ *adj & mf* Paraguayan.
paraíso ➤ *m* paradise.
paralelo ➤ *adj & m* parallel.
parálisis ➤ *f* paralysis ■ **p. cerebral** cerebral palsy.
paralizar §02 ➤ *tr* to paralyze ➤ *reflex* to become paralyzed.
parámetro ➤ *m* parameter.
parapeto ➤ *m* parapet.
parar ➤ *intr (cesar)* to stop ■ **ir a p.** to end up • **p. en** to end up, result in • **sin p.** nonstop ➤ *tr (detener)* to stop ➤ *reflex (detenerse)* to stop; AMER. to stand up ■ **p. a** to stop, pause (to).
parásito, a ➤ *adj* parasitic ➤ *m* parasite.
parcela ➤ *f* parcel, plot.
parche ➤ *m* patch.
parcial ➤ *adj* partial.
pardo, a ➤ *adj* brown.
parecer[1] ➤ *m* opinion.
parecer[2] §09 ➤ *intr* to seem; *(semejarse)* to resemble, seem like ■ **al p.** apparently • **así parece** so it seems ➤ *reflex* to look alike ■ **p. a** to look like.
parecido, a ➤ *adj* similar ■ **ser p. a** to resemble, be like ➤ *m* similarity.
pared ➤ *f* wall.
parentesco ➤ *m* kinship; *(lazo)* tie.
paréntesis ➤ *m* parenthesis ■ **entre p.** in parentheses.
pariente, a ➤ *mf* relative, relation.
parir ➤ *intr & tr* to give birth (to).
parlamento ➤ *m* parliament.
paro ➤ *m* stoppage, standstill; COM. unemployment ■ **p. laboral** strike.
parpadear ➤ *intr (párpados)* to blink; *(luz)* to flicker.
párpado ➤ *m* eyelid.
parque ➤ *m* park; AUTO. parking lot ■ **p. de atracciones** amusement park.
parquear ➤ *tr* AMER. to park.
parra ➤ *f* grapevine.
párrafo ➤ *m* paragraph.
parrilla ➤ *f* grill.
parrillada ➤ *f* CUL. grilled seafood.
párroco ➤ *m* parish priest.
parroquia ➤ *f* parish.
parte ➤ *f* part; *(porción)* portion; *(cantidad asignada)* share; *(sitio)* place, spot ■ **de p. de** on behalf of • **¿de p. de quién?** who's calling? • **en alguna p.** somewhere • **en cualquier p.** anywhere • **en gran p.** for the most part • **en ninguna p.** nowhere • **en** *or* **por todas partes** everywhere • **la mayor p.** the majority • **p. por p.** bit by bit • **por mi p.** as far as I am concerned • **por otra p.** on the other hand.
participación ➤ *f* participation.
participar ➤ *tr* to inform ➤ *intr* to participate, take part ■ **p. en** to share in.
participio ➤ *m* participle.
particular ➤ *adj (privado)* private; *(especial)* particular, special ➤ *mf* individual; *(asunto)* matter, point.
partidario, a ➤ *adj & mf* partisan.
partido, a ➤ *adj* divided ➤ *m* POL. party; SPORT. game ■ **sacar p. de** to benefit from ➤ *f* departure ■ **p. de matrimonio** marriage certificate.
partir ➤ *tr (dividir)* to divide, split; *(romper)* to break, crack open ➤ *intr* to leave ■ **a p. de** as of, starting from.
parto ➤ *m* childbirth, delivery.
pasa ➤ *f* raisin ■ **p. de Corinto** currant.
pasadizo ➤ *m* passage.
pasado, a ➤ *adj* past, gone by; *(anterior)* last ■ **p. de moda** old-fashioned • **p. mañana** day after tomorrow ➤ *m* past.
pasaje ➤ *m* passage.
pasajero, a ➤ *adj* passing, fleeting ➤ *mf* passenger, traveler.
pasamano ➤ *m* handrail.
pasaporte ➤ *m* passport.
pasar ➤ *tr* to pass, hand; *(atravesar)* to cross; *(ir más allá)* to go beyond; *(disfrutar)* to spend, pass; *(sufrir)* to suffer, undergo; *(aprobar)* to pass ■ **p. lista** to call roll • **pasarla bien, mal** to have a good, bad time ➤ *intr* to pass, go by; *(entrar)* to come in; *(ocurrir)* to happen, occur ■ **p. de** *(exceder)* to exceed, surpass; *(edad)* to be over • **p. de moda** to go out of fashion • **p. por** to stop by ➤ *reflex (olvidarse)* to forget; *(deslizar)* to run; *(excederse)* to go too far.
pasarela ➤ *f (puentecillo)* footbridge; *(de desfile de modas)* runway.
pasatiempo ➤ *m* pastime.
Pascua ➤ *f* Easter ■ *pl* Christmastime.
pasear ➤ *intr* to go for a walk ➤ *tr* to take for a walk.
paseo ➤ *m (caminata)* stroll; *(a caballo, coche)* ride; *(avenida)* avenue ■ **dar un p.** *(andar)* to go for a walk; *(en coche)* to go for a ride.
pasillo ➤ *m* corridor, hall(way).
pasión ➤ *f* passion.
pasivo, a ➤ *adj* passive.
paso ➤ *m* step; EQUIT. gait; *(camino)* passage; GEOG. pass; *(pisada)* footstep; *(en el baile)* step ■ **abrir p. a** to make way for • **aflojar el p.** to slow down • **apretar el p.** to go faster • **a pocos pasos** at a short distance • **ceder el p.** to step aside • **p. de peatones** cross-walk • **p. por p.** step by step.
pasta ➤ *f* paste ■ **p. de dientes** tooth-paste ■ *pl* noodles, pasta.
pastel ➤ *m* CUL. *(dulce)* cake; *(de carne, queso)* pie.
pastelería ➤ *f* pastry shop.
pastilla ➤ *f (de jabón)* bar, cake; MED. lozenge, drop; *(de menta)* mint.
pastor ➤ *m* pastor; *(ovejero)* shepherd.
pata ➤ *f* ZOOL. *(pie)* paw, foot; *(pierna)* leg ■ **meter la p.** to put one's foot in it • **tener mala p.** to be unlucky.
patada ➤ *f* kick.
patalear ➤ *intr (pisar)* to stamp, stomp.
patata ➤ *f* potato.
patente ➤ *adj & f* patent.
paternal ➤ *adj* paternal.
patín ➤ *m* skate ■ **p. de hielo** ice skate • **p. de ruedas** roller skate.
patinaje ➤ *m* skating ■ **p. sobre hielo** ice skating • **p. sobre ruedas** roller skating.
patinar ➤ *intr* to skate; *(un vehículo)* to skid; *(resbalar voluntariamente)* to slide; *(resbalar sin querer)* to slip.
patinazo ➤ *m* skid.
patio ➤ *m* patio, courtyard.
pato ➤ *m* duck.
patria ➤ *f* homeland ■ **madre p.** motherland.
patrimonio ➤ *m* patrimony, heritage.
patriota ➤ *mf* patriot.
patriótico, a ➤ *adj* patriotic.
patrocinar ➤ *tr* to sponsor, patronize.
patrón, ona ➤ *mf* RELIG. patron saint; *(jefe)* boss ➤ *m (modelo)* pattern; *(unidad)* standard.
patrono, a ➤ *mf (jefe)* boss; *(empresario)* employer.
patrulla ➤ *f* squad, patrol.
paulatino, a ➤ *adj* gradual.
pausa ➤ *f* pause, break.
pavimento ➤ *m* pavement.
pavo ➤ *m* turkey ■ **p. real** peacock.
pavor ➤ *m* fright, terror.
payaso ➤ *m* clown, buffoon.
paz ➤ *f* peace; *(calma)* peacefulness.
peaje ➤ *m* toll.
peatón, ona ➤ *mf* pedestrian.
peca ➤ *f* freckle.
pecado ➤ *m* sin.
pecar ➤ *intr* to sin.
pecera ➤ *f* fishbowl, aquarium.
pecho ➤ *m* chest; *(busto)* breast; *(seno)* bosom, breast.
pechuga ➤ *f (del ave)* breast.
peculiar ➤ *adj* peculiar.
pedagogía ➤ *f* pedagogy.
pedal ➤ *m* (foot) pedal.
pedazo ➤ *m* piece ■ **a pedazos** in pieces.
pediatra ➤ *mf* pediatrician.
pediatría ➤ *f* pediatrics.
pedido ➤ *m* order, request ■ **hacer un p.** to place an order.
pedir §32 ➤ *tr* to ask, request; *(demandar)* to demand; *(mendigar)* to beg; *(comida, etc.)* to order ■ **p. prestado** to borrow.
pega ➤ *f* gluing, sticking; FIG. snag.
pegajoso, a ➤ *adj* adhesive, sticky.
pegamento ➤ *m* glue, adhesive.
pegar §31 ➤ *tr* to glue; *(golpear)* to hit ■ **no p. un ojo** not to sleep a wink • **p. un susto** to frighten ➤ *intr (adherir)* to adhere, stick; *(golpear)* to hit; *(armonizar)* to go together ➤ *reflex* CUL. *(quemarse)* to stick to the pan.
peinado ➤ *m* hair style.
peinar ➤ *tr* to comb ➤ *reflex* to comb one's hair.
peine ➤ *m* comb.
pelado, a ➤ *adj (con el pelo cortado)* shorn; *(frutos)* peeled; *(pobre)* broke ➤ *m* haircut; *(esquileo)* shearing; *(pobre)* pauper ➤ *f* crew cut.
pelar ➤ *tr (pelo)* to cut; *(fruto)* to peel.
peldaño ➤ *m* step, stair; *(de escala)* rung.
pelea ➤ *f* fight.
pelear ➤ *intr* to fight, quarrel.
peletería ➤ *f* fur shop; *(pieles)* furs.
película ➤ *f* film; CINEM. movie, film ■ **de p.** COLL. fabulous.
peligro ➤ *m* danger.
peligroso, a ➤ *adj* dangerous.
pelirrojo, a ➤ *adj* red-haired, red-headed ➤ *mf* redhead.
pellejo ➤ *m (de animal)* hide; *(piel)* skin ■ **jugarse el p.** to risk one's neck.
pellizcar ➤ *tr* to pinch.
pellizco ➤ *m* pinch.
pelmazo ➤ *mf* COLL. bore.
pelo ➤ *m (cabello)* hair; ZOOL. *(piel)* fur, coat; *(del tejido)* nap ■ **por los pelos** by the skin of one's teeth • **tomar a alguien el p.** to pull someone's leg.
pelota ➤ *f* ball.
peluca ➤ *f* wig.
peluche ➤ *f* plush.
peludo, a ➤ *adj* hairy, shaggy.

peluquería ➤ *f (para hombres)* barber shop; *(para mujeres)* beauty parlor.
peluquero, a ➤ *mf* hairdresser; *(para hombres)* barber.
pena ➤ *f (castigo)* punishment; *(aflicción)* sorrow ▪ **dar p.** to grieve • **p. de muerte** death penalty • **¡qué p.!** what a shame! • **valer la p.** to be worthwhile.
pendiente ➤ *adj (colgante)* hanging; *(sin solucionar)* pending ➤ *m (arete)* earring ➤ *f (cuesta)* slope.
penetrante ➤ *adj (que penetra)* penetrating; *(inteligencia)* acute; *(voz, mirada)* piercing; *(frío)* biting.
penetrar ➤ *tr & intr* to penetrate.
penicilina ➤ *f* penicillin.
península ➤ *f* peninsula.
pensamiento ➤ *m* thought; *(idea)* idea.
pensar §33 ➤ *tr (considerar)* to think about, consider; *(creer)* to think, believe; *(planear)* to intend ➤ *intr* to think ▪ **p. en** *or* **sobre** to think about.
pensativo, a ➤ *adj* pensive.
pensión ➤ *f (en un hotel)* room and board; *(de retiro)* pension; *(casa)* boarding house.
penúltimo, a ➤ *adj & mf* penultimate.
penumbra ➤ *f* shadow; PHYS. penumbra.
peña ➤ *f (roca)* boulder; *(círculo)* group.
peñón ➤ *m* craggy rock.
peón ➤ *m* unskilled laborer; *(de ajedrez)* pawn.
peor ➤ *adj* worse, worst ▪ **cada vez p.** worse and worse ➤ *adv* worse ▪ **p. que p.** *or* **tanto p.** worse still ➤ *mf* worse, worst ▪ **lo p.** the worst thing.
pepino ➤ *m* cucumber.
pequeño, a ➤ *adj* small; *(corto)* short; *(joven)* young ➤ *mf* child ▪ **de p.** as a child.
pera ➤ *f* pear.
percance ➤ *m* mishap.
percha ➤ *f* hanger, coat hanger.
percibir ➤ *tr (distinguir)* to perceive, sense; *(cobrar)* to collect, receive.
percusión ➤ *f* percussion.
perder §34 ➤ *tr* to lose; *(desperdiciar)* to miss ▪ **echar a p.** to spoil • **p. de vista** to lose sight of ➤ *intr* to lose ➤ *reflex* to lose, mislay; *(desorientarse)* to get lost; *(dejar de ser útil)* to go to waste; *(arruinarse)* to go astray ▪ **p. de vista** to disappear.
pérdida ➤ *f* loss, waste ▪ **pérdidas y ganancias** profit and loss.
perdiz ➤ *f* partridge.
perdón ➤ *m* pardon ▪ **¡p.!** sorry!
perdonar ➤ *tr* to pardon, forgive; *(la vida)* to spare.
perecer §09 ➤ *intr* to perish, die.
peregrinación ➤ *f* pilgrimage.
peregrino, a ➤ *mf* pilgrim.
perejil ➤ *m* parsley.
perenne ➤ *adj* perennial.
pereza ➤ *f* laziness.
perezoso, a ➤ *adj & mf* lazy (person).
perfección ➤ *f* perfection.
perfeccionar ➤ *tr (hacer perfecto)* to make perfect; *(mejorar)* to improve.
perfeccionista ➤ *adj & mf* perfectionist.
perfectamente ➤ *adv* perfectly ▪ **¡p.!** right!
perfecto, a ➤ *adj* perfect.
perfil ➤ *m* profile; *(contorno)* outline ▪ **de p.** in profile.
perforar ➤ *tr* to perforate.
perfumar ➤ *tr* to perfume.
perfume ➤ *m* perfume; *(aroma)* fragrance.
pericia ➤ *f* skill, expertise.
periferia ➤ *f* periphery.
periódico, a ➤ *adj* periodic(al) ➤ *m* newspaper.
periodismo ➤ *m* journalism.
periodista ➤ *mf* journalist.
periquito ➤ *m* parakeet.
perjudicar §47 ➤ *tr* to damage, harm.
perjudicial ➤ *adj* harmful, detrimental.
perjuicio ➤ *m (material)* damage; *(moral)* injury; FIN. loss.
perla ➤ *f* pearl.
permanecer §09 ➤ *intr* to stay, remain.
permanente ➤ *adj* permanent ➤ *f* permanent wave.
permiso ➤ *m* permission; *(documento)* permit ▪ **con (su) p.** excuse me • **p. de conducir** driver's license.
permitir ➤ *tr* to permit, let ▪ **permítame** allow me ➤ *reflex* to be permitted *or* allowed.
pero ➤ *conj* but.
perpendicular ➤ *adj & f* perpendicular.
perpetuo, a ➤ *adj* perpetual.
perplejo, a ➤ *adj* perplexed.
perro, a ➤ *mf* dog ➤ *f* bitch.
persecución ➤ *f (tormento)* persecution; *(seguimiento)* pursuit, chase.
perseguir §42 ➤ *tr (seguir)* to pursue, chase; *(acosar)* to persecute.
persiana ➤ *f* blind, shade.
persistir ➤ *intr* to persist.
persona ➤ *f* person ▪ **por p.** per person, each.
personaje ➤ *m* celebrity; LIT. character.
personal ➤ *adj* personal ➤ *m* personnel, staff.
perspectiva ➤ *f* perspective; *(vista)* view.
perspicaz ➤ *adj* sharp, keen; *(sagaz)* shrewd.
persuadir ➤ *tr* to persuade.
persuasión ➤ *f* persuasion.
pertenecer §09 ➤ *intr* to belong (*a* to).
pertinaz ➤ *adj* obstinate, tenacious.
perturbación ➤ *f* disturbance.
peruano, a ➤ *adj & mf* Peruvian.
perverso, a ➤ *adj* wicked.
pervertir §43 ➤ *tr* to pervert.
pesa ➤ *f* weight ▪ *pl* dumbbells, weights.
pesadilla ➤ *f* nightmare.
pesado, a ➤ *adj* heavy; *(molesto)* annoying; *(fatigante)* tedious.
pésame ➤ *m* condolence ▪ **dar el p.** to express condolences.
pesar[1] ➤ *m (pena)* sorrow; *(arrepentimiento)* regret ▪ **a p. de** in spite of, despite • **a p. de uno** against one's will.
pesar[2] ➤ *tr* to weigh; FIG. to weigh, consider ➤ *intr (tener peso)* to weigh; *(ser pesado)* to weigh a lot; *(ser importante)* to carry weight ▪ **pese a quien le pese** say what they will.
pesca ➤ *f* fishing.
pescadería ➤ *f* fish market.
pescado ➤ *m* CUL. fish.
pescador, a ➤ *mf* fisherman/woman.
pescar §47 ➤ *tr* to fish (for).
pescuezo ➤ *m (de animal)* neck.
peseta ➤ *f* FIN. peseta.
pesimista ➤ *adj* pessimistic ➤ *mf* pessimist.
pésimo, a ➤ *adj* very bad, terrible.
peso ➤ *m* weight; FIN. peso.
pestaña ➤ *f* eyelash.
peste ➤ *f* plague; *(olor)* stench.
pétalo ➤ *m* petal.
petición ➤ *f* petition.
petróleo ➤ *m* petroleum, oil.
petrolero ➤ *m* oil tanker.
pez ➤ *m* ZOOL. fish.
pezón ➤ *m* nipple.
pezuña ➤ *f* hoof.
piadoso, a ➤ *adj* pious.
pianista ➤ *mf* pianist.
piano ➤ *m* piano.
picadillo ➤ *m* chopped meat.
picador ➤ *m* TAUR. picador.
picadura ➤ *f* bite.
picante ➤ *adj* spicy; *(chiste)* risqué.
picaporte ➤ *m (barrita)* latch; *(aldaba)* doorknocker.
picar §47 ➤ *tr (morder)* to bite; *(comer)* to nibble; *(quemar)* to sting; *(cortar)* to mince; *(estimular)* to arouse, pique ➤ *intr (escocer)* to itch; *(morder)* to sting; *(calentar)* to be hot ➤ *reflex (fruto)* to rot; *(vino)* to turn sour; *(irritarse)* to get annoyed.
picarón, ona ➤ *adj* COLL. mischievous ➤ *mf* COLL. rascal.
pico ➤ *m (de aves)* beak; *(punta)* tip; *(herramienta)* pick; *(cima)* peak ▪ **veinte dólares y p.** twenty-odd dollars • **son las ocho y p.** it is a little after eight.
pie ➤ *m* foot; *(base)* base, stand ▪ **al p. de la letra** to the letter • **a p.** on foot • **de p.** upright.
piedad ➤ *f* piety; *(lástima)* pity.
piedra ➤ *f (peña)* stone, rock; *(granizo)* hailstone.
piel ➤ *f* skin; *(con pelo)* fur, pelt; *(cuero)* leather; BOT. peel ▪ **de p.** *(de cuero)* leather; *(abrigo)* fur (coat) ▪ **p. de gallina** goose bumps.
pienso ➤ *m* fodder.
pierna ➤ *f* leg.
pieza ➤ *f* piece; *(de maquinaria)* part; *(habitación)* room ▪ **de una p.** solid • **p. de repuesto** spare part.
pijama *or* **piyama** ➤ *m* pajamas.
pila ➤ *f (recipiente)* basin; *(de cocina)* sink; *(montón)* pile; ELEC. battery ▪ **nombre de p.** Christian name.
píldora ➤ *f* pill.
pillar ➤ *tr* to catch, get caught.
pilotar *or* **pilotear** ➤ *tr* to pilot.
piloto ➤ *mf* pilot; AUTO. driver ➤ *m (llama)* pilot light ➤ *adj* pilot, model.
pimentón ➤ *m* paprika.
pimienta ➤ *f (especia)* pepper ▪ **p. negra** black pepper.
pimiento ➤ *m* BOT. (bell) pepper; *(pimentón)* paprika ▪ **p. verde** green pepper.
pinar ➤ *m* pine grove.
pincel ➤ *m* brush.
pinchar ➤ *tr* to puncture; FIG. to annoy.
pinchazo ➤ *m* puncture.
pingüino ➤ *m* penguin.
pino ➤ *m* pine (tree).
pintar ➤ *tr* to paint; *(describir)* to depict ➤ *intr* to paint ➤ *reflex* to put on make-up.
pinto, a ➤ *adj* speckled ➤ *f (mancha)* spot; COLL. *(aspecto)* look; *(medida)* pint ▪ **tener p. de** COLL. to look like.
pintor, a ➤ *mf* painter.
pintoresco, a ➤ *adj* picturesque.
pintura ➤ *f* painting; *(color)* paint.
pinza ➤ *f (de langosta)* claw ▪ *pl (tenacillas)* tweezers; *(tenazas)* tongs.
piña ➤ *f (del pino)* pine cone; *(ananás)* pineapple.
piñón ➤ *m* pine nut.
piojo ➤ *m* louse.
pionero, a ➤ *mf & adj* pioneer.
pipa[1] ➤ *f (para fumar)* pipe.
pipa[2] ➤ *f* pip, seed.
pirámide ➤ *f* pyramid.
piraña ➤ *f* AMER. piranha.
pirata ➤ *mf & adj* pirate; COMPUT. hacker ▪ **p. aéreo** hijacker.
pisada ➤ *f (acción)* step, footstep; *(huella)* footprint.
pisapapeles ➤ *m* paperweight.
pisar ➤ *tr* to step *or* walk on.
piscina ➤ *f* swimming pool.
piso ➤ *m (suelo)* ground; *(de una habitación)* floor; *(planta)* floor, story.
pisotear ➤ *tr* to trample.
pisotón ➤ *m* ▪ **dar un p.** to step on someone's foot.
pista ➤ *f (huella)* trail; SPORT. racetrack; AER. runway; *(indicio)* clue.
pistacho ➤ *m* pistachio (nut).
pistola ➤ *f* pistol.
pitar ➤ *intr* to blow a whistle, whistle.
pitillo ➤ *m* cigarette.
pito ➤ *m* whistle.
pizarra ➤ *f (roca)* slate; *(pizarrón)* blackboard ▪ **p. electrónica** COMPUT. bulletin board.
pizca ➤ *f* pinch ▪ **ni p.** not (at all).
placa ➤ *f* plaque; *(chapa)* plate; COMPUT. chip ▪ **p. de circultos** COMPUT. circuit board • **p. de matrícula** license plate.
placer ➤ *m* pleasure.
plaga ➤ *f* plague; BOT. blight.
plagio ➤ *m* plagiarism.
plan ➤ *m* plan; *(proyecto)* project; *(programa)* program ▪ **p. de estudios** curriculum, course of study.
plana ➤ *f (página)* page ▪ **de primera p.** front-page (news).
plancha ➤ *f (lámina)* sheet; *(utensilio)* iron ▪ **a la p.** grilled.
planchar ➤ *tr* to iron (clothes).
planeador ➤ *m* glider.
planeta ➤ *m* planet.
planetario, a ➤ *adj* planetary ➤ *m* planetarium.
planicie ➤ *f* GEOG. plain.
planificación ➤ *f* planning.
planilla ➤ *f* AMER. *(formulario)* form.
plano, a ➤ *adj (llano)* level, even; *(chato)* flat ➤ *m* map chart.
planta ➤ *f* plant; *(del pie)* sole; *(piso)* floor ▪ **p. baja** ground floor, first floor.
plantar ➤ *tr* to plant, sow; *(colocar)* to put ➤ *reflex* to stand firm.
plantear ➤ *tr* to expound; *(planear)* to outline; *(proponer)* to propose.
plantilla ➤ *f* insole.
plástico, a ➤ *adj & m* plastic.
plata ➤ *f* silver; AMER. money.
plataforma ➤ *f* platform.
plátano ➤ *m* banana; *(grande)* plantain.
platea ➤ *f* orchestra seat *or* section.
platillo ➤ *m* saucer ▪ **p. volador** flying saucer.
plato ➤ *m* plate, dish; CUL. course.
playa ➤ *f* beach.
plaza ➤ *f* plaza, square; *(mercado)* marketplace; *(sitio)* place; *(empleo)* position ▪ **p. de toros** bullring.
plazo ➤ *m (término)* term, period; *(pago)* installment ▪ **a corto p.** short-term • **a largo p.** long-term • **comprar a plazos** to buy on credit.
plegable ➤ *adj* folding.
plegar §35 ➤ *tr* to pleat; *(doblar)* to fold.
pleito ➤ *m* lawsuit; *(disputa)* quarrel.
pleno, a ➤ *adj* full ▪ **en p. día** in broad daylight ➤ *m* joint session.
pliegue ➤ *m* fold; SEW. pleat.
plomero ➤ *m* AMER. plumber.
plomo ➤ *m* lead; ELEC. fuse ▪ **a p.** plumb.
pluma ➤ *f* feather; *(estilográfica)* pen.
población ➤ *f* population; *(lugar)* locality; *(ciudad)* city; *(pueblo)* town.
poblado ➤ *m (habitantes)* population; *(ciudad)* city; *(pueblo)* town.
pobre ➤ *adj* poor; *(necesitado)* needy ➤ *mf* poor person, pauper.
pobreza ➤ *f* poverty; *(escasez)* lack.
pocillo ➤ *m* cup.
poco, a ➤ *adj* little ▪ **p. tiempo** short while ▪ *pl* few • **pocas veces** not very often, rarely ➤ *m* little ▪ **dentro de p.** soon • **un p. de** a little, some ▪ *pl* few ➤ *adv (con escasez)* little, not much; *(en corta duración)* not long; *(no muy)* not very ▪ **falta p. para** it will not be long before • **hace p.** a short time ago • **p. a p.** little by little • **p. después** a little after • **por p.** almost.
poder[1] ➤ *m* power.
poder[2] §36 ➤ *tr* to be able to ➤ *intr* to be able ▪ **puede que . . .** it is possible that . . . • **¿puedes ir?** can you go?
poderoso, a ➤ *adj* powerful.
podrido, a ➤ *adj* rotten.
podrir ➤ *tr & reflex* to rot, putrefy.
poema ➤ *m* poem.
poesía ➤ *f* poetry.
poeta ➤ *mf* poet.
polea ➤ *f* pulley.
polémico, a ➤ *adj* polemic(al).
polen ➤ *m* pollen.
policía ➤ *f* police (force) ➤ *m* policeman ➤ *f* policewoman.
polilla ➤ *f* moth.
politécnico, a ➤ *adj* polytechnic.
político, a ➤ *adj* political; *(de parentesco)* -in-law ➤ *mf* politician ➤ *f* politics; *(modo de obrar)* policy.
póliza ➤ *f (de seguros)* insurance policy; *(contrato)* contract; *(sello)* stamp.
pollo ➤ *m* chicken; *(cría)* chick.
polo ➤ *m* pole ▪ **p. sur** South Pole • **p. norte** North Pole.
polución ➤ *f* pollution.
polvo ➤ *m* dust; *(substancia pulverizada)* powder ▪ **en. p.** powdered.
polvoriento, a ➤ *adj* dusty.
pomelo ➤ *m* grapefruit.
pómulo ➤ *m* cheekbone.
ponche ➤ *m* punch.
ponchera ➤ *f* punch bowl.
poner §37 ➤ *tr* to put, place; *(disponer)* to set; *(instalar)* to set up; *(nombrar)* to give; ORNIT. to lay (an egg); THEAT. to put on; *(imponer)* to levy; *(causar)* to cause to be, put ▪ **p. al día** to bring up to date • **p. en venta** to put up for sale • **p. la mesa** to set the table • **p. por escrito** to put in writing ➤ *reflex (colocarse)* to put *or* place oneself; *(vestirse)* to put on; ASTRON. to set; *(dedicarse)* to apply oneself ▪ **p. a** to begin to • **p. de acuerdo** to reach an agreement • **p. de pie** to stand up • **p. en camino** to set out.
poniente ➤ *m* west.
popa ➤ *f* stern.
popular ➤ *adj* popular, well-liked; *(música)* folk.
popularidad ➤ *f* popularity.
póquer ➤ *m* poker.
por ➤ *prep* for, by ▪ **caminar p. la calle** to walk along the street • **entrar p.** to enter through • **enviar p.** to send by • **escrito p.** written by • **extenderse p.** to extend throughout • **hacerlo p. necesidad** to do it out of necessity • **pasar p. el café** to pass by the cafe • **p. acá** *or* **aquí** around here • **p. ahí** *or* **allí** around there • **p. ciento** per cent • **p. cierto** indeed • **p. completo** completely • **p. correo** by mail • **p. desgracia** unfortunately • **¡p. Dios!** for Heaven's sake! • **p. eso** therefore • **p. la noche** at night • **p. la tarde** in the after-

noon • **p. lo bajo** softly • **p. lo menos** at least • **p. lo tanto** therefore • **p. medio de** through • **p. otra parte** *or* **p. lo demás** on the other hand • **¿p. qué?** why? • **p. si acaso** in case • **p. sí mismo** by oneself • **p. supuesto** of course • **p. todos lados** everywhere • **p. valor de** in the amount of.

porcelana ➤ *f* porcelain.

porcentaje ➤ *m* percentage.

porción ➤ *f* portion.

pormenor ➤ *m* detail, particular.

pornográfico, a ➤ *adj* pornographic.

poro ➤ *m* interstice; BIOL. pore.

porque ➤ *conj* because.

porqué ➤ *m* reason (*de* for), cause.

porquería ➤ *f* filth; *(basura)* garbage.

porra ➤ *f* club.

porrazo ➤ *m (golpe)* blow; *(choque)* bump.

portaaviones ➤ *m* aircraft carrier.

portada ➤ *f* title page; *(tapa)* cover.

portaequipajes ➤ *m* AUTO. trunk; *(rejilla)* luggage rack.

portal ➤ *m* entrance hall; *(porche)* porch.

portarse ➤ *reflex* to behave.

portátil ➤ *adj* portable ➤ *m* laptop (computer).

portavoz ➤ *mf* spokesman/woman.

portazo ➤ *m (de puerta)* slam ■ **dar un p.** to slam the door.

portería ➤ *f* concierge's office; SPORT. goal.

portero, a ➤ *mf* concierge; *(de vivienda)* janitor; SPORT. goalkeeper.

pórtico ➤ *m* portico.

porvenir ➤ *m* future.

posada ➤ *f* inn.

posar ➤ *intr* to pose ➤ *reflex (las aves)* to perch ➤ *tr* to put, lay.

posdata ➤ *f* postscript.

poseer §31 ➤ *tr* to possess.

posesión ➤ *f* possession.

posibilidad ➤ *f* possibility ■ *pl* chances.

posible ➤ *adj* possible ■ **hacer (todo) lo p.** to do everything possible • **lo antes p.** as soon as possible.

posición ➤ *f* position.

positivo, a ➤ *adj* positive.

posponer §37 ➤ *tr (poner detrás)* to put behind; *(diferir)* to postpone.

postal ➤ *adj* postal ■ **giro p.** money order ➤ *f* postcard.

poste ➤ *m* post ■ **p. indicador** signpost.

posterior ➤ *adj (ulterior)* subsequent (*a* to), later; *(trasero)* rear, back.

posteriormente ➤ *adv* later (on).

postigo ➤ *m (contraventana)* shutter; *(de ciudad)* side gate.

postizo, a ➤ *adj* false; *(de quitapón)* detachable ■ **brazo p.** artificial arm.

postre ➤ *m* dessert.

póstumo, a ➤ *adj* posthumous.

postura ➤ *f* posture; *(posición)* position.

potable ➤ *adj* potable, drinkable.

potaje ➤ *m* stew.

potencia ➤ *f* power ■ **p. mundial** world power.

potente ➤ *adj* powerful.

potro ➤ *m* colt; SPORT. horse.

pozo ➤ *m* well; *(hoyo)* pit.

practicar §47 ➤ *tr* to practice; *(hacer)* to perform, carry out.

práctico, a ➤ *adj* practical; *(conveniente)* useful ➤ *m* MARIT. pilot ➤ *f* practice; *(experiencia)* experience.

prado ➤ *m* meadow.

pragmático, a ➤ *adj* pragmatic.

preámbulo ➤ *m (prólogo)* preamble; *(rodeo)* digression.

precario, a ➤ *adj* precarious.

precaución ➤ *f* precaution; *(prudencia)* caution ■ **por p.** as a precaution.

precavido, a ➤ *adj* cautious.

precedente ➤ *adj* preceding ➤ *m* precedent ■ **sentar un p.** to set a precedent.

precepto ➤ *m* precept.

precio ➤ *m* price, cost.

precioso, a ➤ *adj (de valor)* precious, valuable; *(lindo)* lovely.

precipicio ➤ *m* precipice, cliff.

precipitación ➤ *f* precipitation.

precipitar ➤ *tr (lanzar)* to hurl; *(apresurar)* to hasten ➤ *reflex* to hurry; *(lanzarse)* to rush headlong.

precisamente ➤ *adv* precisely.

precisar ➤ *tr (explicar)* to explain; *(fijar)* to set; *(necesitar)* to need.

precisión ➤ *f* precision.

preciso, a ➤ *adj* necessary; *(fijo)* precise; *(exacto)* exact; *(claro)* distinct.

precoz ➤ *adj* precocious.

predecir ➤ *tr* to predict.

predicado ➤ *m* GRAM., LOG. predicate.

predicar §47 ➤ *tr* to preach.

predicción ➤ *f* prediction.

predilecto, a ➤ *adj* favorite.

predisponer §37 ➤ *tr* to predispose.

predominar ➤ *intr* to prevail.

preescolar ➤ *adj* preschool.

preferencia ➤ *f* preference.

preferible ➤ *adj* preferable.

preferir §43 ➤ *tr* to prefer.

prefijo ➤ *m* prefix; TELEC. area code.

pregunta ➤ *f* question ■ **hacer una p.** to ask a question.

preguntar ➤ *tr* to ask ■ **p. por** *(noticias)* to inquire about; *(persona)* to ask for ➤ *reflex* to wonder.

prehistórico, a ➤ *adj* prehistoric.

prejuicio ➤ *m* prejudice.

preliminar ➤ *adj & m* preliminary.

prematuro, a ➤ *adj* premature.

premeditado, a ➤ *adj* premeditated.

premiar ➤ *tr (recompensar)* to reward; *(en certamen)* to award a prize to.

premio ➤ *m (recompensa)* reward; *(en certamen)* prize; COM., FIN. premium.

prenatal ➤ *adj* prenatal.

prenda ➤ *f* article of clothing.

prendedor ➤ *m* clasp; JEWEL. pin.

prender ➤ *tr (clavar)* to fasten; AMER. *(con fuego)* to light; *(un aparato)* to turn *or* switch on ■ **p. fuego a** to set fire to ➤ *intr (planta)* to take root; *(fuego)* to catch fire; *(vacuna)* to take (effect).

prensa ➤ *f* press.

preñado, a ➤ *adj* pregnant.

preocupación ➤ *f* preoccupation; *(ansiedad)* worry, anxiety.

preocupar ➤ *tr* to preoccupy; *(inquietar)* to worry ➤ *reflex* to worry *(con, de, por* about); *(cuidarse)* to take care.

preparación ➤ *f* preparation.

preparar ➤ *tr & reflex* to prepare (oneself).

preposición ➤ *f* preposition.

prepotente ➤ *adj* arrogant.

presa ➤ *f (en la caza)* prey; *(dique)* dam.

presagiar ➤ *tr* to presage.

presagio ➤ *m (señal)* omen; *(adivinación)* premonition.

prescindir ➤ *intr* to do without.

presencia ➤ *f* presence.

presenciar ➤ *tr* to witness.

presentación ➤ *f* presentation; *(exhibición)* exhibition.

presentar ➤ *tr* to present; *(mostrar)* to show; *(introducir)* to introduce ➤ *reflex (mostrarse)* to present oneself; *(venir)* to show up; *(dar el nombre)* to introduce oneself.

presente ➤ *adj* present ■ **tener p.** to keep in mind ➤ *m* GRAM. present.

presentimiento ➤ *m* premonition.

preservar ➤ *tr* to preserve.

preservativo ➤ *m* condom.

presidente, a ➤ *mf* president; *(de reunión)* chairman/woman.

presidio ➤ *m* prison.

presidir ➤ *tr (dirigir)* to preside over; *(predominar)* to dominate.

presión ➤ *f* pressure ■ **olla a p.** pressure cooker • **p. arterial** blood pressure.

presionar ➤ *tr (apretar)* to press; *(hacer presión)* to put pressure on.

preso, a ➤ *mf* prisoner.

préstamo ➤ *m* loan.

prestar ➤ *tr* to lend ■ **p. atención** to pay attention ➤ *reflex (consentir)* to consent; *(ser apto para)* to lend itself (*a, para* to); *(ofrecerse)* to offer.

prestigio ➤ *m* prestige.

presumido, a ➤ *adj* conceited.

presumir ➤ *tr* to presume ➤ *intr* ■ **p. de** to think *or* fancy oneself.

presuntuoso, a ➤ *adj & mf* presumptuous *or* conceited (person).

presupuesto ➤ *m* budget estimate.

pretender ➤ *tr (intentar)* to try, attempt; *(a una mujer)* to court.

pretendiente, a ➤ *mf (al trono)* claimant ➤ *m* suitor.

pretensión ➤ *f* claim; AMER. pretention; *(vanidad)* pretentiousness.

pretérito, a ➤ *adj & m* past.

pretexto ➤ *m* pretext.

prevenir §52 ➤ *tr (impedir)* to prevent; *(avisar)* to forewarn.

previo, a ➤ *adj* previous, prior.

previsto, a ➤ *adj* foreseen.

primario, a ➤ *adj* primary.

primavera ➤ *f (estación)* spring.

primer ➤ *adj contr of* **primero.**

primero, a ➤ *adj* first; *(fundamental)* basic ■ **de primera** first-class • **en primer lugar** first of all ➤ *mf* first; *(el mejor)* best ➤ *adv* first.

primitivo, a ➤ *adj & mf* primitive.

primo, a ➤ *mf* cousin • **p. hermano** *or* **carnal** first cousin.

primogénito, a ➤ *adj & mf* first-born.

primoroso, a ➤ *adj* beautiful, exquisite.

princesa ➤ *f* princess.

principal ➤ *adj* principal, main.

príncipe ➤ *m* prince.

principio ➤ *m* beginning; *(fundamento)* principle ■ **a p.** *or* **principios de** at the beginning of • **al p.** at first.

pringar §31 ➤ *tr (ensuciar)* to get grease on; *(empapar)* to dip in fat.

prioridad ➤ *f* priority.

prisa ➤ *f (apuro)* haste; *(velocidad)* speed; *(urgencia)* urgency ■ **a** *or* **de p.** quickly • **andar** *or* **estar de p.** to be in a hurry • **dar** *or* **meter p. a alguien** to rush someone • **darse p.** to hasten, hurry (up) • **tener p.** to be in a hurry (*por, en* to).

prisión ➤ *f* prison.

prisionero, a ➤ *mf* prisoner.

prismáticos ➤ *mpl* binoculars.

privado, a ➤ *adj* private ■ **vida p.** privacy.

privar ➤ *tr* to deprive ➤ *reflex* to abstain (*de* from).

privilegio ➤ *m* privilege.

pro ➤ *mf* profit, benefit ■ **en p. de pro,** in favor of • **el p. y el contra** pro and con.

proa ➤ *f* prow, bow.

probabilidad ➤ *f* probability.

probable ➤ *adj* probable.

probador ➤ *m* fitting room.

probar §11 ➤ *tr (ensayar)* to test; *(ropa)* to try on; *(comida)* to taste ➤ *intr* to try ➤ *reflex* to try on.

probeta ➤ *f* test tube.

problema ➤ *m* problem.

proceder ➤ *intr (originarse)* to originate (*de* in); *(ir con orden)* to proceed; *(portarse)* to behave; *(continuar)* to go on *or* ahead with.

procedimiento ➤ *m* procedure.

procesamiento ➤ *m* COMPUT. processing ■ **p. de texto** word processing.

procesar ➤ *tr* LAW to prosecute; COMPUT. to process.

procesión ➤ *f* procession.

proceso ➤ *m* process; LAW *(causa)* trial.

proclamar ➤ *tr & reflex* to proclaim (oneself).

procurador, a ➤ *mf (apoderado)* proxy; *(abogado)* attorney.

procurar ➤ *tr (intentar)* to endeavor; *(obtener)* to obtain ➤ *reflex* to obtain.

prodigio ➤ *m (persona)* prodigy; *(fenómeno)* wonder.

prodigioso, a ➤ *adj* marvelous.

producción ➤ *f* production ■ **p. en serie** mass production.

producir §14 ➤ *tr* to produce; *(ocasionar)* to cause; FIN. to yield ➤ *reflex* to take place.

productividad ➤ *f* productivity.

productivo, a ➤ *adj* productive; *(lucrativo)* lucrative.

producto ➤ *m* product; COM. *(beneficio)* profit.

productor, a ➤ *adj* productive, producing ➤ *mf* producer.

proeza ➤ *f* feat.

profano, a ➤ *adj* profane.

profesión ➤ *f* profession.

profesional ➤ *adj & mf* professional.

profesor, a ➤ *mf (de escuela)* teacher; *(de universidad)* professor.

profesorado ➤ *m* faculty.

profetizar §02 ➤ *tr* to prophesy.

profundidad ➤ *f* depth ■ **dos metros de p.** two meters deep.

profundo, a ➤ *adj (hondo)* deep; *(intenso)* profound.

progenitor ➤ *m* progenitor ■ *pl* ancestors; *(padres)* parents.

programa ➤ *m* program ■ **p. de estudios** curriculum.

programación ➤ *f* programming.

programador, a ➤ *mf* programmer.

programar ➤ *tr* to plan; COMPUT. to program.

progresar ➤ *intr* to progress.

progresivo, a ➤ *adj* progressive.

progreso ➤ *m* progress.

prohibido, a ➤ *adj* prohibited.

prohibir ➤ *tr* to prohibit, forbid ■ **se prohibe fumar** no smoking.

prole ➤ *f* progeny.

proliferar ➤ *intr* to proliferate.

prólogo ➤ *m* prologue.

prolongado, a ➤ *adj* prolonged.

prolongar §31 ➤ *tr* to prolong; *(alargar)* to lengthen ➤ *reflex* to extend; *(durar más tiempo)* to last longer.

promedio ➤ *m* average ■ **por p.** on average.

promesa ➤ *f* promise.

prometer ➤ *tr* to promise ➤ *intr* to be promising ➤ *reflex* to promise oneself, expect; *(novios)* to become engaged.

prometido, a ➤ *m* fiancé ➤ *f* fiancée.

prominente ➤ *adj* prominent.

promoción ➤ *f* promotion.

promocionar ➤ *tr* to promote.

promover §54 ➤ *tr* to promote; *(fomentar)* to foster; *(provocar)* to cause.

pronombre ➤ *m* pronoun.

pronosticar §47 ➤ *tr* to predict.

pronóstico ➤ *m* prediction ■ **p. del tiempo** weather forecast.

pronto, a ➤ *adj (veloz)* quick; *(diligente)* prompt ➤ *adv (velozmente)* quickly ■ **de p.** suddenly.

pronunciación ➤ *f* pronunciation.

pronunciar ➤ *tr* to pronounce; *(discurso)* to deliver.

propaganda ➤ *f* propaganda; COM. advertising ■ **hacer p.** to advertise.

propagar §31 ➤ *tr & reflex* to propagate; *(difundir)* to spread.

propenso, a ➤ *adj* prone (*a* to).

propiamente ➤ *adv* ■ **p. dicho** strictly speaking.

propicio, a ➤ *adj* propitious.

propiedad ➤ *f* property; *(posesión)* ownership; *(heredad)* estate ■ **p. intelectual** copyright.

propietario, a ➤ *mf* owner, proprietor.

propina ➤ *f* tip, gratuity.

propio, a ➤ *adj* own; selfsame; *(conveniente)* proper, suitable; *(característico)* typical.

proponer §37 ➤ *tr (sugerir)* to propose; *(presentar)* to nominate ➤ *reflex* to intend to do.

proporción ➤ *f* proportion.

proporcional ➤ *adj* proportional.

proporcionar ➤ *tr* to provide.

proposición ➤ *f* proposition; *(propuesta)* proposal.

propósito ➤ *m (intención)* intention; *(objetivo)* purpose ■ **a p.** *(por cierto)* by the way; *(adrede)* deliberately.

propuesta ➤ *f* proposal.

propulsión ➤ *f* propulsion ■ **p. delantera** front wheel drive.

prórroga ➤ *f* extension.

prorrumpir ➤ *intr* to burst (*en* into).

prosa ➤ *f* prose.

proseguir §42 ➤ *tr & intr* to pursue, carry on with.

prospecto ➤ *m* prospectus, brochure.

prosperar ➤ *intr* to prosper.

prosperidad ➤ *f* prosperity.

próspero, a ➤ *adj* prosperous.

prostituto, a ➤ *mf* prostitute.

protagonista ➤ *mf* protagonist.

protección ➤ *f* protection.

protector, a ➤ *adj* protective ➤ *mf* protector; *(patrocinador)* patron.

proteger §20 ➤ *tr* to protect.

proteína ➤ *f* protein.

protesta ➤ *f* protest.

protestante ➤ *adj & mf* Protestant.

protestar ➤ *tr & intr* to protest.

protocolo ➤ *m* protocol.

provecho ➤ *m (beneficio)* benefit; *(ganancia)* profit ■ **¡buen p.!** COLL. enjoy your meal!

proveedor, a ➤ *mf* supplier.

proveer §27 ➤ *tr* to provide (*de* with).

proveniente ➤ *adj* proceeding (*de* from).

provenir §52 ➤ *intr* to come (*en* from).

proverbio ➤ *m* proverb.

providencial ➤ *adj* providential.

provincia ➤ *f* province.

provisión ➤ *fpl* supplies.

provisional ➤ *adj* temporary.

provocar §47 ➤ *tr (incitar)* to provoke; *(irritar)* to annoy; *(despertar)* to rouse; *(causar)* to cause.

provocativo, a ➤ *adj* inviting, tempting.

próximamente ➤ *adv* soon, before long.

proximidad ➤ *f* proximity.

próximo, a ➤ *adj (cercano)* near; *(siguiente)* next.

proyección ➤ *f* projection; CINEM.

screening.
proyectar ➤ *tr (planear)* to plan; *(sombra)* to cast; CINEM. to show.
proyectil ➤ *m* projectile, missile.
proyecto ➤ *m* project.
proyector ➤ *m* CINEM. projector.
prudencia ➤ *f* prudence.
prudente ➤ *adj* prudent.
prueba ➤ *f (razón)* proof, evidence; *(examen)* test ▪ **a p. de agua, balas** waterproof, bulletproof.
psicoanálisis ➤ *m or f* psychoanalysis.
psicología ➤ *f* psychology.
psicólogo, a ➤ *mf* psychologist.
psicópata ➤ *mf* psychopath.
psicosis ➤ *f* psychosis.
psicoterapia ➤ *f* psychotherapy.
psiquíatra *or* **psiquiatra** ➤ *mf* psychiatrist.
psiquiatría ➤ *f* psychiatry.
púa ➤ *f* BOT. thorn; ZOOL. quill.
pubertad ➤ *f* puberty.
publicación ➤ *f* publication.
publicar §47 ➤ *tr* to publish.
publicidad ➤ *f* publicity; *(anuncio)* advertisement ▪ **agencia de p.** advertising agency.
público, a ➤ *adj* public ➤ *m* public; *(auditorio)* audience.
puchero ➤ *m* CUL. stew.
pudín ➤ *m* pudding.
pudor ➤ *m (recato)* modesty, shyness; *(vergüenza)* shame.
pudrir ➤ *tr & reflex* to rot.
pueblo ➤ *m (población)* town; *(nación)* people, nation.
puente ➤ *m* bridge ▪ **p. aéreo** airlift.
puerco, a ➤ *adj* filthy ➤ *m* ZOOL. pig, hog ➤ *f* ZOOL. sow.
pueril ➤ *adj* childish.
puerta ➤ *f* door; *(armazón)* gate.
puerto ➤ *m* port, harbor.
puertorriqueño, a ➤ *adj & mf* Puerto Rican.
pues ➤ *conj* since, as ▪ **¡p. claro!** of course! • **¿p. qué?** so what?
puesto, a ➤ *adj* dressed ➤ *m (sitio)* place; *(de venta)* stall; *(cargo)* position ▪ **p. que** since, as ➤ *f* ASTRON. setting ▪ **p. del sol** sunset • **p. en escena** staging.
pugilista ➤ *mf* boxer.
pulcritud ➤ *f* neatness.
pulcro, a ➤ *adj* neat.
pulga ➤ *f* flea.
pulgada ➤ *f* inch.
pulgar ➤ *adj & m* thumb.
pulir ➤ *tr* to polish.
pulmón ➤ *m* lung.
pulpa ➤ *f* pulp.
púlpito ➤ *m* pulpit.
pulpo ➤ *m* octopus.
pulsar ➤ *tr* to push ➤ *intr* to beat; COMPUT. to click.
pulsera ➤ *f* bracelet; *(de reloj)* watch band.
pulso ➤ *m (latido)* pulse; *(seguridad)* steady hand.
puma ➤ *m* puma, mountain lion.
pundonor ➤ *m* honor, integrity.
punta ➤ *f* point; *(extremidad)* tip; *(clavo)* small nail ▪ **sacar p. a** to sharpen.
puntapié ➤ *m* kick ▪ **echar a puntapiés** to kick out.
puntería ➤ *f* MIL. aim.
puntiagudo, a ➤ *adj* sharp, pointed.
puntilla ➤ *f* tack, brad; SEW. lace trim.
puntilloso, a ➤ *adj* punctilious.
punto ➤ *m* point; *(señal pequeña)* dot; *(sitio)* spot; *(de oración)* period, full stop; *(puntada)* stitch ▪ **dos puntos** colon • **en p.** on the dot, sharp • **p. de vista** point of view, viewpoint • **p. final** period • **p. y coma** semicolon.
puntuación ➤ *f* punctuation; *(calificación)* grade, mark.
puntual ➤ *adj* prompt.
puñado ➤ *m* handful.
puñal ➤ *m* dagger.
puñalada ➤ *f* stab.
puñetazo ➤ *m* punch ▪ *pl* **a p.** with one's fists.
puño ➤ *m* fist; SEW. cuff.
pupa ➤ *f (en los labios)* cold sore.
pupila ➤ *f* ANAT. pupil.
pupitre ➤ *m* desk.
puré ➤ *m* CUL. purée.
pureza ➤ *f* purity.
purga ➤ *f* laxative.
purificar §47 ➤ *tr* to purify.
puro, a ➤ *adj* pure ➤ *m* cigar.
púrpura ➤ *f* purple.
puta ➤ *f* prostitute, whore.
pútrido, a ➤ *adj* putrid.

Q

que ➤ *rel pron* that, which; who, whom ▪ **el** *or* **la q. he** *or* she who, the one that • **las q.** *or* **los q.** those who, the ones that • **lo q.** which, what ➤ *conj* that; *(porque)* because; *(si)* whether ▪ **a q.** I bet that • **hay mucho q. hacer** there is a lot to do • **más q.** more than • **yo q. tú** if I were you.
qué ➤ *adj* which, what ➤ *pron* what ➤ *adv* how ▪ **¡a mí q.!** so what! • **no hay de q.** you're welcome • **¿para q.?** what for? • **¿por q.?** why? • **¿q. pasa?** what's the matter? • **¿q. tal?** how goes it? • **¡q. va!** nonsense!, come on! • **un no sé q.** a certain something • **¿y q.?** so what?
quebrada ➤ *f* ravine; AMER. stream.
quebradizo, a ➤ *adj* brittle, fragile.
quebrado, a ➤ *adj* broken; COM. bankrupt.
quebrar §33 ➤ *tr* to break ➤ *intr* COM. to go bankrupt ➤ *reflex* to be broken.
quedar ➤ *intr* to remain, stay; *(estar)* to be; *(restar)* to be left; MATH. to leave ▪ **q. bien, mal** to come out well, badly; *(ropa)* to look good, bad • **q. en** to agree ➤ *reflex* to stay; *(estar)* to be; *(ponerse)* to become ▪ **q. con** to keep • **q. sin** to run out of.
quehaceres ➤ *mpl* chores.
queja ➤ *f* moan, groan; *(protesta)* complaint.
quejarse ➤ *reflex* to moan; *(lamentarse)* to whine, complain (*de* about).
quema ➤ *f* burning; *(incendio)* fire.
quemadura ➤ *f* burn.
quemar ➤ *tr* to burn ➤ *intr* to be burning hot ➤ *reflex* to burn oneself.
querella ➤ *f* dispute, quarrel; LAW complaint.
querer[1] ➤ *m* love, affection.
querer[2] §38 ➤ *tr* to want; *(amar)* to love ▪ **cuando quiera** at any time • **no q.** to refuse • **sin q.** unintentionally ➤ *intr* to look as if it is going to.
querido, a ➤ *adj* dear, beloved ➤ *mf* darling, dear.
quesadilla ➤ *f* cheese-filled tortilla.
queso ➤ *m* cheese.
quiebra ➤ *f* COM. bankruptcy.
quien ➤ *pron* who, whom; whoever, he *or* she who.
quién ➤ *pron* who, whom ▪ **de q.** *or* **de quiénes** whose.
quienquiera ➤ *pron* whoever, whomever.
quieto, a ➤ *adj (inmóvil)* motionless, still; *(sosegado)* quiet.
quietud ➤ *f* calm, tranquillity.
quilla ➤ *f* keel.
quilo ➤ *m* kilo, kilogram.
química ➤ *f* chemistry.
químico, a ➤ *adj* chemical ➤ *mf* chemist.
quimioterapia ➤ *f* chemotherapy.
quince ➤ *adj & m* fifteen.
quinto, a ➤ *adj & m* fifth ➤ *f* country house.
quiosco ➤ *m* kiosk.
quirófano ➤ *m* operating room.
quirúrgico, a ➤ *adj* surgical.
quitaesmalte ➤ *m* nail polish remover.
quitamanchas ➤ *m* stain remover.
quitanieves ➤ *m* snowplow.
quitar ➤ *tr (apartar)* to take away; *(hurtar)* to rob of; *(restar)* to subtract; *(abrogar)* to repeal; *(prohibir)* to forbid ▪ **q. la mesa** to clear the table ➤ *reflex* to take off; *(mancha)* to come out ▪ **q. de encima** to get rid of.
quizá(s) ➤ *adv* maybe, perhaps.

R

rábano ➤ *m* radish.
rabia ➤ *f* fury, rage; MED. rabies ▪ **dar r.** to infuriate.
rabiar ➤ *intr* to be furious.
rabillo ➤ *m* stem.
rabino ➤ *m* rabbi.
rabioso, a ➤ *adj* furious; MED. rabid.
rabo ➤ *m* tail.
racha ➤ *f* gust; *(suerte)* run (of luck).
racial ➤ *adj* racial.
ración ➤ *f* ration; *(porción)* serving.
racional ➤ *adj* rational.
racionar ➤ *tr* to ration.
rada ➤ *f* MARIT. roads; GEOG. bay, inlet.
radar ➤ *m* radar.
radiación ➤ *f* radiation.
radiactividad ➤ *f* radioactivity.
radiactivo, a ➤ *adj* radioactive.
radiador ➤ *m* radiator.
radiante ➤ *adj* radiant.
radical ➤ *adj & mf* radical.
radicar §47 ➤ *intr* to reside.
radio[1] ➤ *m* MATH. radius; *(rayo)* spoke.
radio[2] ➤ *m or f* radio.
radiocasete ➤ *m* boom box, tape player.
radiografía ➤ *f* radiography; *(imagen)* x-ray.
radioyente ➤ *mf* radio listener.
ráfaga ➤ *f* gust (of wind).
raído, a ➤ *adj* worn, threadbare.
raíz ➤ *f* root; FIG. origin ▪ **bienes raíces** real estate • **r. cuadrada** square root.
raja ➤ *f* crack; *(de melón, etc.)* slice.
rajar ➤ *tr* to crack ➤ *reflex* to crack; COLL. *(acobardarse)* to chicken out.
rallador ➤ *m* grater.
rallar ➤ *tr* to grate.
ralo, a ➤ *adj* thin.
rama ➤ *f* branch ▪ **en r.** raw.
ramillete ➤ *m* bouquet.
ramo ➤ *m (ramillete)* bouquet; *(subdivisión)* branch ▪ **Domingo de Ramos** Palm Sunday.
rampa ➤ *f* ramp.
rana ➤ *f* frog.
rancho ➤ *m* AMER. ranch, farm; *(comida)* mess.
rancio, a ➤ *adj* rancid.
rango ➤ *m* rank; AMER. pomp.
ranura ➤ *f* groove.
rapar ➤ *tr (el pelo)* to crop.
rapaz, a ➤ *mf* youngster ➤ *adj* rapacious.
rape ➤ *m* ▪ **al r.** close-cropped.
rapidez ➤ *f* speed.
rápido, a ➤ *adj* fast, quick ➤ *m (tren)* express train; *(en un río)* rapids ➤ *adv* quickly.
raptar ➤ *tr* to abduct, kidnap.
rapto ➤ *m* kidnaping; *(éxtasis)* rapture.
raqueta ➤ *f* racket; *(para nieve)* snowshoe.
raro, a ➤ *adj* rare, uncommon; *(extraño)* odd ▪ **rara vez** rarely.
ras ➤ *m* ▪ **a r. de** level with.
rascacielos ➤ *m* skyscraper.
rascar §47 ➤ *tr (con la uña)* to scratch ➤ *reflex* to scratch oneself.
rasgar §31 ➤ *tr* to tear, rip.
rasgo ➤ *m (trazo)* stroke; *(carácter)* trait, feature ▪ *pl* features.
rasguñar ➤ *tr* to scratch.
rasguño ➤ *m* scratch.
raso, a ➤ *adj (llano)* flat; *(el cielo)* clear ▪ **cielo r.** ceiling ➤ *m* satin.
raspar ➤ *tr* to scrape (off).
rastrear ➤ *tr* to trail.
rastrillar ➤ *tr* AGR. to rake.
rastrillo ➤ *m* rake.
rastro ➤ *m (pista)* trail; *(señal)* trace.
rasurar ➤ *tr* to shave.
rata ➤ *f* rat.
ratero, a ➤ *mf* thief, pickpocket.
ratificar §47 ➤ *tr* to ratify.
rato ➤ *m* while ▪ **a cada r.** all the time • **al poco r.** shortly after • **de r. en r.** from time to time • **un buen r.** quite some time.
ratón ➤ *m* ZOOL., COMPUT. mouse.
ratonero ➤ *m* mousetrap.
raudo, a ➤ *adj* swift.
raya ➤ *f (lista)* stripe; *(línea)* line; *(en el pelo)* part; *(pliegue)* crease; GRAM., TELEC. dash ▪ **a rayas** striped.
rayar ➤ *tr* to draw lines on ➤ *intr (lindar)* to be next to; *(amanecer)* to dawn; *(arañar)* to scratch.
rayo ➤ *m* ray; *(de rueda)* spoke; *(relámpago)* lightning.
rayón ➤ *m* rayon.
raza ➤ *f* race; *(de animales)* breed.
razón ➤ *f* reason; *(cómputo)* rate ▪ **dar la r. a alguien** to side with someone • **tener r.** to be right.
razonable ➤ *adj* reasonable.
razonar ➤ *intr* to reason ➤ *tr* to give reasons for.
reacción ➤ *f* reaction.
reaccionar ➤ *intr* to react.
reajuste ➤ *m* readjustment.
real[1] ➤ *adj* real.
real[2] ➤ *adj* royal.
realidad ➤ *f* reality ▪ **en r.** actually • **r. virtual** virtual reality.
realizar §02 ➤ *tr* to realize; *(ejecutar)* to accomplish ➤ *reflex* to come true.
reanimar ➤ *tr* to revive ➤ *reflex* to recover.
reanudar ➤ *tr* to resume ➤ *reflex* to begin again.
rebaja ➤ *f (acción)* reduction; *(descuento)* discount.
rebajar ➤ *tr (reducir)* to reduce; *(bajar)* to lower; *(humillar)* to humiliate ➤ *reflex* to degrade oneself.
rebanada ➤ *f* slice (of bread).
rebaño ➤ *m* herd.
rebasar ➤ *tr* to surpass ➤ *intr* to overflow.
rebelarse ➤ *reflex* to rebel.
rebelde ➤ *adj* rebellious ➤ *mf* rebel.
rebeldía ➤ *f* rebelliousness.
rebelión ➤ *f* rebellion.
rebosar ➤ *intr & reflex* to overflow (*de* with).
rebotar ➤ *intr (pelota)* to bounce.
rebozo ➤ *m* shawl.
rebuscado, a ➤ *adj* pedantic, affected.
rebuznar ➤ *intr* to bray.
recado ➤ *m (mensaje)* message; *(mandado)* errand.
recaída ➤ *f* relapse.
recalcar §47 ➤ *tr (insistir)* to stress.
recalentar §33 ➤ *tr* to reheat.
recambio ➤ *m* spare part.
recapacitar ➤ *tr* to reconsider.
recargado, a ➤ *adj* overloaded; FIG. overdone; ELEC. recharged.
recargar §31 ➤ *tr* to overload; FIG. to overdecorate; ELEC. to recharge.
recatado, a ➤ *adj* modest.
recaudador, a ➤ *mf* tax collector.
recaudar ➤ *tr* to collect.
recelar ➤ *tr* to suspect.
receloso, a ➤ *adj* suspicious.
recepción ➤ *f* reception; *(en un hotel)* front desk.
recepcionista ➤ *mf* receptionist.
receptor, a ➤ *m* receiver.
receta ➤ *f* MED. prescription; CUL. recipe.
recetar ➤ *tr* to prescribe.
rechazar §02 ➤ *tr* to reject.
rechinar ➤ *intr (hacer ruido)* to grate; *(los dientes)* to grind.
recibimiento ➤ *m* reception; *(vestíbulo)* (entrance) hall.
recibir ➤ *tr & intr* to receive ➤ *reflex* ▪ **r. de** to graduate as.
recibo ➤ *m* receipt ▪ **acusar r. de** to acknowledge receipt of.
reciclaje ➤ *m* recycling.
reciclar ➤ *tr* to recycle.
recién ➤ *adv* recently ▪ **r. nacido** newborn.
reciente ➤ *adj* recent; *(moderno)* modern.
recientemente ➤ *adv* recently.
recinto ➤ *m* place.
recio, a ➤ *adj (vigoroso)* strong; *(abultado)* bulky; *(lluvia)* heavy.
recipiente ➤ *m* container.
recíproco, a ➤ *adj* reciprocal.
recital ➤ *m* MUS. recital; LIT. reading.
recitar ➤ *tr* to recite.
reclamación ➤ *f (petición)* claim; *(protesta)* complaint.
reclamar ➤ *tr (pedir)* to claim; *(exigir)* to demand ➤ *intr* to protest.
reclinar ➤ *tr* to lean *or* rest on ➤ *reflex* to recline.
recluir §10 ➤ *tr* to seclude.
recluso, a ➤ *adj (encerrado)* secluded; *(preso)* imprisoned ➤ *mf* prisoner.
recluta ➤ *f* recruitment ➤ *mf* recruit.
recobrar ➤ *tr & reflex* to recover.
recodo ➤ *m* bend.
recoger §20 ➤ *tr (volver a coger)* to pick up; *(juntar)* to gather; *(coleccionar)* to save; AGR. to harvest.
recomendación ➤ *f* recommendation.
recomendar §33 ➤ *tr* to recommend.
recompensa ➤ *f* reward.
reconciliar ➤ *tr & reflex* to reconcile.
reconocer §09 ➤ *tr* to recognize; *(identificar)* to identify; *(agradecer)* to appreciate; *(examinar)* to examine.
reconocimiento ➤ *m* recognition; *(gratitud)* gratitude; *(examinación)* examination; MED. checkup.
reconstrucción ➤ *f* reconstruction; CONSTR. rebuilding.
reconstruir §10 ➤ *tr* to reconstruct; CONSTR. to rebuild.
recopilación ➤ *f* compilation.
recopilar ➤ *tr* to compile.
récord ➤ *m & adj* record.
recordar §11 ➤ *tr* to remember; *(avisar)* to remind ➤ *intr* to remember ➤ *reflex* ▪ **r. que** to remind oneself that.
recorrer ➤ *tr* to travel (through).

recorrido ➤ *m* (*viaje*) journey; (*trayecto*) path; (*de cartero*) route.

recortar ➤ *tr* to cut out.

recorte ➤ *m* newspaper clipping.

recostar §11 ➤ *tr* to lean (on) ➤ *reflex* to lie down.

recreo ➤ *m* (*acción*) recreation; (*en escuela*) recess ▪ de r. pleasure.

recriminar ➤ *intr & reflex* to recriminate (each other).

rectángulo ➤ *adj* rectangular ➤ *m* rectangle.

rectificar §47 ➤ *tr* (*enderezar*) to straighten; (*corregir*) to rectify.

recto, a ➤ *adj* (*derecho*) straight; GEOM. right ➤ *adv* straight.

rector, a ➤ *mf* (*de universidad*) president ▪ *m* (*cura*) priest.

recuento ➤ *m* count, recount.

recuerdo ➤ *m* (*memoria*) memory; (*regalo*) souvenir ▪ *pl* regards.

recuperación ➤ *f* recovery.

recuperar ➤ *tr* (*recobrar*) to recover; (*reconquistar*) to win back; (*el tiempo*) to make up for ➤ *reflex* to recover.

recurrir ➤ *intr* to turn *or* appeal (to); (*volver*) to return *or* revert (to).

recurso ➤ *m* recourse ▪ *pl* resources.

red ➤ *f* net; (*de tiendas*) chain; (*conspiración*) network ▪ R. Internet, Net.

redacción ➤ *f* writing; (*oficina*) editorial office; (*personal*) editorial staff.

redactar ➤ *tr* to draft; (*revisar*) to edit.

redactor, a ➤ *mf* writer; (*revisor*) editor ▪ r. jefe editor in chief.

redondel ➤ *m* circle; TAUR. arena.

redondo, a ➤ *adj* round ▪ a la r. around.

reducción ➤ *f* reduction.

reducir §14 ➤ *tr* to reduce; (*sujetar*) to subjugate ➤ *reflex* to be reduced; (*venir a ser*) to boil down (a to).

redundante ➤ *adj* redundant.

reelegir §37 ➤ *tr* to reelect.

reembolsar ➤ *tr* to reimburse.

reembolso ➤ *m* reimbursement ▪ enviar contra r. to send C.O.D.

reemplazar §02 ➤ *tr* to replace.

referencia ➤ *f* reference.

referir §43 ➤ *tr* to refer; (*contar*) to relate, tell ➤ *reflex* to refer (a to).

refinar ➤ *tr* to refine.

refinería ➤ *f* refinery.

reflector, a ➤ *adj* reflecting ➤ *m* spotlight.

reflejar ➤ *tr* to reflect ➤ *reflex* to be reflected.

reflejo ➤ *m* reflection; PHYSIOL. reflex; (*brillo*) gleam.

reflexionar ➤ *intr & tr* to reflect (en, sobre on).

reflexivo, a ➤ *adj* reflective; GRAM. reflexive.

reforestación ➤ *f* AMER. reforestation.

reforma ➤ *f* reform; (*modificación*) alteration.

reformar ➤ *tr* to reform; (*mejorar*) to improve; (*restaurar*) to renovate; (*modificar*) to alter ➤ *reflex* to reform.

reforzar §22 ➤ *tr* to reinforce.

refrán ➤ *m* saying.

refrescante ➤ *adj* refreshing.

refrescar §47 ➤ *tr* to refresh ➤ *intr & reflex* to become cool; (*tomar fuerzas*) to refresh (oneself).

refresco ➤ *m* (*alimento*) refreshment; (*bebida*) soft drink.

refrigeración ➤ *f* refrigeration; (*de aire*) air conditioning.

refrigerador ➤ *m* refrigerator.

refrigerar ➤ *tr* to refrigerate.

refuerzo ➤ *m* reinforcement.

refugiar ➤ *tr* to give refuge ➤ *reflex* to take refuge.

refugio ➤ *m* refuge.

refunfuñar ➤ *intr* to grumble.

regadera ➤ *f* watering can.

regalar ➤ *tr* (*dar*) to give (as a present); (*donar*) to give away.

regaliz ➤ *m* licorice.

regalo ➤ *m* present, gift.

regañadientes ➤ a r. COLL. grudgingly.

regañar ➤ *intr* to quarrel, argue ➤ *tr* COLL. to scold.

regar §35 ➤ *tr* to water; FIG. to strew.

regata ➤ *f* regatta.

regatear ➤ *tr & intr* to bargain (for).

regateo ➤ *m* haggling.

regazo ➤ *m* lap.

regeneración ➤ *f* regeneration.

régimen ➤ *m* regime; MED. diet.

regio, a ➤ *adj* regal; FIG. magnificent.

región ➤ *f* region.

regional ➤ *adj* regional.

registrar ➤ *tr* (*inspeccionar*) to examine; (*en un registro*) to register; (*rebuscar*) to search ➤ *reflex* to register.

registro ➤ *m* register; (*búsqueda*) search; (*oficina*) registry.

regla ➤ *f* (*para trazar*) ruler; (*norma*) rule; (*modelo*) model; (*menstruación*) period ▪ poner algo en r. to put *or* set something straight.

reglamentario, a ➤ *adj* prescribed.

reglamento ➤ *m* (*reglas*) rules.

regocijar ➤ *tr* to delight ➤ *reflex* to be delighted.

regocijo ➤ *m* joy.

regresar ➤ *tr, intr & reflex* to return.

regresión ➤ *f* regression.

regreso ➤ *m* return ▪ estar de r. to be back.

regular[1] ➤ *adj* regular; (*aceptable*) fairly good; (*mediano*) average ➤ *adv* so-so.

regular[2] ➤ *tr* to regulate, control.

regularidad ➤ *f* regularity.

rehabilitación ➤ *f* rehabilitation.

rehabilitar ➤ *tr* to rehabilitate.

rehacer §24 ➤ *tr* to redo, remake.

rehén ➤ *mf* hostage.

rehogar §31 ➤ *tr* CUL. to brown.

rehuir §10 ➤ *tr* to avoid ➤ *reflex* to flee or shrink from.

rehusar ➤ *tr* to refuse.

reimprimir §55 ➤ *tr* to reprint.

reina ➤ *f* queen.

reinar ➤ *tr* to reign.

reincidencia ➤ *f* relapse; CRIMIN. recidivism.

reincidir ➤ *intr* to relapse.

reiniciar ➤ *tr* COMPUT. to reboot.

reino ➤ *m* kingdom.

reír §39 ➤ *intr & reflex* to laugh (at).

reiterar ➤ *tr* to reiterate.

reja ➤ *f* (*de ventana*) grating.

rejilla ➤ *f* grille; (*de un horno*) fire grate; RAIL. luggage rack.

relación ➤ *f* relation; (*conexión*) connection; (*relato*) account, report ▪ con or en r. a in relation to.

relacionado, a ➤ *adj* related (con to).

relacionar ➤ *tr* to relate ➤ *reflex* to be related; (*amigos*) to make friends.

relajación ➤ *f* relaxation.

relajar ➤ *tr & reflex* to relax.

relámpago ➤ *m* lightning; FIG. flash.

relatar ➤ *tr* to narrate.

relato ➤ *m* narration; (*cuento*) story.

relegar §31 ➤ *tr* to relegate.

relevar ➤ *tr* to relieve (*de* from).

relevo ➤ *m* relief; SPORT. relay.

religión ➤ *f* religion.

religioso, a ➤ *adj* religious ➤ *m* monk ➤ *f* nun.

relinchar ➤ *intr* to neigh.

reliquia ➤ *f* relic.

rellano ➤ *m* landing.

rellenar ➤ *tr* to refill; (*completamente*) to fill up; CUL. to stuff.

relleno, a ➤ *adj* stuffed ➤ *m* stuffing.

reloj ➤ *m* clock; (*de pulsera*) watch.

relojería ➤ *f* jewelry store.

reluciente ➤ *adj* shining.

relucir §28 ➤ *intr* to shine.

remache ➤ *m* rivet.

remangar §31 ➤ *tr* to roll *or* tuck up.

remar ➤ *intr* to row.

rematar ➤ *tr* to finish (off).

remate ➤ *m* conclusion; (*toque final*) finishing touch; (*subasta*) auction.

remediar ➤ *tr* to remedy.

remedio ➤ *m* remedy ▪ como último r. as a last resort • no haber (más) r. to be unavoidable • no tener r. to be hopeless.

remendar §33 ➤ *tr* to mend.

remesa ➤ *f* consignment.

remiendo ➤ *m* mending; SEW. patch.

remilgado, a ➤ *adj* affected.

remitente ➤ *mf* sender.

remitir ➤ *tr* to send; (*dinero*) to remit.

remo ➤ *m* oar; (*de canoa*) paddle.

remolcador ➤ *m* AUTO. tow truck; MARIT. tugboat.

remolcar §47 ➤ *tr* to tow.

remolino ➤ *m* (*de agua*) whirlpool; (*de aire*) whirlwind.

remolque ➤ *m* (*acción*) towing; (*vehículo*) tow truck.

remordimiento ➤ *m* remorse.

remoto, a ➤ *adj* remote.

remover §54 ➤ *tr* to move; (*quitar*) to remove; (*mezclar*) to stir ➤ *reflex* to shake.

remuneración ➤ *f* remuneration.

remunerar ➤ *tr* to remunerate.

renacimiento ➤ *m* revival ▪ R. Renaissance.

renacuajo ➤ *m* tadpole.

rencilla ➤ *f* quarrel.

rencor ➤ *m* rancor.

rencoroso, a ➤ *adj* resentful.

rendido, a ➤ *adj* exhausted.

rendija ➤ *f* crack.

rendir §32 ➤ *tr* to yield; (*dar fruto*) to bear; (*cansar*) to tire out ➤ *intr* to yield ➤ *reflex* to surrender, give up.

renglón ➤ *m* line (of text).

renombre ➤ *m* renown.

renovación ➤ *f* (*extensión*) renewal; (*restauración*) renovation.

renovar §11 ➤ *tr* (*extender*) to renew; (*restaurar*) to renovate.

renta ➤ *f* (*ingresos*) income; (*interés*) interest; (*alquiler*) rent.

rentable ➤ *adj* profitable.

renunciar ➤ *tr* to renounce; (a un puesto) to resign; (*no aceptar*) to reject.

reñido, a ➤ *adj* (*enemistado*) at odds; (*difícil*) hard-fought.

reñir ➤ *intr* to quarrel ➤ *tr* (*regañar*) to scold.

reo, a ➤ *mf* LAW defendant.

reparación ➤ *f* repair.

reparar ➤ *tr* to repair; (*remediar*) to redress.

reparo ➤ *m* objection, criticism; (*duda*) misgiving.

repartidor, a ➤ *mf* distributor.

repartir ➤ *tr* (*dividir*) to divide; (*distribuir*) to distribute.

reparto ➤ *m* (*distribución*) distribution; (*entrega*) delivery.

repasar ➤ *tr* to review.

repaso ➤ *m* review.

repelente ➤ *adj* repellent.

repeler ➤ *tr* to repel; (*rechazar*) to reject.

repente ➤ *m* start ▪ de r. suddenly.

repentino, a ➤ *adj* sudden.

repercutir ➤ *intr* to reverberate ▪ r. en to have repercussions on.

repertorio ➤ *m* repertory, repertoire.

repetición ➤ *f* repetition.

repetir §32 ➤ *tr & intr* to repeat.

repicar §47 ➤ *intr* to ring out, peal.

repisa ➤ *f* shelf.

replegar §35 ➤ *tr* to fold over ➤ *reflex* MIL. to retreat.

repleto, a ➤ *adj* full.

réplica ➤ *f* retort; (*copia*) replica.

replicar §47 ➤ *intr* to retort, reply.

repollo ➤ *m* cabbage.

reponer §37 ➤ *tr* to replace; THEAT. to revive ➤ *reflex* to recover.

reportaje ➤ *m* (*artículo*) report; (*de noticias*) news coverage.

reportero, a ➤ *mf* reporter.

reposar ➤ *intr* to rest.

reposo ➤ *m* repose.

repostería ➤ *f* pastry shop, bakery.

reprender ➤ *tr* to reprimand.

represa ➤ *f* dam.

represalia ➤ *f* reprisal.

representación ➤ *f* representation; THEAT. performance.

representante ➤ *mf* representative.

representar ➤ *tr* to represent; (*aparentar*) to appear to be; THEAT. to perform ➤ *intr* to picture.

represión ➤ *f* repression.

reprimenda ➤ *f* reprimand.

reprimir ➤ *tr & reflex* to repress (oneself).

reprochar ➤ *tr* to reproach.

reproducción ➤ *f* reproduction.

reproducir §14 ➤ *tr & reflex* to reproduce.

reptil ➤ *m* reptile.

república ➤ *f* republic.

repuesto ➤ *m* spare (part) ▪ de r. spare.

repugnante ➤ *adj* repugnant.

repugnar ➤ *intr* to detest.

repulsivo, a ➤ *adj* repulsive.

reputación ➤ *f* reputation.

requesón ➤ *m* cottage cheese.

requisar ➤ *tr* to requisition.

requisito ➤ *m* requirement.

res ➤ *f* animal ▪ r. vacuna cow, bull.

resaca ➤ *f* MARIT. undertow; FIG. hangover.

resaltar ➤ *intr* to jut out; FIG. to stand out ▪ hacer r. to stress, emphasize.

resbaladizo, a ➤ *adj* slippery.

resbalar ➤ *intr* to slip; AUTO to skid.

resbalón ➤ *m* slip.

rescatar ➤ *tr* to recover; (*cautivos*) to ransom; (*salvar*) to rescue.

rescate ➤ *m* rescue; (*dinero*) ransom.

rescoldo ➤ *m* embers.

resentimiento ➤ *m* resentment.

reserva ➤ *f* reserve; (*excepción, territorio*) reservation.

reservación ➤ *f* reservation.

reservado, a ➤ *adj* reserved.

reservar ➤ *tr* to reserve ➤ *reflex* to save one's strength *or* oneself.

resfriado ➤ *m* cold.

resfriar §18 ➤ *tr* to cool ➤ *reflex* to catch a cold.

residencia ➤ *f* residence.

residencial ➤ *adj* residential.

residir ➤ *intr* to reside.

resignar ➤ *tr & reflex* to resign (oneself).

resina ➤ *f* resin.

resistencia ➤ *f* resistance.

resistir ➤ *intr* to resist; (*durar*) to endure ➤ *tr* to resist; (*aguantar*) to bear ➤ *reflex* to resist; (*luchar*) to fight; (*negarse*) to refuse (a to).

resolución ➤ *f* resolution.

resolver §54 ➤ *tr* to solve ➤ *reflex* to resolve itself.

resonar §11 ➤ *intr* to resound.

resoplar ➤ *intr* to puff.

resorte ➤ *m* MECH. spring; FIG. resort.

respaldo ➤ *m* back, backing.

respecto ➤ *m* respect ▪ al r. about the matter • r. a *or* de with respect to.

respetar ➤ *tr* to respect.

respeto ➤ *m* respect.

respetuoso, a ➤ *adj* respectful.

respiración ➤ *f* respiration, breathing.

respirar ➤ *intr* to breathe.

resplandecer §09 ➤ *intr* to shine.

resplandor ➤ *m* brightness; (*brillo*) shine; (*esplendor*) splendor.

responder ➤ *tr* to answer ➤ *intr* (*contestar*) to answer; (*replicar*) to answer back; (*reaccionar*) to respond.

responsabilidad ➤ *f* responsibility.

responsable ➤ *adj* responsible.

respuesta ➤ *f* answer.

resta ➤ *f* subtraction.

restablecer §09 ➤ *tr* to reestablish ➤ *reflex* to recover.

restante ➤ *adj* remaining.

restar ➤ *tr* MATH. to subtract; (*quitar*) to take away.

restaurante ➤ *m* restaurant.

restaurar ➤ *tr* to restore.

resto ➤ *m* remainder ▪ *pl* leftovers.

restricción ➤ *f* restriction.

restringir §19 ➤ *tr* to restrict ➤ *reflex* to cut down on.

resucitar ➤ *tr* to resuscitate; (*memoria*) to revive ➤ *intr* to be resuscitated.

resuelto, a ➤ *adj* determined.

resultado ➤ *m* result, outcome.

resultar ➤ *intr* to turn out (*que* that).

resumen ➤ *m* summary ▪ en r. in short.

resumir ➤ *tr* to summarize.

retar ➤ *tr* to challenge.

retazo ➤ *m* (*de tela*) remnant.

retener §46 ➤ *tr* to retain; (*deducir*) to withhold.

retina ➤ *f* retina.

retirada ➤ *f* retreat.

retirado, a ➤ *adj* secluded; (*jubilado*) retired ➤ *mf* retired person.

retirar ➤ *tr* to remove; (*de circulación*) to withdraw; (*retractar*) to retract; (*dinero*) to withdraw ➤ *reflex* to withdraw; (*jubilarse*) to retire.

retiro ➤ *m* retreat.

reto ➤ *m* challenge.

retoque ➤ *m* PHOTOG. retouching; SEW. alteration.

retorcer §48 ➤ *tr* to twist ➤ *reflex* to twist; (*de dolor*) to writhe.

retorno ➤ *m* return.

retraído, a ➤ *adj* aloof, withdrawn.

retrasado, a ➤ *adj* (*tardío*) late; (*persona*) retarded; (*país*) backward.

retrasar ➤ *tr* (*demorar*) to delay; (*aplazar*) to postpone; (*un reloj*) to set back ➤ *reflex* to be late *or* delayed.

retraso ➤ *m* delay ▪ con r. late.

retratar ➤ *tr* to paint a portrait of; (*describir*) to depict.

retrato ➤ *m* portrait; AMER. photograph.

retrete ➤ *m* toilet.

retribución ➤ *f* retribution.

retroactivo, a ➤ *adj* retroactive.

retroceder ➤ *intr* to step back.

retrospectivo, a ➤ *adj & f* retrospective.

retrovisor ➤ *m* rearview mirror.

reumatismo ➤ *m* rheumatism.

reunión ➤ *f* meeting.

reunir ➤ *tr* to gather; *(requisitos)* to fulfill ➤ *reflex (juntarse)* to unite; *(en una reunión)* to meet.
revelación ➤ *f* revelation.
revelar ➤ *tr* to reveal; PHOTOG. to develop.
reventar §33 ➤ *intr (globo)* to burst; *(neumático)* to blow ➤ *reflex* to burst; *(cansarse)* to exhaust oneself.
reventón ➤ *m* burst; AUTO. flat tire.
reverencia ➤ *f* reverence; *(saludo)* bow.
reverso, a ➤ *adj & m* reverse.
revés ➤ *m (envés)* back; *(desgracia)* setback ▪ **al r.** backwards; *(prenda)* inside out • **al r. de** contrary to.
revisar ➤ *tr* to check.
revisión ➤ *f* revision.
revisor, a ➤ *adj* revising, checking ➤ *mf* inspector ▪ **r. de cuentas** auditor.
revista ➤ *f* magazine.
revivir ➤ *intr* to revive.
revolcarse ➤ *reflex (en el suelo)* to roll; *(en el fango)* to wallow.
revoltijo ➤ *m* jumble.
revoltoso, a ➤ *adj* troublemaking ➤ *mf* troublemaker; *(rebelde)* rebel.
revolución ➤ *f* revolution.
revolver §54 ➤ *tr (mezclar)* to mix; *(desordenar)* to mix up ➤ *reflex (dar vueltas)* to turn around.
revólver ➤ *m* revolver.
revuelo ➤ *m* commotion.
revuelta ➤ *f* revolt; *(riña)* quarrel.
revuelto, a ➤ *adj* jumbled; *(inquieto)* turbulent; *(travieso)* mischievous; *(enrevesado)* complicated ▪ **huevos revueltos** scrambled eggs.
rey ➤ *m* king ▪ **día de Reyes** Epiphany.
rezagar §31 ➤ *tr* to leave behind ➤ *reflex* to lag behind.
rezar §02 ➤ *tr* to say ➤ *intr* to pray.
ribera ➤ *f* shore; *(de río)* bank, shore.
rico, a ➤ *adj* rich, wealthy; *(sabroso)* delicious ➤ *mf* rich person.
ridículo, a ➤ *adj* ridiculous ➤ *m* ridiculous situation ▪ **hacer el r.** to make a fool of oneself.
riego ➤ *m* irrigation.
rienda ➤ *f* rein.
riesgo ➤ *m* risk.
rifa ➤ *f* raffle.
rifle ➤ *m* rifle.
rigidez ➤ *f* rigidity.
rígido, a ➤ *adj* stiff.
rigor ➤ *m* rigor ▪ **de r.** de rigueur.
riguroso, a ➤ *adj* rigorous.
rimar ➤ *intr & tr* to rhyme.
rímel ➤ *m* mascara.
rincón ➤ *m* corner.
rinoceronte ➤ *m* rhinoceros.
riña ➤ *f* quarrel.
riñón ➤ *m* kidney.
río ➤ *m* river ▪ **r. abajo** downstream.
riqueza ➤ *f* wealth.
risa ➤ *f* laugh, laughter ▪ **¡qué r.!** how funny!
ristra ➤ *f* string.
risueño, a ➤ *adj* smiling.
ritmo ➤ *m* rhythm.
rizado ➤ *m* curling.
rizar §02 ➤ *tr* to curl.
rizo ➤ *m* ringlet.
robar ➤ *tr* to rob; *(saquear)* to burgle.
roble ➤ *m* oak.
robo ➤ *m* robbery.
robusto, a ➤ *adj* robust.
roca ➤ *f* rock.
rociar §18 ➤ *tr* to sprinkle.
rocío ➤ *m* dew; *(llovizna)* sprinkle.
rocoso, a ➤ *adj* rocky.
rodaja ➤ *f* disc; *(de fruta)* slice.
rodaje ➤ *m* CINEM. filming.
rodar §11 ➤ *intr & tr* to roll; CINEM. to shoot, film.
rodear ➤ *tr* to surround ➤ *reflex* ▪ **r. de** to surround oneself with.
rodeo ➤ *m (camino indirecto)* roundabout way; *(fiesta)* rodeo.
rodilla ➤ *f* knee ▪ **de rodillas** on one's knees.
rodillera ➤ *f* knee pad.
roer ➤ *tr* to gnaw; *(gastar)* to erode.
rogar §08 ➤ *tr* to beg ➤ *intr* to pray.
rojo, a ➤ *adj* red ▪ **ponerse r.** to blush ➤ *m* red.
rollo ➤ *m* roll; *(de cuerda)* coil.
romance ➤ *m* romance.
romano, a ➤ *adj* Roman.
romántico, a ➤ *adj & mf* romantic.
rombo ➤ *m* rhombus.
romero ➤ *m* rosemary.
rompecabezas ➤ *m* jigsaw puzzle; FIG. riddle.
rompeolas ➤ *m* breakwater.
romper §55 ➤ *tr* to break; *(en pedazos)* to tear *or* rip (up); *(cancelar)* to break off ➤ *intr* to break ▪ **r. con** to break up with • **r. en** to burst into (tears, etc.) • **r. por** to break through ➤ *reflex* to break.
ron ➤ *m* rum.
roncar §47 ➤ *intr* to snore.
roncha ➤ *f* welt; *(cardenal)* bruise.
ronco, a ➤ *adj* hoarse; *(áspero)* harsh.
rondar ➤ *intr (vigilar)* to patrol; *(vagar)* to prowl around.
ronquera ➤ *f* hoarseness.
ronquido ➤ *m* snore.
ronronear ➤ *intr* to purr.
roñoso, a ➤ *adj (sucio)* filthy; *(tacaño)* stingy.
ropa ➤ *f* clothes, clothing ▪ **r. interior** underwear.
ropero ➤ *m* closet.
rosa ➤ *f* rose; *(color)* pink ➤ *adj* pink.
rosado, a ➤ *adj* pink; *(vino)* rosé.
rosal ➤ *m* rosebush.
rosario ➤ *m* rosary.
rosbif ➤ *m* roast beef.
rostro ➤ *m* face.
roto, a ➤ *adj* broken; *(quebrado)* smashed; *(papel, tela)* torn, ripped.
rótula ➤ *f* kneecap; MECH. rounded joint.
rotulador, a ➤ *adj* labeling ➤ *m* felt-tipped pen.
rotular ➤ *tr* to label.
rótulo ➤ *m* label.
rotundo, a ➤ *adj (sonoro)* resounding; *(definitivo)* categorical.
rotura ➤ *f* break; *(en papel, tela)* tear.
rozar §02 ➤ *tr* to brush against ➤ *intr* to touch lightly.
rubí ➤ *m* ruby.
rubio, a ➤ *adj & mf* blond(e).
ruborizarse §02 ➤ *reflex* to blush.
rudo, a ➤ *adj* rough.
rueda ➤ *f* wheel.
ruedo ➤ *m* bullring.
ruego ➤ *m* request.
rugido ➤ *m* roar.
rugir §19 ➤ *intr* to roar.
ruido ➤ *m* noise; *(alboroto)* din.
ruidoso, a ➤ *adj* noisy, loud; FIG. smashing.
ruin ➤ *adj* mean, despicable; *(avaro)* stingy; *(animales)* vicious.
ruina ➤ *f* ruin; FIG. fall, downfall.
ruiseñor ➤ *m* nightingale.
ruleta ➤ *f* roulette.
rulo ➤ *m* roller.
rumbo ➤ *m* direction; AER., MARIT. course ▪ **con r. a** bound for.
rumor ➤ *m* murmur; *(chismes)* rumor.
rumorearse ➤ *reflex* to be rumored.
ruptura ➤ *f (acción)* breaking; MED. fracture; *(de relaciones)* breakup.
rural ➤ *adj* rural.
rústico, a ➤ *adj* rustic ➤ *mf* hick.
ruta ➤ *f* route.
rutina ➤ *f* routine.

S

sábado ➤ *m* Saturday; RELIG. Sabbath.
sabana ➤ *f* AMER. savanna(h).
sábana ➤ *f* bed sheet.
saber[1] ➤ *m* knowledge.
saber[2] §40 ➤ *tr* to know; *(cocinar, etc.)* to know how; *(noticia)* to learn ▪ **hacer a.** to inform • **¿qué sé yo?** how should I know? • **que yo sepa** as far as I know • **s. de memoria** to know by heart ➤ *intr* to know ▪ **s. a** to taste like.
sabiduría ➤ *f (prudencia)* wisdom; *(conocimiento)* knowledge.
sabio, a ➤ *adj* wise ➤ *mf* wise person; *(instruido)* learned person, scholar.
sable ➤ *m* saber.
sabor ➤ *m* taste, flavor ▪ **con s. a limón** lemon-flavored.
saborear ➤ *tr* to taste; FIG. to relish.
sabroso, a ➤ *adj* delicious, tasty; *(agradable)* delightful.
sacacorchos ➤ *m* corkscrew.
sacapuntas ➤ *m* pencil sharpener.
sacar §47 ➤ *tr* to take out; *(quitar)* to remove; *(arrancar)* to pull out; *(de un apuro)* to bail out; *(información)* to get out; *(ganar)* to win; *(fotografiar)* to take; SPORT. to serve; CHEM. to extract.
sacarina ➤ *f* saccharin.
sacerdote ➤ *m* priest.
saciar ➤ *tr* to satiate.
saco ➤ *m (bolsa)* bag; AMER. *(chaqueta)* jacket ▪ **s. de dormir** sleeping bag.
sacramento ➤ *m* sacrament.
sacrificar §47 ➤ *tr* to sacrifice; *(ganado)* to slaughter ➤ *reflex* to sacrifice oneself.
sacrificio ➤ *m* sacrifice.
sacrosanto, a ➤ *adj* sacrosanct.
sacudida ➤ *f (acción)* shake; *(sismo)* tremor; *(de explosión)* blast; *(emoción)* jolt ▪ **s. eléctrica** electric shock.
sacudir ➤ *tr (agitar)* to shake; *(quitar el polvo)* to dust; *(un ala)* to flap; *(alterar)* to jolt ➤ *reflex (la ropa)* to shake *or* brush off.
sagaz ➤ *adj* sagacious, astute.
sagrado, a ➤ *adj* sacred.
sal ➤ *f* salt.
sala ➤ *f* living room; MED. hospital ward ▪ **s. de charla** chat room • **s. de clase** classroom • **s. de espectáculos** theater, hall • **s. de espera** waiting room.
salado, a ➤ *adj* salt, salty; *(plato)* salted.
salar ➤ *tr* to salt; *(curar)* to cure.
salario ➤ *m* wage.
salchicha ➤ *f* sausage.
saldar ➤ *tr* COM. to pay off.
saldo ➤ *m (cifra)* balance; *(mercancías)* remnants.
salero ➤ *m* saltshaker; *(gracia)* wit.
salida ➤ *f (acción)* departure; *(abertura)* exit; *(escapatoria)* way out; *(ocurrencia)* witty remark ▪ **dar s. a** to vent • **s. del sol** sunrise.
salir §41 ➤ *intr* to leave; *(a la calle)* to go out; *(aparecer)* to come out; *(el sol)* to rise; *(libro)* to come out; *(oportunidad)* to come *or* turn up; *(cálculo)* to work out; COMPUT. to log off *or* out ▪ **s. bien, mal** to turn out well, badly • **s. con** to go out with, date ➤ *reflex (derramarse)* to leak; *(rebosar)* to boil over ▪ **s. con la suya** to get one's own way • **s. del tema** to digress.
saliva ➤ *f* saliva, spit.
salmón ➤ *m* salmon.
salobre ➤ *adj* briny.
salón ➤ *m (sala grande)* hall ▪ **s. de conferencias** lecture hall ▪ **s. de belleza** beauty parlor • **s. de té** tearoom.
salpicar §47 ➤ *tr* to splash, splatter; *(rociar)* to sprinkle; *(motear)* to fleck.
salsa ➤ *f* sauce, gravy.
saltamontes ➤ *m* grasshopper.
saltar ➤ *intr (brincar)* to jump; *(levantarse)* to jump up; *(dar saltitos)* to hop; *(lanzarse)* to jump (*a* into); *(salir con ímpetu)* to bound ▪ **s. sobre** to pounce on ➤ *tr (atravesar)* to jump over; *(omitir)* to skip over.
salto ➤ *m* jump, leap ▪ **a saltos** by leaps and bounds.
salud ➤ *f* health, well-being ▪ **estar bien, mal de s.** to be in good, bad health ➤ *interj* COLL. *(al estornudar)* (God) bless you!; *(brindis)* cheers!
saludable ➤ *adj* healthy.
saludar ➤ *tr* to greet; *(honrar)* to salute ▪ **Le saluda atentamente** Yours truly.
saludo ➤ *m* greeting ▪ *pl* regards.
salvación ➤ *f* salvation.
salvadoreño, a ➤ *adj & mf* Salvadoran.
salvaguardar ➤ *tr* to safeguard.
salvaje ➤ *adj (planta, animal)* wild; *(feroz)* savage; *(primitivo)* uncivilized ➤ *mf* savage.
salvamento ➤ *m* rescue.
salvapantallas ➤ *m* screen saver.
salvar ➤ *tr (librar)* to save; *(resolver)* to overcome; *(recorrer)* to cover ➤ *reflex* to escape.
salvavidas ➤ *m* life preserver ➤ *mf* lifeguard.
salvia ➤ *f* BOT. sage.
salvo, a ➤ *adj* safe ▪ **a s.** safe (and sound) • **a s. de** safe from ➤ *adv* except (for), save ▪ **s. que** unless.
san ➤ *adj contr of* **santo.**
sanar ➤ *tr* to heal ➤ *intr* to recover (from illness); *(herida)* to heal.
sanción ➤ *f* sanction.
sancionar ➤ *tr* to sanction.
sandalia ➤ *f* sandal.
sándalo ➤ *m* sandalwood.
sandía ➤ *f* watermelon.
sangrar ➤ *tr & intr* to bleed.
sangre ➤ *f* blood ▪ **a s. fría** in cold blood • **pura s.** thoroughbred.
sangría ➤ *f (bebida)* sangria.
sangriento, a ➤ *adj* bloody; *(manchado)* blood-stained; *(cruel)* cruel.
sanguinario, a ➤ *adj* bloodthirsty.
sanguíneo, a ➤ *adj* blood ▪ **grupo s.** blood group.
sanitario, a ➤ *adj* sanitary.
sano, a ➤ *adj* healthy ▪ **s. y salvo** safe and sound.
santidad ➤ *f* sanctity, holiness.
santo, a ➤ *adj* holy ➤ *mf* saint ➤ *m (imagen)* image of a saint; *(festividad)* saint's day.
santuario ➤ *m* sanctuary; *(intimidad)* privacy.
sapo ➤ *m* toad.
saque ➤ *m (tenis)* serve; *(fútbol)* kick ▪ **s. de banda** throw-in.
saquear ➤ *tr* to plunder.
sarampión ➤ *m* measles.
sarcasmo ➤ *m* sarcasm.
sardina ➤ *f* sardine.
sargento ➤ *m* sergeant.
sarpullido ➤ *m* rash.
sarro ➤ *m* crust; DENT. tartar.
sartén ➤ *f* frying pan.
sastre ➤ *m* tailor.
satélite ➤ *adj & m* satellite.
satén *or* **satín** ➤ *m* satin.
sátira ➤ *f* satire.
satisfacción ➤ *f* satisfaction.
satisfacer §24 ➤ *tr* to satisfy; *(deuda)* to pay.
satisfecho, a ➤ *adj* satisfied.
sauce ➤ *m* willow ▪ **s. llorón** weeping willow.
sazón ➤ *f* CUL. seasoning ▪ **en s.** *(fruta)* in season; FIG. at the right moment.
sazonar ➤ *tr* to season.
se ➤ *reflex pron* himself, herself, etc. ▪ **se están mirando en el espejo** they're looking at themselves in the mirror • **se aman** they love each other ➤ *indef pron* one, they ▪ **se dice que** they say that ➤ *aux pron* ▪ **se venden libros aquí** books are sold here ➤ *pers pron* ▪ **se lo dijo a él** she said it to him • **él se lo robó a ellos** he stole it from them.
secador ➤ *m* hair dryer.
secadora ➤ *f* clothes dryer.
secar §47 ➤ *tr* to dry ➤ *reflex* to dry (out); *(persona)* to dry oneself, dry off; *(río)* to dry up, run dry; BOT. to wither.
sección ➤ *f* section.
seco, a ➤ *adj* dry; *(desecado)* dried; *(corto y brusco)* sharp ▪ **limpiar en s.** to dry-clean.
secretaria ➤ *f* secretary.
secretario ➤ *m* secretary.
secreto, a ➤ *adj & m* secret ▪ **en s.** secretly • **guardar un s.** to keep a secret.
secta ➤ *f* sect.
sector ➤ *m* sector.
secuencia ➤ *f* sequence.
secuestrar ➤ *tr (personas)* to kidnap; *(vehículos)* to hijack.
secuestro ➤ *m (de personas)* kidnapping; *(de vehículos)* hijacking.
secundario, a ➤ *adj & m* secondary ▪ **escuela s.** high school.
sed ➤ *f* thirst.
seda ➤ *f* silk.
sedal ➤ *m* fishing line.
sedativo, a ➤ *adj & m* sedative.
sede ➤ *f (del gobierno)* seat; *(de organización)* headquarters.
sedentario, a ➤ *adj* sedentary.
sedimento ➤ *m* sediment.
sedoso, a ➤ *adj* silky.
seducir §14 ➤ *tr* to seduce.
segar §35 ➤ *tr* to harvest.
seglar ➤ *adj* secular ➤ *mf* layman/woman.
segmento ➤ *m* segment.
seguibola ➤ *f* COMPUT. trackball.
seguidamente ➤ *adv* next.
seguido, a ➤ *adj* consecutive ➤ *adv* often ▪ **en seguida** immediately, right away.
seguidor, a ➤ *mf* follower.
seguir §42 ➤ *tr* to follow; *(venir después)* to come after; *(continuar)* to keep *or* go on ➤ *intr* to continue.
según ➤ *prep* according to ➤ *adv* depending on.
segundero ➤ *m* second hand.
segundo, a ➤ *adj* second ▪ **de s. clase** second-class • **s. enseñanza** secondary education ➤ *m* second.
seguramente ➤ *adv (ciertamente)* certainly; *(probablemente)* probably.
seguridad ➤ *f* security, safety ▪ **con toda s.** with absolute certainty • **de s.** safety.
seguro, a ➤ *adj* safe; *(cierto)* certain, sure; *(confiable)* trustworthy; *(firme)* stable ➤ *m* insurance; *(dispositivo)*

safety catch ▪ s. de vida life insurance ➤ *adv* certainly, for sure.
seis ➤ *adj & m* six ▪ las s. six o'clock.
selección ➤ *f* selection.
seleccionar ➤ *tr* to select.
selecto, a ➤ *adj* select.
sello ➤ *m* stamp; *(de documento)* seal.
selva ➤ *f* woods; *(jungla)* jungle.
semáforo ➤ *m* traffic light.
semana ➤ *f* week ▪ entre s. during the week • s. laboral working week.
semanal ➤ *adj* weekly.
semanario ➤ *m* weekly publication.
sembrar §33 ➤ *tr* to sow.
semejante ➤ *adj* similar ➤ *mf* fellow man.
semestre ➤ *m* six months, semester.
semilla ➤ *f* seed.
seminario ➤ *m* seminary.
sémola ➤ *f* semolina.
sencillez ➤ *f* simplicity.
sencillo, a ➤ *adj* simple, easy; *(sin adorno)* plain; *(ingenuo)* naive.
senda ➤ *f or* **sendero** ➤ *m* path.
seno ➤ *m (pecho)* breast; FIG. bosom.
sensación ➤ *f* sensation; *(impresión)* feeling.
sensacional ➤ *adj* sensational.
sensato, a ➤ *adj* sensible.
sensibilidad ➤ *f* sensibility; *(emotividad, susceptibilidad)* sensitivity.
sensible ➤ *adj* sensitive.
sensitivo, a ➤ *adj* sensitive.
sensualidad ➤ *f* sensuality.
sentar §33 ➤ *tr* to seat; *(establecer)* to set ➤ *intr (la comida)* to agree with; *(la ropa)* to fit ➤ *reflex* to sit (down).
sentencia ➤ *f* LAW *(juicio)* sentence.
sentido ➤ *m* sense; *(conciencia)* consciousness; *(dirección)* direction ▪ doble s. double meaning • tener s. to make sense.
sentimental ➤ *adj* sentimental.
sentimiento ➤ *m (emoción)* sentiment; *(pesar)* sorrow.
sentir[1] ➤ *m (sentimiento)* feeling; *(opinión)* opinion.
sentir[2] §43 ➤ *tr* to feel; *(experimentar)* to experience; *(lamentar)* to regret ▪ lo siento I'm sorry ➤ *intr* to feel ➤ *reflex* to feel ▪ s. como en (su) casa to feel at home.
seña ➤ *f (indicio)* sign; *(marca)* mark ▪ hacer señas to signal.
señal ➤ *f (marca)* sign; *(seña)* reminder; *(vestigio)* trace; *(aviso)* signal.
señalar ➤ *tr* to mark; *(indicar)* to point (at); FIG. to signal, announce.
señor, a ➤ *m (dueño, noble)* lord; *(caballero)* gentleman ▪ (el) s. Márquez Mr. Márquez • siéntese, s. sit down, sir ➤ *f (dueña, noble)* lady; *(esposa)* wife ▪ (la) s. Pérez Mrs. Pérez • buenos días, s. good morning, ma'am.
señorita ➤ *f* young lady ▪ (la) s. García Miss García.
señorito ➤ *m* young man.
separación ➤ *f* separation.
separar ➤ *tr* to separate; *(partir)* to divide ➤ *reflex* to separate.
septentrional ➤ *adj* northern(ly).
septiembre ➤ *m* September.
séptimo, a ➤ *adj & m* seventh.
sepulcro ➤ *m* sepulcher.
sepultura ➤ *f* grave.
sequía ➤ *f* drought.
séquito ➤ *m* entourage.
ser[1] ➤ *m* being ▪ s. humano human being • s. vivo living creature.
ser[2] §44 ➤ *aux* to be ➤ *intr* to be ▪ a *or* de no s. por if it were not for • a no s. que unless • así sea so be it • no sea que lest • o sea *or* esto es that is to say • o sea que in other words • sea como sea one way or the other • sea lo que sea be that as it may • s. de to be made of; *(tener origen)* to be *or* come from; *(suceder)* to become of; *(corresponder)* to be suitable for ▪ ya sea . . . ya sea either . . . or.
sereno, a ➤ *adj* calm.
serial ➤ *adj & m* serial.
serie ➤ *f* series ▪ fabricar *or* producir en s. to mass-produce.
seriedad ➤ *f* seriousness; *(comportamiento)* dependability.
serio, a ➤ *adj* serious.
sermón ➤ *m* sermon.
serpiente ➤ *f* snake ▪ s. de cascabel rattlesnake.
serranía ➤ *f* mountains.
serrano, a ➤ *adj* mountain ➤ *mf* mountain-dweller, highlander.
serrucho ➤ *m* saw.
servicio ➤ *m* service; *(retrete)* bathroom ▪ al s. de in the service of • prestar un s. to perform a service.
servidor, a ➤ *mf* servant ➤ *m* COMPUT. server.
servidumbre ➤ *f* staff of servants; *(esclavitud)* slavery.
servilleta ➤ *f* napkin.
servir §32 ➤ *intr* to serve ▪ no s. para nada to be useless • s. de to act *or* serve as • s. para to be used for ➤ *tr* to serve ➤ *reflex* to make use of.
sesenta ➤ *adj & m* sixty.
sesión ➤ *f* session, meeting.
seso ➤ *m* brain; FIG. sense.
setenta ➤ *adj & m* seventy.
seto ➤ *m* fence ▪ s. vivo hedge.
seudónimo ➤ *m* pseudonym.
severidad ➤ *f* severity, harshness.
severo, a ➤ *adj* severe.
sexo ➤ *m* sex; *(órganos)* genitals.
sexto, a ➤ *adj & m* sixth.
sexual ➤ *adj* sexual.
si ➤ *conj* if, whether ▪ como si as if • por si acaso just in case • si bien although • si no if not, otherwise.
sí[1] ➤ *pron* himself, herself, etc. ▪ dar de sí to give of oneself • de sí *or* en sí in itself • fuera de sí beside oneself • para sí to oneself • sí mismo oneself.
sí[2] ➤ *adv* yes; *(en votación)* aye; *(ciertamente)* certainly ▪ creo que sí I think so ➤ *m* yes; *(consentimiento)* consent, permission ▪ dar el sí to say yes.
sico- *see* **psico-**.
SIDA ➤ *m* AIDS.
siderurgia ➤ *f* iron and steel industry.
sidra ➤ *f* alcoholic cider.
siempre ➤ *adv* always ▪ como s. as always • de s. usual • para *or* por s. forever • s. jamás forever and ever • s. que every time; *(a condición de)* provided that • s. y cuando provided that.
sien ➤ *f* temple.
sierra ➤ *f* saw; GEOL. mountain range.
siesta ➤ *f* afternoon nap.
siete ➤ *adj & m* seven ▪ las s. seven o'clock.
sigiloso, a ➤ *adj (secreto)* secretive; *(prudente)* discreet.
sigla ➤ *f* acronym.
siglo ➤ *m* century.
significado ➤ *m* meaning.
significar §47 ➤ *tr* to mean.
significativo, a ➤ *adj* significant.
signo ➤ *m* sign; *(de puntuación)* mark ▪ s. de admiración exclamation point • s. de interrogación question mark.
siguiente ➤ *adj* following, next.
sílaba ➤ *f* syllable.
silba ➤ *f* hissing, booing.
silbar ➤ *intr* to whistle; *(sisear)* to hiss.
silbato *or* **silbido** ➤ *m* whistle.
silencio ➤ *m* silence.
silencioso, a ➤ *adj* quiet, silent.
silicona ➤ *f* silicone.
silla ➤ *f (asiento)* chair; *(para montar)* saddle ▪ s. de ruedas wheelchair.
sillón ➤ *m* armchair.
silueta ➤ *f* outline.
silvestre ➤ *adj (planta, animal)* wild.
simbólico, a ➤ *adj* symbolic(al).
símbolo ➤ *m* symbol.
simetría ➤ *f* symmetry.
simétrico, a ➤ *adj* symmetric(al).
simiente ➤ *f* seed.
similar ➤ *adj* similar.
similitud ➤ *f* similarity.
simpatía ➤ *f (afecto)* liking; *(afinidad)* sympathy, affinity; *(amabilidad)* congeniality ▪ tener s. a *or* por to like.
simpático, a ➤ *adj* nice, likable.
simpatizar §02 ➤ *intr* to get along (together).
simple ➤ *adj* simple; *(fácil)* easy ➤ *mf* simpleton.
simulacro ➤ *m* pretense.
simular ➤ *tr* to feign.
simultáneo, a ➤ *adj* simultaneous.
sin ➤ *prep* without; *(fuera de)* not including.
sinagoga ➤ *f* synagogue.
sinceridad ➤ *f* sincerity.
sincero, a ➤ *adj* sincere.
sincronizar §02 ➤ *tr* to synchronize.
sindicato ➤ *m* labor *or* trade union.
sinfonía ➤ *f* symphony.
singular ➤ *adj* single; *(excepcional)* unique; *(peculiar)* peculiar ➤ *m* GRAM. singular.
siniestro, a ➤ *adj (izquierdo)* left, left-hand; *(perverso)* wicked; *(funesto)* fateful ➤ *m* disaster.
sino[1] ➤ *m* fate.
sino[2] ➤ *conj* but; *(excepto)* except ▪ no sólo . . . s. not only . . . but also.
sinónimo, a ➤ *adj* synonymous ➤ *m* synonym.
sinsabor ➤ *m* discontent; *(pena)* grief.
sintético, a ➤ *adj* synthetic.
sintetizador ➤ *m* synthesizer.
síntoma ➤ *m* symptom.
sintonía ➤ *f* tuning (in).
sintonizador ➤ *m* tuner.
sintonizar §02 ➤ *tr* to tune (in) ▪ s. con to be tuned to.
sinvergüenza ➤ *adj & mf* shameless *or* brazen (person).
siquiera ➤ *conj* even though, if only ➤ *adv* at least ▪ ni s. not even.
sirena ➤ *f* siren; MYTH. mermaid ▪ s. de niebla foghorn.
sirvienta ➤ *f* maid.
sirviente ➤ *m* servant.
sismógrafo ➤ *m* seismograph.
sistema ➤ *m* system ▪ con s. systematically • s. métrico metric system • s. nervioso nervous system.
sitio ➤ *m (localidad)* site; *(lugar)* place; MIL. siege ▪ s. web website.
situación ➤ *f* situation; *(estado)* position.
situar §45 ➤ *tr* to place.
smoking ➤ *m* tuxedo.
snob ➤ *adj* snobbish ➤ *mf* snob.
sobaco ➤ *m* armpit.
soberanía ➤ *f* sovereignty.
soberano, a ➤ *adj & mf* sovereign.
soberbio, a ➤ *adj (orgulloso)* arrogant; *(magnífico)* superb ➤ *f* arrogance.
sobornar ➤ *tr* to bribe.
sobra ➤ *f* excess ▪ de s. superfluous, extra ▪ *pl* leftovers.
sobrante ➤ *adj* remaining ➤ *m* surplus.
sobrar ➤ *intr (estar de más)* to be more than enough; *(quedar)* to remain; *(ser inútil)* to be superfluous.
sobre[1] ➤ *m* envelope.
sobre[2] ➤ *prep (encima)* above, over; *(en)* on, on top of; *(superior a)* above, over; *(acerca de)* about, on; *(además de)* on top of, over.
sobrecoger §20 ➤ *tr* to scare ➤ *reflex* to be scared.
sobreentendido, a ➤ *adj* understood.
sobrehumano, a ➤ *adj* superhuman.
sobremesa ➤ *f* after-dinner conversation.
sobrenatural ➤ *adj* supernatural.
sobrepasar ➤ *intr* to surpass.
sobreponer §37 ➤ *tr* to superimpose ➤ *reflex* to control oneself; *(vencer)* to triumph.
sobresaliente ➤ *adj* outstanding ➤ *m* highest mark.
sobresalir §41 ➤ *intr (resaltar)* to project; *(sobrepujar)* to be outstanding.
sobresalto ➤ *m* fright.
sobrevenir §52 ➤ *intr* to occur unexpectedly.
sobreviviente ➤ *adj* surviving ➤ *mf* survivor.
sobrevivir ➤ *intr* to survive.
sobrino, a ➤ *m* nephew ➤ *f* niece.
sobrio, a ➤ *adj (sin beber)* sober; *(conservador)* moderate.
socavón ➤ *m* cave-in.
sociable ➤ *adj* sociable.
social ➤ *adj* social.
socialista ➤ *adj & mf* socialist.
sociedad ➤ *f* society ▪ s. anónima corporation.
socio, a ➤ *mf (asociado)* member; *(accionista)* business associate.
sociología ➤ *f* sociology.
socorrer ➤ *tr* to aid.
socorro ➤ *m (apoyo)* aid; *(provisiones)* supplies ➤ *interj* help!
sofá ➤ *m* sofa.
sofisticado, a ➤ *adj* sophisticated.
sofocar §47 ➤ *tr (asfixiar)* to suffocate; *(un fuego)* to put out ➤ *reflex* to suffocate; FIG. to get embarrassed.
sofreír §39 ➤ *tr* to fry lightly.
sofrito ➤ *m* lightly-fried mixture of seasonings.
soga ➤ *f* rope.
sol ➤ *m* sun, sunlight ▪ al ponerse el s. at sunset • al salir el s. at sunrise • hacer s. to be sunny • tomar el s. to sunbathe.
solamente ➤ *adv* only.
solapa ➤ *f* flap; *(de chaqueta)* lapel.
solar[1] ➤ *adj* solar.
solar[2] ➤ *m (terreno)* lot; *(bajo construcción)* building site.
soldado ➤ *mf* soldier.
soldar §11 ➤ *tr* to solder, weld.
soleado ➤ *adj* sunny.
soledad ➤ *f (aislamiento)* solitude; *(sentirse solo)* loneliness.
solemne ➤ *adj* solemn.
soler §54 ➤ *intr* to be in the habit of; *(ser frecuente)* to tend to ▪ suelo llegar tarde I usually arrive late.
solicitante ➤ *mf* petitioner.
solicitar ➤ *tr* to request; *(gestionar)* to apply for; *(atraer)* to attract.
solicitud ➤ *f* application; *(petición)* request ▪ a s. de at the request of.
solidaridad ➤ *f* solidarity.
sólido, a ➤ *adj* solid.
solitario, a ➤ *adj* lone, solitary.
sollozar §02 ➤ *intr* to sob.
sollozo ➤ *m* sob.
solo, a ➤ *adj* alone; *(único)* sole; *(aislado)* lonely ▪ a solas alone.
sólo ➤ *adv* only.
solomillo ➤ *m* sirloin.
soltar §11 ➤ *tr* to let go of; *(liberar)* to free; *(irrumpir)* to let out; *(decir)* to blurt out ➤ *reflex* to become proficient; *(relajarse)* to loosen up.
soltero, a ➤ *adj* single ➤ *m* bachelor ➤ *f* unmarried woman.
solterón, ona ➤ *adj* old and unmarried ➤ *m* confirmed bachelor ➤ *f* spinster; COLL. old maid.
soluble ➤ *adj* CHEM. soluble.
solución ➤ *f* solution; *(desenlace)* ending.
solucionar ➤ *tr* to solve.
sombra ➤ *f* shade; *(imagen)* shadow ▪ dar s. to cast a shadow.
sombrero ➤ *m* hat.
sombrilla ➤ *f* parasol.
sombrío, a ➤ *adj (lugar)* gloomy; *(persona)* sullen.
someter ➤ *tr* to subjugate; *(subordinar)* to subordinate; *(entregar)* to submit ▪ s. a prueba to test • s. a tratamiento to put under treatment ➤ *reflex* to surrender ▪ s. a to undergo.
somnífero ➤ *m* sleeping pill.
sonajero ➤ *m* rattle.
sonar[1] ➤ *m* TECH. sonar.
sonar[2] §11 ➤ *intr (producir sonido)* to sound; *(tintinear)* to ring; *(parecer)* to sound like ➤ *reflex* to blow.
sondeo ➤ *m (encuesta)* poll.
sonido ➤ *m* sound.
sonoro, a ➤ *adj (sonido)* sound; *(resonante)* deep, sonorous.
sonreír §39 ➤ *intr & reflex* to smile.
sonrisa ➤ *f* smile.
sonrojarse ➤ *reflex* to blush.
soñador, a ➤ *adj* dreamy ➤ *mf* dreamer.
soñar §11 ➤ *tr & intr* to dream ▪ ¡ni soñarlo! not on your life! • s. con to dream of *or* about.
sopa ➤ *f* soup.
sopero, a ➤ *adj* soup ➤ *f* soup tureen.
soplar ➤ *intr* to blow ➤ *tr (mover el viento)* to blow (away); *(velas)* to blow out; *(globos)* to blow up.
soplo ➤ *m* blow; FIG. instant.
soportar ➤ *tr (sostener)* to support; *(sufrir)* to bear.
soporte ➤ *m* support; *(base)* stand.
sorber ➤ *tr (beber)* to sip; *(absorber)* to absorb.
sorbete ➤ *m* sherbet.
sorbo ➤ *m* sip; *(trago)* swallow, gulp.
sordo, a ➤ *adj* deaf; *(silencioso)* muffled ➤ *mf* deaf person.
sordomudo, a ➤ *adj & mf* deaf-mute.
sorprendente ➤ *adj* surprising.
sorprender ➤ *tr* to take by surprise; *(asombrar)* to surprise.
sorpresa ➤ *f* surprise.
sorpresivo, a ➤ *adj* unexpected.
sortear ➤ *tr* to draw lots for; *(rifar)* to raffle; *(evitar)* to avoid.
sorteo ➤ *m* drawing; *(rifa)* raffle.
sortija ➤ *f (anillo)* ring.
sosegar §35 ➤ *tr & intr* to calm (down) ➤ *reflex* to calm down.
sosiego ➤ *m* tranquility, quiet.
soso, a ➤ *adj (de poco sabor)* tasteless; *(sin sal)* unsalted.
sospecha ➤ *f* suspicion.
sospechar ➤ *tr* to suspect ➤ *intr* to be suspicious.
sospechoso, a ➤ *adj* suspicious.
sostén ➤ *m (apoyo)* support; *(prenda)*

bra ■ **s. de familia** breadwinner.

sostener §46 ➤ *tr (sustentar)* to support; *(sujetar)* to hold (up); *(defender)* to uphold ➤ *reflex* to hold oneself up; *(mantenerse)* to support oneself.

sótano ➤ *m* basement.

Sr. ➤ *m* Mr.

Sra. ➤ *f* Mrs.

standard ➤ *adj & m* standard ■ **s. de vida** standard of living.

su, sus ➤ *adj* one's, his, her, your, its, their.

suave ➤ *adj* soft; *(liso)* smooth; *(dulce)* sweet; *(tranquilo)* gentle.

suavizar §02 ➤ *tr* to soften; *(hacer plano)* to smooth; *(moderar)* to temper ➤ *reflex* to soften; *(volver plano)* to become smooth.

subalterno, a ➤ *adj & mf* subordinate.

subasta ➤ *f* auction.

subconsciente ➤ *adj & m* subconscious (mind).

subdesarrollado, a ➤ *adj* underdeveloped.

subdirector, a ➤ *mf* assistant manager.

súbdito, a ➤ *mf (de un monarca)* subject; *(ciudadano)* citizen.

subestimar ➤ *tr* to underestimate.

subir ➤ *tr* to climb, go up; *(llevar arriba)* to take *or* carry up; *(levantar, aumentar)* to raise; COMPUT. to upload ➤ *intr* to rise; *(ascender)* to go up ■ **s. a** *(montar)* to get on *or* into; *(alcanzar)* to come *or* amount to ➤ *reflex* to go up ■ **s. a** to get on *or* into.

súbito, a ➤ *adj* sudden ■ **de s.** suddenly.

sublevarse ➤ *reflex* to revolt.

sublime ➤ *adj* sublime.

submarinismo ➤ *m* scuba diving.

submarino, a ➤ *adj & m* submarine.

subordinado, a ➤ *adj & mf* subordinate.

subrayar ➤ *tr (señalar)* to underline; *(poner énfasis)* to emphasize.

subscri- *see* **suscri-**.

subsecretario, a ➤ *mf* assistant secretary; POL. undersecretary.

subsidiario, a ➤ *adj* subsidiary.

subsidio ➤ *m* subsidy; *(ayuda)* aid.

subsistencia ➤ *f* subsistence.

subsistir ➤ *intr* to subsist.

substan-, substi- *see* **sustan-, susti-**.

subterráneo, a ➤ *adj* underground ➤ *m (tren)* subway.

suburbano, a ➤ *adj* suburban.

suburbio ➤ *m (arrabal)* suburb; *(barrio pobre)* slum, shantytown.

subvención ➤ *f* subsidy.

suceder ➤ *intr* to follow; *(ocurrir)* to occur ➤ *reflex* to follow one another.

sucesión ➤ *f* succession.

sucesivamente ➤ *adv* successively.

sucesivo, a ➤ *adj* consecutive ■ **en lo s.** in the future.

suceso ➤ *m* event; *(transcurso)* course; *(resultado)* outcome.

sucesor, a ➤ *mf* successor.

suciedad ➤ *f* dirt, filth.

sucio, a ➤ *adj* dirty.

suculento, a ➤ *adj* succulent.

sucumbir ➤ *intr* to succumb.

sucursal ➤ *f* branch (office); *(de empresa)* subsidiary.

Sudamérica ➤ *f* South America.

sudamericano, a ➤ *adj & mf* South American.

sudar ➤ *intr* to sweat.

sudeste ➤ *adj* southeastern ➤ *m* southeast.

sudoeste ➤ *adj* southwestern ➤ *m* southwest.

sudor ➤ *m* sweat.

suegra ➤ *f* mother-in-law.

suegro ➤ *m* father-in-law ■ *pl* in-laws.

suela ➤ *f* sole.

sueldo ➤ *m* salary ■ **a s.** on a salary.

suelo ➤ *m (tierra)* ground; *(piso)* floor.

suelto, a ➤ *adj* loose; *(desatado)* untied; *(sin pareja)* odd ■ **venderse s.** *(por peso)* to be sold in bulk; *(por separado)* to be sold singly ➤ *m (dinero)* loose change.

sueño ➤ *m* sleep; *(representación)* dream ■ **quitar el s.** to keep awake • **tener s.** to be sleepy.

suerte ➤ *f (destino)* fate; *(fortuna)* luck ■ **buena, mala s.** good, bad luck • **tener s.** to be lucky.

suéter ➤ *m* sweater.

suficiente ➤ *adj* sufficient.

sufrimiento ➤ *m* suffering.

sufrir ➤ *tr (padecer)* to suffer; *(experimentar)* to undergo; *(soportar)* to endure ➤ *intr (padecer)* to suffer; *(preocuparse)* to worry.

sugerencia ➤ *f* suggestion.

sugerir §43 ➤ *tr* to suggest.

sugestión ➤ *f* suggestion.

sugestionar ➤ *tr (influenciar)* to influence; *(hipnotizar)* to hypnotize.

suicida ➤ *adj* suicidal ➤ *mf* suicide.

suicidarse ➤ *reflex* to commit suicide.

suicidio ➤ *m* suicide.

sujetador, a ➤ *adj* fastening ➤ *m (sostén)* bra.

sujetapapeles ➤ *m* paper clip.

sujetar ➤ *tr* to fasten; *(agarrar)* to grasp; *(dominar)* to subject.

sujeto, a ➤ *adj* fastened ➤ *m* subject.

suma ➤ *f* sum; MATH. *(adición)* addition; *(cantidad)* amount of money.

sumamente ➤ *adv* extremely.

sumar ➤ *tr* to add (up); to add up to ➤ *reflex* ■ **s. a** to be added to.

sumergible ➤ *adj & m* submersible.

sumergir §19 ➤ *tr* to submerge ➤ *reflex* to dive, submerge ■ **s. en** to become immersed *or* absorbed in.

suministrar ➤ *tr* to supply.

suministro ➤ *m* supply ■ **s. a domicilio** home delivery.

sumiso, a ➤ *adj (sometido)* submissive; *(obediente)* obedient.

sumo, a ➤ *adj* greatest ■ **a lo sumo** at (the) most.

suntuoso, a ➤ *adj* sumptuous.

superar ➤ *tr (sobrepujar)* to surpass; *(dificultades)* to overcome.

superdotado, a ➤ *adj & mf* exceptionally gifted (child).

superficial ➤ *adj* superficial.

superficie ➤ *f* surface; GEOM. area.

superfino, a ➤ *adj* extra fine.

superfluo, a ➤ *adj* superfluous.

superior ➤ *m* superior ➤ *adj (de más altura)* upper; *(más alto)* higher; *(excelente)* superior.

superioridad ➤ *f (calidad)* superiority; *(autoridad)* higher authority.

supermercado ➤ *m* supermarket.

supersónico, a ➤ *adj* supersonic.

supersticioso, a ➤ *adj* superstitious.

supervisar ➤ *tr* to supervise.

supervivencia ➤ *f* survival.

suplantar ➤ *tr* to supplant.

suplementario, a *or* **suplemental** ➤ *adj* supplemental, supplementary.

suplemento ➤ *m* supplement.

suplencia ➤ *f* replacement.

suplente ➤ *adj* substitute; SPORT. reserve ➤ *mf* replacement; SPORT. reserve player; THEAT. understudy.

suplicar §47 ➤ *tr* to implore.

suplicio ➤ *m (tortura)* torture; *(castigo corporal)* corporal punishment.

suplir ➤ *tr (compensar)* to make up for; *(reemplazar)* to replace.

suponer §37 ➤ *tr* to suppose; *(imaginar)* to imagine; *(traer consigo)* to entail ■ **ser de s.** to be likely.

supositorio ➤ *m* suppository.

supremo, a ➤ *adj* supreme; *(definitivo)* final.

suprimir ➤ *tr* to eliminate.

supuesto, a ➤ *adj (fingido)* assumed; *(que se supone)* supposed; *(imaginario)* imaginary; *(hipotético)* hypothetical ■ **por s.** of course ➤ *m* supposition.

sur ➤ *adj* southern, southerly ➤ *m* south.

surco ➤ *m* trench; AGR. furrow.

surgir §19 ➤ *intr (surtir)* to shoot up; *(aparecer)* to arise.

surtido, a ➤ *adj* assorted ➤ *m* selection.

surtidor ➤ *m (chorro)* spout; *(fuente)* fountain ■ **s. de gasolina** filling station.

susceptible *or* **susceptivo, a** ➤ *adj* susceptible; *(quisquilloso)* sensitive.

suscitar ➤ *tr* to stir up.

suscribir §55 ➤ *tr & reflex* to subscribe (to).

suscripción ➤ *f* subscription.

suspender ➤ *tr* to suspend; *(colgar)* to hang; *(interrumpir)* to interrupt; *(un estudiante)* to fail.

suspensión ➤ *f* suspension.

suspenso ➤ *m* EDUC. failing mark ■ **de s.** suspense • **en s.** pending, outstanding.

suspicacia ➤ *f* distrust.

suspicaz ➤ *adj* distrustful.

suspirar ➤ *intr* to sigh.

suspiro ➤ *m* sigh.

sustancia ➤ *f* substance.

sustantivo, a ➤ *adj* substantive ➤ *m* noun.

sustento ➤ *m (alimento)* sustenance; *(medios)* livelihood.

sustitución ➤ *f* substitution.

sustituir §10 ➤ *tr* to substitute.

sustituto, a ➤ *adj & mf* substitute.

susto ➤ *m* fright, scare.

sustracción ➤ *f* subtraction.

sustraer §49 ➤ *tr* to subtract.

susurrar ➤ *intr* to whisper.

susurro ➤ *m* whisper.

sutil ➤ *adj* subtle; *(perspicaz)* sharp.

suyo, a ➤ *adj* his, her, your, their; of his, hers, yours, *or* theirs ➤ *pron* his, hers, yours, theirs ■ **lo s.** one's share • **los suyos** one's friends *or* family • **salirse con la s.** COLL. to get one's way.

T

tabaco ➤ *m* tobacco.

taberna ➤ *f* tavern.

tabique ➤ *m* partition.

tabla ➤ *f (de madera)* board; *(lista)* table ■ **t. de planchar** ironing board • **t. de surf** surfboard.

tablero ➤ *m* board ■ **t. de ajedrez** chess board • **t. de dibujo** drawing board • **t. de instrumentos** instrument panel; AUTO. dashboard.

tablón ➤ *m* thick plank.

taburete ➤ *m* stool.

tacaño, a ➤ *adj* stingy ➤ *mf* miser.

tachar ➤ *tr* to cross out.

tacón ➤ *m* heel.

táctico, a ➤ *adj* tactical ➤ *f* tactics.

tacto ➤ *m (sentido)* (sense of) touch; *(delicadeza)* tact.

tajada ➤ *f* CUL. slice.

tajo ➤ *m (corte)* cut, slash.

tal ➤ *adj* such (a); *(cierto)* certain ■ **t. cual** such as • **t. vez** perhaps, maybe ➤ *pron* such a thing; *(alguno)* some, someone ■ **fulano de t.** so-and-so • **t. para cual** COLL. two of a kind ➤ *adv* thus, so ■ **con t. que** provided that • **¿qué t.?** COLL. how goes it?

tala ➤ *f (de árboles)* felling.

talante ➤ *m* mood ■ **hacer algo de buen, mal t.** to do something willingly, unwillingly.

talar ➤ *tr (un árbol)* to fell, cut down.

talco ➤ *m* talc; PHARM. talcum powder.

talega ➤ *f* sack.

talento ➤ *m* talent.

talla ➤ *f (estatura)* height; *(medida)* size; *(escultura)* wood carving.

tallar ➤ *tr* to carve; *(en metal)* to engrave; JEWEL. to cut; ARTS to sculpt.

tallarín ➤ *m* noodle.

talle ➤ *m* waist.

taller ➤ *m (de obreros)* shop; *(de artistas)* studio ■ **t. de reparaciones** AUTO. body shop.

tallo ➤ *m* stem.

talón ➤ *m* heel; *(comprobante)* receipt; *(de cheque)* stub.

talonario ➤ *m (de recibos)* receipt book; *(de cheques)* checkbook.

tamaño ➤ *m (dimensión)* size; *(volumen)* volume ■ **del t. de** as large as • **t. natural** life-size.

tambalear ➤ *intr* to stagger.

también ➤ *adv* also, too; *(asimismo)* likewise.

tambor ➤ *m* drum.

tamiz ➤ *m* sieve.

tampoco ➤ *adv* neither, nor.

tampón ➤ *m* ink pad; PHARM. tampon.

tan ➤ *adv* so, as ■ **t. pronto como** as soon as • **t. siquiera** at least • **t. sólo** only.

tanque ➤ *m* tank; *(barco)* tanker.

tanto, a ➤ *adj* so much, so many ➤ *pron* that ■ **por (lo) t.** therefore • **t. como** *or* **cuanto** as much as ➤ *m (cantidad)* certain amount; *(en deportes)* point ■ **entre t.** in the meantime • **no ser para t.** not to be so bad • **otro t.** the same thing • **t. por ciento** per cent • **y tantos** and some, odd ➤ *adv* ■ **t. como** as much as • **t. más** all the more • **t. mejor** all the better • **t. que** so much that.

tapa ➤ *f (de olla)* lid; *(de libro)* cover; *(bocado)* hors d'oeuvre.

tapar ➤ *tr* to cover (up); *(cerrar)* to plug up ➤ *reflex* to cover oneself up.

tapete ➤ *m* table runner.

tapia ➤ *f* mud *or* adobe wall; *(cerca)* (adjoining) wall.

tapiz ➤ *m* tapestry.

tapizar §02 ➤ *tr (muebles)* to upholster.

tapón ➤ *m (de botellas)* cork; *(de tonel)* plug.

taponar ➤ *tr* to plug.

taquilla ➤ *f* THEAT. *(ventanilla)* box office; *(cantidad)* receipts.

tardanza ➤ *f* delay.

tardar ➤ *intr (demorarse)* to delay; *(durar)* to take; *(tomar tiempo)* to take a long time; *(llegar tarde)* to be late.

tarde ➤ *f* afternoon, (early) evening ■ **buenas tardes** good afternoon ➤ *adv (a hora avanzada)* late ■ **lo más t.** at the latest.

tarea ➤ *f* task ■ *pl* homework.

tarifa ➤ *f (tasa)* tariff; *(precio)* fare.

tarjeta ➤ *f* card ■ **t. de crédito** credit card • **t. de identidad** identity card • **t. postal** post card.

tarro ➤ *m (vasija)* jar; *(de lata)* tin can.

tarta ➤ *f* pie, tart.

tartamudear ➤ *intr* to stammer.

tartamudo, a ➤ *mf* stammerer.

tartera ➤ *f* baking pan.

tasa ➤ *f* rate ■ **t. aduanera** customs duty.

tasar ➤ *tr (poner precio)* to set the price of; *(valorar)* to appraise.

tatuaje ➤ *m* tattoo.

taurino, a ➤ *adj* taurine, of bulls.

tautología ➤ *f* tautology.

taxi ➤ *m* taxi.

taxista ➤ *mf* taxi driver.

taza ➤ *f* cup; *(contenido)* cupful; *(de fuente)* basin; *(de retrete)* bowl.

tazón ➤ *m* large cup; *(cuenco)* bowl.

te ➤ *pron* [informal] you; to, for, *or* from you ■ **cálmate** calm yourself.

té ➤ *m* tea.

teatro ➤ *m* theater.

techo ➤ *m* roof; *(cielo raso)* ceiling.

tecla ➤ *f* key.

teclado ➤ *m* keyboard.

técnico, a ➤ *adj* technical ➤ *mf* technician ➤ *f* technique.

tecnología ➤ *f* technology.

tedio ➤ *m* tedium.

teja ➤ *f (mosaico)* tile; *(de techo)* slate.

tejado ➤ *m* roof.

tejer ➤ *intr (con telar)* to weave; *(hacer punto)* to knit.

tejido ➤ *m* fabric.

tela ➤ *f (paño)* fabric; *(de araña)* web.

telar ➤ *m (para tejer)* loom.

telaraña ➤ *f* spider web.

telefonear ➤ *tr* to phone.

teléfono ➤ *m* telephone ■ **t. celular** cellular telephone, cell phone.

telegrama ➤ *m* telegram.

teleobjetivo ➤ *m* telephoto lens.

telescopio ➤ *m* telescope.

televisión ➤ *f* television.

televisor ➤ *m* television (set).

telex ➤ *m* telex.

telón ➤ *m* THEAT. curtain.

tema ➤ *m* subject.

temblar §33 ➤ *intr* to tremble; *(de frío)* to shiver; *(de miedo)* to quiver.

temblor ➤ *m* tremor; AMER. earthquake.

temer ➤ *tr & intr* to fear ■ **t. a** to be afraid of.

temerario, a ➤ *adj* reckless.

temor ➤ *m* fear; *(recelo)* foreboding.

temperamento ➤ *m* temperament.

temperatura ➤ *f* temperature.

tempestad ➤ *f* storm.

templado, a ➤ *adj (moderado)* moderate; *(tibio)* lukewarm; *(el clima)* mild.

templo ➤ *m* temple.

temporada ➤ *f (del año)* season; *(período)* period ■ **fuera de t.** off-season • **t. baja** off season, slow season.

temporal ➤ *adj* temporary ➤ *m* storm.

temprano, a ➤ *adj & adv* early.

tenaz ➤ *adj* tenacious.

tenaza(s) ➤ *f(pl)* pliers.

tendencia ➤ *f* tendency.

tender §34 ➤ *tr (extender)* to spread (out); *(alargar)* to stretch out; *(ropa)* to hang out; *(cable)* to lay; *(puente)* to build ➤ *intr* to tend *(a* to) ➤ *reflex* to lie down.

tendero, a ➤ *mf* shopkeeper.

tendón ➤ *m* tendon.

tenebroso, a ➤ *adj (sombrío)* dark; *(secreto)* shady; *(oscuro)* obscure.

tenedor ➤ *m* fork.

tener §46 ➤ *tr* to have; *(contener)* to contain; *(edad)* to be; *(cumplir)* to keep, fulfill ■ **t. calor, frío** to be hot, cold • **t. celos** to be jealous • **t. cuidado** to be careful • **t. en cuenta** to take into account • **t. éxito** to succeed • **t. ganas de** to feel like • **t. hambre, sed** to be

hungry, thirsty • **t. miedo** to be afraid • **t. presente** to bear in mind • **t. prisa** to be in a hurry • **t. que** to have to • **t. razón** to be right • **t. sueño** to be sleepy • **t. suerte** to be lucky ➤ *reflex* to steady oneself ▪ **t. de pie** to stand up • **t. por** to consider oneself.
teniente ➤ *mf* lieutenant.
tenis ➤ *m* tennis ▪ **t. de mesa** table tennis.
tenista ➤ *mf* tennis player.
tenor ➤ *m* MUS. tenor.
tensar ➤ *tr* to stretch.
tensión ➤ *f* tension; *(emocional)* stress ▪ **t. arterial** blood pressure.
tenso, a ➤ *adj* tense; *(nervios, relaciones)* strained; *(emocionalmente)* stressed.
tentación ➤ *f* temptation.
tentar §33 ➤ *tr (seducir)* to tempt; *(intentar)* to try.
tenue ➤ *adj (delgado)* thin; *(luz)* soft.
teñir ➤ *tr* to dye; FIG. to imbue.
teoría ➤ *f* theory.
terapia ➤ *f* therapy.
tercer ➤ *adj contr of* **tercero.**
tercero, a ➤ *adj & m* third.
tercio, a ➤ *adj & m* third.
terciopelo ➤ *m* velvet.
terco, a ➤ *adj* stubborn.
tergiversar ➤ *tr* to distort.
terminal ➤ *adj & m* terminal.
terminar ➤ *tr* to end ➤ *intr* to come to an end ▪ **t. de** *(acabar de)* to have just; *(concluir)* to finish • **t. en** to end up in • **t. por** to end up ➤ *reflex* to come to an end.
término ➤ *m* end; *(palabra, tiempo)* term ▪ **en buenos términos con** on good terms with • **t. medio** MATH. average; *(compromiso)* middle ground.
termómetro ➤ *m* thermometer.
termostato ➤ *m* thermostat.
ternera ➤ *f* female calf; CUL. veal.
ternero ➤ *m* male calf.
ternura ➤ *f* tenderness.
terquedad ➤ *f* stubbornness.
terracota ➤ *f* terra cotta.
terraza ➤ *f* terrace; veranda.
terremoto ➤ *m* earthquake.
terreno, a ➤ *adj* earthly; *(terrenal)* worldly ➤ *m (tierra)* land; *(campo)* piece of land, ground.
terrestre ➤ *adj* terrestrial.
terrible ➤ *adj* terrible.
territorial ➤ *adj* territorial.
territorio ➤ *m* territory; *(comarca)* zone.
terrón ➤ *m* clod; *(de azúcar)* lump.
terror ➤ *m* terror.
terrorista ➤ *adj & mf* terrorist.
terso, a ➤ *adj* clear; *(estilo)* smooth.
tertulia ➤ *f* social gathering ▪ **t. literaria** literary circle.
tesis ➤ *f* thesis; *(opinión)* theory.
tesoro ➤ *m (dinero)* treasure; *(fondos públicos)* treasury.
testamento ➤ *m* will, testament.
testarudo, a ➤ *adj* stubborn.
testificar §47 ➤ *tr* to testify (to).
testigo ➤ *mf* witness.
testimonio ➤ *m* testimony.
tétano(s) ➤ *m* tetanus.
tetera ➤ *f* teapot.
textil ➤ *adj & m* textile.
texto ➤ *m* text; *(libro)* textbook.
tez ➤ *f* complexion.
ti ➤ *pron* you, yourself (informal).
tía ➤ *f* aunt ▪ **t. abuela** great-aunt.
tibio, a ➤ *adj* lukewarm.
tiburón ➤ *m* shark.
tic ➤ *m* tic.
tiempo ➤ *m* time; *(época)* times; *(ocasión)* moment; *(estación)* season; METEOROL. weather ▪ **a t.** in *or* on time • **con t.** *(por adelantado)* in advance; *(en el momento oportuno)* in good time • **de t. en t.** from time to time • **fuera de t.** at the wrong time • **ganar t.** to save time • **perder el t.** to waste time • **t. atrás** some time ago.
tienda ➤ *f* shop ▪ **ir de tiendas** to go shopping • **t. de campaña** tent.
tienta ➤ *f* ▪ **a tientas** gropingly.
tierno, a ➤ *adj (afectuoso)* loving; *(blando)* soft; *(carne)* tender.
tierra ➤ *f* land; *(suelo)* ground; *(patria)* country ▪ **t. adentro** inland • **t. de nadie** no man's land.
tieso, a ➤ *adj* stiff, rigid; *(terco)* stubborn.
tigre ➤ *m* tiger ▪ **t. americano** jaguar.
tijera(s) ➤ *f(pl)* scissors.
tilo ➤ *m* linden.
timar ➤ *tr* to cheat.
timbre ➤ *m* buzzer; *(sonido)* ring; *(sonoridad)* timbre.
timidez ➤ *f* timidity.
tímido, a ➤ *adj* timid.
timo ➤ *m* swindle.
timón ➤ *m* MARIT. rudder.
tímpano ➤ *m* MUS. kettledrum; ANAT. eardrum.
tina ➤ *f* bathtub.
tinieblas ➤ *fpl* darkness.
tinta ➤ *f* ink.
tinte ➤ *m (colorante)* dye; *(color)* tint.
tinto ➤ *m* red wine; AMER. black coffee.
tintorería ➤ *f* dry cleaner's shop.
tío ➤ *m* uncle ▪ **t. abuelo** great-uncle ▪ *pl* aunt and uncle.
tiovivo ➤ *m* merry-go-round.
típico, a ➤ *adj* typical.
tiple ➤ *mf* MUS. soprano.
tipo ➤ *m (clase)* kind; *(modelo)* type; *(figura)* figure; *(persona)* guy; PRINT. type; COM. rate.
tira ➤ *f* strip.
tiranía ➤ *f* tyranny.
tirante ➤ *adj (tenso)* tight; *(relaciones)* strained ➤ *m (correa)* strap; ARCHIT. tie beam; TECH. brace ▪ *pl* suspenders.
tirar ➤ *tr* to throw; *(desechar)* to throw away; *(derribar)* to knock down; *(disparar)* to fire; *(trazar)* to draw ➤ *intr (hacia sí)* to pull, draw; *(chimenea)* to draw; *(torcer)* to turn, go ▪ **t. de** to pull (at), tug (on) ➤ *reflex* to throw oneself; *(tenderse)* to lie down.
tiritar ➤ *intr* to shiver.
tiro ➤ *m (lanzada)* throw; *(disparo)* shot; *(caballos)* team (of horses); *(de chimenea)* draft.
tisana ➤ *f* infusion.
títere ➤ *m* puppet.
titubear ➤ *intr* to hesitate.
titular[1] ➤ *m* PRINT. headline ➤ *mf* holder (of a passport, office).
titular[2] ➤ *tr* to entitle ➤ *intr* to receive a title ➤ *reflex* EDUC. to receive one's degree.
título ➤ *m* title; *(encabezado)* heading; *(diploma)* degree ▪ **a t. de** by way of.
tiza ➤ *f* chalk.
tiznar ➤ *tr* to smudge; FIG. to stain.
toalla ➤ *f* towel.
toallero ➤ *m* towel rack.
tobillo ➤ *m* ankle.
tobogán ➤ *m (para niños)* slide; *(para mercancías)* chute; *(trineo)* sled.
tocado ➤ *m* hairdo.
tocador ➤ *m* dressing room ▪ **artículos de t.** toiletries.
tocar §47 ➤ *tr* to touch; *(palpar)* to feel; *(manosear)* to handle; *(hacer sonar)* to sound; *(tañer)* to ring; MUS. to play; *(aludir)* to touch on ▪ **t. fondo** to hit bottom ➤ *intr (corresponder)* to be up to, fall to; *(recibir)* to get; *(caer en suerte)* to win; *(a la puerta)* to knock; *(llegar el momento)* to be time ▪ **¿a quién le toca?** whose turn is it?
tocino ➤ *m* bacon; *(cerdo)* salt pork.
todavía ➤ *adv* still; *(sin embargo)* nevertheless; *(aún)* even ▪ **t. no** not yet.
todo, a ➤ *adj* all; *(cada)* each, every; *(entero)* whole, entire ▪ **t. el mundo** everybody ➤ *m* whole, all ▪ **ante t.** first of all • **con t.** still • **sobre t.** above all • **t. está listo** everything is ready ▪ *pl* everybody, everyone ➤ *adv* all.
toldo ➤ *m* awning.
tolerancia ➤ *f* tolerance.
tolerar ➤ *tr* to tolerate.
toma ➤ *f (acción)* taking; *(captura)* capture; *(dosis)* dose; *(entrada)* intake; ELEC. plug.
tomar ➤ *tr* to take; *(capturar)* to capture; *(comer, beber)* to eat, drink, have ▪ **t. en cuenta** to take into account • **t. parte** to participate • **t. partido** to take sides • **t. prestado** to borrow.
tomate ➤ *m* tomato.
tomillo ➤ *m* thyme.
tonel ➤ *m* barrel.
tonelada ➤ *f* ton.
tonelaje ➤ *m* tonnage.
tónico, a ➤ *adj & m* MED. tonic ➤ *f* MUS. tonic ▪ **dar la t.** to set the tone.
tono ➤ *m* tone.
tontería ➤ *f* foolishness; *(acción)* foolish action; *(dicho)* stupid remark ▪ **decir tonterías** to talk nonsense.
tonto, a ➤ *adj* foolish ➤ *mf* fool.
topar ➤ *tr* to bump (into).
tope ➤ *m (extremo)* butt, end; MECH. catch, stop; AUTO. bumper; *(choque)* collision.
tópico ➤ *m* topic.
topo ➤ *m* ZOOL. mole.
torbellino ➤ *m* whirlwind.
torcer §48 ➤ *tr* to twist; *(doblar)* to bend; *(la cara)* to contort; MED. to sprain ➤ *intr* to turn.
torear ➤ *tr & intr* to fight (bulls).
toreo ➤ *m* bullfighting.
torero ➤ *m* bullfighter.
tormenta ➤ *f* storm.
tormento ➤ *m* torment.
tormentoso, a ➤ *adj* stormy.
tornillo ➤ *m* screw.
torno ➤ *m* lathe ▪ **en t. a** around • **t. de alfarero** potter's wheel.
toro ➤ *m* bull ▪ *pl* bullfight.
torpe ➤ *adj* clumsy; *(necio)* stupid.
torre ➤ *f* tower; *(de petróleo)* oil derrick; *(de ajedrez)* rook, castle.
torrente ➤ *m* torrent.
torso ➤ *m* torso.
torta ➤ *f* cake; COLL. *(bofetada)* slap.
tortazo ➤ *m* COLL. blow.
tortícoli(s) ➤ *m* stiff neck.
tortilla ➤ *f* CUL. omelet; AMER. tortilla.
tortuga ➤ *f* turtle.
tortura ➤ *f* torture.
tos ➤ *f* cough, coughing ▪ **acceso de t.** coughing fit.
tosco, a ➤ *adj* crude, coarse.
toser ➤ *intr* to cough.
tostada ➤ *f* toast.
tostador, a ➤ *m or f* toaster.
tostar §11 ➤ *tr (pan)* to toast; *(café)* to roast.
total ➤ *adj & m* total ➤ *adv* so, in short.
tótem ➤ *m* totem.
tóxico, a ➤ *adj* toxic ➤ *m* poison.
tozudo, a ➤ *adj* stubborn.
traba ➤ *f* obstacle.
trabajador, a ➤ *adj* hard-working ➤ *mf* worker.
trabajar ➤ *intr* to work ▪ **t. de** to work as ➤ *tr* to work; AGR. to till.
trabajo ➤ *m* work; *(labor)* labor; *(tarea)* job; *(esfuerzo)* trouble ▪ **costar t.** to be hard • **t. a destajo** piecework.
trabalenguas ➤ *m* tongue twister.
trabar ➤ *tr* to start up ➤ *reflex* to get tangled up ▪ **trabársele a uno la lengua** to get tongue-tied.
tracción ➤ *f* traction ▪ **t. delantera** front-wheel drive.
tractor ➤ *m* tractor.
tradición ➤ *f* tradition.
tradicional ➤ *adj* traditional.
traducción ➤ *f* translation.
traducir §14 ➤ *tr* to translate.
traductor, a ➤ *mf* translator.
traer §49 ➤ *tr* to bring; *(causar)* to bring about; *(llevar)* to wear.
traficante ➤ *adj* dealing ➤ *mf* dealer.
tráfico ➤ *m* traffic.
tragaluz ➤ *m* skylight.
tragar §31 ➤ *intr & tr* to swallow.
tragedia ➤ *f* tragedy.
trágico, a ➤ *adj* tragic.
trago ➤ *m (bebida)* drink; *(porción)* gulp ▪ **de un t.** in one shot.
traición ➤ *f* treason.
traicionar ➤ *tr* to betray.
traidor, a ➤ *adj* traitorous ➤ *mf* traitor.
traje ➤ *m (vestido)* dress; *(conjunto)* suit; THEAT. costume ▪ **t. de baño** bathing suit • **t. de luces** bullfighter's costume.
trama ➤ *f (de novela)* plot.
trámite ➤ *m* procedure ▪ *pl* formalities.
tramo ➤ *m (de terreno)* stretch; *(de una escalera)* flight.
trampa ➤ *f* trap ▪ **hacer trampas** to cheat.
trampolín ➤ *m (del gimnasta)* trampoline; *(del nadador)* diving board.
tramposo, a ➤ *adj* cheating ➤ *mf* swindler.
tranquilidad ➤ *f* tranquility.
tranquilizante ➤ *adj* tranquilizing ➤ *m* tranquilizer.
tranquilizar §02 ➤ *tr* to quiet ➤ *reflex* to be quieted.
tranquilo, a ➤ *adj* tranquil ▪ **¡déjame t.!** leave me alone!
transacción ➤ *f* COM. transaction; *(acuerdo)* settlement.
transatlántico, a ➤ *adj* transatlantic ➤ *m* ocean liner.
transbordador ➤ *m* ferry ▪ **t. espacial** space shuttle.
transbordo ➤ *m* transshipment.
transcontinental ➤ *adj* transcontinental.
transcurrir ➤ *intr* to elapse.
transcurso ➤ *m* course.
transeúnte ➤ *mf* passerby.
transferencia ➤ *f* transfer(ence).
transferir §43 ➤ *tr* to transfer.
transformación ➤ *f* transformation.
transformador, a ➤ *adj* transforming ➤ *m* ELEC. transformer.
transformar ➤ *tr* to transform; SPORT. to convert ➤ *reflex* to be transformed.
transfusión ➤ *f* transfusion.
transición ➤ *f* transition.
transistor ➤ *m* transistor.
transitable ➤ *adj* passable.
transitivo, a ➤ *adj* transitive.
tránsito ➤ *m* traffic ▪ **de t.** in transit.
transitorio, a ➤ *adj* temporary.
transmisión ➤ *f* transmission; RAD., TELEV. broadcast.
transmisor ➤ *m* ELEC. transmitter.
transmitir ➤ *tr* to transmit; RAD., TELEV. to broadcast.
transoceánico, a ➤ *adj* transoceanic.
transparente ➤ *adj (un objeto)* transparent; *(evidente)* obvious.
transpiración ➤ *f* perspiration.
transplantar ➤ *tr* to transplant.
transportar ➤ *tr* to transport.
transporte ➤ *m* transport.
transversal ➤ *adj* transverse ➤ *f* side street.
tranvía ➤ *m* streetcar.
trapo ➤ *m* rag ▪ *pl* clothing.
tráquea ➤ *f* trachea.
tras ➤ *prep (después de)* after; *(detrás de)* behind.
trasatlántico, a ➤ *adj* transatlantic.
trascendencia ➤ *f* PHILOS. transcendence; *(importancia)* significance.
trascendental ➤ *adj* PHILOS. transcendental; *(importante)* very significant.
trasero, a ➤ *adj* back, rear ➤ *m* ANAT. bottom; ZOOL. rump ➤ *f* back, rear.
trasladar ➤ *tr (mover)* to move; *(a un empleado)* to transfer ➤ *reflex* to change residence, move.
traslado ➤ *m (de un empleado)* transfer; *(mudanza)* change of residence.
trasnochar ➤ *intr* to stay up all night.
traspasar ➤ *tr (perforar)* to pierce; *(atravesar)* to cross.
traspié ➤ *m* stumble.
trasplantar ➤ *tr* to transplant ➤ *reflex* to uproot oneself.
trasplante ➤ *m* transplant.
trastienda ➤ *f* stock room.
trasto ➤ *m* piece of junk.
trastornar ➤ *tr (perturbar)* to disrupt; *(inquietar)* to worry; *(enloquecer)* to drive mad ➤ *reflex* to go mad.
trastorno ➤ *m* upset.
tratado ➤ *m* treatise; POL. treaty.
tratamiento ➤ *m* treatment.
tratar ➤ *tr* to treat; *(manejar)* to handle; *(dar el tratamiento de)* to address as; *(comerciar)* to manage; CHEM. to process; MED. to treat ➤ *intr* ▪ **t. con** to have dealings with • **t. de** *(discutir)* to be about; *(procurar)* to try to ➤ *reflex* to treat each other.
trato ➤ *m* treatment; *(título)* form of address; *(relaciones)* dealings; *(negocio)* trade; *(convenio)* agreement ▪ **¡t. hecho!** COLL. it's a deal!
trauma ➤ *m* trauma.
traumático, a ➤ *adj* traumatic.
través ➤ *m* slant; *(torcimiento)* bend ▪ **a t. de** across, through • **al** *or* **de t.** across, crosswise.
travesía ➤ *f (distancia)* distance across; *(viaje)* crossing; *(viento)* crosswind.
travesura ➤ *f* mischief.
travieso, a ➤ *adj* mischievous.
trayecto ➤ *m (distancia)* distance; *(recorrido)* route, way.
trazar §02 ➤ *tr (diseñar)* to design; *(bosquejar)* to outline, trace; *(discurrir)* to draw up (plans).
trébol ➤ *m* BOT. clover; ARCHIT. trefoil ▪ *pl (naipes)* clubs.
trece ➤ *adj & m* thirteen.
trecho ➤ *m* distance, stretch; *(de tiempo)* spell ▪ **de t. en t.** at intervals.
treinta ➤ *adj & m* thirty.
tremendo, a ➤ *adj* tremendous; *(horrendo)* horrible.
tren ➤ *m* train.
trenza *or* **trencilla** ➤ *f* braid.
trepar ➤ *intr* to climb.
tres ➤ *adj & m* three ▪ **las t.** three o'clock.
treta ➤ *f* trick, ruse; SPORT. feint.

triángulo ➤ *m* triangle.
tribu ➤ *f* tribe.
tribuna ➤ *f* rostrum; SPORT. bleachers.
tribunal ➤ *m (lugar)* court; *(magistrados)* bench ■ **t. de menores** juvenile court.
tributo ➤ *m* tribute; *(impuesto)* tax.
tríceps ➤ *adj & m* triceps.
triciclo ➤ *m* tricycle.
tricolor ➤ *adj* tricolor.
tridimensional ➤ *adj* three-dimensional.
trigo ➤ *m* wheat.
trillizo, a ➤ *adj* triple ➤ *mf* triplet.
trimestral ➤ *adj* quarterly.
trimestre ➤ *m (tres meses)* quarter; *(pago)* quarterly payment; *(revista)* quarterly.
trinchar ➤ *tr* to carve.
trinchera ➤ *f* MIL. trench.
trineo ➤ *m* sled, sleigh.
trío ➤ *m* trio.
tripa ➤ *f* intestine; *(panza)* belly, tummy ■ *pl* innards.
triple ➤ *adj & m* triple.
trípode ➤ *m* tripod ➤ *adj* three-legged.
tripulación ➤ *f* crew.
tripulante ➤ *mf* crew member.
tripular ➤ *tr* AVIA., MARIT. to man.
triquiñuela ➤ *f* COLL. trick, ruse.
triste ➤ *adj* sad; *(melancólico)* melancholy, gloomy.
tristeza ➤ *f* sadness.
triturar ➤ *tr* to crush.
triunfador, a ➤ *adj* triumphant ➤ *mf* winner.
triunfar ➤ *intr* to win; FIG. to succeed.
triunfo ➤ *m* triumph; FIG. success.
trivial ➤ *adj* trivial.
triza ➤ *f* piece, shred ■ **hacer trizas** to tear to pieces.
trocear ➤ *tr* to divide into pieces.
trofeo ➤ *m* trophy.
trole ➤ *m* trolley.
tromba ➤ *f* waterspout.
trombón ➤ *m* trombone.
trompa ➤ *f* MUS. horn; ZOOL. trunk.
trompeta ➤ *f* trumpet.
tronchar ➤ *tr (un árbol)* to fell; *(romper)* to split.
tronco ➤ *m* ANAT., BOT. trunk ■ **dormir como un t.** COLL. to sleep like a log.
trono ➤ *m* throne.
tropa(s) ➤ *f(pl)* troops.
tropel ➤ *m* confusion ■ **en t.** in a mad rush.
tropezar §17 ➤ *intr* to stumble, trip; *(cometer un error)* to slip up ■ **t. con** COLL. to bump into.
tropezón ➤ *m* stumble; *(desliz)* slip ■ **a tropezones** by fits and starts.
tropical ➤ *adj* tropical.
trópico, a ➤ *adj* tropical ➤ *m* tropic ■ **t. de Cáncer, Capricornio** Tropic of Cancer, Capricorn.
tropiezo ➤ *m (obstáculo)* stumbling block; *(traspiés)* stumble; *(desliz)* slip.
trozo ➤ *m* piece, chunk.
trucha ➤ *f* trout.
truco ➤ *m* trick.
trueno ➤ *m* thunder.
trufa ➤ *f* truffle.
tú ➤ *pron* you (informal).
tu, tus ➤ *adj* your (informal).
tubería ➤ *f (serie)* pipes; *(tubo)* pipe; *(instalación)* plumbing.
tubo ➤ *m* tube ■ **t. de desagüe** drainpipe • **t. de escape** exhaust pipe.
tuerca ➤ *f* MECH. nut.
tufo ➤ *m* fume.
tulipán ➤ *m* tulip.
tullido, a ➤ *adj* crippled.
tumba ➤ *f* tomb, grave.
tumbar ➤ *tr (derribar)* to knock down; COMPUT. to crash ➤ *reflex* to lie down.
tumbona ➤ *f* deck chair.
tumor ➤ *m* tumor.
tumulto ➤ *m* tumult.
tunante ➤ *adj* crooked ➤ *mf* rascal.
túnel ➤ *m* tunnel.
túnica ➤ *f* tunic.
tupé ➤ *m* toupee.
tupido, a ➤ *adj* thick, dense.
turbar ➤ *tr* to upset; *(desconcertar)* to embarrass ➤ *reflex* to be upset.
turbiedad ➤ *f* muddiness.
turbina ➤ *f* turbine.
turbio, a ➤ *adj* muddy ➤ *mpl* sediment.
turbulencia ➤ *f* turbulence.
turbulento, a ➤ *adj* turbulent.
turismo ➤ *m* tourism.
turista ➤ *mf* tourist.
turístico, a ➤ *adj* tourist.
turnar ➤ *intr & reflex* to take turns.
turno ➤ *m (vez)* turn; *(de obreros)* shift ■ **de t.** on duty • **t. de día** *or* **de noche** day *or* night shift.
turquesa ➤ *f* turquoise.
turrón ➤ *m* nougat.
tutear ➤ *tr* to address as *tú*.
tutela ➤ *f (de personas)* guardianship; *(dirección)* guidance.
tuteo ➤ *m* addressing as *tú*.
tutor, a ➤ *mf* guardian.
tuyo, a ➤ *adj & pron* yours (informal) ■ **lo t.** your affair • **los tuyos** your people • **un pariente t.** a relative of yours.

U

u ➤ *conj var of* o used before *(h)o*.
ubicación ➤ *f* location.
ubicar §47 ➤ *tr* AMER. to locate ➤ *reflex* to be located.
Ud., Uds. ➤ *pron abbrev of* usted, ustedes.
úlcera ➤ *f* ulcer.
últimamente ➤ *adv* ultimately; *(recientemente)* lately.
último, a ➤ *adj (final)* last; *(de dos)* latter; *(más reciente)* latest, most recent; *(mejor)* finest; *(definitivo)* last; COM. lowest ■ **estar a lo ú.** de to be nearly at the end of • **por ú.** lastly.
ultraje ➤ *m* insult, outrage.
ultramar ➤ *m* overseas country.
ultramarino ➤ *mpl* imported foods; *(tienda)* grocery store.
ultrasonido ➤ *m* ultrasound.
ultratumba ➤ *f* otherworld.
ultravioleta ➤ *adj* ultraviolet.
ulular ➤ *intr* to howl.
umbilical ➤ *adj* umbilical.
umbral ➤ *m* threshold.
un ➤ *contr of* **uno.**
unánime ➤ *adj* unanimous.
unanimidad ➤ *f* unanimity ■ **por u.** unanimously.
undécimo, a ➤ *adj & m* eleventh.
único, a ➤ *adj (solo)* only, sole; *(sin igual)* unique ➤ *mf* only one ■ **lo ú.** only thing.
unidad ➤ *f (acuerdo)* unity; *(armonía)* harmony; MATH., MIL., TECH. unit ■ **u. de disco** COMPUT. disk drive.
unido, a ➤ *adj (juntos)* united, joined; *(familia)* close, tight.
unificar ➤ *tr* to unify.
uniforme ➤ *adj & m* uniform.
unilateral ➤ *adj* unilateral.
unión ➤ *f* union.
unir ➤ *tr* to unite ➤ *reflex* to join.
unísono ➤ *m* unison ■ **al u.** in unison.
universal ➤ *adj* universal.
universidad ➤ *f* university.
universitario, a ➤ *adj* university ➤ *mf* university student.
universo ➤ *m* universe.
uno, a ➤ *m* one ➤ *adj* one ■ **la u.** one o'clock • **u. que otro** a few ■ *pl* some, a few ■ **u. diez horas** about ten hours ➤ *indef pron* one, you; *(alguien)* somebody ■ **cada u.** each one, every one • **u. a otro** *or* **con otro** each other, one another • **u. a** *or* **por u.** one at a time • **u. y otro** both • **u. tras otro** one after another ■ *pl* **u. a otros** one another • **u.** cuantos a few, some ➤ *indef art* a, an.
untar ➤ *tr (engrasar)* to grease; *(manchar)* to smear; to spread; MED. to rub.
uña ➤ *f* fingernail; *(del pie)* toenail ■ **comerse las uñas** to bite one's nails.
urbanización ➤ *f* urbanization, city planning; *(desarrollo)* development.
urbano, a ➤ *adj* urban.
urbe ➤ *f* large city.
urgencia ➤ *f* urgency ■ **con u.** urgently.
urgente ➤ *adj* urgent.
urgir §19 ➤ *intr* to be urgent.
urna ➤ *f* urn; *(arca)* ballot box ■ **acudir** *or* **ir a las urnas** to go to the polls.
urraca ➤ *f* magpie.
urticaria ➤ *f* MED. hives.
uruguayo, a ➤ *adj & mf* Uruguayan.
usado, a ➤ *adj (deteriorado)* worn-out; *(de segunda mano)* secondhand.
usar ➤ *tr (emplear)* to use; *(ropa)* to wear ➤ *reflex* to be used.
uso ➤ *m* use; *(costumbre)* custom.
usted ➤ *pron* you (formal) ■ **de u.** yours • **hablar** *or* **tratar de u.** to use the polite form of address ■ *pl* you, all of you.
usual ➤ *adj* usual.
usuario, a ➤ *mf* user.
utensilio ➤ *m* utensil.
útil ➤ *adj* useful ➤ *m* tool, utensil ■ *pl* implements • **ú. de pesca** fishing tackle.
utilidad ➤ *f* usefulness.
utilizar §02 ➤ *tr* to utilize.
uva ➤ *f* grape ■ **u. pasa** raisin.

V

vaca ➤ *f* cow; CUL. beef.
vacaciones ➤ *fpl* ■ **estar de v.** to be on vacation.
vacante ➤ *adj* vacant ➤ *f* vacancy.
vaciar §18 ➤ *tr & reflex* to empty.
vacilación ➤ *f* hesitation.
vacilar ➤ *intr* to hesitate.
vacío, a ➤ *adj* empty; *(desocupado)* vacant; *(hueco)* hollow ➤ *m* emptiness; *(hueco)* hollow; PHYS. vacuum ■ **envasado al v.** vacuum-packed.
vacuna ➤ *f* vaccine.
vacunar ➤ *tr* to vaccinate.
vacuo, a ➤ *adj* vacuous, empty.
vadear ➤ *tr (un río)* to ford; *(a pie)* to wade across; FIG. to overcome.
vado ➤ *m (de un río)* ford.
vagabundo, a ➤ *adj & mf* vagabond.
vagar §31 ➤ *intr* to wander.
vago, a ➤ *adj* vague; *(holgazán)* lazy ➤ *m* loafer, idler.
vagón ➤ *m* RAIL. car, coach ■ **v. cama** sleeping car.
vaho ➤ *m* steam.
vaina ➤ *f* BOT. pod; *(molestia)* nuisance.
vainilla ➤ *f* vanilla.
vajilla ➤ *f* tableware.
vale ➤ *m* voucher; *(recibo)* receipt; *(bueno)* all right, OK.
valentía ➤ *f* bravery.
valer §50 ➤ *intr* to be of value; *(ser válido)* to be valid; *(servir)* to be useful ■ **más vale** it is better ➤ *tr (tener un valor de)* to be worth; *(costar)* to cost ■ **v. la pena** to be worthwhile ➤ *reflex* to manage for oneself ■ **v. de** to make use of ➤ *m* worth.
valeroso, a ➤ *adj* courageous, brave.
validación ➤ *f* validation.
validar ➤ *tr* to validate.
valiente ➤ *adj* courageous, brave.
valioso, a ➤ *adj* valuable.
valla ➤ *f* fence.
valle ➤ *m* valley.
valor ➤ *m (cualidad)* worth; *(precio)* price; *(importancia)* importance; *(coraje)* valor ■ *pl* COM. securities • **v. inmuebles** real estate.
valoración ➤ *f* appraisal.
vals ➤ *m* waltz.
válvula ➤ *f* valve; RAD. tube.
vampiro ➤ *m* vampire.
vandalismo ➤ *m* vandalism.
vanguardia ➤ *f* MIL. vanguard; ARTS, LIT. avant-garde.
vanidad ➤ *f* vanity.
vanidoso, a ➤ *adj* vain, conceited.
vano, a ➤ *adj* vain; *(frívolo)* frivolous; *(vanidoso)* conceited ■ **en v.** in vain.
vapor ➤ *m (gas)* steam; *(vaho)* vapor; *(buque)* steamship ■ **al v.** CUL. steamed.
vaporizador ➤ *m* vaporizer.
vaquero, a ➤ *m* cowboy ➤ *f* cowgirl.
vara ➤ *f (palo)* stick; *(rama)* rod; *(bastón)* staff.
variable ➤ *adj & f* variable.
variación ➤ *f* variation.
variado, a ➤ *adj* varied.
variante ➤ *adj* varying ➤ *f* variant.
variar §18 ➤ *tr & intr* to vary.
varicela ➤ *f* chicken pox.
variedad ➤ *f* variety ■ *pl (cosas diversas)* miscellany; THEAT. variety show.
varilla ➤ *f* rod ■ **v. mágica** magic wand.
vario, a ➤ *adj* varied; *(cambiadizo)* varying ■ *pl* several ➤ *mf* ■ *pl* several.
varón ➤ *m (hombre)* male; *(niño)* boy.
vasectomía ➤ *f* vasectomy.
vasija ➤ *f* container.
vaso ➤ *m* glass.
vasto, a ➤ *adj* vast, immense.
vaticinar ➤ *tr* to predict.
vatio ➤ *m* watt.
vecindad ➤ *f (vecindario)* neighbors; *(cercanías)* neighborhood, vicinity.
vecindario ➤ *m* neighborhood.
vecino, a ➤ *adj* next ➤ *mf* neighbor.
veda ➤ *f* prohibition; HUNT. closed season.
vedado, a ➤ *adj* prohibited ➤ *m* game preserve.
vegetación ➤ *f* vegetation.
vegetal ➤ *adj & m* vegetable.
vegetariano, a ➤ *adj & mf* vegetarian.
vehemente ➤ *adj* vehement.
vehículo ➤ *m* vehicle; MED. carrier.
veinte ➤ *adj & m* twenty.
vejez ➤ *f* old age.
vejiga ➤ *f* ANAT. bladder.
vela[1] ➤ *f (vigilia)* vigil; *(luz)* candle ■ **en v.** awake.
vela[2] ➤ *f* MARIT. sail ■ **barco de v.** sailboat.
velar ➤ *tr* to keep watch over ➤ *intr* to stay awake ➤ *reflex* PHOTOG. to blur.
velero ➤ *m* sailboat.
veleta ➤ *f* weather vane.
vello ➤ *m (pelo)* hair; *(pelusilla)* fuzz.
velo ➤ *m* veil.
velocidad ➤ *f* velocity, speed; AUTO. gear ■ **v. máxima** *or* **límite de v.** speed limit.
velocímetro ➤ *m* speedometer.
veloz ➤ *adj* swift.
vena ➤ *f* vein.
venado ➤ *m* stag, deer; CUL. venison.
vencedor, a ➤ *adj* winning ➤ *mf* winner.
vencer §51 ➤ *tr* to defeat; *(aventajar)* to overcome ➤ *intr (ganar)* to win; COM. *(cumplirse un plazo)* to expire; *(una deuda)* to fall due.
vencido, a ➤ *adj* defeated; COM. *(una deuda)* due; *(cumplido)* expired.
venda ➤ *f or* **vendaje** ➤ *m* bandage.
vendar ➤ *tr* to bandage.
vendaval ➤ *m* gale.
vendedor, a ➤ *mf* vendor, seller; *(de tienda)* salesperson.
vender ➤ *tr & reflex* to sell ■ **se vende** for sale.
vendimia ➤ *f* grape harvest.
veneno ➤ *m* poison.
venenoso, a ➤ *adj* poisonous.
venezolano, a ➤ *adj & mf* Venezuelan.
venganza ➤ *f* vengeance.
vengar §31 ➤ *tr & reflex* to avenge (oneself) ■ **v. de alguien** to take revenge on someone.
venir §52 ➤ *intr* to come; *(llegar)* to arrive; *(ropa)* to fit ■ **el año que viene** next year ➤ *reflex* ■ **v. abajo** *or* **por tierra** *or* **al suelo** to collapse, fall down.
venta ➤ *f* sale.
ventaja ➤ *f* advantage; *(en una carrera)* head start, lead.
ventana ➤ *f* window.
ventanal ➤ *m* large window.
ventanilla ➤ *f (de vehículo)* window; *(taquilla)* box office.
ventilación ➤ *f* ventilation.
ventilador ➤ *m* fan.
ventilar ➤ *tr (un lugar)* to air out.
ventisca ➤ *f* blizzard.
ventolera ➤ *f* gust of wind.
ver §53 ➤ *tr* to see; *(mirar)* to look at; *(televisión, películas)* to watch; *(visitar)* to visit; *(examinar)* to examine; *(observar)* to observe ■ **a v.** let's see • **tener que v. con** to have to do with • **veremos** we'll see ➤ *reflex (ser visto)* to be seen; *(ser obvio)* to be obvious *or* clear; *(visitarse)* to see one another; *(encontrarse)* to meet ■ **estar por v.** to remain to be seen • **véase** see.
veracidad ➤ *f* veracity.
veraneante ➤ *mf* summer resident.
veranear ➤ *intr* to spend the summer.
veraneo ➤ *m* vacationing ■ **ir de v.** to go on vacation • **lugar de v.** summer resort.
veraniego, a ➤ *adj (del verano)* summer; *(ligero)* light, flimsy.
verano ➤ *m* summer.
verbo ➤ *m* GRAM. verb.
verdad ➤ *f* truth; *(veracidad)* truthfulness ■ **de v.** truly; *(verdadero)* real • **¿de v.?** really? • **¿v.?** is that so?
verdadero, a ➤ *adj* true, real.
verde ➤ *adj* green; *(inmaduro)* unripe; ➤ *m* green.
verdura ➤ *f (legumbre)* vegetable; *(follaje)* greenery.
vereda ➤ *f* trail, path; AMER. sidewalk.
veredicto ➤ *m* verdict.
vergonzoso, a ➤ *adj* shameful; *(tímido)* shy ➤ *mf* shy person.
vergüenza ➤ *f* shame; *(timidez)* shyness ■ **darle v. a uno** to embarrass • **tener v.** to be ashamed.
verificar §47 ➤ *tr (la verdad)* to verify; *(una máquina)* to check.
verja ➤ *f (de cerca)* railings; *(de ventana)* grating.
vermut *or* **vermú** ➤ *m* vermouth.
verosímil ➤ *adj* probable.

verruga ➤ f wart.
versión ➤ f version.
verso ➤ m verse.
vértebra ➤ f vertebra.
vertebrado, a ➤ adj & m vertebrate.
vertedero ➤ m (desaguadero) drain; (de basura) garbage dump.
verter §34 ➤ tr (derramar) to spill; (lágrimas, sangre) to shed; (vaciar) to empty out ➤ intr to flow.
vertical ➤ adj & f vertical.
vértice ➤ m apex.
vertiente ➤ f (declive) slope; (manantial) spring.
vertiginoso, a ➤ adj dizzying, giddy.
vértigo ➤ m vertigo ■ tener v. to feel dizzy.
vestíbulo ➤ m vestibule; THEAT. lobby.
vestido ➤ m dress ■ v. de noche evening gown.
vestigio ➤ m vestige.
vestir §32 ➤ tr to dress; (llevar) to wear ■ intr (ir vestido) to dress ➤ reflex to get dressed; (ir vestido) to dress.
vestuario ➤ m wardrobe; (cuarto) dressing room; SPORT. locker room.
veterano, a ➤ adj & mf veteran.
veterinario, a ➤ adj veterinary ➤ mf veterinarian ➤ f veterinary medicine.
veto ➤ m veto ■ poner el v. a to veto.
vez ➤ f time; (turno) turn ■ a la v. at the same time ■ algunas veces sometimes • a veces at times ■ cada v. every time • cada v. que whenever • de una v. all at once • de v. en cuando from time to time • en v. de instead of • muchas veces often • otra v. again • tal v. perhaps.
vía ➤ f (camino) road; (ruta) route; RAIL. (carril) track ■ en vías de in the process of • v. aérea airway.
viajar ➤ intr to travel.
viaje ➤ m trip ■ ¡buen v.! bon voyage! • ir de v. to go on a trip • v. de ida y vuelta round trip.
viajero, a ➤ adj traveling ➤ mf traveler.
víbora ➤ f viper.
vibración ➤ f vibration.
vibrar ➤ intr to vibrate.
vicepresidente, a ➤ mf vice president; (en reunión) vice chairman/woman.
viceversa ➤ adv vice versa.
vicio ➤ m vice; (fumar, etc.) bad habit.
vicioso, a ➤ adj depraved.
víctima ➤ f victim.
victoria ➤ f victory; (éxito) success.
vid ➤ f grapevine.
vida ➤ f life; (duración) lifetime; (sustento) living ■ así es la v. such is life.
video or **vídeo** ➤ m video ■ v. juego video game.
videocámara ➤ f videocamera, camcorder.
videocasete ➤ m videocassette.
vidriera ➤ f window; (de colores) stained-glass window.
vidrio ➤ m glass.
viejo, a ➤ adj old ➤ m old man ■ pl old folks ➤ f old woman.
viento ➤ m wind ■ hacer v. to be windy.
vientre ➤ m (abdomen) belly; (matriz) womb; (intestino) bowels.
viernes ➤ m Friday.
viga ➤ f (madero) beam; (de metal) girder ■ v. transversal crossbeam.
vigencia ➤ f force ■ en v. in force.
vigésimo, a ➤ adj & m twentieth.
vigilante ➤ mf guard, watchman.
vigilar ➤ tr to watch over.
vigor ➤ m vigor ■ en v. in force or effect.
vil ➤ adj vile, base.
villa ➤ f (pueblo) village; (casa) villa.
vinagre ➤ m vinegar.
vinagrera ➤ f vinegar bottle ■ pl cruets.
vinagreta ➤ f vinaigrette.

vinatero, a ➤ mf wine merchant.
vínculo ➤ m link.
vino ➤ m wine ■ v. tinto red wine.
viña ➤ f or **viñedo** ➤ m vineyard.
viñeta ➤ f vignette.
violación ➤ f violation; (sexualmente) rape.
violar ➤ tr to violate; (sexualmente) to rape.
violencia ➤ f violence.
violento, a ➤ adj violent.
violeta ➤ f & adj violet.
violín ➤ m violin ➤ mf violinist.
violinista ➤ mf violinist.
violón ➤ m double bass, bass viol ➤ mf double bass player.
violonc(h)elo ➤ m cello.
virar ➤ tr MARIT. (de rumbo) to turn ➤ intr to swerve.
viril ➤ adj virile.
virtud ➤ f virtue; (eficacia) ability.
virtuoso, a ➤ adj virtuous ➤ mf virtuoso.
viruela ➤ f smallpox.
virus ➤ m virus.
visa ➤ f AMER. visa.
visera ➤ f visor.
visibilidad ➤ f visibility.
visible ➤ adj visible; COLL. decent.
visillo ➤ m window curtain.
visión ➤ f vision; (vista) eyesight.
visita ➤ f visit; (persona) visitor ■ hacer una v. or ir de v. to pay a visit.
visitar ➤ tr & reflex to visit (one another).
vislumbrar ➤ tr to glimpse.
visón ➤ m mink.
víspera ➤ f eve ■ en v. de on the eve of ■ pl RELIG. vespers.
vistazo ➤ m glance ■ dar un v. a to take a glance at.
visto, a ➤ adj ■ bien, mal v. proper, improper • por lo v. apparently ➤ f (visión) sight; (buena, mala) eyesight; (panorama) view; (cuadro) scene; (vistazo) look, glance ■ corto de v. nearsighted • hasta la v. so long.
vistoso, a ➤ adj colorful.
vitalicio, a ➤ adj life ■ miembro v. member for life.
vitalidad ➤ f vitality.
vitamina ➤ f vitamin.
vitorear ➤ tr to cheer.
vítreo, a ➤ adj vitreous.
vitrina ➤ f (caja) display case; (de tienda) window.
viudo, a ➤ m widower ➤ f widow.
vivaracho, a ➤ adj COLL. lively.
vivaz ➤ adj quick-witted; BOT. perennial.
víveres ➤ mpl provisions.
vivero ➤ m BOT. nursery; (de peces) fish hatchery; (de moluscos) farm.
vivienda ➤ f housing; (casa) house.
vivir ➤ intr to live ■ ¡viva! hurrah! ➤ tr to live; (experimentar) to go through.
vivo, a ➤ adj (con vida) alive; (brillante) vivid; (listo) sharp ■ al rojo v. red-hot • en v. TELEC. live.
vocabulario ➤ m vocabulary.
vocación ➤ f vocation.
vocal ➤ adj vocal ➤ mf board or committee member ➤ f vowel.
vocalista ➤ mf vocalist.
vocero, a ➤ mf spokesman/woman.
vociferar ➤ tr & intr to shout.
volante ➤ adj flying ➤ m AUTO. steering wheel; (papel) flier; (juego) badminton.
volar §11 ➤ intr to fly; (irse volando) to fly away; (desaparecer) to disappear; (divulgarse) to spread quickly ➤ tr to blow up.
volcán ➤ m volcano.
volcar ➤ tr to dump ➤ intr to overturn

➤ reflex (derribarse) to tip over; (entregarse) to do one's utmost.
voltaje ➤ m voltage.
voltear ➤ tr to turn over; (dar la vuelta) to turn around.
voltio ➤ m volt.
volumen ➤ m volume.
voluminoso, a ➤ adj voluminous.
voluntad ➤ f (facultad) will; (firmeza) willpower ■ fuerza de v. willpower.
voluntario, a ➤ adj voluntary ➤ mf volunteer.
volver §54 ➤ tr to turn; (dar vuelta) to turn around; (colchón, etc.) to turn over; (prenda) to turn inside out; (al propio sitio) to return; (restablecer) to restore ■ v. la espalda a alguien to turn one's back on someone ➤ intr to return; (reanudar) to get back ■ v. a to . . . again ➤ reflex (darse vuelta) to turn around; (hacerse) to become ■ v. atrás (desdecirse) to back down; (no cumplir) to back out • v. loco to go crazy.
vomitar ➤ tr to vomit; (decir) to spew; (un secreto) to spill ➤ intr to vomit.
vómito ➤ m vomit.
voraz ➤ adj voracious.
vos ➤ pron you, thou, ye; S. AMER. you (singular, informal).
vosotros, as ➤ pron you, yourselves (plural, informal).
votación ➤ f voting; (voto) vote.
votante ➤ adj voting ➤ mf voter.
votar ➤ intr to vote; RELIG. to make a vow ➤ tr to vote.
voto ➤ m vote.
voz ➤ f voice; (rumor) rumor ■ a media v. in a low voice • a una v. unanimously • a voces shouting • dar voces to shout • en v. alta (al leer) aloud; (a gritos) in a loud voice • tener la v. ronca to be hoarse.
vuelo ➤ m flight.
vuelta ➤ f (giro) turn; (regreso) return; (repetición) recurrence; SPORT. lap ■ a la v. on the way back • a la v. de la esquina around the corner • a v. de correo by return mail ■ dar or darse una v. to take a walk • de ida y v. round-trip • estar de v. to be back.
vuestro, a ➤ poss adj [informal] (su) your; (suyo) (of) yours ■ los vuestros or las vuestras yours.
vulgar ➤ adj common; (grosero) vulgar.
vulgaridad ➤ f vulgarity.
vulnerable ➤ adj vulnerable.

W

wat ➤ m watt.
web ➤ m or f COMPUT. Web.
whisky ➤ m whiskey.

X

xenofobia ➤ f xenophobia.
xilófono ➤ m xylophone.

Y

y ➤ conj and ■ ¿y bien? and then? • y eso que even though • ¿y qué? so what?
ya ➤ adv (finalmente) already; (ahora) now; (pronto) soon; (en seguida) right away; (por último) now ■ ya no no longer • ya que since ➤ conj now, at times ➤ interj I see!
yacer ➤ intr to lie.
yacimiento ➤ m GEOL. deposit ■ y. petrolífero oil field.
yarda ➤ f yard.
yate ➤ m yacht.
yegua ➤ f mare.
yema ➤ f yolk; BOT. bud ■ y. del dedo finger tip.
yerba ➤ f grass; (droga) marijuana.
yermo, a ➤ adj barren ➤ m desert.

yerno ➤ m son-in-law.
yeso ➤ m GEOL. gypsum; ARTS, CONSTR. plaster; ARTS, MED. plaster cast.
yo ➤ pron I ■ soy yo it's I or me • yo mismo I myself ➤ m ego.
yodo ➤ m iodine.
yoga ➤ m yoga.
yogur(t) ➤ m yogurt.
yuca ➤ f AMER., CUL. manioc; BOT. yucca.
yugo ➤ m (arreo) yoke; (opresión) oppression; (carga pesada) burden; MARIT. transom.
yugular ➤ adj & f jugular.

Z

zafar ➤ tr reflex to escape (de from).
zaguán ➤ m front hall, vestibule.
zalamería ➤ f flattery.
zalamero, a ➤ adj flattering ➤ mf flatterer.
zamarra ➤ f sheepskin; (chaqueta) sheepskin jacket.
zambo, a ➤ adj & mf bowlegged (person).
zambullir ➤ reflex (en el agua) to dive; (esconderse) to duck out of sight.
zanahoria ➤ f carrot.
zancada ➤ f stride.
zancadilla ➤ f (caída) tripping; COLL. (engaño) trick; (trampa) trap.
zanco ➤ m stilt.
zancón, ona ➤ adj COLL. long-legged.
zancudo, a ➤ adj long-legged; ORNITH. wading ➤ fpl wading birds ➤ m AMER. mosquito.
zanja ➤ f ditch, trench.
zapatear ➤ tr (golpear) to hit with the shoe; (bailar) to tap-dance ➤ intr to tap one's feet.
zapatería ➤ f shoe store.
zapatero, a ➤ mf shoemaker, cobbler; (venta) shoe seller.
zapatilla ➤ f (pantufla) slipper; (de baile) dancing shoe.
zapato ➤ m shoe.
zar ➤ m czar.
zarandear ➤ tr to shake ➤ reflex to be on the go.
zarcillo ➤ m earring; BOT. tendril.
zarina ➤ f czarina.
zarpa ➤ f claw, paw.
zarpar ➤ tr to weigh ➤ intr to set sail.
zarpazo ➤ m scratch, lash of a paw.
zarza ➤ f bramble.
zarzamora ➤ f blackberry.
zarzuela ➤ f Spanish comic opera.
zenit ➤ m zenith.
zigzag ➤ m zigzag.
zócalo ➤ m (de pared) baseboard; ARCHIT. plinth; AMER. public square.
zodiaco ➤ m zodiac.
zona ➤ f zone; (distrito) district.
zonificar §47 ➤ tr to zone.
zoo ➤ m zoo.
zoológico, a ➤ adj zoological ■ jardín z. zoo.
zoom ➤ m zoom lens.
zopilote ➤ m buzzard.
zoquete ➤ m chunk of wood; (tonto) dummy, blockhead.
zorra ➤ f fox; (hembra) vixen.
zorro ➤ m fox.
zozobra ➤ f capsizing, sinking.
zueco ➤ m clog, wooden shoe.
zumbar ➤ intr (un insecto) to buzz; (los oídos) to ring.
zumbido ➤ m (de insecto) buzzing; (de los oídos) ringing.
zumo ➤ m juice.
zurdo, a ➤ adj & mf left-handed (person).
zurra ➤ f tanning; (paliza) thrashing.
zurrar ➤ tr to tan; (pegar) to beat, thrash.

Inglés/Español

A

a ➤ *art indef* un, una ■ **a cat** un gato.
aback ➤ *adv* ■ **to be taken a.** quedar desconcertado.
abandon ➤ *tr* abandonar; *(to desert)* desertar, dejar.
abbey ➤ *s* abadía, convento.
abbreviation ➤ *s (act)* abreviación *f; (form)* abreviatura.
abdomen ➤ *s* abdomen *m*, vientre *m*.
abide◊ ➤ *tr* tolerar, soportar ➤ *intr* permanecer, continuar ■ **to a. by** cumplir con, acatar.
ability ➤ *s (skill)* capacidad *f*, habilidad *f; (talent)* aptitud *f; (power)* facultad *f*.
able ➤ *adj* capaz, hábil ■ **to be a. to** poder, ser capaz (de).
abnormal ➤ *adj* anormal.
abnormality ➤ *s* anormalidad *f*.
aboard ➤ *adv & prep* a bordo (de) ■ **all a.!** ¡pasajeros al tren!
abolish ➤ *tr* abolir, eliminar.
abolition ➤ *s* abolición *f*.
abortion ➤ *s* aborto.
about ➤ *prep (concerning)* acerca de, sobre; *(with regard to)* con respecto a ■ **a. two o'clock** alrededor de las dos • **to be a. to** estar al punto de ➤ *adv* casi.
above ➤ *adv* encima; *(in a text)* más arriba ■ **a. all** sobre todo • **from a.** desde lo alto ➤ *prep (over)* sobre, por encima de; *(greater than)* superior a.
abreast ➤ *adv* en una línea ■ **to keep a. of** mantenerse al corriente de.
abroad ➤ *adv* en el extranjero ■ **to go a.** ir al extranjero.
abrupt ➤ *adj (curt)* brusco; *(sudden)* repentino.
abscess ➤ *s* absceso.
absence ➤ *s* ausencia, falta.
absent ➤ *adj* ausente; *(lacking)* que falta; *(distracted)* abstraído ➤ *tr* ■ **to a. oneself from** ausentarse de.
absent-minded ➤ *adj* distraído.
absolute ➤ *adj* absoluto; *(unconditional)* total.
absorb ➤ *tr* absorber; *(shock)* amortiguar.
abstinence ➤ *s* abstinencia.
abstract ➤ *adj* abstracto.
absurd ➤ *adj* absurdo, ridículo.
abundant ➤ *adj* abundante.
abuse ➤ *tr* abusar de; *(to hurt)* maltratar; *(to berate)* insultar ➤ *s* abuso; *(injury)* maltrato; *(sexual)* violación *f*.
abusive ➤ *adj (abusing)* abusivo; *(insulting)* injurioso, insultante.
abyss ➤ *s* abismo.
academic ➤ *adj* académico, universitario ➤ *s* catedrático/a.
academy ➤ *s* academia.
accelerate ➤ *tr* acelerar.
accelerator ➤ *s* acelerador *m*.
accent ➤ *s* acento.
accept ➤ *tr* aceptar; *(to admit)* admitir.
acceptable ➤ *adj* aceptable, admisible.
access ➤ *s* acceso, entrada.
accessible ➤ *adj* accesible.
accessory ➤ *s* accesorio; DER. cómplice *mf* ➤ *adj* accesorio, adjunto.
accident ➤ *s* accidente *m; (chance)* casualidad *f* ■ **by a.** por casualidad.
accommodate ➤ *tr* hacer un favor a, complacer ➤ *intr* adaptarse.
accommodations ➤ *spl* alojamiento.
accompany ➤ *tr & intr* acompañar(se).
accomplice ➤ *s* cómplice *mf*.
accomplish ➤ *tr* lograr, realizar.
accord ➤ *s* acuerdo, convenio ■ **in a. with** de acuerdo con • **of one's own a.** de propia voluntad.
accordance ➤ *s* acuerdo *f*, conformidad *f* ■ **in a. with** de conformidad con.
according to ➤ *prep* conforme a, según.
accordion ➤ *s* acordeón *m*.
account ➤ *s (report)* relato, informe *m; (explanation)* explicación *f*, motivo; COM. cuenta ■ **to give an a. of (oneself)** dar buena cuenta de (sí) • **to take into a.** tomar en cuenta ➤ *intr* ■ **to a. for** dar razón de.
accountant ➤ *s* contador/a, contable *mf*.
accumulate ➤ *tr & intr* acumular(se), amontonar(se).
accuracy ➤ *s* exactitud *f*, precisión *f*.
accurate ➤ *adj* exacto, preciso.
accuse ➤ *tr* acusar.
accustom ➤ *tr* acostumbrar (*to* a).
accustomed ➤ *adj* acostumbrado, habitual ■ **a. to** acostumbrado a.
ace ➤ *s* as *m*.
ache ➤ *intr* doler ■ **to a. for** anhelar, ansiar ➤ *s* dolor *m*.
achieve ➤ *tr* llevar a cabo, lograr.
achievement ➤ *s* logro, hazaña.
acid ➤ *s & adj* ácido.
acknowledge ➤ *tr* admitir; *(to recognize)* reconocer; *(a gift)* agradecer ■ **to a. receipt of** acusar recibo de.
acne ➤ *s* acné *m*.
acorn ➤ *s* bellota.
acoustic(al) ➤ *adj* acústico ■ **acoustics** *ssg* acústica.
acquaint ➤ *tr* familiarizar, poner al corriente ■ **to be acquainted** conocerse • **to be acquainted with** conocer, estar al corriente de.
acquaintance ➤ *s (knowledge)* conocimiento; *(person)* conocido/a.
acquire ➤ *tr* adquirir, obtener.
acre ➤ *s* acre *m*.
acrobatic ➤ *adj* acrobático.
acronym ➤ *s* siglas.
across ➤ *prep (through)* por, a través de; *(on the other side of)* al *o* en el otro lado de ➤ *adv (on the other side)* a través, del otro lado; *(crosswise)* en cruz ■ **to be ten feet a.** tener diez pies de ancho • **to come** *o* **run a.** encontrarse con • **to go a.** atravesar, cruzar.
acrylic ➤ *adj* acrílico.
act ➤ *intr* actuar, hacer algo; *(to behave)* conducirse, comportarse; *(to perform)* hacer un papel, actuar ■ **to a. like** *o* **as if** hacer como que • **to a. on** *o* **upon** influir en, obrar sobre ➤ *tr* representar, hacer el papel de ➤ *s* acto, hecho; TEAT. acto; *(a law)* ley *f*, decreto.
action ➤ *s* acción *f; (act)* acto, hecho; *(motion)* movimiento; *(activity)* actividad *f; (effect)* influencia, efecto ■ **to put out of a.** inutilizar • **to take a.** tomar medidas ■ *pl* conducta.
activate ➤ *tr* activar, agitar.
active ➤ *adj* activo, en movimiento; *(energetic)* enérgico, vigoroso.
activity ➤ *s* actividad *f*.
actor ➤ *s* actor/a.
actress ➤ *s* actriz *f*.
actual ➤ *adj* real, verdadero.
actually ➤ *adv* en realidad.
acute ➤ *adj* agudo; *(sensitive)* sagaz, perspicaz; *(critical)* grave.
ad ➤ *s* FAM. anuncio, publicidad *f*.
adage ➤ *s* adagio, proverbio.
adapt ➤ *tr & intr* adaptar(se).
adaptable ➤ *adj* adaptable.
adaptation ➤ *s* adaptación *f*.
adapter ➤ *s* adaptador *m*.
add ➤ *tr* añadir, agregar; MAT. sumar ■ **to a. up** sumar.
addict ➤ *tr* ■ **addicted to** adicto a; FAM. entregado a ➤ *s* adicto/a; FAM. fanático/a.
addiction ➤ *s* vicio; FAM. afición *f*.
addictive ➤ *adj* que forma hábito.
addition ➤ *s* adición *f*; MAT. suma ■ **in a.** además, también.
additional ➤ *adj* adicional.
additive ➤ *adj & s* aditivo.
address ➤ *s (postal)* dirección *f*, señas; *(lecture)* discurso ■ **home a.** (dirección de) domicilio ➤ *tr (a person)* dirigirse a; *(a group)* dar un discurso a; *(a letter)* dirigir.
adequate ➤ *adj* adecuado.
adhesion ➤ *s* adhesión *f*.
adhesive ➤ *adj & s* adhesivo.
adjective ➤ *s* adjetivo.
adjoining ➤ *adj* contiguo.
adjust ➤ *tr* ajustar; *(to fix)* arreglar; *(to adapt)* adaptar ➤ *intr* ajustarse.
adjustable ➤ *adj* ajustable.
adjustment ➤ *s* ajuste *m; (fixing)* arreglo; COM. liquidación *f* (de una cuenta).
administer ➤ *tr* administrar; *(to manage)* dirigir, manejar.
administration ➤ *s* administración *f*, manejo; POL. gobierno.
admiral ➤ *s* almirante *mf*.
admiration ➤ *s* admiración *f*.
admire ➤ *tr* admirar.
admission ➤ *s* admisión *f; (fee)* entrada; *(acceptance)* ingreso (al foro, universidad).
admit ➤ *tr (to let in)* admitir, dar entrada a; *(to confess)* confesar.
admittance ➤ *s* acceso, entrada.
adolescent ➤ *s & adj* adolescente *mf*.
adopt ➤ *tr* adoptar.
adopted ➤ *adj (a child)* adoptivo; *(assumed)* adoptado.
adoption ➤ *s* adopción *f*.
adorable ➤ *adj* adorable.
adore ➤ *tr* adorar.
adult ➤ *s* adulto/a ■ *pl* mayores.
adulthood ➤ *s* edad adulta.
advance ➤ *tr* avanzar, adelantar; *(to propose)* proponer ➤ *intr* avanzar; *(to improve)* hacer progresos ➤ *s* avance *m*, adelanto; *(progress)* progreso ➤ *adj* adelantado, anticipado.
advanced ➤ *adj (in level, degree)* avanzado, superior; *(in time, ability)* adelantado.
advantage ➤ *s* ventaja ■ **to take a. of** *(to make use of)* aprovechar, valerse de.
adventure ➤ *s* aventura.
adventurous ➤ *adj* aventurero.
adverb ➤ *s* adverbio.
adversity ➤ *s* adversidad *f*.
advertise ➤ *tr* anunciar ■ **to a. for** buscar por medio de avisos ➤ *intr* hacer publicidad.
advertisement ➤ *s* anuncio, publicidad *f*.
advice ➤ *s* consejo.
advisable ➤ *adj* prudente.
advise ➤ *tr* dar consejo a, aconsejar.
adviser ➤ *s* consejero/a, asesor/a.
aerial ➤ *s* antena.
aerie ➤ *s* aguilera.
aerobic ➤ *adj* aeróbico.
aerosol ➤ *s* aerosol *m*.
affair ➤ *s (business)* asunto; *(liaison)* amorío.
affect[1] ➤ *tr* afectar, influir en.
affect[2] ➤ *tr* fingir, simular.
affection ➤ *s* afecto, cariño.
affectionate ➤ *adj* afectuoso, cariñoso.
affinity ➤ *s* afinidad *f*, semejanza.
affirm ➤ *tr* afirmar, aseverar.
affix ➤ *tr* pegar, adherir.
afflict ➤ *tr* afligir, acongojar ■ **to be afflicted with** padecer de, sufrir de.
affluence ➤ *s* riqueza, opulencia.
affluent ➤ *adj* rico, opulento.
afford ➤ *tr (to spare)* poder disponer de; *(to risk)* afrontar.
affordable ➤ *adj* que se puede comprar *o* dar.
affront ➤ *tr* afrentar, insultar ➤ *s* afrenta, insulto.
afloat ➤ *adj & adv* a flote, flotando.
afraid ➤ *adj* asustado, atemorizado ■ **to be a. (of)** tener miedo (de *o* a) • **to be a. that** temer que.
Africa ➤ *s* África.
African ➤ *adj & s* africano/a.
African-American ➤ *adj & s* afroamericano/a.
after ➤ *prep (in place, order)* después de, detrás de; *(in time)* después de; *(in pursuit of)* en pos, tras; *(at the end of)* al cabo de ■ **a. all** al fin y al cabo • **day a. day** día tras día ➤ *conj* después (de) que ➤ *adv* después; *(behind)* atrás.
aftereffect ➤ *s* consecuencia.
afternoon ➤ *s* tarde *f* ■ **good a.!** ¡buenas tardes!
afterward(s) ➤ *adv* después, luego.
again ➤ *adv* otra vez, de nuevo ■ **a. and a.** una y otra vez • **and then a.** por otra parte • **as much a.** otro tanto más • **never a.** nunca más • **now and a.** de vez en cuando.
against ➤ *prep* contra.
age ➤ *s* edad *f; (era)* época, era ■ **middle a.** edad mediana • **of a.** mayor de edad • **old a.** vejez • **under a.** menor de edad ➤ *tr & intr* envejecer(se).
agency ➤ *s (means)* medio; *(business)* agencia; POL. ministerio.
agenda ➤ *s* agenda, temario.
agent ➤ *s* agente *mf*, representante *mf*.
aggravate ➤ *tr (to worsen)* agravar, empeorar; *(to annoy)* irritar.
aggression ➤ *s* agresión *f*.
aggressive ➤ *adj* agresivo.
agile ➤ *adj* ágil, ligero.
agility ➤ *s* agilidad *f*, ligereza.
aging ➤ *s* añejamiento.
agitated ➤ *adj* agitado, inquieto.
ago ➤ *adj & adv* hace ■ **how long a.?** ¿cuánto tiempo hace? • **two years a.** hace dos años.
agony ➤ *s (pain)* dolor *m*, tortura; *(anguish)* angustia, tormento.
agree ➤ *intr (to consent)* consentir, acceder a; *(to concur)* estar de acuerdo, coincidir; *(to match)* corresponder a; GRAM. concordar ■ **don't you a.?** ¿no le parece? • **to a. on** ponerse de acuerdo con • **to a. that** quedar en • **to a. with one** sentarle bien.
agreeable ➤ *adj (pleasant)* agradable; *(willing to agree)* complaciente.
agreed ➤ *adj* convenido, entendido.
agreement ➤ *s (accord)* conformidad *f; (contract)* acuerdo, pacto ■ **in a. with** de acuerdo con • **to enter into an a.** firmar un contrato.
agricultural ➤ *adj* agrícola.
agriculture ➤ *s* agricultura.
ahead ➤ *adv* delante, al frente, adelante; *(in advance)* por adelantado ■ **a. of** antes que • **go a.!** ¡adelante! • **to be a. of** llevar ventaja a • **to get a.** progresar.
aid ➤ *tr & intr* ayudar ➤ *s* ayuda, auxilio ■ **first a.** primeros auxilios.
AIDS ➤ *s* SIDA.
ailment ➤ *s* dolencia, enfermedad *f*.
aim ➤ *tr (a weapon)* apuntar ➤ *intr (to aspire)* aspirar ➤ *s (of a weapon)* puntería; *(goal)* meta.
air ➤ *s* aire *m* ■ **a. conditioning** aire acondicionado • **a. letter** carta aérea ➤ *tr* orear, ventilar.
aircraft ➤ *s* nave aérea ■ **a. carrier** portaaviones.
airfare ➤ *s* tarifa aérea.
airfield ➤ *s* campo de aviación.
airlift ➤ *s* puente aéreo ➤ *tr* transportar por vía aérea.
airline ➤ *s* aerolínea.
airliner ➤ *s* avión *m* de pasajeros.
airmail ➤ *s* ■ **by a.** por vía aérea.
airplane ➤ *s* avión *m*, aeroplano.
airport ➤ *s* aeropuerto, aeródromo.
airsick ➤ *adj* mareado (en avión).
airtight ➤ *adj* hermético.
aisle ➤ *s* pasillo; *(of church)* nave *f*.
ajar ➤ *adv & adj* entreabierto.
alarm ➤ *s* alarma, temor *m* ■ **a. clock** despertador ➤ *tr* alarmar.
album ➤ *s* álbum *m; (record)* elepé *m*.
alcohol ➤ *s* alcohol *m*.
alcoholic ➤ *adj & s* alcohólico/a.
alert ➤ *adj* alerta ➤ *s* alarma ■ **to be on the a.** estar sobre aviso ➤ *tr (to warn)* alertar; *(to inform)* poner sobre aviso.
algebra ➤ *s* álgebra.
alias ➤ *s* alias *m*.
alibi ➤ *s* DER. coartada, alibí *m*.
alien ➤ *adj (foreign)* extranjero; *(unfamiliar)* extraño ➤ *s* extranjero/a; CIENC. FIC. ser *m* de otro planeta.
alight ➤ *intr (bird)* posarse; *(from a vehicle)* bajar, apearse.
alike ➤ *adj* semejante, parecido ➤ *adv* igualmente, de la misma manera.
alive ➤ *adj* vivo ■ **to come a.** FIG. cobrar vida.
all ➤ *adj* todo ➤ *pron* todo(s), todo el mundo ■ **above a.** sobre todo • **after a.** al fin y al cabo • **a. in a.** en resumen • **not at a.** en absoluto; *(you're welcome)* no hay de qué ➤ *s* todo ■ **that's a.** eso es todo ➤ *adv* completamente ■ **a. along** siempre • **a. around** por todas partes • **a. at once** de repente • **a. but** casi • **a. of a sudden** de repente • **a. over** *(finished)* terminado; *(everywhere)* por todas partes • **a. right** bueno; *(uninjured)* ileso, sin daño; *(very well)* muy bien; *(yes)* sí.
all-around ➤ *adj* completo.
allergic ➤ *adj* alérgico.
allergy ➤ *s* alergia.
alley ➤ *s* callejón *m*.
allied ➤ *adj* aliado.
alligator ➤ *s* caimán *m*.
allocate ➤ *tr* destinar, asignar.
allotment ➤ *s* lote *m*, porción *f*.
all-out ➤ *adj* extremo, máximo.
allow ➤ *tr (to permit)* dejar, permitir; *(to give)* conceder, dar; *(to admit)* confesar, admitir; *(to discount)* deducir ■ **a. me** permítame • **to a. for** tener en cuenta • **to a. oneself** darse el gusto de.
allowance ➤ *s* permiso; *(rebate)* rebaja; *(money)* dinero de bolsillo ■ **to make a. for** tener en cuenta.
all-purpose ➤ *adj* de uso múltiple.
all-right ➤ *adj* bueno, excelente.
allusion ➤ *s* alusión *f*.
ally ➤ *tr & intr* unir(se), aliar(se) ➤ *s* aliado/a.
almond ➤ *s* almendra.
almost ➤ *adv* casi, por poco.
alone ➤ *adj* solo; *(with nothing added)* solamente ■ **let a.** sin mencionar • **to leave** *o* **let a.** no molestar, dejar en paz • **to stand a.** ser único ➤ *adv (only)* sólo, solamente; *(by oneself)* a solas.
along ➤ *adv (in line with)* a lo largo de; *(forward)* adelante; *(with one)* consigo

■ all a. desde el principio • a. with junto con • to get a. with someone llevarse bien con alguien • to go a. with aceptar ➤ *prep* a lo largo de, por.

alongside ➤ *adv & prep* a lo largo (de), junto (a).

aloud ➤ *adv* en voz alta.

alphabet ➤ *s* alfabeto.

alphabetic(al) ➤ *adj* alfabético.

alpine ➤ *adj* alpino.

already ➤ *adv* ya.

also ➤ *adv* también, además.

altar ➤ *s* altar *m* ■ **a. boy** monaguillo.

alter ➤ *tr* alterar, cambiar; COST. arreglar ➤ *intr* transformarse.

alteration ➤ *s* alteración *f*; COST. arreglo.

altercation ➤ *s* altercado, disputa.

alternate ➤ *tr & intr* alternar ➤ *adj* alterno ➤ *s* sustituto, suplente *mf.*

alternately ➤ *adv* alternativamente, por turno.

alternative ➤ *s* alternativa ➤ *adj* alternativo.

although ➤ *conj* aunque, si bien.

altitude ➤ *s* altitud *f.*

altogether ➤ *adv (entirely)* enteramente, del todo; *(all told)* en total.

aluminum ➤ *s* aluminio.

always ➤ *adv* siempre.

am ➤ *vea* **be** *en tabla de verbos.*

amateur ➤ *adj & s* amateur *mf.*

amaze ➤ *tr* asombrar, sorprender.

amazing ➤ *adj* asombroso.

ambassador ➤ *s* embajador/a.

amber ➤ *s* ámbar *m* ➤ *adj* ambarino.

ambient ➤ *adj* ambiente.

ambition ➤ *s* ambición *f*, afán *m.*

ambitious ➤ *adj* ambicioso.

ambulance ➤ *s* ambulancia.

America ➤ *s* América; *(U.S.A.)* Norteamérica.

American ➤ *adj* americano/a; *(of U.S.A.)* norteamericano/a.

amicable ➤ *adj* amigable.

ammunition ➤ *s* municiones *f.*

among(st) ➤ *prep* entre, en medio de.

amorous ➤ *adj* amativo.

amount ➤ *s* cantidad *f* ➤ *intr* ■ **to a. to** subir a.

ample ➤ *adj* extenso, amplio.

amplifier ➤ *s* amplificador *m.*

amputate ➤ *tr* amputar.

amuse ➤ *tr* entretener, divertir ■ **to a. oneself** divertirse, entretenerse.

amusement ➤ *s (pastime)* entretenimiento; *(laughter)* risa.

amusing ➤ *adj* entretenido, divertido.

an ➤ *art indef* un, una ■ **an eye** un ojo.

analysis ➤ *s* análisis *m.*

analyst ➤ *s* analista *mf.*

analyze ➤ *tr* analizar; PSIC. psicoanalizar.

anarchy ➤ *s* anarquía.

anatomic(al) ➤ *adj* anatómico.

anatomize ➤ *tr* anatomizar.

anatomy ➤ *s* anatomía.

ancestor ➤ *s* antepasado/a.

ancestral ➤ *adj* ancestral.

ancestry ➤ *s* linaje *m*, abolengo.

anchor ➤ *s* ancla; TELEV. anunciador/a ➤ *intr* anclar ➤ *tr* sujetar, asegurar.

anchovy ➤ *s* anchoa.

ancient ➤ *adj* antiguo.

and ➤ *conj* y, e ■ **try a.** come trata de venir • **go a. see** anda a ver.

anesthesia ➤ *s* anestesia.

anesthetic ➤ *s & adj* anestésico.

anew ➤ *adv* nuevamente, de nuevo.

angel ➤ *s* ángel *m.*

anger ➤ *s* ira, enojo ➤ *tr & intr* enojar(se).

angle ➤ *s* ángulo.

angler ➤ *s* pescador/a (de caña).

angrily ➤ *adv* con enojo, con ira.

angry ➤ *adj* enojado, enfadado ■ **to make (someone) a.** enojar (a alguien).

anguish ➤ *s* angustia, congoja.

animal ➤ *adj & s* animal *m.*

ankle ➤ *s* tobillo.

annex ➤ *s* anexo.

anniversary ➤ *s* aniversario.

announce ➤ *tr* anunciar, declarar.

announcement ➤ *s* anuncio, declaración *f.*

announcer ➤ *s* anunciador/a, locutor/a.

annoy ➤ *tr* molestar, fastidiar.

annoying ➤ *adj* molesto, irritante.

annual ➤ *adj* anual ➤ *s (yearbook)* anuario; BOT. planta anual.

anomaly ➤ *s* anomalía.

anonymity ➤ *s* anonimato.

anonymous ➤ *adj* anónimo.

another ➤ *adj* otro; *(different)* (otro) distinto; *(additional)* más ■ **a. one** otro más • **a. time** otro día ➤ *pron* otro ■ **one a.** uno(s) a otro(s).

answer ➤ *s* respuesta, contestación *f*; *(solution)* solución *f* ➤ *intr* responder ■ **answering machine** contestador automático (de teléfono) ➤ *tr* contestar a; *(correctly)* solucionar (problema, enigma) ■ **to a. the telephone** contestar el teléfono.

ant ➤ *s* hormiga.

antacid ➤ *adj & s* antiácido.

antelope ➤ *s* antílope *m.*

antenna ➤ *s* RAD., ZOOL. antena.

anthem ➤ *s* RELIG. antífona ■ **national a.** himno nacional.

anthology ➤ *s* antología.

antibiotic ➤ *s & adj* antibiótico.

antibody ➤ *s* anticuerpo.

anticipate ➤ *tr (to foresee)* anticipar, prever; *(to expect)* esperar, contar con.

anticipation ➤ *s (act)* anticipación *f*; *(eagerness)* ilusión *f.*

anticlimactic ➤ *adj* decepcionante.

antifreeze ➤ *s* anticongelante *m.*

antihistamine ➤ *s* antihistamínico.

antique ➤ *adj* antiguo ➤ *s* antigüedad *f.*

antiseptic ➤ *adj & s* antiséptico.

anxiety ➤ *s* ansiedad *f*, ansia; PSIC. angustia.

anxious ➤ *adj (worried)* ansioso, inquieto; *(eager)* deseoso, anhelante.

any ➤ *adj* cualquier ■ **a. minute** pronto • **at a. cost** a toda costa • **in a. case** de todos modos • **there isn't a. reason** no hay ninguna razón ➤ *pron* alguno, cualquiera; *(negative)* ninguno ■ **if a.** si los hay ➤ *adv* algo ■ **a. longer** todavía • **do you feel a. better?** ¿te sientes algo mejor? • **I don't feel a. better** no me siento nada mejor.

anybody ➤ *pron* cualquiera, cualquier persona ■ **did you see a?** ¿viste a alguien? • **I didn't see a.** no vi a nadie.

anyhow ➤ *adv (even so)* de todos modos; *(carelessly)* de cualquier manera.

anymore ➤ *adv* ■ **do you skate a.?** ¿patinas todavía? • **I don't skate a.** ya no patino más.

anyone ➤ *vea* **anybody.**

anyplace ➤ *vea* **anywhere.**

anything ➤ *pron* algo ■ **a. else?** ¿algo más? • **are you doing a. now?** ¿estás haciendo algo ahora? • **I can't see a.** no veo nada • **like a.** FAM. a más no poder • **take a. you like** toma todo lo que quieras.

anytime ➤ *adv* a cualquier hora, en cualquier momento.

anyway ➤ *adv (in any case)* de cualquier manera; *(even so)* de todos modos.

anywhere ➤ *adv (affirmative)* dondequiera; *(negative)* en, a, *o* por ninguna parte; *(interrogative)* en alguna parte.

apart ➤ *adv* aparte ■ **a. from** aparte de • **to come a.** desprenderse • **to fall a.** descomponerse • **to keep a.** apartar, separar • **to take a.** desarmar.

apartment ➤ *s* departamento, apartamento ■ **a. house** casa *o* edificio de departamentos.

ape ➤ *s* mono.

apéritif ➤ *s* aperitivo.

apologetic ➤ *adj* lleno de disculpas.

apologize ➤ *intr* disculparse (*for* por, de) (*to* con).

apology ➤ *s* disculpa.

apostrophe ➤ *s* GRAM. apóstrofo.

appall ➤ *tr* pasmar, horrorizar.

appalling ➤ *adj* pasmoso, horrendo.

apparatus ➤ *s* aparato; *(mechanism)* mecanismo.

apparent ➤ *adj (seeming)* aparente; *(perceptible)* evidente, claro.

apparently ➤ *adv* aparentemente, por lo visto.

appeal ➤ *s (plea)* súplica; *(a call for)* llamada; *(petition)* petición *f*; *(charm)* atracción *f*, encanto; DER. apelación *f*, recurso ➤ *intr* DER. recurrir a, apelar a; *(to be attractive)* tener atractivo para ➤ *tr* llevar a un tribunal superior.

appealing ➤ *adj* atrayente.

appear ➤ *intr* aparecer; *(to present oneself)* presentarse; *(on the stage)* actuar; *(in court)* comparecer.

appearance ➤ *s (act)* aparición *f*; *(looks)* aspecto, apariencia; *(pretense)* pretensión *f*, simulación *f* ■ **to make an a.** hacer acto de presencia ■ *pl* apariencias, exterioridad.

appendicitis ➤ *s* apendicitis *f.*

appendix ➤ *s* apéndice *m.*

appetite ➤ *s* apetito, apetencia.

appetizer ➤ *s* aperitivo.

applaud ➤ *tr & intr* aplaudir.

applause ➤ *s* aplauso.

apple ➤ *s* manzana ■ **a. tree** manzano.

appliance ➤ *s* aparato ■ **household a.** aparato electrodoméstico.

applicant ➤ *s* aspirante *mf.*

application ➤ *s (act)* aplicación *f*; *(relevance)* correspondencia, pertinencia; *(diligence)* esmero; *(request)* solicitación *f*; *(form)* solicitud *f*, aplicación.

apply ➤ *tr* aplicar; *(to use)* emplear, usar (*to* para) ■ **to a. oneself to** aplicarse a ➤ *intr* ser pertinente ■ **to a. for** solicitar (empleo, admisión).

appoint ➤ *tr* nombrar.

appointment ➤ *s (act)* nombramiento, designación *f*; *(post)* puesto, cargo; *(date)* cita, compromiso.

appreciate ➤ *tr (to recognize)* darse cuenta de; *(to value)* apreciar, estimar; *(to be grateful for)* agradecer ➤ *intr* subir de precio *o* valor.

appreciation ➤ *s* apreciación *f*, reconocimiento; *(gratitude)* gratitud *f*; COM. valorización *f.*

apprehensive ➤ *adj* aprensivo.

apprentice ➤ *s* aprendiz/a.

apprenticeship ➤ *s* aprendizaje *m.*

approach ➤ *intr* aproximarse, acercarse ➤ *tr* aproximarse a, acercarse a; *(to make overtures to)* abordar ➤ *s (act)* acercamiento; *(access)* acceso.

approaching ➤ *adj (upcoming)* venidero, próximo; *(nearing)* que se acerca.

appropriate ➤ *adj* apropiado.

approval ➤ *s* aprobación *f*, sanción *f* ■ **on a.** a prueba.

approve ➤ *tr* aprobar.

approximate ➤ *adj* aproximado.

apricot ➤ *s* albaricoque *m.*

April ➤ *s* abril *m.*

apron ➤ *s* delantal *m.*

apt ➤ *adj (suitable)* apropiado, acertado; *(inclined)* propenso; *(bright)* apto, listo.

aptitude ➤ *s* aptitud *f*, capacidad *f.*

aquarium ➤ *s* acuario.

aqueduct ➤ *s* acueducto.

aquifer ➤ *s* acuífero.

Arabic numeral ➤ *s* número arábigo.

arbitration ➤ *s* arbitraje *m.*

arbor ➤ *s* enramada, pérgola.

arc ➤ *s* arco.

arcade ➤ *s* arcada; *(gallery)* galería.

arch ➤ *s* arco ➤ *tr & intr* arquear(se).

archaeology ➤ *s* arqueología.

arched ➤ *adj* arqueado, enarcado.

archer ➤ *s* arquero/a (de arco y flecha).

archery ➤ *s* tiro de arco y flecha.

archetype ➤ *s* arquetipo, prototipo.

archipelago ➤ *s* archipiélago.

architect ➤ *s* arquitecto/a.

architecture ➤ *s* arquitectura.

archway ➤ *s* arcada, arco.

arctic ➤ *adj* frígido, glacial.

are ➤ *vea* **be** *en tabla de verbos.*

area ➤ *s* área; *(region)* zona, región *f* ■ **a. code** prefijo telefónico.

aren't ➤ *contr de* **are not.**

Argentine *o* **Argentinian** ➤ *adj & s* argentino/a.

argue ➤ *tr (a case)* argüir, presentar ➤ *intr (to debate)* argumentar, argüir (en favor o en contra de algo); *(to quarrel)* disputar, discutir.

argument ➤ *s* discusión *f*, debate *m*; *(quarrel)* pelea, disputa; *(contention)* razonamiento, argumento.

arid ➤ *adj* árido, seco.

arise◊ ➤ *intr (to get up)* levantarse; *(to originate)* surgir, originarse.

aristocrat ➤ *s* aristócrata *mf.*

arithmetic ➤ *s* aritmética.

arm[1] ➤ *s* ANAT. brazo.

arm[2] ➤ *s* MIL. arma ➤ *tr* armar.

armband ➤ *s* brazalete *m*, brazal *m.*

armchair ➤ *s* sillón *m*, butaca.

armoire ➤ *s* armario, ropero.

armor ➤ *s* armadura; *(metal plating)* blindaje *m.*

armored ➤ *adj* acorazado, blindado.

armory ➤ *s* armería, arsenal.

armpit ➤ *s* axila.

army ➤ *s* ejército.

aroma ➤ *s* aroma *m*, fragancia.

around ➤ *adv (in all directions)* por todos lados, en derredor; *(in a circle)* alrededor; *(here and there)* por aquí, por allá; *(in circumference)* de circunferencia ■ **all a.** por todos lados • **to get a.** *(person)* viajar; *(news)* divulgarse • **to have been a.** tener experiencia ➤ *prep (about)* cerca de, alrededor de; *(encircling)* alrededor de; *(here and there)* por todos lados, en torno de ■ **a. the corner** a la vuelta de la esquina.

arrange ➤ *tr* arreglar, ordenar; *(to settle upon)* fijar (fechas, convenios); *(to plan)* preparar; MÚS. arreglar.

arrangement ➤ *s* arreglo; *(order)* disposición *f*; *(agreement)* convenio ■ *pl* planes, medidas.

arrears ➤ *spl* ■ **to be in a.** estar atrasado en pagos de deuda.

arrest ➤ *tr (to halt)* detener, parar; *(to seize)* arrestar, detener; *(one's attention)* cautivar ➤ *s* arresto, detención *f* ■ **under a.** detenido.

arrival ➤ *s* llegada, arribo.

arrive ➤ *intr* llegar.

arrow ➤ *s* flecha.

arson ➤ *s* incendio premeditado.

art ➤ *s* arte *m*; *(skill)* destreza, técnica ■ **fine arts** bellas artes.

artery ➤ *s* arteria.

arthritis ➤ *s* artritis *f.*

artichoke ➤ *s* alcachofa.

article ➤ *s* artículo.

articulate ➤ *adj* articulado; *(well-spoken)* claro ➤ *tr (a word)* articular, enunciar; *(to form a joint)* articular.

artifact ➤ *s* artefacto.

artificial ➤ *adj* artificial.

artisan ➤ *s* artesano/a, artífice *mf.*

artist ➤ *s* artista *mf.*

artistic ➤ *adj* artístico.

as ➤ *adv (equally)* así de, tan; *(for example)* (tal) como ■ **as . . . as** tan . . . como ➤ *conj* igual que, como; *(while)* mientras; *(because)* ya que ■ **as if** como si • **as if to** como para • **as it were** por así decirlo • **as long as** *(since)* ya que; *(on the condition that)* siempre y cuando; *(while)* mientras • **as to** en cuanto a • **as yet** hasta ahora ➤ *prep* como ■ **as a rule** por regla general • **as for** en cuanto a.

ascend ➤ *tr & intr* subir.

ascent ➤ *s (act)* subida, ascención *f*; *(in rank)* ascenso; *(upward slope)* cuesta.

ash[1] ➤ *s (from fire)* ceniza.

ash[2] ➤ *s* BOT. fresno.

ashamed ➤ *adj* avergonzado ■ **to be a.** tener vergüenza.

ashore ➤ *adv* a *o* en tierra ■ **to go a.** bajar a tierra, desembarcar.

ashtray ➤ *s* cenicero.

Asia ➤ *s* Asia.

Asian ➤ *adj & s* asiático/a.

aside ➤ *adv* al lado, a un lado ■ **a. from** a no ser por • **joking a.** bromas aparte.

ask ➤ *tr* preguntar; *(to request)* solicitar, pedir; *(to demand)* exigir; *(to invite)* invitar ■ **to a. a favor** pedir un favor • **to a. a question** hacer una pregunta ➤ *intr* preguntar *(about, after* por) ■ **to a. for** pedir.

asleep ➤ *adj* dormido ■ **to fall a.** dormirse, quedarse dormido.

asparagus ➤ *s* espárrago.

aspect ➤ *s* aspecto.

aspirin ➤ *s* aspirina.

assassin ➤ *s* asesino/a.

assassinate ➤ *tr* asesinar.

assault ➤ *s* asalto, ataque *m* ➤ *tr & intr* asaltar, atacar.

assemble ➤ *tr* congregar, reunir; MEC. armar, montar ➤ *intr* congregarse.

assembly ➤ *s* asamblea, congreso; MEC. montaje *m* ■ **a. line** línea de montaje.

assess ➤ *tr (to appraise)* avaluar, tasar (*at* en); *(to levy)* gravar, multar; *(to evaluate)* evaluar, juzgar.

asset ➤ *s (item)* posesión *f*, bien *m*; *(advantage)* ventaja ■ *pl* bienes, activo.

assign ➤ *tr* asignar.

assignment ➤ *s* tarea, deber *m.*

assist ➤ *tr & intr* asistir, auxiliar ➤ *s* ayuda, auxilio.

assistance ➤ *s* asistencia, ayuda.

assistant ➤ *s & adj* ayudante *mf*, auxiliar *mf.*

associate ➤ *tr & intr* asociar(se) ■ **to a. with someone** juntarse *o* tratarse con alguien ➤ *s* socio/a.

association ➤ *s* asociación *f.*

assorted ➤ *adj* surtido, variado.

assortment ➤ *s* surtido.

assume ➤ *tr* asumir; *(to arrogate)* arrogarse (un derecho); *(to presume)*

presumir, suponer.
assurance ➤ s garantía, promesa; *(self-confidence)* aplomo.
assure ➤ tr asegurar.
asterisk ➤ s asterisco.
asthma ➤ s asma.
asthmatic ➤ adj & s asmático/a.
astonish ➤ tr asombrar.
astonishing ➤ adj asombroso.
astray ➤ adv por mal camino ■ **to go a.** extraviarse • **to lead a.** descarriar.
astride ➤ adv a horcajadas (sobre).
astrology ➤ s astrología.
astronaut ➤ s astronauta *mf.*
astronomy ➤ s astronomía.
astrophysics ➤ ssg astrofísica.
at ➤ prep en, a, por, de ■ **at noon** al mediodía • **at right angles** en ángulo recto • **don't laugh at me!** ¡no te rías de mí! • **to be angry at something** estar enfadado por algo.
athlete ➤ s atleta *mf* ■ **a.'s foot** pie de atleta.
athletic ➤ adj atlético ■ **athletics** ssg o pl atletismo.
atlas ➤ s atlas *m.*
atmosphere ➤ s atmósfera.
atom ➤ s átomo ■ **a.** o **atomic bomb** bomba atómica.
atomic ➤ adj atómico.
attach ➤ tr *(to fasten)* ligar, sujetar; *(to bond)* unir, pegar; *(to ascribe)* dar, atribuir (importancia, significado).
attaché ➤ s agregado/a ■ **a. case** portafolio, maletín.
attack ➤ tr atacar, agredir; FIG. acometer (tarea, problema) ➤ intr ir al ataque ➤ s ataque *m,* agresión *f.*
attacker ➤ s agresor/a, asaltante *mf.*
attain ➤ tr lograr, conseguir.
attempt ➤ tr intentar, tratar de ➤ s *(try)* intento, prueba; *(attack)* atentado.
attend ➤ tr *(to go to)* atender, asistir a; *(to take care of)* atender, cuidar ■ **to a.** to prestar atención a.
attendance ➤ s asistencia.
attendant ➤ s asistente/a, mozo/a.
attention ➤ s atención *f; (attentiveness)* cuidado ■ **to pay a. (to)** prestar atención (a) ■ pl cortesías, atenciones.
attentive ➤ adj atento.
attic ➤ s desván *m,* guardilla.
attitude ➤ s actitud *f.*
attorney ➤ s abogado/a, apoderado/a ■ **a. general** fiscal o procurador/a general.
attract ➤ tr & intr atraer.
attraction ➤ s atracción *f; (allure)* atractivo.
attractive ➤ adj atractivo, atrayente.
attribute ➤ tr atribuir ➤ s atributo.
auction ➤ s subasta, remate *m* ➤ tr subastar, rematar.
auctioneer ➤ s subastador/a.
audible ➤ adj audible, oíble.
audience ➤ s *(public)* auditorio, público; *(formal hearing)* audiencia.
audio ➤ adj ■ **a. frequency** audiofrecuencia ➤ s TELEV. transmisión *f* o recepción *f* del sonido.
audio-visual ➤ adj audiovisual.
auditorium ➤ s auditorio.
August ➤ s agosto.
aunt ➤ s tía.
Australia ➤ s Australia.
Australian ➤ adj & s australiano/a.
authentic ➤ adj auténtico.
author ➤ s autor/a ➤ tr escribir.
authoritarian ➤ adj & s autoritario/a.
authority ➤ s autoridad *f; (expert)* experto/a, perito/a ■ **on good a.** de buena tinta.
authorize ➤ tr autorizar.
autobiography ➤ s autobiografía.
autograph ➤ s autógrafo ➤ tr autografiar.
automatic ➤ adj automático ■ **a. rifle** fusil ametrallador ➤ s arma automática.
automobile ➤ s automóvil *m.*
automotive ➤ adj automotor, automotriz; *(industry)* automovilístico.
autonomy ➤ s autonomía.
autopsy ➤ s autopsia.
autumn ➤ s otoño.
auxiliary ➤ adj auxiliar.
available ➤ adj disponible.
avalanche ➤ s avalancha.
avenue ➤ s avenida.
average ➤ s promedio ■ **on the a.** por término medio ➤ adj (de término) medio; *(ordinary)* regular.
aversion ➤ s aversión *f.*
aviation ➤ s aviación *f.*
avocado ➤ s aguacate *m,* palta.
avoid ➤ tr evitar.
await ➤ tr & intr esperar, aguardar.
awake◊ ➤ tr & intr despertar(se) ➤ adj despierto.
award ➤ tr premiar; *(legally)* adjudicar ➤ s *(prize)* premio, recompensa; *(decision)* decisión *f,* fallo.
aware ➤ adj consciente, percatado ■ **to be a. of** o **that** tener conciencia de o que • **to become a.** of enterarse de.
away ➤ adv lejos de, a ■ **far a.** lejos • **right a.** inmediatamente ➤ adj ausente, fuera; *(at a distance)* lejano.
awesome ➤ adj pasmoso, asombroso.
awful ➤ adj *(terrible)* pavoroso; *(atrocious)* atroz, horrible; *(great)* enorme.
awfully ➤ adv *(atrociously)* muy mal; *(very)* muchísimo, muy.
awhile ➤ adv un rato, algún tiempo.
awkward ➤ adj *(clumsy)* torpe, desmañado; *(embarrassing)* embarazoso; *(shape)* inconveniente.
awning ➤ s toldo.
ax(e) ➤ s hacha.
axis ➤ s eje *m.*
axle ➤ s eje *m,* árbol *m.*

B

baby ➤ s bebé *m,* nene *mf* ➤ tr mimar, consentir.
baby-sit ➤ intr cuidar niños.
bachelor ➤ s soltero; EDUC. *(degree)* bachillerato; *(graduate)* bachiller *m.*
back ➤ s espalda; *(animal)* lomo, espinazo; *(reverse side)* envés *m,* revés *m* ➤ adv (hacia) atrás ■ **b. and forth** de acá para allá • **in b. of** detrás de, tras de • **to go** o **come b.** volver, regresar ➤ adj de atrás, posterior ■ **b. talk** impertinencia(s) ➤ tr mover hacia atrás; *(to support)* respaldar, apoyar ■ **to b. up** *(vehicle)* dar marcha atrás; *(drain)* atascar(se); COMPUT. hacer una copia de reserva (de) ➤ intr moverse hacia atrás ■ **to b. down** echarse atrás • **to b. out** volverse atrás.
backache ➤ s dolor *m* de espalda.
backfire ➤ s petardeo ➤ intr AUTO. petardear; *(scheme)* salir al revés.
background ➤ s fondo, trasfondo; *(of events)* antecedentes *m; (experience)* experiencia.
backing ➤ s respaldo (moral, económico).
backlash ➤ s FIG. reacción *f.*
backlog ➤ s acumulación *f* (de trabajo, pedidos).
backpack ➤ s mochila.
backrest ➤ s respaldo (de un asiento).
backstage ➤ adv entre bastidores.
backup ➤ s reserva; *(support)* respaldo; COMPUT. copia de reserva ➤ adj suplente, de reserva.
backward(s) ➤ adv hacia o para atrás ■ **to do something b.** hacer algo al revés • **to fall b.** caerse de espaldas • **to know backwards and forwards** saberse al dedillo ➤ adj hacia atrás; *(motion)* de retroceso; *(reverse)* al revés; *(place, era)* atrasado.
bacon ➤ s tocino ■ **to bring home the b.** FAM. ganar el pan.
bacteria ➤ spl bacteria.
bad ➤ adj malo; *(check)* sin fondos; *(naughty)* desobediente ■ **a b. cold** un catarro fuerte • **to feel b.** *(ill)* sentirse mal; *(sad)* estar triste • **to go b.** echarse a perder • **too b.!** ¡qué lástima!, ¡mala suerte! ➤ s lo malo ➤ adv ■ **it hurts bad** FAM. me duele mucho ■ **to be b. off** FAM. estar mal.
badge ➤ s distintivo, insignia.
badly ➤ adv mal; *(very much)* mucho, con urgencia ■ **to take something b.** tomar a mal algo.
badminton ➤ s volante *m.*
baffle ➤ tr confundir ➤ s deflector *m.*
bag ➤ s bolsa, saco; *(purse)* bolso, cartera; *(suitcase)* valija, maletín *m* ■ pl equipaje ➤ tr meter en una bolsa; FAM. *(to capture)* coger, pescar.
baggage ➤ s equipaje *m,* maletas; MIL. bagaje *m.*
baggy ➤ adj bombacho.
bagpipe ➤ s gaita.
bail ➤ s fianza, caución *f* ■ **out on b.** en libertad bajo fianza ➤ tr ■ **to b. out** sacar de apuros.
bait ➤ s cebo, carnada ➤ tr poner el cebo en (anzuelo, trampa); *(to torment)* atormentar.
bake ➤ tr cocer al horno ➤ intr cocerse ➤ s cocción *f* (al horno).
baker ➤ s panadero/a.
bakery ➤ s panadería.
baking ➤ s cocción *f* ■ **b. powder** levadura en polvo • **b. soda** bicarbonato de sodio.
balance ➤ s *(scale)* balanza; *(equilibrium)* equilibrio ■ **b. due** saldo deudor • **b. sheet** balance • **off b.** en desequilibrio • **to throw off b.** desconcertar ➤ tr balancear, equilibrar; *(to counterbalance)* compensar, contrarrestar ■ **to b. the books** pasar balance ➤ intr equilibrarse.
balcony ➤ s balcón *m;* TEAT. galería, paraíso.
bald ➤ adj calvo; *(blunt)* categórico, sin rodeos ■ **to go b.** quedarse calvo.
baldness ➤ s calvicie *f.*
balk ➤ intr *(to stop)* plantarse; *(to refuse)* oponerse (at a).
ball[1] ➤ s bola; DEP. pelota, balón *m* ■ **b. bearing** cojinete de bolas • **to be on the b.** JER. estar atento.
ball[2] ➤ s baile *m* de etiqueta ■ **to have a b.** JER. pasarla muy bien.
ballerina ➤ s bailarina (de ballet).
ballet ➤ s ballet *m.*
balloon ➤ s globo ➤ intr hincharse, inflarse.
ballot ➤ s papeleta (electoral) ■ **b. box** urna electoral ➤ intr votar.
ballpark ➤ s estadio ■ **in the b.** FAM. aproximado.
ball-point pen ➤ s bolígrafo.
ban ➤ tr prohibir, proscribir ➤ s prohibición *f,* proscripción *f.*
banana ➤ s plátano, banana ■ **b. tree** plátano, banano ■ pl JER. chiflado.
band[1] ➤ s banda, faja; *(stripe)* franja; JOY. anillo (de boda) ➤ tr fajar, atar.
band[2] ➤ s banda; *(gang)* cuadrilla; MÚS. *(military)* banda; *(jazz)* orquesta; *(rock)* conjunto ➤ tr & intr ■ **to b. together** agrupar(se), juntar(se).
bandage ➤ s venda ➤ tr vendar.
bandit ➤ s bandido, bandolero/a.
bang ➤ s *(explosion)* estallido; *(loud slam)* golpe *m,* golpetazo; JER. *(thrill)* emoción *f,* excitación *f* ➤ tr golpear ■ **to b. up** estropear ➤ intr detonar; *(to crash)* chocar *(into* con) ➤ interj *(shot)* ¡pum!; *(blow)* ¡zas!
banister ➤ s barandilla, baranda.
bank[1] ➤ s *(of a river)* ribera, orilla; *(of snow)* montón *m* ➤ tr *(a fire)* cubrir; *(a road)* peraltar; AVIA. inclinar.
bank[2] ➤ s COM. banco; *(in gambling)* banca ■ **b. account** cuenta bancaria • **b. note** billete de banco ➤ intr ■ **to b. on** contar con, confiar en.
banker ➤ s banquero/a.
bankrupt ➤ adj COM. insolvente ■ **to go b.** declararse en quiebra, quebrar ➤ tr hacer quebrar, arruinar.
bankruptcy ➤ s quiebra, bancarrota.
banner ➤ s bandera, estandarte *m;* ➤ adj sobresaliente.
banquet ➤ s banquete *m.*
baptism ➤ s bautismo.
baptistery ➤ s baptisterio.
baptize ➤ tr bautizar.
bar ➤ s barra; *(of soap)* pastilla; *(of chocolate)* tableta; *(obstacle)* obstáculo; *(tavern)* bar *m; (counter)* mostrador *m; (legal profession)* abogacía ➤ tr *(to fasten)* cerrar con barras; *(to obstruct)* obstruir; *(to exclude)* excluir; *(to prohibit)* prohibir ➤ prep ■ **b. none** sin excepción.
barbaric ➤ adj bárbaro.
barbecue ➤ s barbacoa, parrillada ➤ tr asar a la parrilla.
barber ➤ s barbero, peluquero/a.
barbershop ➤ s barbería, peluquería.
bare ➤ adj desnudo; *(head)* descubierto; *(feet)* descalzo; *(empty)* desprovisto, vacío ■ **to lay b.** revelar ➤ tr desnudar; *(to reveal)* descubrir.
barefoot(ed) ➤ adv & adj descalzo.
barely ➤ adv apenas.
bargain ➤ s *(deal)* pacto, convenio; *(good buy)* ganga ■ **into the b.** por añadidura ➤ intr negociar; *(to haggle)* regatear ■ **to b. for** o **on** esperar.
barge ➤ s barcaza, gabarra ➤ intr ■ **to b. in** entremeterse • **to b. into** irrumpir en.
bark[1] ➤ s ladrido ➤ tr & intr ladrar.
bark[2] ➤ s BOT. corteza.
barkeep(er) ➤ s barman *m.*
barn ➤ s *(for grain)* granero; *(for livestock)* establo.
barometer ➤ s barómetro.
baroque ➤ adj & s barroco.
barracks ➤ spl cuartel *m.*
barrage ➤ s MIL. bombardeo, cortina de fuego; FIG. *(burst)* andanada.
barrel ➤ s barril *m,* tonel *m; (of a gun)* cañón *m* ➤ intr ir a gran velocidad.
barren ➤ adj estéril, infecundo; *(land)* yermo.
barrette ➤ s pasador *m.*
barricade ➤ s barricada, barrera.
barrier ➤ s barrera, valla.
barroom ➤ s bar *m.*
bartender ➤ s camarero/a, barman *m.*
base ➤ s base *f;* ARQ. basa ■ **to be off b.** estar equivocado ➤ adj de la base ➤ tr ■ **to b. (up)on** basar en o sobre.
baseball ➤ s béisbol *m; (ball)* pelota.
basement ➤ s sótano.
bash FAM. ➤ tr golpear ➤ s golpazo, porrazo; *(party)* fiesta, parranda.
basic ➤ adj básico ➤ s base *f.*
basin ➤ s palangana, jofaina; *(washbowl)* pila, pileta.
basis ➤ s base *f,* fundamento ■ **on the b. of** en base a.
bask ➤ intr gozar, complacerse.
basket ➤ s cesta, canasta; DEP. cesto.
basketball ➤ s baloncesto, básquetbol *m,* básquet *m; (ball)* pelota, balón *m.*
bas-relief ➤ s bajo relieve.
bass[1] ➤ s *(fish)* róbalo.
bass[2] ➤ s MÚS. bajo.
bat ➤ s DEP. bate *m;* ZOOL. murciélago ➤ tr golpear; DEP. batear ■ **not to b. an eye** no pestañear.
batch ➤ s CUL. hornada; *(lot)* partida, lote *m; (group)* grupo, tanda.
bath ➤ s baño; *(bathroom)* cuarto de baño ■ pl casa de baños.
bathe ➤ intr bañarse ➤ tr bañar; *(to wash)* lavar; *(to flood)* inundar.
bathing suit ➤ s traje *m* de baño.
bathrobe ➤ s bata, albornoz *m.*
bathroom ➤ s cuarto de baño.
bathtub ➤ s bañera.
batter[1] ➤ tr *(to beat)* golpear, apalear.
batter[2] ➤ s CUL. pasta; DEP. bateador/a.
battery ➤ s ELEC., MIL. batería; *(dry cell)* pila; *(storage)* acumulador *m;* DER. asalto.
battle ➤ s batalla ➤ intr & tr combatir.
battleship ➤ s acorazado.
bawl ➤ intr llorar ■ **to b. out** regañar.
bay ➤ s GEOG. bahía.
be◊ ➤ intr *(inherent quality, time, possession, passive voice)* ser ■ **ice is cold** el hielo es frío • **what time is it?** ¿qué hora es? • **is it yours?** ¿es tuyo? ➤ *(location, impermanence)* estar ■ **where are you?** ¿dónde estás? • **my coffee is cold** mi café está frío ➤ *(age, physical sensation)* tener; *(weather)* haber, hacer ■ **as it were** por así decirlo • **so be it** así sea • **there is** o **are** hay.
beach ➤ s playa ➤ tr varar.
beacon ➤ s faro; *(radio)* radiofaro.
bead ➤ s cuenta, abalorio; *(drop)* gota ■ pl RELIG. rosario.
beak ➤ s pico.
beam ➤ s *(of light)* haz *m,* rayo; ARQ. viga; RAD. onda dirigida ➤ tr emitir, dirigir ➤ intr *(to smile)* sonreír radiantemente.
bean ➤ s habichuela, judía, frijol *m; (seed)* haba; *(of coffee)* grano ■ **to spill the beans** FAM. descubrir el pastel.
bear[1]◊ ➤ tr *(to support)* sostener; *(to carry, display)* llevar; *(to endure)* aguantar; *(a baby)* dar a luz; *(fruit)* producir, dar ■ **to b. in mind** tener en cuenta • **to b. mention** merecer mencionarse • **to b. out** corroborar • **to b. with** tener paciencia con ➤ intr producir, rendir; *(to pressure)* pesar ■ **to b. on** relacionarse con • **to b. right** girar a la derecha • **to b. up** resistir • **to bring to b.** aplicar.
bear[2] ➤ s ZOOL. oso.
bearable ➤ adj soportable.
beard ➤ s barba.
bearded ➤ adj barbudo.
bearing ➤ s *(poise)* porte *m;* AER., MARÍT. rumbo; MEC. cojinete *m* ■ pl **to get one's b.** orientarse.
beast ➤ s bestia, bruto ■ **b. of burden** bestia de carga.
beat◊ ➤ tr *(to hit)* golpear; *(to pound, flap, stir)* batir; *(to defeat)* vencer, derrotar; *(to surpass)* superar a; *(a drum)* tocar ■ **b. it!** ¡lárgate! • **to b. back** o **off** repeler ➤ intr latir, pulsar ➤ s latido,

pulsación *f; (tempo)* compás *m.*
beautiful ➤ *adj* bello, hermoso.
beauty ➤ *s* belleza, hermosura.
beaver ➤ *s* castor *m.*
because ➤ *conj* porque ■ **b. of** a causa de, por.
become ➤ *intr (to turn into)* llegar a ser, convertirse en; *(angry, etc.)* hacerse, ponerse, volverse ■ **what has b. of George?** ¿qué se ha hecho de Jorge?
bed ➤ *s* cama, lecho; *(of flowers)* macizo ■ **b. and board** pensión completa • **to go to b.** acostarse.
bedbug ➤ *s* chinche *f.*
bedding ➤ *s* ropa de cama.
bedroom ➤ *s* dormitorio, alcoba.
bedspread ➤ *s* cubrecama *m,* colcha.
bedtime ➤ *s* hora de acostarse.
bee ➤ *s* abeja; FAM. *(contest)* concurso.
beef ➤ *s* carne *f* de res.
beefsteak ➤ *s* bistec *m,* biftec *m.*
beep ➤ *s* sonido agudo ➤ *intr & tr* sonar con sonido agudo.
beeper ➤ *s* buscapersonas *m.*
beer ➤ *s* cerveza ■ **dark, light b.** cerveza negra, dorada.
beet ➤ *s* remolacha.
beetle ➤ *s* escarabajo.
before ➤ *adv* antes ■ **to go b.** ir delante (de) ➤ *prep (in time)* antes de *o* que; *(in space)* delante de; *(in front of)* ante ➤ *conj* antes de que.
beg ➤ *tr & intr (for charity)* mendigar, pedir (limosna); *(to entreat)* suplicar, rogar ■ **to b. pardon** pedir perdón.
beggar ➤ *s* mendigo/a, pobre *mf.*
begin✧ ➤ *tr & intr* empezar, comenzar ■ **to b. by** empezar por • **to b. with** para empezar.
beginner ➤ *s* principiante/a, novato/a.
beginning ➤ *s* comienzo, principio; *(source)* origen *m* ■ **b. with** a partir de.
begrudge ➤ *tr (to envy)* envidiar; *(to give reluctantly)* dar de mala gana.
behalf ➤ *s* ■ **in b. of** para, a favor de • **on b. of** en nombre de.
behave ➤ *tr & intr* portarse, comportarse; *(properly)* portarse bien.
behavior ➤ *s* comportamiento.
behind ➤ *adv (in back)* atrás, detrás; *(late)* atrasado; *(slow)* con retraso ➤ *prep* detrás de ■ **b. schedule** atrasado ➤ *s* FAM. trasero, nalgas.
being ➤ *s* existencia; *(creature)* ser *m.*
belated ➤ *adj* atrasado, tardío.
belch ➤ *intr & tr* eructar; *(smoke, fire)* arrojar, vomitar ➤ *s* eructo.
belfry ➤ *s* campanario.
belief ➤ *s* creencia, fe *f; (conviction)* convicción *f,* opinión *f.*
believable ➤ *adj* creíble.
believe ➤ *tr* creer ■ **to make b.** fingir.
believer ➤ *s* creyente *mf.*
belittle ➤ *tr* menospreciar.
bell ➤ *s* campana;; *(of a door)* timbre *m* ■ **to ring a b.** FIG. sonarle a uno
bellboy *o* **bellhop** ➤ *s* botones *m.*
belligerent ➤ *adj & s* beligerante *mf.*
belly ➤ *s* vientre *m;* FAM. *(paunch)* panza, barriga ■ **b. laugh** carcajada.
bellyache ➤ *s* dolor *m* de barriga; JER. *(gripe)* queja ➤ *intr* JER. quejarse.
bellybutton ➤ *s* FAM. ombligo.
belong ➤ *intr* deber estar, corresponder ■ **to b. to** *(as property)* pertenecer a, ser de; *(as a member)* ser miembro de; *(as part of)* corresponder a.
belongings ➤ *spl* efectos personales.
below ➤ *adv* abajo ➤ *prep* (por) debajo de ■ **b. zero** bajo cero.
belt ➤ *s* cinturón *m,* cinto; TEC. *(band)* correa.
bench ➤ *s* banco; DER. tribunal *m.*
bend✧ ➤ *tr (the head)* inclinar; *(the knee, object)* doblar; *(one's back)* encorvar ➤ *intr* ■ **to b. down** *o* **over** encorvarse ➤ *s* curva; *(turn)* vuelta, recodo.
beneath ➤ *prep* (por) debajo de; *(under)* bajo; *(unworthy)* indigno de ➤ *adv* abajo; *(underneath)* debajo.
beneficial ➤ *adj* provechoso.
benefit ➤ *s* beneficio; *(advantage)* ventaja ■ *pl* asistencia ➤ *tr* beneficiar ➤ *intr* ■ **to b. from** sacar provecho de.
bent ➤ *adj* doblado, torcido.
bereavement ➤ *s* luto, duelo.
beret ➤ *s* boina.
berry ➤ *s* baya.
berserk ➤ *adj* frenético, loco ■ **to go b.** volverse loco.
berth ➤ *s (on train)* litera; *(on ship)* camarote *m* ■ **to give a wide b.** evitar.
beside ➤ *prep* junto a, al lado de ■ **to be b. the point** no venir al caso.
besides ➤ *adv* además; *(otherwise)* por otro lado, aparte de eso ➤ *prep* además de; *(except)* aparte de, fuera de.
best ➤ *adj* mejor ■ **b. man** padrino (de una boda) ➤ *adv* mejor ■ **which do you like b.?** ¿cuál te gusta más? ➤ *s* el mejor, lo mejor ■ **at b.** a lo más.
bet✧ ➤ *s* apuesta ■ **to be a sure b.** ser cosa segura ➤ *tr* apostar ■ **I b. . . .** FAM. seguro que . . . ➤ *intr* ■ **I b.!** FAM. ¡ya lo creo! • **you b.!** FAM. ¡claro!
betray ➤ *tr* traicionar; *(to inform on)* delatar; *(a secret)* revelar.
betrayal ➤ *s* traición *f,* delación *f; (of a secret)* revelación *f.*
better ➤ *adj* mejor ■ **the b. part of** la mayor parte de • **to be b.** to valer más, ser mejor ➤ *adv* mejor ■ **all the b.** *o* **so much the b.** tanto mejor • **b. and b.** cada vez mejor • **b. off** en mejores condiciones • **we had b. go** más vale que nos vayamos • **to get b.** mejorar ➤ *tr & intr* mejorar(se) ➤ *s* el mejor.
between ➤ *prep* entre ■ **b. now and then** de aquí a entonces ➤ *adv* en medio, de por medio ■ **far b.** a grandes intervalos • **in b.** mientras tanto.
beverage ➤ *s* bebida.
beware ➤ *intr* tener cuidado ■ **b. of** cuidado con ➤ *interj* ¡cuidado!
bewilder ➤ *tr* aturdir, dejar perplejo.
beyond ➤ *prep* más allá, fuera de ■ **b. (a) doubt** fuera de duda • **b. help** sin remedio • **it's b. me** no alcanzo a comprender ➤ *adv* más lejos, más allá.
bias ➤ *s* inclinación *f; (prejudice)* prejuicio ➤ *tr* predisponer, influenciar ■ **to be biased** ser parcial.
bib ➤ *s* babero; *(of an apron)* peto.
Bible ➤ *s* Biblia.
bicycle ➤ *s* bicicleta ➤ *intr* montar *or* ir en bicicleta.
bid✧ ➤ *tr (to order)* ordenar, mandar; *(in cards)* declarar ■ **to b. goodbye to** decir adiós a ➤ *intr* hacer una oferta ➤ *s (offer)* licitación *f,* oferta.
bifocals ➤ *spl* anteojos bifocales.
big ➤ *adj* gran, grande; *(older)* mayor; *(important)* importante ■ **b. shot** *o* **wheel** pez gordo ➤ *adv* ■ **to make it b.** tener gran éxito • **to talk b.** jactarse.
big-hearted ➤ *adj* generoso.
bike ➤ *s* bici *f; (motorcycle)* moto *f.*
biker ➤ *s* motociclista *mf.*
bilingual ➤ *adj* bilingüe.
bill[1] ➤ *s (invoice)* cuenta, factura; *(bank note)* billete *m;* POL. proyecto de ley ■ **b. of exchange** letra de cambio • **b. of fare** carta, menú • **b. of sale** boleto de compra y venta.
bill[2] ➤ *s (beak)* pico; *(visor)* visera.
billboard ➤ *s* cartelera.
billfold ➤ *s* billetera, cartera.
billiards ➤ *ssg* billar *m.*
billing ➤ *s* publicidad *f.*
billion ➤ *s* E.U. [10^9] mil millones *m;* G.B. [10^{12}] billón *m.*
bin ➤ *s (box)* cajón *m; (container)* recipiente *m,* compartimiento.
bind✧ ➤ *tr (to tie)* amarrar, atar; *(a wound)* vendar; *(morally, legally)* obligar, comprometer a ➤ *intr (to be tight)* apretar; *(a mix)* aglutinarse ➤ *s* ■ **to be in a b.** estar en un aprieto.
binder ➤ *s (notebook cover)* carpeta.
binding ➤ *adj* DER. obligatorio; *(promise)* que compromete a uno.
binocular ➤ *adj* binocular ■ **binoculars** *spl* gemelos, prismáticos.
biography ➤ *s* biografía.
biologic(al) ➤ *adj* biológico.
biologist ➤ *s* biólogo/a.
biology ➤ *s* biología.
birch ➤ *s* abedul *m.*
bird ➤ *s* pájaro; *(large)* ave *f* ■ **birds of a feather** lobos de la misma camada • **odd b.** bicho raro.
birdcage ➤ *s* jaula.
birth ➤ *s* nacimiento; *(ancestry)* linaje *m;* MED. parto ■ **b. control** control de la natalidad • **by b.** de nacimiento • **to give b.** to dar a luz a.
birthday ➤ *s* cumpleaños ■ **on one's 15th b.** al cumplir los 15 años.
birthplace ➤ *s* lugar *m* de nacimiento.
biscuit ➤ *s* bizcocho; G.B. galletita.
bishop ➤ *s* obispo; *(in chess)* alfil *m.*
bison ➤ *s* bisonte *m.*
bit[1] ➤ *s* pedacito, trocito; *(moment)* ratito ■ **a b. larger** un poco más grande • **a good b.** bastante • **a little b.** un poquito • **b. by b.** poco a poco • **not a b.** en absoluto.
bit[2] ➤ *s (drill)* broca, barrena; *(of a bridle)* freno, bocado.
bit[3] ➤ *s* COMPUT. bit *m,* bitio.
bite✧ ➤ *tr & intr* morder; *(insects, snakes, fish)* picar ➤ *s* mordisco, dentellada; *(wound)* mordedura; *(sting, in fishing)* picada ■ **a b. to eat** FAM. un piscolabis.
bitter ➤ *adj* amargo; *(wind, cold)* cortante; *(resentful)* amargado ■ **to the b. end** hasta vencer o morir.
bitterness ➤ *s* amargura; *(resentment)* rencor *m.*
bizarre ➤ *adj* extravagante, extraño.
black ➤ *s* negro; *(person)* negro/a, persona negra ■ **in b. and white** por escrito ➤ *adj* negro; *(gloomy)* sombrío ■ **b. eye** ojo a la funerala • **b. market** mercado negro, estraperlo.
blackberry ➤ *s* zarzamora.
blackbird ➤ *s* mirlo.
blackboard ➤ *s* pizarra, pizarrón *m.*
blacklist ➤ *s & tr* (poner en la) lista negra.
blackmail ➤ *s* chantaje *m* ➤ *tr* chantajear.
blackout ➤ *s (of a city)* apagón *m;* MED. desmayo, pérdida de la memoria; *(of news)* supresión *f.*
blacksmith ➤ *s* herrero/a.
bladder ➤ *s* vejiga.
blade ➤ *s* hoja; *(razor, skate)* cuchilla; *(propeller, fan)* aleta; *(grass)* brizna.
blame ➤ *tr* ■ **to be to b. for** tener la culpa de • **to b. on** echar la culpa a ➤ *s* culpa ■ **to put the b. on** echar la culpa a.
blameless ➤ *adj* libre de culpa.
blameworthy ➤ *adj* censurable.
bland ➤ *adj (mild)* suave; *(dull)* insulso.
blank ➤ *adj (paper, tape)* en blanco; *(wall)* liso; *(look)* vago; *(mind)* vacío ■ **b. check** cheque en blanco; FIG. carta blanca • **to go b.** quedarse en blanco ➤ *s (space)* blanco, vacío; *(form)* formulario (en blanco).
blanket ➤ *s* manta, frazada ➤ *adj* general, comprensivo.
blare ➤ *intr* resonar ➤ *s* estruendo.
blast ➤ *s* explosión *f; (shock)* onda de choque ■ **(at) full b.** a todo vapor • **to have a b.** JER. pasarla muy bien ➤ *tr (to blow up)* volar; FAM. *(to criticize)* criticar ■ **to b. off** despegar.
blasted ➤ *adj* FAM. condenado, maldito.
blastoff *o* **blast-off** ➤ *s* lanzamiento.
blaze ➤ *s (glare)* resplandor *m; (fire)* fuego, hoguera ➤ *intr* arder ■ **blazing with (lights, colors)** resplandeciente de (luces, colores).
blazer ➤ *s* chaqueta deportiva.
bleach ➤ *tr* blanquear; *(clothes)* colar; *(hair)* de(s)colorar ➤ *s* de(s)colorante *m; (for clothes)* lejía.
bleachers ➤ *spl* gradas.
bleak ➤ *adj* desolado, frío; *(dreary)* sombrío; *(prospect)* poco prometedor.
bleed✧ ➤ *intr* sangrar, perder sangre; *(colors)* correrse ➤ *tr* desangrar a.
blemish ➤ *tr* manchar, mancillar ➤ *s* mancha; *(flaw)* tacha.
blend✧ ➤ *tr & intr* mezclar(se) ➤ *s* mezcla.
blender ➤ *s* licuadora, batidora.
bless✧ ➤ *tr* bendecir ■ **b. my soul!** *o* **b. me!** ¡válgame Dios! • **to b. with** dotar de.
blessed ➤ *adj* bendito, santo.
blessing ➤ *s* bendición *f; (benefit)* ventaja; *(approval)* aprobación *f.*
blind ➤ *adj* ciego; *(street)* sin salida ■ **b. date, navigation** cita, navegación a ciegas • **b. spot** ángulo muerto; FIG. punto flaco ➤ *s* persiana ➤ *adv* a ciegas ➤ *tr* cegar; *(to dazzle)* deslumbrar.
blindfold ➤ *tr* vendar los ojos a ➤ *s* venda.
blinding ➤ *adj* cegador, deslumbrante.
blindly ➤ *adv* ciegamente, a ciegas.
blindness ➤ *s* ceguera.
blink ➤ *intr* parpadear, pestañear; *(signal)* brillar intermitentemente ➤ *tr* abrir y cerrar ➤ *s* parpadeo, pestañeo ■ **on the b.** JER. descompuesto.
blinker ➤ *s* intermitente *m.*
bliss ➤ *s* dicha, felicidad *f.*
blister ➤ *s* ampolla; BOT. verruga ➤ *tr & intr* ampollar(se).
blizzard ➤ *s* ventisca; FIG. torrente *m.*
bloc ➤ *s* bloque *m.*
block ➤ *s* bloque *m; (of a city)* cuadra, manzana; DEP., MED., PSICOL. bloqueo, obstrucción *f* ■ **b. and tackle** aparejo de poleas ➤ *tr (to obstruct)* bloquear, obstruir (tráfico, avance); MED., PSICOL. obstruir, interrumpir.
blockade ➤ *s* bloqueo ➤ *tr* bloquear.
blockage ➤ *s* obstrucción *f.*
blond(e) ➤ *s & adj* rubio/a.
blood ➤ *s* sangre *f; (kinship)* parentesco ■ **b. count** recuento globular • **b. relation** consanguíneo • **b. test** análisis de sangre • **b. type** tipo sanguíneo.
bloodshot ➤ *adj* inyectado de sangre.
bloody ➤ *adj* sangriento; G.B., JER. maldito, infame.
bloom ➤ *s* flor *f; (vigor)* lozanía ➤ *intr* florecer.
blossom ➤ *s* flor *f* ➤ *intr* florecer.
blot ➤ *s* mancha, borrón *m* ➤ *tr* ■ **to b. out** borrar.
blotch ➤ *s* mancha, manchón *m.*
blouse ➤ *s* blusa.
blow[1]✧ ➤ *intr* soplar; *(a horn)* sonar; *(a tire)* reventarse ■ **to b. over** *(storm)* pasar; *(scandal)* olvidarse • **to b. up** *(to explode)* explotar; *(with anger)* encolerizarse ➤ *tr* soplar; *(instrument)* tocar; *(the nose)* sonarse; *(a fuse)* fundir; *(a tire)* reventar ■ **to b. away** llevarse • **to b. down** derribar • **to b. out** soplar, apagar • **to b. up** *(to destroy)* volar; *(to inflate)* inflar; FOTOG. ampliar ➤ *s* soplido, soplo.
blow[2] ➤ *s* golpe *m; (setback)* revés *m* ■ **to come to blows** agarrarse a puñetazos.
blowdryer ➤ *s* secador *m* de cabello.
blowout ➤ *s* AUTO. reventón *m,* pinchazo.
blowup ➤ *s* explosión *f;* FOTOG. ampliación *f.*
blue ➤ *s* azul *m* ■ **out of the b.** de repente ■ *pl* melancolía; MÚS. jazz melancólico ➤ *adj* azul; *(gloomy)* tristón, melancólico ■ **b. jeans** pantalones vaqueros.
bluff[1] ➤ *intr* farolear, aparentar ➤ *s* engaño, farol *m* ■ **to call someone's b.** desenmascarar.
bluff[2] ➤ *s (cliff)* acantilado; *(river bank)* ribera escarpada.
blunder ➤ *s* error craso, metida de pata ➤ *intr (to move)* andar a tropezones; *(to err)* cometer un error craso.
blunt ➤ *adj* desafilado; *(frank)* franco, brusco ➤ *tr* desafilar, embotar.
blur ➤ *tr* empañar, nublar ➤ *intr* oscurecerse, ponerse borroso ➤ *s* borrón *m,* manchón *m.*
blush ➤ *intr* ruborizarse, sonrojarse ➤ *s* rubor *m,* sonrojo.
board ➤ *s* madero, tabla; *(for games)* tablero; *(meals)* pensión *f; (council)* junta, consejo ■ **above b.** honesto • **on b.** a bordo ➤ *tr* embarcar(se) en ➤ *intr* hospedarse con comida.
boarder ➤ *s* pensionista *mf.*
boardinghouse ➤ *s* pensión *f.*
boast ➤ *intr* jactarse, alardear ➤ *s* jactancia.
boat ➤ *s (small craft)* bote *m,* barca; *(ship)* barco, buque *m* ■ **in the same b.** en la misma situación.
boating ➤ *s* paseo en bote.
bodice ➤ *s* cuerpo, corpiño.
bodily ➤ *adj* corporal ➤ *adv* corporalmente.
body ➤ *s* cuerpo; *(corpse)* cadáver *m; (organization)* organismo; *(of water)* masa; AUTO. carrocería ■ **b. and soul** completamente, con toda el alma.
bodyguard ➤ *s* guardaespaldas *mf.*
bog ➤ *s* pantano, ciénaga ➤ *tr & intr* ■ **to b. down** empantanar(se), atascar(se).
bogus ➤ *adj* falso, fraudulento.
boil ➤ *tr & intr* (hacer) hervir; *(to cook)* cocer ■ **to b. down (to)** reducirse (a) • **to b. over** *(pot)* rebosar (al hervir); *(person)* enfurecerse ➤ *s* hervor *m.*
boiler ➤ *s* caldera.
boiling ➤ *adj* hirviente ■ **b. point** FÍS. punto de ebullición.
bold ➤ *adj* intrépido.
Bolivian ➤ *adj & s* boliviano/a.
bolt ➤ *s* MEC. tornillo, perno; *(lock)* cerrojo, pestillo ➤ *tr (to lock)* echar el cerrojo a, cerrar con pestillo; *(to fasten)* sujetar con tornillos *o* pernos ➤ *intr (to dash off)* fugarse.
bomb ➤ *s* bomba; JER. *(failure)* fracaso, fiasco ➤ *tr* bombardear.
bomber ➤ *s* bombardero.
bombing ➤ *s* bombardeo.

bombshell ➤ s MIL., FIG. bomba.
bond ➤ s lazo, atadura; DER. fianza, garantía; FIN. bono, obligación *f* ■ **in b.** en depósito, afianzado ■ *pl* cadenas ➤ *tr & intr* unir(se).
bone ➤ s hueso; *(of fish)* espina ➤ *tr* deshuesar; *(fish)* quitar las espinas a.
bonfire ➤ s fogata, hoguera.
bonnet ➤ s *(hat)* gorra, cofia; G.B., AUTO. capó.
bonus ➤ s plus *m*, sobresueldo.
bony ➤ *adj* óseo; *(fish)* espinoso.
boo ➤ s abucheo, rechifla ➤ *interj* ¡bú! ➤ *intr & tr* abuchear (a), rechiflar (a).
book ➤ s libro ■ **by the b.** según las reglas ➤ *tr (a suspect)* asentar, registrar; *(to reserve)* reservar.
bookcase ➤ s estantería para libros.
booking ➤ s *(engagement)* contratación *f*; *(reservation)* reservación *f*, reserva.
bookkeeper ➤ s tenedor/a de libros.
bookkeeping ➤ s teneduría de libros, contabilidad *f*.
booklet ➤ s folleto.
bookshelf ➤ s estante *m* para libros.
bookstore ➤ s librería.
boom ➤ s *(sound)* estampido, trueno; COM. auge *m* ➤ *intr* tronar, retumbar; COM. estar en auge.
boost ➤ *tr (to lift)* alzar, levantar; *(to increase)* aumentar ➤ s *(push)* impulso; *(increase)* aumento.
boot ➤ s bota; G.B. *(trunk)* portaequipajes *m* ■ **to b.** FAM. además ➤ *tr (to kick)* patear; COMPUT. iniciar, arrancar.
booth ➤ s *(compartment)* cabina; *(stand)* puesto, quiosco.
booze ➤ s FAM. bebida alcohólica.
border ➤ s frontera; *(edge)* borde *m*, orilla ➤ *intr* ■ **to b. on** lindar con; FIG. aproximarse a.
borderline ➤ s frontera ➤ *adj* dudoso.
bore ➤ *tr* aburrir ➤ s *(person)* pesado/a, pelmazo *mf*; *(thing)* pesadez *f*.
boredom ➤ s aburrimiento.
boring ➤ *adj* aburrido, pesado.
born ➤ *adj* nato ■ **a b. fool** un tonto de nacimiento • **a b. liar** un mentiroso innato • **to be b.** nacer.
borough ➤ s municipio.
borrow ➤ *tr* tomar prestado.
boss ➤ s supervisor/a, capataz *mf* ➤ *tr* dirigir, mandar.
bossy ➤ *adj* mandón.
botanic(al) ➤ *adj* botánico.
botany ➤ s botánica.
both ➤ *pron & adj* ambos, los dos ■ **b. of us, you** nosotros, vosotros dos ➤ *conj* ■ **he is b. strong and healthy** él es fuerte y sano además.
bother ➤ *tr & intr* molestar(se) *(about, with,* por) ➤ s molestia, fastidio.
bothersome ➤ *adj* molesto, fastidioso.
bottle ➤ s botella; *(baby's)* biberón *m* ■ **to hit the b.** JER. beber ➤ *tr* embotellar.
bottleneck ➤ s FIG. embotellamiento.
bottom ➤ s fondo; *(of a list)* final *m*; *(foot)* pie *m*; *(of sea, river)* lecho; FAM. *(buttocks)* trasero.
bough ➤ s rama.
boulder ➤ s canto rodado.
bounce ➤ *intr* rebotar ■ **to b. back** recuperarse ➤ s salto, brinco; *(rebound)* rebote *m*; *(springiness)* elasticidad *f*.
bound[1] ➤ *adj (tied)* atado, amarrado; *(obliged)* obligado ■ **it is b. to happen** tiene forzosamente que ocurrir.
bound[2] ➤ *adj* ■ **b. for** con destino a.
boundary ➤ s límite *m*, frontera.
bounds ➤ *spl* límite *m* ■ **out of b.** DEP. fuera de la cancha; *(behavior)* fuera de los límites.
bouquet ➤ s *(of flowers)* ramillete *m*; *(of wine)* buqué *m*.
bow[1] ➤ s MARIT. proa.
bow[2] ➤ *intr (to stoop)* inclinarse, doblegarse; *(to submit)* someterse ■ **to b. out** retirarse, renunciar ➤ s *(obeisance)* reverencia; *(greeting)* saludo.
bow[3] ➤ s ARM., MÚS. arco; *(knot)* lazo ■ **b. tie** corbata de lazo.
bowel ➤ s intestino ■ *pl* entrañas.
bowl[1] ➤ s *(dish)* fuente *f*, cuenco; *(washbasin)* jofaina; *(toilet)* taza, DEP. estadio.
bowl[2] ➤ *intr* DEP. jugar a los bolos ■ **to b. over** derribar; FIG. pasmar.
bowling ➤ s bolos ■ **b. alley** bolera.
box[1] ➤ s caja; *(large)* cajón *m*; *(small)* estuche *m*; *(pigeonhole)* casilla; TEAT. palco ■ **b. office** taquilla, boletería • **b. spring** colchón de resortes ➤ *tr* ■ **to b.** in encerrar.
box[2] ➤ s *(blow)* bofetada, cachete *m* ➤ *tr* abofetear ➤ *intr* DEP. boxear.
boxer ➤ s boxeador/a, púgil *m*.
boxing ➤ s boxeo ■ **b. glove** guante de boxeo.
boy ➤ s muchacho, chico; *(child)* niño; *(son)* hijo.
boycott ➤ *tr* boicotear ➤ s boicot *m*.
boyfriend ➤ s FAM. novio.
bra ➤ s sostén *m*, corpiño.
bracelet ➤ s brazalete *m*, pulsera.
bracket ➤ s soporte *m*, escuadra; *(category)* categoría, grupo.
brag ➤ *tr & intr* jactarse (de) ➤ s jactancia, alarde *m*.
braid ➤ *tr* trenzar ➤ s *(plait)* trenza; *(trim)* galón *m*.
brain ➤ s cerebro ■ **b. child** FAM. invento, creación ■ *pl* CUL. sesos; *(intelligence)* cabeza • **to rack one's b.** devanarse los sesos.
brainwash ➤ *tr* lavar el cerebro.
brainy ➤ *adj* FAM. inteligente, listo.
brake ➤ s freno ➤ *tr* frenar ➤ *intr* aplicar el freno.
branch ➤ s rama; *(division)* ramo, rama; *(of a river)* brazo; F.C. ramal *m* ➤ *intr* ■ **to b. out** extenderse.
brand ➤ s COM. marca (de fábrica); *(style)* modo, manera; *(type)* clase *f*; *(on cattle)* marca (de hierro) ➤ *tr (cattle)* marcar, herrar; *(to stigmatize)* calificar de, tildar de.
brand-new ➤ *adj* flamante.
brandy ➤ s coñac *m*, aguardiente *m*.
brass ➤ s latón *m*; FAM. *(gall)* descaro ■ *pl* MÚS. cobres.
brat ➤ s niño/a malcriado/a, mocoso/a.
brave ➤ *adj* valiente, bravo ➤ s guerrero indio ➤ *tr* afrontar; *(to defy)* desafiar.
bravery ➤ s valentía, valor *m*.
brawl ➤ s pelea ➤ *intr* pelear.
Brazilian ➤ *adj & s* brasileño/a.
breach ➤ s *(of law)* violación *f*; *(of promise)* incumplimiento; *(of relations)* ruptura ➤ *tr* MIL. abrir brecha en; DER. violar.
bread ➤ s pan *m*; JER. *(money)* plata.
breadbasket ➤ s panera; *(region)* granero.
breadth ➤ s *(width)* anchura; *(scope)* extensión *f*.
breadwinner ➤ s sostén *m* de la familia.
break◇ ➤ *tr* romper; *(to damage)* estropear; *(a law)* infringir, violar; *(spirit, will)* quebrantar; *(a record)* batir ■ **to b. off** romper • **to b. open** abrir forzando • **to b. up** *(to put an end to)* acabar, terminar; *(to upset)* quebrantar ➤ *intr* romperse; *(to become unusable)* estropearse; *(the heart)* partirse; *(the voice)* fallar ■ **to b. away** separarse; *(to escape)* escaparse • **to b. down** *(to malfunction)* averiarse; *(physically)* debilitarse; *(emotionally)* abatirse • **to b. even** salir sin ganar o perder • **to b. out** *(to escape)* escaparse; *(to erupt)* estallar • **to b. through** atravesar, abrirse paso ➤ s ruptura, rompimiento; *(crack)* grieta, raja; *(gap)* abertura; *(pause)* intervalo, pausa; *(sudden dash)* salida, arrancada; *(escape)* fuga, evasión *f* ■ **at the b. of day** al amanecer • **lucky b.** coyuntura feliz • **to give someone a b.** dar una oportunidad a alguien • **to take a b.** descansar • **without a b.** sin parar.
breakdown ➤ s MEC. avería; MED. colapso, depresión *f*.
breakfast ➤ s desayuno ➤ *intr* desayunar, tomar el desayuno.
break-in ➤ s *(illegal entry)* entrada forzada; *(testing)* periodo de prueba.
breakthrough ➤ s adelanto, progreso.
breakup ➤ s separación *f*; *(of marriage, firm)* disolución *f*, desintegración *f*.
breast ➤ s pecho; *(of a woman)* pecho, seno; *(of a fowl)* pechuga.
breastbone ➤ s esternón *m*.
breast-feed ➤ *tr* amamantar.
breath ➤ s respiración *f*, aliento; *(of an animal)* hálito ■ **out of b.** sin aliento • **short of b.** corto de resuello • **under one's b.** en voz baja • **to waste one's b.** gastar saliva en balde.
breathe ➤ *tr & intr* respirar ■ **to b. in, out** inhalar, exhalar.
breather ➤ s FAM. respiro, pausa.
breathing ➤ s respiración *f*.
breathless ➤ *adj* sin aliento; *(panting)* jadeante; *(amazed)* sin resuello.
breathtaking ➤ *adj* impresionante.
breech ➤ s ANAT. trasero; ARM. recámara ■ *pl* calzones; FAM. pantalones.
breed◇ ➤ *tr* engendrar; *(to raise, bring up)* criar ➤ *intr* reproducirse ➤ s *(strain)* raza; *(type)* casta, especie *f*.
breeder ➤ s criador/a.
breeding ➤ s crianza, educación *f*.
breeze ➤ s brisa; FAM. *(easy task)* paseo.
brew ➤ *tr (beer)* fabricar; *(tea)* preparar ➤ *intr (to loom)* amenazar ➤ s infusión *f*; FAM. *(beer)* cerveza.
brewery ➤ s cervecería.
bribe ➤ s soborno ■ **to take bribes** dejarse sobornar ➤ *tr* sobornar.
brick ➤ s ladrillo.
bride ➤ s novia, desposada.
bridegroom ➤ s novio, desposado.
bridesmaid ➤ s dama de honor.
bridge ➤ s puente *m* ■ **to burn one's bridges** quemar las naves.
bridle ➤ s brida ➤ *tr* embridar; *(passions)* refrenar, dominar.
brief ➤ *adj (in time)* breve; *(in length)* corto ➤ s sumario, resumen *m*; DER. escrito ■ **in b.** en resumen ■ *pl* calzoncillos ➤ *tr* informar.
briefcase ➤ s portafolio, cartera.
bright ➤ *adj* brillante; *(color)* subido; *(smart)* inteligente, despierto ➤ **brights** *spl* AUTO. luces altas *o* de carretera.
brighten ➤ *tr & intr* aclarar(se), iluminar(se); *(with joy)* alegrar(se).
brightness ➤ s claridad *f*, brillantez *f*.
brilliant ➤ *adj* brillante; *(inventive)* genial.
brim ➤ s borde *m*; *(of a hat)* ala ➤ *intr* estar lleno hasta el tope ■ **to b. over** desbordarse.
bring◇ ➤ *tr* traer; *(to carry)* llevar ■ **to b. about** causar, provocar • **to b. back** *(to return)* devolver; *(a memory)* traer (a la mente) • **to b. in** *(to harvest)* recoger; *(money)* rendir, producir • **to b. off** conseguir, lograr hacer • **to b. on** ocasionar, causar • **to b. oneself to** resignarse a • **to b. up** *(children)* criar, educar; *(a topic)* plantear.
brink ➤ s borde *m*, margen *f* ■ **on the b. of** a punto de.
brisk ➤ *adj (energetic)* enérgico, vigoroso; *(invigorating)* estimulante.
bristle ➤ s cerda ➤ *intr* ■ **to b. with** estar lleno *o* erizado de.
britches ➤ *spl* FAM. pantalones *m*.
British ➤ *adj* británico.
brittle ➤ *adj* quebradizo, frágil.
broad ➤ *adj (wide)* ancho; *(spacious)* extenso, amplio; *(general)* general ■ **in b. daylight** en pleno día.
broadcast ➤ *tr* RAD. emitir, radiar; TELEV. transmitir, televisar; *(to make known)* difundir ➤ s transmisión *f*, emisión *f*; *(program)* programa *m*.
broccoli ➤ s brécol *m*, bróculi *m*.
brochure ➤ s folleto.
broil ➤ *tr* asar a la parrilla.
broiler ➤ s parrilla; *(chicken)* pollo para asar.
broken ➤ *adj* roto, quebrado; *(out of order)* descompuesto; *(health, law)* quebrantado; *(spirit)* sumiso; *(heart)* destrozado.
broker ➤ s agente *mf*, corredor/a de bolsa.
bronchitis ➤ s bronquitis *f*.
bronze ➤ s bronce *m* ➤ *adj* de bronce; *(color)* bronceado ➤ *tr* broncear.
brooch ➤ s broche *m*.
brood ➤ s ORNIT. nidada; FIG. progenie *f*.
brook ➤ s arroyo.
broom ➤ s escoba; BOT. retama.
broth ➤ s caldo.
brother ➤ s hermano; *(fellow member)* compañero; RELIG. hermano.
brother-in-law ➤ s cuñado, hermano político.
brow ➤ s frente *f*; *(eyebrow)* ceja.
brown ➤ s marrón *m*, castaño ➤ *adj* marrón; *(hair)* castaño; *(skin, sugar)* moreno ➤ *tr & intr* CUL. dorar(se).
browse ➤ *intr (shop)* curiosear; *(book)* hojear un libro; *(to graze)* pacer ➤ *tr (Internet)* navegar (por).
browser ➤ s COMPUT. navegador *m*, explorador *m*.
bruise ➤ s *(skin)* magulladura, contusión *f*, *(fruit)* daño ➤ *tr* magullar; *(fruit)* dañar; *(feelings)* herir.
brunch ➤ s combinación de desayuno y almuerzo.
brunette ➤ *adj & s* morena.
brush ➤ s cepillo; *(paintbrush)* brocha; *(artist's)* pincel *m*; *(encounter)* encuentro ➤ *tr* cepillar; *(to graze)* rozar al pasar ■ **to b. up** repasar, retocar.
brutal ➤ *adj* brutal, bestial.
brute ➤ s bestia ➤ *adj* bruto; *(cruel)* brutal.
bubble ➤ s burbuja; *(of soap)* pompa ■ **b. gum** chicle de globo ➤ *intr* burbujear ■ **to b. over with** rebosar de.
buck[1] ➤ s ZOOL. macho; *(deer)* ciervo ➤ *intr (horse)* botar, corcovear.
buck[2] ➤ s JER. dólar *m*.
bucket ➤ s cubo, balde *m* ■ **to kick the b.** FAM. estirar la pata.
buckle[1] ➤ s *(fastener)* hebilla ➤ *tr & intr* abrochar(se) ■ **to b. down to** dedicarse con empeño a.
buckle[2] ➤ *tr & intr (to bend)* combar(se).
bud ➤ s *(shoot)* brote *m*, yema; *(flower)* capullo ➤ *intr (plant)* echar brotes; *(flower)* brotar; FIG. estar en cierne.
budge ➤ *tr & intr (object)* mover(se) un poco; *(person)* (hacer) ceder.
budget ➤ s presupuesto ➤ *tr* presupuestar.
buffalo ➤ s búfalo; *(bison)* bisonte *m*.
buffet ➤ s *(sideboard)* aparador *m*; *(restaurant)* cantina, buffet *m*.
bug ➤ s insecto, bicho; FAM. microbio; *(defect)* defecto, falla (en un sistema); JER. *(enthusiast)* entusiasta *mf* ➤ *tr* JER. fastidiar, importunar.
buggy ➤ s calesa; *(baby carriage)* coche *m* de niño.
bugle ➤ s clarín *m*, corneta.
build◇ ➤ *tr* construir, edificar; *(to make)* hacer ➤ *intr* ■ **to b. up** *(to increase)* aumentar; *(to intensify)* intensificarse ➤ s talle *m*, figura.
builder ➤ s constructor/a.
building ➤ s edificio, casa.
built-up ➤ *adj* urbanizado.
bulb ➤ s BOT. bulbo; *(lamp)* bombilla.
bulge ➤ s protuberancia, bulto ➤ *intr & tr* hinchar(se), abultar.
bulk ➤ s volumen *m*, tamaño; *(largest part)* grueso ■ **in b.** *(loose)* a granel, suelto; *(in large amounts)* en grandes cantidades.
bulky ➤ *adj (massive)* voluminoso; *(unwieldy)* pesado.
bull ➤ s toro; *(elephant, seal)* macho; JER. tontería ■ **b. session** FAM. tertulia ➤ *adj* macho ■ **b. market** mercado en alza.
bulldog ➤ s buldog *m*, dogo.
bulldozer ➤ s bulldozer *m*, excavadora.
bullet ➤ s bala.
bulletin ➤ s boletín *m*; *(report)* comunicado ■ **b. board** tablero de anuncios; COMPUT. pizarra (electrónica), tablero.
bulletproof ➤ *adj* a prueba de balas.
bullfight ➤ s corrida de toros.
bullfighter ➤ s torero.
bullring ➤ s plaza de toros.
bull's-eye ➤ s *(target)* blanco; *(shot)* acierto ■ **to hit the b.** dar en el blanco.
bully ➤ s matón *m*, abusador/a ➤ *tr* intimidar, amedrentar ➤ *intr* abusar.
bum ➤ s vagabundo/a; *(loafer)* vago/a, holgazán/ana ➤ *tr & intr* gorronear, sablear ■ **to b. around** vagar ➤ *adj* FAM. sin valor, inútil; *(sore)* dolorido.
bumblebee ➤ s abejorro.
bump ➤ *tr* topar, chocar contra ■ **to b. into** tropezarse con ➤ s choque *m*, topetón *m*; *(swelling)* hinchazón *f*, chichón *m*; *(in a road)* bache *m*.
bumper ➤ s parachoques *m*.
bumpy ➤ *adj (uneven)* desigual, accidentado; *(jolty)* agitado, sacudido.
bun ➤ s bollo, panecillo; *(hair)* moño.
bunch ➤ s *(of grapes)* racimo; *(of flowers)* ramillete *m*; *(group)* montón *m* ➤ *tr & intr* agrupar(se), juntar(se).
bundle ➤ s bulto, fardo; *(papers)* fajo ➤ *tr (to tie)* atar; *(to wrap)* envolver ➤ *intr* ■ **to b. up** arroparse, abrigarse.
bunion ➤ s juanete *m*.
bunk ➤ s litera.
bunny ➤ s FAM. conejo, conejito.
buoy ➤ s boya.
burden ➤ s carga ➤ *tr (to load)* cargar; *(to oppress)* agobiar.
bureau ➤ s *(dresser)* tocador *m*; POL. departamento; *(business)* agencia.
bureaucracy ➤ s burocracia.
burger ➤ s FAM. hamburguesa.
burglar ➤ s ladrón/ona ■ **b. alarm** alarma antirrobo.

burglarize ➤ *tr* robar (casa, tienda).
burglary ➤ *s* robo con allanamiento de morada.
burial ➤ *s* entierro ■ **b. ground** cementerio, camposanto.
burn◊ ➤ *tr* quemar; *(a building)* incendiar ■ **to b. down** incendiar • **to b. oneself out** JER. agotarse • **to b. up** *(to consume)* consumir; FAM. *(to enrage)* enfurecer ➤ *intr* quemarse, arder; *(building)* consumirse; *(light bulb)* estar encendido; *(with fever)* arder; *(with passion)* consumirse ■ **to b. out** *(fire)* apagarse; *(fuse, bulb)* quemarse, fundirse ➤ *s* quemadura.
burner ➤ *s* quemador *m*, mechero.
burning ➤ *adj (hot)* ardiente, abrasador; *(passionate)* ardiente; *(urgent)* urgente.
burp ➤ *s* eructo ➤ *intr* eructar ➤ *tr* hacer eructar (a un niño).
burrow ➤ *s* madriguera.
bursar ➤ *s* tesorero.
burst ➤ *intr (to break open)* estallar, reventarse; *(to explode)* explotar ■ **to b. in** interrumpir • **to b. into flame(s)** estallar en llamas • **to b. out** *(to exclaim)* exclamar; *(crying, laughing)* echarse a ➤ *tr* reventar ■ **to b. into** *(a room)* irrumpir en; *(tears, laughter)* desatarse en • **to b. with** rebosar de ➤ *s* reventón *m*, explosión *f*; *(of gunfire)* ráfaga; *(of energy)* explosión; *(of applause)* salva.
bury ➤ *tr* enterrar; FIG. sepultar.
bus ➤ *s* autobús *m*, ómnibus *m* ➤ *tr* transportar en autobús.
bush ➤ *s (shrub)* arbusto; *(thicket)* maleza; *(land)* matorral *m*.
business ➤ *s (establishment)* comercio, negocio; *(firma)* firma, empresa; *(commerce)* negocios; *(matter, concern)* asunto ■ **that's none of your b.** eso no es cosa tuya • **to mean b.** no andar con juegos.
businesslike ➤ *adj* metódico, serio.
businessman ➤ *s* hombre *m* de negocios, comerciante *m*.
businesswoman ➤ *s* mujer *f* de negocios, comerciante *f*.
bust[1] ➤ *s* ARTE., ANAT. busto.
bust[2] FAM. ➤ *tr* romper; *(to damage)* descomponer; *(to arrest)* arrestar ➤ *intr* romperse, descomponerse ➤ *s (flop)* chasco, fracaso; COM. quiebra; *(arrest)* arresto; *(raid)* redada, batida.
bustle ➤ *intr* apresurarse ➤ *s* bullicio, animación *f*.
busy ➤ *adj* atareado, ocupado; *(place)* animado; *(telephone)* ocupado.
busybody ➤ *s* entremetido/a.
but ➤ *conj* pero, mas; *(rather)* sino; *(nevertheless)* no obstante, sin embargo; *(except)* excepto ■ **cannot (help) b.** no poder menos que • **none b.** solamente ➤ *adv* solamente ■ **all b.** casi • **to do nothing b.** no hacer más que ➤ *prep* ■ **b. for** a no ser por.
butcher ➤ *s* carnicero/a ■ **b. shop** carnicería ➤ *tr (animals)* matar; FAM. *(to botch)* chapucear.
butler ➤ *s* mayordomo.
butt[1] ➤ *tr & intr* topar ■ **to b. in(to)** FAM. entremeterse en ➤ *s* topetazo.
butt[2] ➤ *s (of a rifle)* culata; *(cigarette end)* colilla; FAM. *(buttocks)* trasero.
butter ➤ *s* mantequilla ➤ *tr* untar con mantequilla ■ **to b. up** lisonjear.
butterfly ➤ *s* mariposa ■ **to have butterflies in one's stomach** tener cosquillas en el estómago.
buttock ➤ *s* nalga ■ *pl* trasero.
button ➤ *s* botón *m*; *(badge)* insignia ■ **on the b.** FAM. correcto, exacto ➤ *tr & intr* abotonar(se), abrochar(se).
buttonhole ➤ *s* ojal *m*.
buy◊ ➤ *tr* comprar ■ **to b. off** sobornar • **to b. up** acaparar ➤ *intr* hacer compras ➤ *s* compra; FAM. *(bargain)* ganga.
buyer ➤ *s* comprador/a.
buzz ➤ *intr* zumbar; *(buzzer)* sonar; *(to ring)* tocar el timbre ➤ *s* zumbido; *(murmur)* murmullo; FAM. *(phone call)* telefonazo ■ **b. saw** sierra circular.
by ➤ *prep* por, de ■ **by birth** de nacimiento • **by mail** por correo • **by night** de noche • **by noon** para el mediodía • **by the bed** junto a la cama • **by the by** de paso, a propósito • **by the dozen** por docena • **by the rules** de acuerdo con las reglas • **by the way** de paso, entre paréntesis • **by this time** *(hour)* a esta hora; *(point)* a estas alturas • **day by day** día a día • **made by** hecho por ➤ *adv (nearby)* cerca, al lado de; *(aside)* a un lado, aparte ■ **by and by** *(soon)* pronto; *(after a while)* más tarde • **by and large** en términos generales • **by then** para entonces.
bye(-bye) ➤ *interj* FAM. ¡adiós!, ¡chau!
by-pass ➤ *s* carretera de circunvalación ■ **coronary b.** desviación coronaria ➤ *tr* evitar, pasar por alto.
bystander ➤ *s* espectador/a, circunstante *mf*.
byte ➤ *s* byte *m*, octeto.

C

cab ➤ *s* taxi *m*; *(of vehicle)* cabina.
cabbage ➤ *s* col *f*, berza.
cabdriver ➤ *s* taxista *mf*.
cabin ➤ *s* barraca, choza; *(of ship)* camarote *m*; *(of plane)* cabina.
cabinet ➤ *s* armario; POL. consejo *o* gabinete *m* de ministros.
cable ➤ *s* cable *m*; *(cablegram)* cablegrama *m*; TELEV. televisión *f* por cable ■ **c. car** funicular ➤ *tr & intr* cablegrafiar.
cablevision ➤ *s* televisión *f* por cable.
cache ➤ *s* escondrijo; *(goods)* reserva ➤ *tr* guardar en un escondrijo.
cactus ➤ *s* cactus *m*, cacto.
cadaver ➤ *s* cadáver *m*.
cafeteria ➤ *s* cafetería.
caffeine ➤ *s* cafeína.
cage ➤ *s* jaula ➤ *tr* enjaular.
cake ➤ *s* pastel *m*; *(sponge)* bizcocho; *(of soap)* pastilla ■ **to take the c.** FAM. ser el colmo ➤ *tr & intr* endurecer(se).
calculate ➤ *tr* calcular ➤ *intr* hacer cálculos.
calculation ➤ *s* cálculo.
calculator ➤ *s* calculadora.
calendar ➤ *s* calendario.
calf[1] ➤ *s* becerro, ternero; *(of whale, elephant)* cría.
calf[2] ➤ *s* ANAT. pantorrilla.
call ➤ *tr* llamar; *(a meeting)* convocar; *(to label)* calificar (de) ■ **to c. back** hacer volver; TEL. volver a llamar • **to c. off** cancelar • **to c. oneself** llamarse • **to c. together** convocar, reunir • **to c. to mind** evocar • **to c. up** telefonear; MIL. llamar a las armas ➤ *intr (to yell)* llamar, gritar; ORNIT., ZOOL. reclamarse ■ **to c. for** necesitar • **to c. on** *(to visit)* visitar a; *(to appeal)* recurrir a; *(God)* invocar • **to c. out** gritar ➤ *s* llamada; ORNIT., ZOOL. reclamo, canto; *(of bugle)* toque *m*; *(short visit)* visita; *(summons, appeal)* llamamiento ■ **on c.** de guardia • **port of c.** puerto de escala.
caller ➤ *s* visita, visitante *mf*.
calling ➤ *s* vocación *f* ■ **c. card** tarjeta de visita.
callus ➤ *s* callo ➤ *intr* encallecerse.
calm ➤ *adj* sereno, tranquilo ➤ *s* calma ➤ *tr & intr* aplacar(se), calmar(se).
calorie ➤ *s* caloría.
came ➤ *vea* **come** *en tabla de verbos.*
camel ➤ *s* camello.
camera ➤ *s* FOTOG. cámara, máquina; CINEM. cámara.
camp ➤ *s* campo; *(encampment)* campamento ➤ *intr & tr* acampar.
campaign ➤ *intr & s* (hacer una) campaña.
campanile ➤ *s* campanario.
camper ➤ *s* campista *mf*; AUTO. caravana.
campfire ➤ *s* hoguera de campamento.
campground ➤ *s* camping *m*.
campsite ➤ *s* camping *m*.
campus ➤ *s* ciudad universitaria.
can[1] ➤ *aux. (to be able to)* poder; *(to know how to)* saber ■ **he c. cook** él sabe cocinar.
can[2] ➤ *s (tin)* lata; *(for trash)* tacho, cubo ■ **c. opener** abrelatas ➤ *tr* enlatar; JER. *(to fire)* despedir.
Canadian ➤ *adj & s* canadiense *mf*.
canal ➤ *s* canal *m*.
canary ➤ *s* canario.
cancel ➤ *tr* anular, cancelar; *(a stamp)* matar ➤ *s* cancelación *f*, anulación *f*.
cancellation ➤ *s* cancelación *f*; *(of stamp)* matasellos *m*.
cancer ➤ *s* cáncer *m*.
candid ➤ *adj* franco; *(not posed)* espontáneo.
candidate ➤ *s* candidato/a.
candle ➤ *s* vela, bujía; *(in church)* cirio.
candlestick ➤ *s* candelero.
candy ➤ *s* caramelo ■ **c. store** confitería.
cane ➤ *s* bastón *m*; *(switch)* vara; *(plant)* caña; *(wicker)* mimbre *m* ➤ *tr* golpear con una vara.
canebrake ➤ *s* cañaveral *m*.
canned ➤ *adj* enlatado; FAM. *(taped)* grabado.
cannery ➤ *s* fábrica de conservas.
cannibal ➤ *s* caníbal *mf*, antropófago/a.
cannon ➤ *s* cañón *m*.
canoe ➤ *intr & s* (ir en) canoa.
canopy ➤ *s* dosel *m*; *(of leaves, stars)* bóveda.
canteen ➤ *s (store, cafeteria)* cantina; *(flask)* cantimplora.
canvas ➤ *s* lona; *(painting)* lienzo; *(sails)* velamen *m*.
canyon ➤ *s* cañón *m*.
cap ➤ *s* gorro, gorra; *(cover)* tapa; *(limit)* tope *m* ➤ *tr* cubrir; *(to complete)* terminar ■ **to c. off** culminar.
capable ➤ *adj* capaz.
capacity ➤ *s* capacidad *f* ■ **in the c. of** en calidad de.
cape[1] ➤ *s* GEOG. cabo.
cape[2] ➤ *s (garment)* capa.
capital[1] ➤ *s (city)* capital *f*; *(assets, wealth)* capital *m*; IMPR. *(letter)* mayúscula ■ **c. punishment** pena capital *o* de muerte ➤ *adj (foremost)* capital; *(excellent)* excelente.
capital[2] ➤ *s* ARQ. capitel *m*.
capitol ➤ *s* capitolio.
capsule ➤ *s* cápsula.
captain ➤ *s* capitán/ana ➤ *tr* capitanear.
caption ➤ *s* leyenda; TELEV. subtítulo.
capture ➤ *tr* capturar; *(a prize)* ganar ➤ *s* captura.
car ➤ *s* AUTO. coche *m*, carro; F.C. coche *m*, vagón *m*; *(tramcar)* tranvía *m*.
caramel ➤ *s* caramelo.
caravan ➤ *s* caravana.
carbon ➤ *s* carbono ■ **c. copy** copia al carbón • **c. dioxide** bióxido de carbono • **c. paper** papel carbón.
carburetor ➤ *s* carburador *m*.
card ➤ *s (playing)* naipe *m*, carta; *(greeting)* tarjeta; *(post)* (tarjeta) postal *f*; *(index)* ficha; *(ID)* carnet *m* ■ *pl* naipes • **it's in the c.** está escrito.
cardboard ➤ *s* cartón *m*.
cardigan ➤ *s* chaqueta de punto.
cardinal ➤ *adj* cardinal ➤ *s* ORNIT., RELIG. cardenal *m*.
care ➤ *s (worry)* inquietud *f*, preocupación *f*; *(grief)* pena; *(charge)* cargo; *(caution)* cuidado ■ **(in) c. of** para entregar a • **to take c. (not to)** tener cuidado (de que no) • **to take c. of** *(person)* cuidar de; *(thing)* (pre)ocuparse de ➤ *intr (to be concerned)* preocuparse; *(to mind)* importar ■ **I don't c.** no me importa • **to c. for** cuidar • **to c. to** tener ganas de, querer.
career ➤ *s* carrera, profesión *f*.
carefree ➤ *adj* despreocupado.
careful ➤ *adj* cauteloso; *(thorough)* cuidadoso ■ **to be c.** tener cuidado.
careless ➤ *adj* descuidado; *(unconcerned)* indiferente; *(offhand)* espontáneo.
caress ➤ *s* caricia ➤ *tr* acariciar.
cargo ➤ *s* carga, cargamento.
Caribbean ➤ *adj & s* caribeño/a.
carnation ➤ *s* clavel *m*.
carnival ➤ *s (season)* carnaval *m*; *(fair)* feria, parque *m* de atracciones.
carol ➤ *s* villancico.
carpenter ➤ *s* carpintero/a.
carpentry ➤ *s* carpintería.
carpet ➤ *s* alfombra ➤ *tr* alfombrar.
carriage ➤ *s* carruaje *m*, coche *m*; *(posture)* porte *m* ■ **baby c.** cochecito de niños.
carrot ➤ *s* zanahoria.
carry ➤ *tr* llevar; *(a disease)* transmitir; MAT. llevarse ■ **to c. on** *(conversation)* mantener; *(business)* dirigir • **to c. out** realizar, llevar a cabo • **to c. through** completar, llevar a cabo.
carsick ➤ *adj* mareado.
cart ➤ *s* carro; *(handcart)* carretilla ➤ *tr* acarrear; *(to lug)* arrastrar ■ **to c. away** *o* **off** llevar.
carton ➤ *s* caja de cartón.
cartoon ➤ *s (political)* caricatura; *(film)* dibujos animados.
cartridge ➤ *s* cartucho; *(cassette)* casete *m*; *(ink refill)* repuesto ■ **c. belt** cartuchera.
carve ➤ *tr* CUL. trinchar; ARTE. *(to sculpt)* tallar, cincelar; *(to engrave)* grabar ■ **to c. out** labrar.
carving ➤ *s* talla, escultura.
cascade ➤ *s* cascada ➤ *intr* caer en forma de cascada.
case[1] ➤ *s* caso; *(example)* ejemplo; DER. causa, pleito ■ **a c. of honor** una cuestión de honor • **c. history** hoja clínica • **in any c.** en todo caso • **in no c.** de ningún modo • **in that c.** en tal caso • **just in c.** por si acaso.
case[2] ➤ *s (box)* caja; *(outer covering)* estuche *m*; *(slipcover)* funda.
cash ➤ *s* efectivo ■ **c. register** caja registradora • **to pay (in) c.** pagar al contado ➤ *tr* hacer efectivo, cobrar ■ **to c. in** convertir en efectivo.
cashbox ➤ *s* caja.
cashier ➤ *s* cajero/a ■ **c.'s check** cheque de caja.
casino ➤ *s* casino.
cask ➤ *s* barril *m*, tonel *m*.
casserole ➤ *s* cazuela, cacerola.
cassette ➤ *s (film)* cartucho; *(tape)* casete *m*.
cast◊ ➤ *tr (to hurl)* tirar, arrojar; *(anchor, vote)* echar; *(glance)* volver, dirigir; *(light, shadow)* proyectar; CINEM. *(roles)* repartir; *(actor)* asignar una parte a; METAL. moldear ■ **to c. aside** *o* **away** desechar, descartar • **to c. doubt (up)on** poner en duda ➤ *s* tirada, lanzamiento; *(of dice)* tirada; *(appearance)* apariencia; METAL. molde *f*, forma; MED. enyesadura; CINEM., TEAT. reparto ■ **c. iron** hierro fundido.
castle ➤ *s* castillo.
casual ➤ *adj* casual; *(occasional)* irregular; *(indifferent)* despreocupado; *(informal)* informal.
casualty ➤ *s* accidente *m*; *(victim)* accidentado, víctima; MIL. baja.
cat ➤ *s* gato ■ **to let the c. out of the bag** revelar un secreto.
catacombs ➤ *spl* catacumbas.
catalog(ue) ➤ *s* catálogo ➤ *tr* catalogar.
catapult ➤ *s* catapulta ➤ *tr* catapultar.
catastrophe ➤ *s* catástrofe *f*.
catastrophic ➤ *adj* catastrófico.
catch◊ ➤ *tr* coger, agarrar; *(to capture)* prender, capturar; *(animals)* atrapar, cazar; *(fish)* pescar; *(bus, train)* alcanzar, tomar; *(to snag, hook)* engancharse *(on* en); *(an illness)* coger, contraer; *(to surprise)* sorprender ■ **to c. up on** ponerse al corriente en cuanto a • **to c. up with** alcanzar ➤ *intr (to become hooked)* engancharse; *(to snag)* enredarse ■ **to c. on** *(to understand)* comprender; *(a fad)* volverse muy popular ➤ *s (act)* cogida; *(lock)* cerradura; *(in hunting)* presa; *(in fishing)* pesca; *(capture)* captura.
catcher ➤ *s* DEP. receptor/a.
catching ➤ *adj* contagioso.
category ➤ *s* categoría.
cater ➤ *intr* abastecer de comida ■ **to c. to** intentar satisfacer los deseos de.
caterpillar ➤ *s* oruga.
cathedral ➤ *s* catedral *f*.
catholic ➤ *adj* general, universal ■ **C.** *adj & s* católico/a.
cattle ➤ *s* ganado vacuno.
cauliflower ➤ *s* coliflor *f*.
cause ➤ *s* causa; *(reason)* motivo, razón *f* ➤ *tr* causar, provocar.
caution ➤ *s* cautela, precaución *f*; *(warning)* advertencia ➤ *tr* advertir, amonestar.
cautious ➤ *adj* cauteloso, precavido.
cave ➤ *s* cueva ➤ *intr* ■ **to c. in** *(to collapse)* derrumbarse; *(to yield)* ceder.
cave-in ➤ *s* hundimiento, socavón *m*.
cavern ➤ *s* caverna.
cavity ➤ *s* cavidad *f*; ODONT. caries *f*.
CD ➤ *s* disco compacto, CD *m*.
cease ➤ *tr (to stop)* dejar de; *(to discontinue)* suspender ■ **c. fire!** MIL. ¡alto el fuego! ➤ *intr* cesar ➤ *s* cese *m* ■ **without c.** incesantemente.
ceiling ➤ *s* cielo raso, techo.
celebrate ➤ *tr* celebrar; *(an occasion)* festejar, conmemorar ➤ *intr* festejarse.
celebration ➤ *s* celebración *f*.
celebrity ➤ *s* celebridad *f*.
celery ➤ *s* apio.
celestial ➤ *adj (of the sky)* celeste; *(divine)* celestial.
celibacy ➤ *s* celibato.
celibate ➤ *adj & s* célibe *mf*.
cell ➤ *s* celda; BIOL., ELEC., POL. célula ■ **c. phone** celular *m*.
cellar ➤ *s* sótano; *(of wines)* bodega.

cello ➤ *s* violoncelo.
cellular ➤ *adj* celular ■ **c. telephone** teléfono celular, celular *m.*
cement ➤ *s* cemento; *(glue)* pegamento ■ **c. mixer** hormigonera ➤ *tr* unir con cemento; *(to glue)* pegar; FIG. cimentar.
cemetery ➤ *s* cementerio.
censorship ➤ *s* censura.
censure ➤ *s* censura ➤ *tr* censurar.
cent ➤ *s* centavo, céntimo.
center ➤ *s* centro ➤ *tr* centrar.
centigrade ➤ *adj* centígrado.
centimeter ➤ *s* centímetro.
centipede ➤ *s* ciempiés *m.*
central ➤ *adj* central.
Central American ➤ *adj & s* centroamericano/a.
centric ➤ *adj* céntrico, central.
centrifuge ➤ *s* centrifugadora.
century ➤ *s* siglo.
ceramic ➤ *s (clay)* arcilla, barro; *(porcelain)* porcelana ■ **ceramics** *sg* cerámica.
cereal ➤ *s* cereal *m.*
ceremony ➤ *s* ceremonia.
certain ➤ *adj (definite)* cierto; *(sure)* seguro; *(some)* algunos, ciertos ■ **for c.** por cierto • **to make c.** asegurarse.
certainly ➤ *adv* cierto; *(of course)* por supuesto; *(without fail)* seguro.
certainty ➤ *s* certeza; *(fact)* cosa segura.
certificate ➤ *s* certificado, partida.
certify ➤ *tr & intr* certificar.
chain ➤ *s* cadena ■ **c. saw** sierra de cadena • **c. store** sucursal de una cadena de tiendas ➤ *tr* encadenar.
chair ➤ *s* silla; *(chairman/woman)* presidente/a; EDUC. cátedra ■ **c. lift** telesilla ➤ *tr* presidir.
chairman ➤ *s* presidente *m.*
chalk ➤ *s* MIN. creta; *(marker)* tiza ➤ *tr* marcar, escribir (con tiza) ■ **to c. up** apuntarse (tanto, victoria).
challenge ➤ *s* desafío, reto; DER. recusación *f* ➤ *tr* desafiar, retar; *(to contest)* disputar; DER. recusar.
challenging ➤ *adj* arduo, difícil.
chamber ➤ *s* cámara ■ *pl* despacho (de un juez).
champagne ➤ *s* champaña *m.*
champion ➤ *s* campeón/ona ➤ *tr* abogar por.
championship ➤ *s* campeonato.
chance ➤ *s* casualidad *f; (luck)* suerte *f; (opportunity)* oportunidad *f; (possibility)* posibilidad *f; (risk)* riesgo ➤ *intr* suceder, acaecer ➤ *tr* arriesgar ➤ *adj* casual, fortuito.
chancellor ➤ *s* canciller *mf.*
chandelier ➤ *s* araña.
change ➤ *tr & intr* cambiar (de); *(clothes, color)* mudar (de); *(to transform)* convertir(se) ➤ *s* cambio; *(substitution)* relevo; *(of clothing)* muda; *(money)* cambio, vuelto; *(coins)* suelto ■ **for a c.** para variar • **keep the c.** quédese con el vuelto.
changeable ➤ *adj* cambiable; *(inconstant)* variable.
changeover ➤ *s* cambio.
channel ➤ *s* canal *m; (riverbed)* cauce *m; (groove)* ranura ➤ *tr* canalizar.
chant ➤ *s* canto; RELIG. cántico ➤ *tr & intr* cantar, salmodiar.
chaos ➤ *s* caos *m.*
chaotic ➤ *adj* caótico.
chapel ➤ *s* capilla.
chapter ➤ *s* capítulo; *(of a club)* sección *f.*
character ➤ *s* carácter *m;* LIT. *(role)* personaje *m,* papel *m;* FAM. *(guy)* tipo ■ **in c.** característico.
characteristic ➤ *adj* característico ➤ *s* característica.
charcoal ➤ *s* carbon *m* vegetal; DIB. carboncillo.
charge ➤ *tr (to entrust)* encargar, encomendar; *(to accuse)* acusar; COM. *(a price)* pedir, cobrar; *(on credit)* cargar; MIL. atacar; ELEC. cargar ➤ *s (management)* cargo; *(accusation)* acusación *f; (burden)* carga, peso; *(cost)* costo; *(tax)* impuesto; ARM., ELEC., MIL. carga ■ **in c. of** encargado de • **to be in c.** ser el encargado • **to take c.** asumir el mando.
charitable ➤ *adj* caritativo.
charity ➤ *s* caridad *f,* beneficencia; *(institution)* beneficencia.
charm ➤ *s* encanto; *(amulet)* amuleto ➤ *tr* encantar.
charming ➤ *adj* encantador.
chart ➤ *s* MARÍT. carta de navegación ➤ *tr* trazar.
charter ➤ *s* POL. carta; *(of organization)* estatutos ■ **c. flight** vuelo fletado ➤ *tr (to rent)* fletar.
chase ➤ *tr* perseguir *(after* a) ■ **to c. away** *o* **off** ahuyentar • **to c. out** echar fuera ➤ *s* persecución *f* ■ **the c.** *(sport)* la cacería; *(quarry)* caza, presa.
chasm ➤ *s* abismo.
chassis ➤ *s* chasis *m.*
chat ➤ *intr* charlar, platicar; COMPUT. charlar, chatear ➤ *s* charla, plática; COMPUT. charla, chat *m* ■ **c. room** sala *o* canal de charla.
chatter ➤ *intr* parlotear, chacharear; *(teeth)* castañetear ➤ *s* cháchara.
chauffeur ➤ *s* chófer *mf* ➤ *tr* conducir.
chauvinist ➤ *s* chauvinista *mf.*
cheap ➤ *adj* barato; *(inferior)* de mala calidad; *(tawdry)* charro; *(stingy)* tacaño ➤ *adv* barato.
cheat ➤ *tr (to swindle)* defraudar, estafar; *(to deceive)* engañar ➤ *intr* hacer trampa; *(on exam)* copiar.
check ➤ *s (halt)* detención *f; (restraint)* freno; *(verification)* chequeo; *(mark)* marca, señal *f; (bill)* cuenta (de restaurante); *(bank draft)* cheque *m* ➤ *interj* ¡jaque! ➤ *tr (to halt)* detener; *(to restrain)* refrenar; *(to verify)* verificar; *(hat, coat)* depositar; *(luggage)* facturar ■ **to c. out** FAM. comprobar • **to c. up on** comprobar, verificar • **to c. with** consultar con ➤ *intr* ■ **to c. in (to)** registrarse (en un hotel) • **to c. out (of)** pagar la cuenta y marcharse (de un hotel).
checkbook ➤ *s* chequera, talonario.
checkers ➤ *spl* damas.
checkerboard ➤ *s* tablero de damas.
checkmate ➤ *s* jaque y mate *m.*
check-out ➤ *s (exit)* salida (de hotel, supermercado); *(inspection)* inspección *f.*
checkpoint ➤ *s* lugar *m* de inspección.
checkroom ➤ *s* guardarropa *m; (for luggage)* consigna.
checkup ➤ *s* chequeo, reconocimiento médico general.
cheek ➤ *s* mejilla; *(impudence)* descaro.
cheeky ➤ *adj* descarado, caradura.
cheer ➤ *tr (to gladden)* animar, alegrar; *(to encourage)* alentar; *(to shout)* vitorear, ovacionar ■ **to c. on** animar, alentar ➤ *intr* aplaudir ■ **c. up!** ¡ánimo! • **to c. up** alegrarse ➤ *s* alegría, ánimo; *(shout)* viva, hurra ■ *pl* **c.!** ¡salud!
cheerful ➤ *adj* alegre.
cheese ➤ *s* queso.
cheesecake ➤ *s* quesadilla.
chef ➤ *s* cocinero/a, jefe/a de cocina.
chemical ➤ *adj* químico ➤ *s* sustancia química.
chemist ➤ *s* químico/a; G.B. *(pharmacist)* farmacéutico.
chemistry ➤ *s* química.
cherry ➤ *s* cereza ■ **c. tree** cerezo.
chess ➤ *s* ajedrez *m.*
chessboard ➤ *s* tablero de ajedrez.
chest ➤ *s* pecho; *(box)* cofre *m,* arca *m; (dresser)* cómoda.
chestnut ➤ *s* castaña ■ **c. tree** castaño ➤ *adj* castaño, marrón.
chew ➤ *tr & intr* masticar, mascar ■ **to c. out** regañar • **to c. over** rumiar.
chewing ➤ *s* masticación *f* ■ **c. gum** chicle, goma de mascar.
chick ➤ *s* polluelo; JER. *(girl)* chavala.
chicken ➤ *s* gallina, pollo ■ **c. pox** varicela ➤ *adj* FAM. miedoso, cobarde ➤ *intr* ■ **to c. out** acobardarse.
chickpea ➤ *s* garbanzo.
chief ➤ *s* jefe/a ■ **c. executive** primer mandatorio • **c. justice** presidente del tribunal ➤ *adj* principal.
chiefly ➤ *adv* principalmente.
child ➤ *s* niño/a; *(offspring)* hijo/a.
childhood ➤ *s* niñez *f,* infancia.
childish ➤ *adj* infantil, pueril.
children ➤ *pl de* **child.**
Chilean ➤ *adj & s* chileno/a.
chili ➤ *s* chile *m,* ají *m.*
chill ➤ *s* frío; *(shiver)* escalofrío ■ **to catch a c.** resfriarse ➤ *adj* frío ➤ *tr* enfriar; *(food)* refrigerar.
chilly ➤ *adj* frío.
chime ➤ *s* carillón *m; (sound)* repique *m* ■ *pl* carillón ➤ *intr* repicar ■ **to c. in** intervenir (en una conversación).
chimney ➤ *s* chimenea; *(of a lamp)* tubo de vidrio.
chimpanzee ➤ *s* chimpancé *m.*
chin ➤ *s* barbilla, mentón *m* ■ **to keep one's c. up** no desanimarse.
china ➤ *s* china, porcelana; *(crockery)* loza.
chip ➤ *s* pedacito, trozo; *(splinter)* astilla; *(in china)* desportilladura; *(in gambling)* ficha; ELECTRÓN. placa ■ *pl* patatas fritas ➤ *tr* hacer astillas; *(to chop)* picar ➤ *intr* ■ **to c. in** contribuir.
chiropractor ➤ *s* quiropráctico/a.
chisel ➤ *s* cincel *m* ➤ *tr* cincelar; FAM. *(to cheat)* estafar.
chlorine ➤ *s* cloro.
chocolate ➤ *adj & s* (de) chocolate *m.*
choice ➤ *s* elección *f,* selección *f; (option)* opción *f; (assortment)* surtido; *(alternative)* alternative ■ **by c.** por gusto ➤ *adj* escogido, superior.
choir ➤ *s* coro.
choke ➤ *tr* estrangular, ahogar; *(to suffocate)* sofocar ■ **to c. back** ahogar • **to c. down** tragar con asco ➤ *intr* sofocarse, ahogarse; *(on food)* atragantarse; *(to clog)* atorarse ■ **to c. up** FAM. emocionarse ➤ *s* sofocación *f,* ahogo; AUTO. estrangulador *m.*
cholera ➤ *s* cólera *m.*
cholesterol ➤ *s* colesterol *m.*
choose◊ ➤ *tr* elegir, escoger; *(to prefer)* preferir ➤ *intr* ■ **to do as one chooses** hacer lo que quiere.
chop ➤ *tr* cortar; *(to mince)* picar ■ **to c. down** talar • **to c. up** cortar en trozos ➤ *s* corte *m,* tajo; CUL. chuleta.
chopper ➤ *s* FAM. helicóptero.
choppy ➤ *adj* picado, agitado.
chopsticks ➤ *spl* palillos chinos.
chord ➤ *s* MÚS. acorde *m;* GEOM. cuerda.
chore ➤ *s* quehacer *m,* faena.
choreographer ➤ *s* coreógrafo/a.
chorus ➤ *s* coro; *(refrain)* estribillo ■ **in c.** al unísono.
chosen ➤ *adj & s* elegido, escogido.
christen ➤ *tr* bautizar.
christening ➤ *s* bautismo, bautizo.
Christian ➤ *adj & s* cristiano/a ■ **C. name** nombre de pila.
Christmas ➤ *s* Navidad *f.*
chrome ➤ *s* cromo.
chrysanthemum ➤ *s* crisantemo.
chubby ➤ *adj* rechoncho.
chunk ➤ *s* pedazo, trozo.
church ➤ *s* iglesia.
churn ➤ *s* mantequera ➤ *tr* agitar, revolver ■ **to c. out** producir en profusión ➤ *intr* agitarse, revolverse.
chute ➤ *s* rampa, tobogán *m.*
cicada ➤ *s* cigarra.
cider ➤ *s* sidra.
cigar ➤ *s* cigarro, puro.
cigarette ➤ *s* cigarrillo.
cinema ➤ *s* cine *m.*
cinematography ➤ *s* cinematografía.
cinnamon ➤ *s* canela.
circle ➤ *s* círculo; *(orbit)* órbita; *(turn)* vuelta ■ **to come full c.** volver al punto de partida ➤ *tr (to draw)* hecer un círculo alrededor de; *(to revolve around)* girar alrededor de ➤ *intr* dar vueltas.
circuit ➤ *s* circuito ■ **c. board** placa *o* tarjeta de circuitos • **c. breaker** cortacircuitos.
circular ➤ *adj & s* circular *f.*
circulate ➤ *tr & intr* circular.
circulation ➤ *s* circulación *f.*
circumference ➤ *s* circunferencia.
circumstance ➤ *s* circunstancia ■ *pl* situación, posición • **under no c.** de ninguna manera.
circus ➤ *s* circo.
citadel ➤ *s* ciudadela.
cite ➤ *tr* citar.
citizen ➤ *s* ciudadano/a.
citizenship ➤ *s* ciudadanía.
city ➤ *s* ciudad *f* ■ **c. hall** ayuntamiento.
civil ➤ *adj* civil ■ **c. service** administración pública.
civilian ➤ *adj & s* civil *mf.*
civilization ➤ *s* civilización *f.*
civilize ➤ *s* civilizar.
claim ➤ *tr* reclamar; *(to state)* afirmar ➤ *s* reclamación *f; (assertion)* afirmación *f; (right)* derecho, título; DER. demanda.
clam ➤ *s* almeja.
clamp ➤ *s* TEC. grapa, abrazadera; CARP. cárcel *f* ➤ *tr* sujetar con abrazadera ■ **to c. down on** FAM. reprimir.
clap ➤ *intr* dar palmadas ➤ *s* aplauso; *(tap)* palmada; *(bang)* estampido.
clapping ➤ *s* aplausos; *(in time)* palmadas.
claret ➤ *s* clarete *m.*
clarinet ➤ *s* clarinete *m.*
clarity ➤ *s* claridad *f.*
clash ➤ *intr* chocar ➤ *s (noise)* estruendo; *(collision)* choque *m; (conflict)* desacuerdo.
clasp ➤ *s (device)* cierre *m,* broche *m; (hug)* abrazo; *(of the hands)* apretón *m* ➤ *tr (to hug)* abrazar; *(to clutch)* agarrar; *(the hand)* apretar.
class ➤ *s* clase *f* ■ **c. of 2003** promoción de 2003 ➤ *tr* clasificar.
classic ➤ *adj & s* clásico.
classical ➤ *adj* clásico.
classify ➤ *tr* clasificar.
classmate ➤ *s* compañero/a de clase.
classroom ➤ *s* aula, sala de clase.
clause ➤ *s* cláusula *f;* GRAM. oración *f.*
claw ➤ *s* garra; *(of cat)* uña; *(of crab)* tenaza, pinza ➤ *tr & intr* arañar.
clay ➤ *s* arcilla.
clean ➤ *adj* limpio; *(pure)* puro; *(total)* completo, radical ➤ *adv* limpiamente; FAM. completamente ■ **to come c.** confesarlo todo ➤ *tr* limpiar; *(fish)* escamar y abrir ■ **to c. out** *(to empty out)* vaciar; *(to use up)* agotar • **to c. up** acabar con (un asunto) ➤ *intr* limpiar(se) ■ **to c. house** FIG. poner las cosas en orden • **to c. up** FAM. ganarse una fortuna.
cleaner ➤ *s* limpiador *m,* quitamanchas *m* ■ **c.'s** tintorería.
cleaning ➤ *s* limpieza.
cleanliness ➤ *s* limpieza, aseo.
clear ➤ *adj* claro; *(sky, view)* despejado; *(air, water)* transparente; *(evident)* evidente; *(conscience)* limpio, tranquilo ■ **c. of** libre de • **c. profit** beneficio neto • **to make oneself c.** explicar claramente ➤ *adv* claro, con claridad ■ **to stand c.** mantenerse aparte ➤ *tr (to make clear)* aclarar; *(to unobstruct)* despejar; *(a path, way)* abrir; *(the table)* levantar; *(to remove)* quitar; *(the throat)* aclararse; *(to exonerate)* limpiar; *(to acquit)* absolver; *(a check)* compensar; *(customs)* sacar de la aduana ■ **to c. up** *(doubt)* disipar; *(mystery)* aclarar ➤ *intr* aclararse; *(sky)* despejarse ■ **to c. out** largarse ➤ *s* ■ **in the c.** fuera de sospecha.
clearance ➤ *s (removal)* despejo; *(sale)* liquidación *f,* saldo; *(leeway)* espacio, margen *m; (by customs)* despacho.
clearly ➤ *adv* claramente; *(evidently)* evidentemente; *(of course)* claro.
clench ➤ *tr* apretar ➤ *s* apretón *m.*
clergy ➤ *s* clero.
clergyman ➤ *s* clérigo.
clerical ➤ *adj* de oficina; RELIG. clerical.
clerk ➤ *s (in office)* oficinista *mf; (in store)* dependiente *mf;* DER. escribano/a, amanuense *mf.*
clever ➤ *adj (bright)* listo, inteligente; *(witty)* ingenioso; *(skillful)* hábil.
click ➤ *s* chasquido, ruidito seco; COMPUT. clic *m,* pinche *m* ➤ *intr* chasquear; COMPUT. pulsar, pinchar ➤ *tr (tongue)* chasquear; *(heels)* taconear.
client ➤ *s* cliente *mf.*
cliff ➤ *s* acantilado, precipicio.
climate ➤ *s* clima *m.*
climax ➤ *s* culminación *f;* LIT., RET. climax *m* ➤ *intr* culminar.
climb ➤ *tr & intr* subir; *(to scale)* escalar, trepar ■ **to c. down** descender, bajar ➤ *s* subida, ascenso.
climber ➤ *s* alpinista *mf,* andinista *mf.*
cling◊ ➤ *intr (to hold fast)* asirse, agarrarse; *(to stick)* pegarse.
clinic ➤ *s* clínica.
clip[1] ➤ *tr* recortar; *(to trim)* podar.
clip[2] ➤ *s (fastener)* sujetador *m; (for paper)* sujetapapeles *m; (for hair)* horquilla; *(of rifle)* cargador *m* ➤ *tr* sujetar.
clipper ➤ *s (shears)* tijeras; MARÍT. clíper *m* ■ *pl* tijeras • **nail c.** cortaúñas.
clipping ➤ *s* recorte *m.*
cloak ➤ *s* capa, manto ➤ *tr* encubrir.
cloakroom ➤ *s* guardarropa *m.*
clock ➤ reloj *m* (de pie, de mesa); DEP. cronómetro ➤ *tr* cronometrar.
clockwise ➤ *adv & adj* en el sentido de las agujas del reloj.
cloister ➤ *s* claustro; RELIG. monasterio, convento ➤ *tr* enclaustrar.
clone ➤ *s* clon *m* ➤ *tr & intr* clonar(se), reproducir(se) asexualmente.
close ➤ *adj* cercano; *(relationship)* íntimo; *(similar)* parecido; *(contest)* reñido; *(rigorous)* minucioso; *(atten-*

tion) total ■ **a c. resemblance** un gran parecido • **at c. range** a quemarropa, de cerca • **c. call** FAM. escape difícil ➤ *tr* cerrar; *(letter)* concluir; *(session)* levantar; *(gap, distance)* acortar ■ **to c. down** cerrar definitivamente • **to c. in** rodear, cercar • **to c. up** *(shop)* cerrar; *(opening)* tapar ➤ *intr* cerrarse; *(shop)* cerrar; *(story, show)* terminarse, concluirse ➤ *s* final *m*, conclusión *f* ■ **to bring to a c.** terminar ➤ *adv* cerca ■ **c. at hand** a mano • **c. by** muy cerca • **c. to** muy cerca de, junto a • **c. together** muy juntos • **to come c.** acercarse.

closed-circuit television ➤ *s* televisión *f* en circuito cerrado.

closet ➤ *s* armario, ropero.

clot ➤ *s* coágulo ➤ *intr* cuajarse.

cloth ➤ *s* tela, paño; *(strip)* trapo ■ **the c.** el clero.

clothes ➤ *spl* ropa, vestimenta.

clothesline ➤ *s* cuerda para tender ropa.

clothespin ➤ *s* pinza para tender ropa.

clothing ➤ *s* ropa, indumentaria.

cloud ➤ *s* nube *f*; *(shadow)* sombra ■ **under a c.** bajo sospecha ➤ *tr & intr* nublar(se), anublar(se) ■ **to c. over** *o* **up** nublarse.

cloudy ➤ *adj* nublado; *(liquid)* turbio.

clove ➤ *s (spice)* clavo de especia; *(of garlic)* diente *m*.

clover ➤ *s* trébol *m*.

clown ➤ *s* payaso/a ➤ *intr* payasear.

club ➤ *s (cudgel)* porra; *(golf)* palo; *(in cards)* trébol *m*, basto; *(association)* club *m* ➤ *tr* aporrear.

clue ➤ *s* pista, indicio; *(in puzzle)* indicación *f* ■ **I haven't a c.** no tengo ni idea.

clumsy ➤ *adj* torpe; *(unwieldy)* incómodo; *(unrefined)* crudo.

clutch ➤ *tr* agarrar, asir ➤ *s (grasp)* apretón *m*; MEC. embrague *m* ■ **in the c.** en situación crítica ■ *pl* FIG. garras.

clutter ➤ *s* desorden *m* ➤ *tr* ■ **to be cluttered with** estar atestado con.

coach ➤ *s (carriage)* coche *m*, carruaje *m*; *(bus)* ómnibus *m*; AVIA. clase económica; *(trainer)* entrenador/a ➤ *tr & intr (to tutor)* dar lecciones suplementarias; *(to train)* entrenar.

coal ➤ *s* carbón *m*, hulla; *(ember)* ascua.

coarse ➤ *adj (inferior)* basto; *(uncouth)* vulgar; *(rough)* áspero, tosco; *(grainy)* granular.

coast ➤ *s* costa ■ **c. guard** guardacostas • **the c. is clear** no hay moros en la costa ➤ *intr (to slide)* deslizarse; *(bicycle, car)* rodar sin impulso.

coat ➤ *s (overcoat)* abrigo; *(jacket)* saco, chaqueta; *(of animal)* piel *f*, pelo; *(paint)* mano *f*, capa ➤ *tr (to cover)* revestir; *(to paint)* dar una capa.

coating ➤ *s (layer)* capa, mano *f*; *(gold, silver)* baño, revestimiento.

cob ➤ *s* elote *m*, mazorca.

cobblestone ➤ *s* piedra redonda ■ **c. pavement** empedrado.

cobweb ➤ *s* telaraña.

cocaine ➤ *s* cocaína.

cock ➤ *s (rooster)* gallo; *(male bird)* macho; *(faucet)* grifo, llave *f*; ARM. martillo ➤ *tr* ARM. amartillar; *(a hat)* inclinar (hacia arriba).

cockpit ➤ *s* cancha; AVIA. cabina.

cockroach ➤ *s* cucaracha.

cocktail ➤ *s* cóctel *m*.

cocoa ➤ *s* cacao.

coconut ➤ *s* coco ■ **c. palm** cocotero.

cod *or* **codfish** ➤ *s* bacalao.

code ➤ *s* código; *(cipher)* clave *f*, cifra ➤ *tr* codificar; *(a message)* cifrar.

coed ➤ *s* FAM. ➤ *s* alumna de una universidad mixta ➤ *adj* coeducacional.

coffee ➤ *s* café *m* ■ **c. shop** café, cafetería • **c. table** mesa de café *o* de centro.

coffeepot ➤ *s* cafetera.

coffin ➤ *s* ataúd *m*.

cog ➤ *s* MEC. diente *m*.

cognac ➤ *s* coñac *m*.

coil ➤ *s* rollo; *(single)* anillo, vuelta; ELEC. bobina ➤ *tr & intr* enrollar(se), enroscar(se).

coin ➤ *s* moneda.

coincide ➤ *intr* coincidir.

coincidence ➤ *s (identicalness)* coincidencia; *(chance)* casualidad *f*.

cola ➤ *s* cola (nuez, bebida).

colander ➤ *s* colador *m*.

cold ➤ *adj* frío ■ **c. cream** crema para el cutis • **c. cuts** fiambres • **c. feet** JER. miedo • **c. sore** afta (labial) • **out c.** sin conocimiento • **to be c.** *(object)* estar frío; *(person)* tener frío; *(weather)* hacer frío ➤ *adv (unprepared)* sin preparación, en seco ■ **to know c.** saber al dedillo ➤ *s* frío; MED. catarro, resfriado ■ **to catch (a) c.** resfriarse.

coldness ➤ *s.* frío, frialdad *f*.

colic ➤ *s* cólico.

coliseum ➤ *s* coliseo.

collaborate ➤ *intr* colaborar.

collaboration ➤ *s* colaboración *f*; *(treason)* colaboracionismo.

collage ➤ *s* collage *m*, montaje *m*.

collapse ➤ *intr* caerse, derrumbarse; *(person)* desplomarse; *(business)* fracasar; *(to fold)* plegarse ➤ *s* derrumbe *f*; *(business)* fracaso; MED. colapso.

collar ➤ *s* collar *m*; *(of shirt)* cuello ➤ *tr (an animal)* poner un collar a; FAM. *(to nab)* agarrar, detener.

collarbone ➤ *s* clavícula.

collate ➤ *tr (texts)* colacionar; *(pages)* ordenar.

colleague ➤ *s* colega *mf*.

collect ➤ *tr (to gather)* juntar, reunir; *(as hobby)* coleccionar; *(payments)* recaudar ➤ *adj & adv (telephone call)* de cobro revertido.

collection ➤ *s* colección *f*; *(heap)* acumulación *f*; *(of money)* cobro; *(donation)* colecta.

collector ➤ *s* MEC. colector *m*; *(of taxes)* recaudador/a; *(of bills)* cobrador/a; *(as hobby)* coleccionista *mf*.

college ➤ *s* universidad *f*; *(department)* facultad *f*; RELIG. colegio.

collide ➤ *intr* chocar.

collision ➤ *s* choque *m*.

colloquial ➤ *adj* familiar.

cologne ➤ *s* colonia (perfume).

Columbian ➤ *adj & s* colombiano/a.

colon[1] ➤ *s* GRAM. dos puntos.

colon[2] ➤ *s* ANAT. colon *m*.

colonel ➤ *s* coronel *mf*.

colonial ➤ *adj (of a colony)* colonial; *(colonizing)* colonizador ➤ *s* colono/a.

colony ➤ *s* colonia.

color ➤ *s* color *m* ■ **c. photography** cromofotografía • **in c.** en colores • **off c.** verde ➤ *tr* colorear; *(to dye)* teñir; *(to distort)* alterar, embellecer.

colored ➤ *adj* coloreado, de color; *(person)* de color.

colorful ➤ *adj (vivid)* de gran colorido; *(picturesque)* pintoresco.

colour G.B. ➤ *var de* **color.**

column ➤ *s* columna.

coma ➤ *s* coma *m*.

comb ➤ *s* peine *m* ➤ *tr* peinar ■ **to c. one's hair** peinarse.

combination ➤ *s* combinación *f*; *(mix)* mezcla.

combine ➤ *tr & intr* combinar(se); *(to mix)* mezclar.

come◊ ➤ *intr* venir; *(to arrive at, extend to)* llegar ■ **to c. across** encontrarse con • **to c. along** *(to accompany)* acompañar; *(to progress)* progresar • **to c. back** volver • **to c. before** preceder • **to c. between** interponerse entre • **to c. by** *(to visit)* hacer una visita; *(to obtain)* obtener, lograr • **to c. down** bajar • **to c. in** *(to enter)* entrar; *(to figure into)* figurar, entrar • **to c. of** resultar de, suceder por • **to c. off** *(to detach)* soltarse, separarse; *(to acquit oneself)* salir (bien, mal) • **to c. out** salir; *(book)* publicarse; *(to result)* resultar (bien, mal); *(stain)* quitarse; *(truth)* salir a la luz, revelarse • **to c. to** *(to revive)* recobrar los sentidos, volver en sí; *(to amount to)* reducirse a • **to c. up** subir; *(to arise)* presentarse, surgir; *(to be mentioned)* ser mencionado ➤ *interj* ¡venga!, ¡ven! ■ **c. again?** ¿cómo? • **c. in!** ¡adelante!, ¡pase! • **c. on!** FAM. *(hurry up!)* ¡apúrate!; *(you're kidding!)* ¡no me digas!

comeback ➤ *s* réplica, respuesta ingeniosa ■ **to make a c.** restablecerse.

comedian ➤ *s* cómico/a.

comedy ➤ *s* comedia.

come-on ➤ *s* aliciente *m*, incentivo.

comfort ➤ *tr* confortar, consolar; *(to relieve)* aliviar ➤ *s* confort *m*; *(relief)* alivio; *(ease)* comodidad *f*.

comfortable ➤ *adj (easy)* confortable, cómodo; FAM. *(sufficient)* adecuado.

comforter ➤ *s (person)* consolador/a; *(quilt)* edredón *m*.

comic ➤ *adj & s* cómico ■ **c. book** revista de historietas ilustradas • **c. strip** tira cómica.

comical ➤ *s* cómico.

coming ➤ *adj* venidero ➤ *s* venida.

comma ➤ *s* GRAM. coma.

command ➤ *tr* mandar; *(to rule)* regir; *(to deserve)* infundir ➤ *intr* mandar, dar órdenes ➤ *s* mando; *(order)* orden *f*; *(mastery)* dominio; MIL. comando ■ **at one's c.** a la disposición de uno • **under the c. of** al mando de.

commemorate ➤ *tr* conmemorar.

commence ➤ *tr & intr* comenzar.

comment ➤ *s* comentario; *(remark)* observación *f* ➤ *intr* comentar.

commentary ➤ *s* comentario.

commentator ➤ *s* locutor/a.

commerce ➤ *s* comercio.

commercial ➤ *adj* comercial ➤ *s* RAD., TELEV. anuncio.

commission ➤ *s* comisión *f*; MIL. nombramiento ■ **out of c.** fuera de servicio ➤ *tr* MIL. nombrar; *(to order)* encargar, mandar a hacer.

commit ➤ *tr* cometer; *(to entrust)* encomendar; *(to confine)* internar ■ **to c. oneself** comprometerse.

commitment ➤ *s (pledge)* compromiso; *(institutionalization)* internamiento, reclusión *f*; *(obligation)* obligación *f*.

committee ➤ *s* comité *m*, comisión *f*.

commodity ➤ *s* mercancía.

common ➤ *adj* común; *(widespread)* general; *(frequent)* usual, frecuente; *(quality)* mediocre, inferior ■ **c. cold** resfriado, catarro • **c. law** derecho consuetudinario • **c. sense** sentido común ➤ *s* ejido, campo comunal.

commonwealth ➤ *s (people)* comunidad *f*; *(state)* rebública.

commotion ➤ *s* tumulto, alboroto.

communal ➤ *adj* comunal.

commune ➤ *s* POL. comuna; *(community)* vivienda colectiva.

communicate ➤ *tr & intr* comunicar(se).

communication ➤ *s* comunicación *f*.

communion ➤ *s* comunión *f*.

communism ➤ *s* comunismo.

communist ➤ *s* comunista *mf*.

community ➤ *s* comunidad *f*.

commute ➤ *tr* conmutar ➤ *intr* viajar diariamente al lugar en que se trabaja ➤ *s* viaje diario.

commuter ➤ *s* persona que viaja diariamente (esp. al trabajo).

compact[1] ➤ *adj* compacto; *(concise)* conciso ■ **c. disk** disco compacto, CD ➤ *tr* comprimir ➤ *s* polvera; AUTO. automóvil compacto.

compact[2] ➤ *s* pacto, convenio.

companion ➤ *s* compañero/a.

company ➤ *s* compañía; *(group)* grupo; *(guests)* invitado(s) ■ **to keep c. with** asociarse con.

comparative ➤ *adj* comparativo; *(relative)* relativo.

compare ➤ *tr & intr* (poderse) comparar ■ **as compared with** comparado con ➤ *s* ■ **beyond c.** incomparable.

comparison ➤ *s* comparación *f* ■ **by c.** en comparación.

compartment ➤ *s* compartimiento.

compass ➤ *s* brújula, compás *m* ■ **c.** *o pl* GEOM. compás.

compatible ➤ *adj* compatible.

compel ➤ *tr* compeler, obligar; *(respect, belief)* imponer.

compelling ➤ *adj* obligatorio; *(evidence)* incontestable; *(need)* apremiante.

compensate ➤ *tr* compensar; COM. indemnizar.

compensation ➤ *s* compensación *f*; COM. indemnización *f*.

compete ➤ *intr* competir ■ **to c. in** concursar *o* tomar parte en.

competent ➤ *adj* competente.

competition ➤ *s* competencia.

competitive ➤ *adj* competitivo; *(person)* competidor.

competitor ➤ *s* competidor/a.

compile ➤ *tr* compilar, recopilar.

complain ➤ *intr* quejarse (*about* de).

complaint ➤ *s* queja; *(protest)* reclamación *f*; DER. querella, demanda.

complete ➤ *adj* completo; *(thorough)* total; *(utter)* verdadero ➤ *tr* completar, llevar a cabo; *(a form)* llenar.

completion ➤ *s* terminación *f*.

complex ➤ *adj (composite)* compuesto; *(intricate)* complejo ➤ *s* complejo.

complexion ➤ *s (skin)* tez *f*; *(character)* aspecto, carácter *m*.

compliance ➤ *s (with an order)* acatamiento; *(acquiescence)* conformidad *f* ■ **in c. with** conforme a.

complicated ➤ *adj* complicado.

complication ➤ *s* complicación *f*.

compliment ➤ *s (praise)* elogio; *(honor)* honor *m* ■ *pl* saludos • **with the c. of** obsequio de ➤ *tr* elogiar, felicitar.

comply ➤ *intr (with an order)* acatar, obedecer; *(with a request)* acceder.

component ➤ *s* componente *m*.

compose ➤ *tr & intr* componer ■ **to c. oneself** tranquilizarse.

composed ➤ *adj* sosegado, tranquilo.

composer ➤ *s* compositor/a.

composition ➤ *s* composición *f*.

compound ➤ *adj* compuesto ■ **c. fracture** MED. fractura complicada ➤ *s* compuesto.

comprehend ➤ *tr* comprender.

comprehension ➤ *s* comprensión *f*.

comprehensive ➤ *adj (broad)* amplio, general; *(knowledge)* comprensivo.

compress ➤ *tr* comprimir ➤ *s* compresa.

comprise ➤ *tr (to include)* comprender, incluir; *(to consist of)* constar de.

compromise ➤ *s* compromiso, acuerdo ➤ *tr (to endanger)* comprometer ➤ *intr* hacer concesiones.

compulsion ➤ *s* compulsión *f*; *(impulse)* impulso ■ **under c.** a la fuerza.

compulsive ➤ *adj (desire)* incontrolable; *(person)* obsesivo.

compulsory ➤ *adj (coercive)* compulsorio; *(required)* obligatorio.

compute ➤ *tr* computar, calcular.

computer ➤ *s* computadora, ordenador *m* ■ **c. science** informática.

comrade ➤ *s* camarada *mf*.

conceal ➤ *tr* ocultar.

concede ➤ *tr* conceder ➤ *intr* hacer una concesión.

conceited ➤ *adj* vanidoso, engreído.

conceivable ➤ *adj* concebible.

concentrate ➤ *tr & intr* concentrar(se) ➤ *s* concentrado.

concentration ➤ *s* concentración *f* ■ **c. camp** campo de concentración.

concept ➤ *s* concepto.

conception ➤ *s* concepción *f*; *(idea)* concepto.

concern ➤ *tr (to be about)* tratar de; *(to trouble)* preocupar ■ **as concerns** en lo que concierne a • **to c. oneself with** ocuparse de, interesarse por ➤ *s (affair)* asunto; *(interest)* interés *m*; *(worry)* preocupación *f* ■ **to be of no c.** carecer de importancia.

concerned ➤ *adj (interested)* interesado; *(worried)* preocupado.

concert ➤ *s* concierto ■ **in c. with** de concierto con.

concession ➤ *s* concesión *f*.

concise ➤ *adj* conciso, sucinto.

conclude ➤ *tr & intr* concluir.

conclusion ➤ *s* conclusión *f*.

concrete ➤ *adj* concreto; CONSTR. de hormigón ➤ *s* concreto, hormigón *m*.

condemn ➤ *tr* condenar.

condensation ➤ *s* condensación *f*; LIT. versión condensada.

condense ➤ *tr & intr* condensar(se).

condescension ➤ *s* condescendencia.

condition ➤ *s* condición *f*; *(health)* estado de salud ➤ *tr (to qualify, train)* condicionar; *(to make fit)* poner en condiciones; *(to adapt)* acostumbrar.

conditioner ➤ *s* acondicionador *m*.

condom ➤ *s* preservativo, condón *m*.

condominium ➤ *s* condominio.

conduct ➤ *tr* dirigir (negocio, orquesta); *(to carry out)* llevar a cabo, hacer; FÍS. conducir ■ **to c. oneself** conducirse ➤ *s* conducta, comportamiento.

conductor ➤ *s* conductor/a; MÚS. director/a.

cone ➤ *s* cono; CUL. barquillo, cucurucho.

confer ➤ *tr* conferir.

conference ➤ *s (assembly)* conferencia, congreso; *(meeting)* reunión *f*.

confess ➤ *tr* confesar ➤ *intr* confesar; RELIG. confesarse.

confession ➤ *s* confesión *f*.

confetti ➤ *spl* confeti *m*.

confidence ➤ *s* confianza; *(secret)* confidencia.

confident ➤ *s* seguro; *(self-assured)* confiado; *(manner)* de confianza.

confidential ➤ *adj* confidencial.

confine ➤ *tr (person)* confinar, recluir; *(answer)* limitar ➤ *s* ■ *pl* confines.

confirm ➤ *tr* confirmar; POL. ratificar.

confirmed ➤ *adj* confirmado; POL. rati-

ficado; *(inveterate)* habitual.
confiscate ➤ *tr* confiscar.
conflict ➤ *s* conflicto ➤ *intr* contradecirse.
conflicting ➤ *adj* contradictorio.
conform ➤ *intr* conformarse, concordar; *(to standards, rules)* ajustarse.
confront ➤ *tr (to face)* enfrentar, hacer frente a; *(to encounter)* encontrar.
confuse ➤ *tr* confundir.
confused ➤ *adj* confundido, desconcertado; *(disordered)* confuso.
confusing ➤ *adj* confuso.
confusion ➤ *s* confusión *f.*
congested ➤ *adj (by traffic)* congestionado; *(area)* superpoblado; *(chest, nose)* constipado.
congestion ➤ *s* congestión *f.*
congratulate ➤ *tr* felicitar.
congratulation ➤ *s* felicitación *f,* congratulación *f* ■ **congratulations!** ¡felicidades!, ¡enhorabuena!
congregate ➤ *intr & tr* congregar(se).
congress ➤ *s* congreso.
congressman ➤ *s* E.U. diputado de la Cámara de Representantes.
congresswoman ➤ *s* E.U. diputada de la Cámara de Representantes.
conjugate ➤ *tr & intr* conjugar(se).
conjugation ➤ *s* conjugación *f.*
conjunction ➤ *s* conjunción *f* ■ **in c. with** conjuntamente con.
conjure ➤ *tr* ■ **to c. up** *(a spirit)* invocar; *(to evoke)* evocar.
conjurer *or* **conjuror** ➤ *s* mago/a.
connect ➤ *tr* conectar; *(to associate)* vincular, relacionar ➤ *intr* unirse; *(rooms)* comunicarse; *(buses, trains)* hacer combinación.
connection ➤ *s* conexión *f; (buses, trains)* combinación *f* ■ **in c. with** en relación con.
conquer ➤ *tr* conquistar; *(enemy, disease)* vencer ➤ *intr* vencer, triunfar.
conqueror ➤ *s* conquistador/a.
conquest ➤ *s* conquista.
conscience ➤ *s* conciencia.
conscientious ➤ *adj* concienzudo.
conscious ➤ *adj* consciente; *(intentional)* deliberado ■ **to become c.** volver en sí • **to become c. of** darse cuenta de.
consecutive ➤ *adj* consecutivo.
consent ➤ *intr* consentir ➤ *s* consentimiento.
consequence ➤ *s* consecuencia; *(importance)* importancia ■ **in c.** por consiguiente.
conservation ➤ *s* conservación *f.*
conservative ➤ *adj* conservador; *(moderate)* moderado; *(cautious)* prudente ➤ *s* conservador/a.
conservatory ➤ *s (for plants)* invernadero; *(school)* conservatorio.
conserve ➤ *tr* conservar.
consider ➤ *tr & intr* considerar ■ **to c. oneself** considerarse.
considerable ➤ *adj* considerable.
considerate ➤ *adj* considerado, atento.
consideration ➤ *s* consideración *f* ■ **out of c. for** por respeto a.
consign ➤ *tr* consignar.
consignment ➤ *s* consignación *f.*
consist ➤ *intr* consistir *(of, in* en).
consistent ➤ *adj (in agreement)* coherente; *(uniform)* consistente.
consolation ➤ *s* consolación *f,* consuelo.
console[1] ➤ *tr* consolar.
console[2] ➤ *s* gabinete *m* (de radio o televisor); TEC. tablero de mando.
consonant ➤ *adj & s* consonante *f.*
conspicuous ➤ *adj* destacado, evidente ■ **to be c.** destacar(se).
constable ➤ *s* alguacil *mf;* G.B. policía *mf.*
constant ➤ *adj & s* constante *f.*
constipation ➤ *s* estreñimiento.
constitute ➤ *tr* constituir.
constitution ➤ *s* constitución *f.*
construct ➤ *tr* construir.
construction ➤ *s* construcción *f; (structure)* estructura.
consul ➤ *s* cónsul *mf.*
consulate ➤ *s* consulado.
consult ➤ *tr & intr* consultar.
consultant ➤ *s* consultor/a.
consume ➤ *tr* consumir; *(food)* tragar; *(time, effort)* tomar ■ **to be consumed with** consumirse de.
consumer ➤ *s* consumidor/a.
consumption ➤ *s* consumo; MED. consunción *f.*
contact ➤ *s* contacto; *(connection)* relación *f* ■ **c. lens** lente de contacto ➤ *tr* ponerse en contacto con.
contagious ➤ *adj* contagioso.
contain ➤ *tr* contener ■ **to c. oneself** contenerse.
container ➤ *s* recipiente *m,* envase *m;* COM. contenedor *m.*
contaminate ➤ *tr* contaminar.
contemplate ➤ *tr* contemplar; *(to intend)* pensar, proyectar.
contemporary ➤ *adj & s* contemporáneo, coetáneo.
contempt ➤ *s* desprecio, desdén *m;* DER. desacato.
contend ➤ *intr* contender ➤ *tr* mantener, sostener.
content[1] ➤ *s* contenido; *(meaning)* significado ■ *pl* contenido, materia.
content[2] ➤ *adj* contento, satisfecho ➤ *s* satisfacción *f.*
contented ➤ *adj* contento, satisfecho.
contest ➤ *s (struggle)* contienda; *(competition)* competencia, concurso ➤ *tr* cuestionar, impugnar.
contestant ➤ *s* contendiente *mf.*
context ➤ *s* contexto.
continent ➤ *adj & s* continente *m.*
continental ➤ *adj* continental.
contingent ➤ *adj* contingente, eventual ■ **to be c. on** depender de.
continual ➤ *adj* continuo.
continuation ➤ *s* continuación *f.*
continue ➤ *tr & intr* continuar ■ **to be continued** continuará.
continuous ➤ *adj* continuo.
contraception ➤ *s* contracepción *f.*
contraceptive ➤ *adj & s* anticonceptivo.
contract ➤ *s* contrato ➤ *tr (to agree to)* contratar; *(to acquire)* contraer ➤ *intr* contraerse, encogerse.
contraction ➤ *s* contracción *f.*
contradict ➤ *tr* contradecir.
contradiction ➤ *s* contradicción *f.*
contrary ➤ *adj* contrario; *(ornery)* terco ➤ *s* lo contrario, lo opuesto ➤ *adv* ■ **c. to** en contra de.
contrast ➤ *tr & intr* (hacer) contrastar ➤ *s* contraste *m* ■ **in c.** por contraste • **in c. to** a diferencia de.
contribute ➤ *tr & intr* contribuir.
contribution ➤ *s* contribución *f.*
contributor ➤ *s* contribuidor/a.
contrive ➤ *tr* inventar, idear ■ **to c. to** conseguir (hacer algo).
contrived ➤ *adj* artificial.
control ➤ *tr* controlar, dirigir ■ **to c. oneself** dominarse ➤ *s* control *m; (restraint)* dominio ■ **to be in c.** tener el mando • **to get out of c.** desmandarse ■ *pl* mandos, controles.
convalescence ➤ *s* convalecencia.
convenience ➤ *s (suitability)* conveniencia; *(comfort)* comodidad *f* ■ **at your c.** cuando guste.
convenient ➤ *adj (suitable)* conveniente; *(handy)* útil.
convent ➤ *s* convento.
convention ➤ *s* convención *f; (custom)* costumbre *f,* regla convencional.
conversation ➤ *s* conversación *f* ■ **to make c.** dar conversación, platicar.
converse ➤ *intr* conversar.
convert ➤ *tr & intr* convertir(se) ➤ *s* converso/a.
converter ➤ *s* convertidor *m.*
convertible ➤ *adj* convertible ➤ *s* AUTO. descapotable *m.*
convey ➤ *tr* transportar, llevar; *(a meaning)* comunicar, dar a entender.
convict ➤ *tr* condenar ➤ *s* convicto/a.
convince ➤ *tr* convencer.
convoke ➤ *tr* convocar.
convolution ➤ *s* enrollamiento.
convoy ➤ *s* convoy *m.*
cook ➤ *tr* cocinar, guisar ■ **to c. up** FAM. inventar ➤ *intr (food)* cocinarse; *(chef)* cocinar ➤ *s* cocinero/a.
cookbook ➤ *s* libro de cocina.
cookie *or* **cooky** ➤ *s* galleta (dulce).
cooking ➤ *adj & s* (de) cocina.
cool ➤ *adj* fresco; *(calm)* tranquilo; *(unenthusiastic)* frío; JER. fenomenal ■ **to keep c.** no perder la calma ➤ *tr & intr* refrescar(se), enfriar(se); *(passions)* entibiar(se) ■ **c. it!** JER. ¡cálmate! ➤ *s* frescor *m* ■ **to keep, lose one's c.** conservar, perder la serenidad.
coolant ➤ *s* líquido refrigerante.
cooler ➤ *s* enfriador *m.*
coolness ➤ *s* frescor *m,* fresco; *(calmness)* calma; *(indifference)* frialdad *f.*
coop ➤ *s* gallinero ➤ *tr* ■ **to c. up** enjaular.
cooperate ➤ *intr* cooperar.
cooperative ➤ *adj (joint)* cooperativo; *(helpful)* servicial ➤ *s* cooperativa.
cop ➤ *s* FAM. policía *mf.*
cope ➤ *intr* FAM. arreglárselas *(with* para); *(to face up)* hacer frente *(with* a).
copier ➤ *s* copiadora.
copper ➤ *s* cobre *m* ➤ *adj* (de) cobre; *(color)* cobrizo.
copy ➤ *s* copia; *(book, magazine)* ejemplar *m* ➤ *tr* copiar, sacar en limpio; *(to imitate)* imitar.
coral ➤ *adj & s* (de) coral *m.*
cord ➤ *s* cuerda; ELEC. cordón *m.*
cordial ➤ *adj* amable ➤ *s* cordial *m.*
cordless ➤ *adj* inalámbrico, sin cable.
cordon ➤ *s* cordón *m* ➤ *tr* ■ **to c. off** acordonar.
corduroy ➤ *s* pana ■ *pl* pantalones de pana.
core ➤ *s (essence)* corazón *m,* médula; *(center)* núcleo, foco; *(of fruit)* corazón ➤ *tr* quitar el corazón de.
cork ➤ *s* corcho ➤ *tr* encorchar.
corkscrew ➤ *s* sacacorchos *m.*
corn[1] ➤ *s* maíz *m* ■ **c. flakes** copos de maíz.
corn[2] ➤ *s* MED. callo, callosidad *f.*
corner ➤ *s* esquina; *(inside)* rincón *m; (of eye)* rabillo; *(of mouth)* comisura ■ **to cut corners** hacer economías • **to turn the c.** doblar la esquina; FIG. pasar el punto crítico ➤ *tr (to trap)* arrinconar; COM. monopolizar.
cornice ➤ *s* cornisa.
cornmeal ➤ *s* harina de maíz.
corny ➤ *adj (mawkish)* sensiblero; *(joke)* demasiado obvio.
corporal[1] ➤ *adj* corporal ■ **c. punishment** castigo corporal.
corporal[2] ➤ *s* MIL. cabo *mf.*
corps ➤ *s* cuerpo.
corpse ➤ *s* cuerpo, cadáver *m.*
correct ➤ *tr* corregir; *(to remedy)* remediar; *(to adjust)* ajustar ➤ *adj* correcto ■ **to be c.** tener razón.
correction ➤ *s* corrección *f; (punishment)* castigo; *(adjustment)* ajuste *m.*
correspond ➤ *intr* corresponder; *(to write)* escribirse.
correspondence ➤ *s* correspondencia ■ **c. course** curso por correspondencia.
correspondent ➤ *s* correspondiente *mf;* PERIOD. corresponsal *mf* ➤ *adj* correspondiente.
corridor ➤ *s* pasillo, corredor *m.*
corrugated ➤ *adj (cardboard)* corrugado, ondulado; *(metal)* acanalado.
corrupt ➤ *adj* corrompido; *(dishonest)* corrupto ➤ *tr & intr* corromper(se).
corruption ➤ *s* corrupción *f.*
cosmetic ➤ *s & adj* cosmético.
cost◊ ➤ *s* costo, coste *m; (in time, effort)* costa ■ **at all costs** *o* **at any c.** cueste lo que cueste ■ *pl* gastos; *(risks)* riesgos ➤ *intr* costar.
Costa Rican ➤ *adj & s* costarricense *mf,* costarriqueño/a.
costly ➤ *adj* caro; FIG. costoso.
costume ➤ *s (dress)* traje *m; (disguise)* máscara, disfraz *m* ■ *pl* TEAT. vestuario ➤ *tr* vestir, disfrazar.
cot ➤ *s* catre *m.*
cottage ➤ *s* casa de campo, chalet *m* ■ **c. cheese** requesón, cuajada.
cotton ➤ *s* algodón *m.*
couch ➤ *s* sofá *m* ➤ *tr* expresar.
cough ➤ *intr* toser ➤ *tr* ■ **to c. up** escupir; JER. *(money)* soltar ➤ *s* tos *f* ■ **c. drop** pastilla para la tos.
could ➤ *vea* **can** *en tabla de verbos.*
council ➤ *s* consejo, junta; RELIG. concilio ■ **city c.** concejo municipal.
council(l)or ➤ *s* consejero/a.
counsel(l)or ➤ *s (adviser)* consejero/a; *(lawyer)* abogado/a.
count ➤ *tr* contar; *(to deem)* considerar ■ **to c. against** pesar contra • **to c. for** valer por • **to c. in** incluir • **to c. on** contar con • **to c. out** excluir ➤ *intr* contar; *(to matter)* valer ➤ *s (act)* cuenta; *(number)* cómputo, cálculo.
countdown ➤ *s* cuenta atrás.
counter ➤ *s* mostrador *m; (of a kitchen)* tablero; *(chip, token)* ficha.
counteract ➤ *tr* contrarrestar.
counterclockwise ➤ *adv & adj* en sentido contrario de las agujas del reloj.
counterfeit ➤ *tr* falsificar ➤ *adj* contrahecho, falso ➤ *s* falsificación *f,* imitación *f; (money)* moneda falsa.
counterproductive ➤ *adj* contraproducente.
counting ➤ *s* cuenta, contaje *m.*
country ➤ *s* país *m; (rural area)* campo; *(homeland)* patria ■ **c. house** casa de campo, quinta.
countryside ➤ *s* campo, paisaje *m.*
county ➤ *s* condado, distrito.
couple ➤ *s* par *m; (of people)* pareja; *(several)* unos cuantos ➤ *tr* juntar; TEC. acoplar.
coupon ➤ *s* cupón *m.*
courage ➤ *s* coraje *m,* valor *m* ■ **to take c.** animarse.
courageous ➤ *adj* valiente.
courier ➤ *s* correo, mensajero/a.
course ➤ *s (flow, path)* curso; *(duration)* transcurso; *(of a meal)* plato; *(of studies)* programa *m; (subject)* curso ■ **in due c.** a su debido tiempo • **of c. (not)** claro (que no) • **to change c.** cambiar de rumbo ➤ *intr* correr.
court ➤ *s (royal)* corte *f; (of law)* tribunal *m;* DEP. cancha ■ **c. order** orden judicial ➤ *tr (to curry favor)* cortejar; *(to woo)* enamorar.
courteous ➤ *adj* cortés, atento.
courthouse ➤ *s* palacio de justicia.
courtroom ➤ *s* sala de justicia.
courtship ➤ *s* corte *f; (period)* noviazgo.
courtyard ➤ *s* patio.
cousin ➤ *s* primo/a ■ **first, second c.** primo/a hermano/a, segundo/a.
cover ➤ *tr* cubrir; *(with a lid)* tapar; *(a subject)* tratar; *(to encompass)* abarcar; *(to insure)* asegurar ■ **to c. up** disimular, encubrir ➤ *s* cubierta; *(lid)* tapa; *(of a magazine)* portada; *(bedspread)* sobrecama; *(shelter)* refugio; *(table setting)* cubierto ■ **c. charge** precio del cubierto • **to take c.** refugiarse, ponerse a cubierto • **under c.** clandestinamente ■ *pl* ropa de cama.
coveralls ➤ *spl* mono.
cow ➤ *s* vaca; *(whale, elephant)* hembra.
coward ➤ *s* cobarde *mf.*
cowardice ➤ *s* cobardía.
cowardly ➤ *adj* cobarde ➤ *adv* cobardemente.
cowboy ➤ *s* vaquero.
cozy ➤ *adj* cómodo, calentito.
crab ➤ *s* cangrejo; *(louse)* ladilla.
crabby ➤ *adj* de malas pulgas.
crack ➤ *intr (to break)* romperse; *(to snap)* chasquear; *(bones, knuckles)* crujir; *(to split)* rajarse, agrietarse ■ **to c. down** tomar medidas represivas • **to c. up** *(to wreck)* estrellarse; *(mentally)* chiflarse; *(to laugh)* morirse de risa ➤ *tr* romper; *(to break open)* partir; *(eggs, nuts)* cascar; *(to solve)* solucionar; FAM. *(a joke)* contar ➤ *s (snap)* chasquido; *(of a whip)* restallido; *(split)* rajadura, grieta; *(slit)* rendija ➤ *adj* experto; *(marksman)* certero.
cracker ➤ *s* galleta (salada).
crackpot ➤ *s* chiflado/a, excéntrico/a.
cradle ➤ *s* cuna ➤ *tr* mecer en los brazos.
craft ➤ *s* habilidad *f,* arte *m; (guile)* astucia; *(trade)* oficio; *(boat)* embarcación *f; (airplane)* avión *m.*
craftsman ➤ *s* artesano/a.
craftsmanship ➤ *s* arte *m,* destreza.
cram ➤ *tr (to force)* meter a la fuerza; *(to stuff)* abarrotar, rellenar.
cramp MED. ➤ *s* calambre *m* ■ *pl* retortijones ➤ *intr* ■ **to c. up** acalambrarse.
cramped ➤ *adj* apretado, apiñado.
crane ➤ *s* ORNIT. grulla; TEC. grúa ➤ *tr* estirar (el cuello).
crash ➤ *intr* estrellarse, chocar; *(to break)* hacerse pedazos; *(to resound)* retumbar; COMPUT. colgar, caer ➤ *tr* estrellar; COMPUT. tumbar ➤ *s (noise)* estrépito; *(collision)* choque *m,* colisión *f;* AVIA. caída; COM. *(failure)* ruina; COMPUT. fallo (de sistema).
crash-land ➤ *intr* hacer un aterrizaje forzoso.
crate ➤ *s* cajón *m* ➤ *tr* encajonar.
crave ➤ *tr* ansiar, morirse por.
craving ➤ *s* anhelo, antojo.
crawl ➤ *intr* arrastrarse, reptar; *(baby)* gatear; *(skin)* erizarse ➤ *s* gateado; DEP. crol *m* ■ **at a c.** a paso de tortuga.
crayon ➤ *s & tr* (dibujar al) crayón *m.*
craze ➤ *tr* enloquecer ➤ *s* moda.
crazy ➤ *adj* loco; *(foolish)* de locos, dis-

paratado ■ to be c. about *(person)* estar loco por; *(fad)* estar loco con • to go c. volverse loco.
creak ➤ *intr* crujir, chirriar ➤ *s* crujido, chirrido.
cream ➤ *s* crema ■ c. cheese queso crema • whipped c. nata montada.
crease ➤ *s* pliegue *m; (of trousers)* filo, raya ➤ *tr* plegar.
create ➤ *tr* crear; *(to cause)* producir.
creation ➤ *s* creación *f.*
creator ➤ *s* creador/a.
creature ➤ *s* criatura; *(being)* ente *m,* ser *m; (animal)* bestia, bicho.
credentials ➤ *s* credenciales *f.*
credible ➤ *adj* creíble.
credit ➤ *s* crédito; *(merit)* mérito; *(recognition)* reconocimiento; TEN. haber *m* ■ c. card, line tarjeta, límite de crédito • on c. a crédito ■ *pl* títulos de crédito ➤ *tr (to recognize)* otorgar reconocimiento; *(to attribute)* atribuir.
creek ➤ *s* riachuelo, arroyo ■ up the c. FAM. en apuros.
creep✧ ➤ *intr* arrastrarse, deslizarse; *(to crawl)* gatear; BOT. trepar ■ to c. by pasar lentamente ➤ *s* gateado; *(pace)* paso lento; JER. desgraciado/a, cretino/a ■ *pl* FAM. escalofrío, pavor.
creepy ➤ *adj* FAM. horripilante.
cremate ➤ *tr* incinerar.
crematorium ➤ *s* crematorio.
crepe *o* **crêpe** ➤ *s* crepé *m;* CUL. panqueque *m* ■ c. paper papel crepé.
crest ➤ *s* cresta; *(on a helmet)* penacho, cimera; HER. timbre *m.*
crew ➤ *s* AVIA., MARÍT. tripulación *f;* MIL. dotación *f; (of workers)* equipo ■ c. cut pelado al cepillo.
crib ➤ *s* cuna ➤ *tr* FAM. plagiar ➤ *intr* usar una chuleta.
cricket ➤ *s* ENTOM. grillo.
crime ➤ *s* crimen *m* ■ c. rate criminalidad.
criminal ➤ *adj & s* criminal *mf* ■ c. record antecedentes penales.
crimson ➤ *s* carmesí *m.*
cripple ➤ *s* lisiado/a, cojo/a ➤ *tr* lisiar, tullir; FIG. inutilizar, estropear.
crisis ➤ *s* crisis *f.*
crisp ➤ *adj (crunchy)* tostado, crujiente; *(fresh)* fresco; *(precise)* preciso, claro.
critic ➤ *s* crítico/a.
critical ➤ *adj* crítico; *(carping)* criticón ■ in c. condition grave • to be c. of criticar.
critically ➤ *adv* gravemente.
criticism ➤ *s* crítica.
criticize ➤ *tr & intr* criticar.
crockery ➤ *s* vajilla de barro, loza.
crocodile ➤ *s* cocodrilo.
crocus ➤ *s* azafrán *m.*
crook ➤ *s* ángulo; FAM. *(thief)* tramposo/a, ladrón/ona.
crooked ➤ *adj (road, thief)* torcido; *(nose)* corvo; *(back)* encorvado.
crop ➤ *s* cosecha; *(variety)* cultivo ➤ *tr* cortar, recortar ■ to c. up surgir.
cross ➤ *s* cruz *f; (mixture)* mezcla ➤ *tr* cruzar; FAM. *(to oppose)* contrariar ■ to c. off *o* out tachar • to c. one's arms cruzarse de brazos • to c. oneself santiguarse • to c. over atravesar ➤ *intr* cruzarse ➤ *adj* transversal; *(angry)* de mal humor ■ c. section sección transversal; FIG. muestra representativa.
cross-country ➤ *adj* a campo traviesa; *(flight, drive)* a través del país.
cross-eyed ➤ *adj* bizco.
crossing ➤ *s* cruce *m; (ford)* vado; F.C. paso a nivel.
cross-reference ➤ *s* remisión *f.*
crossroad ➤ *s* vía transversal *f* ■ *pl* encrucijada.
crossword puzzle ➤ *s* crucigrama *m.*
crotch ➤ *s (of tree)* horquilla; ANAT. entrepiernas.
crouch ➤ *intr* agacharse, acuclillarse.
crow[1] ➤ *s* ORNIT. cuervo.
crow[2]✧ ➤ *intr* cantar, cacarear ➤ *s* canto, cacareo.
crowbar ➤ *s* pata de cabra, palanca.
crowd ➤ *s* multitud *f,* muchedumbre *f; (spectators)* público; *(clique)* gente *f* ➤ *intr* apiñarse, amontonarse.
crowded ➤ *adj* lleno, concurrido; *(cramped)* apiñado.
crown ➤ *s* corona; *(of a hat, tree)* copa; *(summit, honor)* cima ➤ *tr* coronar ■ to c. it all para rematar.
crucial ➤ *adj* crucial, decisivo.
crude ➤ *adj (vulgar)* ordinario, grosero; *(rough)* tosco, basto; *(raw)* crudo, bruto ➤ *s (oil)* (petróleo) crudo.
cruel ➤ *adj* cruel, despiadado.
cruelty ➤ *s* crueldad *f.*
cruet ➤ *s* vinagrera, aceitera.
cruise ➤ *intr (to sail)* navegar; *(car)* circular; *(to patrol)* patrullar ➤ *s* crucero.
crumb ➤ *s* miga, migaja.
crumble ➤ *tr & intr* desmigajar(se); FIG. desmoronar(se).
crummy *o* **crumby** ➤ *adj (miserable)* malísimo; *(cheap)* de mala muerte.
crumple ➤ *tr & intr (to crush)* arrugar(se); *(to collapse)* derribar(se).
crunch ➤ *tr* triturar ➤ *intr* crujir ➤ *s* crujido; FAM. *(crisis)* aprieto, crisis *f.*
crunchy ➤ *adj* crujiente.
crusade ➤ *s & intr* (hacer una) cruzada.
crush ➤ *tr (to squash, defeat)* aplastar; *(to squeeze)* exprimir; *(to grind)* triturar, moler ➤ *s* aplastamiento; *(infatuation)* enamoramiento.
crust ➤ *s (bread, pie)* corteza; *(coating, scab)* costra; *(layer)* capa.
crutch ➤ *s* muleta; FIG. sostén *m.*
cry ➤ *intr* llorar; *(to shout)* gritar; *(animals)* aullar ■ to c. for clamar por • to c. over lamentarse por ➤ *s* grito; *(weeping)* llanto; *(entreaty)* petición *f; (peddler's call)* pregón *m.*
crystal ➤ *s* cristal *m* ➤ *adj* de cristal; *(transparent)* cristalino.
cub ➤ *s* cachorro; *(novice)* novato/a.
Cuban ➤ *adj & s* cubano/a.
cube ➤ *s* cubo; *(of sugar)* terrón *m.*
cubicle ➤ *s* compartimiento.
cuckoo ➤ *s (bird)* cuco, cuclillo; *(call)* cucú *m* ➤ *adj* loco, chiflado.
cucumber ➤ *s* pepino.
cuddle ➤ *tr & intr* acurrucar(se).
cuddly ➤ *adj* mimoso.
cue[1] ➤ *s (stick)* taco.
cue[2] ➤ *s* TEAT. pie *m,* señal *f.*
cuff ➤ *s (shirt)* puño; *(pant)* bajos, vuelta ■ c. links gemelos, yugos • off the c. FAM. de improviso.
cuisine ➤ *s* cocina, arte culinario.
culinary ➤ *adj* culinario.
culprit ➤ *s* culpable *mf.*
cult ➤ *s* culto; *(sect)* secta.
cultivate ➤ *tr* cultivar.
cultural ➤ *adj* cultural.
culture ➤ *s* cultura; AGR., BIOL. cultivo.
cultured ➤ *adj* culto; *(pearl)* de cultivo.
cumbersome ➤ *adj* incómodo.
cunning ➤ *adj* astuto, taimado ➤ *s* astucia, habilidad *f.*
cup ➤ *s* taza; DEP. copa ➤ *tr* ahuecar.
cupboard ➤ *s (cabinet)* aparador *m; (closet)* alacena.
curb ➤ *s (of a street)* bordillo; *(restraint)* freno ➤ *tr* refrenar.
cure ➤ *s* cura ➤ *tr & intr* curar(se).
curiosity ➤ *s* curiosidad *f.*
curious ➤ *adj* curioso ■ to be c. to tener deseos de.
curl ➤ *tr & intr* rizar(se), ensortijar(se); ■ to c. up acurrucarse ➤ *s* riza, crespo; *(of smoke)* voluta.
curly ➤ *adj* rizado, crespo.
currency ➤ *s* moneda, dinero (corriente) ■ foreign c. divisas.
current ➤ *adj (present-day)* actual; *(in progress)* corriente, en curso; *(edition)* último ■ c. events actualidades ➤ *s* corriente *f* ■ alternating, direct c. corriente alterna, continua.
currently ➤ *adv* actualmente.
curriculum ➤ *s* programa *m* de estudios ■ c. vitae historial profesional.
curry ➤ *s* CUL. (salsa de) cari *m.*
curse✧ ➤ *s* maldición *f; (scourge)* desgracia, calamidad *f* ➤ *tr* maldecir; *(to afflict)* desgraciar, afligir; *(to swear at)* insultar a ➤ *intr* decir malas palabras.
cursor ➤ *s* cursor *m.*
curtain ➤ *s* cortina; TEAT. telón *m.*
curve ➤ *s* curva ➤ *intr* curvear; *(surface)* doblarse.
cushion ➤ *s* cojín *m,* almohadilla ➤ *tr (to pad)* acolchar; *(a blow)* amortiguar.
custard ➤ *s* natilla ■ caramel c. flan *m.*
custom ➤ *s* costumbre *f* ■ *pl* aduana • to go through c. pasar la aduana ➤ *adj* hecho a la medida.
customary ➤ *adj* acostumbrado, usual.
customer ➤ *s* cliente *mf.*
cut✧ ➤ *tr* cortar; *(to divide)* dividir, repartir; *(to omit)* omitir, excluir; *(to fell)* talar; *(to carve)* tallar; *(the size of)* reducir, acortar; *(time)* abreviar; *(prices)* rebajar; FAM. *(classes)* faltar a ■ c. it out! ¡basta ya! • to c. back reducir, disminuir • to c. off *(to sever)* cortar; *(to shut off)* parar • to c. out *(to remove)* cortar; *(designs)* recortar; *(to delete)* suprimir • to c. up partir ➤ *intr* cortar ■ to be c. out for estar hecho para • to c. down on reducir(se), aminorar • to c. in *(a line of people)* colarse; *(to interrupt)* interrumpir • to c. loose JER. hablar *o* actuar sin cuidarse ➤ *s* corte *m; (reduction)* reducción *f; (discount)* rebaja; FAM. *(share)* tajada, parte *f;* CINEM. corte ■ a c. above mejor que.
cutback ➤ *s* reducción *f.*
cute ➤ *adj* mono; *(contrived)* afectado ■ to get c. with hacerse el listo con.
cuticle ➤ *s* cutícula.
cutlery ➤ *s* cubiertos.
cutlet ➤ *s* chuleta.
cutting ➤ *s* recorte *m* ➤ *adj* cortante; *(remark)* mordaz.
cyberspace ➤ *s* ciberespacio.
cycle ➤ *s* ciclo ➤ *intr* ocurrir cíclicamente; *(to go)* ir en bicicleta.
cyclist ➤ *s (bicycle)* ciclista *mf; (motorcycle)* motociclista *mf.*
cylinder ➤ *s* cilindro.
cynic ➤ *adj & s* cínico/a.
cyst ➤ *s* quiste *m.*

D

dad ➤ *s* FAM. papá *m.*
daddy ➤ *s* FAM. papacito, papito.
daffodil ➤ *s* narciso.
daily ➤ *adj & s* diario ➤ *adv* diariamente, cada día.
dairy ➤ *s* lechería ■ d. farm granja lechera.
daisy ➤ *s* margarita.
dam ➤ *s (barrier)* presa; *(reservoir)* embalse *m* ➤ *tr* embalsar, represar.
damage ➤ *s* daño; *(mechanical)* avería; FIG. perjuicio ■ *pl* daños y perjuicios ➤ *tr & intr* dañar(se), estropear(se).
damn ➤ *tr* condenar; *(to swear at)* maldecir ➤ *interj* ■ d. (it)! ¡maldito sea!, ¡maldición! ➤ *s* ■ I don't give a d. no me importa un comino ➤ *adj* maldito ➤ *adv* FAM. muy.
damnation ➤ *s* condenación *f* ➤ *interj* ¡maldición!
damned ➤ *adj* condenado, maldito ➤ *adv* FAM. muy, sumamente ➤ *s* ■ the d. los condenados.
damp ➤ *adj* húmedo ➤ *s* humedad *f; (gas)* mofeta ➤ *tr* humedecer; *(a fire)* apagar; *(to discourage)* desanimar.
dampen ➤ *tr* humedecer; *(spirit, zeal)* deprimir, disminuir.
dampness ➤ *s* humedad *f.*
dance ➤ *tr & intr* bailar ➤ *s* baile *m.*
dancer ➤ *s* bailador/a; *(ballet)* bailarín/ina.
dandelion ➤ *s* diente *m* de león.
dandruff ➤ *s* caspa.
danger ➤ *s* peligro.
dangerous ➤ *adj* peligroso.
dare ➤ *intr* osar, atreverse ➤ *tr* retar, desafiar ■ I d. say me parece probable ➤ *s* desafío, reto.
daring ➤ *adj* temerario, audaz ➤ *s* audacia, atrevimiento.
dark ➤ *adj* oscuro; *(skin)* moreno, morocho; *(dismal)* triste; *(evil)* siniestro; *(unknown)* misterioso ➤ *s* oscuridad *f; (nightfall)* anochecer *m,* noche *f* ■ to be in the d. no estar informado.
darkness ➤ *s* oscuridad *f.*
darling ➤ *s* querido/a, amado/a; *(favorite)* predilecto/a ➤ *adj* querido, amado; FAM. adorable.
dart ➤ *intr* correr, lanzarse ➤ *tr* lanzar, arrojar ➤ *s* dardo, saeta.
dash ➤ *tr (to smash)* estrellar, romper; *(to spoil)* arruinar, frustrar ■ to d. off hacer rápidamente ➤ *intr* correr, lanzarse ■ to d. in, out entrar, salir corriendo ➤ *s (bit)* pizca; *(rush)* prisa; *(race)* carrera corta; AUTO. salpicadero.
dashboard ➤ *s* salpicadero.
data ➤ *spl o sg* información *f,* datos ■ d. bank base *o* banco de datos • d. processing procesamiento de datos • d. processor ordenador, computadora.
database ➤ *s* base *f* de datos.
date[1] ➤ *s* fecha; *(appointment)* cita, compromiso; *(companion)* acompañante *mf* ➤ *tr & intr* fechar; *(socially)* salir (con) ■ to d. back to remontar(se) a • to d. from datar de.
date[2] ➤ *s (fruit)* dátil *m* ■ d. palm datilero.
daughter ➤ *s* hija.
daughter-in-law ➤ *s* nuera, hija política.
dawdle ➤ *intr* demorarse.
dawn ➤ *s* amanecer *m,* alba ➤ *intr* amanecer ■ it dawned on me caí en la cuenta.
day ➤ *s* día *m; (workday)* jornada; *(epoch)* época ■ day-care center guardería • d. in, d. out día tras día • the d. after al día siguiente • the d. before . . . la víspera de . . . • these days hoy en día.
daybreak ➤ *s* amanecer *m,* alba.
daylight ➤ *s* luz *f* del día; *(dawn)* amanecer *m; (daytime)* día *m.*
daytime ➤ *s* día *m.*
dead ➤ *adj* muerto; *(dull)* triste, aburrido; ELEC. sin corriente; *(battery)* descargado ■ d. center, weight punto, peso muerto • d. end callejón sin salida ➤ *s* muerto ■ the d. los muertos • the d. of night, winter plena noche, pleno invierno.
dead-end ➤ *adj* sin salida.
deadline ➤ *s* fecha tope, plazo.
deadly ➤ *adj* mortífero, mortal; *(dull)* pesado.
deaf ➤ *adj* sordo.
deafness ➤ *s* sordera.
deal✧ ➤ *tr* repartir, distribuir ➤ *intr* comerciar (*in* en) ■ to d. with COM. tratar con; *(a situation)* enfrentarse con; *(to treat)* tratar de *o* sobre ➤ *s (agreement)* arreglo, convenio; *(in cards)* reparto; FAM. *(dealings)* trato ■ a good *o* great d. mucho • big d.! ¡gran cosa! • it's a d.! ¡trato hecho!
dealer ➤ *s* negociante *mf,* traficante *mf.*
dealings ➤ *spl (business)* negocios; *(relations)* trato.
dean ➤ *s* EDUC. decano/a; RELIG. deán *m.*
dear ➤ *adj* querido; *(esteemed)* estimado; *(precious)* valioso; *(costly)* caro ■ D. Sir Estimado señor mío ➤ *adv* caro ➤ *s* querido/a.
death ➤ *s* muerte *f* ■ d. certificate partida de defunción • d. penalty pena de muerte • d. rate índice de mortalidad • to put to d. ejecutar.
debate ➤ *tr & intr* discutir, debatir ➤ *s* discusión *f,* debate *m.*
debit ➤ *s* débito, debe *m* ■ d. balance saldo deudor ➤ *tr* cargar en cuenta.
debt ➤ *s* deuda.
debtor ➤ *s* deudor/a.
decade ➤ *s* decenio, década.
decay ➤ *intr* pudrirse, descomponerse; *(a tooth)* cariarse; FÍS. desintegrarse; FIG. decaer ➤ *s* descomposición *f; (of a tooth)* caries *f;* FÍS. desintegración *f; (of morals)* decadencia.
deceased ➤ *adj & s* difunto/a.
deceit ➤ *s* engaño, fraude *m.*
deceive ➤ *tr & intr* engañar.
December ➤ *s* diciembre *m.*
decent ➤ *adj* decente; *(kind)* bueno.
decide ➤ *tr & intr* decidir.
decimal ➤ *s & adj* decimal *m* ■ d. point coma.
decision ➤ *s* decisión *f.*
decisive ➤ *adj* decisivo.
deck ➤ *s* cubierta; *(of cards)* baraja ■ to clear the d. prepararse para la acción.
declaration ➤ *s* declaración *f.*
declare ➤ *tr* declarar ➤ *intr* hacer una declaración.
decline ➤ *tr* rehusar ➤ *intr (to slope)* inclinarse; *(health)* deteriorarse.
decongestant ➤ *s* descongestionante *m.*
decorate ➤ *tr* decorar; *(with medals)* condecorar.
decoration ➤ *s* decoración *f; (medal)* condecoración *f.*
decorative ➤ *adj* decorativo.
decorator ➤ *s* decorador/a.
decrease ➤ *intr & tr* disminuir, reducir ➤ *s* disminución *f.*
dedicate ➤ *tr* dedicar.
dedication ➤ *s* dedicación *f; (inscription)* dedicatoria.
deduct ➤ *tr* restar, substraer.
deduction ➤ *s* deducción *f.*
deed ➤ *s* acto, hecho; *(feat)* proeza; DER. *(title)* escritura (de propiedad) ➤ *tr* traspasar por escritura.
deem ➤ *tr* considerar, juzgar.
deep ➤ *adj* profundo; *(colors)* subido; MÚS. bajo, grave ■ d. down en el fondo • to go off the d. end ponerse histérico • two meters d. dos metros de profundidad ➤ *adv* profundamente, en lo más hondo ➤ *s* profundidad *f; (of*

night, winter) lo más profundo.
deer ➤ *s* ciervo, venado.
defeat ➤ *tr* derrotar, vencer ➤ *s (loss)* derrota; *(failure)* fracaso.
defect ➤ *s* defecto ➤ *intr* desertar.
defective ➤ *adj* defectuoso; *(subnormal)* deficiente; GRAM. defectivo.
defend ➤ *tr* defender; *(to justify)* justificar ➤ *intr* hacer una defensa.
defendant ➤ *s* acusado/a.
defender ➤ *s* defensor/a.
defense ➤ *s* defensa.
defiant ➤ *adj* provocador, desafiante.
deficient ➤ *adj* deficiente, carente.
deficit ➤ *s* déficit *f.*
define ➤ *tr* definir.
definite ➤ *adj* definido; *(certain)* definitivo; *(explicit)* claro, explícito.
definitely ➤ *adv* definitivamente.
definition ➤ *s* definición *f; (of power, authority)* limitación *f.*
deformed ➤ *adj* deforme, desfigurado.
defrost ➤ *tr & intr* descongelar(se).
defy ➤ *tr* desafiar; *(to resist)* resistir.
degenerate ➤ *adj & s* degenerado/a ➤ *intr* degenerar.
degree ➤ *s* grado; EDUC. título ■ **by degrees** gradualmente, poco a poco • **to a certain d.** hasta cierto punto • **to take a d. in** licenciarse en.
dejected ➤ *adj* desanimado.
delay ➤ *tr (to postpone)* postergar; *(to make late)* retrasar, demorar ➤ *intr* demorarse, tardar ➤ *s* demora, retraso.
delegate ➤ *s* delegado/a ➤ *tr* delegar.
delegation ➤ *s* delegación *f.*
delete ➤ *tr* tachar, suprimir.
deliberate ➤ *adj* deliberado; *(slow)* pausado ➤ *intr & tr* deliberar.
delicacy ➤ *s* delicadeza; *(fine food)* manjar *m,* gollería.
delicate ➤ *adj* delicado.
delicatessen ➤ *s* fiambrería.
delicious ➤ *adj* delicioso.
delight ➤ *s* deleite *m; (person, thing)* encanto ➤ *tr* deleitar, encantar.
delighted ➤ *adj* encantado.
delightful ➤ *adj* delicioso, encantador.
delinquent ➤ *adj* delincuente; *(in payment)* moroso ➤ *s* delincuente *mf.*
deliver ➤ *tr (to free)* liberar; *(to hand over)* entregar; *(a blow, speech)* dar; *(baby)* asistir al parto de ➤ *intr* cumplir (*on* con); *(to give birth)* alumbrar ■ **we d.** entregamos a domicilio.
delivery ➤ *s* entrega; *(release)* liberación *f; (birth)* parto; *(style)* elocución *f.*
delude ➤ *tr* engañar, despistar.
delusion ➤ *s* engaño, ilusión *f.*
deluxe *o* **de luxe** ➤ *adj* de lujo, lujoso.
demand ➤ *tr (to ask for)* demandar; *(to claim, require)* reclamar, exigir ➤ *s (request)* solicitud *f; (claim)* reclamación *f; (requirement)* necesidad *f;* COM. demanda ■ **on d.** COM. a la vista • **to be in d.** ser popular.
demanding ➤ *adj* exigente.
democracy ➤ *s* democracia.
democrat ➤ *s* demócrata *mf.*
democratic ➤ *adj* democrático.
demolish ➤ *tr* demoler, derribar.
demolition ➤ *s* demolición *f.*
demonstrate ➤ *tr* demostrar ➤ *intr* protestar, manifestarse.
demonstration ➤ *s* demostración *f; (rally)* manifestación *f.*
demonstrative ➤ *adj* demostrativo; *(expressive)* expresivo, efusivo.
demonstrator ➤ *s* manifestante *mf.*
demoralize ➤ *tr* desmoralizar.
den ➤ *s (lair)* cubil *m; (study)* estudio.
denial ➤ *s* negativa; *(disavowal)* repudio; DER. denegación *f.*
denim ➤ *s* denim *m,* dril *m* de algodón.
denomination ➤ *s* denominación *f; (sect)* secta.
denounce ➤ *tr* denunciar.
dense ➤ *adj* denso.
dent ➤ *s* abolladura, mella ➤ *tr & intr* abollar(se), mellar(se).
dental ➤ *adj* dental.
dentist ➤ *s* dentista *mf.*
denture ➤ *s* dentadura postiza.
deny ➤ *tr* negar; *(to withhold)* rehusar; *(to repudiate)* repudiar ■ **to d. oneself** privarse de.
deodorant ➤ *s* desodorante *m.*
depart ➤ *intr* marcharse, irse; *(train, bus)* salir ➤ *tr* partir de.
department ➤ *s* departamento; POL. ministerio ■ **d. store** gran almacén.
departure ➤ *s* partida, salida; *(deviation)* desviación *f.*
depend ➤ *intr* ■ **to d. (up)on** *(as a dependent, consequence)* depender de; *(to trust)* confiar en, fiar; *(to count on)* contar con.
dependable ➤ *adj (trustworthy)* (digno) de confianza; *(reliable)* seguro.
dependent ➤ *adj* ■ **d. (up)on** dependiente de ➤ *s* persona a cargo.
depict ➤ *tr* representar, pintar.
deplorable ➤ *adj* deplorable.
deplore ➤ *tr* deplorar, desaprobar.
deposit ➤ *tr* depositar; COM. *(down payment)* dar de señal ➤ *s* depósito; *(down payment)* señal *f,* entrada.
depot ➤ *s (bus, train)* estación *f; (warehouse)* almacén *m,* depósito.
depress ➤ *tr* deprimir, desanimar; *(button)* presionar; *(prices)* bajar.
depressed ➤ *adj* deprimido; *(economy)* deprimido.
depression ➤ *s (a hollow)* cavidad *f,* hueco; ECON., MED. depresión *f.*
deprive ➤ *tr* privar (*of* de).
deprived ➤ *adj* pobre, necesitado.
depth ➤ *s* profundidad *f; (most intense part)* lo más profundo; *(color)* intensidad *f* ■ **in d.** a fondo.
deputy ➤ *s* delegado/a; POL. diputado/a.
derail ➤ *tr & intr* (hacer) descarrilar.
derelict ➤ *s (person)* vago/a; *(ship)* derrelicto ➤ *adj (remiss)* remiso; *(property)* abandonado.
derive ➤ *tr & intr* derivar (*from* de).
descend ➤ *tr & intr* descender.
descendant ➤ *s* descendiente *mf.*
descent ➤ *s* descenso; *(slope)* declive *m; (lineage)* descendencia.
describe ➤ *tr* describir.
description ➤ *s* descripción *f.*
desert[1] ➤ *s* desierto ➤ *adj* desértico.
desert[2] ➤ *tr* abandonar; MIL. desertar de ➤ *intr* desertar.
deserve ➤ *tr & intr* merecer(se).
design ➤ *tr (to invent)* idear; *(a plan)* diseñar; *(pattern)* dibujar ➤ *intr* hacer diseños ➤ *s* diseño; ARQ. plano; *(intention)* propósito ■ **by d.** intencionalmente • **to have designs on** poner las miras en.
designer ➤ *s* diseñador/a.
desirable ➤ *adj* deseable.
desire ➤ *tr* desear ➤ *s* deseo.
desk ➤ *s* escritorio; *(at school)* pupitre *m; (in hotel)* recepción *f; (counter, booth)* mesa.
desktop publishing ➤ *s* autoedición *f.*
despair ➤ *s* desesperación *f* ➤ *intr* desesperar(se).
desperation ➤ *s* desesperación *f.*
despicable ➤ *adj* odioso, vil.
despise ➤ *tr* despreciar.
despite ➤ *prep* a pesar de, no obstante.
dessert ➤ *s* CUL. postre *m.*
destination ➤ *s* destino.
destine ➤ *tr* destinar.
destiny ➤ *s* destino.
destitute ➤ *adj* indigente.
destroy ➤ *tr* destruir.
destruction ➤ *s* destrucción *f.*
destructive ➤ *adj* destructivo, destructor ■ **d. of** *o* **to** perjudicial para.
detach ➤ *tr* separar, desprender.
detachable ➤ *adj* desmontable.
detached ➤ *adj* separado; *(aloof)* indiferente, despreocupado.
detachment ➤ *s* separación *f; (impartiality)* objetividad *f.*
detail ➤ *s* detalle *m,* pormenor *m;* MIL. destacamento ➤ *tr* detallar.
detailed ➤ *adj* detallado, minucioso.
detain ➤ *tr (to delay)* retardar, demorar; *(in custody)* detener.
detect ➤ *tr* percibir, detectar.
detective ➤ *s* detective *mf.*
detector ➤ *s* detector *m.*
detention ➤ *s* detención *f.*
deter ➤ *tr* impedir.
detergent ➤ *s* detergente *m.*
deteriorate ➤ *intr* empeorar, degenerar.
determination ➤ *s* determinación *f; (resolve)* resolución *f;* DER. decisión *f.*
determine ➤ *tr* determinar ➤ *intr* decidir.
determined ➤ *adj* determinado.
deterrent ➤ *s* agente disuasivo ➤ *adj* impeditivo.
detour ➤ *s* desvío ➤ *tr & intr* desviar(se).
develop ➤ *tr* desarrollar; *(the body)* fortalecer; *(an ability)* formar; *(land)* urbanizar; FOTOG. revelar ➤ *intr* desarrollarse; *(to advance)* progresar.
development ➤ *s* desarrollo; *(event)* suceso; FOTOG. revelado.
deviate ➤ *intr* desviarse.
device ➤ *s* dispositivo, aparato.
devil ➤ *s* diablo ■ **d.'s advocate** abogado del diablo.
devise ➤ *tr (to conceive)* idear, concebir; *(to contrive)* trazar, tramar.
devote ➤ *tr* dedicar, consagrar.
devoted ➤ *adj (loving)* afectuoso; *(dedicated)* devoto; *(ardent)* fervoroso.
devotion ➤ *s* devoción *f.*
devour ➤ *tr* devorar.
dew ➤ *s* rocío ■ **d. point** punto de condensación.
diabetes ➤ *s* diabetes *f.*
diabetic ➤ *adj & s* diabético/a.
diagnosis ➤ *s* diagnóstico.
diagonal ➤ *adj & s* diagonal *f.*
diagram ➤ *s* diagrama *m* ➤ *tr* representar con un diagrama.
dial ➤ *s (scale, clock)* esfera, cuadrante *m;* RAD., TELEV. dial *m,* botón *m* selector ■ **d. tone** TEL. tono para marcar ➤ *tr* TEL. marcar (un número).
dialect ➤ *s* dialecto.
dialogue ➤ *s* diálogo.
diameter ➤ *s* diámetro.
diamond ➤ *s (jewel, cards)* diamante *m; (shape)* rombo.
diaper ➤ *s* pañal *m* ➤ *tr* poner el pañal a.
diarrhea ➤ *s* diarrea.
diary ➤ *s* diario.
dice ➤ *spl* dados ➤ *tr* picar en cubitos.
dictate ➤ *tr (letter)* dictar; *(policy)* imponer ➤ *intr* mandar ➤ *s* mandato ■ *pl* dictados.
dictation ➤ *s* dictado.
dictator ➤ *s* dictador/a.
dictionary ➤ *s* diccionario.
did ➤ *vea* **do** *en la tabla de verbos.*
didn't ➤ *contr de* **did not.**
die ➤ *intr* morir; *(to lose force)* apagarse, disminuir; *(to become extinct)* extinguirse, desaparecer.
diesel engine ➤ *s* motor *m* diesel.
diet ➤ *s & intr* (estar a) dieta.
differ ➤ *intr* disentir, diferenciar (*with* de) ■ **to d. from** diferenciarse de.
difference ➤ *s* diferencia ■ **it makes no d.** da lo mismo • **what d. does it make?** ¿qué más da?
different ➤ *adj* diferente, distinto.
difficult ➤ *adj* difícil.
difficulty ➤ *s* dificultad *f* ■ *pl* apuros.
dig◊ ➤ *tr* cavar, excavar; *(well, tunnel)* hacer, abrir ■ **to d. in(to)** hincar, hundir en • **to d. out** *(hole)* excavar; *(object)* extraer • **to d. up** *(object)* extraer, desenterrar; *(facts)* descubrir ➤ *intr* cavar ■ **to d. for** buscar • **to d. in** atrincherarse; FAM. *(to eat)* atacar ➤ *s (with the elbow)* codazo; *(gibe)* pulla; ARQUEOL. excavación *f.*
digest ➤ *tr & intr* digerir(se) ➤ *s* compendio, sinopsis *f.*
digestion ➤ *s* digestión *f.*
digit ➤ *s* ANAT. dedo; MAT. dígito.
digital ➤ *adj* digital.
dignity ➤ *s* dignidad *f.*
dilapidated ➤ *adj* desvencijado.
dilute ➤ *tr* diluir, desleír ➤ *adj* diluido.
dim ➤ *adj (dark)* oscuro; *(lights)* bajo, débil; *(outline)* borroso; *(memory)* vago; *(person)* de pocas luces ■ **to take a d. view of** ver de modo poco favorable ➤ *tr* oscurecer; *(lights)* bajar ➤ *intr* oscurecerse; *(lights)* perder intensidad; *(outline, memory)* borrarse.
dime ➤ *s* E.U. moneda de diez centavos.
dimension ➤ *s* dimensión *f.*
diminish ➤ *tr & intr* disminuir(se).
din ➤ *s* estrépito; *(of a crowd)* clamoreo.
dine ➤ *intr* cenar.
diner ➤ *s* comensal *mf;* F.C. vagón *m* restaurante; *(restaurant)* restaurante *m* popular.
dinghy ➤ *s* bote *m* (de remo).
dingy ➤ *adj* sórdido, sucio.
dining ➤ *adj* ■ **d. car** vagón restaurante • **d. hall** refectorio • **d. room** comedor.
dinner ➤ *s* cena; *(at noon)* comida (principal); *(formal)* banquete *m* ■ **d. jacket** smoking.
dinosaur ➤ *s* dinosaurio.
dip ➤ *tr (to immerse)* sumergir, meter; *(to lower)* inclinar, bajar ➤ *intr (to plunge)* sumergirse; *(prices, road)* bajar ■ **to d. into** *(a subject)* meterse en; *(a book)* hojear; *(savings)* echar mano a ➤ *s* immersión *f; (swim)* chapuzón *m; (slope, drop)* bajada; *(hollow)* depresión *f;* CUL. salsa.
diphtheria ➤ *s* difteria.
diploma ➤ *s* diploma *m.*
diplomacy ➤ *s* diplomacia.
diplomat ➤ *s* diplomático/a.
direct ➤ *tr* dirigir; *(to order)* ordenar ➤ *adj* directo; *(candid)* franco ➤ *adv* directamente.
direction ➤ *s* dirección *f; (order)* orden *f* ■ *pl* instrucciones.
directly ➤ *adv* directamente; *(immediately)* inmediatamente.
director ➤ *s* director/a.
directory ➤ *s* directorio ■ **telephone d.** guía telefónica • **d. assistance** información telefónica.
dirt ➤ *s* tierra; *(grime)* mugre *f; (filth)* suciedad; *(smut)* porquería.
dirty ➤ *adj* sucio; *(joke)* verde; *(language)* grosero ■ **d. language** groserías • **d. trick** mala jugada • **d. work** trabajo pesado ➤ *tr & intr* ensuciar(se).
disability ➤ *s* discapacidad *f,* incapacidad *f,* invalidez *f.*
disable ➤ *tr* discapacitar, incapacitar; *(vehicle)* averiar.
disabled ➤ *adj* discapacitado, incapacitado; *(vehicle)* averiado.
disadvantage ➤ *s* desventaja, inconveniente *m.*
disagree ➤ *intr* no estar de acuerdo, estar en desacuerdo; *(food)* sentar mal; *(to quarrel)* reñir.
disagreeable ➤ *adj* desagradable.
disagreement ➤ *s* desacuerdo; *(quarrel)* riña.
disappear ➤ *intr* desaparecer.
disappearance ➤ *s* desaparición *f.*
disappoint ➤ *tr* decepcionar, desilusionar; *(to fail to please)* defraudar.
disappointing ➤ *adj* decepcionante.
disappointment ➤ *s* desilusión *f,* decepción *f; (in love)* desengaño.
disapproval ➤ *s* desaprobación *f.*
disapprove ➤ *tr* desaprobar.
disarm ➤ *tr & intr* desarmar(se).
disaster ➤ *s* desastre *m.*
disc ➤ *s* disco ■ **d. jockey** animador/a.
discard ➤ *tr (cards)* descartar; *(clothing, books)* desechar ➤ *intr* descartarse ➤ *s* descarte *m.*
discharge ➤ *tr* descargar; *(soldiers)* licenciar; *(patients)* dar de alta; *(pus)* arrojar; *(duty)* desempeñar, ejecutar ➤ *s* descarga; *(emission)* escape *m; (secretion)* secreción *f; (flow)* flujo; *(from hospital)* alta; *(of soldiers)* licenciamiento.
disciple ➤ *s* discípulo/a.
discipline ➤ *s* disciplina; *(punishment)* castigo ➤ *tr* disciplinar; *(to punish)* castigar.
disclose ➤ *tr* divulgar, revelar.
disco ➤ *s* (baile *m* de) discoteca.
discomfort ➤ *s* molestia, malestar *m.*
disconnected ➤ *adj* desconectado; *(unrelated)* sin relación; *(illogical)* inconexo.
discontented ➤ *adj* descontento.
discontinue ➤ *tr* discontinuar.
discount ➤ *tr* descontar ➤ *s* descuento, rebaja ■ **d. rate** tasa de descuento.
discourage ➤ *tr* desanimar, desalentar; *(to hinder)* no fomentar ■ **to d. from** disuadir *o* recomendar que no.
discourse ➤ *s* discurso ➤ *intr* conversar (*on* sobre).
discover ➤ *tr* descubrir.
discovery ➤ *s* descubrimiento.
discreet ➤ *adj* discreto.
discretion ➤ *s* discreción *f* ■ **at the d. of** a juicio de, según el deseo de.
discrimination ➤ *s (prejudice)* discriminación *f; (perception)* discernimiento; *(distinction)* distinción *f.*
discuss ➤ *tr (to talk over)* hablar de *o* sobre; *(formally)* discutir, tratar.
discussion ➤ *s (conversation)* discusión *f; (discourse)* disertación *f.*
disease ➤ *s* enfermedad *f.*
disembark ➤ *tr & intr* desembarcar.
disfigure ➤ *tr* desfigurar, afear.
disgrace ➤ *s* deshonra; *(ignominy)* ignominia ➤ *tr* deshonrar.
disgraceful ➤ *adj* vergonzoso.
disguise ➤ *s* disfraz *m* ➤ *tr* disfrazar.
disgust ➤ *tr* repugnar, asquear ➤ *s* repugnancia, asco.
disgusted ➤ *adj* asqueado, repugnado.
disgusting ➤ *adj* repugnante, asqueroso.
dish ➤ *s* plato; RAD., TELEV. disco (de

antena) ➤ *tr* ■ **to d. out** *(food)* servir; *(advice, abuse)* repartir, dar.
dishonest ➤ *adj* deshonesto, deshonrado; *(dealings)* fraudulento.
dishonor ➤ *s* deshonra; *(shame)* vergüenza ➤ *tr* deshonrar.
dishwasher ➤ *s* lavaplatos *m.*
disillusion ➤ *tr* desilusionar.
disillusionment ➤ *s* desilusión *f.*
disincentive ➤ *s* falta de incentivo.
disinfect ➤ *tr* desinfectar.
disinfectant ➤ *s & adj* desinfectante *m.*
disk ➤ *s* disco ■ **d. drive** COMPUT. unidad de disco • **d. jockey** animador/a.
diskette ➤ *s* disco, diskette *m.*
dislike ➤ *tr* tener aversión a, no gustarle a uno ➤ *s* antipatía, aversión *f.*
dislocate ➤ *tr* dislocar.
dismal ➤ *adj* triste, deprimente.
dismantle ➤ *tr (to tear down)* desmantelar; *(to disassemble)* desarmar.
dismay ➤ *tr (to upset)* consternar; *(to dishearten)* desalentar ➤ *s* consternación *f,* desaliento.
dismiss ➤ *tr* dar permiso para salir; *(employee)* despedir; *(officials)* destituir.
dismissal ➤ *s* despido; *(official)* destitución *f;* DER. desestimación *f.*
disobedient ➤ *adj* desobediente.
disobey ➤ *tr & intr* desobedecer.
disorder ➤ *s* desorden *m;* MED. trastorno ➤ *tr* desordenar.
disorganize ➤ *tr* desorganizar.
dispatch ➤ *tr* despachar ➤ *s* despacho; *(speed)* diligencia.
dispel ➤ *tr* disipar.
disperse ➤ *tr & intr* dispersar(se).
displace ➤ *tr* desplazar; *(to supplant)* substituir, suplantar ■ **displaced person** persona expatriada.
display ➤ *tr* exhibir, mostrar; *(to show off)* ostentar ➤ *s* exhibición *f; (ostentation)* ostentación *f;* COMPUT. representación *f* visual.
displease ➤ *tr & intr* desagradar.
disposal ➤ *s* disposición *f; (of waste)* eliminación *f* ■ **at your d.** a su disposición.
dispose ➤ *tr* disponer ■ **to d. of** *(property, business)* despachar; *(waste)* eliminar, desechar.
disposed ➤ *adj* dispuesto.
disposition ➤ *s* disposición *f.*
dispute ➤ *tr* disputar; *(to doubt)* cuestionar; *(in court)* litigar, contender ➤ *intr* disputar, discutir; *(to quarrel)* pelear ➤ *s (debate)* disputa; *(conflict)* conflicto; *(quarrel)* pelea, riña.
disqualify ➤ *tr* descalificar.
disregard ➤ *tr* no hacer caso de, desatender ➤ *s* desatención *f,* negligencia.
disrespect ➤ *s* falta de respeto, descortesía ➤ *tr* faltar el respeto.
disrupt ➤ *tr* interrumpir.
disruption ➤ *s* interrupción *f.*
dissatisfaction ➤ *s* descontento.
dissertation ➤ *s (discourse)* disertación *f; (thesis)* tesis *f.*
dissolve ➤ *tr & intr* disolver(se).
dissuade ➤ *tr* disuadir.
distance ➤ *s* distancia; *(stretch)* trecho, tirada; *(coolness)* reserva ■ **at** *o* **from a d.** a (la) distancia • **in the d.** a lo lejos ➤ *tr* alejar, distanciar.
distant ➤ *adj* distante, alejado; *(in relationship)* lejano; *(aloof)* reservado.
distasteful ➤ *adj* desagradable.
distinct ➤ *adj* distinto; *(clear)* claro; *(unquestionable)* marcado, indudable.
distinction ➤ *s* distinción *f.*
distinctive ➤ *adj* distintivo.
distinguish ➤ *tr & intr* distinguir.
distort ➤ *tr* distorsionar; *(to misrepresent)* tergiversar, alterar.
distortion ➤ *s* distorsión *f; (misrepresentation)* tergiversación *f.*
distract ➤ *tr* distraer.
distraction ➤ *s* distracción *f.*
distraught ➤ *adj* aturdido, turbado.
distress ➤ *s (suffering)* aflicción *f,* pena; *(anxiety)* ansiedad *f* ➤ *tr* afligir.
distribute ➤ *tr* distribuir.
distribution ➤ *s* distribución *f,* reparto.
distributor ➤ *s* distribuidor/a.
district ➤ *s* región *f,* comarca; *(of a city)* zona, barrio; POL. distrito ■ **d. attorney** fiscal • **d. court** tribunal federal.
distrust ➤ *s* desconfianza, recelo ➤ *tr* desconfiar de, sospechar.
disturb ➤ *tr (to alter)* perturbar; *(to upset)* turbar, trastornar; *(to interrupt)* interrumpir; *(to bother)* molestar ■ **do not d.** no molestar.
disturbance ➤ *s* perturbación *f; (worry)* trastorno; *(interruption)* interrupción *f; (bother)* molestia; *(disorder)* desorden *m; (riot)* disturbio.
ditch ➤ *s* zanja; *(irrigation)* acequia; *(drainage)* canal *m; (of a road)* cuneta ➤ *tr* FAM. abandonar.
dive✧ ➤ *intr (headfirst)* zambullirse (de cabeza); DEP. saltar; *(scuba)* bucear; *(to plummet)* caer a plomo ➤ *s (headfirst)* zambullida; DEP. salto; *(plane)* picado; *(submarine)* sumersión *f.*
diver ➤ *s* DEP. saltador/a; *(underwater)* buzo, buceador/a.
diversion ➤ *s* diversión *f.*
diversity ➤ *s* diversidad *f,* variedad *f.*
divert ➤ *tr* divertir; *(to turn aside)* desviar.
divide ➤ *tr & intr* dividir(se) ■ **to d. up** *(to apportion)* repartir.
dividend ➤ *s* dividendo.
divine ➤ *adj* divino.
diving ➤ *s* DEP. salto; *(scuba)* buceo ■ **d. board** trampolín • **d. suit** escafandra.
division ➤ *s* división *f; (section)* sección *f,* departamento.
divorce ➤ *s* divorcio ➤ *tr & intr* divorciarse (de).
divorcé ➤ *s* divorciado ■ **divorcée** divorciada.
dizziness ➤ *s* vértigo, mareo.
dizzy ➤ *adj* mareado; *(speed, height)* vertiginoso ➤ *tr* marear, dar vértigo.
do✧ ➤ *tr* hacer; *(dishes)* fregar; *(justice, homage)* rendir, tributar; *(to work on)* trabajar en; JER. *(drugs)* tomar, usar ■ **to do again** *o* **over** volver a hacer, hacer de nuevo • **to do away with** eliminar • **to do in** JER. *(to kill)* liquidar; *(to exhaust)* agotar, cansar • **what can I do for you?** ¿en qué puedo servirle? ➤ *intr (to perform)* obrar, actuar; *(to get along)* andar, irle a uno; *(to serve the purpose)* servir ■ **how do you do?** ¿cómo está usted? • **that will do!** ¡basta ya! ➤ *s (hairdo)* peinado.
dock ➤ *s* muelle *m,* embarcadero ➤ *tr & intr (ship)* (hacer) atracar al muelle; *(spacecraft)* acoplar(se).
doctor ➤ *s* médico/a, doctor/a; EDUC. doctor/a ➤ *tr (to treat)* tratar, atender; *(to falsify)* adulterar.
doctorate ➤ *s* doctorado.
document ➤ *s* documento ➤ *tr* documentar, probar con documentos.
documentary ➤ *adj & s* documental *m.*
dodge ➤ *tr* esquivar ➤ *intr* echarse a un lado ➤ *s* regate *m.*
does ➤ *vea* **do** *en tabla de verbos.*
dog ➤ *s* perro; *(scoundrel)* canalla *mf* ➤ *tr* perseguir, seguir.
doll ➤ *s* muñeca.
dollar ➤ *s* dólar *m.*
dolphin ➤ *s* ZOOL. delfín *m; (fish)* dorado.
domain ➤ *s* dominio; FIG. campo.
dome ➤ *s* cúpula, domo.
domestic ➤ *adj* doméstico; *(home-loving)* casero; ECON. nacional.
dominant ➤ *adj & s* dominante *f.*
dominate ➤ *tr & intr* dominar.
Dominican ➤ *adj & s* dominicano/a.
dominion ➤ *s* dominio.
domino ➤ *s (game piece)* ficha ■ *pl (game)* dominó.
donate ➤ *tr* donar.
donation ➤ *s (act)* donación *f; (gift)* donativo.
done ➤ *adj* terminado, hecho; CUL. cocido, hecho ■ **d. for** FAM. vencido • **well d.!** ¡muy bien!
donkey ➤ *s* burro, asno.
donor ➤ *s* donador/a, donante *mf.*
don't ➤ *contr de* **do not.**
door ➤ *s* puerta; AUTO. portezuela.
doorbell ➤ *s* timbre *m.*
doorknob ➤ *s* perilla.
doorman ➤ *s* portero.
doormat ➤ *s* felpudo, estera.
doorway ➤ *s* puerta, entrada.
dope ➤ *s* FAM. narcótico, droga; JER. *(dolt)* tonto/a; *(information)* datos.
dorm ➤ *s* FAM. *(room)* dormitorio; *(building)* residencia para estudiantes.
dormitory ➤ *s (room)* dormitorio; *(building)* residencia.
dosage ➤ *s* dosificación *f; (amount)* dosis *f.*
dose ➤ *s* dosis *f* ➤ *tr* medicinar.
dot ➤ *s* punto ■ **d. matrix** matriz de puntos • **on the d.** FAM. *(on time)* a la hora; *(o'clock)* en punto ➤ *tr* poner el punto a; *(to scatter)* salpicar ■ **dotted line** línea de puntos.
double ➤ *adj* doble ■ **d. take** reacción tardía • **d. talk** lenguaje ambiguo ➤ *s* doble *m* ■ **on the d.** FAM. con toda rapidez ➤ *tr* doblar; *(to repeat)* redoblar ➤ *intr* doblarse, duplicarse ■ **to d. as** servir también como • **to d. back** volver uno sobre sus pasos ➤ *adv* doble, doblemente.
doublebreasted ➤ *adj* cruzado.
doubt ➤ *tr* dudar; *(to distrust)* desconfiar de ➤ *intr* dudar ➤ *s* duda ■ **beyond d.** fuera de duda • **in d.** dudoso • **no d.** sin duda.
doubtful ➤ *adj* dudoso.
doubtless ➤ *adv* sin duda.
dough ➤ *s* masa, pasta; JER. *(money)* plata.
doughnut ➤ *s* buñuelo.
dove ➤ *s* paloma; FIG. pacifista *mf.*
down[1] ➤ *adv (downward)* (hacia) abajo; *(in writing)* por escrito; COM. *(in advance)* como adelanto ■ **d. and out** pobrísimo • **d. with . . .!** ¡abajo . . .! ➤ *adj* que va hacia abajo; *(depressed)* deprimido; COM. inicial, a cuenta ■ **to be d. on** tenerle inquina a ➤ *prep* abajo ■ **d. the centuries** a través de los siglos ➤ *s* descenso, caída.
down[2] ➤ *s (feathers)* plumón *m.*
downhill ➤ *adv* cuesta abajo ■ **to go d.** deteriorarse; *(health)* debilitarse.
download ➤ *tr* bajar, descargar.
downpour ➤ *s* chaparrón *m,* aguacero.
downright ➤ *adj* absoluto, completo ➤ *adv* completamente, categóricamente.
downstairs ➤ *adv & adj* en *o* del piso de abajo ■ **to go d.** bajar (de un piso a otro) ➤ *spl* planta baja.
downtown ➤ *adv & s* (hacia *o* en el) centro de una ciudad ➤ *adj* del centro.
downward(s) ➤ *adv* hacia abajo ➤ *adj* descendente.
doze ➤ *intr* dormitar ➤ *s* sueño ligero.
dozen ➤ *s & adj* docena (de).
drab ➤ *adj* ordinario, monótono.
draft ➤ *s* corriente *f* de aire; *(of a chimney)* tiro; *(sketch)* bosquejo; *(written)* borrador *m,* versión *f;* MIL. conscripción *f,* quinta; COM. giro ■ **on d.** de barril ➤ *tr (a bill)* hacer un anteproyecto de; *(a writing)* hacer un borrador de; MIL. quintar, reclutar ➤ *adj (horse)* de tiro; *(beer)* de barril.
drag ➤ *tr* arrastrar; *(river, lake)* dragar ■ **to d. out** alargar interminablemente ➤ *intr* arrastrar(se) ■ **to d. on** hacerse interminable ➤ *s (act)* arrastre *m; (hindrance)* estorbo; JER. *(bore)* pesado; *(puff)* chupada, pitada ■ **in d.** JER. vestido de mujer (un hombre, o vice versa) • **main d.** JER. calle principal.
dragon ➤ *s* dragón *m.*
dragonfly ➤ *s* libélula.
drain ➤ *tr* drenar, desaguar; *(to drink)* beber; *(to empty)* vaciar ➤ *intr* desaguarse, vaciarse ➤ *s* desagüe *m,* desaguadero.
drama ➤ *s* drama *m.*
dramatic ➤ *adj* dramático.
drape ➤ *tr (to cover)* cubrir; *(to hang)* colgar; *(arms, legs)* echar ➤ *spl* cortinas.
drastic ➤ *adj* drástico.
draw✧ ➤ *tr (to pull)* tirar de, halar; *(to lead)* llevar; *(to attract)* atraer; *(liquid, gun, conclusion)* sacar; *(fire, criticism)* provocar; *(cards)* robar; ARTE. dibujar ■ **to d. attention** llamar la atención • **to d. out** *(information)* sonsacar; *(to prolong)* prolongar • **to d. up** preparar ➤ *intr (to take in air)* tirar; DEP. *(to tie)* empatar; ARTE. dibujar ■ **to d. back** echarse para atrás ➤ *s (attraction)* atracción *f; (air intake)* tiro; *(tie)* empate *m.*
drawback ➤ *s* desventaja.
drawer ➤ *s* cajón *m,* gaveta.
drawing ➤ *s* dibujo; *(lottery)* sorteo.
dread ➤ *s* pavor *m,* terror *m; (anticipation)* aprensión *f* ➤ *tr* temer ➤ *adj* espantoso, terrible.
dreadful ➤ *adj* espantoso, terrible.
dream✧ ➤ *s* sueño; *(daydream)* ensueño ➤ *tr & intr* soñar *(of, about* con); *(to daydream)* soñar despierto ■ **to d. up** inventar.
dreary ➤ *adj (bleak)* deprimente, sombrío; *(dull)* monótono, aburrido.
drench ➤ *tr* empapar.
dress ➤ *s (garment)* vestido, traje *m; (apparel)* vestimenta, ropa ➤ *tr* vestir; *(to decorate)* decorar; *(hair)* peinar, arreglar; *(wounds)* curar ➤ *intr* vestirse ■ **to d. up** vestirse de etiqueta.
dresser ➤ *s* cómoda, tocador *m.*
dressing ➤ *s* MED. vendaje *m; (sauce)* aliño, salsa; *(stuffing)* relleno ■ **d. gown** bata.
dressy ➤ *adj* elegante.
dribble ➤ *intr (to trickle)* gotear; *(to drool)* babear; DEP. *(soccer)* gambetear; *(basketball)* driblar ➤ *tr* echar a gotas; DEP. gambetear, driblar.
drift ➤ *intr* ser arrastrado por la corriente; *(to roam)* vagar, vagabundear; *(snow, sand)* amontonarse ➤ *s (of sand, snow)* pila, montón *m; (general idea)* dirección *f,* rumbo ■ **to get the d.** FAM. caer en la cuenta.
drill ➤ *s (tool)* torno, taladro; *(oil rig)* perforadora; *(machine)* taladradora; *(exercises)* ejercicios repetitivos ➤ *intr & tr* taladrar, perforar; *(to teach)* enseñar por medio de repetición.
drink✧ ➤ *tr & intr* beber, tomar ■ **to d. to** brindar por • **to d. up** FAM. bebérselo todo ➤ *s* bebida; *(swallow)* trago.
drinkable ➤ *adj* potable.
drinking ➤ *s* beber *m; (habit)* bebida.
drip ➤ *tr* echar (a gotas) ➤ *intr* gotear ➤ *s* gota; *(sound)* goteo, goteadero.
drive✧ ➤ *tr (a vehicle)* conducir, guiar; *(passengers)* llevar; *(to compel)* forzar, obligar; *(a nail)* clavar ■ **to d. away** *o* **off** alejar, apartar • **to d. out** echar ➤ *intr* ir en coche ➤ *s (ride)* vuelta en coche; *(journey)* viaje *m; (road)* carretera, camino; *(vigor)* vigor *m,* energía; MEC. transmisión *f;* AUTO. tracción *f;* COMPUT. unidad *f* de disco.
driver ➤ *s* chofer *mf,* conductor/a; COMPUT. controlador *m.*
driveway ➤ *s* camino de entrada.
driving ➤ *adj (impelling)* impulsor, motriz; *(rain)* torrencial; AUTO. de conducción ➤ *s* acción *f* de conducir.
drizzle ➤ *intr* lloviznar, garuar ➤ *s* llovizna, garúa.
droop ➤ *intr* inclinarse; *(trees, eyelids)* caerse; *(shoulders)* encorvarse; *(spirits)* desanimarse.
drop ➤ *s* gota; *(trace)* poco, pizca; *(lozenge)* pastilla; *(fall)* bajada, caída; *(height of fall)* altura; *(in prices)* baja; *(in value, quality)* disminución *f; (abyss)* precipicio; *(by parachute)* lanzamiento ➤ *intr (to fall)* caer a tierra, desplomarse; *(temperature, prices)* bajar; *(value, quality)* disminuir ■ **to d. behind** quedarse atrás • **to d. in** *o* **by** pasar (por casa de alguien) • **to d. out** dejar de participar ➤ *tr (to let fall)* dejar caer, soltar; *(to let go of)* soltar; *(plan)* abandonar; *(habit)* dejar de; *(hint)* soltar; *(voice, prices)* bajar; *(bombs)* lanzar.
dropout ➤ *s* estudiante *mf* que abandona sus estudios; *(from society)* persona que rechaza a la sociedad.
dropper ➤ *s* gotero, cuentagotas *m.*
drought ➤ *s* sequía, seca.
drown ➤ *tr & intr* ahogar(se).
drowsy ➤ *adj* soñoliento.
drug ➤ *s* droga; MED. medicamento; *(narcotic)* narcótico ■ **d. addict** drogadicto ➤ *tr* MED. dar medicamento; *(with a narcotic)* drogar, narcotizar; *(food, drink)* poner una droga en.
druggist ➤ *s* farmacéutico/a, boticario/a.
drugstore ➤ *s* farmacia, botica.
drum ➤ *s* cilindro, tambor *m; (barrel)* tonel *m;* MÚS. tambor ■ *pl* MÚS. batería ➤ *intr & tr* tocar (el tambor); *(fingers)* tamborilear (con) ■ **to d. up** conseguir.
drummer ➤ *s* baterista *mf,* tambor *mf.*
drunk ➤ *adj* ebrio, borracho ■ **to get d.** emborracharse ➤ *s (drunkard)* borracho/a; *(bout)* juerga.
dry ➤ *adj* seco; *(arid)* árido; *(thirsty)* sediento; *(boring)* pesado; *(wit, style)* agudo, satírico ■ **d. cleaner's** tintorería, tinte • **to run d.** secarse, agotarse ➤ *tr & intr* secar(se), desecar(se).
dry-clean ➤ *tr* limpiar en seco.
dryer ➤ *s (clothes)* secador *m; (hair)* secadora.
dual ➤ *adj* dual, doble.
dub ➤ *tr* MÚS. mezclar; CINEM. doblar.
dubious ➤ *adj (doubtful)* dudoso,

incierto; *(questionable)* sospechoso.

duck[1] ➤ *s* pato; *(female)* pata.

duck[2] ➤ *tr (head)* agachar; *(to dodge)* eludir, evadir ➤ *intr* agacharse.

due ➤ *adj (payable)* pagadero; *(amount)* sin pagar; *(just)* debido, merecido; *(sufficient)* suficiente ■ **d. date** vencimiento • **d. process** proceso legal correspondiente • **d. to** debido a ➤ *s (comeuppance)* merecido; *(reward)* recompensa ■ *pl* cuota ➤ *adv* ■ **d. north** derecho hacia el norte.

duel ➤ *intr & s* (batirse en) duelo.

duet ➤ *s* dueto, dúo.

dull ➤ *adj (stupid)* torpe; *(blunt)* desafilado, romo; *(sound, pain)* sordo; *(boring)* aburrido; *(color, sound)* apagado ➤ *tr & intr* desafilar(se), enromar(se); *(pain)* aliviar(se).

duly ➤ *adv* debidamente.

dumb ➤ *adj (mute)* mudo; FAM. *(stupid)* tonto, estúpido.

dump ➤ *tr* tirar, deshacerse de; *(to empty)* vaciar, descargar ➤ *intr* caerse, desplomarse ➤ *s* vertedero, muladar *m; (depot)* depósito; JER. *(unkept place)* pocilga ■ **d. truck** volquete ■ *pl* FAM. abatimiento.

dune ➤ *s* duna.

duplex ➤ *s* apartamento de dos pisos; *(house)* casa de dos viviendas.

duplicate ➤ *s* duplicado, copia ■ **in d.** por duplicado ➤ *tr* copiar, duplicar; *(on a machine)* multicopiar.

durable ➤ *adj* duradero ■ **d. goods** productos no perecederos.

duration ➤ *s* duración *f.*

during ➤ *prep* durante.

dusk ➤ *s* crepúsculo ■ **at d.** al atardecer.

dust ➤ *s* polvo ➤ *intr* limpiar el polvo.

dusty ➤ *adj* polvoriento.

duty ➤ *s* deber *m,* obligación *f; (task)* función *f; (tax)* impuesto, arancel *m* ■ **in the line of d.** en cumplimiento del deber • **to be on (off) d.** (no) estar de servicio.

duty-free ➤ *adj & adv* exento de derechos de aduana.

dwarf ➤ *s* enano/a ➤ *tr* achicar.

dwell✧ ➤ *intr* morar ■ **to d. on** detenerse en.

dwelling ➤ *s* residencia, morada.

dye ➤ *s* tintura, tinte *m* ➤ *tr* teñir, colorar.

dynamic ➤ *adj* dinámico ■ **dynamics** ➤ *s* dinámica.

dynamite ➤ *s* dinamita.

dynamo ➤ *s* dínamo *f.*

E

each ➤ *adj* cada ➤ *pron* cada uno ■ **e. other** uno a otro • **to e. his own** cada uno con su gusto ➤ *adv* por persona, cada uno.

eager ➤ *adj (avid)* ansioso, ávido; *(desirous)* deseoso, ardiente.

eagle ➤ *s* águila.

ear[1] ➤ *s* oreja; *(organ of hearing)* oído ■ • **to give** *o* **lend an e. to** prestar atención a.

ear[2] ➤ *s* BOT. espiga, mazorca.

earache ➤ *s* dolor *m* de oído.

early ➤ *adj* temprano; *(near the beginning)* primero; *(premature)* prematuro; *(primitive)* primitivo ■ **e. bird** FAM. *(riser)* madrugador; *(arrival)* persona que llega temprano ➤ *adv (soon)* temprano, pronto; *(before)* antes; *(in advance)* con anticipación; *(prematurely)* prematuramente ■ **bright and e.** muy temprano.

earmuff ➤ *s* orejera.

earn ➤ *tr* ganar; *(to deserve)* merecer; *(to acquire)* obtener; *(interest)* devengar.

earnest ➤ *adj* sincero, serio ■ **en e.** en serio.

earnings ➤ *spl (salary)* sueldo; *(income)* ingresos; *(profits)* utilidades *f.*

earphone ➤ *s* auricular *m.*

earring ➤ *s* pendiente *m,* arete *m.*

earth ➤ *s* tierra; *(world)* mundo ■ **down to e.** sensato, realista • **E.** Tierra.

earthquake ➤ *s* terremoto, temblor *m.*

ease ➤ *s (comfort)* comodidad *f; (relief)* alivio; *(naturalness)* desenvoltura; *(facility)* facilidad *f* ■ **at e.** cómodo; MIL. en posición de descanso • **to put at e.** poner cómodo • **with e.** fácilmente ➤ *tr & intr (pain)* aliviar(se); *(pressure)* descargar(se); *(tension)* relajar(se); *(to loosen)* aflojar(se) ■ **to e. in(to)** (hacer) entrar con cuidado • **to e. up on** tratar con menos rigor.

easel ➤ *s* caballete *m.*

easily ➤ *adv* fácilmente; *(possibly)* muy probablemente.

east ➤ *s* este *m,* oriente *m* ➤ *adj* del este, oriental ➤ *adv* al este, hacia el este.

Easter ➤ *s* Pascua de Resurrección; *(period)* Semana Santa ■ **E. Sunday** domingo de Pascua.

eastern ➤ *adj* oriental, del este.

easterner ➤ *s* habitante *mf* del este.

eastward ➤ *adv* hacia el este.

easy ➤ *adj* fácil; *(free from worry)* tranquilo; *(comfortable)* cómodo; *(simple)* sencillo; *(unhurried)* lento, pausado ■ **e. chair** sillón • **to be on e. street** vivir acomodado ➤ *adv* fácilmente ■ **e. does it** con calma • **to come e.** costar poco esfuerzo • **to go e. on** FAM. *(to use moderately)* usar con moderación; *(to be lenient to)* no tratar con mucha severidad • **to take it e.** FAM. *(to relax)* descansar; *(to stay calm)* no agitarse.

easygoing ➤ *adj* despreocupado, descuidado; *(tolerant)* tolerante.

eat✧ ➤ *tr* comer; *(lunch, dinner)* tomar (el almuerzo, la cena); JER. *(to annoy)* molestar, fastidiar ■ **to e. away** corroer, carcomer • **to e. up** *(to devour)* comérselo todo; *(to use up)* gastar; *(to enjoy)* deleitarse en ➤ *intr* comer, alimentarse ■ **to e. (away) at** roer, corroer • **to e. out** comer fuera (de casa).

ebb ➤ *s* menguante *f* ➤ *intr* menguar.

eccentric ➤ *adj & s* excéntrico/a.

echo ➤ *s* eco ➤ *tr* repetir; *(to imitate)* imitar ➤ *intr* producir eco, resonar.

eclipse ➤ *s* eclipse *m* ➤ *tr* eclipsar.

ecological ➤ *adj* ecológico.

ecology ➤ *s* ecología.

economic ➤ *adj* económico ■ **economics** *ssg* economía.

economical ➤ *adj* económico.

economize ➤ *intr* economizar (*on* en).

economy ➤ *s* economía *f* ■ **e. car** automóvil económico.

ecosystem ➤ *s* ecosistema *m.*

Ecuadorian ➤ *adj & s* ecuatoriano/a.

edge ➤ *s (cutting side)* filo, corte *m; (border, rim)* borde *m; (boundary)* límite *m; (of table, coin)* canto; *(farthest part)* extremidad *f;* FAM. *(advantage)* ventaja ■ **to be on e.** tener los nervios de punta • **to be on the e. of** estar al borde *o* al punto de ➤ *tr (to border)* bordear ■ **to e. out** vencer por un margen pequeño ➤ *intr* andar *o* moverse cautelosamente.

edible ➤ *adj & s* comestible *m.*

edict ➤ *s* edicto.

edit ➤ *tr (to draft)* redactar; *(to correct)* corregir, editar; *(edition)* preparar; *(a publication)* dirigir; CINEM. montar.

editing ➤ *s (of text)* redacción *f; (correction)* corrección *f,* revisión *f; (of a publication)* dirección *f; (of film)* montaje *m.*

edition ➤ *s* edición *f; (number of copies)* tiraje *m,* tirada; FIG. versión *f.*

editor ➤ *s* editor/a; *(supervisor)* redactor/a jefe; CINEM. montador/a ■ **e. in chief** jefe/a de redacción, redactor/a en jefe.

editorial ➤ *adj & s* editorial *m.*

educate ➤ *tr* educar.

educated ➤ *adj (cultured)* culto; *(schooled)* educado.

education ➤ *s* educación *f.*

educational ➤ *adj (institution, staff)* docente; *(instructive)* educativo.

eel ➤ *s* anguila.

effect ➤ *s* efecto; *(result)* resultado ■ **for e.** para impresionar • **in e.** *(in fact)* efectivamente; *(virtually)* casi • **to be in e.** estar vigente • **to go into e.** entrar en vigor • **to take e.** *(medication)* surtir efecto; *(laws, schedule)* entrar en vigor ■ *pl* bienes, pertenencias ➤ *tr* efectuar, realizar.

effective ➤ *adj* efectivo; *(striking)* impresionante; *(operative)* vigente.

efficiency ➤ *s* eficiencia; FAM. *(apartment)* apartamento de un cuarto con cocina y baño; MEC. rendimiento.

efficient ➤ *adj* eficaz, eficiente.

effort ➤ *s* esfuerzo; *(achievement)* obra ■ **to spare no e.** hacer todo lo posible.

egg ➤ *s* huevo; BIOL. óvulo ■ **bad e.** JER. calavera • **good e.** JER. buen tipo • **to put all one's eggs in one basket** jugárselo todo en una carta ➤ *tr* ■ **to e. on** incitar.

eggplant ➤ *s* berenjena.

eggshell ➤ *s* cascarón *m.*

eight ➤ *s & adj* ocho ■ **e. hundred** ochocientos • **e. o'clock** las ocho.

eighteen ➤ *s & adj* dieciocho.

eighth ➤ *s & adj* octavo.

eighty ➤ *s & adj* ochenta *m.*

either ➤ *pron & adj* uno u otro, cualquiera de los dos; *(negative)* ni uno ni otro, ninguno de los dos ➤ *conj* ■ **e. we go now, or we stay** o nos vamos ahora o nos quedamos ➤ *adv* tampoco.

elastic ➤ *adj & m* elástico.

elbow ➤ *s* codo ■ **e. grease** FAM. energía física ➤ *tr* dar un codazo.

elder ➤ *adj* mayor ➤ *s (old person)* mayor *mf; (leader)* anciano/a.

elderly ➤ *adj* mayor (de edad).

eldest ➤ *adj* mayor ■ **the e.** el mayor.

elect ➤ *tr & intr* elegir ➤ *adj* electo ■ **the e.** los elegidos.

election ➤ *s (choice)* elección *f;* POL. elecciones.

electric(al) ➤ *adj* eléctrico.

electrician ➤ *s* electricista *mf.*

electricity ➤ *s* electricidad *f.*

electrify ➤ *tr* electrizar; *(a building, town)* electrificar.

electrocute ➤ *tr* electrocutar.

electron ➤ *s* electrón *m.*

electronic ➤ *adj* electrónico ■ **electronics** *ssg* electrónica.

elegance ➤ *s* elegancia.

elegant ➤ *adj* elegante.

element ➤ *s* elemento ■ *pl (weather)* los elementos.

elemental ➤ *adj* elemental.

elementary ➤ *adj* elemental ■ **e. school** escuela primaria.

elephant ➤ *s* elefante *m.*

elevation ➤ *s* elevación *f;* GEOG. altitud *f.*

elevator ➤ *s* ascensor *m.*

eleven ➤ *s & adj* once *m* ■ **e. o'clock** las once.

eleventh ➤ *s & adj* undécimo; *(part)* onzavo.

eligible ➤ *adj* elegible.

eliminate ➤ *tr* eliminar.

else ➤ *adj & adv* ■ **all** *o* **everything e.** todo lo demás • **anybody** *o* **anyone e.** cualquier otro; *(negative)* ningún otro • **anything e.** algo más; *(negative)* nada más • **anywhere e.** *(place)* en cualquier otra parte; *(direction)* a cualquier otra parte; *(negative) (place)* a ningún otro lugar; *(in existence)* en ningún otro lugar • **everyone e.** todos los demás • **how e.?** ¿de qué otro modo? • **nobody** *o* **no one e.** nadie más • **nothing e.** nada más • **nowhere e.** en *o* a ninguna otra parte • **or e.** si no • **what e.?** ¿qué más? • **where e.?** ¿en o a qué otro sitio? • **who e?** ¿quién más?

elude ➤ *tr* eludir, esquivar.

e-mail ➤ *s* correo electrónico, e-mail *m* ➤ *tr* enviar *o* mandar por e-mail.

emancipate ➤ *tr* emancipar.

embark ➤ *tr & intr* embarcar(se) ■ **to e. on** lanzarse a.

embarrass ➤ *tr (to disconcert)* desconcertar, turbar; *(to shame)* avergonzar.

embarrassing ➤ *adj* desconcertante.

embarrassment ➤ *s (shame)* vergüenza, turbación *f; (trouble)* embarazo; *(confusion)* desconcierto.

embassy ➤ *s* embajada.

embrace ➤ *tr* abrazar; *(to accept eagerly)* aprovecharse de ➤ *intr* abrazarse ➤ *s* abrazo.

embroider ➤ *tr* bordar; *(a story)* exagerar ➤ *intr* hacer bordado.

embroidery ➤ *s* bordado.

emerald ➤ *s* esmeralda.

emerge ➤ *intr* emerger, surgir.

emergency ➤ *s* emergencia; MED. caso de urgencia; *(need)* necesidad *f* urgente ■ **e. landing** aterrizaje forzoso.

emigrant ➤ *s* emigrante *mf.*

emigrate ➤ *intr* emigrar.

emit ➤ *tr* emitir.

emotion ➤ *s* emoción *f.*

emotional ➤ *adj* emocional; *(scene, person)* emotivo.

emperor ➤ *s* emperador *m.*

emphasis ➤ *s* énfasis *m.*

emphasize ➤ *tr* enfatizar, hacer hincapié en.

empire ➤ *s* imperio.

employ ➤ *tr* emplear ■ **to be employed** tener empleo ➤ *s* empleo.

employee ➤ *s* empleado/a.

employer ➤ *s* empleador/a.

employment ➤ *s* empleo.

empower ➤ *tr* autorizar.

emptiness ➤ *s* vacío; *(of a person, words)* vacuidad *f.*

empty ➤ *adj* vacío; *(place)* desierto; *(devoid)* falto ➤ *tr* vaciar; *(to vacate)* dejar vacío, desalojar; *(to unload)* descargar ➤ *intr* vaciarse ■ **to e. into** desembocar en ➤ *s* envase vacío.

enable ➤ *tr* capacitar; *(to make possible)* posibilitar; DER. autorizar.

enact ➤ *tr* promulgar; TEAT. representar.

enamel ➤ *s* esmalte *m* ➤ *tr* esmaltar.

encase ➤ *tr* encerrar, encajonar.

enchanting ➤ *adj* encantador.

encircle ➤ *tr* rodear, circundar.

enclose ➤ *tr* encerrar; *(a document)* adjuntar; *(to fence in)* cercar ■ **enclosed herewith** encontrará adjunto.

enclosure ➤ *s* encierro; *(land)* cercado; *(document)* adjunto, documento; *(fence)* cerco, valla.

encounter ➤ *s* encuentro; *(clash)* choque *m* ➤ *tr* encontrar.

encourage ➤ *tr* animar, alentar; *(to embolden)* fortalecer; *(to foster)* fomentar.

encouragement ➤ *s* ánimo, aliento; *(incentive)* incentivo.

encyclopedia ➤ *s* enciclopedia.

end ➤ *s (tip)* extremo, punta; *(boundary)* límite *m; (conclusion)* fin *m,* final *m; (outcome)* desenlace *m; (goal)* propósito ■ **at the e. of** al cabo de • **e. to e.** punta con punta • **in the e.** al fin, al final • **on e.** *(upright)* de pie, derecho; *(nonstop)* sin parar; *(hair)* de punta • **to bring (come) to an e.** terminar(se), acabar(se) ➤ *tr* acabar, concluir; *(to destroy)* destruir ➤ *intr* terminar(se), acabar(se) ■ **to e. up** ir a parar.

endanger ➤ *tr* poner en peligro.

endeavor ➤ *s (effort)* esfuerzo, empeño; *(attempt)* intento ➤ *intr* intentar.

ending ➤ *s* conclusión *f,* fin *m; (of a story)* desenlace *m,* final *m.*

endive ➤ *s* escarola, endibia.

endless ➤ *adj* interminable; *(infinite)* infinito; *(continuous)* continuo.

endorse ➤ *tr* endosar; *(to support)* apoyar; *(to approve)* sancionar.

endorsement ➤ *s* endoso; *(approval)* aprobación *f; (support)* apoyo.

endow ➤ *tr* dotar.

endowment ➤ *s* dotación *f.*

endurance ➤ *s* resistencia, aguante *m.*

endure ➤ *tr* resistir, aguantar; *(to tolerate)* tolerar ➤ *intr* aguantarse, resistir; *(to last)* durar.

enemy ➤ *s & adj* enemigo/a.

energetic ➤ *adj* enérgico.

energy ➤ *s* energía.

enforce ➤ *tr (a law)* hacer cumplir *o* respetar; *(to impose)* imponer.

engage ➤ *tr (to hire)* emplear; *(to reserve)* contratar; *(to engross)* cautivar ➤ *intr* ■ **to e.** in ocuparse en.

engaged ➤ *adj (employed)* empleado; *(busy)* ocupado; *(reserved)* contratado; *(betrothed)* comprometido; MEC. engranado ■ **to be e.** *(busy)* estar ocupado; *(betrothed)* estar comprometido • **to get e.** prometerse.

engagement ➤ *s* compromiso; *(appointment)* cita; MIL. batalla, combate *m.*

engine ➤ *s* máquina, motor *m;* F.C. locomotora.

engineer ➤ *s* ingeniero/a; F.C. maquinista *mf* ➤ *tr* maniobrar, maquinar.

engineering ➤ *s* ingeniería.

English ➤ *adj* inglés ➤ *s (idioma)* inglés *m* ■ **the E.** los ingleses.

Englishman/woman ➤ *s* inglés/esa.

engrave ➤ *tr* grabar; *(on stone)* tallar.

engraving ➤ *s* grabado.

enjoy ➤ *tr* gozar (de), disfrutar (de) ■ **I e. swimming** me gusta nadar • **to e. oneself** divertirse, pasarlo bien.

enjoyable ➤ *adj* agradable, encantador; *(fun)* divertido.

enjoyment ➤ *s* placer *m,* goce *m;* disfrute *m.*

enlarge ➤ *tr* agrandar, aumentar; *(to magnify)* magnificar; FOTOG. ampliar ➤ *intr* agrandarse.

enlighten ➤ *tr* iluminar, ilustrar; *(to inform)* aclarar.

enormous ➤ *adj* enorme.

enough ➤ *adj* bastante, suficiente ■ **to be e.** bastar ➤ *adv* bastante ■ **sure e.** en efecto ➤ *s* lo bastante, lo suficiente ■ **e. is e.** basta y sobra • **to have had e.** *(to be satisfied)* estar satisfecho; *(to be*

tired of) estar harto ➤ *interj* ¡basta! ■ e. of this! ¡basta ya!
enrich ➤ *tr* enriquecer; AGR. abonar.
enrol(l) ➤ *tr & intr* registrar(se), inscribir(se); *(a student)* matricular(se).
enrol(l)ment ➤ *s* inscripción *f*; *(in school)* matriculación *f*; *(record)* registro.
ensure ➤ *tr* asegurar, garantizar.
entail ➤ *tr* implicar, comportar; DER. vincular.
enter ➤ *tr* entrar en; *(to penetrate)* penetrar en; *(to participate in)* participar en; *(to embark upon)* emprender; *(to obtain admission to)* ingresar, entrar a; *(in a register)* asentar, anotar ➤ *intr* entrar; *(to register)* inscribirse, matricularse ■ **to e. into** *(a contract)* celebrar, concertar; *(to begin)* iniciar.
enterprise ➤ *s* empresa; *(initiative)* iniciativa.
entertain ➤ *tr* divertir, entretener; *(an idea)* considerar ■ **to e. oneself** divertirse ➤ *intr* recibir invitados.
entertainer ➤ *s* artista *mf.*
entertaining ➤ *adj* entretenido, divertido.
entertainment ➤ *s* entretenimiento, diversion *f*; *(show)* espectáculo.
enthusiasm ➤ *s* entusiasmo.
enthusiast ➤ *s* entusiasta *mf.*
enthusiastic ➤ *adj* entusiástico.
entire ➤ *adj* entero, total; *(in one piece)* intacto.
entirety ➤ *s* totalidad *f.*
entitle ➤ *tr* titular; *(to give a right)* dar derecho a ■ **to be entitled to** tener derecho a.
entrance ➤ *s* entrada.
entrée *or* **entree** ➤ *s* *(admittance)* entrada; CUL. plato principal.
entrepreneur ➤ *s* empresario/a.
entry ➤ *s* entrada; *(in a register)* registro; DEP. competidor *m*; *(teneduría)* asiento.
enumerate ➤ *tr* enumerar.
envelop ➤ *tr* envolver.
envelope ➤ *s* sobre *m*; *(wrapping)* envoltura; *(cover)* cobertura.
envious ➤ *adj* envidioso.
environment ➤ *s* medio ambiente; *(atmosphere)* ambiente *m.*
envy ➤ *s* envidia; *(object)* cosa *o* persona envidiada ➤ *tr* envidiar, tener envidia de ➤ *intr* sentir envidia.
epidemic ➤ *adj* epidémico ➤ *s* MED. epidemia; FIG. ola.
episode ➤ *s* episodio.
epoch ➤ *s* época.
equal ➤ *adj* igual; *(evenhanded)* equitativo ■ **all things being e.** si todo sigue igual • **to be e. to** ser igual que; *(capable)* ser apto para ➤ *s* igual *mf* ■ **e. sign** signo de igualdad • **without e.** sin par ➤ *tr* ser igual a; *(to match)* igualar.
equality ➤ *s* igualdad *f.*
equalize ➤ *tr & intr* igualar.
equally ➤ *adj* igualmente, por igual.
equation ➤ *s* ecuación *f.*
equator ➤ *s* ecuador *m.*
equip ➤ *tr* equipar; FIG. preparar.
equipment ➤ *s* equipo; *(tools)* avíos.
equivalent ➤ *adj & s* equivalente *m.*
erase ➤ *tr* borrar.
eraser ➤ *s* goma, borrador *m.*
erect ➤ *adj* erecto, erguido; *(hair)* erizado ➤ *tr (to construct)* erigir, construir; *(to raise, establish)* levantar.
erode ➤ *tr & intr* erosionar(se), desgastar(se); *(to corrode)* corroer(se).
erosion ➤ *s* erosión *f.*
erotic ➤ *adj* erótico.
err ➤ *intr* errar, equivocarse.
errand ➤ *s* mandado, recado.
erratic ➤ *adj* irregular; *(eccentric)* excéntrico, extravagante.
error ➤ *s* error *m.*
escalator ➤ *s* escalera mecánica.
escape ➤ *intr* escaparse ➤ *s* escapatoria.
escort ➤ *s* escolta; *(companion)* acompañante *m* ➤ *tr* acompañar, escoltar.
especially ➤ *adv* especialmente.
essay ➤ *tr* ensayar ➤ *s* ensayo.
essence ➤ *s* esencia ■ **in e.** esencialmente.
essential ➤ *adj & s* (elemento) esencial.
establish ➤ *tr* establecer; *(to prove)* demostrar; *(facts)* verificar.
establishment ➤ *s* establecimiento ■ **E.** iglesia oficial; POL. clase dirigente.
estate ➤ *s (land)* hacienda, finca; *(property)* propiedad *f*; DER. testamentaría ■ **real e.** bienes raíces.
esteem ➤ *tr* estimar ➤ *s* estimación *f*, aprecio.
estimate ➤ *tr* estimar ➤ *s* estimación *f*; *(of costs)* presupuesto ■ **rough e.** cálculo aproximado.
eternal ➤ *adj* eterno.
eternity ➤ *s* eternidad *f.*
ethical ➤ *adj* ético, moral.
ethnic ➤ *adj* étnico.
etiquette ➤ *s* etiqueta, protocolo.
Europe ➤ *s* Europa.
European ➤ *adj & s* europeo/a.
evacuate ➤ *tr* evacuar ➤ *intr* retirarse.
evade ➤ *tr* evitar, evadir.
evaluate ➤ *tr* evaluar; *(to appraise)* tasar, valorar.
evaluation ➤ *s* evaluación *f*, valoración *f*; *(judgment)* opinión *f.*
evaporate ➤ *tr & intr* evaporar(se).
evaporation ➤ *s* evaporación *f.*
eve ➤ *s* víspera; *(before a feast)* vigilia ■ **on the e. of** en vísperas de.
even ➤ *adj (flat)* plano, llano; *(level)* a nivel; *(uniform)* regular; *(score)* empatado; MAT. par ■ **to get e.** desquitarse • **to break e.** cubrir los gastos ➤ *adv* todavía, aun ■ **e.** as justo cuando • **e. if** *o* **though** aunque • **e. so** aun así • **I didn't e. cry** ni siquiera lloré ➤ *tr (to level)* emparejar, nivelar; *(to make equal)* igualar.
evening ➤ *s* tarde *f*; *(dusk)* anochecer *m*, noche *f* ■ **e. class** clase nocturna • **e. dress** *(for men)* traje de etiqueta; *(for women)* traje de noche • **good e.!** ¡buenas noches!
event ➤ *s* suceso, acontecimiento; *(outcome)* resultado; DEP. evento ■ **in any e.** en todo caso • **in the e. of** en caso de (que).
eventual ➤ *adj* final.
eventually ➤ *adv* con el tiempo, a la larga.
ever ➤ *adv* siempre; *(at any time)* alguna vez; *(at all)* jamás ■ **as e.** como siempre • **better than e.** mejor que nunca • **e. since** *(from the time)* desde que; *(since then)* desde entonces • **for e. and e.** por siempre jamás • **hardly e.** casi nunca • **not e.** nunca.
every ➤ *adj* cada; *(all)* todo(s) ■ **e. day** todos los días • **e. other day** cada dos días.
everyday ➤ *adj* diario, cotidiano; *(usual)* común; *(clothes)* de todos los días.
everyone *o* **everybody** ➤ *pron* cada uno, cada cual; *(all)* todos, todo el mundo ■ **e. for himself** cada cual por su cuenta.
everything ➤ *pron* todo.
everywhere ➤ *adv* en, a *o* por todas partes; *(wherever)* dondequiera que.
evidence ➤ *s* prueba; *(data)* hechos, datos; *(testimony)* declaración *f* ■ **to be in e.** estar a la vista • **to give e.** declarar como testigo • **to show e. of** presentar señales de ➤ *tr* evidenciar, probar.
evident ➤ *adj* evidente.
evil ➤ *adj* malo, malvado; *(harmful)* nocivo, perjudicial; *(influence)* pernicioso ➤ *s* mal, maldad *f*; *(harm)* perjuicio; *(immorality)* perversidad *f.*
evolution ➤ *s* evolución *f.*
ewe ➤ *s* oveja hembra.
exact ➤ *adj* exacto.
exactly ➤ *adv* exactamente; *(wholly)* precisamente; *(time)* en punto; *(quite true)* es verdad, así es.
exaggerate ➤ *tr & intr* exagerar.
exaggeration ➤ *s* exageración *f.*
exam ➤ *s* FAM. examen *m.*
examination ➤ *s* examen *m*; DER. interrogatorio; *(inquiry)* investigación *f* ■ **to take an e.** sufrir un examen.
examine ➤ *tr* examinar; *(to scrutinize)* escudriñar; DER. interrogar.
example ➤ *s* ejemplo ■ **to set an e.** dar ejemplo.
excavate ➤ *tr* excavar; *(ruins)* desenterrar.
exceed ➤ *tr* exceder; *(limits, authority)* propasarse en, excederse en.
exceedingly ➤ *adv* extremadamente.
excel ➤ *tr* superar, aventajar ➤ *intr* distinguirse.
excellent ➤ *adj* excelente.
except ➤ *prep* excepto, menos ■ **e. for** *(were it not for)* a no ser por; *(apart from)* aparte de ➤ *conj (only)* sólo que; *(otherwise than)* sino ■ **e. that** salvo *o* excepto que ➤ *tr* exceptuar, excluir.
exception ➤ *s* excepción *f.*
exceptional ➤ *adj* excepcional.
excerpt ➤ *s* extracto ➤ *tr* extractar ■ **to e. from** citar de.
excess ➤ *s* exceso ➤ *adj* excesivo.
excessive ➤ *adj* excesivo.
exchange ➤ *tr* cambiar, intercambiar; *(glances, words)* cruzar; *(prisoners, goods)* canjear ➤ *s* cambio, intercambio; *(of prisoners, goods)* canje *m*; COM. bolsa ■ **e. rate** tipo de cambio • **in e. for** a cambio de.
excise tax ➤ *s* impuesto indirecto.
excite ➤ *tr* excitar; *(to thrill)* entusiasmar, emocionar.
excited ➤ *adj* excitado; *(emotions)* agitado; *(thrilled)* entusiasmado.
excitement ➤ *s* emoción *f*, agitación *f*; *(enthusiasm)* entusiasmo.
exciting ➤ *adj* emocionante.
exclaim ➤ *intr* exclamar ➤ *tr* gritar.
exclamation ➤ *s* exclamación *f* ■ **e. point** signo de admiración.
exclude ➤ *tr* excluir.
exclusive ➤ *adj* exclusivo; *(select)* selecto ■ **e. rights** exclusividad.
excursion ➤ *s* excursión *f*, paseo.
excuse ➤ *tr* excusar, disculpar; *(to exempt)* dispensar *(from* de) ■ **e. me** *(I'm sorry!)* ¡discúlpeme!; *(pardon me)* con permiso ➤ *s* excusa ■ **to make excuses (for)** dar excusas (por).
execute ➤ *tr* ejecutar; *(to do)* hacer; *(to validate)* formalizar.
execution ➤ *s* ejecución *f*; *(validation)* legalización *f.*
executive ➤ *s* ejecutivo/a; POL. presidente/a, jefe/a de estado; *(branch)* poder ejecutivo ➤ *adj* ejecutivo.
exempt ➤ *tr* eximir *(from* de) ➤ *adj* exento.
exemption ➤ *s* exención *f.*
exercise ➤ *s* ejercicio ■ *pl (ceremony)* ceremonia ➤ *tr (to use)* usar de, proceder con; *(to drill)* ejercitar, entrenar; *(rights)* ejercer ➤ *intr* ejercitarse.
exert ➤ *tr (strength)* emplear; *(influence)* ejercer.
exertion ➤ *s (of strength)* empleo; *(of influence)* ejercicio; *(effort)* esfuerzo.
exhaust ➤ *tr* agotar; *(to tire)* cansar ➤ *s* AUTO. escape *m*; *(fumes)* gases *m* de escape ■ **e. pipe** tubo de escape.
exhaustion ➤ *s* agotamiento.
exhibit ➤ *tr* exhibir; *(at a show)* exponer; *(emotion, trait)* manifestar ➤ *intr* exponer ➤ *s (display)* exhibición *f*; *(object)* objeto exhibido.
exhibition ➤ *s* exhibición *f.*
exhibitor ➤ *s* expositor/a.
exile ➤ *s* exilio, destierro; *(persona)* desterrado/a ➤ *tr* exiliar, desterrar.
exist ➤ *intr* existir, ser; *(to live)* vivir.
existence ➤ *s* existencia; *(life)* vida *f.*
existing ➤ *adj* existente.
exit ➤ *s* salida ➤ *intr* salir.
exorbitant ➤ *adj* exorbitante.
expand ➤ *tr & intr* extender(se); *(to enlarge)* expandir(se); FÍS. dilatar(se).
expanse ➤ *s* extensión *f.*
expansion ➤ *s* expansión *f*; FÍS. dilatación *f*; *(of a town)* ensanche *m*; *(of an idea)* ampliación.
expect ➤ *tr (to await)* esperar; *(to require)* contar con.
expectation ➤ *s* expectación *f*, expectativa; *(prospect)* esperanza.
expedition ➤ *s* expedición *f.*
expel ➤ *tr* expeler; *(to dismiss)* echar, expulsar.
expenditure ➤ *s* desembolso, gasto.
expense ➤ *s* gasto ■ **at the e. of** a expensas de ■ *pl* expensas.
expensive ➤ *adj* costoso, caro.
experience ➤ *s* experiencia ➤ *tr (to undergo)* experimentar; *(to feel)* sentir.
experienced ➤ *adj* experimentado.
experiment ➤ *s* experimento ➤ *intr* experimentar *(on* en).
expert ➤ *s & adj* experto/a, perito/a.
expertise ➤ *s* pericia.
expiration ➤ *s (end, death)* expiración *f*; *(lapse)* caducidad *f*; *(breath)* espiración *f*; COM. vencimiento.
expire ➤ *intr* expirar; *(to lapse)* vencer, caducar; *(to exhale)* espirar.
explain ➤ *tr* explicar ➤ *intr* dar explicaciones.
explanation ➤ *s* explicación *f.*
explode ➤ *intr* explotar, estallar ➤ *tr* hacer explotar; *(to detonate)* detonar; *(to disprove)* desbaratar.
exploit ➤ *s* hazaña, proeza ➤ *tr* explotar.
exploration ➤ *s* exploración *f.*
explore ➤ *tr* explorar; FIG. investigar.
explorer ➤ *s* explorador/a.
explosion ➤ *s* explosión *f.*
explosive ➤ *adj & s* explosivo.
export ➤ *tr* exportar ➤ *s* exportación *f.*
expose ➤ *tr* exponer; *(to reveal)* revelar; *(to unmask)* desenmascarar.
express ➤ *tr* expresar; *(to show)* manifestar ➤ *adj* expreso; *(explicit)* explícito; *(mail)* de entrega inmediata ➤ *adv* por expreso ➤ *s* transporte rápido; *(train)* expreso, rápido.
expression ➤ *s* expresión *f*; *(sign)* señal *f*; *(gesture)* gesto.
expressway ➤ *s* autopista.
extend ➤ *tr* extender; *(road, visit)* prolongar; *(hand, arm)* alargar; *(to enlarge)* agrandar, ampliar ■ **to e. an invitation** invitar ➤ *intr* extenderse; *(to reach)* alcanzar.
extension ➤ *s* extensión *f*; *(expansion)* ampliación *f*; *(annex)* anexo; *(continuation)* prolongación *f*; FIN. prórroga.
extensive ➤ *adj* extensivo, extenso.
extent ➤ *s* extensión *f*; *(degree)* grado ■ **to a certain e.** hasta cierto punto.
exterior ➤ *adj (outer)* exterior; *(external)* externo ➤ *s* exterior *m.*
external ➤ *adj* externo; *(exterior, foreign)* exterior.
extinct ➤ *adj* extinto, desaparecido; *(inactive)* inactivo.
extra ➤ *adj* extra; *(additional)* adicional ➤ *s* extra *m* ➤ *adv* excepcionalmente.
extract ➤ *tr* extraer; *(to excerpt)* extractar ➤ *s* extracto.
extraordinary ➤ *adj* extraordinario.
extravagant ➤ *adj* pródigo; *(wasteful)* derrochador; *(exorbitant)* costoso.
extreme ➤ *adj* extremo; *(extraordinary)* excepcional; *(drastic)* drástico ➤ *s* extremo ■ **to go to extremes** tomar medidas extremas.
extremely ➤ *adv* extremadamente.
eye ➤ *s* ojo ■ **e. shadow** sombreador • **to catch someone's e.** llamar la atención de alguien • **to keep an e. on** vigilar • **to roll one's eyes** poner los ojos en blanco • **to see e. to e.** estar de acuerdo ➤ *tr* ojear, mirar.
eyeball ➤ *s* globo ocular.
eyebrow ➤ *s* ceja.
eyeglasses ➤ *spl* lentes *m.*
eyelash ➤ *s* pestaña.
eyelid ➤ *s* párpado.
eyesight ➤ *s* vista ■ **within e.** al alcance de la vista.

F

fable ➤ *s* fábula.
fabric ➤ *s* tela.
fabulous ➤ *adj* fabuloso.
face ➤ *s* cara; *(façade)* frente *m*; *(of a clock)* esfera ■ **f. down, up** boca abajo, arriba • **f. value** FIN. valor nominal • **in the f. of** frente a • **to lose f.** desprestigiarse • **to save f.** salvar las apariencias ➤ *tr* mirar hacia; *(building, window)* dar a; *(to confront)* hacer frente a ■ **to be faced with** enfrentarse con • **to f. up to** encararse con, enfrentarse a.
facility ➤ *s* facilidad *f* ■ *pl* COM. facilidades; *(buildings)* instalaciones; *(public toilet)* servicio, baño.
fact ➤ *s* hecho ■ **in fact** en realidad ■ *pl* datos, información.
factor ➤ *s* factor *m.*
factory ➤ *s* fábrica.
faculty ➤ *s (ability)* facultad *f*; EDUC. profesorado.
fade ➤ *intr (light)* palidecer; *(flower)* marchitarse; *(color)* desteñirse.
fail ➤ *intr* fracasar; *(motor, health, support)* fallar; *(to be inadequate)* faltar; *(in school)* aplazarse; COM. quebrar ■ **to f. to** *(to be unsuccessful in)* no alcanzar a; *(to neglect to)* dejar de ➤ *tr* fallar, frustrar; *(course, exam)* salir mal en ➤ *s* ■ **without f.** sin falta.
failing ➤ *s* falla, defecto.
failure ➤ *s* fracaso; *(person)* fracasado/a; *(weakening)* deterioro; ELEC. apagón *m*; COM. quiebra.
faint ➤ *adj (indistinct)* borroso; *(slight)* vago, ligero; *(dizzy)* mareado; *(weak)* débil ➤ *s* desmayo ➤ *intr* desmayarse.
fair¹ ➤ *adj* imparcial; *(just)* justo; *(mediocre)* regular; *(weather)* bueno; *(sky)* despejado ■ **f. enough!** ¡vale! • **f. play** juego limpio ➤ *adv* honrado.
fair² ➤ *s (exhibition)* exposición *f*, feria.

fairly ➤ *adv (justly)* justamente, equitativamente; *(moderately)* bastante.
fairy ➤ *s* hada ▪ **f. tale** cuento de hadas.
faith ➤ *s (confidence)* confianza; *(belief)* fe *f* ▪ **in good, bad f.** de buena, mala fe.
faithful ➤ *adj* fiel.
fake ➤ *adj* falso, fraudulento ➤ *s* impostor/a; *(fraud)* engaño; *(forgery)* falsificación *f* ➤ *tr* falsificar; *(to feign)* fingir.
fall◊ ➤ *intr* caer(se); *(prices, temperature)* bajar ▪ **to f. behind** quedarse atrás • **to f. down** *o* **over** caer(se) • **to f. for** FAM. *(person)* volverse loco por; *(trick)* tragarse • **to f. off** *(to come loose)* desprenderse; *(to decrease)* disminuir, decaer • **to f. through** fracasar ➤ *s* caída; *(autumn)* otoño; *(reduction)* bajada, descenso; *(decline)* decadencia, ruina ▪ *pl* catarata, cascada.
fallout ➤ *s* lluvia radioactiva; *(side effects)* consecuencias.
false ➤ *adj* falso; *(hope)* infundado; *(teeth)* postizo ▪ **f. pretense** intención fraudulenta • **f. start** salida mala *o* nula • **f. step** paso en falso ➤ *adv* falsamente, con falsedad; *(wrong)* mal.
fame ➤ *s* fama, renombre *m.*
familiar ➤ *adj* familiar, conocido; *(intimate)* de confianza; *(forward)* confianzudo ▪ **to be f. with** conocer.
familiarity ➤ *s* familiaridad *f; (impropriety)* atrevimiento ▪ *pl* libertades.
familiarize ➤ *tr* familiarizar.
family ➤ *s* familia ▪ **f. name** apellido.
famine ➤ *s* hambre *f.*
famous ➤ *adj* famoso.
fan[1] ➤ *s (hand)* abanico; *(electric)* ventilador *m* ➤ *tr* abanicar.
fan[2] ➤ *s* FAM. *(enthusiast)* aficionado/a.
fanatic ➤ *s & adj* fanático/a.
fancy ➤ *s* fantasía; *(whim)* capricho ➤ *adj* adornado; *(superior)* fino ➤ *tr* imaginar; *(to like)* gustarle a uno; *(to suppose)* suponer.
fantastic ➤ *adj* fantástico.
fantasy ➤ *s* fantasía.
far ➤ *adv* lejos ▪ **as f. as I am concerned** por mi parte • **f. away** *o* **f. off** (a lo) lejos • **f. different** muy diferente • **f. from** lejos de • **f. from it** al contrario • **f. more** mucho más • **how f.?** ¿a qué distancia? • **to go f.** realizar mucho • **to go too f.** pasarse de la raya ➤ *adj* lejano; POL. extremo ▪ **a f. cry** una gran diferencia.
faraway ➤ *adj* lejano.
farce ➤ *s* farsa.
fare ➤ *s* pasaje *m; (food)* comida.
farewell ➤ *s & interj* adiós *m.*
farm ➤ *s* granja, finca ➤ *tr* cultivar ➤ *intr* labrar la tierra, ser agricultor.
farmer ➤ *s* granjero/a.
farmhouse ➤ *s* granja, cortijo.
farmyard ➤ *s* corral *m.*
farther ➤ *adv (in space)* más lejos; *(in time)* más adelante; *(degree)* más.
farthest ➤ *adj* más remoto ➤ *adv* más lejos.
fascinate ➤ *tr* fascinar.
fascination ➤ *s* fascinación *f.*
fashion ➤ *s* manera; *(style)* moda ▪ **in f.** de moda • **to go out of f.** pasar de moda.
fashionable ➤ *adj* de moda; *(elegant)* elegante.
fast[1] ➤ *adj* rápido; *(clock)* adelantado ➤ *adv* rápidamente; *(securely)* firmemente.
fast[2] ➤ *s* ayuno ➤ *intr* ayunar.
fasten ➤ *tr* fijar; *(to tie)* atar; *(to close)* cerrar.
fastener ➤ *s* sujetador *m*, cierre *m.*
fat ➤ *s* grasa; CUL. manteca ➤ *adj* gordo; *(thick)* grueso; *(large)* grande ▪ **to get f.** ponerse gordo, engordar.
fatal ➤ *adj* fatal, mortal.
fate ➤ *s* destino.
father ➤ *s* padre *m* ➤ *tr* engendrar.
father-in-law ➤ *s* suegro.
fatigue ➤ *s* fatiga ➤ *tr* fatigar.
fattening ➤ *adj* que engorda.
fatty ➤ *adj* graso, adiposo.
fatuous ➤ *adj* fatuo.
faucet ➤ *s* grifo, llave *f.*
fault ➤ *s* culpa; *(shortcoming)* defecto; ELEC., GEOL. falla ▪ **to be at f.** tener la culpa • **to find f.** criticar.
faulty ➤ *adj* defectuoso.
favor ➤ *s* favor *mf* ▪ **to be in f. of** estar a favor de ➤ *tr* favorecer; *(to be partial to)* preferir.
favorable ➤ *adj* favorable.
favorite ➤ *adj & s* favorito/a.
fear ➤ *s* miedo ➤ *tr & intr* tener miedo (de), temer.
fearful ➤ *adj* temeroso; FAM. *(dreadful)* tremendo.
fearless ➤ *adj* intrépido, audaz.
feast ➤ *s* banquete *m* ➤ *tr & intr* banquetear.
feat ➤ *s* proeza, hazaña.
feather ➤ *s* pluma ▪ *pl* plumaje.
feature ➤ *s* característica, rasgo; CINEM. película principal ▪ *pl* facciones, rasgos ➤ *tr* presentar.
February ➤ *s* febrero.
fed ➤ *adj* ▪ **f. up with** harto de.
federation ➤ *s* federación *f.*
fee ➤ *s* honorarios; *(fixed)* cuota.
feeble ➤ *adj* débil.
feed◊ ➤ *tr* dar de comer a; *(to nourish, supply)* alimentar ➤ *intr* comer.
feedback ➤ *s* información *f;* ELECTRÓN. realimentación *f*, retroacción *f.*
feel◊ ➤ *tr* sentir; *(to touch)* tocar; *(to sense)* percibir ➤ *intr* sentir (por tacto); *(emotionally)* sentirse, estar; *(to seem)* parecer ▪ **to f. like** FAM. *(to want to)* tener ganas de; *(to the touch)* parecer (como) • **to f. smooth, rough** ser suave, áspero al tacto • **to f. up to** FAM. sentirse con ánimos para ➤ *s (touch)* tacto; *(perception)* sensación *f; (atmosphere)* atmósfera.
feeling ➤ *s (touch)* tacto; *(sensation)* sensación *f; (emotion)* emoción *f; (impression)* impresión *f; (premonition)* presentimiento ▪ *pl* sensibilidades • **ill f.** malos sentimientos.
fellow ➤ *s* compañero; *(guy)* tipo ➤ *adj* ▪ **f. citizens** (con)ciudadanos • **f. worker** compañero de trabajo.
fellowship ➤ *s* comunidad *f* (de intereses, ideas); EDUC. beca.
felt ➤ *adj & s* (de) fieltro.
female ➤ *adj* del sexo femenino; BIOL., MEC. hembra ➤ *s* mujer *f;* BIOL. hembra.
feminine ➤ *adj & s* femenino.
fence ➤ *s* cerca, valla, empalizada ➤ *tr* cercar, vallar; *(to close off)* encerrar.
fend ➤ *tr* ▪ **to f. off** *(blow)* parar; *(attack)* repeler ➤ *intr* ▪ **to f. for oneself** valerse por sí mismo.
fender ➤ *s* AUTO. guardafango.
ferocious ➤ *adj* feroz.
ferry ➤ *tr* transportar en barco *o* avión ➤ *s* transbordador *m.*
fertile ➤ *adj* fértil; BIOL. fecundo.
fertilize ➤ *tr* abonar; BIOL. fecundar.
fertilizer ➤ *s* fertilizante *m*, abono.
festival ➤ fiesta; *(art, film)* festival *m.*
festive ➤ *adj* festivo, de fiesta.
festivity ➤ *s* festividad *f* ▪ *pl* diversiones.
fetch ➤ *tr* ir a buscar.
fever ➤ *s* fiebre *f.*
feverish ➤ *adj* febril.
few ➤ *adj* pocos ▪ **a f.** unos • **every f.** cada dos o tres ➤ *s & pron* pocos ▪ **a f.** unos cuantos • **quite a f.** muchos.
fiancé ➤ *s* novio, prometido ▪ **fiancée** novia, prometida.
fiber ➤ *s* fibra.
fiction ➤ *s* ficción *f.*
fiddle FAM. ➤ *s* violín *m* ➤ *intr* tocar el violín ▪ **to f. around** perder el tiempo • **to f. with** juguetear con.
fidget ➤ *intr* moverse, no estarse quieto.
field ➤ *s* campo; *(profession)* profesión *f* ▪ **f. glasses** gemelos • **f. of view** campo visual • **f. trip** excursión.
fieldwork ➤ *s* trabajo en el terreno.
fierce ➤ *adj* feroz; *(hard-fought)* reñido; *(ardent)* furioso.
fiery ➤ *adj (blazing)* llameante; *(hot)* abrasador; FIG. enardecido.
fifteen ➤ *s & adj* quince *m.*
fifth ➤ *adj & s* quinto.
fifty ➤ *adj & s* cincuenta *m.*
fig ➤ *s* higo ▪ **f. tree** higuera.
fight◊ ➤ *intr* luchar, pelear; *(to box)* boxear; *(to argue)* reñir ▪ **to f. back** defenderse ➤ *tr* luchar con *o* contra; *(to resist)* combatir; *(a battle)* dar ➤ *s* lucha; *(combat)* combate *m; (quarrel)* riña; *(brawl, boxing)* pelea.
fighter ➤ *s* luchador/a, combatiente *mf; (boxer)* boxeador *m.*
figure ➤ *s* figura; *(number)* cifra; *(price)* precio; *(illustration)* dibujo; *(silhouette)* silueta ▪ **f. of speech** figura, tropo ▪ *pl* cálculos ➤ *tr* computar, calcular; *(to depict)* figurar ▪ **to f. out** *(to solve)* resolver ➤ *intr* hacer cálculos; *(to appear)* figurar.
file[1] ➤ *s* archivo; *(for cards)* fichero; COMPUT. archivo, fichero; *(folder)* carpeta; MIL. fila ▪ **f. server** servidor de archivos • **to be on f.** estar archivado ➤ *tr* archivar; *(to put in order)* clasificar ➤ *intr* marchar en fila.
file[2] ➤ *s (tool)* lima ➤ *tr* limar.
filet ➤ *s* filete *m.*
fill ➤ *tr* llenar; *(a tooth)* empastar ▪ **to f. in** *o* **out** *(a form)* llenar; *(to complete)* completar con (información, detalles).
fillet ➤ *s* filete *m.*
filling ➤ *s* relleno; ODONT. empaste *m* ▪ **f. station** gasolinera.
film ➤ *s* película ➤ *tr (an event)* filmar; *(a scene)* rodar ➤ *intr* rodar.
filter ➤ *s* filtro ➤ *tr & intr* filtrar(se).
filth ➤ *s* mugre *f*, suciedad *f.*
filthy ➤ *adj* sucio, mugriento.
fin ➤ *s* aleta.
final ➤ *adj* último, final ➤ *s* DEP. final *f;* EDUC. examen *m* final.
finally ➤ *adv* finalmente, por último.
finance ➤ *s* finanzas ▪ *pl* finanzas, fondos ➤ *tr* financiar.
financial ➤ *adj* financiero.
find◊ ➤ *tr* encontrar; *(to notice)* hallar; *(to discover)* descubrir ▪ **to f. out** averiguar, descubrir ➤ *intr* ▪ **to f. out about** informarse sobre ➤ *s* descubrimiento, hallazgo.
fine[1] ➤ *adj* fino; *(skillful)* excelente; *(weather)* bueno ▪ **f. arts** bellas artes • **that's f.!** ¡está bien! ➤ *adv* FAM. muy bien.
fine[2] ➤ *s* multa ➤ *tr* multar.
finger ➤ *s* dedo ▪ **index f.** (dedo) índice • **little f.** (dedo) meñique • **not to lift a f.** no mover un dedo • **ring f.** (dedo) anular ➤ *tr (to handle, play)* tocar.
fingernail ➤ *s* uña.
fingerprint ➤ *s* huella digital ➤ *tr* tomar las huellas digitales.
fingertip ➤ *s* punta *o* yema del dedo.
finish ➤ *tr* acabar (con); *(to terminate)* terminar ▪ **to f. up** acabar, terminar ➤ *intr* acabar, terminar ➤ *s* final *m*, fin *m; (substance)* pulimento; *(perfection)* perfección *f.*
fir ➤ *s* abeto.
fire ➤ *s* fuego; *(destructive)* incendio ▪ **f. department, engine** cuerpo, camión de bomberos • **f. escape** salida de urgencia • **to be on f.** estar en llamas • **to set on f.** prenderle fuego a ➤ *tr* encender; *(to arouse)* enardecer; FAM. *(to hurl)* tirar, arrojar; *(from a job)* despedir ➤ *intr* disparar (*on* contra).
firearm ➤ *s* arma de fuego.
firecracker ➤ *s* cohete *m*, petardo.
fireman *o* **firefighter** ➤ *s* bombero/a.
fireplace ➤ *s* hogar *m*, chimenea *m.*
firewood ➤ *s* leña.
fireworks ➤ *spl* fuegos artificiales.
firm[1] ➤ *adj & adv* firme.
firm[2] ➤ *s* COM. firma, casa.
firmament ➤ *s* firmamento.
firmness ➤ *s* firmeza.
first ➤ *adj* primero; *(elementary)* primario; *(outstanding)* sobresaliente; *(principal)* principal ▪ **f. aid** primeros auxilios • **f. name** nombre de pila ➤ *adv* primero; *(before anything else)* antes; *(firstly)* en primer lugar ▪ **at f.** en un principio ➤ *s* primero; *(beginning)* principio.
first-class ➤ *adj* de primera clase; *(first-rate)* de primera categoría ➤ *adv* en primera.
fish ➤ *s* pez *m; (food)* pescado ➤ *intr* pescar ▪ **to go fishing** ir de pesca.
fisherman ➤ *s* pescador *m.*
fishhook ➤ *s* anzuelo.
fishing ➤ *s* pesca ▪ **f. ground** zona de pesca • **f. rod** caña de pescar.
fist ➤ *s* puño.
fit[1] ➤ *tr (to go on, in)* entrar en; *(to put on, in)* colocar, meter; *(to alter, adjust, match)* ajustar; *(to suit)* sentar bien ➤ *intr* caber; *(part, piece)* ajustar, encajar; *(clothes)* sentar bien ▪ **to f. in with** *(people)* congeniar con; *(things)* cuadrar con ➤ *adj (healthy)* sano; *(competent)* idóneo ▪ • **to keep f.** mantenerse en buen estado físico • **to see f.** juzgar conveniente ➤ *s* ajuste *m*, encaje *m; (clothes)* corte *m*, entalladura.
fit[2] ➤ *s* ataque *m;* MED. convulsión *f.*
fitting ➤ *adj* apropiado, oportuno; *(proper)* justo.
five ➤ *s & adj* cinco ▪ **f. hundred** quinientos • **f. o'clock** las cinco.
fix ➤ *tr* fijar; *(to repair)* componer; *(hair)* arreglar; *(meal)* preparar ➤ *s* apuro, aprieto.
flag ➤ *s* bandera ➤ *tr (taxi, bus)* hacer parar con señales a.
flake ➤ *s* escama, hojuela; *(snowflake)* copo ➤ *intr (skin)* descamarse; *(paint)* desprenderse en escamillas.
flame ➤ *s* llama; FAM. *(sweetheart)* novio/a ➤ *intr* arder, llamear.
flammable ➤ *adj* inflamable.
flank ➤ *s* costado ➤ *tr* flanquear.
flannel ➤ *s* franela.
flap ➤ *s (of wings)* aleteo; *(of flags)* ondulación *f; (of envelopes)* solapa ➤ *tr & intr (wings)* aletear; *(arms)* agitar.
flare ➤ *intr* llamear; *(to glow)* brillar; *(in anger)* encolerizarse; *(conflict)* estallar ➤ *s* llamarada; *(signal)* señal luminosa.
flare-up ➤ *s* llamarada repentina; *(outburst)* estallido.
flash ➤ *tr (to emit)* lanzar, despedir ➤ *intr (to sparkle)* brillar, destellar ➤ *s* destello, resplandor *m;* FOTOG. flash *m; (of lightning)* relámpago ▪ **f. bulb** lámpara de flash.
flashlight ➤ *s* linterna eléctrica.
flask ➤ *s* frasco.
flat[1] ➤ *adj (level)* plano, llano; *(smooth)* liso, raso; *(tasteless)* soso; *(tire)* desinflado; *(color)* sin brillo; MÚS. *(key)* bemol ➤ *s* plano, superficie *f; (tire)* pinchazo; MÚS. bemol *m.*
flat[2] ➤ *s (apartment)* apartamento.
flatten ➤ *tr* allanar ➤ *intr* achatarse.
flatter ➤ *tr* adular; *(to suit)* favorecer.
flattery ➤ *s* lisonja, halago.
flavor ➤ *s* gusto, sabor *m* ➤ *tr* condimentar, aderezar.
flavoring ➤ *s* condimento, aderezo.
flaw ➤ *s* imperfección *f*, defecto.
flea ➤ *s* pulga ▪ **f. market** mercado de pulgas, mercado de artículos usados.
flee◊ ➤ *intr* huir, escaparse.
fleet ➤ *s (of ships)* flota.
flesh ➤ *s* carne *f; (of fruits)* pulpa.
flex ➤ *tr & intr* doblar(se).
flick ➤ *s* golpecito; *(of tail)* coleada; *(of fingers)* capirotazo; FAM. *(film)* película ➤ *tr* golpear rápida y ligeramente.
flight[1] ➤ *s* vuelo; *(of stairs)* tramo ▪ **f. attendant** aeromozo/a • **to take f.** alzar el vuelo.
flight[2] ➤ *s* huida, fuga.
flimsy ➤ *adj* insubstancial, endeble; *(excuse)* flojo.
fling◊ ➤ *tr* arrojar, tirar.
flint ➤ *s* pedernal *m.*
flip ➤ *tr* lanzar, tirar; *(coin)* echar (a cara o cruz) ▪ **to f. over** dar la vuelta a.
flirt ➤ *intr* flirtear, coquetear ➤ *s (man)* galanteador *m; (woman)* coqueta.
float ➤ *tr* hacer flotar, poner a flote ➤ *intr* flotar ➤ *s* flotador *m; (buoy)* boya.
flock ➤ *s (of birds)* bandada; ZOOL., RELIG. rebaño ➤ *intr* congregarse ▪ **to f. to** llegar en tropel a.
flood ➤ *s* inundación *f; (torrent)* torrente *m* ➤ *tr & intr* inundar(se).
floodlight ➤ *s* luz *f* de proyector.
floor ➤ *s* piso; *(of dance hall)* pista.
flop ➤ *s* FAM. fracaso ➤ *tr* dejar caer (pesadamente) ➤ *intr* dejarse caer; *(to move about)* agitarse; FAM. fracasar.
floppy ➤ *adj* flojo, blando ▪ **f. disk** disco flexible (de memoria auxiliar).
florist ➤ *s* florista *mf.*
flour ➤ *s* harina ➤ *tr* enharinar.
flourish ➤ *intr* florecer ➤ *s* floreo.
flow ➤ *intr* fluir; ELEC., FIG. correr; *(to gush)* manar ➤ *s* flujo.
flower ➤ *s* flor *f* ▪ **f. shop** florería ➤ *intr* florecer, dar flor.
flu ➤ *s* FAM. gripe *f.*
fluent ➤ *adj* perfecto; *(fluid)* fluyente ▪ **to be f. in** dominar.
fluently ➤ *adv* con soltura.
fluff ➤ *s (down)* pelusa; FIG. nadería.
fluid ➤ *s & adj* fluido, líquido ▪ **f. ounce** onza líquida.
flunk ➤ *intr* FAM. sacar suspenso.
fluorescent ➤ *adj* fluorescente.
flush[1] ➤ *intr (to blush)* ruborizarse ➤ *tr* limpiar con agua ➤ *s (gush)* chorro; *(blush)* rubor *m.*
flush[2] ➤ *tr (toilet)* hacer funcionar.
flute ➤ *s* MÚS. flauta.
flutter ➤ *intr* revolotear, aletear; *(heart)* palpitar ➤ *tr* agitar, mover ➤ *s* revoloteo, aleteo; MED. palpitación *f.*

fly¹✧ ➤ *intr* volar; *(hair, flag)* ondular; *(to flee)* huir; *(sparks, chips)* saltar ➤ *tr* hacer volar; *(to pilot)* pilotear ➤ *s (of trousers)* bragueta.
fly² ➤ *s* mosca.
foam ➤ *s* espuma ➤ *intr* hacer espuma.
foamy ➤ *adj* espumoso.
focus ➤ *s* foco ■ **in f.** enfocado • **out of f.** desenfocado ➤ *tr* enfocar.
fog ➤ *s* neblina, niebla.
foggy ➤ *adj* neblinoso; FIG. ofuscado.
foghorn ➤ *s* sirena de niebla.
foil¹ ➤ *tr* frustrar, hacer fracasar.
foil² ➤ *s (sheet)* lámina fina de metal.
fold ➤ *tr* doblar, plegar; *(arms)* cruzar ➤ *intr* plegarse ➤ *s* pliegue *m.*
folder ➤ *s* carpeta.
folding ➤ *adj* plegable.
foliage ➤ *s* follaje *m.*
folk ➤ *s* pueblo *f* ■ *pl* **folks** gente; FAM. *(relatives)* familia.
follow ➤ *tr* seguir; *(rules)* observar; *(to understand)* comprender ■ **to f. through** llevar a cabo ➤ *intr* seguir.
follower ➤ *s (disciple)* discípulo/a; *(supporter)* partidario/a.
following ➤ *adj* siguiente ➤ *s* adherentes *mf.*
folly ➤ *s* tontería.
fond ➤ *adj* cariñoso ■ **to be f. of** *(person)* tener cariño a; *(thing)* ser aficionado a.
font ➤ *s* fuente *f;* RELIG. pila bautismal.
food ➤ *s* comida; *(nourishment)* alimento ■ **f. poisoning** intoxicación alimenticia.
fool ➤ *s* tonto/a, necio/a ➤ *tr* engañar ➤ *intr* ■ **to f. around** jugar (sin propósito).
foolish ➤ *adj* tonto, absurdo.
foot ➤ *s* pie *m;* ZOOL. pata; *(base)* base *f* ■ **by** *o* **on f.** a pie • **to put one's f. down** ponerse firme • **to put one's f. in one's mouth** meter la pata.
football ➤ *s* fútbol americano; *(ball)* pelota; G.B. fútbol; *(ball)* balón *m.*
footprint ➤ *s* huella.
footstep ➤ *s* pisada.
for ➤ *prep* para, por; *(destination)* para, hacia; *(beneficiary)* para; *(exchange)* por; *(duration)* por; *(on account of)* de, por ■ **as f.** en cuanto a • **f. all that** con todo • **to be f.** estar de parte de ➤ *conj* ya que, pues, porque.
forbid ➤ *tr* prohibir.
forbidden ➤ *adj* prohibido.
force ➤ *s* fuerza ■ **by f.** por la fuerza • **in f.** DER. vigente, en vigor ➤ *tr* compeler, obligar; *(to impose)* imponer ■ **to f. back** *(to repel)* rechazar.
fore ➤ *adj* delantero.
forearm ➤ *s* antebrazo.
foreboding ➤ *s* presentimiento.
forecast ➤ *tr & intr* pronosticar ➤ *s* pronóstico.
forecaster ➤ *s* pronosticador/a.
forefather ➤ *s* antepasado.
forefront ➤ *s* vanguardia.
foreground ➤ *s* primer plano.
forehead ➤ *s* frente *f.*
foreign ➤ *adj* extranjero; *(trade)* exterior.
foreigner ➤ *s* extranjero/a, forastero/a.
foreman ➤ *s* capataz *m;* DER. presidente *m* de un jurado.
foremost ➤ *adj* primero.
forensic ➤ *adj* forense.
forerunner ➤ *s* precursor/a.
foresee ➤ *tr* prever, anticipar.
foresight ➤ *s* previsión *f.*
forest ➤ *s* bosque *m,* selva.
foretell ➤ *tr* predecir.
forever ➤ *adv* por *o* para siempre, eternamente.
foreword ➤ *s* prólogo, prefacio.
forge ➤ *s* forja, fragua ➤ *tr* fraguar, forjar; *(to counterfeit)* falsificar.
forgery ➤ *s* falsificación *f.*
forget ➤ *tr & intr* olvidar, olvidarse de ■ **f. to** olvidarse de.
forgetful ➤ *adj* olvidadizo.
forgive ➤ *tr & intr* perdonar.
forgotten ➤ *adj* olvidado.
fork ➤ *s* tenedor *m; (of a road)* bifurcación *f* ➤ *intr* bifurcarse.
form ➤ *s* forma; *(figure)* figura; *(type)* clase *f,* tipo; *(document)* formulario ■ **f. letter** circular ➤ *tr* formar; *(to model)* moldear ➤ *intr* formarse.
formal ➤ *adj* formal; *(official)* oficial; *(dress)* de etiqueta ➤ *s* ceremonia de etiqueta; *(attire)* traje *m* de etiqueta.
formality ➤ *s* formalidad *f.*
formally ➤ *adv* formalmente; *(officially)* oficialmente.
format ➤ *s* formato ➤ *tr* COMPUT. *(a diskette)* formatear.
formation ➤ *s* formación *f.*
former ➤ *adj (earlier)* antiguo; *(of two)* anterior.
formerly ➤ *adv* anteriormente, antes.
formula ➤ *s* fórmula.
fort ➤ *s* fuerte *m.*
fortify ➤ *tr* fortificar.
fortress ➤ *s* fortaleza.
fortunate ➤ *adj* afortunado ■ **to be f.** *(person)* tener suerte.
fortunately ➤ *adv* afortunadamente.
fortune ➤ *s* fortuna; *(good luck)* suerte *f.*
forty ➤ *adj & s* cuarenta *m.*
forward ➤ *adj (bold)* descarado; *(progressive)* avanzado ➤ *adv* hacia adelante ■ **to look f. to** anticipar ➤ *s* DEP. delantero ➤ *tr (mail)* reexpedir.
fossil ➤ *s & adj* fósil *m.*
foul ➤ *adj (revolting)* asqueroso; *(polluted)* contaminado; *(obscene)* obsceno, grosero ➤ *s* DEP. falta.
found ➤ *tr (to establish)* fundar.
foundation ➤ *s* fundación *f; (base)* fundamento; CONSTR. cimientos.
founder ➤ *s* fundador/a.
fountain ➤ *s* fuente *f; (for drinking)* surtidor *m.*
four ➤ *s & adj* cuatro ■ **f. hundred** cuatrocientos • **f. o'clock** las cuatro.
fourteen ➤ *s & adj* catorce *m.*
fourth ➤ *adj & s* cuarto.
fowl ➤ *s* aves *f* (en general); *(domesticated)* ave de corral.
fox ➤ *s* zorra, zorro ➤ *tr* embaucar.
fraction ➤ *s* MAT. fracción *f,* quebrado; *(bit)* porción minúscula, pizca.
fracture ➤ *s* fractura ➤ *tr & intr* fracturar(se).
fragile ➤ *adj* frágil.
fragment ➤ *s* fragmento.
fragrance ➤ *s* fragancia, perfume *m.*
fragrant ➤ *adj* fragrante.
frail ➤ *adj* débil.
frame ➤ *s* armadura, armazón *f; (border)* cerco, marco; *(glasses)* montura ■ **f. of mind** estado de animo *f* ➤ *tr (picture)* enmarcar, encuadrar.
framework ➤ *s* armadura, esquéleto; *(system)* sistema *m.*
frank ➤ *adj* franco, sincero.
frantic ➤ *adj* desesperado; *(pace)* frenético.
fraternity ➤ *s* (con)fraternidad *f; (organization)* asociación estudiantil masculina.
fraud ➤ *s* fraude *m; (person)* impostor/a.
fray ➤ *tr & intr* desgastar(se).
freckle ➤ *s* peca.
freckled ➤ *adj* pecoso.
free ➤ *adj* libre; *(gratis)* gratis, gratuito ➤ *adv* libremente; *(gratis)* gratis ➤ *tr* libertar, poner en libertad.
freedom ➤ *s* libertad *f.*
freeway ➤ *s* autopista.
freeze✧ ➤ *intr* helarse, congelarse ■ **to f. over** helarse ➤ *tr* helar; *(food, assets)* congelar ➤ *s* congelación *f.*
freezer ➤ *s* congelador *m.*
freezing ➤ *adj* glacial ■ **it's f. cold** hace un frío tremendo ➤ *s* congelación *f.*
freight ➤ *s* carga, flete *m.*
French ➤ *adj & s* francés *m* ■ **F. fries** papas fritas.
frequent ➤ *adj* frecuente ➤ *tr* frecuentar.
frequently ➤ *adv* frecuentemente.
fresco ➤ *s* fresco.
fresh ➤ *adj* fresco; *(new)* nuevo.
freshen ➤ *tr & intr* refrescar ■ **to f. up** refrescarse, asearse.
freshman ➤ *s* estudiante *mf* de primer año; *(novice)* novato.
fret ➤ *intr (to worry)* preocuparse.
friction ➤ *s* fricción *f.*
Friday ➤ *s* viernes *m.*
fridge ➤ *s* FAM. refrigerador *m,* nevera.
fried ➤ *adj* frito.
friend ➤ *s* amigo/a.
friendly ➤ *adj* amable, simpático.
friendship ➤ *s* amistad *f.*
fright ➤ *s* miedo, susto.
frighten ➤ *tr & intr* asustar(se).
frightening ➤ *adj* espantoso.
frill ➤ *s* farala *m* ■ *pl* FAM. adornos.
fringe ➤ *s (trim)* franja; *(flounce)* fleco ■ **f. benefits** beneficios suplementarios.
frog ➤ *s* rana.
from ➤ *prep* de, desde.
frond ➤ *s* fronda.
front ➤ *s* frente *m* ■ **from the f.** por delante, de frente • **in f. of** delante de, frente a, en frente de ➤ *adj* delantero, frontal ■ **f. door** puerta de entrada • **f. page** primera plana ➤ *tr (to face)* dar frente a; *(to confront)* hacer frente a ➤ *intr* ■ **to f. on(to)** dar frente a.
frontier ➤ *s* frontera.
frost ➤ *s* escarcha; *(freezing weather)* helada.
frostbite ➤ *s* congelación *f.*
frosty ➤ *adj* muy frío, de helada; *(welcome)* frío, glacial.
froth ➤ *s* espuma.
frown ➤ *s* ceño, entrecejo ➤ *intr* fruncir el entrecejo.
frozen ➤ *adj* helado; *(food, assets)* congelado.
fruit ➤ *s* fruta; BOT. fruto.
fruitcake ➤ *s* torta de frutas.
fruitful ➤ *adj* fructuoso, fructífero.
frustrate ➤ *tr* frustrar.
fry ➤ *tr & intr* freír(se) ■ **frying pan** sartén.
fuel ➤ *s* combustible *m* ■ **f. oil** aceite fuel *o* combustible.
fugitive ➤ *adj & s* fugitivo/a.
fulfill ➤ *tr (requirements)* llenar; *(contract, promise)* cumplir (con); *(ambition)* realizar.
full ➤ *adj* lleno; *(complete)* completo; *(maximum)* máximo; *(entire)* entero; *(total)* total ■ **to be f.** *(person)* estar satisfecho; *(hotel)* no tener lugar ➤ *adv* muy ➤ *s* ■ **in f.** completamente • **to pay in f.** pagar íntegramente.
full-scale ➤ *adj* de tamaño natural; *(all-out)* en gran escala, a todo dar.
full-size(d) ➤ *adj* de tamaño natural.
full-time ➤ *adj* de jornada completa.
fully ➤ *adv* completamente.
fume ➤ *s* humo, tufo ■ *pl* gases, humo ➤ *intr* enfurecerse.
fun ➤ *s* diversión *f* ■ **for f.** *(as a joke)* en broma, bromeando; *(to have fun)* para divertirse • **in f.** en broma, bromeando • **to be f.** ser divertido • **to have f.** divertirse • **to make f. of** burlarse de.
function ➤ *s* función *f; (ceremony)* acto, ceremonia ➤ *intr* funcionar.
fund ➤ *s* fondo ■ *pl* fondos ➤ *tr (to finance)* costear.
funeral ➤ *s* funeral(es).
funnel ➤ *s* embudo; *(stack)* chimenea.
funny ➤ *adj (amusing)* divertido, cómico, gracioso; *(odd)* raro, extraño ➤ **funnies** *spl* tiras cómicas.
fur ➤ *s* pelo, pelaje *m; (pelt)* piel *f.*
furious ➤ *adj* furioso.
furnace ➤ *s* horno.
furnish ➤ *tr (room, house)* amueblar; *(supplies)* suministrar.
furnishings ➤ *spl* mobiliario.
furniture ➤ *s* muebles *m* ■ **a piece of f.** un mueble.
further ➤ *adj (more distant)* más lejano *o* alejado; *(additional)* más ➤ *adv (extent, degree)* más; *(distance)* más lejos ■ **f. back** *(space)* más atrás.
furthermore ➤ *adv* además.
furthest ➤ *adj* más lejano.
fury ➤ *s* furia.
fuse¹ ➤ *s (wick)* mecha.
fuse² ➤ *tr & intr* fundir(se) ➤ *s* ELEC. fusible *m,* plomo ■ **f. box** caja de fusibles *o* plomos • **to blow a f.** ELEC. fundir(se) un plomo.
fuss ➤ *s (commotion)* alboroto ■ **to kick up** *o* **to make a f.** armar un lío ➤ *intr* inquietarse *(over* por).
fussy ➤ *adj* irritable; *(baby)* llorícón; *(fastidious)* quisquilloso, melindroso; *(meticulous)* concienzudo.
future ➤ *s* futuro, porvenir *m.*
fuzzy ➤ *adj* velloso, velludo; *(indistinct)* borroso; *(confused)* confuso.

G

gabardine ➤ *s* gabardina.
gadget ➤ *s* FAM. artilugio, dispositivo.
gaffe ➤ *s* metida de pata.
gag ➤ *s* mordaza; FAM. *(joke)* chiste *m.*
gain ➤ *tr* ganar; *(strength, momentum)* cobrar ➤ *intr* aumentar ➤ *s* ganancia; *(increase)* aumento.
gait ➤ *s* paso.
gala ➤ *adj & s* (de) gala, (de) fiesta.
galaxy ➤ *s* galaxia.
gale ➤ *s* vendaval *m.*
gallant ➤ *adj* galante.
gallery ➤ *s* galería.
gallon ➤ *s* galón *m.*
gallop ➤ *s* galope *m* ➤ *intr* galopar.
gambit ➤ *s* estratagema, maniobra.
gamble ➤ *intr* jugar ➤ *tr (to bet)* jugar, apostar; *(to risk)* arriesgar ➤ *s (bet)* jugada; *(risk)* riesgo.
gambler ➤ *s* jugador/a.
gambling ➤ *s* juego.
game ➤ *s* juego; *(of checkers, etc.)* partida; *(of baseball, etc.)* partido ➤ *adj (plucky)* valeroso; *(willing)* listo.
gang ➤ *s* pandilla; *(laborers)* cuadrilla ➤ *intr* ■ **to g. up on** atacar en grupo.
gangster ➤ *s* gángster *mf.*
gap ➤ *s* boquete *m,* hueco; *(blank)* espacio; *(of time)* intervalo.
garage ➤ *s* garaje *m.*
garbage ➤ *s* basura; FIG. porquería.
garden ➤ *s* jardín *m; (for vegetables)* huerto ➤ *intr* cultivar el huerto.
gardener ➤ *s* jardinero/a.
gardening ➤ *s* jardinería.
gargle ➤ *intr* hacer gárgaras.
garland ➤ *s* guirnalda.
garlic ➤ *s* ajo.
garment ➤ *s* prenda de vestir.
gas ➤ *s* gas *m; (gasoline)* gasolina ■ **g. mask** máscara antigás • **g. station** gasolinera ➤ *tr* asfixiar con gas.
gash ➤ *s* cuchillada, tajo.
gasoline ➤ *s* gasolina, nafta.
gasp ➤ *intr (in surprise)* quedar boquiabierto; *(to pant)* jadear ➤ *s* jadeo; *(surprise)* grito ahogado.
gate ➤ *s* puerta; *(of iron)* verja.
gateway ➤ *s* pórtico; FIG. camino.
gather ➤ *tr* reunir, juntar; *(to amass)* acumular ➤ *intr* reunirse, congregarse; *(to accumulate)* amontonarse.
gathering ➤ *s* asamblea, reunión *f.*
gaudy ➤ *adj* llamativo, chillón.
gauge ➤ *s* TEC. calibrador *m;* ARM. calibre *m* ➤ *tr* evaluar; *(to determine)* determinar.
gaunt ➤ *adj* macilento, demacrado.
gauze ➤ *s* gasa.
gay ➤ *adj* alegre; *(sexually)* gay, homosexual ➤ *s* homosexual *mf.*
gaze ➤ *intr* mirar con fijeza, contemplar ➤ *s* mirada fija.
gazette ➤ *s* gaceta.
gear ➤ *s* MEC. engranaje *m;* AUTO. marcha; *(assembly)* tren *m; (equipment)* equipo, aparejos; FAM. *(belongings)* cosas ■ **in g.** engranado.
geese ➤ *pl de* **goose.**
gel ➤ *s* gel *m.*
gem ➤ *s* piedra preciosa.
gender ➤ *s* GRAM. género; *(sex)* sexo.
general ➤ *adj* general ■ **in g.** por lo general ➤ *s* MIL. general *mf.*
generally ➤ *adv* generalmente.
generation ➤ *s* generación *f.*
generator ➤ *s* generador *m.*
generosity ➤ *s* generosidad *f.*
generous ➤ *adj* generoso.
genius ➤ *s* genio.
gentle ➤ *adj* amable; *(tender)* dulce; *(mild)* suave.
gentleman ➤ *s* caballero.
gentleness ➤ *s (mildness)* suavidad *f; (tameness)* mansedumbre *f.*
genuine ➤ *adj (authentic)* genuino; *(sincere)* sincero.
geographic(al) ➤ *adj* geográfico.
geography ➤ *s* geografía.
geology ➤ *s* geología.
geometric(al) ➤ *adj* geométrico.
geometry ➤ *s* geometría.
germ ➤ *s* BIOL., FIG. germen *m;* MED. *(microbe)* microbio.
gesticulate ➤ *intr* gesticular.
gesture ➤ *s* gesto.
get✧ ➤ *tr (to obtain)* obtener, conseguir; *(to receive)* recibir; *(to seize)* agarrar; *(flu, cold)* coger, contraer; *(to bring)* traer; *(to understand)* comprender ■ **to g. back** recobrar • **to g. down** poner por escrito • **to g. out of** *(information)* sonsacar de; *(pleasure, benefit)* sacar *o* obtener de • **to g. over (with)** acabar con ➤ *intr (to become)* ponerse, hacer ■ **to g. along** *(in years)* ponerse viejo; *(to be friendly)* llevarse bien *(with* con) • **to g. around** to encontrar tiempo para • **to g. back** volver • **to g. back at** vengarse de • **to g. into** *(car)* subir a; *(bed, trouble)* meterse en; *(a habit)* adquirir • **to g. off** *(train, horse)* apearse; *(work)* salir (del trabajo); *(to escape punishment)* librarse • **to g. on** *(train, horse)* montar en • **to g. out of** *(bed, chair)* levantarse de; *(town)* alejarse de; *(obligation)* librarse de; *(trouble)* sacarse de; *(the way)* quitarse

(de en medio) • to g. **through** *(exam)* aprobrar; *(to finish)* terminar; *(to arrive)* llegar a su destino (provisiones, mensaje) • to g. **up** *(to stand up)* levantarse, ponerse de pie; *(out of bed)* levantarse (de la cama).
geyser ➤ *s* geiser *m.*
ghastly ➤ *adj* horrible, horroroso.
ghetto ➤ *s* ghetto.
ghost ➤ *s* fantasma *m* ■ **g. town** pueblo desierto.
giant ➤ *adj & s* gigante *m.*
giddy ➤ *adj* mareado; *(causing dizziness)* vertiginoso; *(frivolous)* frívolo.
gift ➤ *s* regalo, obsequio; *(talent)* talento, aptitud *f.*
gifted ➤ *adj* dotado.
gigantic ➤ *adj* gigantesco.
giggle ➤ *intr* reírse tontamente.
gimmick ➤ *s* truco.
gin ➤ *s* ginebra.
ginger ➤ *s* jengibre *m.*
giraffe ➤ *s* jirafa.
girdle ➤ *s* faja.
girl ➤ *s* muchacha, chica; *(child)* niña; *(daughter)* hija.
girlfriend ➤ *s* amiga; *(sweetheart)* novia.
give◊ ➤ *tr* dar; *(a gift)* regalar; *(an illness)* transmitir, contagiar; *(medicine, sacraments)* administrar; *(to yield)* ceder; *(dance, party)* dar ■ **to g. away** *(secret, plot)* contar, revelar; *(to sell cheaply)* regalar • **to g. back** devolver • **to g. up** abandonar, renunciar a (intento, tarea); *(to hand over)* entregar; *(to stop)* dejar de; *(to consider as lost)* dar por perdido • **to g. in** *(to collapse)* ceder, caerse; *(to accede)* acceder; *(to admit defeat)* darse por vencido.
given ➤ *adj* dado ■ **g. name** nombre de pila • **g. that** dado que.
glacier ➤ *s* glaciar *m.*
glad ➤ *adj* alegre, contento.
glamour ➤ *s* encanto, hechizo.
glamourous ➤ *adj* elegante, hechicero.
glance ➤ *intr* echar un vistazo *o* una mirada (*at* a) ➤ *s* vistazo, mirada.
gland ➤ *s* glándula.
glaring ➤ *adj* *(light)* deslumbrador; *(error)* patente, manifiesto.
glass ➤ *s* vidrio, cristal *m; (drinking vessel)* vaso; *(mirror)* espejo ■ *pl (eyeglasses)* lentes, anteojos; *(binoculars)* gemelos • **dark g.** lentes oscuros.
gleam ➤ *s* destello ➤ *intr* destellar.
glee ➤ *s* regocijo, alegría ■ **g. club** orfeón.
glide ➤ *intr* deslizarse; AVIA. planear.
glider ➤ *s* planeador *m.*
glimmer ➤ *s & intr* (lucir con) luz trémula.
glimpse ➤ *s* ojeada ➤ *tr* vislumbrar.
glitter ➤ *s* centello ➤ *intr* centellear.
gloat ➤ *intr* regodearse.
global ➤ *adj* mundial; *(total)* global.
globe ➤ *s* globo (terrestre).
gloom ➤ *s* *(partial)* penumbra; *(total)* tinieblas *f; (melancholy)* melancolía.
gloomy ➤ *adj* *(dark)* oscuro; *(melancholy)* triste; *(pessimistic)* pesimista.
glorious ➤ *adj* glorioso; *(magnificent)* esplendoroso; FAM. magnífico.
glory ➤ *s* gloria.
gloss ➤ *s* lustre *m,* brillo.
glossy ➤ *adj* lustroso, brillante.
glove ➤ *s* guante *m* ■ **g. compartment** guantera.
glow ➤ *intr* resplandecer, brillar ➤ *s* resplandor *m,* brillo.
glue ➤ *s* pegamento ➤ *tr* pegar.
glutton ➤ *s* glotón/ona.
gnat ➤ *s* jején *m.*
gnaw ➤ *tr & intr* roer.
go◊ ➤ *intr* ir; *(to proceed)* seguir adelante; *(to leave)* irse, marcharse; *(to function)* funcionar, andar ■ **to go after** seguir a • **to go before** preceder, ir antes • **to go by** *(to pass by)* pasar por; *(time)* pasar • **to go down** *(to descend)* bajar; *(the sun)* ponerse; *(a ship)* hundirse; *(airplane)* caerse • **to go into** *(to enter)* entrar en; *(to fit)* caber *o* encajar en; *(a profession)* dedicarse a • **to go off** *(gun)* dispararse; *(bomb)* hacer explosión; *(to sound)* sonar • **to go on** continuar, seguir • **to go out** *(to exit, socially)* salir; *(light)* apagarse • **to go over** *(to rehearse)* ensayar; *(to review)* repasar • **to go under** *(to fail)* fracasar ➤ *s* *(try)* intento; *(energy)* energía ■ **on the go** en actividad.
goal ➤ *s* meta; *(score)* gol *m,* tanto ■ **g. line** línea de gol • **g. post** poste.
goalkeeper *o* **goalie** ➤ *s* portero/a.
goat ➤ *s* cabra, macho cabrío ■ **to get someone's g.** molestar a alguien.
god ➤ *s* dios; *(idol)* ídolo ■ **G.** Dios.
goddaughter ➤ *s* ahijada.
goddess ➤ *s* diosa.
godfather ➤ *s* padrino.
godmother ➤ *s* madrina.
godson ➤ *s* ahijado.
goggles ➤ *spl* gafas, anteojos.
going ➤ *s* ida, partida ➤ *adj* actual.
goings-on ➤ *spl* actividades *f.*
gold ➤ *s* oro ➤ *adj* *(made of gold)* de oro; *(golden)* dorado.
golden ➤ *adj* dorado; *(voice, epoch)* de oro; *(hair)* rubio; *(opportunity)* excelente ■ **g. mean** justo medio.
goldfish ➤ *s* pez *m* de colores.
golf ➤ *s* golf *m* ➤ *intr* jugar al golf.
golfer ➤ *s* golfista *mf.*
gone ➤ *vea* **go** *en tabla de verbos* ➤ *adj* *(past)* pasado, ido.
good ➤ *adj* bueno; *(beneficial)* beneficioso; *(valid)* válido; *(pleasant)* agradable; *(favorable)* favorable ■ **to be g. at** tener capacidad *o* talento para • **to be no g.** ser inútil • **to have a g. time** pasarlo bien ➤ *s* bien *m; (goodness)* bondad *f* ■ **for g.** para siempre ■ *pl (wares)* bienes; *(merchandise)* mercancías, géneros ➤ *adv* FAM. bien ■ **to feel g.** *(satisfied)* estar satisfecho; *(well)* sentirse bien ➤ *interj* ¡bueno!, ¡muy bien!
goodby(e) ➤ *interj* ¡adiós!, ¡hasta luego! ➤ *s* adiós, despedida.
good-looking ➤ *adj* bien parecido.
goodness ➤ *s* bondad *f.*
goose ➤ *s* ganso.
gorge ➤ *s* *(ravine)* desfiladero ➤ *tr* ■ **to g. oneself** hartarse y atiborrarse.
gorgeous ➤ *adj* hermosísimo.
gorilla ➤ *s* gorila *m.*
gospel ➤ *s* evangelio.
gossip ➤ *s* chismes *m; (gossiper)* chismoso/a ■ **g. column** noticias sociales.
got, gotten ➤ *vea* **got** *en tabla de verbos.*
Gothic ➤ *adj* gótico.
gourmet ➤ *s* gastrónomo/a.
govern ➤ *tr* gobernar; *(to determine)* determinar ➤ *intr* gobernar.
government ➤ *s & adj* (del) gobierno.
governor ➤ *s* gobernador/a; MEC. *(regulator)* regulador automático.
gown ➤ *s* vestido (de etiqueta); *(nightgown)* camisón *m; (judge, etc.)* toga.
grab ➤ *tr (to seize)* agarrar, coger ➤ *intr* ■ **to g at** tratar de arrebatar ➤ *s* ■ **to make a g. at** tratar de agarrar • **up for grabs** disponible.
grace ➤ *s* gracia; *(at table)* bendición *f* de la mesa ➤ *tr* adornar, embellecer.
graceful ➤ *adj* agraciado, elegante.
gracious ➤ *s* amable, cortés *m.*
grade ➤ *s* *(degree, rank)* grado; EDUC. *(class)* año, curso; *(mark)* nota ➤ *tr* clasificar; *(an exam)* calificar.
gradual ➤ *adj* gradual.
graduate ➤ *tr & intr* graduar(se) ■ **to g. as** recibirse de ➤ *adj & s* graduado/a, diplomado/a.
graduation ➤ *s* graduación *f; (commencement)* entrega de diplomas.
graffiti ➤ *spl* graffiti *m.*
graft[1] AGR., MED. ➤ *tr & intr* injertar(se) ➤ *s* injerto.
graft[2] ➤ *s* *(crime)* concusión *f,* extorsión *f.*
grain ➤ *s* grano; *(cereals)* cereales *m.*
gram ➤ *s* gramo.
grammar ➤ *s* gramática ■ **g. school** escuela primaria.
grand ➤ *adj* grandioso, magnífico ■ **g. jury** jurado de acusación • **g. piano** piano de cola.
grandaunt ➤ *s* tía abuela.
grandchild ➤ *s* nieto/a.
granddaughter ➤ *s* nieta.
grandfather ➤ *s* abuelo ■ **g. clock** reloj de pie *o* de caja.
grandma ➤ *s* FAM. abuelita.
grandmother ➤ *s* abuela.
grandpa ➤ *s* FAM. abuelito.
grandson ➤ *s* nieto.
grant ➤ *tr* conceder; *(to bestow)* otorgar; *(to admit)* admitir ■ **to take it for granted** dar por sentado ➤ *s* *(funding)* subvención *f; (scholarship)* beca; DER. *(transfer)* cesión *f.*
grape ➤ *s* uva.
grapefruit ➤ *s* toronja, pomelo.
graph ➤ *s* gráfico, diagrama *m.*
graphic ➤ *adj* gráfico ➤ *spl* *(drawing)* dibujo lineal; ARTE. artes gráficas; COMPUT. gráficos.
grasp ➤ *tr (to seize)* agarrar, asir; *(to comprehend)* captar ➤ *s* *(grip)* apretón *m;* FIG. comprensión *f.*
grass ➤ *s* hierba; *(lawn)* césped *m;* JER. *(marijuana)* yerba.
grasshopper ➤ *s* saltamontes *m.*
grate[1] ➤ *tr* CUL. rallar; FIG. irritar ➤ *intr* *(teeth, hinge)* rechinar.
grate[2] ➤ *s* reja, verja; *(for coals)* parrilla.
grateful ➤ *adj* agradecido.
grater ➤ *s* rallador *m.*
gratitude ➤ *s* gratitud *f.*
grave[1] ➤ *s* tumba.
grave[2] ➤ *adj* grave, serio.
gravel ➤ *s* grava.
graveyard ➤ *s* cementerio.
gravity ➤ *s* gravedad *f; (solemnity)* solemnidad *f.*
gravy ➤ *s* *(sauce)* salsa.
gray ➤ *s* gris *m* ➤ *adj* gris; *(hair)* cano.
graze[1] ➤ *intr (to feed)* pacer, pastar ➤ *tr* apacentar.
graze[2] ➤ *tr & intr (to touch)* rozar.
grease ➤ *s* grasa ➤ *tr* engrasar.
greasy ➤ *adj* *(coated)* engrasado; *(fatty)* grasoso; *(dirty)* grasiento.
great ➤ *adj* grande; FAM. magnífico ■ *s* grande *m* ➤ *adv* FAM. muy bien.
great-grandchild ➤ *s* bisnieto/a.
great-grandfather ➤ *s* bisabuelo.
great-grandmother ➤ *s* bisabuela.
greatly ➤ *adv* muy, mucho.
greed ➤ *s* *(for wealth)* codicia, avaricia; *(for food)* gula, glotonería.
greedy ➤ *adj* *(avaricious)* codicioso; *(gluttonous)* glotón *m; (eager)* ávido.
green ➤ *s* verde *m* ■ *pl* verduras ➤ *adj* verde; *(raw)* inexperto.
greenhouse ➤ *s* invernadero.
greet ➤ *tr* dar la bienvenida, saludar.
greeting ➤ *s* saludo.
greyhound ➤ *s* galgo.
grief ➤ *s* pena; *(trouble)* desgracia.
grieve ➤ *tr* dar pena, afligir ➤ *intr* apenarse; *(to mourn)* lamentarse.
grill ➤ *tr* asar a la parrilla ➤ *s* *(rack)* parrilla; *(food)* asado.
grim ➤ *adj* *(forbidding)* imponente; *(ghastly)* macabro; *(gloomy)* lúgubre.
grime ➤ *s* mugre *f.*
grimy ➤ *adj* mugriento.
grin ➤ *intr* sonreír ➤ *s* sonrisa abierta.
grind◊ ➤ *tr* *(to crush)* triturar, pulverizar; *(coffee, wheat)* moler; *(teeth)* hacer rechinar ■ **to g. down** *(to wear away)* desgastar; *(to oppress)* oprimir.
grip ➤ *s* *(of hands)* apretón *m; (control)* control *m; (handle)* asidero ■ **to have a good g. on** tener un buen dominio de ➤ *tr (to seize)* agarrar; *(to clasp)* apretar ➤ *intr* agarrarse.
groan ➤ *intr* gemir ➤ *s* gemido.
grocer ➤ *s* tendero/a, almacenero/a.
grocery ➤ *s* tienda de comestibles, almacén *m.*
groin ➤ *s* ANAT. ingle *f.*
groom ➤ *s* mozo de caballos; *(bridegroom)* novio ➤ *tr* *(horses)* cuidar; *(oneself)* arreglarse, acicalarse.
groove ➤ *s* ranura; *(of a record)* surco.
gross ➤ *adj* *(income, weight)* bruto; *(error, ignorance)* craso; *(vulgar)* grosero ➤ *s* total *m; (12 dozen)* gruesa.
grotesque ➤ *adj* grotesco.
grotto ➤ *s* gruta.
ground ➤ *s* tierra, suelo; *(area)* terreno, campo ■ **g. floor** planta baja • **to break new g.** marcar nuevos rumbos • **to give, gain g.** ceder, ganar terreno ■ *pl (land)* terreno; *(basis)* base; *(cause)* motivo ➤ *adj* triturado; *(coffee, wheat)* molido.
groundwork ➤ *s* fundamento, base *f.*
group ➤ *s* grupo ➤ *tr & intr* agrupar(se).
grow◊ ➤ *tr* cultivar; *(beard, hair)* dejar(se) crecer ➤ *intr* *(business, industry)* expandirse, agrandarse; *(to increase)* aumentar; *(person)* madurar ■ **to g. dark** oscurecerse • **to g. old** envejecer • **to g. up** crecer.
growl ➤ *s* gruñido ➤ *intr* gruñir.
grown ➤ *adj* mayor, adulto.
grown-up ➤ *adj & s* adulto/a.
growth ➤ *s* crecimiento; *(development)* desarrollo; *(increase)* aumento.
grubby ➤ *adj* sucio.
grudge ➤ *tr* escatimar, dar a regañadientes ➤ *s* rencor *m.*
gruel(l)ing ➤ *adj* abrumador.
gruesome ➤ *adj* horrible, horrendo.
grumble ➤ *intr* quejarse, gruñir.
grumpy ➤ *adj* malhumorado.
grunt ➤ *intr* gruñir ➤ *s* gruñido.
guarantee ➤ *s* garantía ➤ *tr* garantizar; *(to promise)* prometer.
guard ➤ *tr* guardar; *(to protect)* proteger; *(to watch over)* custodiar ➤ *s* *(sentinel, soldier)* guardia *mf; (troops)* guardia *f; (escort)* escolta; DEP. defensa *mf* ■ **off g.** desprevenido • **to be on g.** MIL. estar de guardia.
guardian ➤ *s* guardián/ana; *(of an orphan)* tutor/a, curador/a.
Guatemalan ➤ *adj & s* guatemalteco/a.
guess ➤ *tr & intr (to suppose)* suponer; *(correctly)* adivinar ■ **I g. so** supongo que sí ➤ *s* conjetura, suposición *f.*
guest ➤ *s* *(at home)* invitado/a; *(at hotel)* huésped/a.
guidance ➤ *s* *(direction)* dirección ■ **under the g. of** guiado por.
guide ➤ *s* guía *mf; (book, device)* guía *f* ➤ *tr* guiar.
guidebook ➤ guía.
guilty ➤ *adj* culpable.
guinea pig ➤ *s* conejillo de Indias, cui *m.*
guitar ➤ *s* guitarra.
gulf ➤ *s* golfo; *(abyss)* abismo.
gulp ➤ *tr* tragar, engullir ➤ *s* trago.
gum[1] ➤ *s* *(sap, glue)* goma; *(for chewing)* chicle *m* ➤ *tr* engomar.
gum[2] ➤ *s* ODONT. encía.
gun ➤ *s* arma de fuego; *(cannon)* cañón *m; (handgun)* pistola; *(rifle)* fusil *m.*
gunshot ➤ *s* tiro.
gush ➤ *intr* brotar, chorrear.
gust ➤ *s* ventolera, ráfaga ➤ *intr* soplar.
gutter ➤ *s* *(street)* cuneta; *(roof)* canalón *m.*
guy ➤ *s* FAM. tipo, tío ■ *pl* muchachos.
gym ➤ *s* FAM. gimnasio.
Gypsy ➤ *adj & s* gitano/a.

H

habit ➤ *s* costumbre *f; (addiction)* dependencia ■ **to be in the h. of** acostumbrarse de.
habitat ➤ *s* hábitat *m.*
hack ➤ *tr* cortar; COMPUT. hackear ■ **h. into** COMPUT. sabotear ➤ *s* tos seca.
hacker ➤ *s* hacker *mf,* pirata *mf.*
had ➤ *vea* **have** *en tabla de verbos.*
haddock ➤ *s* abadejo.
haggle ➤ *intr* regatear.
hail ➤ *s* *(ice)* granizo; *(barrage)* lluvia, andanada ➤ *intr* granizar.
hailstone ➤ *s* granizo.
hair ➤ *s* pelo, cabello ■ **gray h.** canas • **h. style** peinado.
hairbrush ➤ *s* cepillo (para el pelo).
haircut ➤ *s* corte *m* de pelo.
hairdresser ➤ *s* peluquero/a.
hairpin ➤ *s* horquilla.
hairy ➤ *adj* peludo; JER. *(hazardous)* espinoso.
half ➤ *s* mitad *f;* DEP. tiempo ■ **and a h.** y medio • **in h.** por la mitad • **h. brother, sister** hermanastro/a ➤ *adj & adv* medio, a medias.
halfway ➤ *adv (partially)* a medias ■ **to meet h.** hacer concesiones.
hall ➤ *s* corredor *m; (lobby)* vestíbulo; *(auditorium)* sala.
hallway ➤ *s* pasillo, corredor *m.*
halt ➤ *s* *(stop)* alto, parada; *(pause)* interrupción *f* ➤ *tr & intr* parar(se) ■ **halt!** ¡alto!
halve ➤ *tr* partir *o* reducir a la mitad; *(a number)* dividir por dos.
ham ➤ *s* jamón *m.*
hamburger ➤ *s* hamburguesa.
hammer ➤ *s* martillo ➤ *tr* martillar.
hammock ➤ *s* hamaca.
hamster ➤ *s* hámster *m.*
hand ➤ *s* mano *f; (of clock, gauge)* aguja, manecilla ■ **by h.** a mano • **(close) at h.** muy cerca, a mano • **on h.** disponible • **on the one (other) h.** por una (otra) parte • **to be an old h. at** tener mucha experiencia en • **to clap one's hands** batir palmas • **to give** *o* **lend a h. (with)** echar una mano (a) • **to have a h. in** tener parte en • **to shake hands** darse la mano ➤ *tr* entregar, dar ■ **to h. down** transmitir; *(verdict)* dictar • **to h. in** presentar • **to h. out** *(to administer)* dar; *(to distribute)* repartir.
handbag ➤ *s* cartera, bolso.

handbook ➤ *s* manual *m.*
handcuff ➤ *s* esposas ➤ *tr* esposar.
handful ➤ *s* puñado.
handicap ➤ *s* DEP. hándicap *m; (hindrance)* obstáculo; *(physical, mental)* discapacidad *f,* minusvalía ➤ *tr (to impede)* poner en desventaja.
handicapped ➤ *adj* discapacitado, minusválido; *(hindered)* obstaculizado.
handicraft ➤ *s* destreza manual; *(occupation, product)* (artículo de) artesanía.
handkerchief ➤ *s* pañuelo.
handle ➤ *tr* tocar, andar con; *(conveyance)* manejar, dirigir; *(to deal with)* encargarse de; *(to cope with)* poder con ➤ *s* mango; *(of door)* manija; *(grip)* asa, asidero.
handmade ➤ *adj* hecho a mano.
handout ➤ *s* limosna; *(leaflet)* folleto.
handrail ➤ *s* pasamano, barandilla.
handshake ➤ *s* apretón *m* de manos.
handsome ➤ *adj* guapo, bien parecido; FIG. liberal, generoso.
handwriting ➤ *s* escritura; *(style)* letra.
handy ➤ *adj* mañoso; *(accessible)* a mano; *(useful)* conveniente.
hang◇ ➤ *tr* suspender, colgar; *(one's head)* bajar, inclinar ■ **to h. up** *(to delay)* demorar; *(telephone)* colgar ➤ *intr* colgar; *(to be executed)* ser ahorcado; *(in air)* flotar ■ **to h. around** *o* **out** FAM. haraganear • **to h. on** *(to wait)* esperar; *(to persevere)* persistir.
hanger ➤ *s* colgadero, percha.
hangout ➤ *s* guarida, punto de reunión.
hangover ➤ *s* resaca.
hang-up ➤ *s* FAM. complejo, problema *m.*
happen ➤ *intr (to come to pass)* pasar, suceder; *(to take place)* producirse, ocurrir ■ **to h. to be** dar la casualidad de ser *o* estar.
happiness ➤ *s* felicidad *f,* dicha.
happy ➤ *adj* feliz, dichoso ■ **h. birthday!** ¡feliz cumpleaños!, ¡felicidades!
harass ➤ *tr* acosar; *(to annoy)* molestar.
harbor ➤ *s* puerto, bahía ➤ *tr (hopes)* abrigar; *(doubt)* guardar.
hard ➤ *adj* duro, sólido; *(firm)* firme; *(resistant)* resistente; *(difficult)* difícil, arduo; *(robust)* fuerte ■ **h. cash** metálico • **h. line** postura firme • **h. luck** mala suerte ➤ *adv (intensely)* mucho; *(vigorously)* con fuerza.
hard-boiled ➤ *adj (egg)* duro.
hard disk ➤ *s* disco rígido *o* duro.
harden ➤ *tr & intr* endurecer(se).
hardly ➤ *adv* apenas ■ **h. ever** casi nunca.
hardship ➤ *s* sufrimiento; *(privation)* penuria.
hardware ➤ *s* (artículos de) ferretería; COMPUT. equipo, maquinaria, hardware *m* ■ **h. store** ferretería.
hare ➤ *s* liebre *f.*
harm ➤ *s* daño, perjuicio ➤ *tr* hacer daño.
harmful ➤ *adj* perjudicial.
harmless ➤ *adj* inocuo.
harmonica ➤ *s* armónica.
harmonious ➤ *adj* armonioso.
harmony ➤ *s* armonía.
harness ➤ *s* arreos ➤ *tr (horse)* enjaezar; *(energy)* aprovechar, utilizar.
harp ➤ *s* arpa ➤ **to h. on** machacar.
harsh ➤ *adj* áspero; *(stern)* severo.
harvest ➤ *s* cosecha; *(of grapes)* vendimia ➤ *tr & intr* cosechar.
has ➤ *vea* **have** *en tabla de verbos.*
hassle FAM. ➤ *s* jaleo ➤ *tr* fastidiar, molestar.
haste ➤ *s* prisa.
hasty ➤ *adj* apresurado; *(rash)* precipitado.
hat ➤ *s* sombrero.
hatch[1] ➤ *s* trampa; MARÍT. escotilla.
hatch[2] ➤ *intr* salir del cascarón ➤ *tr (a plot)* tramar.
hatchet ➤ *s* hacha.
hate ➤ *tr* odiar ➤ *intr* sentir odio ➤ *s* odio.
hatred ➤ *s* odio.
haul ➤ *intr & tr* halar, tirar (de) ➤ *s* ■ **over the long h.** a la larga.
have◇ ➤ *tr* tener; *(to possess)* poseer; *(in mind)* retener; *(disease)* sufrir de; *(good time)* pasar; *(baby)* dar a luz ■ **to be had** JER. ser engañado • **to h. to do with** tener que ver con ➤ *aux* haber.
havoc ➤ *s* estragos.
hawk ➤ *s* halcón *m.*
hay ➤ *s* heno ■ **h. fever** fiebre del heno.
hazard ➤ *s* riesgo, peligro; *(chance)* azar *m* ➤ *tr* arriesgar; *(a guess)* aventurar.
haze ➤ *s* niebla ligera.
hazelnut ➤ *s* avellana.
hazy ➤ *adj* nebuloso.
he ➤ *pron* él ➤ *s* varón *m.*
head ➤ *s* cabeza; *(sense)* inteligencia; *(chief)* jefe *m* ■ **h. start** ventaja • **to be over one's h.** estar (algo) fuera de la capacidad de uno • **to go to one's h.** subírsele a la cabeza ■ *pl* cara (de moneda) • **h. or tails** cara o cruz ➤ *tr* encabezar ➤ *intr* dirigirse ■ **to h. back** regresar • **to h. for** ir con rumbo a ➤ *adj* principal, central.
headache ➤ *s* dolor *m* de cabeza.
headlight ➤ *s* faro, luz delantera.
headline ➤ *s* titular *m.*
headmaster ➤ *s* EDUC. director *m.*
headmistress ➤ *s* EDUC. directora.
headphones ➤ *spl* auriculares *m.*
headquarters ➤ *spl* cuartel *m* general; *(police)* jefatura; COM. oficina central.
headwaiter ➤ *s* jefe *m* de comedor.
headway ➤ *s* ■ **to make h.** avanzar, progresar.
heal ➤ *tr* curar ➤ *intr* sanar.
health ➤ *s* salud *f* ■ **h. food** alimentos naturales ■ **h. insurance** seguro médico.
healthy ➤ *adj* sano; *(air, place)* saludable, salubre.
heap ➤ *s* montón ➤ *tr* amontonar.
hear◇ ➤ *tr* oír; *(to listen to)* escuchar; *(to know)* enterarse de ➤ *intr* oír ■ **to h. from** tener noticias de.
hearing ➤ *s* oído; DER. audiencia ■ **h. aid** audífono.
hearse ➤ *s* carroza fúnebre.
heart ➤ *s* corazón *m; (in cards)* corazón, copa ■ **at h.** en el fondo • **h. failure** colapso (cardiaco) • **to lose h.** descorazonarse • **to one's h.'s content** hasta saciarse • **to take h.** cobrar ánimo • **with all** *o* **from one's h.** de todo corazón.
heartbeat ➤ *s* latido.
heartbreak ➤ *s* angustia, pena.
heartburn ➤ *s* acedía.
hearth ➤ *s* hogar *m.*
hearty ➤ *adj* cordial, sincero; *(robust)* robusto; *(appetite)* bueno; *(meal)* abundante.
heat ➤ *s* calor *m;* DEP. carrera; *(for building)* calefacción *f* ■ **h. rash** miliaria • **h. stroke** insolación ➤ *tr & intr* calentar(se); *(to excite)* acalorar(se) ■ **to h. up** recalentarse.
heater ➤ *s* estufa, calentador *m.*
heating calefacción *f.*
heave ➤ *tr* alzar (con esfuerzo); *(to hurl)* arrojar; *(sigh)* exhalar.
heaven ➤ *s* cielo ■ **for h.'s sake!** ¡por Diós! ■ *spl* cielo • **good h.!** ¡cielos!
heavy ➤ *adj* pesado; *(rain)* fuerte; *(grave)* serio; *(heart)* oprimido.
hectic ➤ *adj* ajetreado.
hedge ➤ *s* seto (vivo) ➤ *tr* encerrar (con us seto) ■ **to h. against** cubrirse contra.
heed ➤ *tr* hacer caso (a, de) ➤ *s* ■ **to pay h. to** prestar atención a.
heedless ➤ *adj* descuidado, incauto.
heel ➤ *s* talón *m; (of shoe)* tacón *m.*
hefty ➤ *adj* pesado; *(strong)* robusto.
height ➤ *s* altura, alto; *(summit)* cumbre *f; (of folly)* colmo; *(of person)* estatura.
heir ➤ *s* heredero/a.
heiress ➤ *s* heredera (de una fortuna).
helicopter ➤ *s* helicóptero.
hell ➤ *s* infierno ■ **to h. with it!** ¡al diablo! • **to raise h.** armar una de todos los diablos • **what, who the h. . . .?** ¿qué, quién diablos . . .?
hello ➤ *interj* ¡hola!
helm ➤ *s* timón *m.*
helmet ➤ *s* casco.
help ➤ *tr* ayudar; *(to relieve)* aliviar ■ **to h. oneself to** *(food)* servirse ➤ *intr* ser útil ■ **to h. out** dar una mano ➤ *s* ayuda.
helper ➤ *s* ayudante *mf.*
helpful ➤ *adj* útil; *(kind)* amable.
helping ➤ *s* ración *f.*
helpless ➤ *adj* indefenso; *(powerless)* incapaz.
hem ➤ *s* dobladillo.
hemorrhage ➤ *s & intr* (sufrir una) hemorragia.
hen ➤ *s* gallina.
hepatitis ➤ *s* hepatitis *f.*
her ➤ *pron* la, le, ella ■ **I saw h.** la ví • **for h.** para ella ➤ *adj* su, de ella.
herb ➤ *s* hierba ■ *pl* finas hierbas.
herd ➤ *s & tr* (reunir en) manada.
here ➤ *adv* aquí; *(to this place)* acá ■ **that's neither h. nor there** eso no viene al caso.
heredity ➤ *s* herencia.
heritage ➤ *s* herencia.
hermit ➤ *s* ermitaño/a.
hero ➤ *s* héroe *m;* LIT. protagonista *mf.*
heroic ➤ *adj* heróico.
heroine ➤ *s* heroina; LIT. protagonista.
herpes ➤ *s* herpes *m.*
herring ➤ *s* arenque *m.*
hers ➤ *pron* (el) suyo, el de ella.
herself ➤ *pron* ■ **by h.** sola • **she h.** ella misma • **she hurt h.** se lastimó.
hesitant ➤ *adj* vacilante.
hesitate ➤ *intr* vacilar; *(not to dare)* no atreverse.
hesitation ➤ *s* indecisión *f; (vacillation)* titubeo.
hey ➤ *interj* ¡eh!, ¡oiga!
hi ➤ *interj* ¡hola!
hiccup ➤ *s* hipo ➤ *intr* tener hipo, hipar.
hide[1]◇ ➤ *tr* ocultar, esconder; *(to conceal)* disimular; *(to cover up)* tapar ➤ *intr* esconderse; *(to seek refuge)* refugiarse.
hide[2] ➤ *s* cuero.
hideaway ➤ *s* escondite *m; (retreat)* retiro.
hideous ➤ *adj* espantoso; *(atrocious)* atroz.
hide-out ➤ *s* escondite *m.*
hiding ➤ *s* ■ **in h.** escondido.
high ➤ *adj* alto; *(wind, fever)* fuerte; *(voice)* agudo; *(advanced)* avanzado; *(crime)* grave; JER. drogado ■ **h. jump** salto de altura • **h. priority** primera importancia • **h. school** escuela secundaria • **h. tide** pleamar • **two feet h.** dos pies de altura ➤ *adv* en lo alto, alto ■ **to look h. and low** buscar por todas partes ➤ *s* altura; *(gear)* directa.
highchair ➤ *s* silla alta para niños.
higher ➤ *adj* más alto; *(greater)* mayor; *(advanced)* superior.
highlands ➤ *spl* tierras altas, sierra.
highlight ➤ *s* toque *m* de luz; *(event)* suceso *o* atracción *f* principal ➤ *tr* iluminar; *(to emphasize)* destacar.
highly ➤ *adv* altamente; *(extremely)* extremadamente; *(well)* muy bien.
high-pitched ➤ *adj* agudo; *(voice)* chillón.
high-rise ➤ *s* edificio de muchos pisos.
high-tech ➤ *adj* de tecnología avanzada.
highway ➤ *s* carretera, autopista.
hijack ➤ *tr* secuestrar.
hijacker ➤ *s* secuestrador/a; *(of plane)* pirata *mf* aéreo.
hijacking ➤ *s* secuestro; *(of plane)* piratería aérea.
hike ➤ *intr* caminar ➤ *s* caminata.
hiker ➤ *s* excursionista *mf.*
hill ➤ *s* colina; *(heap)* montón *m.*
hilly ➤ *adj* montuoso.
him ➤ *pron* le, lo, él ■ **I know h.** lo conozco • **to h.** a él.
himself ➤ *pron* ■ **by h.** solo • **he h.** él mismo • **he hit h.** se golpeó.
hinder ➤ *tr* impedir, obstaculizar.
hinge ➤ *s* bisagra.
hint ➤ *s* insinuación *f; (tip)* sugerencia ➤ *tr & intr* ■ **to h. (at)** insinuar.
hip ➤ *s* ANAT. cadera.
hippopotamus ➤ *s* hipopótamo.
hire ➤ *tr* emplear; *(to rent)* alquilar ➤ *s* ■ **for h.** se alquila.
his ➤ *adj* su, de él ➤ *pron* (el) suyo, el de él.
Hispanic ➤ *adj & s* hispano/a.
hiss ➤ *s* siseo ➤ *tr & intr* silbar.
historic(al) ➤ *adj* histórico.
history ➤ *s* historia.
hit◇ ➤ *tr* golpear; *(to collide with)* chocar contra *o* con ➤ *s* golpe *m; (collision)* choque *m; (success)* éxito.
hitch ➤ *tr* enganchar ■ **to h. a ride** FAM. hacerse llevar en automovil ➤ *intr* FAM. *(to hitchhike)* hacer autostop.
hitchhike ➤ *intr* hacer autostop.
hitchhiker ➤ *s* autostopista *mf.*
hive ➤ *s* colmena; *(colony)* enjambre *m.*
hoarse ➤ *adj* ronco.
hoax ➤ *s* engaño, trampa.
hobby ➤ *s* pasatiempo, afición *f.*
hobo ➤ *s* vago, vagabundo.
hockey ➤ *s* hockey *m.*
hoe ➤ *s* azada ➤ *tr & intr* azadonar.
hog ➤ *s* cerdo, puerco ➤ *tr* acaparar.
hold◇ ➤ *tr* asir, agarrar; *(to take)* tener; *(to support)* sostener; *(to secure)* sujetar; *(for questioning)* tener bajo custodia; *(to keep)* retener; *(to control)* contener; *(to occupy)* ocupar; *(meeting)* celebrar; *(elections)* convocar ■ **to h. back** *(to repress)* reprimir, contener • **to h. down a job** mantener un trabajo • **to h. off** alejar • **to h. one's own** defenderse • **to h. to** hacer cumplir • **to h. up** FAM. *(to delay)* atrasar; *(to rob)* atracar; *(to stop)* detener ➤ *intr* asirse, agarrarse; *(to be firm)* sostenerse; *(to be valid)* seguir en vigor ■ **to h. off** demorarse • **to h. on** *(to grip)* agarrarse bien; *(to wait)* aguardar, esperar • **to h. out** *o* **up** *(to last)* durar; *(to resist)* aguantar ➤ *s (grip)* asidero; *(influence)* influencia ■ **to get h. of** *(to grasp)* coger; *(to obtain)* conseguir • **to get h. of oneself** dominarse.
holdup ➤ *s (delay)* demora; *(robbery)* asalto, atraco (a mano armada).
hole ➤ *s* hueco; *(in ground)* hoyo; *(in road)* bache *m; (small)* agujero.
holiday ➤ *s* día feriado; RELIG. día de fiesta.
hollow ➤ *adj* hueco; *(empty)* vacío ➤ *s* hueco; FIG. vacío.
holly ➤ *s* acebo.
holy ➤ *adj* sacro; *(revered)* venerable; *(saintly)* santo, pío ■ **h. day** fiesta de guardar.
home ➤ *s* casa; *(residence)* domicilio; *(household)* hogar *m* ■ **to feel at h.** sentirse a gusto ➤ *adj* casero; *(native)* natal; *(team)* de casa ■ **h. page** página inicial • **h. run** DEP. jonrón ➤ *adv* ■ **at h.** en casa • **to be h.** estar (en casa).
homeless ➤ *adj* sin hogar.
homely ➤ *adj* sin atractivo; *(plain)* sencillo, rústico.
homemade ➤ *adj* hecho en casa.
homesick ➤ *adj* nostálgico.
hometown ➤ *s* ciudad *f* de origen.
homeward ➤ *adj* de vuelto, de regreso ➤ *adv* hacia casa.
homework ➤ *s* deberes *m,* tareas escolares.
homosexual ➤ *adj & s* homosexual *mf.*
Honduran ➤ *adj & s* hondureño/a.
honest ➤ *adj* honesto; *(sincere)* franco.
honesty ➤ *s* honestidad *f; (integrity)* honradez *f; (truthfulness)* veracidad *f.*
honey ➤ *s* miel *f; (darling)* tesoro.
honeymoon ➤ *s & intr* (pasar la) luna de miel.
honk ➤ *tr & intr* tocar (la bocina) ➤ *s* bocinazo; *(goose)* graznido.
honor ➤ *s* honor ➤ *tr* honrar; *(check)* aceptar; *(contract)* cumplir.
honorable ➤ *adj* honorable; *(praiseworthy)* honroso; *(honest)* honrado.
hood ➤ *s* capucha; *(of car)* capó.
hoof ➤ *s* pezuña.
hook ➤ *s* gancho; *(for fishing)* anzuelo ■ **off the h.** *(telephone)* descolgado ➤ *tr* enganchar ■ **to get hooked on** enviciarse con.
hooked ➤ *adj* ganchudo; *(addicted)* adicto.
hop ➤ *intr* brincar; *(to skip)* saltar con un pie ➤ *s* brinco.
hope ➤ *intr* esperar ➤ *s* esperanza.
hopeful ➤ *adj* esperanzado; *(promising)* prometedor.
hopeless ➤ *adj* desesperado.
horizon ➤ *s* horizonte *m.*
horizontal ➤ *adj & s* horizontal *f.*
hormonal ➤ *adj* hormonal.
hormone ➤ *s* hormona.
horn ➤ *s* cuerno; AUTO., TEC. bocina.
horrible ➤ *adj* horrible.
horrify ➤ *tr* horrorizar.
horror ➤ *s* horror *m* ■ **h. film** película de miedo.
horse ➤ *s* caballo.
horseback ➤ *adv* a caballo.
hose ➤ *s* medias; *(for water)* manguera.
hospitable ➤ *adj* hospitalario; *(receptive)* receptivo.
hospital ➤ *s* hospital *m.*
hospitality ➤ *s* hospitalidad *f.*
hospitalize ➤ *tr* hospitalizar.
host ➤ *s (at a meal)* anfitrión *m; (of inn)* mesonero/a; TELEV. presentador/a.
hostage ➤ *s* rehén *mf.*
hostel ➤ *s* albergue *m* (para jóvenes).
hostess ➤ *s (host)* anfitriona; *(waitress)* camarera; *(stewardess)* azafata.
hostile ➤ *adj* hostil.

hostility ➤ *s* hostilidad.
hot ➤ *adj* caliente; *(climate)* cálido; *(spicy)* picante; *(temper)* vivo ■ **h. line** línea de emergencia.
hotel ➤ *s* hotel *m.*
hound ➤ *s* podenco ➤ *tr* acosar.
hour ➤ *s* hora.
hourly ➤ *adj* por hora ➤ *adv* a cada hora.
house ➤ *s* casa ➤ *tr* alojar; *(to shelter)* proteger; *(to contain)* contener.
household ➤ *s* casa.
housekeeping ➤ *s* manejo de una casa.
housewarming ➤ *s* fiesta para el estreno de una casa.
housewife ➤ *s* ama de casa.
housework ➤ *s* quehaceres domésticos.
housing ➤ *s* vivienda.
how ➤ *adv* cómo; *(in what condition)* qué tal; *(to what extent)* cuánto, qué ■ **h. about . . .?** ¿qué te parece . . .? • **h. do you do?** ¿cómo está usted? • **h. old are you?** ¿cuántos años tienes? ➤ *conj* cómo; *(that)* que.
however ➤ *adv* de cualquier modo; *(to whatever degree)* por . . . que ■ **h. much** por más *o* por mucho que ➤ *conj* no obstante.
howl ➤ *intr* aullar ➤ *tr* gritar ➤ *s* aullido.
huddle ➤ *intr* apiñarse ➤ *s* grupo.
hug ➤ *tr* abrazar ➤ *s* abrazo.
huge ➤ *adj* enorme.
hull ➤ *s (shell)* cáscara; MARÍT. casco.
hum ➤ *tr & intr* tararear ➤ *s* zumbido.
human ➤ *adj & s* (ser) humano ■ **h. being** ser humano.
humanity ➤ *s* humanidad *f; (humanness)* naturaleza humana.
humble ➤ *adj* humilde.
humid ➤ *adj* húmedo.
humidity ➤ *s* humedad *f.*
humiliate ➤ *tr* humillar.
humiliation ➤ *s* humillación *f.*
humor ➤ *s* humor *m.*
humorous ➤ *adj* cómico.
hunch ➤ *s (feeling)* corazonada.
hundred ➤ *s & adj* cien, ciento; MAT. centena ■ *pl* centenares.
hunger ➤ *s* hambre *f* ➤ *intr* tener hambre (*for, after* de).
hungry ➤ *adj* hambriento.
hunt ➤ *tr* cazar ➤ *s* caza.
hunter ➤ *s* cazador/a.
hunting ➤ *s* cacería ➤ *adj* de caza.
hurdle ➤ *s* valla; FIG. barrera.
hurl ➤ *tr* lanzar.
hurricane ➤ *s* huracán *m.*
hurry ➤ *intr* darse prisa ■ **to h. up** apresurarse ➤ *tr* apurar; *(to rush)* dar prisa a ➤ *s* prisa; *(urgency)* apuro ■ **to be in a h. (to)** tener prisa (por).
hurt✧ ➤ *tr* hacer daño ➤ *intr* doler ➤ *s (harm)* daño; *(anguish)* angustia.
husband ➤ *s* marido.
hush ➤ *tr & intr* callar(se) ➤ *s* silencio.
hustle ➤ *tr* empujar; FAM. *(to hurry)* apurar ➤ *s* FAM. ajetreo.
hut ➤ *s* choza.
hydrant ➤ *s* boca de agua.
hydrogen ➤ *s* hidrógeno.
hygiene ➤ *s* higiene *f.*
hygienic ➤ *adj* higiénico.
hymn ➤ *s* himno.
hyphen ➤ *s* guión *m.*
hypocrisy ➤ *s* hipocresía.
hypocrite ➤ *s* hipócrita *mf.*
hysteric ➤ *s* histérico.
hysterical ➤ *adj* histérico.

I

I ➤ *pron* yo ➤ *s* yo, ego.
ice ➤ *s* hielo ■ **i. cream** helado • **i.-cream cone** helado de cucurucho • **i. cube** cubito de hielo ➤ *tr* helar; *(a cake)* escarchar.
iceberg ➤ *s* iceberg *m.*
ice-skate ➤ *intr* patinar sobre hielo.
icicle ➤ *s* carámbano.
icing ➤ *s* alcorza, escarchado.
icon ➤ *s* icono.
icy ➤ *adj* helado; *(person, look)* glacial.
idea ➤ *s* idea.
ideal ➤ *adj & s* ideal *m.*
identical ➤ *adj* idéntico.
identification ➤ *s* identificación *f* ■ **i. card, papers** carnet, documentos de identidad.
identify ➤ *tr & intr* identificar(se).
identity ➤ *s* identidad *f* ■ **i. card, papers** tarjeta, documentos de identidad.
idiom ➤ *s* modismo.
idiot ➤ *s* idiota *mf.*
idiotic ➤ *adj* idiota.
idle ➤ *adj* ocioso; *(threat)* vano.
idol ➤ *s* ídolo.
idolize ➤ *tr* idolatrar.
if ➤ *conj* si ■ **if and when** siempre y cuando • **if at all** si es que.
ignite ➤ *tr & intr* encender(se).
ignition ➤ *s* AUTO. encendido.
ignorance ➤ *s* ignorancia.
ignorant ➤ *adj* ignorante.
ignore ➤ *tr (to disregard)* no hacer caso de; *(to leave out)* pasar por alto.
ill ➤ *adj* enfermo, malo ➤ *s* mal *m.*
illegal ➤ *adj* ilegal ➤ *s* inmigrante *mf* ilegal.
illegible ➤ *adj* ilegible.
illiterate ➤ *s & adj* analfabeto/a.
illness ➤ *s* enfermedad *f.*
illuminate ➤ *tr* iluminar.
illusion ➤ *s* ilusión *f.*
illustrate ➤ *tr & intr* ilustrar.
illustration ➤ *s* ilustración *f.*
image ➤ *s* imagen *f.*
imagination ➤ *s* imaginación *f.*
imagine ➤ *tr* imaginar; *(to suppose)* imaginarse.
imbecile ➤ *adj & s* imbécil *mf.*
imitate ➤ *tr* imitar.
imitation ➤ *s* imitación *f.*
immature ➤ *adj* inmaduro.
immediate ➤ *adj* inmediato.
immense ➤ *adj* inmenso, enorme.
immigrant ➤ *s* inmigrante *mf.*
immigration ➤ *s* inmigración *f.*
immortal ➤ *adj & s* inmortal *mf.*
immune ➤ *adj* inmune (*from* de).
immunize ➤ *tr* inmunizar.
impact ➤ *s* impacto, choque *m; (influence)* efecto.
impatience ➤ *s* impaciencia.
impatient ➤ *adj* impaciente.
impel ➤ *tr* impeler, impulsar.
imperial ➤ *adj* imperial.
imperative ➤ *adj* imperioso.
impersonate ➤ *tr* hacerse pasar por.
impersonator ➤ *s* imitador/a.
impertinent ➤ *adj* impertinente.
impetus ➤ *s* ímpetu *m,* impulso.
implant ➤ *tr* implantar ➤ *s* MED. injerto.
implement ➤ *s* utensilio, instrumento ➤ *tr* poner en práctica.
implication ➤ *s* implicación *f; (inference)* inferencia.
implied ➤ *adj* implícito.
imply ➤ *tr (to entail)* implicar; *(to hint)* dar a entender, insinuar.
impolite ➤ *adj* descortés.
import ➤ *tr* importar ➤ *s* artículo importado; *(business)* importación *f.*
importance ➤ *s* importancia.
important ➤ *adj* importante.
importer ➤ *s* importador/a.
impose ➤ *tr* imponer ➤ *intr* ■ **to i. (up)on** abusar de.
imposing ➤ *adj* imponente.
imposition ➤ *s (act)* imposición *f; (unfair demand)* abuso.
impossibility ➤ *s* imposibilidad *f.*
impossible ➤ *adj* imposible.
impostor ➤ *s* impostor/a.
impractical ➤ *adj* poco práctico.
impress ➤ *tr* impresionar ■ **I was not impressed** no me pareció gran cosa.
impression ➤ *s* impresión *f; (memory)* idea ■ **to be under the i. that** tener la impresión de que.
impressive ➤ *adj* impresionante.
imprison ➤ *tr* aprisionar.
improbable ➤ *adj* improbable.
improper ➤ *adj* impropio; *(indecorous)* incorrecto, indebido.
improve ➤ *tr & intr* mejorar(se).
improvement ➤ *s* mejora; *(in school)* progreso; *(in health)* mejoría.
improvise ➤ *tr & intr* improvisar.
impudent ➤ *adj* impudente, descarado.
impulse ➤ *s* impulso.
impulsive ➤ *adj* impetuoso.
impurity ➤ *s* impureza.
in ➤ *prep* en, dentro de, por; *(time)* a, por, durante, de; *(arrival)* a; *(method)* a, en, por; *(with verbs)* al, mientras ➤ *adv (inside)* (a)dentro ■ **is the doctor in?** ¿está el médico? • **to be in on** tomar parte en; *(to know)* estar enterado de • **to have it in for someone** FAM. tenerle antipatía a alguien ➤ *adj* FAM. *(fashionable)* de moda.
inability ➤ *s* incapacidad *f.*
inaccessible ➤ *adj* inaccesible.
inaccuracy ➤ *s* inexactitud *f.*
inaccurate ➤ *adj* inexacto.
inadequacy ➤ *s* inadecuación *f; (insufficiency)* insuficiencia.
inadequate ➤ *adj* inadecuado; *(insufficient)* insuficiente.
inappropriate ➤ *adj* impropio.
inaugurate ➤ *tr* inaugurar.
inauguration ➤ *s* inauguración *f.*
incapable ➤ *adj* incapaz; *(incompetent)* incompetente.
incentive ➤ *s* incentivo.
inch ➤ *s* pulgada ■ **i. by i.** poco a poco ➤ *intr* avanzar poco a poco.
incident ➤ *adj & s* incidente *m.*
incite ➤ *tr* incitar.
incitement ➤ *s* incitación *f.*
inclination ➤ *s* inclinación *f; (tendency)* tendencia; *(preference)* gusto.
incline ➤ *tr & intr* inclinar(se) ■ **to be inclined to** estar dispuesto a.
include ➤ *tr* incluir, abarcar.
inclusive ➤ *adj (including)* inclusive; *(comprehensive)* inclusivo.
income ➤ *s* ingresos *m; (on investments)* renta; *(profit)* utilidades *f* ■ **i. tax** impuesto sobre la renta.
incompatible ➤ *adj* incompatible.
incompetent ➤ *adj & s* (persona) incompetente.
incomplete ➤ *adj* incompleto.
inconceivable ➤ *adj* inconcebible.
inconsiderate ➤ *adj* desconsiderado.
inconsistency ➤ *s* inconsecuencia.
inconsistent ➤ *adj* inconsecuente.
inconspicuous ➤ *adj* no conspicuo.
inconvenience ➤ *s* inconveniencia; *(bother)* molestia ➤ *tr* incomodar.
inconvenient ➤ *adj* inconveniente; *(bothersome)* molesto.
incorporate ➤ *tr* incorporar, incluir.
incorrect ➤ *adj* incorrecto.
increase ➤ *tr & intr* aumentar ➤ *s* aumento; *(in prices)* subida, alza; *(in production)* incremento.
increasing ➤ *adj* creciente.
increasingly ➤ *adv* cada vez más.
incredible ➤ *adj* increíble.
incurable ➤ *adj* incurable.
indecent ➤ *adj* indecente.
indecisive ➤ *adj (inconclusive)* dudoso; *(irresolute)* indeciso, irresoluto.
indeed ➤ *adv (truly)* verdaderamente; *(in fact)* en efecto; *(of course)* claro ■ **i.?** ¿de verdad? • **that is i. a luxury** eso sí que es lujo ➤ *interj* de veras, verdad.
indefinite ➤ *adj* indefinido.
Indian ➤ *adj & s* indio/a.
independence ➤ *s* independencia.
independent ➤ *adj & s* independiente *mf.*
index ➤ *s* índice *m* ■ **i. card** ficha, tarjeta.
indicate ➤ *tr* indicar.
indication ➤ *s* indicación *f; (sign)* indicio.
indicator ➤ *s* indicador *m.*
indifference ➤ *s* indiferencia.
indifferent ➤ *adj* indiferente.
indigestion ➤ *s* indigestión *f.*
indignant ➤ *adj* indignado.
indirect ➤ *adj* indirecto.
indiscreet ➤ *adj* indiscreto.
indiscriminate ➤ *adj* sin criterio; *(random)* al azar.
indisposed ➤ *adj (slightly ill)* indispuesto; *(averse)* averso.
indistinguishable ➤ *adj* indistinguible.
individual ➤ *adj* individual; *(style, manner)* particular ➤ *s* individuo.
individuality ➤ *s* individualidad *f,* particularidad *f.*
indoor ➤ *adj* interior, interno.
indoors ➤ *adv* dentro, bajo techo.
induce ➤ *tr* ocasionar; *(childbirth)* provocar.
indulge ➤ *tr (to pamper)* consentir, mimar; *(to gratify)* satisfacer.
indulgent ➤ *adj* indulgente.
industrial ➤ *adj* industrial.
industry ➤ *s* industria; *(diligence)* diligencia.
inedible ➤ *adj* incomestible.
ineffective ➤ *adj* ineficaz.
inefficient ➤ *adj* ineficiente, ineficaz.
inept ➤ *adj* inepto, incapaz.
inequality ➤ *s* desigualdad *f.*
inevitable ➤ *adj* inevitable.
inexcusable ➤ *adj* inexcusable.
inexpensive ➤ *adj* barato.
inexperienced ➤ *adj* inexperto.
inexplicable ➤ *adj* inexplicable.
infallible ➤ *adj* infalible.
infamous ➤ *adj* infame.
infancy ➤ *s* infancia.
infant ➤ *s* infante *mf,* niño/a.
infantry ➤ *s* infantería.
infatuated ➤ *adj* locamente enamorado; *(foolish)* encaprichado.
infatuation ➤ *s* encaprichamiento.
infect ➤ *tr* infectar.
infection ➤ *s* infección *f.*
infectious ➤ *adj* infeccioso.
inferior ➤ *adj & s* inferior *mf.*
inferiority ➤ *s* inferioridad *f.*
infest ➤ *tr* infestar, plagar.
infinite ➤ *adj & s* infinito.
infinitive ➤ *s* infinitivo.
infinity ➤ *s* infinidad *f;* MAT. infinito.
infirm ➤ *adj* débil, enfermizo.
infirmary ➤ *s* enfermería.
inflame ➤ *tr* inflamar.
inflammable ➤ *adj* inflamable.
inflammation ➤ *s* inflamación *f.*
inflate ➤ *tr* inflar.
inflation ➤ *s* inflación *f.*
inflexible ➤ *adj* inflexible.
inflict ➤ *tr* infligir, causar.
influence ➤ *s* influencia, influjo ➤ *tr* influir en, ejercer influencia sobre.
influential ➤ *adj* influyente.
influenza ➤ *s* influenza.
influx ➤ *s* afluencia, entrada.
inform ➤ *tr* informar, avisar.
informal ➤ *adj (casual)* familiar, llano; *(unofficial)* extraoficial; *(agreement)* no legalizado.
information ➤ *s* información *f; (data)* datos ■ **for your i.** para su conocimiento.
informative ➤ *adj* informativo.
infuriate ➤ *tr* enfurecer.
infusion ➤ *s* infusión *f.*
ingenious ➤ *adj* ingenioso.
ingenuity ➤ *s* ingenio.
ingest ➤ *tr* ingerir.
ingratitude ➤ *s* ingratitud *f.*
ingredient ➤ *s* ingrediente *m.*
inhabit ➤ *tr* habitar, vivir en.
inhabitant ➤ *s* habitante *mf.*
inhale ➤ *tr* aspirar; *(smoke)* tragar; MED. inhalar ➤ *intr* aspirar aire.
inherit ➤ *tr* heredar.
inheritance ➤ *s* herencia.
inhibit ➤ *tr* inhibir; *(to prevent)* impedir; *(to prohibit)* prohibir.
inhibition ➤ *s* inhibición *f.*
inhospitable ➤ *adj* inhospitalario; *(barren)* inhóspito.
initial ➤ *adj & s* inicial *f* ■ *spl (person)* iniciales; *(organization)* siglas.
initiative ➤ *s* iniciativa.
inject ➤ *tr* inyectar.
injection ➤ *s* inyección *f.*
injure ➤ *tr* lastimar, herir.
injury ➤ *s* herida.
injustice ➤ *s* injusticia.
ink ➤ *s* tinta.
inland ➤ *adj* (del) interior ➤ *adv* tierra adentro.
in-law ➤ *s* pariente político.
inmate ➤ *s (of asylum)* asilado/a; *(prisoner)* preso/a.
inn ➤ *s* posada, hostería.
inner ➤ *adj* interior ■ **i. tube** cámara.
innocence ➤ *s* inocencia.
innocent ➤ *adj & s* inocente *mf.*
inoculate ➤ *tr* inocular.
inoculation ➤ *s* inoculación *f.*
inpatient ➤ *s* paciente *mf* internado en un hospital.
input ➤ *s* COMPUT., ELEC. entrada ➤ *tr* COMPUT. entrar, ingresar.
inquire ➤ *tr & intr* preguntar (por).
inquiry ➤ *s* pregunta; *(investigation)* investigación *f,* inquisición *f.*
inquisitive ➤ *adj (prying)* preguntón, inquisitivo; *(curious)* curioso.
insane ➤ *adj* loco.
insanity ➤ *s* locura.
inscribe ➤ *tr* inscribir.
inscription ➤ *s* inscripción *f.*
insect ➤ *s* insecto.
insecticide ➤ *s* insecticida *m.*
insecure ➤ *adj* inseguro.
insensitive ➤ *adj* insensible.
insert ➤ *tr (into)* insertar, introducir; *(between)* intercalar.
inside ➤ *s* interior *m,* parte *f* de adentro ■ **i. out** al revés ■ *pl* FAM. entrañas ➤ *adj (inner)* interior, interno ■ *adv (within)* dentro, adentro; *(on the inner side)* por dentro ➤ *prep* dentro de.
insight ➤ *s* perspicacia.
insignificant ➤ *adj* insignificante.
insincere ➤ *adj* insincero.
insist ➤ *intr* insistir.
insistence ➤ *s* insistencia.

insistent ➤ *adj* insistente.
insolence ➤ *s* insolencia, descaro.
insolent ➤ *adj* insolente, descarado.
insomnia ➤ *s* insomnio.
inspect ➤ *tr* inspeccionar.
inspection ➤ *s* inspección *f.*
inspector ➤ *s* inspector/a.
inspiration ➤ *s* inspiración *f.*
inspire ➤ *tr* inspirar, motivar; *(emotion)* infundir ■ **to i. with** llenar de.
install ➤ *tr* instalar.
installment ➤ *s* plazo, pago ■ **i. plan** pago a plazos.
instance ➤ *s (example)* ejemplo, muestra; *(case)* caso ■ **for i.** por ejemplo.
instant ➤ *s* instante *m*, momento ➤ *adj* inmediato; *(success)* instantáneo.
instantly ➤ *adv* inmediatamente.
instead ➤ *adv* en su lugar; *(rather than)* en cambio ■ **i. of** en vez de.
instinct ➤ *s* instinto.
instinctive ➤ *adj* instintivo.
institute ➤ *tr* instituir ➤ *s* instituto.
institution ➤ *s* institución *f.*
instruct ➤ *tr* instruir; *(to order)* dar instrucciones, mandar.
instruction ➤ *s* instrucción *f.*
instructor ➤ *s* instructor/a.
instrument ➤ *s* instrumento.
insufficient ➤ *adj* insuficiente.
insulate ➤ *tr* aislar.
insulation ➤ *s* aislamiento.
insulin ➤ *s* insulina.
insult ➤ *tr* insultar ➤ *s* insulto.
insurance ➤ *s* seguro; FIG. seguridad *f.*
insure ➤ *tr* asegurar.
insured ➤ *s* asegurado.
intact ➤ *adj* intacto.
integral ➤ *adj & s* integral *f.*
intellect ➤ *s* intelecto.
intellectual ➤ *adj & s* intelectual *mf.*
intelligence ➤ *s* inteligencia.
intelligent ➤ *adj* inteligente.
intelligible ➤ *adj* inteligible.
intend ➤ *tr (to plan)* proponerse; *(to mean)* pensar, tener intención de.
intense ➤ *adj* intenso.
intensify ➤ *tr & intr* intensificar(se).
intensity ➤ *s* intensidad *f.*
intensive ➤ *adj* intensivo.
intent ➤ *s* intención *f*, propósito.
intention ➤ *s* intención *f.*
intentional ➤ *adj* intencional.
intercept ➤ *tr* interceptar.
interchange ➤ *s* intercambio; *(highway junction)* empalme *m.*
interchangeable ➤ *adj* intercambiable.
intercom ➤ *s* sistema *m* de intercomunicación.
interest ➤ *s* interés *m* ■ **in one's own i.** en beneficio propio • **to be of i.** ser interesante ➤ *tr* interesar.
interesting ➤ *adj* interesante.
interfere ➤ *intr* interferir; *(to meddle)* entrometerse ■ **to i. with** obstruir.
interference ➤ *s* interferencia.
interior ➤ *adj & s* interior *m.*
intermediary ➤ *s* intermediario/a.
intermediate ➤ *adj* intermedio.
intermission ➤ *s* intermisión *f*; TEAT. intermedio, entreacto.
intern ➤ *s* interno/a, médico/a residente.
internal ➤ *adj* interno; *(domestic)* interior, nacional.
international ➤ *adj* internacional.
Internet ➤ *s* Internet *m*, Red *f.*
interpret ➤ *tr* interpretar.
interpreter ➤ *s* intérprete *mf.*
interrogate ➤ *tr* interrogar.
interrogation ➤ *s* interrogación *f.*
interrupt ➤ *tr* interrumpir.
interruption ➤ *s* interrupción *f.*
intersect ➤ *tr & intr* cruzarse.
intersection ➤ *s* intersección *f.*
interval ➤ *s* intervalo.
intervene ➤ *intr* intervenir.
intervention ➤ *s* intervención *f.*
interview ➤ *s* entrevista ➤ *tr & intr* entrevistar(se).
interviewer ➤ *s* entrevistador/a.
intimate ➤ *adj & s* íntimo/a.
into ➤ *prep* en, a, dentro de, contra.
intolerable ➤ *adj* intolerable.
intoxicate ➤ *tr* embriagar.
intransitive ➤ *adj & s* (verbo) intransitivo.
intricate ➤ *adj* complejo, intrincado.
intrigue ➤ *s* intriga ➤ *intr & tr* intrigar.
introduce ➤ *tr* presentar; *(to bring into use)* introducir.
introduction ➤ *s* introducción *f*; *(of people)* presentación *f.*
intrude ➤ *tr* meter por fuerza (en) ➤ *intr (to meddle)* inmiscuirse, entrometerse; *(to interrupt)* molestar.
intruder ➤ *s* intruso/a.
intrusion ➤ *s* intrusión *f.*
intuition ➤ *s* intuición *f.*
inundate ➤ *tr* inundar.
inundation ➤ *s* inundación *f.*
invade ➤ *tr* invadir.
invader ➤ *s* invasor/a.
invalid[1] ➤ *adj & s* inválido/a.
invalid[2] ➤ *adj* nulo.
invaluable ➤ *adj* inestimable.
invariable ➤ *adj* invariable.
invent ➤ *tr* inventar.
invention ➤ *s* invención *f*; *(new device)* invento; *(skill)* inventiva.
inventor ➤ *s* inventor/a.
inventory ➤ *s* inventario.
inversion ➤ *s* inversión *f.*
invest ➤ *tr (money)* invertir; *(effort)* dedicar.
investigate ➤ *tr* investigar.
investigation ➤ *s* investigación *f.*
investigator ➤ *s* investigador/a.
investment ➤ *s* inversión *f.*
investor ➤ *s* inversionista *mf.*
invisible ➤ *adj* invisible.
invitation ➤ *s* invitación *f.*
invite ➤ *tr* invitar; *(for food, drink)* convidar; *(a response)* solicitar; *(trouble)* provocar, buscar.
inviting ➤ *adj* atrayente, tentador.
invoice ➤ *s* factura ➤ *tr* facturar.
involve ➤ *tr (to include)* comprender, incluir; *(to entail)* implicar.
involved ➤ *adj* complicado, enredado.
involvement ➤ *s* participación *f.*
inward(s) ➤ *adj* interior, interno ➤ *adv* hacia adentro.
iodine ➤ *s* yodo.
iris ➤ *s (of the eye)* iris *m*; BOT. lirio.
iron ➤ *s* hierro; *(for clothes)* plancha ➤ *tr & intr* planchar ■ **to i. out** allanar.
ironic(al) ➤ *adj* irónico.
ironing ➤ *s* planchado ■ **i. board** tabla de planchar.
irony ➤ *s* ironía.
irrational ➤ *adj* irracional.
irregular ➤ *adj* irregular.
irrelevance *or* **irrelevancy** ➤ *s* improcedencia, falta de pertinencia.
irrelevant ➤ *adj* inaplicable, improcedente ■ **to be i.** no venir al caso.
irrespective ➤ *adj* ■ **i. of** sin tener en cuenta, no obstante.
irretrievable ➤ *adj (not recoverable)* irrecuperable; *(mistake)* irreparable.
irrigate ➤ *tr* irrigar.
irritable ➤ *adj* irritable.
irritate ➤ *tr* irritar.
irritating ➤ *adj* irritante, molesto.
irritation ➤ *s* irritación *f.*
is ➤ *vea* **be** *en tabla de verbos.*
island ➤ *s* isla; *(in a street)* isleta.
isolate ➤ *tr* aislar.
isolation ➤ *s* aislamiento.
issue ➤ *(magazine)* edición *f*; *(result)* consecuencia; *(matter)* cuestión *f* ➤ *intr* salir ➤ *tr (magazine)* publicar; *(stamps, money)* emitir.
it ➤ *pron* lo, la, le ■ **it's cold** hace frío • **it is good** es bueno • **it is raining** llueve, está lloviendo.
italic ➤ *s & adj* cursiva.
itch ➤ *s* picazón *f* ➤ *intr* picar ➤ *tr* dar picazón; *(to scratch)* rascarse.
itchy ➤ *adj* que da picazón.
item ➤ *s* artículo; *(on an agenda)* punto; *(of a document)* item *m.*
its ➤ *adj* su ■ **its flavor** su sabor.
it's ➤ *contr de* **it is.**
itself ➤ *pron* ■ (all) **by i.** solo • **it turns i. off automatically** se apaga automáticamente • **of** *o* **in i.** de sí • **the book i.** el libro mismo.
ivory ➤ *s* marfil *m.*
ivy ➤ *s* hiedra, yedra.

J

jab ➤ *tr* golpear ➤ *s* pinchazo; *(with elbow)* codazo; *(punch)* golpe corto.
jack ➤ *s (in cards)* sota; MEC. gato, cric *m* ➤ *tr* ■ **to j. up** alzar con el gato; *(prices)* aumentar.
jacket ➤ *s* saco, chaqueta.
jade ➤ *s* MIN. jade *m.*
jagged ➤ *adj* dentado.
jail ➤ *s* cárcel *f* ➤ *tr* encarcelar.
jam[1] ➤ *tr & intr (to lock)* atascar(se), trabar(se) ■ **jammed with** atestado de ➤ *s (blockage)* atasco; FIG. aprieto.
jam[2] ➤ *s* CUL. mermelada.
January ➤ *s* enero.
jar[1] ➤ *s (jug)* jarra; *(pot)* tarro, pote *m.*
jar[2] ➤ *tr & intr* sacudir(se) ■ **to j. with** no concordar con ➤ *s* choque *m.*
jaundice ➤ *s* ictericia.
jaw ➤ *s* mandíbula.
jazz ➤ *s* jazz *m.*
jealous ➤ *adj* celoso; *(suspicious)* receloso; *(envious)* envidioso ■ **to be j. of** tener celos de.
jealousy ➤ *s* celos *m*, envidia.
jeans ➤ *s* jeans *m*, pantalones vaqueros.
jeer ➤ *intr (to mock)* burlarse (*at* de); *(to boo)* abuchear ➤ *s (mockery)* mofa, burla; *(boo)* abucheo.
jelly ➤ *s* jalea.
jeopardize ➤ *tr* poner en peligro.
jerk ➤ *tr* dar un tirón a, tironear de ➤ *s* tirón *m*, sacudida; FAM. pelmazo *mf.*
jet ➤ *s (spurt)* chorro; *(airplane)* jet *m*; *(engine)* reactor *m.*
Jew ➤ *s* judío/a.
jewel ➤ *s* joya.
jewel(l)er ➤ *s* joyero.
jewelry ➤ *s* joyas, alhajas.
Jewish ➤ *adj* judío.
jingle ➤ *tr & intr* (hacer) cascabelear *o* tintinear.
jitters ➤ *spl* ■ **to give someone the j.** poner nervioso a alguien.
job ➤ *s (task)* tarea; *(work)* trabajo; *(employment)* empleo.
jobless ➤ *adj* sin trabajo.
jog ➤ *tr (to push)* empujar levemente; *(the memory)* refrescar ➤ *intr* correr despacio ➤ *s* paso lento.
jogger ➤ *s* persona que corre despacio para hacer ejercicio.
join ➤ *tr* juntar, unir; *(a cause)* abrazar; *(political party)* afiliarse a ➤ *intr* juntarse, unirse ■ **to j. in** participar en.
joint ➤ *s* junta, unión *f*; JER. cigarrillo de marihuana ➤ *adj* (en) común; *(collective)* mutuo ■ **j. ownership** propiedad en común.
joke ➤ *s* chiste *m*; *(amusing remark)* gracia; *(prank)* broma ➤ *intr* contar chistes ■ **to j. around** bromear.
joker ➤ *s* bromista *mf*; *(cards)* comodín *m.*
jolly ➤ *adj* alegre.
jolt ➤ *tr & intr* sacudir(se) ➤ *s* sacudida.
jostle ➤ *intr & tr* empujar, dar empellones ➤ *s* empujón *m*, empellón *m.*
jot ➤ *tr* ■ **to j. down** anotar, apuntar.
journal ➤ *s* diario; *(periodical)* revista.
journalist ➤ *s* periodista *mf.*
journey ➤ *s* viaje *m*; *(distance)* jornada.
joy ➤ *s* alegría.
joyful ➤ *adj* alegre, jubiloso.
joystick ➤ *s* AVIA. palanca de mando; *(game)* palanca de juego, joystick *m.*
judge ➤ *tr & intr* juzgar ➤ *s* juez *mf*; *(in a contest)* árbitro/a.
judg(e)ment ➤ *s (good sense)* juicio; *(ruling)* opinión *f*; DER. decisión *f.*
jug ➤ *s (jar)* jarra, cántaro.
juggle ➤ *tr* hacer malabares con ➤ *intr* hacer juego de manos.
juggler ➤ *s* malabarista *mf.*
juice ➤ *s* jugo, zumo *f.*
juicy ➤ *adj* jugoso.
July ➤ *s* julio.
jumble ➤ *tr* mezclar ➤ *s* revoltijo.
jumbo ➤ *s* coloso ➤ *adj* enorme.
jump ➤ *intr* saltar; *(to be startled)* sobresaltarse ■ **to j. at** *(a chance)* aprovechar ➤ *tr* saltar (por encima de) ➤ *s* salto; *(leap)* brinco ■ **to get** *o* **have a j. on** adelantarse a.
jumpy ➤ *adj* nervioso.
junction ➤ *s* juntura; F.C., ELEC. empalme *m.*
June ➤ *s* junio.
jungle ➤ *s* selva, jungla.
junior ➤ *adj* más joven; *(for children)* juvenil; *(in rank)* subalterno ➤ *s* joven *mf*, menor *mf*; *(rank)* subordinado.
junk ➤ *s* FAM. trastos viejos, cachivaches *m* ➤ *tr* desechar.
juror ➤ *s* jurado, miembro *mf* del jurado.
jury ➤ *s* jurado, tribunal *m.*
just ➤ *adj (fair, right)* justo ➤ *adv (recently)* recién ■ **j. about** *(not quite)* casi • **j. about to** a punto de • **j. as if** lo mismo que si • **j. in case** por si acaso • **j. in time to** *o* **for** justo a tiempo para • **j. so** a su gusto, ni más ni menos • **not j. yet** todavía no • **to have j.** acabar de.
justice ➤ *s* justicia.
justify ➤ *tr* justificar.
juvenile ➤ *adj* joven, juvenil; *(immature)* infantil ➤ *s* joven *mf* ■ **j. court** tribunal de menores.

K

kangaroo ➤ *s* canguro ■ **k. court** tribunal desautorizado.
karat ➤ *s* quilate *m.*
kayak ➤ *s* kayac *m*, kayak *m.*
keel ➤ *s* quilla.
keen ➤ *adj* agudo; *(interest)* vivo ■ **to be k. on** tener entusiasmo por.
keep✧ ➤ *tr* quedarse con; *(to put aside)* guardar; *(a family)* sostener; *(in a place)* guardar; *(order, tradition)* mantener; *(diary, accounts)* llevar ■ **to k. away** mantener alejado • **to k. from** *(to prevent)* impedir; *(to conceal)* ocultar • **to k. out** no dejar entrar ■ **to k. up** *(to continue)* proseguir; *(to maintain)* mantener ➤ *intr (food)* conservarse ■ **k. off** prohibido pasar • **to k. on** continuar • **to k. quiet** quedarse callado ➤ *s (care)* custodia.
kennel ➤ *tr & s* (meter en la) perrera.
kernel ➤ grano.
kerosene *o* **kerosine** ➤ *s* queroseno.
ketchup ➤ *s* salsa de tomate.
kettle ➤ *s* marmita; *(teakettle)* tetera.
key[1] ➤ *s* llave *f*; *(code, solution)* clave *f*; *(of a piano, keyboard)* tecla ■ **off k.** desafinado ➤ *adj* clave, importante.
key[2] ➤ *s* GEOG. cayo.
keyboard ➤ *s* teclado.
khaki ➤ *s* caqui *m.*
kick ➤ *tr* patear, dar un puntapié a; *(animals)* dar coces a; DEP. patear; *(a goal)* marcar, meter ■ **to k. out** echar a patadas ➤ *s* patada, puntapié *m*; *(animal)* coz *f* ■ *pl* sensación *f* • **for k.** por diversión.
kickoff ➤ *s* DEP. saque *m* inicial; FIG. comienzo.
kid ➤ *s (goat)* cabrito; FAM. niño ➤ *tr & intr* FAM. bromear *o* jugar (con).
kidnap ➤ *tr* secuestrar, raptar.
kidnapper ➤ *s* secuestrador/a, raptor/a.
kidnapping ➤ *s* secuestro, rapto.
kidney ➤ *s* riñón *m.*
kill ➤ *tr* matar ➤ *s (hunting)* cacería; *(final blow)* acabamiento.
killer ➤ *s* asesino/a.
kilo ➤ *s* kilo.
kilogram ➤ *s* kilogramo, kilo.
kilometer ➤ *s* kilómetro.
kind[1] ➤ *adj* bueno, afable; *(thoughtful)* amable.
kind[2] ➤ *s* tipo, clase *f* ■ **in k.** del mismo modo • **k. of** FAM. un poco.
kindergarten ➤ *s* jardín *m* de infantes.
kindly ➤ *adj* bondadoso ➤ *adv* bondadosamente.
kindness ➤ *s* bondad *f*; *(favor)* favor *m.*
king ➤ *s* rey *m.*
kingdom ➤ *s* reino.
kiosk ➤ *s* quiosco.
kiss ➤ *tr* besar, dar un beso a ➤ *intr* besarse ➤ *s* beso.
kit ➤ *s (set of tools)* equipo, conjunto ■ **first-aid k.** botiquín *m.*
kitchen ➤ *s* cocina.
kitchenette ➤ *s* cocina pequeña.
kite ➤ *s (toy)* cometa.
kitten ➤ *s* gatito.
knapsack ➤ *s* mochila.
knee ➤ *s* rodilla.
kneel✧ ➤ *intr* arrodillarse.
knife ➤ *s* cuchillo ➤ *tr* apuñalar.
knife-edge ➤ *s* filo.
knight ➤ *s* caballero; *(in chess)* caballo.
knit✧ ➤ *tr & intr* tejer, hacer punto ➤ *s* prenda de punto.
knitting ➤ *s* tejido, labor *f* de punto.
knitwear ➤ *s* artículos de punto.
knob ➤ *s* tirador *m*; *(dial)* botón *m.*
knock ➤ *tr (to hit)* golpear, pegar ■ **to k. down** derribar, tumbar • **to k. out** *(a person)* dejar sin sentido; *(in boxing)* poner fuera de combate; *(power)* cortar • **to k. over** tirar (vasa, lámpara) ➤ *intr (at the door)* golpear, llamar ■ **to k. against** chocar contra ➤ *s (blow)* golpe *m*; *(rap)* toque *m*, llamada.
knocker ➤ *s* aldaba, picaporte.
knot ➤ *s* nudo ➤ *tr & intr* anudar(se).
know✧ ➤ *tr* saber; *(a person, place)* conocer ■ **to get to k. someone** llegar a conocer a alguien • **to let someone k.** hacer saber a alguien • **to k. how to** saber ➤ *intr* saber.
know-how ➤ *s* habilidad *f.*
knowledge ➤ *s (understanding)* conocimiento; *(information)* conocimientos

■ **without my k.** sin saberlo yo.
known ➤ *adj* conocido.
knuckle ➤ *s* nudillo.

L

lab ➤ *s* laboratorio.
label ➤ *s* rótulo, etiqueta ➤ *tr* rotular, marcar; *(to describe)* describir.
labor ➤ *s* trabajo, labor *f*; *(task)* tarea, faena; *(workers)* mano *f* de obra ■ **l. union** sindicato • **to be in l.** estar de parto ➤ *intr* trabajar.
laboratory ➤ *s* laboratorio.
laborer ➤ *s* trabajador/a, obrero/a; *(unskilled)* peón *m*, jornalero/a.
lace ➤ *s* encaje *m*; *(trim)* puntilla; *(shoelace)* cordón *m* ➤ *tr* encordonar.
lack ➤ *s* *(deficiency)* falta, carencia; *(need)* escasez *f* ➤ *tr* carecer de, faltar.
lad ➤ *s* joven *m*, muchacho.
ladder ➤ *s* escalera.
ladle ➤ *s & tr* (servir con) cucharón *m*.
lady ➤ *s* dama; *(married)* señora.
ladybug ➤ *s* mariquita.
lake ➤ *s* lago.
lamb ➤ *s* cordero; *(dear)* amor *m*.
lame ➤ *adj* cojo; *(excuse)* débil.
lamp ➤ *s* lámpara.
lamppost ➤ *s* poste *m* de farol.
land ➤ *s* tierra; *(tract)* campo, terreno; *(country)* tierra, país *m* ■ *pl* tierras, posesiones ➤ *intr* *(boat)* arribar ➤ *tr & intr* *(to unload, disembark)* desembarcar; *(plane)* aterrizar.
landing ➤ *s* *(plane)* aterrizaje *m*; *(of a staircase)* descanso.
landlord/lady ➤ *s* propietario/a.
landscape ➤ *s* paisaje *m*.
landslide ➤ *s* derrumbe *m* (de tierra).
lane ➤ *s* *(path)* senda, vereda; *(road)* camino; *(of a highway)* vía, carril *m*.
language ➤ *s* lenguaje *m*; *(tongue)* lengua, idioma *m*.
lantern ➤ *s* linterna.
lap[1] ➤ *s* *(of body)* falda, regazo.
lap[2] ➤ *s* *(of a race)* vuelta a la pista; *(swimming)* largo; *(segment)* etapa.
lapel ➤ *s* solapa.
laptop ➤ *s* (computadora) portátil.
large ➤ *adj & adv* grande ■ **by and l.** por lo general.
largely ➤ *adv* en gran parte.
lark ➤ *s* ORNIT. alondra.
laser ➤ *s* láser *m*.
last[1] ➤ *adj* *(final, newest)* último; *(past)* pasado ■ **l. name** apellido • **l. night** anoche ➤ *adv* el último, en último lugar; *(most recently)* la última vez; *(finally)* por último, finalmente ➤ *s* el último; *(the end)* final *m*.
last[2] ➤ *intr* durar; *(to survive)* sobrevivir.
last-minute ➤ *adj* de última hora.
latch ➤ *s & tr* (cerrar con) pestillo.
late ➤ *adj* *(behind schedule)* atrasado; *(former)* antiguo; *(dead)* fallecido ■ **to get l.** hacerse tarde ➤ *adv* tarde.
latecomer ➤ *s* rezagado/a.
lately ➤ *adv* últimamente.
later ➤ *adj* posterior ➤ *adv* más tarde ■ **l. on** luego, después.
latest ➤ *adj & s* (lo) último ■ **at the l.** a más tardar.
Latin America ➤ *s* Latinoamérica.
Latin American ➤ *adj & s* Latinoamericano/a.
latter ➤ *adj* último.
laugh ➤ *intr* reír(se) ■ **to l. at** *(with amusement)* reírse con; *(to ridicule)* reírse de ➤ *s* risa.
laughter ➤ *s* risa(s).
launch ➤ *tr* lanzar; *(a ship)* botar ➤ *s* lanzamiento; *(of ship)* botadura.
laundry ➤ *s* *(soiled)* ropa sucia; *(clean)* ropa limpia; *(place)* lavandería.
lavatory ➤ *s* servicios, baño.
law ➤ *s* ley *f*; *(code)* fuero, código; *(study)* derecho.
lawful ➤ *adj* legal, lícito.
lawn ➤ *s* césped *m* ■ **l. mower** cortacéspedes.
lawsuit ➤ *s* pleito, juicio.
lawyer ➤ *s* abogado/a.
lay◊ ➤ *tr* poner; *(to cause to lie)* acostar; *(eggs)* poner ■ **to be laid up** guardar cama • **to l. down** dictar, establecer • **to l. off** despedir • **to l. out** *(to plan)* proyectar; *(to spread out)* preparar ➤ *intr* poner huevos ■ **to l. over** pararse.
layer ➤ *s* capa.
layman/woman ➤ *s* lego/a, seglar *mf*.
layoff ➤ *s* despido.
layover ➤ *s* escala, parada.
lazy ➤ *adj* perezoso.
lead[1]◊ ➤ *tr* *(to guide)* guiar, conducir; *(to command)* dirigir, mandar ➤ *intr* estar a la cabeza; *(to go first)* enseñar el camino; *(to command)* mandar ➤ *s* *(position)* primer lugar *m*, delantera; *(margin)* ventaja; *(clue)* pista ■ **in the l.** a la cabeza, primero • **to take the l.** tomar la delantera ➤ *adj* principal.
lead[2] ➤ *s* plomo.
leader ➤ *s* jefe/a, líder *mf*.
leading ➤ *adj* primero; *(main)* principal.
leaf ➤ *s* hoja ■ **gold l.** pan de oro.
leaflet ➤ *s* folleto, panfleto.
league ➤ *s* liga.
leak ➤ *intr* *(container)* salirse; *(roof, faucet)* gotear ➤ *tr* divulgar ➤ *s* *(faucet, roof)* gotera; *(gas)* salida, escape; *(disclosure)* divulgación *f*.
lean[1]◊ ➤ *intr* inclinarse; *(to rest on)* apoyarse, reclinarse ■ **to l. back** recostarse ➤ *tr* *(to rest)* apoyar, recostar.
lean[2] ➤ *adj* *(thin)* flaco; *(meat)* magro.
leap◊ ➤ *intr & tr* saltar (por encima de) ➤ *s* salto, brinco.
learn◊ ➤ *tr* aprender; *(to find out)* saber, enterarse de ➤ *intr* aprender; *(from mistakes)* escarmentar ■ **to l. how to** aprender a.
learner ➤ *s* principiante/a.
learning ➤ *s* aprendizaje *m*; *(knowledge)* saber *m*, erudición *f*.
leash ➤ *s* correa ➤ *tr* atraillar.
least ➤ *adj* menor; *(smallest)* mínimo ➤ *adv & s* (lo) menos ■ **at l.** por lo menos • **not in the l.** en absoluto.
leather ➤ *s* cuero, piel *f*.
leave◊ ➤ *tr* salir de; *(to forget, let stay, result in)* dejar ■ **to l. alone** dejar en paz • **to l. out** omitir ➤ *intr* irse, marcharse; *(to depart)* salir, partir.
lecture ➤ *s* conferencia; *(class)* curso, clase *f* ➤ *intr* dictar conferencia ➤ *tr* dar una conferencia a; *(to scold)* sermonear.
lecturer ➤ *s* conferenciante *mf*, conferencista *mf*.
leek ➤ *s* puerro.
left ➤ *adj* izquierdo ➤ *s* izquierda ➤ *adv* a *o* hacia la izquierda.
left-hand ➤ *adj* a la izquierda.
left-handed ➤ *adj* zurdo.
leftover ➤ *adj* sobrante ■ **leftovers** *spl* sobras, restos.
leg ➤ *s* pierna; *(of animal, chair)* pata.
legal ➤ *adj* legal; *(relating to the law)* jurídico; *(statutory)* legítimo.
legend ➤ *s* leyenda.
legible ➤ *adj* legible.
legitimate ➤ *adj* legítimo; *(lawful)* lícito.
leisure ➤ *s* ocio ■ **l. time** tiempo libre.
lemon ➤ *s* limón *m* ■ **l. tree** limonero.
lemonade ➤ *s* limonada.
lend◊ ➤ *tr* prestar.
length ➤ *s* largo; *(piece)* pedazo, tramo; *(duration)* duración *f*.
lengthen ➤ *tr & intr* alargar(se), estirar(se); *(time)* prolongar(se).
lenient ➤ *adj* indulgente.
lens ➤ *s* lente *m o f*.
lentil ➤ *s* lenteja.
leopard ➤ *s* leopardo.
leotard ➤ *s* malla de bailarines.
less ➤ *adj* menos ■ **l. than** menos de (lo que) ➤ *prep* menos ➤ *adv* menos ■ **l. and l.** cada vez menos ➤ *s* menos *m*.
lesson ➤ *s* lección *f* ■ **to take lessons** tomar clases.
let◊ ➤ *tr* permitir; *(to allow)* dejar ■ **to l. down** bajar; *(to disappoint)* fallar • **to l. go** *(to fire)* despedir; *(to set free)* dejar en libertad; *(to release)* soltar • **to l. in** dejar entrar • **to l. out** dejar salir ➤ *intr* ■ **to l. up** FAM. *(to cease)* cesar; *(to slacken)* disminuirse ➤ *conj* ■ **l. alone** y mucho menos.
letter ➤ *s* carta; *(of alphabet)* letra.
lettuce ➤ *s* lechuga.
level ➤ *s* nivel *m*; *(height)* altura; *(flat land)* llano, llanura ■ **at ground l.** a ras de tierra ➤ *adj* plano, llano; *(horizontal)* a nivel; *(even)* parejo, igual ➤ *tr* nivelar; *(to make flat)* allanar.
lever ➤ *s* palanca.
liability ➤ *s* responsabilidad *f*; *(hindrance)* desventaja.
liable ➤ *adj* responsable; *(obligated)* obligado; *(subject)* sujeto; *(tending to)* susceptible.
liar ➤ *s* mentiroso/a.
liberal ➤ *adj & s* liberal *mf*.
liberty ➤ *s* libertad *f* ■ **at l.** libre, en libertad.
librarian ➤ *s* bibliotecario/a.
library ➤ *s* biblioteca.
license ➤ *s* licencia, permiso; *(card)* carnet *m* ■ **l. plate** patente, placa (de matricula) ➤ *tr* licenciar, autorizar.
lick ➤ *tr* lamer.
licorice ➤ *s* regaliz *m*.
lid ➤ *s* tapa; *(eyelid)* párpado.
lie[1]◊ ➤ *intr* *(to recline)* tenderse, acostarse; *(to be stretched out)* yacer.
lie[2] ➤ *s* mentira ➤ *intr* mentir.
lieutenant ➤ *s* teniente *mf*.
life ➤ *s* vida ■ **l. jacket** chaleco salvavidas • **l. preserver** salvavidas • **true to l.** verosímil.
lifeboat ➤ *s* bote *m* salvavidas.
lifeguard ➤ *s* salvavidas *mf*.
lifetime ➤ *s* vida.
lift ➤ *tr* alzar, levantar; *(to revoke)* revocar ➤ *s* G.B. ascensor *m* ■ **to give someone a l.** llevar a alguien en un vehículo.
liftoff ➤ *s* despegue *m*.
light[1]◊ ➤ *s* luz *f* ■ **l. bulb** bombilla • **to bring to l.** sacar a luz, revelar • **to see the l.** comprender, darse cuenta ➤ *tr* encender; *(to illuminate)* alumbrar, iluminar ➤ *intr* encenderse ■ **to l. up** iluminarse ➤ *adj* *(colors)* claro; *(hair)* rubio; *(bright)* bien iluminado.
light[2] ➤ *adj* *(not heavy)* ligero, liviano; *(rain)* fino; *(food)* ligero ➤ *adv* ligeramente.
lighthouse ➤ *s* faro.
lighting ➤ *s* iluminación *f*, alumbrado.
lighter ➤ *s* encendedor *m*.
lightning ➤ *s* rayo, relámpago.
likable ➤ *adj* agradable, grato.
like[1] ➤ *tr* ■ **I l. to read** me gusta leer • **do you l. to cook?** ¿te gusta cocinar? ➤ *intr* querer ■ **as you l.** como usted quiera.
like[2] ➤ *prep* como ■ **l. this** *o* **that** así ➤ *adj* similar, parecido.
likelihood ➤ *s* probabilidad *f*.
likely ➤ *adj* probable; *(plausible)* verosímil ➤ *adv* probablemente.
likeness ➤ *s* semejanza.
likewise ➤ *adv* del mismo modo, lo mismo; *(also)* además.
liking ➤ *s* afición *f*; *(taste)* gusto.
lily ➤ *s* lirio ■ **l. pad** hoja de nenúfar.
limb ➤ *s* BOT. rama; ANAT. miembro, extremidad *f*.
lime[1] ➤ *s* *(tree, fruit)* lima.
lime[2] ➤ *s* MIN. cal *f*.
limit ➤ *s* límite *m*; *(maximum)* máximo ■ *pl* límites, confines ➤ *tr* limitar.
limited ➤ *adj* limitado ■ **l. company** sociedad anónima ➤ *s* (tren) expreso.
limousine ➤ *s* limosina.
limp ➤ *intr* cojear ➤ *s* cojera.
line[1] ➤ *s* línea; *(mark)* raya; *(row)* hilera, fila; *(queue)* cola; *(verse)* verso; *(brief letter)* letras, líneas ■ **down the l.** en el futuro • **to draw the l.** fijar límites ➤ *tr* rayar, trazar líneas en ➤ *intr* ■ **to l. up** hacer cola.
line[2] ➤ *tr* COST. forrar; TEC. revestir.
linen ➤ *s* lino, hilo; *(goods)* lencería ■ *pl* ropa de cama.
liner ➤ *s* transatlántico.
lineup ➤ *s* fila (de personas); DEP. alineación *f*.
lining ➤ *s* forro.
link ➤ *s* *(chain)* eslabón *m*; FIG., COMPUT. enlace *m* ➤ *tr & intr* *(to unite)* unir(se); *(to connect)* conectar(se).
links ➤ *spl* campo de golf.
lion ➤ *s* león *m*.
lioness ➤ *s* leona.
lip ➤ *s* labio.
lipstick ➤ *s* lápiz *m* labial.
liqueur ➤ *s* licor *m*.
liquid ➤ *s & adj* líquido.
liquor ➤ *s* licor *m*.
list ➤ *s* lista ➤ *tr* enumerar; *(to register)* poner en una lista.
listen ➤ *intr* escuchar; *(to heed advice)* prestar atención.
listener ➤ *s* oyente *mf*.
literary ➤ *adj* literario.
literature ➤ *s* literatura; *(printed material)* folletos, impresos.
litter ➤ *s* ZOOL. camada, cría; *(trash)* basura ➤ *tr & intr* tirar basura (en).
little ➤ *adj* *(small)* pequeño; *(not much)* poco ➤ *adv* *(not much)* poco; *(somewhat)* un poco, algo ■ **l. by l.** poco a poco • **l. did I know that** no me imaginé que ➤ *s* poco; *(short time)* momento.
live ➤ *intr & tr* vivir ■ **to l. it up** FAM. vivir la vida • **to l. off** *(someone)* vivir a expensas de; *(the land)* vivir de • **to l. through** sobrevivir • **to l. with** tolerar ➤ *adj* vivo; RAD., TELEV. en directo.
lively ➤ *adj* vivaz; *(spirited)* alegre; *(keen)* vivo, grande.
liver ➤ *s* ANAT., CUL. hígado.
living ➤ *adj* vivo ■ **l. expenses** gastos de manutención • **l. room** sala de estar ➤ *s* vida ■ **to earn a l.** ganarse la vida.
lizard ➤ *s* lagarto.
load ➤ *s* *(weight)* peso; *(cargo)* carga ■ *pl* FAM. un montón, muchísimo ➤ *tr & intr* cargar(se).
loaf[1] ➤ *s* pan *m*.
loaf[2] ➤ *intr* haranganear, holgazanear.
loafer ➤ *s* holgazán/ana; *(shoe)* mocasín *m*.
loan ➤ *s* préstamo ■ **on l.** prestado ➤ *tr* prestar.
lobby ➤ *s* vestíbulo ➤ *intr* POL. ejercer presiones.
lobster ➤ *s* langosta, bogavante.
local ➤ *adj* local ■ **l. call** TEL. llamada urbana.
locate ➤ *tr* localizar; *(to place)* ubicar.
location ➤ *s* lugar *m*, sitio.
lock[1] ➤ *s* cerradura; *(of a canal)* esclusa ➤ *tr* cerrar con llave ➤ *intr* cerrarse.
lock[2] ➤ *s* *(of hair)* mecha.
locker ➤ *s* armario ■ **l. room** vestuario (de un gimnasio, club).
locksmith ➤ *s* cerrajero/a.
lodge ➤ *s* *(inn)* posada ➤ *tr & intr* alojar(se).
lodger ➤ *s* inquilino/a.
lodging ➤ *s* alojamiento.
log ➤ *s* leño, tronco; AVIA., MARÍT. diario ■ **l. cabin** cabaña de troncos.
logic ➤ *s* lógica.
logical ➤ *adj* lógico.
loin ➤ *s* lomo.
lollipop ➤ *s* pirulí *m*.
loneliness ➤ *s* soledad *f*.
lonely ➤ *adj* solo; *(isolated)* solitario.
long[1] ➤ *adj* largo ■ **l. jump** salto de longitud • **six feet l.** seis pies de largo • **to take a l. time** tardar mucho ➤ *adv* mucho tiempo ■ **as l. as** *(while)* mientras; *(if)* si, siempre y cuando • **how l.?** *(time)* ¿cuánto tiempo?; *(length)* ¿qué largo? • **no longer** ya no ➤ *s* mucho tiempo ■ **before l.** dentro de poco.
long[2] ➤ *intr* ■ **to l. for** añorar • **to l. to** anhelar.
long-distance ➤ *adj & adv* de larga distancia.
long-term ➤ *adj* a largo plazo.
look ➤ *intr* mirar; *(to seem)* parecer ■ **l. out!** ¡cuidado! ➤ *tr* mirar ■ **to l. after** *(someone)* cuidar a, ocuparse de; *(something)* ocuparse de, encargarse de • **to l. for** buscar; *(to expect)* esperar • **to l. forward to** anticipar ➤ *s* *(quick glance)* ojeada, vistazo; *(gaze)* mirada; *(aspect)* aspecto ■ *pl* aspecto.
lookout ➤ *s* *(watch)* vigilancia; *(vantage point)* mirador *m* ■ **to be on the l. for** estar al acecho de.
loose ➤ *adj* *(unfastened)* suelto; *(slack)* flojo; *(not tight)* holgado; *(not packaged)* a granel ■ **to tie up l. ends** FIG. atar cabos ➤ *adv* ■ **to come l.** aflojarse, desatarse • **to turn l.** soltar, libertar ➤ *s* ■ **on the l.** FAM. suelto, en libertad.
loosen ➤ *tr* aflojar; *(to untie)* desatar.
lord ➤ *s* señor *m*.
lose◊ ➤ *tr* perder.
loser ➤ *s* perdedor/a.
loss ➤ *s* pérdida.
lost ➤ *adj* perdido; *(engrossed)* absorto ■ **l. and found** oficina de objetos perdidos • **to get l.** perderse.
lot ➤ *s* *(articles for sale)* lote *m*; *(large amount)* gran cantidad *f*, mucho; *(land)* solar *m*, lote ■ **lots of** cantidades de, mucho.
lotion ➤ *s* loción *f*.
lottery ➤ *s* lotería.
loud ➤ *adj* alto, fuerte; *(noisy)* ruidoso, bullicioso.
loudspeaker ➤ *s* altavoz *m*.
love ➤ *s* amor *m*, cariño; *(lover)* amor; DEP. cero (en tenis) ■ **l.** *o* **with l.** un cariñoso saludo • **to fall in l.** enamorarse ➤ *tr* amar, querer ■ **I l. to travel** me encanta viajar.
lovely ➤ *adj* precioso, bonito.
lover ➤ *s* amante *mf*; *(devotee)* aficionado/a.

low ➤ adj bajo; (in quality) inferior; (humble) humilde ▪ l. tide bajamar ➤ adv bajo ➤ s punto más bajo.

lower ➤ adj más bajo, inferior ➤ tr & intr bajar; (to diminish) disminuir.

lowercase ➤ adj minúsculo.

lowlands ➤ spl tierras bajas.

loyal ➤ adj leal.

loyalty ➤ s lealtad f.

lozenge ➤ s (cough drop) pastilla.

luck ➤ s suerte f ▪ **good l.!** ¡buena suerte! • **to be in l.** estar de suerte ➤ intr ▪ **to l. out** FAM. tener suerte.

lucky ➤ adj afortunado; (fortuitous) fortuito, oportuno.

ludicrous ➤ adj absurdo, ridículo.

luggage ➤ s equipaje m.

lukewarm ➤ adj tibio.

lullaby ➤ s canción f de cuna, nana.

lump ➤ s montón m, masa; (of soil, sugar) terrón m ➤ tr amontonar ▪ **to l. together** juntar.

lunatic ➤ adj loco ➤ s lunático/a.

lunch ➤ s almuerzo ➤ intr almorzar.

luncheon ➤ s almuerzo.

lung ➤ s pulmón m.

luxurious ➤ adj lujoso; (lush) suntuoso.

luxury ➤ s lujo.

lyric ➤ adj lírico ▪ **lyrics** spl MÚS. letra.

M

macaroni ➤ spl macarrones m.

machine ➤ s máquina ▪ **m. gun** ametralladora.

machinery ➤ s maquinaria; (working parts) mecanismo.

mackerel ➤ s caballa.

mad ➤ adj enojado; (insane) loco; (frantic) frenético; (rabid) rabioso ▪ **to be m. at** estar enojado con • **to get m.** enfadarse.

Madam ➤ s señora.

made ➤ adj hecho.

madness ➤ s locura; (fury) rabia.

magazine ➤ s revista.

magic ➤ s magia ➤ adj mágico.

magical ➤ adj mágico.

magician ➤ s mago/a.

magistrate ➤ s magistrado/a.

magnet ➤ s FÍS. imán m.

magnetic ➤ adj magnético.

magnificent ➤ adj magnífico.

magnify ➤ tr aumentar ▪ **magnifying glass** lupa.

mahogany ➤ s caoba.

maid ➤ s (servant) criada; (maiden) doncella ▪ **m. of honor** dama de honor.

maiden ➤ s doncella ▪ **m. name** apellido de soltera.

mail ➤ s correo ▪ **air m.** vía aérea • **m. carrier** cartero/a ➤ tr enviar por correo; (to post) echar al correo.

mailbox ➤ s buzón m.

mailman ➤ s cartero.

main ➤ adj principal; (office) central ▪ **the m. thing** lo principal.

mainframe ➤ s elaborador m central.

maintain ➤ tr mantener; (to repair) cuidar.

maintenance ➤ s mantenimiento; (upkeep) cuidado.

majestic ➤ adj majestuoso.

majesty ➤ s majestad f; (splendor) majestuosidad f.

major ➤ adj mayor; (chief) principal ➤ s EDUC. especialidad f ➤ intr ▪ **to m. in** EDUC. especializarse en.

majority ➤ s mayoría.

make✧ ➤ tr hacer; (to build) construir; (to manufacture) fabricar; (decision) tomar; (food) preparar; (to earn) ganar; (to compel) obligar a ▪ **to m. clear** poner en claro • **to m. easy** facilitar • **to m. into** convertir en • **to m. up** preparar; (story) inventar; (to constitute) integrar ➤ s fabricación f; (style) corte m; (brand) marca.

maker ➤ s fabricante mf.

make-up o **makeup** maquillaje m.

malaria ➤ s malaria, paludismo.

male ➤ adj del sexo masculino; BIOL., MEC. macho ➤ s varón m; BIOL. macho.

malice ➤ s malicia.

malicious ➤ adj malicioso.

malignant ➤ adj maligno.

mall ➤ s paseo, alameda; (for shopping) galería.

malnutrition ➤ s desnutrición f.

malt ➤ s malta; (beer) cerveza de malta.

mammal ➤ s mamífero.

man ➤ s hombre m; (male) varón m; (mankind) el hombre.

manage ➤ tr controlar; (business) dirigir; (to handle) poder con ➤ intr arreglárselas.

manageable ➤ adj manejable; (tame) dócil; (task) realizable.

management ➤ s gerencia; (directors) gerentes mf; (skill) habilidad directiva.

manager ➤ s gerente mf; (agent) apoderado/a.

mandatory ➤ adj obligatorio.

mane ➤ s (of horse) crin f; (of lion) melena.

maneuver ➤ s maniobra ➤ intr maniobrar; (to manipulate) manipular.

mangrove ➤ s mangle m.

mania ➤ s manía.

maniac ➤ s & adj maníaco/a.

manicure ➤ s manicura.

manipulate ➤ tr manipular.

mankind ➤ s género humano.

manmade ➤ adj artificial.

manner ➤ s manera, modo; (bearing) comportamiento ▪ pl modales; (politeness) educación.

manor ➤ s (estate) finca.

mantel o **mantelpiece** ➤ s repisa de la chimenea.

manual ➤ adj & s manual m.

manufacture ➤ tr fabricar ➤ s fabricación f; (product) producto manufacturado.

manufacturer ➤ fabricante mf.

manufacturing ➤ adj manufacturero ➤ s manufactura.

manure ➤ s estiércol m.

manuscript ➤ s manuscrito.

many ➤ adj muchos ▪ **how m.?** ¿cuántos? • **too m.** demasiados ➤ s & pron muchos ▪ **as m. as** (the same number) tantos como; (up to) hasta.

map ➤ s mapa m.

marathon ➤ s maratón m.

marble ➤ s mármol m; (glass ball) canica, bola.

march ➤ intr MIL. marchar ➤ s marcha.

March ➤ s marzo.

mare ➤ s yegua.

margarine ➤ s margarina.

margin ➤ s margen mf.

marine ➤ adj marítimo; BIOL. marino ➤ s soldado mf de marina.

marital ➤ adj matrimonial, marital.

maritime ➤ adj marítimo.

mark ➤ s marca; (grade) nota; (indication) signo; (reference point) señal f ▪ **to hit the m.** dar en el clavo ➤ tr marcar; (a spot) señalar; (to grade) calificar ▪ **to m. down** (prices) rebajar.

markdown ➤ s rebaja.

marker ➤ s marcador m.

market ➤ s mercado; (stock market) bolsa ▪ **m. price** precio corriente ➤ tr vender.

marketing ➤ s comercio; (of new products) mercadeo, marketing m.

marmalade ➤ s mermelada.

maroon ➤ s & adj (color) marrón m, castaño ➤ tr abandonar.

marriage ➤ s matrimonio; (wedding) boda ▪ **m. certificate** partida de matrimonio.

married ➤ adj casado.

marrow ➤ s médula.

marry ➤ tr (to join in marriage) casar; (to take in marriage) casarse con.

marsh ➤ s pantano; (salt) marisma.

marshal ➤ s mariscal m.

marvel ➤ s maravilla ➤ intr maravillarse.

marvellous ➤ adj maravilloso.

mascara ➤ s rimel m.

masculine ➤ adj & s masculino.

mask ➤ s máscara ➤ tr enmascarar.

masking tape ➤ s cinta adhesiva opaca.

masonry ➤ s obra de albañilería.

mass ➤ s masa; (large amount) montón m ➤ adj de las masas • **m. media** medios de comunicación de masa.

Mass o **mass** ➤ s RELIG. misa.

massacre ➤ s masacre f ➤ tr masacrar.

massage ➤ s masaje m ➤ tr dar masajes a.

masseur ➤ s masajista m.

masseuse ➤ s masajista f.

massive ➤ adj masivo; (huge) monumental.

mast ➤ s mástil m; (pole) palo.

master ➤ s maestro; (degree) maestría (título académico entre la licenciatura y el doctorado); (owner) amo; (of household) señor m ➤ adj maestro; (main) principal ➤ tr lograr dominar; (to overcome) superar.

masterpiece ➤ s obra maestra.

mat ➤ s estera; (doormat) esterilla; DEP. colchoneta; (tangled mass) maraña.

match[1] ➤ s par m; DEP. partido ▪ **to be a m. for** poder competir con ➤ tr corresponder a; (to go with) hacer juego con; (to equal) igualar ➤ intr hacer juego.

match[2] ➤ s (for lighting) fósforo.

mate ➤ s compañero; (spouse) conyuge mf ➤ intr (to breed) aparearse.

material ➤ s material m; (cloth) tela ➤ adj material; (noticeable) notable.

maternal ➤ adj maternal; (of one's mother) materno.

maternity ➤ s maternidad f.

math ➤ s matemática(s).

mathematics ➤ ssg matemática(s).

matinée ➤ s matinée f.

matrimonial ➤ adj matrimonial.

matrimony ➤ s matrimonio.

matter ➤ s materia; (concern) cuestión f ▪ **as a m. of fact** de hecho • **for that m.** en cuanto a eso • **what's the m.?** ¿qué pasa? ➤ intr importar.

mattress ➤ s colchón m.

mature ➤ adj maduro ➤ tr & intr madurar.

maturity ➤ s madurez f.

maximum ➤ adj & s máximo.

may ➤ aux (permission) poder; (possibility) ser posible (que) ▪ **come what m.** pase lo que pase • **it m. rain** es posible que llueva • **m. I?** ¿me permite?

May ➤ s mayo.

maybe ➤ adj (perhaps) quizá(s); (possibly) tal vez.

mayonnaise ➤ s mayonesa.

mayor ➤ s alcalde m, alcaldesa.

maze ➤ s laberinto.

me ➤ pron me; (after preposition) mí ▪ **with m.** conmigo.

meadow ➤ s pradera.

meal[1] ➤ s (ground grain) harina.

meal[2] ➤ s comida.

mean[1]✧ ➤ tr (to signify) querer decir; (to intend) tener la intención de; (to allude to) referirse a; (to entail) implicar ➤ intr ▪ **to m. well** tener buenas intenciones.

mean[2] ➤ adj (stingy) tacaño; (malicious) mal intencionado.

mean[3] ➤ punto medio; MAT. (average) promedio ▪ pl medios • **by m. of** por medio de • **by no m.** de ningún modo.

meaning ➤ s sentido; (intent) significado.

meaningful ➤ adj significativo.

meaningless ➤ adj insignificante; (senseless) sin sentido.

meanwhile o **meantime** ➤ adv entretanto, mientras tanto.

measure ➤ s medida ▪ **beyond m.** sin límite • **for good m.** por añadidura ➤ tr medir.

measurement ➤ s medición f; (unit) medida.

meat ➤ s carne f.

meatless ➤ adj sin carne.

mechanic ➤ s mecánico/a ▪ pl mecánica.

mechanical ➤ adj mecánico.

mechanism ➤ s mecanismo.

medal ➤ s medalla.

medalist ➤ s DEP. ganador/a.

media ➤ spl medios.

medical ➤ adj médico.

medication ➤ s medicamento.

medicine ➤ s medicina.

medieval ➤ adj medieval.

mediocre ➤ adj mediocre.

meditate ➤ tr & intr meditar.

medium ➤ s medio ➤ adj mediano.

meet✧ ➤ tr encontrar(se) con; (an arrival) recibir; (to be introduced) conocer; (to confer with) entrevistarse con; (to confront) hacer frente a; (requirements) satisfacer ➤ intr encontrarse, verse; (to join) unirse; (to assemble) reunirse ➤ s DEP. encuentro.

meeting ➤ s reunión f; (rally) mitin m.

melody ➤ s melodía.

melon ➤ s melón m.

melt ➤ tr & intr derretir(se); (to dissolve) disolver(se); FIG. ablandar(se).

member ➤ s miembro.

membrane ➤ s membrana.

memo ➤ s memorándum m.

memorial ➤ s & adj (monumento) conmemorativo.

memory ➤ s memoria; (recollection) recuerdo.

men ➤ pl de **man.**

mend ➤ tr remendar ➤ intr curar, sanar.

menswear ➤ s ropa para hombres.

mental ➤ adj mental; (hospital) psiquiátrico.

mentality ➤ s mentalidad f.

mention ➤ tr mencionar ➤ s mención f.

menu ➤ s menú m, carta.

merchandise ➤ s mercancía.

merchant ➤ s comerciante mf; (shopkeeper) tendero/a.

mercy ➤ s clemencia; (compassion) misericordia.

mere ➤ adj (simple) puro; (no more than) no más que.

merely ➤ adv simplemente; (no more than) no más que.

merge ➤ tr & intr unir(se); COM. fusionar(se).

merger ➤ s unión f; COM. fusión f.

meridian ➤ s meridiano.

merit ➤ mérito ➤ tr & intr merecer.

merry ➤ adj alegre ▪ **M. Christmas** Feliz Navidad.

mesh ➤ s TEJ. malla ➤ intr enredarse; (to harmonize) encajar; MEC. engranar.

mess ➤ s desorden m; (dirty condition) asquerosidad f; (difficulty) lío ▪ **m. hall** comedor ➤ tr ▪ **to m. up** o **make a m. of** desarreglar; (to spoil) echar a perder ➤ intr ▪ **to m. around** FAM. entretenerse • **to m. with** FAM. molestar.

message ➤ s mensaje m.

messenger ➤ s mensajero/a.

messy ➤ adj desordenado; (slovenly) desaseado.

metal ➤ s metal m.

metallic ➤ adj metálico.

meter ➤ s (measurement, verse) metro; (device) contador m.

method ➤ s método.

methodic(al) ➤ adj metódico.

meticulous ➤ adj meticuloso; (overscrupulous) minucioso.

metric ➤ adj métrico.

metropolis ➤ s metrópoli f.

metropolitan ➤ adj metropolitano.

Mexican ➤ adj & s Mexicano/a.

mice ➤ pl de **mouse.**

microbe ➤ s microbio.

microchip ➤ s microchip m.

microphone ➤ s micrófono.

microprocessor ➤ s microprocesador m.

microscope ➤ s microscopio.

microwave ➤ s microonda; (oven) (horno) microondas m.

mid ➤ adj medio ▪ **in mid-May** a mediados de mayo.

midday ➤ s mediodía m.

middle ➤ adj medio; (intermediate) intermedio ➤ s medio ▪ **in the m. of** en medio de.

middle-class ➤ adj de la clase media.

midnight ➤ s medianoche f.

midwife ➤ s comadrona.

might[1] ➤ poder, fuerzas.

might[2] ➤ aux ▪ **it m. rain** es posible que llueva.

migrant ➤ adj migratorio ➤ s emigrante mf; (worker) trabajador/a ambulante.

migrate ➤ intr emigrar.

mild ➤ adj suave; (climate) templado; (cold, cough) leve.

mile ➤ s milla.

mileage ➤ s distancia en millas.

military ➤ adj militar ➤ s las fuerzas armadas.

milk ➤ s leche f ▪ **m. shake** batido de leche • **skim m.** leche desnatada.

mill ➤ s molino; (for spices, coffee) molinillo; (factory) fábrica.

millimeter ➤ s milímetro.

million ➤ s millón m.

millionaire ➤ s millonario/a.

mimic ➤ tr remedar; (resemble) simular ➤ s imitador/a.

mind ➤ s mente f ▪ **to bring to m.** recordar • **to change one's m.** cambiar de opinión • **to come to m.** venir a la memoria • **to have in m.** planear ➤ tr (to heed) prestar atención a; (to obey) obedecer; (to look after) cuidar ▪ **he does not m. the cold** no le molesta el frío ➤ intr ▪ **never m.** no importa.

mine[1] ➤ s mina ▪ **land m.** mina terrestre ➤ tr extraer.

mine[2] ➤ pron (el) mío, (la) mía, etc.

miner ➤ s minero/a.

mineral ➤ s & adj mineral m.

miniature ➤ *adj & s* (en) miniatura.
minicomputer ➤ *s* minicomputadora.
minimum ➤ *s & adj* mínimo ■ **m. wage** salario vital.
minister ➤ *s* POL. ministro/a; RELIG. pastor/a, clérigo/a ➤ *intr* cuidar.
ministry ➤ *s* POL. ministerio; RELIG. sacerdocio.
minor ➤ *adj* menor; *(secondary)* de poca importancia ➤ *s* menor *mf* de edad.
minority ➤ *s* minoría.
mint[1] ➤ *s* casa de moneda ➤ *tr* acuñar.
mint[2] ➤ *s* BOT. menta, hierbabuena; *(candy)* (pastilla de) menta.
minus ➤ *prep* MAT. menos; FAM. *(without)* sin ➤ *adj* MAT. negativo.
minute[1] ➤ *s* minuto; *(moment)* momento.
minute[2] ➤ *adj* diminuto; *(insignificant)* insignificante; *(thorough)* minucioso.
miracle ➤ *s* milagro; FIG. maravilla.
mirror ➤ *s* espejo ➤ *tr* reflejar.
misbehave ➤ *intr* portarse mal.
miscarriage ➤ *s* MED. aborto.
miscellaneous ➤ *adj* misceláneo.
mischief ➤ *s (prank)* travesura; *(perverseness)* malicia.
mischievous ➤ *adj* malicioso; *(playful)* travieso; *(troublesome)* molesto.
miser ➤ *s* avaro/a.
miserable ➤ *adj (unhappy)* desdichado; *(inadequate)* miserable.
misery ➤ *s* miseria; *(unhappiness)* desdicha.
misfortune ➤ *s* mala suerte.
misgiving ➤ *s* duda.
mishandle ➤ *tr (to botch)* manejar mal; *(to maltreat)* maltratar.
mishap ➤ *s* desgracia.
mislead ➤ *tr* descaminar; *(to deceive)* engañar.
misleading ➤ *adj* engañoso.
misplace ➤ *tr (to lose)* extraviar.
misprint ➤ *s* error *m* de imprenta.
miss[1] ➤ *tr* perder; *(not to achieve)* no conseguir; *(a person, place)* echar de menos, extrañar ■ **to m. the point** no comprender ➤ *intr* fallar ■ **to be missing** faltar ➤ *s* fallo; *(failure)* fracaso.
miss[2] ➤ *s* señorita.
missile ➤ *(rock, spear)* proyectil *m;* MIL. misil *m.*
missing ➤ *adj (lost)* perdido; *(absent)* ausente; *(lacking)* que falta.
mission ➤ *s* misión *f;* DIPL. embajada.
misspell ➤ *tr* escribir mal.
mist ➤ *s* neblina.
mistake ➤ *s* error *m* ➤ *tr* interpretar *o* entender mal ■ **to m. . . . for** confundir . . . con.
mistaken ➤ *adj (wrong)* equivocado, errado; *(inexact)* erróneo ■ **to be m.** equivocarse.
Mister ➤ *s* señor *m.*
mistreat ➤ *tr* maltratar.
mistress ➤ *s (of household)* señora; *(lover)* amante *f;* *(owner)* ama.
mistrust ➤ *s* desconfianza ➤ *tr & intr* desconfiar (de).
misty ➤ *adj* nebuloso; *(glass)* empañado.
misunderstand ➤ *tr* entender *o* interpretar mal.
misunderstanding ➤ *s* malentendido; *(disagreement)* desacuerdo.
misuse ➤ *s* mal empleo; *(mistreatment)* maltrato ➤ *tr* emplear mal; *(to mistreat)* maltratar.
mitten ➤ *s* mitón *m,* manopla.
mix ➤ *tr* mezclar; *(a drink)* preparar ■ **to m. up** *(to confuse)* confundir; *(to jumble)* mezclar ➤ *intr* mezclarse; *(to go together)* pegar ➤ *s* mezcla.
mixed ➤ *adj* mezclado; *(conflicting)* contradictorio; *(composite)* mixto.
mixed-up ➤ *adj* FAM. confundido, que no sabe lo que quiere.
mixer ➤ *s (appliance)* batidora.
mixture ➤ *s* mezcla.
mix-up ➤ *s* confusión *f,* lío.
moat ➤ *s* foso (de un castillo).
mob ➤ *s* turba.
mobile ➤ *adj* móvil.
mobility ➤ *s* movilidad *f.*
mock ➤ *tr* mofarse de ➤ *adj* simulado.
mockingbird ➤ *s* sinsonte *m.*
model ➤ *s & adj* modelo *mf.*
moderate ➤ *adj* moderado; *(price)* módico ➤ *s* moderado/a.
moderation ➤ *s* moderación *f.*
modern ➤ *adj & s* moderno.
modernize ➤ *tr & intr* modernizar(se).
modest ➤ *adj* modesto; *(reserved)* recatado; *(in price)* módico.
modesty ➤ *s* modestia; *(decency)* pudor *m;* *(in price)* modicidad *f.*
modification ➤ *s* modificación *f.*
modify ➤ *tr* modificar.
moist ➤ *adj* húmedo.
moisten ➤ *tr & intr* humedecer(se).
moisture ➤ *s* humedad *f.*
mold[1] ➤ *s* molde *m* ➤ *tr* moldear.
mold[2] BIOL. ➤ *s* moho.
moldy ➤ *adj* mohoso; *(musty)* enmohecido.
mole[1] ➤ *s* ANAT. lunar *m.*
mole[2] ➤ *s* ZOOL. topo.
mom ➤ *s* FAM. mamá.
moment ➤ *s* momento.
monarch ➤ *s* monarca *mf.*
monarchy ➤ *s* monarquía.
monastery ➤ *s* monasterio.
Monday ➤ *s* lunes *m.*
monetary ➤ *adj* monetario.
money ➤ *s* dinero; *(currency)* moneda ■ **m. order** giro postal.
monitor ➤ *s* monitor/a; COMPUT., TEC. monitor *m* ➤ *tr (signal, quality)* comprobar.
monk ➤ *s* monje *m.*
monkey ➤ *s* mono.
monologue ➤ *s* monólogo.
monopolize ➤ *tr* monopolizar.
monopoly ➤ *s* monopolio.
monorail ➤ *s* monocarril *m.*
monotonous ➤ *adj* monótono.
monotony ➤ *s* monotonía.
monster ➤ *s* monstruo.
month ➤ *s* mes *m.*
monthly ➤ *adj* mensual ➤ *adv* mensualmente.
monument ➤ *s* monumento.
mood ➤ *s* humor *m* ■ **to be in the m. for** tener ganas de.
moody ➤ *adj* malhumorado.
moon ➤ *s* luna.
moor[1] ➤ *tr* MARÍT. amarrar.
moor[2] ➤ *s* GEOG. terreno pantanoso.
mooring ➤ *s (cable)* amarra.
moose ➤ *s* alce.
mop ➤ *s* fregona; *(of hair)* greña ➤ *tr* fregar.
moped ➤ *s* ciclomotor *m.*
moral ➤ *adj* moral ➤ *s* moraleja ■ *pl* principios morales.
morale ➤ *s* moral *f.*
more ➤ *adj* más; *(greater in quantity)* superior ➤ *s* más ■ **the m. . . . the m. . . .** cuanto más . . . más . . . ➤ *pron* más ➤ *adv* más ■ **m. and m.** cada vez más • **m. or less** más o menos.
moreover ➤ *adv* además.
morning ➤ *s* mañana ■ **good m.!** ¡buenos días! • **in the m.** por la mañana.
mortal ➤ *adj & s* mortal *mf.*
mortality ➤ *s* mortalidad *f.*
mortgage ➤ *s* hipoteca ➤ *tr* hipotecar.
mosaic ➤ *s* mosaico.
mosque ➤ *s* mezquita.
mosquito ➤ *s* mosquito ■ **m. net** mosquitero, toldillo.
moss ➤ *s* musgo.
most ➤ *adj (in quantity)* más . . . que todos los demás; *(in measure)* mayor; *(almost all)* la mayoría de ➤ *s* la mayor parte; *(the majority)* la mayoría ■ **at (the) m.** a lo sumo • **to make the m. of** aprovechar al máximo ➤ *pron* la mayor parte ➤ *adv* más . . . que todos los demás; *(superlative)* más; *(very)* muy ■ **m. of all** sobre todo.
mostly ➤ *adv* en su mayor parte.
motel ➤ *s* motel *m.*
moth ➤ *s* mariposa nocturna; *(clothes moth)* polilla.
mother ➤ *s* madre *f.*
motherhood ➤ *s* maternidad *f.*
mother-in-law ➤ *s* suegra.
motion ➤ *s* movimiento; *(gesture)* ademán *m;* *(proposal)* moción *f* ■ **m. picture** película • **m. sickness** mareo ➤ *intr* hacer señas.
motivation ➤ *s* motivación *f.*
motive ➤ *s* motivo; DER. móvil *m.*
motor ➤ *s* motor *m.*
motorboat lancha motora.
motorcycle ➤ *s* motocicleta, moto *f.*
motorist ➤ *s* automovilista *mf.*
mound ➤ *s* montículo; *(heap)* montón *m.*
mount[1] ➤ *tr* subir (a); *(a horse)* montar ➤ *s* montura; *(base)* soporte *m.*
mount[2] ➤ *s (hill)* monte *m.*
mountain ➤ *s* montaña ■ **m. range** cordillera.
mountaineer ➤ *s* montañero/a.
mountainous ➤ *adj* montañoso.
mourn ➤ *intr & tr* llorar; *(a death)* lamentar(se).
mourning ➤ *s* duelo; *(period)* luto.
mouse ➤ *s* ZOOL., COMPUT. ratón *m.*
mousepad ➤ *s* alfombrilla de ratón.
mouth ➤ *s* boca.
mouthwash ➤ *s* enjuague *m* bucal.
move ➤ *intr* moverse; *(to change position)* cambiar de postura; *(to relocate)* mudarse; *(in a game)* jugar ■ **to m. away** alejarse • **to m. in** instalarse ➤ *tr* mover; *(to reposition)* trasladar; *(to prompt)* impulsar ➤ *s* movimiento; *(change of residence)* mudanza; *(of a piece)* jugada; *(player's turn)* turno; *(step)* paso ■ **on the m.** andando de acá para allá; *(active)* activo.
movement ➤ *s* movimiento.
mover ➤ *s* persona que hace mudanzas ■ *pl* agencia de mudanzas.
movie ➤ *s* película.
moving ➤ *adj* móvil; *(in motion)* en marcha; *(touching)* conmovedor.
mow◊ ➤ *tr* segar.
mower ➤ *s* segador/a; *(machine)* segadora; *(for lawn)* cortacéspedes *m.*
Mr. ➤ *s* Sr.
Mrs. ➤ *s* Sra.
much ➤ *adj* mucho ■ **as m. . . . as** tanto . . . como • **too m.** demasiado ➤ *s* mucho ■ **as m. again** otro tanto • **as m. as** tanto como • **not so m. as** ni siquiera • **so m. the better** tanto mejor • **to make m. of** dar mucha importancia a ➤ *adv* mucho ■ **however m.** por mucho que • **how m.?** ¿cuánto?
mud ➤ *s* barro.
muddle ➤ *tr (to befuddle)* atontar; *(to bungle)* chapucear.
muddy ➤ *adj* fangoso; *(liquid)* turbio ➤ *tr* enfangar; *(liquid)* enturbiar.
mug ➤ *s (cup)* jarra.
mugger ➤ *s* asaltante *mf.*
mugging ➤ *s* asalto (con intento de robo).
muggy ➤ *adj* bochornoso.
mule ➤ *s* mulo.
multimedia ➤ *adj* multimedia.
multiple ➤ *adj* múltiple; MAT. múltiplo ➤ *s* múltiplo.
multiplication ➤ *s* multiplicación *f.*
multiply ➤ *tr & intr* multiplicar(se).
mumble ➤ *tr* mascullar ➤ *intr* balbucir ➤ *s* refunfuño.
mummy ➤ *s (corpse)* momia.
mumps ➤ *spl* paperas *f.*
mural ➤ *s* pintura mural.
murder ➤ *s* asesinato ➤ *tr* asesinar.
murderer ➤ *s* asesino/a.
murmur ➤ *s* murmullo; MED. soplo cardíaco ➤ *tr & intr* murmurar.
muscle ➤ *s* ANAT. músculo.
muscular ➤ *adj* muscular; *(strong)* musculoso.
museum ➤ *s* museo.
mushroom ➤ *s* BOT. hongo; CUL. champiñón *m* ➤ *intr* crecer rápidamente.
music ➤ *s* música.
musical ➤ *adj* de música; *(like music)* musical ➤ *s* comedia musical.
musician ➤ *s* músico/a.
mussel ➤ *s* mejillón *m.*
must ➤ *aux* deber, tener que; *(indicating probability)* deber de.
mustache ➤ *s* bigote(s) *m.*
mustard ➤ *s* mostaza.
musty ➤ *adj* mohoso.
mute ➤ *adj & s* mudo.
mutter ➤ *intr & tr* murmurar.
mutual ➤ *adj* mutuo ■ **m. fund** fondo mutualista (de inversión).
muzzle ➤ *s (snout)* hocico; *(restraint)* bozal *m;* *(gun)* boca ➤ *tr* abozalar; *(to restrain)* amordazar.
my ➤ *adj pos* mi, mis.
myself ➤ *pron* yo mismo; *(reflexive)* me; *(after preposition)* mí (mismo).
mysterious ➤ *adj* misterioso.
mystery ➤ *s* misterio; LIT. novela policíaca.
myth ➤ *s* mito.
mythology ➤ *s* mitología.

N

nail ➤ *s* clavo; *(finger, toe)* uña ➤ *tr* clavar.
naive ➤ *adj* cándido, ingenuo.
naked ➤ *adj* desnudo.
name ➤ *s* nombre *m;* *(surname)* apellido; *(reputation)* fama ■ **full n.** nombre y apellido • **my n. is** me llamo ➤ *tr* llamar; *(to mention)* nombrar.
namely ➤ *adv* es decir, a saber.
nanny ➤ *s* niñera.
nap ➤ *s* siesta ➤ *intr* dormir la siesta.
napkin ➤ *s* servilleta.
narrow ➤ *adj* angosto, estrecho ➤ *tr & intr* estrechar(se).
nasal ➤ *adj* nasal.
nasty ➤ *adj (filthy)* sucio; *(malicious)* malicioso; *(cough, cold)* molesto.
nation ➤ *s* nación *f.*
national ➤ *adj & s* nacional.
nationality ➤ *s* nacionalidad *f.*
native ➤ *adj* nativo, indígeno; *(country, town)* natal; *(language)* materno; *(product)* del país ➤ *s* nativo/a, indígena *mf.*
natural ➤ *adj* natural; *(one's own)* propio ■ **n. resource** recurso natural.
naturally ➤ *adv* naturalmente; *(by nature)* por naturaleza; *(of course)* por supuesto, claro.
nature ➤ *s* (la) naturaleza; *(temperament)* natural *m.*
naughty ➤ *adj* travieso, desobediente.
nausea ➤ *s* náusea; *(disgust)* asco.
nauseate ➤ *tr* dar náuseas a; *(to disgust)* dar asco a.
naval ➤ *adj* naval.
navel ➤ *s* ombligo.
navigate ➤ *intr & tr* navegar.
navigation ➤ *s* navegación *f.*
navy ➤ *s* marina, flota; *(color)* azul marino ■ **the N.** la marina, la armada.
near ➤ *adv* cerca, próximo; *(almost)* casi; *(closely related)* íntimo, cercano ■ **to come n.** acercarse ➤ *adj* próximo; *(relation)* allegado; *(direct)* directo, corto ➤ *prep (close to)* cerca de; *(almost)* casi ➤ *tr & intr* acercarse (a).
nearby ➤ *adj* cercano, próximo ➤ *adv* cerca.
nearly ➤ *adv* casi.
nearsighted ➤ *adj* miope.
neat ➤ *adj (orderly)* ordenado; *(work)* esmerado, bien hecho; *(writing)* claro.
necessary ➤ *adj* necesario.
necessity ➤ *s* necesidad *f.*
neck ➤ *s* cuello; *(of animals)* pescuezo.
necklace ➤ *s* collar *m.*
necktie ➤ *s* corbata.
nectarine ➤ *s* griñón *m,* pelón *m.*
need ➤ *s* necesidad *f;* *(trouble)* apuro ■ **if n. be** si fuera necesario • **to be in n. of** necesitar ➤ *tr* necesitar ➤ *intr* ■ **to n. to** *(to have to)* deber, tener que; *(to be necessary)* ser necesario.
needle ➤ *s* aguja.
needless ➤ *adj* innecesario ■ **n. to say** huelga decir que.
negative ➤ *adj* negativo ➤ *s* negativa; GRAM. negación *f;* FOTOG. negativo.
neglect ➤ *tr* descuidar ■ **to n. to** olvidarse de ➤ *s* descuido, negligencia.
negligence ➤ *s* negligencia.
negligent ➤ *adj* negligente, descuidado.
negotiate ➤ *intr* negociar.
negotiation ➤ *s* negociación *f.*
neigh ➤ *intr* relinchar.
neighbor ➤ *s* vecino/a.
neighborhood ➤ *s* barrio; *(people)* vecindario.
neighboring ➤ *adj* vecino.
neither ➤ *adj* ninguno (de los dos) ➤ *pron* ninguno (de dos), ni uno ni otro ➤ *conj & adv* (ni . . .) tampoco ■ **n. . . . nor** ni . . . ni.
nephew ➤ *s* sobrino.
nerve ➤ *s* nervio; *(courage)* valor *m* ■ **to get on one's nerves** crispar los nervios a uno • **to lose one's n.** acobardarse ■ *pl* nerviosidad.
nervous ➤ *adj* nervioso; *(high-strung)* irritable, excitable.
nest ➤ *s* nido ➤ *intr* anidar.
net[1] ➤ *s* red *f* ■ **N.** Red, Internet.
net[2] ➤ *adj (after deductions)* neto.
netting ➤ *s* red *f.*
network ➤ *s* red *f.*
neutral ➤ *adj* neutral; FÍS., QUÍM. neutro ➤ *s* neutral *mf;* AUTO. punto muerto.
never ➤ *adv* nunca, jamás ■ **n. again** nunca más • **n. ever** nunca jamás.
nevertheless ➤ *adv* sin embargo, no obstante.
new ➤ *adj* nuevo.
newborn ➤ *adj & s* (niño/a) recién nacido/a.
newcomer ➤ *s* recién llegado/a.
news ➤ *s* noticia; *(current events)* noticias, actualidades *f;* *(broadcast)* noti-

ciario.

newscast ➤ *s* noticiario.

newscaster ➤ *s* locutor/a.

newsletter ➤ *s* hoja informativa.

newspaper ➤ *s* periódico, diario.

next ➤ *adj (in time)* próximo; *(adjacent)* de al lado; *(following)* siguiente ➤ *adv* después, luego ■ **n. door** al lado • **n. to** *(beside)* junto a; *(almost)* casi.

nibble ➤ *tr* mordiscar ➤ *s* mordisco.

Nicaraguan ➤ *adj & s* nicaragüense *mf.*

nice ➤ *adj (friendly)* amable, bueno; *(pleasant)* agradable; *(dress, looks)* bonito, lindo ■ **to be n.** to ser amable con • **to have a n. time** pasarlo bien.

nickel ➤ *s* QUÍM. niquel *m; (U.S. coin)* moneda de cinco centavos.

nickname ➤ *s* apodo.

niece ➤ *s* sobrina.

night ➤ *s* noche *f; (nightfall)* anochecer *m* ■ **at** *o* **by n.** de noche • **good n.!** ¡buenas noches! • **last n.** anoche • **n. school** escuela nocturna.

nightclub ➤ *s* club nocturno.

nightgown ➤ *s* camisa de dormir, camisón *m.*

nightingale ➤ *s* ruiseñor *m.*

nightmare ➤ *s* pesadilla.

nighttime ➤ *s* noche *f.*

nine ➤ *s & adj* nueve *m* ■ **n. hundred** novecientos • **n. o'clock** las nueve.

nineteen ➤ *s & adj* diecinueve *m.*

ninety ➤ *s & adj* noventa.

ninth ➤ *s & adj* noveno.

nip ➤ *tr (to pinch)* pellizcar; *(to bite)* morder.

nipple ➤ *s* pezón *m; (on bottle)* tetilla.

nitrogen ➤ *s* nitrógeno.

no ➤ *adv* no ■ **no longer** ya no ➤ *adj* no ■ **by no means** de ninguna manera • **no smoking** prohibido fumar • **no way!** ¡nunca!, ¡jamás! • **to have no hope** no tener ninguna esperanza.

nobility ➤ *s* nobleza.

noble ➤ *adj & s* noble *mf.*

nobody ➤ *pron* nadie ➤ *s* don nadie *m.*

nod ➤ *intr (sleepily)* dar cabezadas; *(in agreement)* asentir con la cabeza; *(in greeting)* saludar con la cabeza ■ **to n. off** dormirse ➤ *tr* inclinar (la cabeza) ➤ *s* inclinación *f* de la cabeza.

noise ➤ *s* ruido.

noisy ➤ *adj* ruidoso.

nominate ➤ *tr* nombrar.

nominee ➤ *s* candidato/a.

none ➤ *pron* nadie, ninguno.

nonetheless ➤ *adv* sin embargo.

nonfat ➤ *adj* sin grasa.

nonfiction ➤ *s* literatura no ficción.

nonnegotiable ➤ *adj* no negociable.

nonresident ➤ *adj & s* no residente *mf,* transeúnte *mf.*

nonsense ➤ *s* disparate(s) *m* ■ **n.!** tonterías • **to talk n.** decir tonterías.

nonstop ➤ *adv* sin parar ➤ *adj (train)* directo; *(plane)* sin escalas.

nontransferable ➤ *adj* intransferible.

noodle ➤ *s* CUL. tallarín *m,* fideo.

noon ➤ *s* mediodía *m.*

nor ➤ *conj* ni ■ **neither rain n. snow** ni lluvia ni nieve.

normal ➤ *adj* normal.

north ➤ *s* norte *m* ➤ *adj* del norte ➤ *adv* al norte, hacia el norte.

North America ➤ *s* Norteamérica.

North American ➤ *adj & s* norteamericano/a.

northeast ➤ *adj & s* (del) nordeste *m.*

northeastern ➤ *adj* del nordeste.

northern ➤ *adj* septentrional, del norte ■ **n. lights** aurora boreal.

northerner ➤ *s* norteño/a.

North Pole ➤ *s* Polo Norte.

northwest ➤ *adj & s* (del) noroeste *m.*

northwestern ➤ *adj* del noroeste.

nose ➤ *s* nariz *f* ■ **on the n.** exacto • **to blow one's n.** sonarse la nariz.

nosebleed ➤ *s* hemorragia nasal.

nostril ➤ *s* ventana ■ *pl* narices.

nosy ➤ *adj* entrometido.

not ➤ *adv* no ■ **n. even** ni siquiera • **n. yet** ya no, todavía no.

notable ➤ *adj & s* notable *mf.*

note ➤ *s* nota; FIN. billete *m* ■ **to make a n. of** tomar nota de ■ *pl* notas, apuntes • **to compare n.** cambiar impresiones ➤ *tr (to notice)* notar, advertir; *(to mention)* señalar.

notebook ➤ *s* cuaderno.

notepaper ➤ *s* papel *m* de escribir.

nothing ➤ *pron* nada ■ **for n.** *(for free)* por nada; *(in vain)* para nada • **n. but** sólo • **to have n. to do with** no tener nada que ver con ➤ *s* nada ■ **to believe in n.** no creer en nada.

notice ➤ *s* atención *f; (warning)* aviso; *(announcement)* anuncio; *(sign)* letrero ■ **at a moment's n.** sin previo aviso • **to give n.** *(to resign)* renunciar ➤ *tr* darse cuenta de.

noticeable ➤ *adj* evidente.

notification ➤ *s* notificación *f,* aviso.

notify ➤ *tr* notificar, avisar.

notion ➤ *s* noción *f,* idea.

noun ➤ *s* sustantivo, nombre *m.*

nourish ➤ *tr* nutrir, alimentar.

novel ➤ *s* novela ➤ *adj* nuevo, original.

novelist ➤ *s* novelista *mf.*

novelty ➤ novedad *f.*

November ➤ *s* noviembre *m.*

now ➤ *adv* ahora; *(immediately)* ahora mismo ■ **right n.!** ¡ahora mismo! ➤ *conj* ■ **n. that** ya que ➤ *s* ■ **by n.** ya.

nowadays ➤ *adv* hoy (en) día.

nowhere ➤ *adv* en, por, *o* a ninguna parte ■ **n. near** muy lejos de ➤ *s* ■ **out of n.** de la nada.

nozzle ➤ *s* boquilla.

nuclear ➤ *adj* nuclear.

nude ➤ *s & adj* desnudo.

nuisance ➤ *s (person)* pesado/a; *(thing)* fastidio, molestia.

numb ➤ *adj* entumecido ➤ *tr* entumecer.

number ➤ *s* número ■ **a n. of** varios ■ *pl (many)* muchos; MAT. números ➤ *tr* numerar.

numeral ➤ *s* número.

numerous ➤ *adj* numeroso.

nun ➤ *s* monja, religiosa.

nurse ➤ *s* enfermero/a ➤ *tr (infant)* criar; *(patient)* cuidar.

nursery ➤ *s* cuarto de los niños; *(center)* guardería infantil; AGR. vivero ■ **n. school** escuela de párvulos.

nut ➤ *s* nuez *f;* MEC. *(for bolts)* tuerca; JER. *(crazy person)* chiflado/a.

nutcracker ➤ *s* cascanueces *m.*

nutmeg ➤ *s* nuez moscada.

nutrition ➤ *s* nutrición *f.*

nylon ➤ *s* nilón *m* ■ *pl* medias de nilón.

O

oak ➤ *s* roble *m.*

oar ➤ *s* remo.

oath ➤ *s* juramento.

oatmeal CUL. gachas de avena.

obedience ➤ *s* obediencia.

obedient ➤ *adj* obediente.

obese ➤ *adj* obeso.

obey ➤ *tr & intr* obedecer.

object[1] ➤ *intr* hacer objeciones; *(to disapprove)* oponerse *(to* a).

object[2] ➤ *s* objeto; *(purpose)* propósito; *(goal)* fin *m;* GRAM. complemento.

objection ➤ *s* objeción *f,* reparo.

objective ➤ *adj & s* objetivo.

obligation ➤ *s* obligación *f.*

oblige ➤ *tr* obligar; *(to do a favor for)* hacer un favor a ■ **to be obliged to** verse obligado a.

obliging ➤ *adj* complaciente.

oblique ➤ *adj* oblicuo.

oblong ➤ *adj* oblongo, rectangular.

obscene ➤ *adj* obsceno.

obscure ➤ *adj* oscuro; *(meaning)* oculto ➤ *tr* ocultar; *(view)* tapar.

observant ➤ *adj* observador.

observation ➤ *s* observación *f.*

observatory ➤ *s* observatorio.

observe ➤ *tr* observar; *(to say)* decir.

observer ➤ *s* observador/a.

obsession ➤ *s* obsesión *f.*

obstacle ➤ *s* obstáculo.

obstinate ➤ *adj* obstinado.

obstruct ➤ *tr* obstruir.

obtain ➤ *tr* obtener.

obvious ➤ *adj* obvio, patente.

obviously ➤ *adv* evidentemente.

occasion ➤ *s* ocasión *f; (event)* acontecimiento ■ **on o.** ocasionalmente.

occasional ➤ *adj* ocasional.

occupant ➤ *s (tenant)* inquilino/a; *(guest)* huésped *mf; (passenger)* pasajero/a.

occupation ➤ *s* ocupación *f.*

occupy ➤ *tr (space)* ocupar; *(time)* emplear ■ **to o. oneself with** entretenerse con.

occur ➤ *intr* ocurrir, suceder; *(to be found)* encontrarse.

occurrence ➤ *s (incident)* suceso.

ocean ➤ *s* océano.

o'clock ➤ *adv* ■ **one o.** la una • **it's ten o.** son las diez.

October ➤ *s* octubre *m.*

octopus ➤ *s* pulpo.

odd ➤ *adj (unusual)* raro, extraño; *(strange)* curioso; MAT. impar, non ■ **o. jobs** chapuces • **o. or even?** ¿pares o nones? • **thirty-o.** treinta y pico.

odds ➤ *spl* ventaja; *(chances)* probabilidades *f* ■ **o. and ends** retazos • **the o. are against it** no es muy probable.

odor ➤ *s* olor *m.*

of ➤ *prep* de ■ **a friend of mine** un amigo mío • **all of them** todos ellos.

off ➤ *adv* lejos, a distancia ■ **o. and on** de vez en cuando • **ten per cent o.** diez por ciento de descuento ➤ *adj (lights)* apagado; *(not operating)* desconectado; *(canceled)* cancelado ■ **in the o. position** en posición de cerrado • **o. chance** posibilidad remota ➤ *prep (from)* de; *(near)* frente a; *(away from)* lejos de; *(down from)* desde, por.

offend ➤ *tr* ofender.

offender ➤ *s* ofensor/a; *(criminal)* infractor/a.

offense ➤ *s* ofensa; *(crime)* delito ■ **no o. (intended)** sin intención de ofender • **to take o. at** ofenderse por.

offensive ➤ *adj* ofensivo ➤ *s* ofensiva.

offer ➤ *tr* ofrecer; *(to propose)* proponer; *(to provide)* proporcionar; *(to present)* presentar ➤ *s* oferta.

offhand ➤ *adv* sin pensarlo ➤ *adj* improvisado; *(manner)* desenvuelto.

office ➤ *s* oficina; *(room)* despacho.

officer ➤ *s* oficial *mf; (police)* agente *mf* de policía.

official ➤ *adj* oficial ➤ *s* oficial *mf,* funcionario/a.

often ➤ *adv* frecuentemente, a menudo ■ **every so o.** alguna que otra vez • **not very o.** pocas veces.

oil ➤ *s* aceite *m; (fuel)* petróleo; *(lubricant)* aceite lubricante ➤ *tr* aceitar, lubricar.

ointment ➤ *s* ungüento, pomada.

O.K. *o* **okay** ➤ *s* autorización *f* ➤ *tr* autorizar ➤ *interj* ¡muy bien!

old ➤ *adj* viejo; *(elderly)* mayor, anciano; *(ancient, former)* antiguo ■ **older** mayor • **oldest** (el, la) mayor.

old-fashioned ➤ *adj* anticuado; *(person)* chapado a la antigua.

olive ➤ *s* oliva, aceituna ■ **o. tree** olivo.

Olympic ➤ *adj* olímpico ■ **Olympics** *spl* juegos olímpicos.

omelet(te) ➤ *s* tortilla.

omit ➤ *tr* omitir.

on ➤ *prep (general)* en; *(on top of)* sobre ➤ *adv* ■ **on and off** de vez en cuando • **on and on** sin parar ➤ *adj (appliance, lights, gas)* encendido; *(faucet)* abierto; *(brakes, alarms)* puesto.

once ➤ *adv (one time)* una vez; *(formerly)* en otro tiempo, antes ■ **at o.** inmediatamente; *(at the same time)* al mismo tiempo • **o. again** otra vez • **o. and for all** de una vez para siempre • **o. in a while** de vez en cuando ➤ *s* una vez ■ **for o.** una vez siquiera.

one ➤ *adj* un, uno ➤ *s* uno; *(unit)* unidad *f* ■ **o. and all** todos • **o. never knows** nunca se sabe • **o. o'clock** la una ➤ *pron* uno ■ **that o.** aquél • **this o.** éste • **which o.?** ¿cuál?

oneself ➤ *pron* sí (mismo), uno (mismo); *(reflexively)* se ■ **by o.** solo • **to be o.** comportarse con naturalidad • **to wash o.** lavarse.

one-way ➤ *adj (street)* de sentido único; *(ticket)* de ida solamente.

onion ➤ *s* cebolla.

online ➤ *adj* en línea, conectado.

onlooker ➤ *s* espectador/a.

only ➤ *adj (sole)* único, solo ➤ *adv (merely)* sólo; *(solely)* únicamente ■ **not o. . . . but also** no sólo . . . sino también.

onward(s) ➤ *adv* hacia adelante.

opaque ➤ *adj* opaco.

open ➤ *adj* abierto; *(uncovered)* descubierto; *(uncapped)* destapado ■ **o. for business** abierto al público • **o. house** recepción general ➤ *tr* abrir; *(to uncover)* destapar ➤ *intr* abrirse; *(to come undone)* desatarse; TEAT. estrenarse ➤ *s* ■ **in the o.** al aire libre • **to bring, come into the o.** sacar, salir a la luz.

open-air ➤ *adj* al aire libre.

opener ➤ *s* abridor *m.*

opening ➤ *s* abertura, orificio; *(breach)* grieta; *(clearing)* claro; *(of a store)* inauguración *f; (job)* puesto.

opera ➤ *s* ópera.

operate ➤ *intr* funcionar; *(to have an effect)* actuar; CIR., MIL. operar ➤ *tr (to drive)* manejar; *(tool)* usar; *(appliance)* accionar; *(business)* manejar.

operation ➤ *s* operación *f; (condition)* funcionamiento.

operative ➤ *adj* operativo; *(law)* en vigor; MED. operatorio.

operator ➤ *s (of a machine)* operario; TEL. telefonista *mf; (of a vehicle)* conductor/a.

opinion ➤ *s* opinión *f.*

opponent ➤ *s* adversario/a.

opportunity ➤ *s* oportunidad *f.*

oppose ➤ *tr* oponerse a.

opposite ➤ *adj* opuesto; *(direction)* contrario; *(across from)* de enfrente; *(opinions)* contrario ■ **on the o. side of** del otro lado de ➤ *s* contrario ➤ *adv* enfrente ➤ *prep* enfrente de, frente a.

opposition ➤ *s* oposición *f; (resistance)* resistencia ■ **to be in o.** to estar en contra de.

oppress ➤ *tr* oprimir; FIG. agobiar.

opt ➤ *intr* optar *(for, to* por).

oppression ➤ *s* opresión *f.*

optician ➤ *s* óptico/a.

optimist ➤ *s* optimista *mf.*

optimistic ➤ *adj* optimista ■ **to feel o.** tener optimismo.

option ➤ *s* opción *f.*

optional ➤ *adj* opcional.

optometrist ➤ *s* optómetra *mf.*

or ➤ *conj* o, u; *(after negative)* ni.

oral ➤ *adj* oral ➤ *s* examen *m* oral.

orange ➤ *s* naranja; *(tree)* naranjo ➤ *adj* anaranjado.

orbit ➤ *s* órbita ➤ *tr* girar alrededor de ➤ *intr* estar en órbita.

orchard ➤ *s* huerto.

orchestra ➤ *s* orquesta.

ordeal ➤ *s* prueba dura.

order ➤ *s* orden *m;* COM. pedido; *(organization)* orden *f* ■ **out of o.** descompuesto ➤ *tr (to command, arrange)* ordenar; *(to request)* pedir ➤ *intr (command)* dar una orden; *(request)* hacer un pedido.

ordinary ➤ *adj* ordinario; *(plain)* corriente, cualquiera; *(average)* medio ■ **out of the o.** fuera de lo común.

ore ➤ *s* mineral *m,* mena.

oregano ➤ *s* orégano.

organ ➤ *s* órgano; *(agency)* organismo.

organic ➤ *adj* orgánico.

organism ➤ *s* organismo.

organization ➤ *s* organización *f.*

organize ➤ *tr & intr* organizar(se).

organizer ➤ *s* organizador/a.

Oriental ➤ *adj & s* oriental *mf.*

origin ➤ *s* origen *m.*

original ➤ *adj & s* original *m.*

originality ➤ *s* originalidad *f.*

ornament ➤ *s* ornamento.

orphan ➤ *s & adj* huérfano/a.

orphanage ➤ *s* orfanato, orfelinato.

ostrich ➤ *s* avestruz *m.*

other ➤ *adj* otro ➤ *s* otro ■ **no o.** ningún otro ➤ *pron* otro ➤ *adv* ■ **o. than** *(differently)* de otro modo; *(anything but)* otra cosa que.

otherwise ➤ *adv (differently)* de otro modo; *(under other circumstances)* de lo contrario, si no; *(in other respects)* por lo demás, a no ser por eso.

ought ➤ *aux (to be obliged)* deber; *(to be wise)* convenir; *(to be likely)* deber de.

ounce ➤ *s* onza.

our ➤ *adj* nuestro, nuestra, etc.

ours ➤ *pron* (el) nuestro, (la) nuestra, etc.

ourselves ➤ *pron* nos ■ **we did it o.** lo hicimos nosotros mismos.

oust ➤ *tr* expulsar.

ouster ➤ *s* expulsión *f.*

out ➤ *adv (away from)* fuera; *(outside)* afuera ■ **all o.** con tesón • **o. and o.** completamente • **to be o.** *(not at home)* no estar en casa; *(sun, moon)* haber salido; *(eliminated)* quedar excluido ➤ *adj* exterior; *(absent)* ausente; *(used up)* agotado; *(extinguished)* apagado; *(not in fashion)* fuera de moda ➤ *prep (through)* por; *(beyond)* fuera de, al otro lado de ■ **o. of** de • **o. of curiosity** por curiosidad • **o. of money** sin dinero • **three o. of four times** tres veces de cada cuatro.

outbreak ➤ *s* brote *m.*

outburst ➤ *s* arranque *m,* estallido.

outcome ➤ *s* resultado, consecuencia.

outdated ➤ *adj* obsoleto, anticuado.

outdo ➤ tr superar.
outdoor ➤ adj al aire libre.
outdoors ➤ adv al aire libre; *(outside)* (a)fuera ➤ s el aire libre.
outer ➤ adj exterior, externo.
outfit ➤ s *(clothing)* conjunto; *(business)* empresa ➤ tr equipar.
outgoing ➤ adj sociable.
outing ➤ s excursión f.
outlast ➤ tr durar más que.
outlet ➤ s salida; *(socket)* tomacorriente m; *(drain)* desagüe m; *(store)* distribuidor m.
outline ➤ s *(contour)* contorno; *(profile)* perfil m; *(shape)* silueta; *(summary)* resumen.
outlook ➤ s punto de vista; *(attitude)* actitud f; *(prospect)* posibilidades f.
outnumber ➤ tr superar en número.
outpatient ➤ s paciente externo/a.
output ➤ s producción f; *(yield)* rendimiento; COMPUT. salida ➤ tr COMPUT. imprimir.
outright ➤ adv *(frankly)* sin reservas; *(straightway)* en el acto ➤ adj *(unqualified)* sin reservas.
outside ➤ s exterior m ■ **from, on the o.** desde, por fuera ➤ adj exterior; *(influence)* de afuera ➤ adv (a)fuera; *(outdoors)* en o a la calle ➤ prep fuera de ■ **o. of** fuera de; *(except)* excepto.
outskirts ➤ spl afueras.
outstanding ➤ adj sobresaliente; *(superior)* excelente; *(unresolved)* pendiente.
outward ➤ adj exterior, externo; *(direction)* hacia afuera; *(journey)* de ida ➤ adv hacia afuera.
oval ➤ adj ovalado, oval ➤ s óvalo.
oven ➤ s horno.
over ➤ prep sobre; *(above)* encima de; *(across, on, higher than)* por encima de; *(more than)* más de o que ■ **o. the border** al otro lado de la frontera • **o. the past two years** durante los dos últimos años • **o. the phone** por teléfono • **to stumble o.** tropezar con ➤ adv *(above)* (por) encima; *(across)* al otro lado, enfrente; allá; *(again)* otra vez, de nuevo ■ **o. again** otra vez • **o. and above** además de • **o. and o.** una y otra vez • **o. here, there** aquí, allá • **o. with** FAM. acabado ➤ adj terminado, acabado.
overall ➤ adj total ➤ adv en general.
overalls ➤ spl mono, overol m.
overboard ➤ adv por la borda ■ **man o.!** ¡hombre al agua!
overcast ➤ adj nublado.
overcharge ➤ tr & intr cobrar demasiado ➤ s precio excesivo.
overcoat ➤ s sobretodo, abrigo.
overcome ➤ tr *(to defeat)* derrotar, conquistar; *(to overwhelm)* abrumar; *(obstacle, difficulty)* superar.
overdo ➤ tr hacer demasiado; *(diet, exercise)* exagerar.
overdraft ➤ s giro en descubierto.
overdraw ➤ tr girar en descubierto.
overdue ➤ adj *(delayed)* retrasado.
overeat ➤ intr comer demasiado.
overflow ➤ intr desbordarse ■ **to o. with** rebosar de ➤ tr desbordar, salirse de; *(to flood)* inundar.
overhead ➤ adj de arriba; *(light)* del techo; *(railway)* elevado ➤ s COM. gastos generales.
overhear ➤ tr oír por casualidad.
overheat ➤ tr & intr recalentar(se).
overlap ➤ tr & intr superponerse (a).
overload ➤ tr sobrecargar.
overlook ➤ tr mirar desde lo alto; *(view, window)* dar a, tener vista a; *(to disregard)* pasar por alto.
overnight ➤ adj *(guests)* por la noche; *(sudden)* repentino ➤ adv durante o por la noche; *(suddenly)* de la noche a la mañana ■ **to stay o.** pasar la noche.
overpass ➤ s paso superior, puente m.
overpay ➤ tr & intr pagar demasiado.
overpower ➤ tr abrumar.
overrate ➤ tr sobrestimar.
overreact ➤ intr reaccionar de modo exagerado.
overrun ➤ tr invadir.
overseas ➤ adv en el o al extranjero ➤ adj extranjero; *(trade)* exterior.
oversee ➤ tr supervisar.
oversight ➤ s descuido, omisión f.
oversleep ➤ intr quedarse dormido.
overtake ➤ tr *(to catch up with)* alcanzar; *(to pass)* pasar.
overtime ➤ s & adv horas extras.
overturn ➤ tr volcar.
overwhelming ➤ adj *(staggering)* abrumador; *(victory)* arrollador; *(majority)* inmenso; *(passion)* irresistible.
overwork ➤ tr & intr (hacer) trabajar demasiado.
owe ➤ tr deber.
owing ➤ adj por pagarse ■ **o. to** debido a.
owl ➤ s lechuza, búho.
own ➤ adj propio ➤ s lo mío, lo tuyo, etc. ■ **on one's o.** *(unaided)* sin ayuda de nadie; *(independently)* por cuenta propia ➤ tr ser dueño de, tener ➤ intr ■ **to o. up** confesar.
owner ➤ s dueño/a, propietario/a.
ox ➤ s buey m.
oxygen ➤ s oxígeno.
oyster ➤ s ostra.

P

pace ➤ s paso; *(speed)* ritmo ➤ tr pasearse por ➤ intr pasear.
pacific ➤ adj pacífico.
pacifier ➤ s chupete m.
pack ➤ s paquete m; *(knapsack)* mochila; *(of cigarettes)* cajetilla; *(of cards)* baraja; *(of dogs)* jauría ➤ tr *(to wrap up)* envolver; *(for shipping)* embalar; *(to put)* poner; *(to package)* empaquetar; *(to cram)* apiñar ➤ intr hacer las maletas; *(people)* apiñarse (*into* en).
package ➤ s paquete m ➤ tr empaquetar.
packed ➤ adj *(crowded)* atestado; *(suitcase)* hecho ■ **p. with** lleno de.
packet ➤ s paquete pequeño.
packing ➤ s embalaje m, envase m.
pact ➤ s pacto, convenio.
pad ➤ s *(cushion)* almohadilla, cojín m; *(stuffing)* relleno; *(of paper)* bloc m.
paddle ➤ s pala, remo ➤ intr remar con pala.
padlock ➤ s & tr (cerrar con) candado.
page[1] ➤ s HIST. paje m ➤ tr llamar.
page[2] ➤ s *(of book)* página.
paid ➤ adj pagado.
pail ➤ s cubo, balde m.
pain ➤ s dolor m; *(distress)* pena.
painful ➤ adj doloroso.
painkiller ➤ s calmante m.
paint ➤ s pintura ➤ tr & intr pintar.
paintbrush ➤ s brocha; ARTE. pincel m.
painter ➤ s pintor/a.
painting ➤ s pintura, cuadro.
pair ➤ s par m; *(persons, animals)* pareja.
pajamas ➤ spl piyama m.
palace ➤ s palacio.
palate ➤ s paladar m.
pale ➤ adj *(complexion)* pálido; *(color)* claro.
palm[1] ➤ s *(of a hand)* palma.
palm[2] ➤ s BOT. palma, palmera.
pamphlet ➤ s folleto.
pan ➤ s cacerola; *(frying pan)* sartén f.
pancake ➤ s panqueque m.
pane ➤ s hoja de vidrio.
panel ➤ s panel m; *(jury)* jurado; *(group)* grupo.
panic ➤ s pánico ➤ tr & intr aterrar(se).
panorama ➤ s panorama m.
pansy ➤ s pensamiento.
pant ➤ intr jadear.
pantheon ➤ s panteón m.
panther ➤ s pantera.
panties ➤ spl bragas, calzones.
pantry ➤ s despensa.
pants ➤ spl pantalones m.
pantyhose ➤ s pantimedia.
paper ➤ s papel m; *(composition)* trabajo escrito; *(newspaper)* periódico ■ **on p.** por escrito • **p. clip** sujetapapeles ■ pl papeles ➤ tr empapelar.
paperback ➤ s libro de bolsillo.
paprika ➤ s paprika, pimentón m.
parachute ➤ s & intr (saltar en) paracaídas m.
parade ➤ s desfile m ➤ intr desfilar.
paradise ➤ s paraíso.
paragraph ➤ s párrafo.
Paraguayan ➤ adj & s paraguayo/a.
parallel ➤ adj paralelo; FIG. análogo.
paralyze ➤ tr paralizar.
parasite ➤ s parásito.
parcel ➤ s paquete m.
parchment ➤ s pergamino.
pardon ➤ tr perdonar; *(an offense)* disculpar ■ **p.** me perdóneme ➤ s perdón m; *(exemption)* indulto ■ **I beg your p.?** ¿cómo?, ¿cómo dijo?
parent ➤ s *(father)* padre m; *(mother)* madre f ■ pl padres.
parish ➤ s parroquia.
park ➤ s parque m ➤ tr & intr *(a vehicle)* estacionar(se).
parking ➤ s aparcamiento, estacionamiento ■ **p. lot** aparcamiento • **p. meter** parquímetro.
parliament ➤ s parlamento.
parliamentary ➤ adj parlamentario.
parlor ➤ s salón m ■ **funeral p.** funeraria • **ice-cream p.** heladería.
parquet ➤ s parqué m.
parrot ➤ s papagayo, loro.
parsley ➤ s perejil m.
part ➤ s parte f; *(of a machine)* pieza; *(role)* papel m ■ **for the most p.** generalmente, por lo general ➤ tr dividir; *(to break)* partir, romper; *(to come between)* apartar ■ **to p. with** deshacerse de ➤ intr separarse, apartarse; *(to leave)* irse ➤ adv en parte.
partake ➤ intr participar (*in*, de).
partial ➤ adj parcial ■ **p. to** partidario de, aficionado a.
participant ➤ s & adj participante mf.
participate ➤ intr participar.
participation ➤ s participación f.
participle ➤ s participio.
particular ➤ adj particular; *(fussy)* exigente, minucioso ➤ s particularidad f, detalle m ■ pl pormenores.
particularly ➤ adv especialmente.
partition ➤ s partición f; *(wall)* tabique m.
partly ➤ adv en parte.
partner ➤ s socio/a; *(in a dance, games)* pareja.
partnership ➤ s sociedad f.
partridge ➤ s perdiz f.
part-time ➤ adj & adv por horas.
party ➤ s fiesta; POL. partido; *(group)* grupo.
pass ➤ intr pasar; *(to cross)* cruzarse; EDUC. aprobar ■ **in passing** de paso • **to p. away** fallecer • **to p. out** desmayarse ➤ tr pasar; *(to exceed)* sobrepasar, superar ■ **to p. on** pasar, transmitir • **to p. out** repartir, distribuir • **to p. over** pasar por alto • **to p. up** *(opportunity)* dejar pasar; *(offer)* rechazar ➤ s paso; *(permit, free ticket)* pase m; *(authorization)* permiso, licencia ■ **to make a p. at** hacer insinuaciones amorosas a.
passable ➤ adj *(road)* transitable; *(work)* aceptable; *(satisfactory)* pasable.
passage ➤ s paso; *(journey, ticket)* pasaje m; *(corridor)* pasillo.
passenger ➤ s pasajero/a, viajero/a.
passing ➤ adj *(transitory)* pasajero, transitorio ■ **p. grade** EDUC. calificación aprobatoria.
passion ➤ s pasión f.
passionate ➤ adj apasionado.
passive ➤ adj pasivo.
passport ➤ s pasaporte m.
password ➤ s MIL. contraseña; COMPUT. clave f, contraseña.
past ➤ adj pasado; *(former)* anterior, último; GRAM. pretérito, pasado ➤ s pasado; *(background)* historia; GRAM. pretérito, pasado ➤ prep *(by)* por delante de; *(on the far side of)* más allá de; *(beyond)* ya no ■ **it's ten p. two** son las dos y diez.
pasta ➤ s (plato de) pasta.
paste ➤ s engrudo ➤ tr *(to stick)* pegar.
pasteurize ➤ tr paste(u)rizar.
pastime ➤ s pasatiempo.
pastry ➤ s pasteles m.
pasture ➤ s pastura.
pat ➤ tr *(to tap)* dar palmaditas o golpecitos a ➤ s palmada, golpecito.
patch ➤ s parche m ➤ tr remendar.
patent ➤ s patente f ➤ tr patentar.
paternal ➤ adj *(fatherly)* paternal; *(on the father's side)* paterno.
path ➤ s *(trail)* sendero, senda; *(track)* camino, pista.
pathetic ➤ adj patético.
pathway ➤ s sendero.
patience ➤ s paciencia.
patient ➤ adj & s paciente mf.
patio ➤ s patio, terraza.
patriot ➤ s patriota mf.
patriotic ➤ adj patriótico.
patrol ➤ s patrulla ➤ tr & intr rondar.
patron ➤ s benefactor/a; *(customer)* cliente mf.
pattern ➤ s *(for sewing)* patrón m; *(design)* diseño, dibujo.
pause ➤ intr *(mentally)* hacer una pausa; *(physically)* pararse, detenerse; *(to hesitate)* vacilar ➤ s pausa; *(rest)* descanso.
pavement ➤ s pavimento.
paving ➤ s pavimentación f.
paw ➤ s pata.
pawn[1] ➤ s *(object)* prenda; *(hostage)* rehén mf ➤ tr empeñar.
pawn[2] ➤ s *(in chess)* peón m; FIG. pelele m.
pay◊ ➤ tr pagar; *(to profit)* compensar; *(visit, compliment)* hacer; *(attention)* prestar ■ **to p. back** *(money)* devolver, reembolsar • **to p. off** *(debts)* liquidar ➤ intr pagar; *(to be profitable)* ser rentable ■ **it pays** vale la pena • **to p. off** merecer la pena ➤ s paga, pago ➤ adj de pago ■ **p. telephone** teléfono público.
payable ➤ adj pagable.
paycheck ➤ s cheque m de pago de sueldo.
payment ➤ s pago.
payoff ➤ s pago; FAM. resultado final.
payroll ➤ s nómina o planilla de pagos.
pea ➤ s guisante m.
peace ➤ s paz f ■ **at p.** *(serene)* en calma, tranquilo.
peaceful ➤ adj pacífico; *(tranquil)* apacible, tranquilo.
peach ➤ s melocotón m, durazno.
peacock ➤ s pavo real.
peak ➤ s punta; *(of a mountain)* cima, cumbre f; *(mountain)* pico; *(maximum)* tope m ➤ intr culminar.
peanut ➤ s cacahuate m, maní m.
pear ➤ s *(tree)* peral m; *(fruit)* pera.
pearl ➤ s perla.
peasant ➤ s campesino/a.
pebble ➤ s guijarro, canto rodado.
pecan ➤ s pacana.
peck ➤ tr & intr *(bird)* picotear ➤ s picotazo.
peculiar ➤ adj peculiar; *(odd)* raro, extraño; *(special)* especial, singular.
pedal ➤ s pedal m ➤ intr pedalear.
pedestrian ➤ s peatón/ona.
peek ➤ intr echar una ojeada; *(furtively)* atisbar ➤ s atisbo, ojeada.
peel ➤ s cáscara, mondadura ➤ tr & intr pelar(se).
peer ➤ intr mirar curiosamente, mirar con atención.
peg ➤ s *(plug, spike)* clavija; *(clothes hook)* percha, gancho.
pen[1] ➤ s pluma; *(ballpoint)* bolígrafo.
pen[2] ➤ s corral m; *(sty)* pocilga ➤ tr acorralar.
penalty ➤ s pena; *(fine)* multa; *(consequences)* consecuencias; FIN. descuento; DEP. castigo, penalty m.
pencil ➤ s lápiz m ■ **p. sharpener** sacapuntas.
pendulum ➤ s péndulo.
penetrate ➤ tr penetrar.
penguin ➤ s pingüino.
penicillin ➤ s penicilina.
peninsula ➤ s península.
penniless ➤ adj sin dinero.
penny ➤ s centavo; G.B. penique m.
pension ➤ s pensión f ➤ tr pensionar.
people ➤ spl gente f; *(nation)* pueblo ■ **thirteen p.** trece personas ➤ ssg *(ethnic group)* pueblo.
pepper ➤ s *(seasoning)* pimienta; *(fruit)* pimiento, chile m ■ **black p.** pimienta negra • **green, red p.** pimiento verde, rojo.
peppermint ➤ s hierbabuena, menta; *(candy)* pastilla de menta.
per ➤ prep por; *(according to)* según ■ **p. capita** por cabeza • **p. se** por sí mismo.
perceive ➤ tr percibir.
percent ➤ adv & ssg por ciento.
percentage ➤ s porcentaje m.
perch[1] ➤ s percha ➤ intr *(to roost)* posarse.
perch[2] ➤ s *(fish)* perca.
percolator ➤ s cafetera de filtro.
perfect ➤ adj perfecto; *(ideal)* ideal ➤ tr perfeccionar.
perfection ➤ s perfección f.
perfectly ➤ adv perfectamente; *(completely)* completamente; *(utterly)* absolutamente.
perforate ➤ tr perforar.
perform ➤ tr *(to do)* ejecutar, hacer; *(a function)* desempeñar; TEAT. representar ➤ intr funcionar; *(to act)* actuar.
performance ➤ s *(doing)* ejecución f; *(of a play)* representación f; *(of a role, musical composition)* interpretación f; *(in a competition)* actuación f; *(functioning)* funcionamiento.
performer ➤ s *(actor)* artista mf; *(musi-

cian) músico/a; *(dancer)* bailarín/ina.
perfume ➤ *s* perfume *m.*
perhaps ➤ *adv* quizá(s).
peril ➤ *s* peligro.
period ➤ *s* período, periodo; *(term)* plazo; *(age, stage)* época; *(class)* hora, clase *f;* DEP. tiempo; *(menstruation)* período, regla; GRAM. punto.
periodical ➤ *adj* periódico ➤ *s* publicación periódica, revista.
peripheral ➤ *adj & s* periférico.
perish ➤ *intr* perecer.
perishable ➤ *adj* perecedero.
perk ➤ *intr* ■ **to p. up** (re)animarse.
perm ➤ *s* permanente *f.*
permanent ➤ *adj & s* permanente *f.*
permission ➤ *s* permiso.
permit ➤ *tr* permitir; *(to give consent to)* dar permiso a, dejar ➤ *s* permiso.
perpendicular ➤ *adj & s* perpendicular *f.*
perpetual ➤ *adj* perpetuo.
persecute ➤ *tr* perseguir.
persecution ➤ *s* persecución *f.*
perseverance ➤ *s* perseverancia.
persevere ➤ *intr* perseverar.
persist ➤ *intr* persistir.
persistent ➤ *adj* persistente.
person ➤ *s* persona.
personal ➤ *adj* personal; *(private)* particular; *(in person)* en persona; *(for one's use)* de uso personal ■ **p. property** bienes muebles.
personality ➤ *s* personalidad *f; (celebrity)* personaje *m,* figura.
personnel ➤ *s* personal *m.*
perspiration ➤ *s* sudor *m.*
perspire ➤ *intr* sudar, transpirar.
persuade ➤ *tr* persuadir.
persuasion ➤ *s* persuasión *f.*
Peruvian ➤ *adj & s* peruano/a.
pessimism ➤ *s* pesimismo.
pessimist ➤ *s* pesimista *mf.*
pest ➤ *s (insect)* insecto; *(person)* pelmazo, persona molesta; *(plant, animal)* plaga, peste *f.*
pester ➤ *tr* molestar, fastidiar.
pet ➤ *s* mascota, animal domesticado ➤ *tr* acariciar.
petal ➤ *s* pétalo.
petition ➤ *s* petición *f.*
petroleum ➤ *s* petróleo.
petticoat ➤ *s* enaguas.
petty ➤ *adj* insignificante, trivial; *(selfish)* mezquino ■ **p. cash** caja chica.
pharmacist ➤ *s* farmacéutico/a.
pharmacy ➤ *s* farmacia.
phase ➤ *s* fase *f* ■ **out of p.** desfasado ➤ *tr* ■ **to p. in, out** introducir, eliminar progresivamente.
pheasant ➤ *s* faisán *m.*
phenomenal ➤ *adj* fenomenal.
phenomenon ➤ *s* fenómeno.
philanthropy ➤ *s* filantropía.
philosopher ➤ *s* filósofo/a.
philosophic(al) ➤ *adj* filosófico.
philosophy ➤ *s* filosofía.
phlegm ➤ *s* flema.
phone FAM. ➤ *s* teléfono ➤ *tr & intr* telefonear, llamar por teléfono.
phonetic ➤ *adj* fonético.
phosphorus ➤ *s* fósforo.
photo ➤ *s* foto *f,* fotografía.
photocopier ➤ *s* fotocopiadora.
photocopy ➤ *tr* fotocopiar ➤ *s* fotocopia.
photograph ➤ *s* fotografía, foto *f* ➤ *tr* fotografiar.
photographer ➤ *s* fotógrafo/a.
photography ➤ *s* fotografía.
phrase ➤ *s* frase *f.*
physical ➤ *adj* físico.
physician ➤ *s* médico/a, facultativo/a.
physicist ➤ *s* físico/a.
physics ➤ *ssg* física.
pianist ➤ *s* pianista *mf.*
piano ➤ *s* piano.
pick ➤ *tr* escoger, elegir; *(to gather)* recoger ■ **to p. apart** destrozar, despedazar • **to p. oneself up** levantarse • **to p. out** escoger • **to p. up** *(to lift)* coger; *(fallen object, mess)* recoger; *(to buy)* comprar; *(to learn)* aprender; *(a habit)* adquirir ➤ *intr* ■ **to p. at** *(food)* picar, picotear • **to p. on** atormentar ➤ *s* elección *f,* selección *f.*
pickle ➤ *s* encurtido ➤ *tr* encurtir.
pickpocket ➤ *s* carterista *mf.*
pickup ➤ *s (collection)* recogida; *(truck)* camioneta; FAM. *(increase)* aumento.
picnic ➤ *s* picnic *m* ➤ *intr* comer al aire libre.
picture ➤ *s (painting)* cuadro, pintura; *(illustration)* ilustración *f; (photograph)* fotografía; *(mental image)* imagen *f* ➤ *tr (to visualize)* imaginar.
picturesque ➤ *adj* pintoresco.
pie ➤ *s (with meat)* empanada; *(with fruit)* pastel *m.*
piece ➤ *s* pedazo; *(in a set)* pieza ■ **in one p.** en buen estado; *(person)* sano y salvo ■ *pl* • **in p.** *(unassembled)* desarmado; *(shattered)* hecho añicos.
pier ➤ *s* muelle *m,* embarcadero.
pierce ➤ *tr* traspasar, perforar.
piercing ➤ *adj (sharp)* agudo; *(look)* penetrante.
piety ➤ *s* piedad *f.*
pig ➤ *s* cerdo, puerco; FAM. glotón/ona.
pigeon ➤ *s* paloma.
piggyback ➤ *adv* a cuestas.
pigtail ➤ *s* coleta, trenza.
pile ➤ *s* pila, montón *m* ➤ *tr* apilar, amontar ➤ *intr* ■ **to p. up** acumularse.
pilgrim ➤ *s* peregrino/a.
pill ➤ *s* píldora.
pillar ➤ *s* pilar *m.*
pillow ➤ *s* almohada.
pillowcase ➤ *s* funda de almohada.
pilot ➤ *s* AVIA. piloto *mf.*
pimple ➤ *s* grano.
pin ➤ *s* alfiler *m; (brooch)* broche *m* ➤ *tr* prender con alfileres.
pinball ➤ *s* pinball *m,* millón *m.*
pincer ➤ *s* pinza ■ *pl* pinzas, tenazas.
pinch ➤ *tr* pellizcar ➤ *intr (shoes)* apretar ➤ *s* pellizco ■ **in a p.** en caso de apuro.
pine ➤ *s* pino ■ **p. cone** piña.
pineapple ➤ *s* piña, ananás *m.*
pink ➤ *s & adj (color)* rosado, rosa.
pinkie ➤ *s* FAM. dedo meñique.
pint ➤ *s* pinta.
pioneer ➤ *s* pionero/a.
pipe ➤ *s (for liquids, gas)* tubería, cañería; *(for tobacco)* pipa.
pipeline ➤ *s (gas)* gasoducto; *(oil)* oleoducto.
pirate ➤ *s* pirata *mf* ➤ *tr (book, software)* piratear.
pistachio ➤ *s (nut)* pistacho.
pit[1] ➤ *s (hole)* hoyo, pozo.
pit[2] ➤ *s* hueso (de frutas) ➤ *tr* deshuesar.
pitch[1] ➤ *s* MIN. alquitrán *m,* brea.
pitch[2] ➤ *tr (to throw)* lanzar, tirar; *(hay)* echar; *(tent)* montar, armar ➤ *s (throw)* lanzamiento; *(of a roof)* pendiente *f;* MÚS. tono; *(intensity)* grado.
pitcher[1] ➤ *s* DEP. lanzador/a.
pitcher[2] ➤ *s* jarra, cántaro.
pitiful ➤ *adj* lastimoso.
pity ➤ *s (compassion)* piedad *f; (regrettable fact)* lástima, pena ➤ *intr & tr* compadecer(se de).
pizza ➤ *s* pizza.
placard ➤ *s* cartel *m,* letrero.
place ➤ *s* lugar *m; (locale)* sitio, local *m; (house)* casa; *(seat)* asiento ■ **all over the p.** por todas partes • **in p.** en orden • **in p. of** en vez de • **out of p.** fuera de lugar • **p. setting** cubierto • **to take p.** tener lugar ➤ *tr* colocar, poner; *(to situate)* situar, ubicar; *(an order, bet)* hacer.
plague ➤ *s* peste *f.*
plain ➤ *adj (obvious)* claro, evidente; *(simple)* sencillo; *(unattractive)* nada atractivo ■ **in p. sight** a la vista de todos • **the p. truth** la pura verdad ➤ *s* llanura, llano ■ *pl* praderas.
plan ➤ *s* plan *m; (schedule)* programa *m* ➤ *tr* planear, proyectar; *(to project)* planificar ■ **to p. to** *o* **on** pensar.
plane ➤ *s* MAT. plano; AVIA. avión *m.*
planet ➤ *s* planeta *m.*
planetarium ➤ *s* planetario.
plank ➤ *s* tablón *m.*
plant ➤ *s* planta; *(factory)* fábrica ➤ *tr* plantar.
plantain ➤ *s* BOT., CUL. plátano.
plantation ➤ *s* plantación *f.*
plaster ➤ *s* yeso; *(of a cast)* escayola.
plastic ➤ *adj & s* plástico.
plate ➤ *s (dish)* plato; *(plaque)* placa; *(of metal)* plancha, lámina.
platform ➤ *s* plataforma; *(railroad)* andén *m;* POL. programa político.
platinum ➤ *s* platino.
platter ➤ *s* fuente *f.*
play ➤ *intr* jugar; *(to pretend)* fingirse ■ **to p. along** cooperar • **to p. around** bromear, tomar el pelo • **to p. fair** jugar limpio ➤ *tr* jugar (a); TEAT. *(a role)* desempeñar; *(to act as)* hacer de; DEP. jugar contra; MÚS. tocar ■ **to p. back** volver a poner (algo grabado) • **to p. down** quitar importancia a ➤ *s* juego; *(drama)* obra ■ **to bring into p.** poner en juego • **p. on words** juego de palabras.
playback ➤ *s* reproducción *f.*
playbill ➤ *s (poster)* cartel *m; (program)* programa *m.*
player ➤ *s* jugador/a; *(actor)* actor *m; (actress)* actriz *f; (musician)* ejecutante *mf,* músico/a.
playground ➤ *s* parque *m* infantil.
play-off ➤ *s* DEP. partido de desempate.
playwright ➤ *s* dramaturgo/a.
plead ➤ *intr* suplicar ■ **to p. guilty, innocent** declararse culpable, inocente.
pleasant ➤ *adj* agradable.
please ➤ *adv* por favor ➤ *tr* agradar, gustar; *(to satisfy)* contentar, complacer ■ **to be pleased with** estar contento con.
pleasing ➤ *adj* agradable.
pleasure ➤ *s* placer *m* ■ **with p.** con gusto.
pleat ➤ *s* pliegue *m.*
plentiful ➤ *adj* abundante, copioso.
plenty ➤ *s* abundancia ➤ *adj* abundante; *(sufficient)* suficiente, bastante ■ **p. of** bastante; *(more than enough)* de sobra ➤ *adv* FAM. muy.
pliers ➤ *s* alicates *m,* tenazas.
plot ➤ *s (of land)* parcela; *(story line)* trama; *(conspiracy)* complot *m* ➤ *tr (a chart, curve)* trazar; *(to scheme)* tramar.
plow ➤ *s* arado; *(snowplow)* quitanieves *m* ➤ *tr (a field)* arar.
pluck ➤ *tr (to pick)* coger; *(a chicken)* desplumar; *(to pull out)* arrancar.
plug ➤ *s* tapón *m;* ELEC. enchufe *m; (spark plug)* bujía ➤ *tr* tapar ■ **to p. in** enchufar ➤ *intr* ■ **p. away at** perseverar en.
plum ➤ *s (tree)* ciruelo; *(fruit)* ciruela; FIG. breva, chollo.
plumber ➤ *s* plomero/a, fontanero/a.
plumbing ➤ *s (pipes)* cañería, tubería; *(trade)* plomería.
plump ➤ *adj* rechoncho, regordete.
plunge ➤ *tr & intr* hundir(se) ➤ *s (dive)* zambullida; *(in prices)* baja vertiginosa.
plunger ➤ *s* desatascador *m.*
plural ➤ *adj & s* plural *m.*
plus ➤ *prep* más ➤ *s* ventaja ➤ *conj* y además.
pneumatic ➤ *adj* neumático.
poach[1] ➤ *tr* cocer a fuego lento, escalfar.
poach[2] ➤ *intr* cazar en vedado.
pocket ➤ *s* bolsillo ➤ *adj* de bolsillo.
pocketknife ➤ *s* navaja, cortaplumas *m.*
poem ➤ *s* poema *m.*
poet ➤ *s* poeta *mf.*
poetic ➤ *adj* poético.
poetry ➤ *s* poesía.
point ➤ *s* punto; *(sharp tip)* punta; *(place)* lugar *m; (reason)* motivo, razón *f;* DEP. punto, tanto; GEOG. punta ■ **at this p.** a estas alturas • **to miss the p.** no comprender • **to the p.** pertinente • **what's the p.?** ¿para qué? ➤ *tr (to aim)* apuntar; *(to show)* indicar ■ **to p. out** señalar ➤ *intr* apuntar.
pointed ➤ *adj* puntiagudo.
pointless ➤ *adj (meaningless)* sin sentido; *(useless)* inútil.
poison ➤ *s* veneno ➤ *tr* envenenar; *(to pollute)* contaminar.
poisonous ➤ *adj* venenoso.
poke ➤ *tr (with elbow)* dar codazo; *(with finger)* dar con la punta del dedo.
poker[1] ➤ *s* atizador *m,* hurgón *m.*
poker[2] ➤ *s (game)* póker *m,* póquer *m.*
polar ➤ *adj* polar ■ **p. bear** oso blanco.
pole[1] ➤ *s (axis)* polo.
pole[2] ➤ *s (post)* poste *m,* palo.
police ➤ *s* policía ■ **p. force** fuerza pública • **p. station** jefatura de policía.
policeman ➤ *s* policía *m.*
policewoman ➤ *s* mujer *f* policía.
policy[1] ➤ *s* POL. política.
policy[2] ➤ *s (written contract)* póliza.
policyholder ➤ *s* asegurado/a.
polish ➤ *tr (to wax)* encerar; *(metals)* bruñir; *(nails)* pintar; *(to refine)* pulir ➤ *s (wax)* cera; *(for metals)* líquido de bruñir; *(for nails)* esmalte *m* ■ **shoe p.** betún.
polite ➤ *adj* cortés; *(refined)* educado.
politeness ➤ *s* cortesía.
political ➤ *adj* político.
politician ➤ *s* político/a.
politics ➤ *ssg* política.
poll ➤ *s (votes)* votación *f; (survey)* encuesta ■ *pl* urnas, centro electoral.
pollen ➤ *s* polen *m.*
pollutant ➤ *s* agente *m* contaminador.
pollute ➤ *tr (to corrupt)* corromper; *(to contaminate)* contaminar.
pollution ➤ *s* contaminación *f.*
polo ➤ *s* polo ■ **p. shirt** polo.
polyester ➤ *s* poliéster *m.*
polytechnic ➤ *adj & s* (instituto) politécnico.
pomegranate ➤ *s* granada.
pond ➤ *s* estanque *m.*
pony ➤ *s* poney *m,* jaca.
ponytail ➤ *s* cola de caballo.
poodle ➤ *s* perro de lanas, caniche *m.*
pool[1] ➤ *s (small pond)* charca; *(puddle)* charco; *(for swimming)* piscina.
pool[2] ➤ *s (in betting)* banco, bolsa; *(game)* billar americano.
poor ➤ *adj* pobre; *(mediocre)* malo, mediocre.
pop ➤ *intr (to explode)* estallar; *(eyes)* abrirse ■ **to p. up** aparecer de repente ➤ *tr* hacer estallar ■ **to p. open** abrir haciendo sonar • **to p. out** asomar ➤ *s* estallido; *(of a cork)* taponazo; *(soda pop)* gaseosa.
popcorn ➤ *s* rosetas *o* palomitas de maíz.
pope *o* **Pope** ➤ papa *m.*
poppy ➤ *s* amapola.
popular ➤ *adj* popular; *(in vogue)* de moda.
popularity ➤ *s* popularidad *f.*
population ➤ *s* población *f.*
porch ➤ *s* porche *m.*
pore ➤ *s* ANAT. poro.
pork ➤ *s* (carne *f*) de cerdo.
port[1] ➤ *s* puerto ■ **p. of call** puerto de escala.
port[2] ➤ *s & adj* (de *o* a) babor *m.*
port[3] ➤ *s (wine)* oporto.
portable ➤ *adj & s* (máquina) portátil.
porter ➤ *s* mozo.
portfolio ➤ *s* cartera.
portion ➤ *s* porción *f,* parte *f* ➤ *tr* dividir ■ **to p. out** repartir.
portrait ➤ *s* retrato.
pose ➤ *intr* posar ■ **to p. as** hacerse pasar por ➤ *tr (question)* plantear; *(threat)* representar ➤ *s* pose *f.*
position ➤ *s* posición *f; (post, job)* puesto; *(point of view)* postura, actitud *f* ➤ *tr* colocar, poner.
positive ➤ *adj* positivo; *(sure)* seguro, cierto ➤ *s* positivo; FOTOG. positiva.
possess ➤ *tr* poseer.
possession ➤ *s* posesión *f* ■ **to get** *o* **take p. of** apoderarse de ■ *pl* posesiones.
possessive ➤ *adj* posesivo.
possibility ➤ *s* posibilidad *f.*
possible ➤ *adj* posible ■ **as much as p.** todo lo posible • **as soon as p.** lo antes posible.
post[1] ➤ *s (pole)* poste *m; (stake)* palo, estaca; COMPUT. mensaje *m,* nota ➤ *tr (poster)* pegar, fijar; COMPUT. enviar.
post[2] ➤ *s* MIL. base *f; (job)* puesto, cargo.
post[3] ➤ *s* G.B. *(mail)* correo ■ **p. card** tarjeta postal • **p. office** correos ➤ *tr* echar al correo.
postage ➤ *s* franqueo ■ **p. stamp** sello (postal), estampilla.
postal ➤ *adj & s* postal *f.*
poster ➤ *s* cartel *m,* afiche *m,* póster *m.*
posterity ➤ *s* posteridad *f.*
postgraduate ➤ *adj & s* postgraduado/a.
postmark ➤ *s* matasellos ➤ *tr* matasellar.
postpone ➤ *tr (to delay)* posponer; *(to put off)* aplazar.
postponement ➤ *s* aplazamiento.
postscript ➤ *s* posdata.
posture ➤ *s* postura ➤ *intr* posar, asumir una pose.
pot ➤ *s* CUL. cazuela, olla; *(flowerpot)* maceta; FAM. *(marijuana)* yerba.
potato ➤ *s* patata, papa ■ **p. chips** papas fritas.
potential ➤ *adj* potencial, posible ➤ *s* posibilidad *f.*
pothole ➤ *s* bache *m.*
potter ➤ *s* alfarero/a.
pottery ➤ *s* alfarería.
potty ➤ *s* FAM. orinal *m* para niños.
pouch ➤ *s* bolsa pequeña, valija.

poultry ➤ *s* aves *f* de corral.
pounce ➤ *intr* *(to spring)* saltar sobre; *(to attack)* abalanzarse sobre.
pound[1] ➤ *s* FIN., FÍS. libra.
pound[2] ➤ *tr* golpear; *(to grind)* moler; *(to crush)* machacar.
pound[3] ➤ *s* *(for dogs)* perrera.
pour ➤ *tr* verter, derramar ➤ *intr* manar; *(to rain)* llover a cántaros.
poverty ➤ *s* pobreza.
powder ➤ *s* polvo; *(cosmetic, medicinal)* polvos ▪ **p. room** tocador, servicios.
power ➤ *s* poder *m*; *(capacity)* capacidad *f*; *(strength)* fuerza; *(nation)* potencia; *(energy)* energía; *(electricity)* corriente *f* ▪ **p. brake** servofreno • **p. line** línea de transmisión eléctrica • **p. steering** servodirección ▪ *pl* poder, capacidad.
powerful ➤ *adj* poderoso; *(strong)* fuerte; *(convincing)* convincente.
practical ➤ *adj* práctico ▪ **p. joke** broma pesada.
practically ➤ *adv* de modo práctico; *(almost)* prácticamente, casi.
practice ➤ *tr* practicar; *(to train in)* ejercitarse *o* entrenarse en; *(a profession)* ejercer ➤ *intr* hacer prácticas ➤ *s* práctica; *(custom)* costumbre *f*; *(of a profession)* ejercicio; *(of a doctor)* clientela; *(of a lawyer)* bufete *m*.
prairie ➤ *s* llanura, planicie *f*.
praise ➤ *s* alabanza ➤ *tr* alabar.
prank ➤ *s* jugarreta, travesura.
prawn ➤ *s* camarón *m*, gamba.
pray ➤ *intr* rezar, orar.
prayer ➤ *s* oración *f*.
preach ➤ *tr & intr* predicar.
precaution ➤ *s* precaución *f*.
precede ➤ *tr & intr* preceder.
preceding ➤ *adj* precedente.
precept ➤ *s* precepto.
precious ➤ *adj* precioso.
precipice ➤ *s* precipicio.
precise ➤ *adj* preciso.
precision ➤ *s* precisión *f*.
precocious ➤ *adj* precoz.
predecessor ➤ *s* predecesor/a; *(ancestor)* antepasado/a.
predicament ➤ *s* apuro.
predict ➤ *tr* predecir; *(to forecast)* pronosticar.
predictable ➤ *adj* previsible; *(behavior)* invariable, constante.
prediction ➤ *s* predicción *f*; *(forecast)* pronóstico.
prefabricate ➤ *tr* prefabricar.
preface ➤ *s* prefacio, prólogo.
prefer ➤ *tr* preferir.
preferable ➤ *adj* preferible.
preference ➤ *s* preferencia.
prefix ➤ *s* prefijo.
pregnancy ➤ *s* embarazo.
pregnant ➤ *adj* encinta, embarazada.
prehistoric(al) ➤ *adj* prehistórico.
prejudice ➤ *s* prejuicio.
preliminary ➤ *adj & s* preliminar *m*.
premature ➤ *adj* prematuro.
première ➤ *s* estreno ➤ *tr & intr* estrenar ➤ *adj* primero.
premise ➤ *s* premisa ▪ *pl* local *m*.
premium ➤ *s* *(prize)* premio, recompensa; *(fee)* prima; *(installment)* prima (de un seguro).
preparation ➤ *s* preparación *f*; *(medicine)* preparado ▪ *pl* preparativos.
prepare ➤ *tr & intr* preparar(se).
prepay ➤ *tr* pagar por adelantado.
preposition ➤ *s* preposición *f*.
prescribe ➤ *tr* prescribir; MED. recetar.
prescription ➤ *s* prescripción *f*; MED. receta.
presence ➤ *s* presencia; *(bearing)* porte *m*, talle *m*; *(confidence)* seguridad *f*.
present[1] ➤ *s* presente *m* ▪ **for the p.** por ahora ➤ *adj* presente; *(month)* corriente; *(year)* en curso ▪ **to be p.** asistir.
present[2] ➤ *tr* presentar; *(a gift)* regalar, obsequiar; *(a case)* exponer; *(a problem)* plantear; *(charges)* formular ➤ *s* presente *m*, regalo.
presentation ➤ *s* presentación *f*; *(of a play)* representación *f*; *(of a case, argument)* exposición *f*.
presently ➤ *adv* *(soon)* dentro de poco; *(now)* actualmente.
preservation ➤ *s* preservación *f*; *(of customs, food)* conservación *f*.
preservative ➤ *adj* preservativo ➤ *s* conservante *m*, preservador *m*.
preserve ➤ *tr* preservar; *(to maintain)* conservar; *(food)* conservar ➤ *s* coto, vedado ▪ *pl* confitura.
preside ➤ *intr* presidir.
presidency ➤ *s* presidencia.
president ➤ *s* presidente/a.
presidential ➤ *adj* presidencial.
press ➤ *tr* *(to bear down on)* apretar; *(to squeeze)* prensar; *(to compress)* comprimir; *(to iron)* planchar ▪ **to be pressed for** estar con apuros de • **to p. one's luck** forzar la suerte ➤ *intr* apretar, ejercer presión ▪ **to p. for** pedir con insistencia • **to p. on** seguir adelante ➤ *s* PERIOD. prensa.
pressure ➤ *s* presión *f*; *(compression)* compresión *f* ▪ **blood p.** presión arterial • **p. cooker** olla de presión ➤ *tr* ejercer presión sobre.
prestige ➤ *s* prestigio.
presume ➤ *tr* suponer.
pretend ➤ *tr & intr* fingir.
pretext ➤ *s* pretexto.
pretty ➤ *adj* lindo; FAM. considerable ▪ **a p. penny** mucho dinero ➤ *adv* bastante ▪ **p. much** más o menos.
prevail ➤ *intr* prevalecer.
prevent ➤ *tr* *(to avoid)* evitar; *(to impede)* impedir.
prevention ➤ *s* prevención *f*.
preview ➤ *s* exhibición *f* preliminar; CINEM. avance *m*.
previous ➤ *adj* previo.
prey ➤ *s* presa; FIG. víctima.
price ➤ *s* precio.
prick ➤ *s* pinchazo; *(of an insect)* picadura ➤ *tr* pinchar.
prickly ➤ *adj* espinoso.
pride ➤ *s* orgullo; *(self-respect)* amor propio ➤ *tr* ▪ **to p. oneself on** estar orgulloso de.
priest ➤ *s* sacerdote *m*, cura *m*.
primarily ➤ *adv* principalmente.
primary ➤ *adj* primario ➤ *s* lo principal; POL. elección primaria.
prime ➤ *adj* primero; *(main)* fundamental ▪ **p. meridian** primer meridiano • **p. minister** primero/a ministro/a • **p. rate** tasa preferida.
primitive ➤ *adj* primitivo.
prince ➤ *s* principe *m*.
princess ➤ *s* princesa.
principal ➤ *adj* principal ➤ *s* *(of a school)* director/a; COM., FIN. principal *m*.
principle ➤ *s* principio ▪ **in p.** en principio • **on p.** por principio.
print ➤ *s* huella; *(letters)* letra; FOTOG. copia; *(engraving)* grabado, estampa ▪ **in p.** impreso, publicado • **out of p.** agotado ➤ *tr* imprimir; *(to publish)* publicar; FOTOG. copiar; *(to write)* escribir con letras de molde.
printer ➤ *s* *(person)* impresor/a; *(machine)* impresora.
printout ➤ *s* salida impresa.
prior ➤ *adj* previo ▪ **p. to** antes de.
priority ➤ *s* prioridad *f*.
prison ➤ *s* cárcel *f*, prisión *f*.
prisoner ➤ *s* prisionero/a, preso/a.
privacy ➤ *s* intimidad *f*.
private ➤ *adj* privado; *(not public)* particular; *(secluded)* solitario ▪ **p. enterprise** sector privado ➤ *s* soldado raso.
privilege ➤ *s* privilegio.
prize ➤ *s* premio.
prizefighter ➤ *s* boxeador *m* profesional.
probable ➤ *adj* probable.
problem ➤ *s* problema *m*.
proceed ➤ *intr* proceder, continuar ➤ *s* ▪ *pl* ganancias.
process ➤ *s* *(treatment)* procedimiento; *(method)* proceso ▪ **in the p.** al hacerlo ➤ *tr* *(an application)* tramitar; COMPUT., DER. procesar.
processing ➤ *s* *(of food)* tratamiento; COMPUT. procesamiento ▪ **data p.** procesamiento de datos; *(science)* informática.
procession ➤ *s* procesión *f*, desfile *m*.
processor ➤ *s* procesador *m*.
proclaim ➤ *tr* proclamar.
procure ➤ *tr* obtener.
produce ➤ *tr* producir; *(to manufacture)* fabricar; *(to give rise to)* causar; *(to show)* exhibir ➤ *s* producto.
producer ➤ *s* productor/a.
product ➤ *s* producto.
production ➤ *s* producción *f*.
productive ➤ *adj* productivo.
profession ➤ *s* profesión *f*.
professional ➤ *adj & s* profesional *mf*; *(expert)* perito/a, experto/a.
professor ➤ *s* profesor/a; *(university)* catedrático/a.
profile ➤ *s* perfil *m*.
profit ➤ *s* beneficio ▪ **to make a p.** *(person)* ganar dinero; *(business)* rendir ganancias ➤ *intr* servir ▪ **to p. by** *o* **from** COM. sacar dinero de; *(to benefit from)* sacar provecho de.
profitable ➤ *adj* beneficioso, provechoso; COM. lucrativo.
program ➤ *s* programa *m* ➤ *tr* programar.
program(m)er ➤ *s* programador/a.
program(m)ing ➤ *s* programación *f*.
progress ➤ *s* progreso ▪ **in p.** en curso • **to make p.** progresar ➤ *intr* progresar; *(to improve)* mejorar.
prohibit ➤ *tr* prohibir.
project ➤ *s* proyecto ➤ *tr* proyectar ➤ *intr* sobresalir.
projectile ➤ *s* proyectil *m*.
projector ➤ *s* proyector *m*.
prolong ➤ *tr* prolongar.
prominent ➤ *adj* prominente; *(eminent)* notable.
promise ➤ *s* promesa ▪ **to break one's p.** faltar a su palabra ➤ *tr* prometer ➤ *intr* hacer una promesa.
promising ➤ *adj* prometedor.
promote ➤ *tr* *(employee, officer)* ascender; *(to further)* promover; *(to advertise)* promocionar.
promotion ➤ *s* ascenso; *(furtherance)* fomento.
prompt ➤ *adj* puntual; *(without delay)* pronto, rápido.
pronoun ➤ *s* pronombre *m*.
pronounce ➤ *tr* pronunciar.
pronunciation ➤ *s* pronunciación *f*.
proof ➤ *s* prueba.
propagate ➤ *tr & intr* propagar(se).
propeller ➤ *s* hélice *f*.
proper ➤ *adj* apropiado; *(right)* debido; *(correct)* correcto.
properly ➤ *adv* apropiadamente; *(strictly)* propiamente; *(correctly)* correctamente.
property ➤ *s* propiedad *f*; *(possessions)* bienes *m*; TEAT. accesorio ▪ **personal p.** bienes muebles.
prophecy ➤ *s* profecía.
prophet ➤ *s* profeta *m*, profetisa.
prophylactic ➤ *adj & s* profiláctico.
proportion ➤ *s* proporción *f* ▪ **out of p.** desproporcionado.
proposal ➤ *s* propuesta.
propose ➤ *tr* proponer; *(to intend)* tener intención de; *(marriage)* ofrecer ➤ *intr* ofrecer matrimonio.
proposition ➤ *s* proposición *f*; FAM. *(matter)* asunto.
prose ➤ *s* prosa.
prosecute ➤ *tr* proseguir; DER. *(a person)* procesar; *(claim, case)* entablar.
prosecutor ➤ *s* fiscal *mf*.
prospect ➤ *s* perspectiva ▪ *pl* perspectivas ➤ *tr* prospectar.
prospector ➤ *s* buscador/a.
prospectus ➤ *s* prospecto.
prosper ➤ *intr* prosperar.
prosperity ➤ *s* prosperidad *f*.
prosperous ➤ *adj* próspero.
protect ➤ *tr* proteger.
protection ➤ *s* protección *f*.
protective ➤ *adj* protector.
protest ➤ *tr & intr* protestar (contra) ➤ *s* protesta.
Protestant ➤ *s & adj* protestante *mf*.
protester ➤ *s* persona que protesta; *(demonstrator)* manifestante *mf*.
proud ➤ *adj* orgulloso; *(arrogant)* soberbio ▪ **to be p. to** tener el honor de.
prove◊ ➤ *tr* probar; *(to test)* poner a prueba ➤ *intr* salir, resultar.
proven ➤ *adj* probado.
proverb ➤ *s* proverbio.
provide ➤ *tr* *(to supply)* suministrar; *(to make available)* proveer.
province ➤ *s* provincia; *(jurisdiction)* competencia.
provincial ➤ *adj* provincial; *(unsophisticated)* provinciano.
provision ➤ *s* provisión *f* ▪ *pl* provisiones.
provoke ➤ *tr* provocar.
prowl ➤ *tr & intr* merodear, rondar.
prudent ➤ *adj* prudente.
prune[1] ➤ *s* *(fruit)* ciruela pasa.
prune[2] ➤ *tr & intr* *(to trim)* podar.
psalm ➤ *s* salmo.
psychiatrist ➤ *s* psiquiatra *mf*.
psychiatry ➤ *s* psiquiatría.
psychological ➤ *adj* psicológico.
psychologist ➤ *s* psicólogo/a.
psychology ➤ *s* psicología.
pub ➤ *s* taberna, cantina.
public ➤ *adj & s* público.
publication ➤ *s* publicación *f*.
publicist ➤ *s* publicista *mf*.
publicity ➤ *s* publicidad *f*.
publish ➤ *tr & intr* publicar.
publisher ➤ *s* editor/a.
puck ➤ *s* DEP. disco.
pudding ➤ *s* budín *m*.
puddle ➤ *s* charco.
Puerto Rican ➤ *s & adj* puertorriqueño/a.
puff ➤ *s* *(of air)* soplo; *(of smoke, steam)* bocanada ➤ *intr* resoplar, resollar.
pull ➤ *tr* tirar de; *(trigger)* apretar ▪ **to p. off** *(to take off)* quitar; *(to carry out)* llevar a cabo • **to p. oneself together** componerse, dominarse • **to p. out** sacar, extraer • **to p. strings** conseguir algo por influencias ➤ *intr* tirar ▪ **to p. ahead** destacarse • **to p. away** dejar atrás • **to p. over** AUTO. parar • **to p. through** *(to survive)* salir de una enfermedad *o* apuro ➤ *s* *(tug)* tirón *m*.
pullout ➤ *s* retirada.
pullover ➤ *s* jersey *m*, suéter *m*.
pulse ➤ *s* pulso.
pump ➤ *s* MEC. bomba; AUTO. surtidor *m* ➤ *tr* bombear; *(blood)* impulsar; *(lever, arm)* mover de arriba abajo.
pumpkin ➤ *s* calabaza.
punch[1] ➤ *s* *(for paper)* perforadora; *(for tickets)* máquina de picar billetes ➤ *tr* *(tickets)* picar; *(metal, leather)* taladrar.
punch[2] ➤ *tr* *(to hit)* dar un puñetazo ➤ *s* puñetazo.
punctual ➤ *adj* puntual.
punctuation ➤ *s* puntuación *f*.
puncture ➤ *tr* perforar; *(a tire)* pinchar ➤ *s* perforación *f*; *(in a tire)* pinchazo.
punish ➤ *tr* castigar.
punishment ➤ *s* castigo.
pupil[1] ➤ *s* *(student)* alumno/a.
pupil[2] ➤ *s* ANAT. pupila.
puppet ➤ *s* marioneta, títere *m*.
puppy ➤ *s* cachorro ▪ **p. love** amor juvenil.
purchase ➤ *tr* comprar ➤ *s* compra ▪ **p. order** orden de compra.
pure ➤ *adj* puro.
purge ➤ *tr* purgar ➤ *s* purga.
purify ➤ *tr* purificar.
purity ➤ *s* pureza.
purple ➤ *s* violeta, morado ➤ *adj* purpúreo, morado.
purpose ➤ *s* objetivo; *(intention)* propósito.
purposely ➤ *adv* adrede, a propósito.
purse ➤ *s* bolso ➤ *tr* *(lips)* apretar.
pursue ➤ *tr* perseguir; *(to strive for)* aspirar a; *(to follow)* seguir, continuar; *(a career)* dedicarse a.
pursuit ➤ *s* persecución *f*; *(activity)* pasatiempo.
push ➤ *tr* empujar; *(to press)* apretar, presionar ➤ *intr* empujar ▪ **to p. ahead** avanzar • **to p. back** retroceder • **to p. forward** avanzar • **to p. on** seguir adelante, continuar ➤ *s* empujón *m*.
put◊ ➤ *tr* poner; *(to insert)* meter; *(to add)* echar ▪ **to p. aside** poner a un lado; *(to save)* guardar • **to p. back** volver a poner en su sitio • **to p. down** *(to let go of)* soltar; *(to suppress)* reprimir; *(to write down)* apuntar; *(to criticize)* poner por los suelos; *(down payment)* hacer un desembolso inicial de • **to p. into words** expresar • **to p. off** *(to postpone)* aplazar, diferir; *(to offend)* dar asco, asquear • **to p. on** TEAT. poner en escena; *(clothes)* ponerse; *(to affect)* afectar • **to p. out** *(to extinguish)* apagar; *(to inconvenience)* molestar; *(to publish)* publicar • **to p. up** *(to build)* levantar, construir; *(to offer)* poner; *(to lodge)* hospedar, alojar • **to p. up with** aguantar.
puzzle ➤ *tr* desconcertar, dejar perplejo ➤ *s* enigma *m*, misterio ▪ **crossword p.** crucigrama • **jigsaw p.** rompecabezas.
pyramid ➤ *s* pirámide *f*.

Q

quack[1] ➤ *s* graznido ➤ *intr* graznar.
quack[2] ➤ *s* *(doctor)* curandero/a.
quake ➤ *intr* temblar ➤ *s* temblor *m*.
qualification ➤ *s* calificación *f*; *(requirement)* requisito; *(restriction)* reserva ▪ *pl* credenciales.
qualified ➤ *adj* *(competent)* capacitado; *(certified)* acreditado.
qualify ➤ *intr* tener las capacidades

necesarias; DEP. clasificarse ■ **to q.** as merecer el título de.
quality ➤ *s (nature, excellence)* calidad *f; (attribute)* cualidad *f.*
quantity ➤ *s* cantidad *f.*
quarrel ➤ *s* pelea, discusión *f* ➤ *intr* pelear, discutir.
quarry[1] ➤ *s (prey)* presa.
quarry[2] ➤ *s (pit)* cantera.
quart ➤ *s* cuarto (de galón).
quarter ➤ *s (fourth part)* cuarto; *(of a dollar)* veinticinco centavos; *(of a year)* trimestre *m; (neighborhood)* barrio ■ **(a) q. past** y cuarto • **(a) q. to** *o* of menos cuarto ■ *pl (residence)* residencia; MIL. cuartel *m.*
quarterly ➤ *s & adj* (publicación *f*) trimestral ➤ *adv* trimestralmente.
quartet ➤ *s* cuarteto.
quartz ➤ *s* cuarzo.
queen ➤ *s* reina; *(in cards, chess)* dama.
queer ➤ *adj (strange)* raro; *(odd)* curioso.
quench ➤ *tr (fire)* apagar; *(thirst)* matar.
query ➤ *s* pregunta.
quest ➤ *s* búsqueda.
question ➤ *s* pregunta; *(issue)* cuestión *f* ■ **beyond q.** fuera de duda • **in q.** en cuestión • **q. mark** signo de interrogación • **to be out of the q.** ser imposible ➤ *tr* preguntar.
questionable ➤ *adj (debatable)* cuestionable; *(dubious)* dudoso.
questionnaire ➤ *s* cuestionario.
quiche ➤ *s* pastel *m* de queso y huevos.
quick ➤ *adj (fast)* rápido; *(bright)* listo.
quiet ➤ *adj (silent)* callado, silencioso; *(calm)* tranquilo ➤ *s (calm)* quietud *f; (silence)* silencio.
quilt ➤ *s* colcha ➤ *tr* acolchar.
quit✧ ➤ *tr (to leave)* salir de; *(a school, job)* abandonar, dejar; *(a habit)* dejar de ➤ *intr (to give up)* desistir; *(to resign)* renunciar.
quite ➤ *adv* totalmente; *(exactly)* exactamente ■ **q. a bit** bastante • **q. a while** un buen rato • **q. long** bastante largo.
quits ➤ *adj* ■ **to call it q.** dejarlo así.
quiz ➤ *tr* interrogar; *(to test)* examinar ➤ *s (test)* prueba, examen *m* ■ **q. show** concurso de televisión.
quota ➤ *s* cuota.
quotation ➤ *s* cita; *(of prices)* cotización *f* ■ **q. marks** comillas.
quote ➤ *tr (words, source)* citar; *(example, price)* dar; FIN. cotizar ➤ *s* ■ **in quotes** entre comillas.

R

rabbi ➤ *s* rabino/a.
rabbit ➤ *s* conejo.
rabies ➤ *s* rabia.
race[1] ➤ *s (people)* raza.
race[2] ➤ *s (contest)* carrera ➤ *intr* correr; *(to compete)* competir; *(engine)* embalarse.
racial ➤ *adj* racial.
racism ➤ *s* racismo.
racist ➤ *adj & s* racista *mf.*
rack ➤ *s (for luggage)* portaequipajes *m; (for hat, coat)* percha.
racket[1] ➤ *s* DEP. raqueta.
racket[2] ➤ *s (noise)* alboroto; *(crime)* negocio ilegal.
radar ➤ *s* radar *m.*
radial ➤ *adj* radial.
radiate ➤ *intr* radiar ➤ *tr* (ir)radiar.
radiator ➤ *s* radiador *m.*
radio ➤ *s* radio *f* ■ **r. station** emisora ➤ *tr & intr* transmitir (un mensaje) por radio.
radioactive ➤ *adj* radiactivo.
radish ➤ *s* rábano.
radius ➤ *s* radio.
raffle ➤ *s* rifa ➤ *tr & intr* rifar.
raft ➤ *s* balsa.
rag ➤ *s* trapo ■ *pl* harapos.
rage ➤ *s* furia ➤ *intr* rabiar; *(storm)* bramar; *(plague, fire)* propagarse.
ragged ➤ *adj (beggar)* andrajoso; *(sleeve)* raído; *(edge)* mellado.
raid ➤ *s* MIL. incursión *f,* ataque sorpresivo; *(by police)* redada ➤ *tr* atacar por sorpresa; *(police)* hacer una redada en.
rail ➤ *s (banister)* barandilla; *(at racetrack)* cerca; F.C. riel *m.*
railing ➤ *s (of balcony)* baranda; *(of stairs)* pasamanos.
railroad ➤ *s* ferrocarril *m* ■ **r. car** vagón • **r. crossing** cruce de ferrocarril • **r. station** estación ferroviaria.
railway ➤ *s* ferrocarril *m; (track)* vía.
rain ➤ *s* lluvia ■ **r. forest** bosque húmedo ➤ *intr* llover ■ **to r. cats and dogs** llover a cántaros.
rainbow ➤ *s* arco iris.
raincoat ➤ *s* impermeable *m.*
raindrop ➤ *s* gota de lluvia.
rainfall ➤ *s (shower)* aguacero; *(precipitation)* precipitación *f.*
rainstorm ➤ *s* tempestad *f* de lluvia.
rainy ➤ *adj* lluvioso.
raise ➤ *tr* levantar; *(window, prices)* subir; *(flag)* izar; *(welt, blister)* producir; *(voice)* alzar; *(children, animals)* criar; *(crop)* cultivar; *(money)* recaudar; *(an army)* reclutar ➤ *s* aumento.
raisin ➤ *s* pasa (de uva).
rake ➤ *s* rastrillo ➤ *tr* rastrillar.
rally ➤ *intr* reunirse; *(to recover)* recuperarse ■ **to r. round** dar apoyo a, adherirse a ➤ *s* reunión *f.*
ram ➤ *s* carnero ➤ *tr (to stuff)* meter a la fuerza; *(to crash into)* chocar con.
ramble ➤ *intr (to walk)* pasear; *(to digress)* divagar ➤ *s* paseo.
rampart ➤ *s* muralla.
ranch ➤ *s* hacienda ■ **r. house** casa de una sola planta ➤ *intr* llevar una hacienda.
rancher ➤ *s* estanciero/a, hacendado/a.
random ➤ *adj* hecho al azar, fortuito.
range ➤ *s (reach)* alcance *m; (variety)* gama; *(stove)* cocina; *(of merchandise)* surtido ■ **at close r.** de cerca.
ranger ➤ *s (of a forest)* guardabosques *mf; (mounted police)* policía *mf.*
rank ➤ *s (in society)* clase *f; (high status)* rango; *(quality)* categoría; MIL. grado ■ *pl* filas • **to join the r. of** unirse con ➤ *tr (in rows)* alinear; *(in order)* clasificar.
ransom ➤ *s* rescate *m* ➤ *tr* rescatar.
rap[1] ➤ *s* golpe seco ➤ *tr & intr* golpear.
rap[2] JER. ➤ *intr* conversar ➤ *s* conversación *f;* MÚS. rap *m.*
rape ➤ *s* violación *f* ➤ *tr* violar.
rapid ➤ *adj* rápido ■ **r. transit** sistema de transporte urbano ■ **rapids** *spl* rápidos.
rapist ➤ *s* violador *m.*
rare[1] ➤ *adj* raro; *(special)* poco común.
rare[2] ➤ *adj* CUL. jugoso, poco hecho.
rascal ➤ *s* tunante *mf,* bribón/ona.
rash[1] ➤ *adj (act)* precipitado; *(person)* impetuoso.
rash[2] ➤ *s* MED. sarpullido; FIG. ola.
raspberry ➤ *s (fruit)* frambuesa.
rat ➤ *s* rata; JER. canalla *mf.*
rate ➤ *s (speed)* velocidad *f; (of change)* coeficiente *m; (percentage)* porcentaje *m;* FIN. interés *m* ■ **at any r.** de todos modos • **at this r.** a este paso • **postal r.** tarifa postal • **r. of exchange** cambio ➤ *tr (to value)* valorar; *(to classify)* clasificar; *(to deserve)* merecer.
rather ➤ *adv (more exactly)* mejor dicho; *(quite)* bastante; *(somewhat)* un poco ■ **I would r.** preferiría • **r. than** en vez de.
ration ➤ *s* ración *f,* porción *f.*
rational ➤ *adj* racional.
rationing ➤ *s* racionamiento.
rattle ➤ *intr (vehicle)* traquetear; *(window, door)* golpetear; *(teeth)* castañetear ➤ *tr (to shake)* sacudir; FAM. poner nervioso ➤ *s* traqueteo; *(of window)* golpe *m; (of baby)* sonajero.
ravenous ➤ *adj* hambriento; *(voracious)* voraz.
ravine ➤ *s* barranco, quebrada.
ravishing ➤ *adj* encantador.
raw ➤ *adj* crudo; *(not refined)* sin refinar, bruto ■ **r. material** materia prima.
rawhide ➤ *s* cuero sin curtir.
ray[1] ➤ *s* rayo; MAT., BOT. radio.
ray[2] *(fish)* raya.
razor ➤ *s* navaja de afeitar ■ **r. blade** cuchilla *u* hoja de afeitar.
reach ➤ *tr* alcanzar; *(to arrive at)* llegar a ■ **to r. out** extender, alargar ➤ *intr* llegar ■ **to r. for** tratar de tomar *o* agarrar ➤ *s* alcance *m.*
react ➤ *intr* reaccionar.
reaction ➤ *s* reacción *f.*
reactor ➤ *s* reactor *m.*
read✧ ➤ *tr & intr* leer ■ **to r. into** atribuir (a) • **to r. over** repasar • **to r. up on** informarse acerca de.
reader ➤ *s* lector/a; *(schoolbook)* libro de lecturas.
readily ➤ *adv (willingly)* de buena gana; *(easily)* con facilidad.
reading ➤ *s* lectura; *(of a text)* versión *f.*
ready ➤ *adj* listo; *(willing)* dispuesto ■ **to get r.** *(to prepare)* preparar(se); *(to fix up)* arreglar(se) ➤ *tr* preparar.
ready-made ➤ *adj* hecho.
ready-to-wear ➤ *adj* hecho, confeccionado ➤ *s* ropa hecha.
real ➤ *adj* real; *(true)* verdadero ■ **r. estate** bienes inmuebles *o* raíces.
realism ➤ *s* realismo.
realistic ➤ *adj* realista.
reality ➤ *s* realidad *f* ■ **virtual r.** COMPUT. realidad virtual.
realize ➤ *tr* darse cuenta de; *(to attain)* realizar; *(a profit)* obtener.
really ➤ *adv (in reality)* en realidad; *(truly)* verdaderamente; *(very)* muy.
realm ➤ *s* reino.
realtor ➤ *s [service mark]* corredor/a *m* de bienes raíces.
realty ➤ *s* bienes *m* raíces.
reap ➤ *tr & intr* cosechar.
reappear ➤ *intr* reaparecer.
rear[1] ➤ *s* parte trasera; *(of a house)* fondo; FAM. *(buttocks)* nalgas ➤ *adj* trasero, de atrás.
rear[2] ➤ *tr (animals)* criar; *(children)* educar ➤ *intr (horse)* encabritarse.
rearing ➤ *s* crianza, cría.
rearview mirror ➤ *s* retrovisor *m.*
reason ➤ *s* razón *f* ■ **for no r.** sin ningún motivo • **the r. why** el porqué • **to have r. to** tener motivos para ➤ *tr & intr* razonar.
reasonable ➤ *adj* razonable.
reasoning ➤ *s* razonamiento.
reassure ➤ *tr* dar confianza a.
rebel ➤ *intr* rebelarse ➤ *s* rebelde *mf.*
rebellion ➤ *s* rebelión *f.*
reboot ➤ *tr* COMPUT. reiniciar.
rebound ➤ *intr* rebotar ➤ *s* rebote *m.*
rebuild ➤ *tr & intr* reconstruir.
recall ➤ *tr* recordar, acordarse de; *(product)* retirar del mercado.
receipt ➤ *s* recibo ■ **on r. of** al recibir ■ *pl* ingresos.
receive ➤ *tr* recibir.
receiver ➤ *s* receptor *m;* DER. *(in bankruptcy)* síndico; TEL. auricular *m.*
recent ➤ *adj* reciente.
reception ➤ *s* recepción *f.*
receptionist ➤ *s* recepcionista *mf.*
recharge ➤ *tr* recargar.
recipe ➤ *s* receta.
recite ➤ *tr & intr* recitar.
reckless ➤ *adj (careless)* imprudente; *(rash)* precipitado.
reckon ➤ *tr* calcular; *(to regard)* considerar.
reclaim ➤ *tr (land)* recobrar; *(swamp)* sanear; *(from waste)* recuperar.
recognize ➤ *tr* reconocer.
recollect ➤ *tr & intr* acordarse (de).
recollection ➤ *s* recuerdo.
recommend ➤ *tr* recomendar.
recommendation ➤ *s* recomendación *f.*
reconstruction ➤ *s* reconstrucción *f.*
record ➤ *tr (facts, data)* registrar; *(thoughts)* apuntar; TEC. grabar ➤ *s (tally)* cuenta; *(testimony)* testimonio; *(of conduct, health)* historial *m; (dossier)* expediente *m; (for phonograph)* disco; *(recording)* grabación *f;* COMPUT. registro, récord *m* ■ **for the r.** para que así conste • **to break the r.** batir el record ■ *pl* archivos.
recorder ➤ *s* grabadora; MÚS. flauta dulce.
recording ➤ *s* grabación *f.*
recover ➤ *tr* recuperar; *(damages)* cobrar ➤ *intr* recuperarse.
recreate ➤ *tr* recrear.
recruit ➤ *tr* contratar; MIL. reclutar ➤ *s* MIL. recluta *mf; (new member)* socio/a nuevo/a.
rectangle ➤ *s* rectángulo.
rectangular ➤ *adj* rectangular.
rector ➤ *s (of a parish)* cura párroco; *(of a university)* rector/a.
recur ➤ *intr* repetirse.
recycle ➤ *tr* reciclar.
red ➤ *s* rojo, colorado ■ **be in the r.** tener pérdidas ➤ *adj* rojo, colorado; *(wine)* tinto ■ **r. tape** trámites, papeleo.
redo ➤ *tr* volver a hacer, rehacer.
reduce ➤ *tr* reducir; COM. rebajar.
reduction ➤ *s* reducción *f,* disminución *f; (discount)* descuento.
redundant ➤ *s* superfluo.
reed ➤ *s (plant, stalk)* caña; MÚS. (instrumento de) lengüeta.
reef ➤ *s* GEOL. arrecife *m,* escollo.
reel ➤ *s (spool)* carrete *m;* CINEM., FOTOG. rollo ➤ *tr* enrollar en un carrete.
reelect ➤ *tr* reelegir.
refer ➤ *tr (to direct to)* remitir; *(to send to)* enviar; *(to submit to)* someter a ➤ *intr* referirse.
referee ➤ *s* árbitro/a ➤ *tr & intr* arbitrar.
reference ➤ *s* referencia; *(allusion)* alusión *f,* mención *f* ■ **r. book** libro de consulta • **with r. to** en cuanto a.
refill ➤ *tr* rellenar ➤ *s* recambio.
refine ➤ *tr* refinar.
refinery ➤ *s* refinería.
reflect ➤ *tr* reflejar ➤ *intr (to think)* reflexionar, meditar.
reflection ➤ *s (image)* reflejo; *(thought)* reflexión *f.*
reflex ➤ *adj & s* reflejo.
reform ➤ *tr & intr* reformar(se) ➤ *s* reforma.
reformation ➤ *s* reforma.
refrain[1] ➤ *intr* abstenerse *(from* de).
refrain[2] ➤ *s* MÚS., POET. estribillo.
refresh ➤ *tr & intr* refrescar(se).
refreshing ➤ *adj* refrescante.
refreshment ➤ *s* refresco.
refrigerator ➤ *s* nevera, frigorífico.
refuge ➤ *s* refugio ■ **to take r. in** refugiarse en.
refugee ➤ *s* refugiado/a.
refund ➤ *tr* reembolsar ➤ *s* reembolso.
refusal ➤ *s* negativa.
refuse[1] ➤ *tr (offer)* no aceptar; *(permission)* negar ➤ *intr* negarse *(to* a).
refuse[2] ➤ *s* desperdicios, basura.
refute ➤ *tr* refutar.
regain ➤ *tr* recuperar, recobrar.
regard ➤ *tr* considerar ■ **regarding** *o* **as regards** con respecto a ➤ *s* consideración *f; (esteem)* aprecio ■ **in** *o* **with r. to** con respecto a • **to send one's regards to** dar recuerdos a • **without r. to** sin tomar en consideración.
regardless ➤ *adv* a pesar de todo; *(come what may)* pase lo que pase.
regime ➤ *s* régimen *m.*
regiment ➤ *s* regimiento.
region ➤ *s* región *f.*
regional ➤ *adj* regional.
register ➤ *s* registro; *(cash register)* registradora ➤ *tr* registrar; *(students)* matricular; *(vehicle)* sacar la matrícula de.
registered ➤ *adj (trademark)* registrado; *(student, vehicle)* matriculado; *(certified)* titulado ■ **r. mail** correo certificado.
registration ➤ *s (of voters)* inscripción *f; (of students, cars)* matrícula.
regret ➤ *tr (to be sorry for)* arrepentirse de; *(to be sorry about)* lamentar ➤ *s (sorrow)* pena; *(remorse)* arrepentimiento ■ *pl* excusas.
regular ➤ *adj* regular; *(usual)* normal; *(customary)* habitual, de costumbre; *(work)* fijo.
regularity ➤ *s* regularidad *f.*
regulate ➤ *tr* regular.
regulation ➤ *s (act)* regulación *f; (rule)* regla ■ *pl* reglamento.
rehearsal ➤ *s* ensayo.
rehearse ➤ *tr & intr* ensayar.
reign ➤ *s* reinado; *(dominance)* dominio ➤ *intr* reinar.
reimburse ➤ *tr* reembolsar.
rein ➤ *s* rienda ■ **to give free r. to** dar rienda suelta a.
reindeer ➤ *s* reno.
reinforce ➤ *tr* reforzar.
reinforcement ➤ *s* refuerzo ■ *pl* MIL. refuerzos.
reinstate ➤ *tr (to office)* restituir, reintegrar; *(to reestablish)* restablecer.
reject ➤ *tr* rechazar.
rejection ➤ *s* rechazo.
rejoice ➤ *tr & intr* regocijar(se).
relate ➤ *tr (to tell)* relatar, contar; *(to associate)* asociar ➤ *intr (to interact)* relacionarse *(with, to* con).
related ➤ *adj* relacionado *(to* con); *(by blood, marriage)* emparentado.
relation ➤ *s* relación *f; (kinship)* parentesco; *(relative)* pariente *mf.*
relationship ➤ *s* relación *f; (kinship)* parentesco; *(tie)* vínculo.
relative ➤ *adj* relativo ➤ *s* pariente *mf.*
relax ➤ *tr & intr* relajar(se).
relaxation ➤ *s* relajación *f.*
relaxed ➤ *adj* relajado.
relay ➤ *s* relevo; *(of messages)* transmisión *f* ➤ *tr* transmitir.
release ➤ *tr (to free)* poner en libertad; *(from one's grip)* soltar; *(film)* estrenar; *(record)* sacar ➤ *s* liberación *f; (of*

film) estreno; *(record)* grabación *f;* *(communiqué)* anuncio.
relevant ➤ *adj* pertinente.
reliable ➤ *adj (person)* de confianza; *(machine)* fiable; *(data, source)* fidedigno.
relic ➤ *s* reliquia.
relief ➤ *s (assistance)* ayuda; *(replacement)* relevo ■ **in r.** en relieve • **what a r.!** ¡qué alivio!
religion ➤ *s* religión *f.*
religious ➤ *adj* religioso; *(pious)* devoto.
relish ➤ *s* entusiasmo; CUL. salsa ➤ *tr* gustar ■ **I don't r. the idea** no me hace ninguna gracia la idea.
reload ➤ *tr & intr* recargar.
reluctant ➤ *adj* poco dispuesto.
rely ➤ *intr* ■ **to r. (up)on** *(to depend)* depender de; *(to trust)* contar con.
remain ➤ *intr* seguir; *(to stay)* quedarse; *(to be left)* quedar.
remainder ➤ *s* resto, residuo.
remaining ➤ *adj* restante.
remark ➤ *tr & intr* comentar (*on* sobre) ➤ *s* comentario.
remarkable ➤ *adj* notable; *(admirable)* extraordinario, admirable.
remedy ➤ *s* remedio ➤ *tr* remediar.
remember ➤ *tr & intr* acordarse (de), recordar.
remind ➤ *tr* recordar.
reminder ➤ *s* aviso, notificación *f.*
remit ➤ *tr* remitir.
remittance ➤ *s* remesa, envío.
remorse ➤ *s* remordimiento.
remote ➤ *adj* remoto; *(relative)* lejano ■ **r. control** control a distancia; *(device)* telemando, mando a distancia.
removal ➤ *s* eliminación *f.*
remove ➤ *tr (to take off, away)* quitar(se); *(to eliminate)* eliminar.
remunerate ➤ *tr* remunerar.
render ➤ *tr (help)* dar; *(service)* prestar.
renew ➤ *tr* renovar; *(to resume)* reanudar.
renounce ➤ *tr* renunciar a.
rent ➤ *s* alquiler *m,* renta ■ **for r.** se alquila ➤ *tr & intr* alquilar(se).
rental ➤ *s (property)* propiedad alquilada ➤ *adj* de alquiler.
reorganize ➤ *tr & intr* reorganizar(se).
repair ➤ *tr* reparar; *(clothes)* remendar ➤ *s* reparación *f* ■ **to be beyond r.** no tener arreglo.
repairman ➤ *s* reparador *m.*
repay ➤ *tr (loan)* pagar; *(favor)* devolver; *(to compensate)* compensar ■ **to r. in kind** pagar con la misma moneda.
repayment ➤ *s* pago, reembolso.
repeat ➤ *tr & intr* repetir ➤ *s* repetición *f;* RAD., TELEV. segunda difusión.
repeated ➤ *adj* repetido.
repel ➤ *tr* repeler.
repent ➤ *intr & tr* arrepentirse (de).
repetition ➤ *s* repetición *f.*
repetitive ➤ *adj* repetitivo.
replace ➤ *tr* reponer; *(to substitute)* reemplazar, suplir.
replacement ➤ *s* reposición *f; (substitution)* reemplazo.
replay ➤ *tr* volver a jugar; *(videotape)* volver a poner ➤ *s* repetición *f.*
replenish ➤ *tr* volver a llenar.
replica ➤ *s* copia.
reply ➤ *tr & intr* contestar, responder ➤ *s* respuesta, contestación *f.*
report ➤ *s (account)* relato; *(official account)* informe *m; (of news)* reportaje *m* ■ **r. card** boletín de notas • **weather r.** boletín meteorológico ➤ *tr* relatar; *(to denounce)* denunciar.
reporter ➤ *s* reportero/a, periodista *mf.*
represent ➤ *tr* representar.
representation ➤ *s* representación *f;* POL. delegación *f.*
representative ➤ *s* representante *mf* ➤ *adj* representativo; *(typical)* típico.
repression ➤ *s* represión *f.*
repressive ➤ *adj* represivo.
reprieve ➤ *tr* conmutar la pena de ➤ *s* conmutación *f;* FIG. alivio temporal.
reprimand ➤ *tr* reprender ➤ *s* reprimenda.
reprint ➤ *s (of book)* reimpresión *f; (of article)* tirada aparte ➤ *tr* reimprimir.
reproach ➤ *tr* reprochar ➤ *s* reproche *m* ■ **above** *o* **beyond r.** intachable.
reproduce ➤ *tr & intr* reproducir(se).
reproduction ➤ *s* reproducción *f.*
reptile ➤ *s* reptil *m;* FIG. canalla *mf.*
republic ➤ *s* república.
republican ➤ *adj & s* republicano/a.
repugnant ➤ *adj* repugnante.
repulsive ➤ *adj* repulsivo.
reputable ➤ *adj* respetable.
reputation ➤ *s* reputación *f.*
request ➤ *tr* solicitar ➤ *s* solicitud *f* ■ **available on r.** disponible a petición.
require ➤ *tr (to need)* requerir, necesitar; *(to demand)* exigir.
requirement ➤ *s* requisito.
requisite ➤ *adj* necesario, indispensable ➤ *s* requisito.
rerun ➤ *s* CINEM., TELEV. reestreno.
rescue ➤ *tr* rescatar, salvar ➤ *s* rescate *m,* salvamento.
research ➤ *s* investigación *f* ➤ *tr & intr* hacer una investigación (sobre).
researcher ➤ *s* investigador/a.
resemble ➤ *tr* parecerse a.
resent ➤ *tr* resentirse por.
resentful ➤ *adj* resentido.
resentment ➤ *s* resentimiento.
reservation ➤ *s (of room, table)* reservación *f; (condition, land)* reserva.
reserve ➤ *tr* reservar ➤ *s* reserva ■ *pl* MIL. reserva ➤ *adj* de reserva.
reserved ➤ *adj* reservado.
reservoir ➤ *s* embalse *m.*
reside ➤ *intr* residir.
residence ➤ *s* residencia.
resident ➤ *s* residente *mf;* MED. interno/a ➤ *adj* residente.
residential ➤ *adj* residencial.
residue ➤ *s* residuo.
resign ➤ *tr* renunciar, dimitir ■ **to r. oneself to** resignarse a ➤ *intr* dimitir.
resignation ➤ *s (act)* renuncia; *(acceptance)* resignación *f.*
resist ➤ *tr & intr* resistir.
resistance ➤ *s* resistencia.
resolution ➤ *s* resolución *f.*
resolve ➤ *tr* resolver ➤ *intr* decidir ➤ *s* resolución *f.*
resort ➤ *intr* ■ **to r. to** recurrir a ➤ *s* lugar *m* de temporado ■ **as a last r.** como último recurso.
resource ➤ *s* recurso, medio.
respect ➤ *tr* respetar ➤ *s* respeto ■ **in that r.** en cuanto a eso.
respectable ➤ *adj* respetable.
respiration ➤ *s* respiración *f.*
respirator ➤ *s* respirador *m.*
respond ➤ *intr* responder.
response ➤ *s* respuesta; *(to a proposal)* acogida; *(to a stimulus)* reacción *f.*
responsibility ➤ *s* responsabilidad *f.*
responsible ➤ *adj* responsable (*for* de, *to* ante).
rest[1] ➤ *s* descanso; *(peace)* tranquilidad *f* ■ **r. room** baño • **to come to r.** pararse ➤ *intr* descansar.
rest[2] ➤ *s* ■ **the r.** *(remainder)* el resto; *(others)* los demás.
restaurant ➤ *s* restaurante *m.*
restful ➤ *adj* quieto, sosegado.
restless ➤ *adj* inquieto, agitado.
restore ➤ *tr (order, relations)* restablecer; *(painting, monarch)* restaurar.
restrict ➤ *tr* restringir, limitar.
restricted ➤ *adj* restringido.
restriction ➤ *s* restricción *f.*
result ➤ *intr* ■ **to r. from, in** resultar de, en ➤ *s* resultado ■ **as a r. of** a causa de.
resume ➤ *tr (talking)* reanudar; *(working)* reasumir.
résumé ➤ *s* currículum vitae *m.*
retail COM. ➤ *s* venta al por menor *o* al detalle ➤ *adj & adv* al por menor, al detalle ➤ *tr & intr* vender(se) al por menor.
retailer ➤ *s* minorista *mf,* detallista *mf.*
retain ➤ *tr* retener; *(lawyer)* contratar; *(sense of humor)* conservar.
retire ➤ *intr (to go to bed)* acostarse; *(to stop working)* jubilarse.
retired ➤ *adj* jubilado.
retirement ➤ *s* jubilación *f.*
retreat ➤ *intr* retirarse ➤ *s* retirada.
retrieve ➤ *tr* recuperar; *(damage)* reparar; *(in hunting)* cobrar.
return ➤ *intr* volver, regresar ➤ *tr* devolver; *(profits, interest)* producir ➤ *s* regreso; *(giving back)* devolución *f; (profits)* ganancia ■ **r. address** dirección del remitente • **r. ticket** billete de vuelta ■ *pl (income)* ingresos; *(in an election)* resultados.
reunion ➤ *s* reunión *f.*
reunite ➤ *tr & intr* reunir(se).
reusable ➤ *adj* que puede volverse a usar.
reuse ➤ *tr* volver a usar.
reveal ➤ *tr* revelar.
revenge ➤ *tr* vengar, vengarse de ➤ *s* venganza ■ **to take r. on** vengarse de.
revenue ➤ ingreso, renta.
reverend ➤ *adj* reverendo ➤ *s* pastor/a.
reverse ➤ *adj* opuesto, contrario ■ **the r. side** *(of a form)* dorso; *(of a page, coin)* reverso ➤ *s* lo opuesto, lo contrario; AUTO. marcha atrás ➤ *tr (order)* invertir; *(to transpose)* transponer; *(policy, direction)* cambiar; DER. revocar.
review ➤ *tr (lesson, text)* repasar; *(film, book)* reseñar, criticar ➤ *s* repaso; *(critique)* crítica.
revise ➤ *tr (to correct)* revisar, corregir; *(to modify)* modificar.
revision ➤ *s* corrección *f; (modification)* modificación *f.*
revive ➤ *tr & intr* resucitar.
revolt ➤ *intr* rebelarse ➤ *s* rebelión *f.*
revolting ➤ *adj* repugnante.
revolution ➤ *s* revolución *f.*
revolutionary ➤ *adj & s* revolucionario/a.
revolve ➤ *tr & intr* (hacer) girar.
revolver ➤ *s* revólver *m.*
reward ➤ *s* recompensa, premio ➤ *tr* recompensar, premiar.
rewrite ➤ *tr* escribir de nuevo.
rheumatism ➤ *s* reumatismo.
rhinestone ➤ *s* diamante falso.
rhinoceros ➤ *s* rinoceronte *m.*
rhyme ➤ *s* rima ➤ *intr & tr* rimar.
rhythm ➤ *s* ritmo.
rib ➤ *s* costilla.
ribbon ➤ *s* cinta.
rice ➤ *s* arroz *m.*
rich ➤ *adj* rico; *(color)* vivo, intenso.
riches ➤ *spl* riquezas.
rid◇ ➤ *tr* librar (*of* de).
riddle ➤ *s (puzzle)* acertijo; *(mystery)* enigma *m.*
ride◇ ➤ *intr* montar; *(to travel)* ir, viajar; *(in a car)* pasearse ➤ *tr (a horse)* montar a; *(a bicycle)* montar en ➤ *s (on horse, car)* paseo; *(trip)* viaje *m; (tour)* vuelta ■ **to give someone a r.** llevar a alguien • **to go for a r.** dar un paseo.
rider ➤ *s (horse)* jinete *mf; (bicycle)* ciclista *mf; (passenger)* viajero/a.
ridiculous ➤ *adj* ridículo.
rifle ➤ *s* rifle *m;* MIL. fusil *m.*
rig ➤ *tr (to equip)* equipar; *(an election)* amañar ➤ *s (gear)* equipo; MARÍT. aparejo ■ **oil. r.** torre de perforación.
right ➤ *adj (just, fair)* justo; *(ethical, correct)* correcto; *(word, time)* exacto; *(conditions)* favorable; *(opposite the left)* derecho ■ **r. angle** ángulo recto • **to be r.** tener razón • **to put r.** arreglar ➤ *s (justice)* justicia; *(good)* (lo) bueno, bien *m; (side, hand)* derecha; *(claim)* derecho; POL. derecha ■ **by rights** de derecho • **r. of way** derecho de paso ➤ *adv (well, correctly)* bien; *(squarely)* en pleno; *(to the right)* a *o* hacia la derecha ■ **r. behind** justo detrás • **r. now** ahora mismo • **to come r. home** regresar derecho a casa.
right-hand ➤ *adj* a la derecha.
right-handed ➤ *adj* que usa la mano derecha.
rightly ➤ *adj* correctamente; *(properly)* con derecho.
rigid ➤ *adj* rígido.
rim ➤ *s* borde *m; (coin)* canto.
rind ➤ *s (fruits)* cáscara; *(cheese)* corteza.
ring[1] ➤ *s* anillo; *(circle)* círculo; *(on finger)* anillo, sortija; *(for bullfights)* ruedo; *(in boxing)* ring *m* ➤ *tr* rodear.
ring[2]◇ ➤ *intr (bells)* repicar; *(telephone, doorbell)* sonar ➤ *tr (a bell, buzzer)* tocar; *(to telephone)* llamar, telefonear ➤ *s (of telephone, buzzer, voice)* timbre *m; (tinkle)* tintineo.
rinse ➤ *tr* enjuagar ➤ *s* enjuague *m.*
riot ➤ *s* motín *m,* disturbio ■ **r. police** guardia de asalto ➤ *intr* amotinarse.
rip ➤ *tr* rasgar, desgarrar ■ **to r. off** arrancar, quitar; JER. *(to rob)* timar, limpiar • **to r. up** desgarrar, destrozar ➤ *intr* rasgarse, desgarrarse ➤ *s* desgarrón *m; (split seam)* descosido ■ **r. tide** corriente turbulenta.
ripe ➤ *adj* maduro.
ripen ➤ *tr & intr* madurar.
rip-off ➤ *s* FAM. timo.
rise◇ ➤ *intr (person, wind, dough)* levantarse; *(buildings, hills, spirits)* elevarse; *(temperature, prices, land)* subir; *(in rank, position)* ascender; *(water level)* crecer; *(voice)* alzarse; *(sun)* salir ➤ *s* subida, ascensión *f; (elevation)* elevación *f; (of prices, temperature, land)* subida; *(in rank)* ascenso; *(in pressure, rate, pitch)* elevación; *(of sun)* salida; COM. alza ■ **to give r. to** ocasionar.
risk ➤ *s* riesgo ➤ *tr* arriesgarse a.
risky ➤ *adj* arriesgado.
rival ➤ *adj & s* rival *mf* ➤ *tr* rivalizar con.
river ➤ *s* río.
road ➤ *s (highway)* carretera; *(street)* calle *f; (route, path)* camino.
roam ➤ *intr & tr* vagar (por).
roar ➤ *intr* rugir; *(bull, wind)* bramar ➤ *s* rugido, bramido; *(of the crowd)* clamor *m; (of laughter)* carcajada.
roast ➤ *tr (meat)* asar; *(coffee, nuts)* tostar ➤ *s* asado; *(cut)* carne *f* para asar ➤ *adj* asado ■ **r. beef** rosbif.
rob ➤ *tr & intr* robar.
robber ➤ *s* ladrón/ona.
robbery ➤ *s* robo.
robe ➤ *s (judge)* toga; *(priest)* sotana; *(bathrobe)* bata.
robot ➤ *s* robot *m,* autómata *m.*
rock[1] ➤ *s* roca; *(stone)* piedra.
rock[2] ➤ *intr (to sway)* balancearse; *(to shake)* estremecerse ➤ *tr (baby, cradle)* mecer; *(to shake)* sacudir ■ **rocking chair** mecedora ➤ *s* MÚS. rock *m.*
rocket ➤ *s* cohete *m.*
rocky ➤ *adj* rocoso.
rod ➤ *s (stick)* vara; *(staff)* bastón *m.*
rodent ➤ *adj & s* roedor *m.*
role *o* **rôle** ➤ *s* papel *m.*
roll ➤ *intr* rodar; *(to wallow)* revolcarse; *(thunder)* retumbar; *(drum)* redoblar ■ **to r. over** dar una vuelta ➤ *tr* ■ **rolling pin** rodillo • **to r. up** *(paper, rug)* enrollar; *(sleeves)* arremangar ➤ *s (of paper, film)* rollo; *(bread)* bollo, panecillo.
roller ➤ *s (cylinder)* rodillo; *(small wheel)* ruedecilla; *(for the hair)* rulo ■ **r. coaster** montaña rusa • **r. skate** patín de ruedas.
Roman *adj & s* romano/a ■ **R. Catholic** católico romano.
romance ➤ *s* romance *m; (novel)* novela romántica; *(love affair)* amores *m; (adventure)* aventura.
romantic ➤ *adj & s* romántico/a.
roof ➤ *s* techo, tejado.
rook ➤ *s (in chess)* torre *f.*
room ➤ *s* habitación *f,* cuarto; *(space, a spot)* sitio ■ **r. and board** pensión completa ■ *pl* alojamiento ➤ *intr* alojarse ■ **rooming house** pensión.
roommate ➤ *s* compañero/a de cuarto.
roomy ➤ *adj* espacioso, amplio.
rooster ➤ *s* gallo.
root ➤ *s* raíz *f* ➤ *intr* echar raíces ➤ *tr* arraigar ■ **to r. out** extirpar.
rope ➤ *s* soga, cuerda ➤ *tr (to tie)* amarrar, atar; *(horses)* coger con lazo ■ **to r. off** acordonar.
rose ➤ *s* rosa ■ **r. garden** rosaleda ➤ *adj* (de color) rosa.
rosebush ➤ *s* rosal *m.*
rosemary ➤ *s* romero.
rot ➤ *tr & intr* pudrir(se) ➤ *s* podredumbre *f.*
rotten ➤ *adj (meat, fruit)* estropeado; *(wood)* carcomido; *(smell, egg)* podrido; *(trick)* malo.
rough ➤ *adj* áspero; *(terrain)* accidentado; *(coarse)* basto, burdo; *(seas)* agitado; *(idea, guess)* aproximado ■ **r. draft** borrador.
round ➤ *adj* redondo ■ **r. trip** viaje de ida y vuelta ➤ *s* círculo; *(of talks, drinks)* ronda ■ **to make one's rounds** *(police, patrol)* hacer la ronda; *(doctor)* hacer las visitas ➤ *tr* ■ **to r. off** redondear • **to r. up** acorralar; *(people)* reunir ➤ *adv* ■ **all year r.** durante todo el año ➤ *prep (the world)* alrededor de; *(the corner)* a la vuelta de.
roundabout ➤ *adj* indirecto.
route ➤ *s (course)* ruta, vía; *(road)* carretera; *(for delivery)* recorrido ➤ *tr* mandar, encaminar.
routine ➤ *s* rutina ➤ *adj* rutinario.
row[1] ➤ *s* línea, fila.
row[2] ➤ *intr (boat)* remar.
row[3] ➤ *s (quarrel)* pelea; *(noise)* jaleo.
rowboat ➤ *s* bote *m* de remos.
royal ➤ *adj* real.
royalty ➤ *s* familia real; *(rank, power)* realeza; *(payment)* derechos de autor.
rub ➤ *tr* frotar (*against* contra); *(to massage)* friccionar ■ **to r. in** *u* on fro-

tar con ➤ *intr* rozar ➤ *s* fricción *f.*

rubber ➤ *s* caucho; *(synthetic)* goma; *(eraser)* goma de borrar; JER. *(condom)* preservativo ▪ **r. band** goma.

rubbish ➤ *s* basura; FIG. tonterías.

rubble ➤ *s* escombros.

ruby ➤ *s* rubí *m.*

rudder ➤ *s* timón *m.*

rude ➤ *adj (crude)* crudo, rudo; *(discourteous)* grosero, descortés.

rug ➤ *s* alfombra.

ruin ➤ *s* ruina ➤ *tr* arruinar; *(crops, party)* estropear.

rule ➤ *s* regla; *(control)* dominio, mando; *(reign)* reinado ▪ **as a (general) r.** por lo regular ▪ *pl* reglamento ➤ *tr* gobernar ▪ **to r. out** excluir, descartar ➤ *intr* gobernar; DER. fallar.

ruler ➤ *s* gobernante *mf; (strip)* regla.

rum ➤ *s* ron *m.*

rumor ➤ *s* rumor *m.*

run✧ ➤ *intr* correr; *(to function)* andar, marchar; *(color, ink)* correrse; POL. presentarse como candidato ▪ **to r. away** fugarse • **to r. in the family** venir de familia • **to r. smoothly** ir sobre ruedas ➤ *tr (race, risk)* correr; *(errand, experiment)* hacer; *(to operate)* hacer funcionar; *(household)* llevar; COMPUT. ejecutar ▪ **to r. into** *(by chance)* encontrarse con; *(to collide with)* chocar contra • **to r. out of** acabársele a uno • **to r. over** atropellar ➤ *s (race)* carrera; *(quick trip)* visita; *(in stockings)* carrera.

runaway ➤ *adj & s* fugitivo/a.

runner ➤ *s* corredor/a.

runner-up ➤ *s* segundo/a.

running ➤ *adj (water)* corriente ▪ **r. start** salida lanzada ➤ *adv* seguido.

run-off ➤ *s (overflow)* derrame *m; (competition)* carrera de desempate.

runway ➤ *s* AVIA. pista.

rural ➤ *adj* rural.

ruse ➤ *s* artimaña, treta.

rush ➤ *intr (to run)* ir de prisa; *(to hurry)* apresurarse, darse prisa; *(to flow)* correr ➤ *tr (a person)* dar prisa, apurar; *(a job)* hacer de prisa; *(an order)* ejecutar urgentemente ➤ *s (haste)* prisa; *(bustle)* bullicio, ajetreo; *(of emotion)* arrebato ▪ **r. hour** hora punta ➤ *adj* urgente.

rust ➤ *s* herrumbre *f* ➤ *tr & intr* oxidar(se).

rustic ➤ *adj & s* rústico/a.

rusty ➤ *adj* oxidado.

rut ➤ *s* carril *m;* FIG. rutina.

rye ➤ *s* centeno.

S

sabotage ➤ *s* sabotaje *m* ➤ *tr* sabotear.

sack ➤ *s* saco.

sacred ➤ *adj* sacro, sagrado.

sacrifice ➤ *s* sacrificio ➤ *tr* sacrificar.

sad ➤ *adj* triste.

sadden ➤ *tr* entristecer.

saddle ➤ *s* silla de montar; *(bicycle)* sillín *m* ➤ *tr* ensillar.

sadness ➤ *s* tristeza.

safe ➤ *adj* seguro ▪ **s. and sound** sano y salvo • **to play it s.** actuar con precaución ➤ *s* caja de caudales.

safely ➤ *adv (without harm)* sin accidente; *(driving)* con cuidado.

safety ➤ *s* seguridad *f* ▪ **s. belt** cinturón de seguridad • **s. pin** imperdible.

saffron ➤ *s* azafrán *m.*

sag ➤ *intr (skin, clothes)* colgar; *(plank)* combarse; *(rope)* aflojarse.

said ➤ *adj* (ante)dicho.

sail ➤ *s* vela ➤ *intr* navegar; *(to travel)* ir en barco; *(to set out)* zarpar ➤ *tr (a boat)* gobernar.

sailboat ➤ *s* barco de vela.

sailing ➤ *s* navegación *f; (sport)* vela.

sailor ➤ *s* marinero/a.

saint ➤ *s* santo/a.

sake ➤ *s* ▪ **for God's** *o* **goodness'** *o* **heaven's s.!** ¡por (el amor de) Dios! • **for your own s.** por tu propio bien.

salad ➤ *s* ensalada.

salary ➤ *s* salario.

sale ➤ *s* venta; *(clearance)* liquidación *f* ▪ **for s.** se vende • **on s.** *(available)* en venta; *(reduced)* en liquidación ▪ *pl* venta • **s. tax** impuesto a las ventas.

salesclerk ➤ *s* dependiente/a.

salesperson ➤ *s* vendedor/a.

saliva ➤ *s* saliva.

salmon ➤ *s* salmón *m.*

salt ➤ *s* sal *f* ▪ **s. water** agua salada ➤ *tr* echar sal a; *(to preserve)* salar.

saltshaker ➤ *s* salero.

salty ➤ *adj* salado.

salute ➤ *tr* saludar ➤ *intr* hacer un saludo ➤ *s* saludo.

Salvadoran ➤ *adj & s* salvadoreño/a.

salvation ➤ *s* salvación *f.*

same ➤ *adj* mismo; *(similar)* igual ➤ *adv* igual ➤ *pron* el mismo; *(thing)* lo mismo ▪ **all the s.** sin embargo.

sample ➤ *s* muestra ➤ *tr* tomar una muestra de.

sand ➤ *s* arena ▪ **s. dune** duna, médano ▪ *pl* arenales.

sandal ➤ *s* sandalia.

sandalwood ➤ *s* sándalo.

sandbar ➤ *s* arrecife *m* de arena.

sandpaper ➤ *s* papel *m* de lija.

sandwich ➤ *s* emparedado, sandwich *m.*

sane ➤ *adj* cuerdo.

sanitary ➤ *adj* sanitario ▪ **s. napkin** paño higiénico.

sanitize ➤ *tr* sanear.

sanity ➤ *s* cordura.

sarcasm ➤ *s* sarcasmo.

sardine ➤ *s* sardina.

satellite ➤ *s* satélite *m.*

satin ➤ *s* raso, satén *m.*

satire ➤ *s* sátira.

satisfaction ➤ *s* satisfacción *f.*

satisfactory ➤ *adj* satisfactorio.

satisfy ➤ *tr* satisfacer; *(requirements)* cumplir con; *(to make do)* contentarse; *(to convince)* convencer ➤ *intr* dar satisfacción.

satisfying ➤ *adj* satisfactorio; *(experience)* agradable; *(food)* sustancioso.

saturate ➤ *tr* saturar.

Saturday ➤ *s* sábado.

sauce ➤ *s* salsa.

saucepan ➤ *s* cacerola.

saucer ➤ *s* platillo.

saucy ➤ *adj* descarado.

sausage ➤ *s* salchicha.

savage ➤ *adj & s* salvaje *mf.*

savanna(h) ➤ *s* sabana.

save ➤ *tr (to rescue)* salvar; *(to keep)* guardar; *(to conserve)* ahorrar; COMPUT. grabar, salvar, guardar ➤ *intr* ahorrar ➤ *s* DEP. parada.

savings ➤ *spl* ahorros ▪ **s. account, bank** cuenta, caja de ahorros.

saw✧ ➤ *s (handsaw)* serrucho; *(machine)* sierra ➤ *tr* (a)serrar.

saxophone ➤ *s* saxófono.

say✧ ➤ *tr* decir; *(prayer)* rezar ▪ **it is said** se dice • **let us s.** digamos • **not to s.** por no decir • **that is to s.** o sea, es decir ➤ *s (opinion)* voz *f; (turn to speak)* uso de la palabra.

saying ➤ *s* dicho.

scab ➤ *s* costra, postilla.

scaffolding ➤ *s* andamiaje *m.*

scald ➤ *tr* escaldar.

scale[1] ➤ *s (of fish, skin)* escama ➤ *tr* escamar.

scale[2] ➤ *s* escala ➤ *tr (to climb)* escalar.

scale[3] ➤ *s (balance)* balanza, báscula; *(tray)* platillo (de balanza).

scallion ➤ *s* cebollino.

scallop ➤ *s (animal, shell)* venera.

scan ➤ *tr (to examine)* escudriñar; *(the horizon)* recorrer con la mirada; COMPUT. escanear.

scandal ➤ *s* escándalo.

scanner ➤ *s* COMPUT. escáner *m.*

scar ➤ *s* cicatriz *f.*

scarce ➤ *adj* escaso.

scarcely ➤ *adv* apenas.

scarcity ➤ *s* escasez *f.*

scare ➤ *tr & intr* asustar(se) ➤ *s* susto.

scarecrow ➤ *s* espantapájaros *m.*

scarf ➤ *s* bufanda.

scarlet ➤ *s & adj* escarlata ▪ **s. fever** escarlatina.

scatter ➤ *tr* dispersar; *(to strew)* esparcir ➤ *intr* dispersarse.

scene ➤ *s* escena; *(place)* lugar ▪ **behind the scenes** TEAT. entre bastidores; FIG. en privado.

scenery ➤ *s* paisaje *m;* TEAT. decorado.

scenic ➤ *adj* del paisaje; *(picturesque)* pintoresco; TEAT. escénico.

scent ➤ *s* olor *m; (trail)* pista.

schedule ➤ *s (timetable)* horario; *(agenda)* calendario ▪ **to be behind s.** *(plane)* llevar retraso; *(work)* estar atrasado • **on s.** a la hora ➤ *tr* fijar el horario de; *(meeting)* programar.

scheme ➤ *s (plan)* proyecto; *(plot)* ardid *m* ➤ *intr* conspirar.

scholar ➤ *s* erudito/a; *(pupil)* escolar *mf.*

scholarship ➤ *s* erudición *f; (financial aid)* beca.

school[1] ➤ *s* escuela; *(for teens)* colegio; *(department)* facultad *f* ▪ **night s.** escuela nocturna • **summer s.** curso(s) de verano • **Sunday s.** escuela dominical ➤ *tr* educar; *(to train)* disciplinar.

school[2] ➤ *s (fish)* cardumen *m.*

schoolbook ➤ *s* libro de texto.

schoolhouse ➤ *s* colegio, escuela.

schoolmate ➤ *s* compañero/a de clase.

schoolroom ➤ *s* aula, sala de clase.

schoolteacher ➤ *s* maestro/a.

science ➤ *s* ciencia ▪ **s. fiction** ciencia ficción.

scientific ➤ *adj* científico.

scientist ➤ *s* científico/a.

scissors ➤ *spl* tijeras *f.*

scold ➤ *tr* regañar ➤ *s* regañón/a.

scooter ➤ *s* patineta, monopatín *m.*

scope ➤ *s (reach)* alcance *m; (freedom)* libertad *f.*

scorch ➤ *tr & intr* quemar(se) ➤ *s* quemadura.

score ➤ *s* DEP. tanteo; EDUC. calificación *f;* MÚS. partitura ▪ **final s.** DEP. resultado • **on that s.** en cuanto a eso • **to keep s.** apuntar los tantos ➤ *tr* DEP. marcar; FAM. *(to get)* conseguir; EDUC. sacar ➤ *intr* FAM. tener éxito; DEP. marcar un tanto; *(to keep score)* tantear.

scorn ➤ *s* desprecio ➤ *tr* despreciar.

scoundrel ➤ *s* canalla *mf.*

scout ➤ *tr* explorar ➤ *s* explorador/a.

scramble ➤ *intr* gatear ➤ *tr* revolver; ELECTRÓN. perturbar ▪ **scrambled eggs** huevos revueltos.

scrap ➤ *s (of paper)* pedazo; *(of fabric)* retazo ▪ *pl (of food)* restos; *(waste)* desechos ➤ *tr* desechar.

scrapbook ➤ *s* álbum *m* de recortes.

scrape ➤ *tr* raspar ➤ *intr* rozar ▪ **to s. by** ir tirando ➤ *s (on skin)* rasguño; *(jam)* lío.

scratch ➤ *tr & intr* rayar(se); *(to claw)* arañar; *(an itch)* rascar(se) ➤ *s* raya; *(on skin)* arañazo ▪ **from s.** de la nada ➤ *adj* ▪ **s. paper** papel (de) borrador.

scream ➤ *intr* chillar ➤ *s* chillido.

screen ➤ *s* pantalla; *(for privacy)* biombo; *(for windows)* (tela) mosquitera ➤ *tr* ocultar; CINEM. proyectar.

screen saver ➤ *s* salvapantallas *m.*

screw ➤ *s* CARP. tornillo ➤ *tr* JER. *(to cheat)* estafar ▪ **to s. down** *o* **on** CARP. atornillar • **to s. up** FAM. arruinar.

screwdriver ➤ *s* destornillador *m.*

scribble ➤ *tr & intr* garabatear ➤ *s* garabatos.

script ➤ *s* letra cursiva; CINEM. guión *m.*

scroll ➤ *s* rollo de pergamino ▪ **s. bar** COMPUT. barra de enrollar ➤ *intr* COMPUT. enrollar.

scrub ➤ *tr* fregar; *(clothes)* restregar.

scrutinize ➤ *tr* escudriñar.

scuba ➤ *s* submarinismo, escafandra autónoma.

sculpt ➤ *tr* esculpir.

sculptor ➤ *s* escultor/a.

sculpture ➤ *s* escultura ➤ *tr* esculpir.

scurvy ➤ *s* escorbuto.

sea ➤ *s* mar *mf* ▪ **at s.** en el mar; FIG. confuso ➤ *adj* marino; *(saltwater)* de mar.

seafood ➤ *s* mariscos; *(fish)* pescado.

seal[1] ➤ *s* sello; *(closure)* cierre *m* ➤ *tr* sellar; *(with wax)* lacrar; *(envelope)* cerrar.

seal[2] ➤ *s* ZOOL. foca.

seam ➤ *s* costura.

seaman ➤ *s* marinero.

seaport ➤ *s* puerto marítimo.

search ➤ *tr & intr* registrar; *(conscience)* examinar ▪ **to s. for** buscar ➤ *s* búsqueda; *(by police)* registro; *(of person)* cacheo ▪ **in s. of** en busca de • **s. engine** buscador • **s. warrant** mandamiento de registro.

seashell ➤ *s* concha marina.

seashore ➤ *s* playa; *(coast)* costa.

seasick ➤ *adj* mareado.

seasickness ➤ *s* mareo.

seaside ➤ *s* costa ▪ **s. resort** estación balnearia.

season ➤ *s (of year)* estación *f; (time)* temporada ▪ **off s.** temporada baja • **s. ticket** abono ➤ *tr (food)* sazonar.

seasoning ➤ *s* aderezo, condimento.

seat ➤ *s* asiento; *(for a show, game)* localidad *f; (of bicycle)* sillín *m; (of government)* sede *f* ▪ **s. belt** cinturón de seguridad ➤ *tr* sentar; *(to accommodate)* tener sitio para.

seating ➤ *s* asientos.

seaweed ➤ *s* alga.

second[1] ➤ *s (time unit)* segundo.

second[2] ➤ *adj* segundo ▪ **every s.** (uno de) cada dos • **s. floor** primer piso (en países hispánicos) ➤ *s* segundo; AUTO. segunda.

secondary ➤ *adj* secundario ▪ **s. education** enseñanza media.

second-class ➤ *adj* de segunda clase ➤ *adv* en segunda (clase).

secret ➤ *adj & s* secreto.

secretary ➤ *s* secretario/a.

section ➤ *s* sección *f.*

secure ➤ *adj* seguro; *(stable)* asegurado ➤ *tr* asegurar; *(to obtain)* conseguir; *(boat)* amarrar.

security ➤ *s* seguridad *f; (of loan)* garantía ▪ **s. guard** guardia ▪ *pl* FIN. valores.

sedation ➤ *s* sedación *f.*

sedative ➤ *s & adj* sedante *m.*

seduce ➤ *tr* seducir.

see✧ ➤ *tr* ver; *(to understand)* entender; *(socially)* verse; *(to consult)* consultar; *(a place)* conocer ▪ **s. you later!** ¡hasta luego! • **to s. off** ir a despedirse de • **to s. to** atender a ➤ *intr* ver ▪ **let's s.** a ver • **to s. fit** creer conveniente.

seed ➤ *s* semilla; *(pip)* pepita ➤ *tr* sembrar.

seek✧ ➤ *tr* buscar; *(fame)* anhelar; *(advice)* solicitar ▪ **to s. out** ir en busca de • **to s. to** tratar de.

seem ➤ *intr* parecer.

seeming ➤ *adj* aparente.

seep ➤ *intr* rezumarse.

see-through ➤ *adj* transparente.

segment ➤ *s* segmento.

segregate ➤ *tr & intr* segregar(se).

segregation ➤ *s* segregación *f.*

seize ➤ *tr* agarrar; *(to possess)* apoderarse de; *(to confiscate)* incautarse de.

seizure ➤ *s (of goods)* embargo; *(of power)* toma; MED. ataque *m.*

seldom ➤ *adv* rara vez.

select ➤ *tr & intr* escoger; *(candidate, team)* seleccionar ➤ *adj* de primera calidad.

selection ➤ *s* selección *f; (collection)* surtido.

self ➤ *s* uno mismo; *(ego)* ego.

self-addressed ➤ *adj* con la dirección del remitente.

self-assured ➤ *adj* seguro de sí mismo.

self-confidence ➤ *s* confianza en sí mismo.

self-conscious ➤ *adj* cohibido.

self-control ➤ *s* dominio de sí mismo.

self-defense ➤ *s* autodefensa; DER. legítima defensa ▪ **in s.** en defensa propia.

self-employed ➤ *adj* que trabaja por cuenta propia.

self-esteem ➤ *s* amor propio.

self-government ➤ *s* autonomía.

selfish ➤ *adj* egoísta.

selfishness ➤ *s* egoísmo.

self-portrait ➤ *s* autorretrato.

self-respect ➤ *s* dignidad *f.*

self-righteous ➤ *adj* santurrón.

self-service ➤ *adj* de autoservicio.

sell✧ ➤ *tr* vender ▪ **to s. off** COM. liquidar ➤ *intr* venderse ▪ **to be sold out** estar agotado.

seller ➤ *s* vendedor/a.

sellout ➤ *s* COM. liquidación *f* total; FAM. traidor/a.

semester ➤ *s* semestre *m.*

semicircle ➤ *s* semicírculo.

semicolon ➤ *s* punto y coma.

semiconductor ➤ *s* semiconductor *m.*

semifinal DEP. ➤ *s* semifinal *f* ➤ *adj* semifinalista.

senate ➤ *s* senado.

senator ➤ *s* senador/a.

send✧ ➤ *tr* mandar; *(letter)* enviar ▪ **to s. away for** ordenar por correo • **to s. back** devolver • **to s. off** *(letter)* echar al buzón; *(person)* ir a despedir ➤ *intr* enviar.

sender ➤ *s* remitente *mf.*

senior ➤ *adj (partner)* principal; *(senator)* más antiguo; *(officer)* superior ▪ **s. citizen** anciano/a ➤ *s* anciano/a; *(student)* estudiante *mf* del último año.

sensational ➤ *adj* sensacional.

sense ➤ *s* sentido; *(feeling)* sensación *f; (consciousness)* sentimiento ▪ **good s.** sentido común • **in a s.** en cierto sentido • **to come to one's senses** recobrar el juicio • **to make s.** tener sentido ➤ *tr (to perceive)* darse cuenta de; *(to detect)* detectar.

senseless ➤ *adj* sin sentido.

sensible ➤ *adj* sensato; *(perceptible)* sensible.
sensitive ➤ *adj* sensible; *(delicate)* delicado ■ **to be s. to** *o* **about** ser susceptible a.
sensual ➤ *adj* sensual.
sentence ➤ *s* GRAM. oración *f,* frase *f;* DER. sentencia ■ **life s.** condena perpetua • **to pass s. on** sentenciar ➤ *tr* sentenciar.
sentry ➤ *s* centinela *mf.*
separate ➤ *tr & intr* separar(se) ➤ *adj* separado; *(different)* distinto.
separation ➤ *s* separación *f.*
September ➤ *s* septiembre *m.*
sequence ➤ *s* sucesión *f; (arrangement)* orden *m; (series)* serie *f.*
sergeant ➤ *s* sargento *mf.*
serial ➤ *adj* ■ **s. number** número de serie ➤ *s* serial *m.*
series ➤ *s* serie *f.*
serious ➤ *adj* serio; *(illness)* grave.
servant ➤ *s* sirviente/a; *(civil)* funcionario/a.
serve ➤ *tr* servir; *(to wait on)* atender ■ **to s. as** *o* **for** servir de • **to s. on** ser miembro de ➤ *intr* servir ➤ *s* DEP. saque *m.*
service ➤ *s* servicio; *(set)* juego ■ **at your s.** a sus órdenes • **diplomatic s.** cuerpo diplomático • **s. charge** recargo por servicios • **to be out of s.** no funcionar ➤ *adj* de servicio; *(military)* militar ➤ *tr* mantener, reparar.
serviceman ➤ *s* militar *m; (repairman)* mecánico.
session ➤ *s* sesión *f; (of legislature)* reunión *f.*
set[1]◊ ➤ *tr* poner; *(to locate)* situar; *(date, price)* fijar; *(record)* establecer; *(example)* dar ■ **to s. back** atrasar • **to s. free** liberar • **to s. off** *(reaction)* iniciar; *(bomb)* hacer estallar; *(alarm)* hacer sonar • **to s. out to** proponerse • **to s. up** *(monument)* levantar; *(machine)* montar; *(business, fund)* crear ➤ *intr (sun)* ponerse ■ **to s. forth** *o* **out** salir, encaminarse ➤ *adj (agreed upon)* señalado; *(price)* fijo; *(opinion)* firme; *(face)* inmóvil; *(determined)* resuelto ■ **all s.** listo • **to be s. on** *(action)* estar empeñado en; *(idea)* estar aferrado a • **to get s.** prepararse.
set[2] ➤ *s (of items)* juego; *(of rules)* serie *f; (people)* grupo; *(works)* colección *f;* TEAT. decorado; RAD. aparato; MAT. conjunto ■ **s. of dishes** vajilla • **television s.** televisor.
setback ➤ *s* revés *m.*
setting ➤ *s (place)* marco; LIT., TEAT. escena, escenario.
settle ➤ *tr (affairs, dispute)* arreglar; *(debt)* saldar; *(territory)* colonizar; *(stomach)* asentar ■ **to s. accounts** ajustar cuentas • **to s. (up)on** decidirse por ➤ *intr (bird, gaze)* posarse; *(dust)* asentarse; *(in a city)* establecerse ■ **to s. down** *(to relax)* calmarse; *(conditions)* normalizarse • **to s. in** instalarse; *(at a job)* acostumbrarse.
settlement ➤ *s (of dispute)* arreglo; *(of problem)* solución *f; (agreement)* acuerdo; *(colony)* poblado.
settler ➤ *s* poblador/a.
seven ➤ *s & adj* siete ■ **s. hundred** setecientos • **s. o'clock** las siete.
seventeen ➤ *s & adj* diecisiete *m.*
seventh ➤ *s & adj* séptimo.
seventy ➤ *s & adj* setenta *m.*
several ➤ *adj & s* varios.
severe ➤ *adj* severo.
severity ➤ *s* severidad *f.*
sew◊ ➤ *tr & intr* coser.
sewage ➤ *s* aguas residuales.
sewer ➤ *s* alcantarilla, cloaca.
sewing ➤ *s* costura ■ **s. machine** máquina de coser.
sex ➤ *s* sexo ■ **to have s.** tener relaciones sexuales.
sexual ➤ *adj* sexual.
sexy ➤ *adj* excitante; *(erotic)* erótico.
shabby ➤ *adj (worn)* raído; *(treatment)* malo, mezquino.
shade ➤ *s* sombra; *(for lamp)* pantalla; *(for window)* persiana; *(hue)* tono; *(of meaning)* matiz *m* ➤ *tr (from light)* resguardar; *(to obscure)* dar sombra a.
shadow ➤ *s* sombra.
shady ➤ *adj* sombreado.
shaft ➤ *s (light)* rayo; *(tool)* mango; *(mine)* pozo; *(elevator)* hueco.
shake◊ ➤ *tr* sacudir; *(bottle)* agitar; *(faith)* hacer vacilar ■ **to s. hands** darse la mano ➤ *intr* temblar.
shall ➤ *aux* ■ **we s. see** veremos • **s. I call?** ¿quiere que llame por teléfono?
shallow ➤ *adj* poco profundo.
shame ➤ *s* vergüenza; *(pity)* lástima ■ **s. on you!** ¡qué vergüenza! ➤ *tr* avergonzar; *(to dishonor)* deshonrar.
shameful ➤ *adj* vergonzoso.
shampoo ➤ *s* champú *m* ➤ *intr* lavarse la cabeza con champú.
shape ➤ *s* forma; *(body)* figura; *(guise)* aspecto; *(condition)* estado ■ **to be in no s. to** no estar en condiciones de *o* para • **to be out of s.** DEP. no estar en forma ➤ *tr* formar.
share ➤ *s* parte *f; (of stock)* acción *f* ➤ *tr & intr* compartir.
shareholder ➤ *s* accionista *mf.*
shark ➤ *s* tiburón *m;* JER. usurero/a.
sharp ➤ *adj (cutting)* afilado; *(pointed)* puntiagudo; *(image)* nítido; *(curve)* cerrado; *(acute)* agudo.
sharpen ➤ *tr* afilar; *(pencil)* sacar punta a; *(appetite)* aguzar.
shatter ➤ *tr & intr* hacer(se) añicos.
shave◊ ➤ *tr & intr* afeitar(se) ➤ *s* afeitado.
shaver ➤ *s* afeitadora.
shawl ➤ *s* chal *m.*
she ➤ *pron* ella ➤ *s* hembra.
shears ➤ *spl* tijeras.
shed[1]◊ ➤ *tr (tears)* derramar; *(water)* verter; *(skin)* mudar.
shed[2] ➤ *s* cobertizo.
sheep ➤ *s* oveja.
sheet ➤ *s (for bed)* sábana; *(paper)* hoja; *(glass)* lámina; *(ice)* capa.
shelf ➤ *s (in closet)* anaquel *m; (shelving)* estante *m.*
shell ➤ *s* concha; *(of crab, turtle)* caparazón *m; (of nuts, eggs)* cáscara; *(of peas)* vaina; ARM. proyectil *m* ➤ *tr (peas)* desvainar; MIL. bombardear.
shellfish ➤ *s* CUL. mariscos.
shelter ➤ *s* cobertizo; *(refuge)* refugio ■ **to take s.** ponerse a cubierto ➤ *tr* proteger ➤ *intr* refugiarse.
shelving ➤ *s* estantería.
shepherd/ess ➤ *s* pastor/a.
sheriff ➤ *s* alguacil *m,* sheriff *m.*
sherry ➤ *s* jerez *m.*
shield ➤ *s* escudo ➤ *tr* escudar; *(to conceal)* tapar.
shift ➤ *tr (load)* pasar; *(to switch)* cambiar de ➤ *intr* cambiar; *(person)* moverse; AUTO. cambiar de velocidad ➤ *s* cambio; *(of workers)* turno ■ **in shifts** por turnos.
shin ➤ *s* espinilla.
shine◊ ➤ *intr* brillar ➤ *tr (to polish)* sacar brillo a; *(light)* dirigir ➤ *s* brillo.
shingle ➤ *s* tablilla ■ *pl* MED. zona.
shiny ➤ *adj* brillante; *(glossy)* lustroso.
ship ➤ *s* barco ➤ *tr* enviar.
shipment ➤ *s* embarque *m; (cargo)* cargamento.
shipping ➤ *s* embarque *m.*
shipwreck ➤ *s* naufragio ➤ *tr* ■ **to be shipwrecked** naufragar.
shipyard ➤ *s* astillero.
shirt ➤ *s* camisa.
shiver ➤ *intr* tiritar ➤ *s* escalofrío.
shock ➤ *s* choque *m; (mental)* golpe *m; (of earthquake)* sacudida ■ **s. absorber** amortiguador ➤ *tr & intr* chocar ■ **to be shocked at** escandalizarse por.
shocking ➤ *adj (disturbing)* horroroso; *(offensive)* indecente.
shoe◊ ➤ *s* zapato ■ **s. polish** betún • **s. store** zapatería ➤ *tr (horse)* herrar.
shoelace ➤ *s* cordón *m.*
shoemaker ➤ *s* zapatero/a.
shoot◊ ➤ *tr (gun)* disparar; *(to wound)* herir; *(to kill)* matar a tiros; *(to execute)* fusilar; CINEM. rodar; FOTOG. fotografiar ■ **to s. down** derribar • **to s. dead** *o* **to death** matar a tiros ➤ *intr (to fire)* disparar; DEP. tirar ■ **to s. up** *(to grow)* espigar; *(prices)* subir de repente; *(sparks)* brotar ➤ *s* BOT. retoño ➤ *interj* ¡miércoles!
shooting ➤ *s* tiro; *(murder)* asesinato.
shop ➤ *s* tienda; *(workshop)* taller *m* ■ **s. window** escaparate ➤ *intr* ir de compras ■ **to s. for** ir a comprar.
shopkeeper ➤ *s* tendero/a.
shopping ➤ *s* compras ■ **s. center** centro comercial • **to go s.** ir de compras.
shore ➤ *s (coast)* orilla; *(beach)* playa.
short ➤ *adj* corto; *(in height)* bajo; *(in amount)* poco ■ **a s. distance from** a poca distancia de • **in s. order** sin demora • **s. circuit** ELEC. cortocircuito • **s. story** cuento • **to be s. of** *(money)* tener poco; *(breath)* faltarle a uno • **to run s. of** agotársele (a uno) ➤ *adv (abruptly)* en seco ■ **to come up s.** quedarse corto • **to fall s. (of)** no alcanzar ➤ *s* cortocircuito ■ **in s.** en resumen ■ *pl* pantalones cortos.
shortage ➤ *s* falta.
shortcut ➤ *s* atajo.
shorten ➤ *tr & intr* acortar(se).
shorthand ➤ *s* taquigrafía.
shortly ➤ *adv* dentro de poco.
shortsighted ➤ *adj* corto de vista.
short-term ➤ *adj* a corto plazo.
shot ➤ *s* disparo; *(try)* tiro; CINEM. plano; FOTOG. foto *f;* MED. inyección *f.*
shotgun ➤ *s* escopeta.
should ➤ *aux (obligation)* deber; *(expectation)* deber de.
shoulder ➤ *s* hombro; *(of road)* orilla ■ **s. bag** bolsa *o* bolso bandolera ➤ *tr* echarse al hombro.
shout ➤ *s* grito ➤ *tr & intr* gritar.
shove ➤ *tr* empujar a ➤ *intr* dar empujones ➤ *s* empujón *m.*
shovel ➤ *s* pala ➤ *tr* traspalar.
show◊ ➤ *tr* mostrar; *(to present)* presentar; *(to prove)* demostrar; *(to manifest)* manifestar; *(to exhibit)* exponer ■ **to s. how to** enseñar a • **to s. off** hacer alarde de ➤ *intr* verse; FAM. *(to come)* aparecer ■ **to s. off** alardear • **to s. up** aparecer ➤ *s* demostración *f;* TELEV. programa *m;* TEAT. espectáculo ■ **fashion s.** desfile de modelos • **s. business** mundo del espectáculo • **s. room** sala de exposición.
shower ➤ *s (rain)* chaparrón *m; (bath)* ducha ➤ *intr* ducharse.
showoff ➤ *s* FAM. presumido/a.
showy ➤ *adj* llamativo.
shred ➤ *s* fragmento ➤ *tr* hacer trizas.
shrewd ➤ *adj* astuto.
shrill ➤ *adj* chillón.
shrimp ➤ *s* camarón *m.*
shrine ➤ *s* relicario.
shrink◊ ➤ *tr & intr* encoger(se) ➤ *s* JER. psiquiatra *mf.*
shrivel ➤ *tr & intr* encoger(se).
shrub ➤ *s* matorral *m.*
shrug ➤ *intr* encogerse de hombros.
shudder ➤ *intr* estremecerse.
shuffle ➤ *tr (cards)* barajar.
shut◊ ➤ *tr & intr* cerrar(se) ■ **to s. off** aislar; *(to turn off)* desconectar • **to s. up** encerrar; *(to silence)* hacer callar; *(to be silent)* callarse la boca.
shutdown ➤ *s* cierre *m.*
shutter ➤ *s* contraventana; FOTOG. obturador *m.*
shuttle ➤ *s* lanzadera; *(vehicle)* vehículo de enlace; AVIA. puente aéreo ■ **space s.** transbordador espacial.
shy ➤ *adj* tímido; *(bashful)* vergonzoso; *(wary)* cauteloso.
shyness ➤ *s* timidez *f.*
sibling ➤ *s* hermano/a.
sick ➤ *adj* enfermo; *(disgusted)* asqueado; *(tired)* cansado ■ **to be s.** vomitar • **to get s.** *(seasick)* marearse; *(to take sick)* ponerse enfermo • **to make s.** dar asco a.
sickness ➤ *s* enfermedad *f; (nausea)* náusea.
side ➤ *s* lado; *(of hill)* ladera; *(of boat)* costado; *(of coin)* cara; *(edge)* borde *m; (team)* facción *f* ■ **by the s. of** al lado de • **on either s.** de cada lado • **s. by s.** juntos • **to take sides** tomar partido ➤ *adj* lateral ■ **s. effect** efecto secundario • **s. view** vista de perfil ➤ *intr* ■ **to s. with** ponerse del lado de.
sidewalk ➤ *s* acera.
sideways ➤ *adv* de lado.
sieve ➤ *s* tamiz *m* ➤ *tr* tamizar.
sift ➤ *tr* cerner; *(to separate)* separar.
sigh ➤ *intr* suspirar ➤ *s* suspiro.
sight ➤ *s* vista; *(vision)* visión *f; (thing to see)* lugar *m* de interés; *(of gun)* mira ■ **s. unseen** sin haberlo visto • **to be (with)in s. of** estar a la vista de ■ *pl* meta • **to set one's s. on** tener el ojo puesto en ➤ *tr* ver; *(to aim)* apuntar.
sightseeing ➤ *s* excursionismo.
sign ➤ *s* seña, signo; *(gesture)* gesto; *(poster)* letrero; *(symbol)* símbolo; *(trace)* huella ➤ *tr* firmar ➤ *intr* hacer señas; *(to write)* firmar ■ **to s. on** *o* **up** alistar(se).
signal ➤ *s* señal *f* ➤ *tr* dar la señal de *o* para; *(to make known)* indicar ➤ *intr* hacer señales.
signature ➤ *s* firma.
significant ➤ *adj* significativo.
signify ➤ *tr* significar.
signpost ➤ *s* poste *m* indicador.
silence ➤ *s* silencio ➤ *tr* hacer callar.
silent ➤ *adj* silencioso; *(mute)* mudo ■ **to be s.** callar.
silicon ➤ *s* silicio.
silicone ➤ *s* silicona.
silk ➤ *s* seda.
silly ➤ *adj* tonto, bobo; *(ridiculous)* ridículo.
silver ➤ *s* plata; *(color)* plateado ➤ *adj* de plata; *(like silver)* plateado ■ **s. plate** platería ➤ *tr* platear.
silverware ➤ *s* (vajilla de) plata.
similar ➤ *adj* similar.
similarity ➤ *s* similitud *f.*
simple ➤ *adj* simple, sencillo.
simplify ➤ *tr* simplificar.
simply ➤ *adv* simplemente, sencillamente.
simultaneous ➤ *adj* simultáneo.
sin ➤ *s* pecado ➤ *intr* pecar.
since ➤ *adv* desde entonces; *(ago)* hace ■ **long s.** hace mucho tiempo ➤ *prep* desde ■ **s. that time** desde entonces ➤ *conj* desde que; *(inasmuch as)* ya que.
sincere ➤ *adj* sincero.
sincerity ➤ *s* sinceridad *f.*
sinful ➤ *adj* pecaminoso.
sing◊ ➤ *tr & intr* cantar.
singer ➤ *s* cantante *mf.*
single ➤ *adj* solo; *(for one)* individual; *(unmarried)* soltero ■ **s. bed** cama para una persona • **s. file** hilera.
singular ➤ *adj & s* singular *m.*
sinister ➤ *adj* siniestro.
sink◊ ➤ *intr* descender; *(ship)* hundirse; ➤ *s (bathroom)* lavabo; *(kitchen)* fregadero.
sip ➤ *tr & intr* sorber ➤ *s* sorbo.
sir ➤ *s* señor *m.*
siren ➤ *s* sirena.
sirloin ➤ *s* solomillo.
sister ➤ *s* hermana.
sister-in-law ➤ *s* cuñada, hermana política.
sit◊ ➤ *intr* sentarse; *(to be at rest)* estar sentado ■ **to s. down** sentarse • **to s. in** participar • **to s. still** no moverse • **to s. up** incorporarse.
site ➤ *s* sitio ➤ *tr* situar.
sitter ➤ *s* persona que cuida niños.
situation ➤ *s* situación *f.*
six ➤ *s & adj* seis *m* ■ **s. hundred** seiscientos • **s. o'clock** las seis.
sixteen ➤ *s & adj* dieciséis *m.*
sixth ➤ *s & adj* sexto.
sixty ➤ *s & adj* sesenta *m.*
size ➤ *s* tamaño; *(of shoes)* número; *(of persons, garments)* talla.
skate ➤ *s* patín *m* ➤ *intr* patinar.
skateboard ➤ *s* monopatín *m.*
skeleton ➤ *s* esqueleto.
sketch ➤ *s* esbozo; *(outline)* bosquejo ➤ *tr* esbozar ➤ *intr* dibujar.
sketchbook ➤ *s* bloc *m* de dibujo.
ski ➤ *s* esquí *m* ■ **s. lift** telesquí ➤ *intr & tr* esquiar.
skid ➤ *s* patinazo, resbalón *m* ➤ *intr* resbalar (rueda, automóvil).
skier ➤ *s* esquiador/a.
skiing ➤ *s* esquí *m* (deporte).
skill ➤ *s* maña; *(art)* técnica; *(experience)* experiencia.
skilled ➤ *adj* mañoso; *(qualified)* especializado.
skillet ➤ *s* sartén *f.*
skim ➤ *tr (milk)* desnatar; *(book)* hojear ➤ *s* ■ **s. milk** leche desnatada.
skin ➤ *s* piel *f* ➤ *tr* despellajar.
skinny ➤ *adj* flaco.
skip ➤ *tr & intr* saltar ■ **to s. over** saltar por encima de ➤ *s* salto.
skirt ➤ *s* falda.
skull ➤ *s* cráneo.
sky ➤ *s* cielo.
skyline ➤ *s* horizonte *m.*
skyscraper ➤ *s* rascacielos *m.*
slack ➤ *adj (loose)* flojo ➤ *intr* aflojarse; *(to be remiss)* ser negligente ➤ *s (of rope)* parte floja ■ *pl* pantalones.
slam ➤ *tr & intr* cerrar(se) de golpe ■ **to s. into** chocar con ➤ *s* golpe *m* fuerte; *(of door)* portazo.
slander ➤ *s* calumnia ➤ *tr* calumniar.
slang ➤ *s* jerga.
slant ➤ *tr & intr* inclinar(se) ➤ *s* inclinación *f;* FIG. interpretación *f.*
slap ➤ *s* palmada; *(on face)* bofetada ➤ *tr* dar una palmada; *(the face)*

abofetar.
slash ➤ *tr* acuchillar; *(prices)* rebajar ➤ *s* tajo.
slate ➤ *s* pizarra.
slaughter ➤ *s* matanza ➤ *tr* matar.
slave ➤ *s* esclavo/a.
slavery ➤ *s* esclavitud *f.*
slay◊ ➤ *tr* matar.
slayer ➤ asesino/a.
sleep◊ ➤ *s* sueño ▪ **go to s.** dormirse ➤ *intr* dormir.
sleeping ➤ *adj* dormido, durmiendo ▪ **s. bag** saco de dormir • **s. car** coche cama • **s. pill** somnífero.
sleepy ➤ *adj* soñoliento.
sleet ➤ *s* aguanieve *f* ➤ *intr* cellisquear.
sleeve ➤ *s* manga.
sleeveless ➤ *adj* sin mangas.
sleigh ➤ *s* trineo.
slender ➤ *adj* delgado; *(svelte)* esbelto.
slew ➤ *s* FAM. montón *m.*
slice ➤ *s (of meat)* tajada; *(of bread)* rebanada; *(of ham)* lonja ➤ *tr* cortar, tajar; *(bread)* rebanar.
slide◊ ➤ *intr* resbalar; *(to coast)* deslizarse ➤ *tr* hacer resbalar ➤ *s (playground)* tobogán *m;* FOTOG diapositiva.
slight ➤ *adj* escaso; *(trifling)* insignificante; *(slender)* delgado ➤ *tr* menospreciar; *(to shirk)* desatender ➤ *s* desaire *m.*
slim ➤ *adj* delgado; *(scant)* escaso ➤ *tr & intr* adelgazar.
sling◊ ➤ *s (weapon)* honda; MED. cabestrillo ➤ *tr* arrojar; *(to hang)* colgar.
slip ➤ *intr (to slide)* deslizarse; *(stealthily)* escabullirse; *(to lose one's balance)* resbalar ▪ **to let s.** decir sin querer • **to s. by** *(time)* correr; *(unnoticed)* pasar inadvertido • **to s. out** salir inadvertido • **to s. up** FAM. equivocarse ➤ *tr* librarse *(from* de) ➤ *s* resbalón *m; (false step)* paso en falso; *(error)* equivocación *f; (lapse)* desliz *m; (undergarment)* combinación *f.*
slipper ➤ *s* zapatilla.
slippery ➤ *adj* resbaladizo.
slit◊ ➤ *s* corte *m* ➤ *tr* hender.
slogan ➤ *s* lema *m;* COM. slogan *m.*
slope ➤ *tr & intr* inclinar(se) ➤ *s* cuesta; *(of roof)* vertiente *f; (inclination)* inclinación *f* ▪ **on a s.** en declive.
sloppy ➤ *adj (messy)* desordenado; *(careless)* chapucero.
slot ➤ *s* ranura; *(on roster)* puesto ▪ **s. machine** máquina tragaperras.
slow ➤ *adj* lento; *(clock)* atrasado; *(mentally)* torpe ▪ **s. motion** cámara lenta ▪ **to be s. to** tardar en ➤ *adv* lentamente ➤ *tr* retrasar, retardar ➤ *intr* ▪ **to s. down** ir más despacio.
slug ➤ *s* ZOOL. babosa.
slum ➤ *s* barrio bajo.
sly ➤ *adj* astuto.
smack ➤ *tr (to strike)* dar un palmada ▪ **to s. one's lips** relamerse ➤ *s (sound)* chasquido; *(blow)* golpe *m.*
small ➤ *adj* pequeño; *(petty)* mezquino ▪ **s. letters** minúsculas • **s. talk** charloteo.
smallpox ➤ *s* viruela.
smart ➤ *adj* listo; *(witty)* ingenioso; *(fashionable)* elegante.
smash ➤ *tr* romper; *(to shatter)* destrozar ➤ *intr* romperse ▪ **to s. into** chocar con • **to s. to pieces** hacerse pedazos ➤ *adj* ▪ **a s. hit** un gran éxito.
smell◊ ➤ *tr* oler ➤ *intr* oler; *(to stink)* apestar ➤ *s* olor *m.*
smile ➤ *s* sonrisa ➤ *intr* sonreír(se).
smock ➤ *s* guardapolvo.
smog ➤ *s* mezcla de humo y niebla.
smoke ➤ *s* humo ▪ **s. detector** detector de humo ➤ *intr* humear; *(tobacco)* fumar ➤ *tr* fumar; *(to preserve)* ahumar ▪ **to s. out** descubrir.
smooth ➤ *adj (fine)* liso; *(soft)* suave; *(calm)* tranquilo ➤ *tr (to level)* alisar; *(to polish)* pulir ▪ **to s. things over** limar asperezas.
smother ➤ *tr* sofocar ➤ *intr* asfixiarse.
smuggle ➤ *tr* pasar de contrabando.
smuggler ➤ *s* contrabandista *mf.*
snack ➤ *s* bocado.
snail ➤ *s* caracol *m.*
snake ➤ *s* serpiente *f.*
snap ➤ *tr & intr* quebrar(se) ▪ **to s. off** desprender(se) • **to s. open, shut** abrir(se), cerrar(se) de golpe ➤ *s (breaking)* rotura; *(clasp)* broche *m* de presión.
snapshot ➤ *s* instantánea.
snarl ➤ *intr* gruñir ➤ *s* gruñido.
snatch ➤ *tr* agarrar, arrebatar; *(purse)* robar ➤ *s (of conversation)* fragmento.
sneaker ➤ *s* zapato de lona.
sneer ➤ *s & intr* (hacer un) gesto de desprecio.
sneeze ➤ *intr* estornudar ➤ *s* estornudo.
sniff ➤ *tr (odor)* olfatear; *(substance)* inhalar ➤ *s* olfateo.
snip ➤ *tr & intr* tijeretear ➤ *s (action)* tijeretazo; *(piece)* recorte *m.*
snore ➤ *intr* roncar ➤ *s* ronquido.
snorkel ➤ *s & intr* (bucear con) tubo de respiración.
snout ➤ *s* hocico.
snow ➤ *s* nieve *f; (snowfall)* nevada ➤ *intr* nevar.
snowball ➤ *s* bola de nieve ➤ *intr* aumentar rápidamente.
snowdrift ➤ *s* ventisquero.
snowfall ➤ *s* nevada.
snowplow ➤ *s* quitanieves *m.*
snug ➤ *adj (cozy)* cómodo; *(warm)* calentito; *(tight)* ajustado.
snuggle ➤ *tr & intr* acurrucar(se).
so ➤ *adv (thus)* así; *(to such an extent)* tan; *(consequently)* por eso; *(likewise)* también; *(so much)* tanto; *(then)* así que ▪ **I hope so** espero que sí • **not so** no es así • **not so much as** ni siquiera • **or so** más o menos • **so far** hasta aquí • **so far so good** por ahora, bien • **so long** tanto (tiempo); *(goodbye)* hasta luego • **so so** así, así ➤ *adj* así ➤ *conj* así que ▪ **so that** para que.
soak ➤ *tr* empapar; *(to immerse)* remojar ▪ **to s. up** absorber ➤ *intr* remojarse; *(to drench)* calar ➤ *s* remojo.
soap ➤ *s* jabón *m* ➤ *tr* (en)jabonar.
soapy ➤ *adj* jabonoso.
sob ➤ *intr* sollozar ➤ *s* sollozo.
sober ➤ *adj* sobrio ➤ *intr* ▪ **to s. up** pasarsele a uno la embriaguez.
soccer ➤ *s* fútbol *m* ▪ **s. ball** balón.
social ➤ *adj* social ▪ **s. services** programa de asistencia social • **s. work** asistencia social ➤ *s* reunión *f.*
socialist ➤ *s & adj* socialista *mf.*
society ➤ *s* sociedad *f.*
sock ➤ *s* calcetín *m.*
socket ➤ *s* ELEC. enchufe *m.*
soda ➤ *s* soda, gaseosa.
sodium ➤ *s* sodio.
sofa ➤ *s* sofá *m.*
soft ➤ *adj (not hard)* blando; *(not loud)* bajo; *(gentle, smooth)* suave ▪ **s. drink** gaseosa.
soft-boiled ➤ *adj (egg)* pasado por agua.
software ➤ *s* software *m.*
soil ➤ *s (land)* tierra ➤ *tr* ensuciar.
soiled ➤ *adj* sucio.
soldier ➤ *s* soldado *mf.*
sold-out ➤ *adj* agotado.
sole[1] ➤ *s (of foot)* planta; *(of shoe)* suela.
sole[2] ➤ *adj (single)* único; *(rights, ownership)* exclusivo.
sole[3] ➤ *s (fish)* lenguado.
solemn ➤ *adj* solemne.
solicit ➤ *tr* solicitar.
solicitor ➤ *s* G.B. abogado/a.
solid ➤ *adj* sólido; *(not hollow)* macizo; *(line)* continuo ➤ *s* sólido.
solidarity ➤ *s* solidaridad *f.*
solitude ➤ *s* soledad *f.*
solo ➤ *adj & s* solo ➤ *adv* a solas ➤ *intr* volar solo.
solution ➤ *s* solución *f.*
solve ➤ *tr* resolver, solucionar.
solvent ➤ *adj* FIN. solvente ➤ *s* (di)solvente *m.*
some ➤ *adj* alguno(s); *(a little)* un poco de ▪ **after s. time** después de cierto tiempo • **s. days ago** hace varios días • **s. other time** otro día ➤ *pron (several)* algunos; *(a little)* un poco, algo ▪ **and then s.** y más todavía.
somebody *o* **someone** ➤ *pron* alguien.
somehow ➤ *adv* de algún modo; *(for some reason)* por alguna razón.
someplace ➤ *adv* en *o* a alguna parte.
somersault ➤ *s & intr* (dar un) salto mortal.
something ➤ *pron & s* algo ▪ **s. or other** una cosa u otra • **to be s. of a . . .** tener algo de . . .
sometime ➤ *adv* alguna vez, algún día.
sometimes ➤ *adv* a veces.
somewhat ➤ *adv* algo.
somewhere ➤ *adv* en o a alguna parte ▪ **s. around** aproximadamente.
son ➤ *s* hijo.
song ➤ *s* canción *f; (act)* canto.
son-in-law ➤ *s* yerno, hijo político.
soon ➤ *adv* pronto; *(early)* temprano ▪ **as s. as** en cuanto, tan pronto como • **how s.?** ¿cuándo? • **s. after** poco después • **sooner or later** tarde o temprano.
soothe ➤ *tr* calmar, tranquilizar; *(pain)* aliviar.
sophisticated ➤ *adj* sofisticado.
sophomore ➤ *s* estudiante *mf* de segundo año.
sore ➤ *adj* dolorido ▪ **s. throat** dolor de garganta • **to be s.** doler ➤ *s (wound)* llaga; *(pain)* dolor *m.*
sorority ➤ *s* asociación estudiantil femenina.
sorrow ➤ *s* pesar.
sorry ➤ *adj (sad)* triste ▪ **I'm s.** lo siento • **to be s.** sentir • **to feel s. for** compadecer ➤ *interj* ¡perdón!
sort ➤ *s (class)* clase *f,* tipo ▪ **s. of** *(rather)* más bien; *(somewhat)* algo • **out of sorts** de mal humor ➤ *tr* clasificar; *(to put in order)* ordenar ▪ **to s. out** *(problems)* resolver.
soul ➤ *s* alma.
sound[1] ➤ *s* sonido ▪ **from the s. of it** al parecer • **s. effects** efectos sonoros ➤ *intr* sonar; *(to seem)* parecer ➤ *tr (instrument)* tocar; *(alarm)* dar.
sound[2] ➤ *adj* en buenas condiciones; *(healthy)* sano; *(economy)* fuerte; *(sleep)* profundo; *(advice)* razonable; DER. válido ▪ **to be s. of mind** estar uno en su sano juicio.
sound[3] ➤ *s* MARÍT. brazo de mar.
soundproof ➤ *adj* a prueba de sonido.
soundtrack ➤ *s* pista *o* banda sonora.
soup ➤ *s* sopa ▪ **s. kitchen** comedor de beneficencia.
soupspoon ➤ *s* cuchara de sopa.
sour ➤ *adj* agrio; *(milk)* cortado; *(smell)* acre.
source ➤ *s* origen *m; (of river)* manantial *m; (of supply, news)* fuente *f.*
south ➤ *s* sur *m* ➤ *adj* del sur ➤ *adv* al sur, hacia el sur.
South America ➤ *s* Sudamérica.
South American ➤ *adj & s* sudamericano/a.
southeast ➤ *adj & s* (del) sudeste *m.*
southeastern ➤ *adj* del sudeste.
southern ➤ *adj* del sur.
southerner ➤ *s* sureño/a.
South Pole ➤ *s* Polo Sur.
southwest ➤ *adj & s* (del) suroeste *m.*
southwestern ➤ *adj* del suroeste.
souvenir ➤ *s* recuerdo.
sovereign ➤ *adj & s* soberano.
sow[1]◊ ➤ *tr* sembrar.
sow[2] ➤ *s (female hog)* cerda.
soy ➤ *s* soja ▪ **s. sauce** salsa de soja.
spa ➤ *s* balneario.
space ➤ *s* espacio; *(place)* sitio, lugar ▪ **outer s.** espacio exterior • **s. age** era espacial • **s. bar** espaciador ➤ *tr* espaciar ➤ *intr* ▪ **to s. out** JER. abstraerse.
spaceship ➤ *s* nave *f* espacial.
spacious ➤ *adj* espacioso, amplio.
spade[1] ➤ *s (digging tool)* pala.
spade[2] ➤ *s (in cards)* espada, pico.
spaghetti ➤ *s* espagueti *m.*
Spaniard ➤ *s* español/a.
Spanish ➤ *adj* español ➤ *s (language)* español *m,* castellano.
Spanish-speaking ➤ *adj* hispanohablante.
spank ➤ *tr* dar una zurra a, zurrar.
spare ➤ *tr (expenses, efforts)* escatimar; *(not to kill, destroy)* perdonar; *(to do without)* prescindir de; *(time)* dar, dedicar; *(feelings)* no herir ▪ **to s.** de sobra ➤ *adj (part)* de repuesto, de recambio; *(extra)* sobrante, de sobra; *(unoccupied)* libre ▪ **s. room** cuarto en desuso ➤ *s* pieza de repuesto.
spark ➤ *s* chispa ➤ *intr* chispear ➤ *tr* provocar.
sparkle ➤ *intr* centellear, brillar.
sparkplug ➤ *s* AUTO. bujía.
sparrow ➤ *s* gorrión *m.*
speak◊ ➤ *intr* hablar; *(in assembly)* tomar la palabra ▪ **to s. out** hablar claro • **to s. up** *(louder)* hablar más fuerte; *(to be heard)* decir lo que uno piensa ➤ *tr (a language)* hablar ▪ **to s. for** *(to recommend)* hablar en favor de; *(on behalf of)* hablar en nombre de • **to s. for itself** ser evidente • **to s. the truth** decir la verdad.
speaker ➤ *s (orator)* orador/a; *(loudspeaker)* altoparlante *m,* altavoz *m.*
spear ➤ *s* lanza.
special ➤ *adj* especial ▪ **s. delivery** entrega inmediata.
specialist ➤ *s* especialista *mf.*
speciality ➤ *s* especialidad *f.*
specialize ➤ *intr* especializarse.
specially ➤ *adv* especialmente.
specialty ➤ *s* especialidad *f.*
species ➤ *s* especie *f.*
specific ➤ *adj* específico.
specify ➤ *tr* especificar.
specimen ➤ *s* muestra, ejemplar *m.*
speck ➤ *s* mancha, mota.
spectacle ➤ *s* espectáculo.
spectacular ➤ *adj* espectacular.
spectator ➤ *s* espectador/a.
speech ➤ *s* habla; *(address)* discurso ▪ **free s.** libertad de expresión.
speed◊ ➤ *s* velocidad *f* ▪ **at full** *o* **top s.** a toda velocidad • **s. limit** velocidad máxima ➤ *intr* ir de prisa, ir corriendo; *(to drive fast)* conducir con exceso de velocidad ▪ **to s. up** acelerar.
speedboat ➤ *s* lancha motora.
speedometer ➤ *s* velocímetro.
spell[1] ➤ *tr* escribir ▪ **how do you s. . . . ?** ¿cómo se escribe . . . ? • **to s. out** deletrear; *(to explain)* explicar.
spell[2] ➤ *s* encanto, hechizo.
spell[3] ➤ *s (of time)* temporada; *(of work)* turno.
spelling ➤ *s* ortografía.
spend◊ ➤ *tr (money)* gastar; *(time)* pasar.
sphere ➤ *s* esfera.
spice ➤ *s* especia; FIG. sabor *m* ➤ *tr* sazonar; FIG. salpimentar.
spicy ➤ *adj* picante.
spider ➤ *s* araña.
spike ➤ *s (nail)* clavo, estaca; *(spine)* púa; *(sharp point)* punta.
spill◊ ➤ *tr & intr (liquid)* derramar(se), verter(se); *(a container)* volcar(se) ▪ **to s. over** salirse.
spin◊ ➤ *tr (thread)* hilar; *(web)* tejer; *(to twirl)* hacer girar, dar vueltas a ➤ *intr (to whirl)* girar, dar vueltas ➤ *s* giro, vuelta; *(in a car)* vuelta, paseo.
spinach ➤ *s* espinaca.
spine ➤ *s* ANAT. espina dorsal; BOT., ZOOL. espina, púa.
spiny ➤ *adj* espinoso.
spiral ➤ *s & intr* (moverse en) espiral *f.*
spirit ➤ *s* espíritu *m; (soul)* alma ▪ *pl* alcohol, licor • **in high** *o* **good s.** de buen humor.
spiritual ➤ *adj & s* espiritual *m.*
spit◊ ➤ *s* saliva; *(act)* escupitajo ➤ *tr & intr* escupir.
spite ➤ *s* rencor ▪ **in s. of** a pesar de, no obstante • **out of s.** por despecho ➤ *tr* despechar.
splash ➤ *tr (to spatter)* salpicar *(with* de); *(to wet)* chapotear ▪ **to s. about** chapotear • **to s. down** amerizar.
splendid ➤ *adj* espléndido.
splinter ➤ *s* astilla ➤ *tr & intr* astillar.
split◊ ➤ *tr (in two)* partir, dividir; *(to crack)* hender; *(to share)* compartir ▪ **to s. off** separar • **to s. up** *(to share)* repartir; *(to separate)* separar ➤ *intr (in two)* partirse; *(cloth)* desgarrarse ➤ *s (crack)* grieta.
spoil◊ ➤ *tr (to damage)* estropear; *(child)* mimar ➤ *intr* estropearse ➤ **spoils** *spl* botín *m.*
spoke ➤ *s (of a wheel)* radio.
spokesperson ➤ *s* portavoz *mf.*
sponge ➤ *s* esponja ➤ *tr* limpiar con esponja; *(money, food)* gorronear.
sponsor ➤ *s* patrocinador *m* ➤ *tr* patrocinar.
spontaneous ➤ *adj* espontáneo.
spool ➤ *s* carrete *m,* bobina.
spoon ➤ *s & tr* (sacar con) cuchara.
sport ➤ *s* deporte *m* ▪ **in s.** en broma • **s. shirt** camisa de sport • **to be a good s.** ser buen/a perdedor/a.
sports ➤ *adj* de sport ▪ **s. car** automóvil deportivo.
sportsman/woman ➤ *s* deportista *mf.*
spot ➤ *s* lugar *m; (stain)* mancha; *(dot)* lunar *m;* TELEV. anuncio ▪ **in a bad** *o* **tight s.** en apuros • **s. remover** quitamanchas • **to put on the s.** poner en un aprieto ➤ *tr* manchar; *(to detect)* notar.
spotless ➤ *adj* inmaculado.
spotlight ➤ *s* foco.
spouse ➤ *s* esposo/a.
spout ➤ *s (for pouring)* pico; *(tube)* caño; *(stream)* chorro ➤ *intr* chorrear.

sprain ➤ *s* torcedura ➤ *tr* torcer.
spray ➤ *s* rociada; MARÍT. espuma ■ **s. can** pulverizador ➤ *tr* rociar.
spread✧ ➤ *tr* extender; *(to move apart)* separar; *(butter)* untar ➤ *intr* esparcirse; *(knowledge)* difundirse; *(to move apart)* separarse ■ **to s. out** extenderse; *(to get wider)* ensancharse ➤ *s* difusión *f; (expanse)* extensión *f.*
spreadsheet ➤ *s* hoja de cálculo.
spring✧ ➤ *intr (to jump)* saltar ■ **to s. forth** brotar • **to s. up** surgir ➤ *s (jump)* salto; *(coil)* resorte *m; (season)* primavera; *(source)* fuente *f.*
springboard ➤ *s* trampolín *m.*
springtime ➤ *s* primavera.
sprinkle ➤ *tr* rociar ➤ *intr (rain)* lloviznar ➤ *s* llovizna.
sprinkler ➤ *s* regadera; *(fire extinguisher)* extintor *m.*
sprout ➤ *intr* brotar ➤ *s* brote *m.*
spur ➤ *s* espuela; FIG. incentivo ➤ *tr* espolear; FIG. estimular.
spurt ➤ *s* chorro ➤ *intr* salir a chorros.
spy ➤ *s* espía *mf* ➤ *intr* ■ **to s. (on)** espiar.
spying ➤ *s* espionaje *m.*
squander ➤ *tr* derrochar.
square ➤ *s* cuadrado; *(in town)* plaza ➤ *adj* cuadrado ■ **s. dance** baile de figuras • **s. deal** FAM. trato justo.
squash[1] ➤ *s* BOT. calabaza.
squash[2] ➤ *tr & intr* aplastar(se).
squat ➤ *intr* ponerse en cuclillas.
squeak ➤ *intr* chirriar ➤ *s* chirrido.
squeal ➤ *intr* chirriar ➤ *s* chillido.
squeeze ➤ *tr* apretar; *(lemon, juice)* exprimir ■ **to s. out** sacar; *(to exclude)* excluir ➤ *s* presión *f.*
squid ➤ *s* calamar *m.*
squint ➤ *intr* entrecerrar los ojos ➤ *s* mirada bizca.
squirrel ➤ *s* ardilla.
squirt ➤ *intr & tr* (dejar) salir a chorros ➤ *s* chorro.
stab ➤ *tr* apuñalar ➤ *s* puñalada; *(wound)* herida; FIG. *(attempt)* intento.
stability ➤ *s* estabilidad *f.*
stable[1] ➤ *adj* estable.
stable[2] ➤ *s (building)* establo.
stack ➤ *s (pile)* pila; FAM. montón *m* ■ *pl* estantes ➤ *tr* amontonar.
stadium ➤ *s* estadio.
staff ➤ *s (personnel)* personal *m; (stick)* báculo, bastón *m.*
stag ➤ *s* ciervo.
stage ➤ *s* plataforma; *(phase)* etapa; TEAT. escena ■ **by stages** progresivamente ➤ *tr* TEAT. representar; *(to arrange)* organizar.
stagger ➤ *intr* tambalearse ➤ *tr (to overwhelm)* asombrar; *(to alternate)* escalonar.
stain ➤ *tr* manchar ➤ *s* mancha.
stainless ➤ *adj* inoxidable.
stair ➤ *s* escalón *m* ■ *pl* escalera.
staircase ➤ *s* escalera.
stake ➤ *s (stick)* estaca; *(interest)* intereses *m* ■ **at s.** en juego ■ *pl (bet)* apuesta ➤ *tr* estacar; *(to risk)* jugarse.
stale ➤ *adj (food)* rancio; *(bread)* duro; *(news)* viejo.
stalk[1] ➤ *s (plant stem)* tallo.
stalk[2] ➤ *tr (to pursue)* acechar.
stall ➤ *s (in barn)* pesebre *m; (booth)* caseta ➤ *intr (to delay)* andar con rodeos; AUTO. calarse.
stammer ➤ *intr* tartamudear ➤ *s* tartamudez *f,* tartamudeo.
stamp ➤ *tr (to affix stamp)* poner un sello a ■ **to s. on** pisar • **to s. out** sofocar ➤ *intr* patear ➤ *s* sello; *(postage)* sello, estampilla; *(official)* timbre *m.*
stand✧ ➤ *intr* estar de pie; *(to rise)* ponerse de pie; *(to place oneself)* ponerse ■ **to s. alone** ser el único • **to s. aside** retirarse • **to s. by** estar listo; *(to look on)* mirar y no hacer nada • **to s. in** *o* **on line** hacer cola • **to s. out** resaltar • **to s. up** levantarse ➤ *tr (to withstand)* tolerar ■ **to s. for** representar • **to s. up to** hacer frente a; *(to last)* resistir ➤ *s (booth)* quiosco; *(counter)* mostrador *m; (pedestal)* pie *m; (for coats, hats)* perchero ■ **to take a s.** adoptar una actitud.
standard ➤ *s* criterio; *(model)* patrón *m* ■ **s. of living** nivel de vida ■ *pl* normas ➤ *adj* standard; *(accepted)* normal ■ **s. time** hora civil.
standby ➤ *s* persona *o* cosa de confianza ■ **s. list** lista de espera.
standing ➤ *s* reputación *f* ➤ *adj* de pie, parado.
standoff ➤ *s* empate *m.*
standpoint ➤ *s* punto de vista.
standstill ➤ *s* parada.
staple ➤ *s (fastener)* grapa ➤ *tr* sujetar con una grapa.
stapler ➤ *s* grapador *m.*
star ➤ *s* estrella ■ **shooting s.** estrella fugaz ■ *pl* ASTROL. astros ➤ *tr (to feature)* presentar como protagonista ➤ *intr* protagonizar.
starboard ➤ *s & adj* (de) estribor *m.*
starch ➤ *s* CUL. fécula; *(stiffener)* almidón *m* ➤ *tr* almidonar.
stare ➤ *intr* mirar fijamente ➤ *s* mirada fija.
start ➤ *intr* empezar; *(to set out)* salir; *(motor)* arrancar ■ **to s. with** para comenzar ➤ *tr* empezar; *(car, machine)* poner en marcha ➤ *s (beginning)* principio; *(place)* salida, punto de partida ■ **to make a fresh s.** empezar de nuevo.
startle ➤ *tr & intr* sobresaltar(se) ➤ *s* sobresalto.
starvation ➤ *s* hambre *f.*
starve ➤ *intr* morirse de hambre ➤ *tr* matar de hambre.
starving ➤ *adj* hambriento.
state ➤ *s* estado ■ **the States** los Estados Unidos ➤ *tr* declarar.
statement ➤ *s* declaración *f;* COM. *(bill)* cuenta; *(report)* estado de cuenta.
statesman/woman ➤ *s* estadista *mf.*
station ➤ *s* estación *f; (social)* rango ■ **police s.** comisaría • **service s.** estación de servicio ➤ *tr* estacionar; *(to post)* apostar.
stationary ➤ *adj* estacionario; *(fixed)* fijo.
stationery ➤ *s* papel y sobres *m.*
statistic ➤ *s* estadística ■ *pl (science)* estadística.
statistical ➤ *adj* estadístico.
statue ➤ *s* estatua.
stature ➤ *s* estatura.
status ➤ *s* posición *f* social; DER. estado.
statute ➤ *s* estatuto.
stay ➤ *intr* quedarse; *(to sojourn)* alojarse ■ **to s. away** ausentarse • **to s. in** quedarse en casa • **to s. up late** acostarse tarde ➤ *s (visit)* estancia; DER. aplazamiento.
steady ➤ *adj* firme; *(stable)* estable; *(reliable)* seguro ➤ *tr & intr* estabilizar(se).
steak ➤ *s* bistec *m; (fish)* filete *m.*
steal✧ ➤ *tr & intr* robar ■ **to s. away** escabullirse ➤ *s* JER. *(bargain)* ganga.
steam ➤ *s* vapor *m* ■ **s. engine** máquina a vapor ➤ *intr* echar vapor; *(to fog up)* empañarse ➤ *tr* CUL. cocer al vapor.
steamer ➤ *(ship)* vapor *m;* CUL. olla de vapor.
steamroller ➤ *s* apisonadora.
steel ➤ *s & adj* (de) acero.
steep ➤ *adj (high)* empinado; *(price)* excesivo.
steeple ➤ *s* torrecilla; *(spire)* aguja.
steer ➤ *tr (boat)* gobernar; *(car)* conducir; FIG. dirigir, guiar ■ **steering wheel** volante • **to s. clear of** evitar.
stem ➤ *s* BOT. tallo.
step ➤ *s* paso; *(sound)* pisada; *(stair, degree)* escalón *m* ■ **s. by s.** paso a paso ■ *pl* escaleras ➤ *intr* ■ **to s. aside** hacerse a un lado • **to s. down** bajar; *(to resign)* renunciar • **to s. in** entrar; *(to intervene)* intervenir • **to s. on** pisar • **to s. out** salir; *(of car)* apearse • **to s. up** subir; *(to increase)* aumentar.
stepbrother ➤ *s* hermanastro.
stepchild ➤ *s* hijastro/a.
stepfather ➤ *s* padrastro.
stepladder ➤ *s* escalera de tijera.
stepmother ➤ *s* madrastra.
stepsister ➤ *s* hermanastra.
stereo ➤ *adj & s* estéreo.
stereotype ➤ *s* estereotipo ➤ *tr* estereotipar.
sterile ➤ *adj* estéril.
sterilize ➤ *tr* esterilizar.
stern[1] ➤ *adj* severo.
stern[2] ➤ *s* MARÍT. popa.
stew ➤ *tr* guisar ➤ *intr* cocerse ➤ *s* guiso ■ **in a s.** agitado.
steward ➤ *s* administrador *m; (domestic)* mayordomo; AVIA. auxiliar *m* de vuelo, aeromozo.
stewardess ➤ *s* azafata, aeromoza.
stick✧ ➤ *s* vara, palo; *(of gum)* barra ■ **s. shift** AUTO. cambio manual ➤ *tr (to impale)* clavar; *(to glue)* pegar ■ **to s. in** introducir • **to s. out** *(tongue)* mostrar; *(head)* asomar ➤ *intr (to cling)* pegarse; *(to jam)* atascarse ■ **to s. around** quedarse • **to s. out** sobresalir • **to s. to** *(promise)* cumplir; *(friend)* ser fiel a; *(facts)* ceñirse a.
stickup ➤ *s* JER. atraco.
sticky ➤ *adj* pegajoso.
stiff ➤ *adj* rígido; *(not limber)* tieso; *(formal)* formal.
stifle ➤ *tr & intr* sofocar(se).
still ➤ *adj (at rest)* inmóvil; *(tranquil)* sosegado; *(waters)* mansa ■ **s. life** naturaleza muerta ➤ *s* foto fija ➤ *adv* quieto; *(nevertheless)* sin embargo ■ **he's s. awake** todavía está despierto • **s. more** aun más.
stillness ➤ *s* quietud *f; (silence)* silencio.
stimulate ➤ *tr* estimular.
sting✧ ➤ *tr & intr* picar ➤ *s* picadura.
stinger ➤ *s* aguijón *m.*
stink✧ ➤ *intr* heder, apestar ➤ *s* hedor *m* ■ **to make** *o* **raise a s.** armar un escándulo.
stipulate ➤ *tr* estipular.
stir ➤ *tr (to mix)* revolver; *(to move)* agitar ■ **to s. up** *(memory)* despertar; *(trouble)* provocar ➤ *intr* moverse.
stirrup ➤ *s* estribo.
stitch ➤ *s* COST. puntada; *(decorative)* punto; MED. punzada.
stock ➤ *s (inventory)* stock *m; (supply)* surtido; *(livestock)* ganado; *(shares)* acciones *f* ■ **in s.** en existencia • **out of s.** agotado • **to take s. of** evaluar ➤ *tr* ■ **to s. up on** abastecerse de ➤ *adj* ■ **s. exchange** *o* **market** bolsa.
stockbroker ➤ *s* corredor/a *m* de bolsa.
stockholder ➤ *s* accionista *mf.*
stocking ➤ *s* media.
stomach ➤ *s* estómago.
stomachache ➤ *s* dolor *m* de estómago.
stone ➤ *s* piedra ➤ *tr* apedrear.
stoned ➤ *adj (drunk)* borracho; *(on drugs)* drogado.
stool ➤ *s* taburete *m.*
stoop ➤ *intr* encorvarse; FIG. condescender.
stop ➤ *tr (to halt)* detener; *(to cease)* dejar de ■ **to s. up** taponar ➤ *intr* detenerse; *(to cease)* cesar ■ **to s. by** *o* **in** hacer una visita corta ➤ *s (place)* parada; *(en route)* escala ■ **s. sign** señal de alto • **to come to a s.** pararse • **to put a s. to** poner fin a.
stoplight ➤ *s* semáforo.
stopover ➤ *s* AVIA., MARÍT. escala.
stopwatch ➤ *s* cronómetro.
storage ➤ *s* almacenamiento.
store ➤ *s* tienda; *(supply)* surtido ■ **department s.** gran almacén ■ *pl* provisiones ➤ *tr* almacenar ■ **to s. up** acumular.
storeroom ➤ *s* despensa, bodega.
stork ➤ *s* cigüeña.
storm ➤ *s* tormenta ➤ *intr* haber tormenta ■ **to s. in, out** entrar, salir violentamente ➤ *tr* asaltar, tomar por asalto.
stormy ➤ *adj* tempestuoso.
story[1] ➤ *s* cuento, relato; *(plot)* trama; *(article)* artículo; *(lie)* mentira.
story[2] ➤ *s (of a building)* piso.
stout ➤ *adj (body)* fornido, corpulento; *(sturdy)* fuerte.
stove ➤ *s* cocina; *(heater)* estufa.
straight ➤ *adj (line)* recto; *(upright, not bent)* derecho; *(honest)* honrado; *(not gay)* heterosexual ➤ *adv* en línea recta; *(without delay)* directamente ■ **s. ahead** en frente; *(forward)* todo seguido • **for three days s.** durante tres días seguidos.
straighten ➤ *tr & intr* enderezar(se) ■ **to s. out** ordenar.
straightforward ➤ *adj (direct)* directo; *(honest)* sincero.
strain ➤ *tr (nerves)* agotar; *(limb)* torcer; *(to sieve)* colar ■ **to s. one's eyes** cansar la vista ➤ *s (effort)* esfuerzo; *(stress)* tensión *f.*
strainer ➤ *s* filtro; CUL. colador *m.*
strait(s) ➤ *s(pl)* GEOG. estrecho(s).
straitjacket ➤ *s* camisa de fuerza.
strange ➤ *adj* desconocido; *(odd)* extraño, raro.
stranger ➤ *s* desconocido/a; *(foreigner)* extranjero/a.
strangle ➤ *tr* estrangular.
strap ➤ *s (strip)* tira, correa; *(band)* banda; *(of a dress)* tirante *m.*
strategic ➤ *adj* estratégico.
strategy ➤ *s* estrategia.
straw ➤ *s* paja; *(for drinking)* pajita.
strawberry ➤ *s* fresa.
stray ➤ *intr* errar ➤ *adj (pet)* extraviado; *(bullet)* perdido.
streak ➤ *s* raya; *(of lightning)* rayo; *(of luck)* racha ➤ *tr* rayar.
stream ➤ *s* arroyo ➤ *intr* correr ■ **to s. in, out** entrar, salir en tropel.
street ➤ *s* calle *f.*
streetcar ➤ *s* tranvía *m.*
strength ➤ *s* fuerza; *(of material)* resistencia; *(intensity)* intensidad *f.*
strengthen ➤ *tr* reforzar ➤ *intr* fortalecerse, intensificarse.
stress ➤ *s (emphasis)* hincapié *m; (tension)* tensión *f;* MED. estrés *m,* fatiga nerviosa; GRAM. énfasis *m.*
stretch ➤ *tr* estirar; *(to extend)* extender; *(wire)* tender ➤ *intr* estirarse; *(shoes)* ensancharse ■ **to s. out** estirarse; *(to lie down)* tumbarse.
stretcher ➤ *s* camilla.
strew✧ ➤ *tr* esparcir.
strict ➤ *adj* estricto.
strictly ➤ *adv* estrictamente ■ **s. speaking** en realidad.
stride✧ ➤ *intr* caminar a grandes pasos ➤ *s* zancada.
strident ➤ *adj* estridente.
strike✧ ➤ *tr* golpear; *(a blow)* asestar; *(to crash into)* chocar con ■ **to s. down** derribar • **to s. up** *(friendship)* trabar; *(conversation)* entablar • **to s. upon** ocurrírsele a uno ➤ *intr* dar golpes; *(to attack)* atacar; *(bell)* sonar; *(to stop work)* declararse en huelga • **to s. out (for)** ponerse en marcha (hacia) ➤ *s (act)* golpe *m; (attack)* ataque *m; (labor)* huelga.
striker ➤ *s* huelguista *mf.*
striking ➤ *adj* notable.
string✧ ➤ *s* cuerda; *(series)* serie *f* ➤ *tr (to thread)* ensartar.
strip[1] ➤ *tr* desnudar; *(bed)* deshacer ■ **to s. off** quitar ➤ *intr* desvestirse.
strip[2] ➤ *s* faja; AER. pista de aterrizaje.
stripe ➤ *s* raya.
striped ➤ *adj* a rayas, rayado.
strive✧ ➤ *intr* esforzarse.
stroke ➤ *s* golpe *m; (in swimming)* brazada; *(with brush)* pincelada; MED. apoplejía ■ **s. of luck** suerte ➤ *tr* acariciar.
stroll ➤ *intr* pasearse ➤ *s* paseo.
stroller ➤ *s* cochecito de niño.
strong ➤ *adj* fuerte.
structure ➤ *s* estructura.
struggle ➤ *intr* luchar ➤ *s* lucha; *(effort)* esfuerzo.
strut ➤ *intr* pavonearse.
stub ➤ *s* tocón *m; (check)* talón *m* ➤ *tr (toe)* tropezar con.
stubborn ➤ *adj* testarudo; *(stain)* duro.
stubbornness ➤ *s* testarudez *f.*
student ➤ *s* estudiante *mf.*
studio ➤ *s* estudio; *(of artist)* taller *m.*
study ➤ *s* estudio ➤ *tr & intr* estudiar.
stuff ➤ *s* material *m; (belongings)* cosas ■ **the same old s.** lo mismo de siempre ➤ *tr* rellenar ■ **to s. oneself** atiborrarse.
stuffing ➤ *s* relleno.
stuffy ➤ *adj* sofocante, mal ventilado; *(congested)* tupido; FAM. pomposo.
stumble ➤ *intr* tropezar ■ **to s. across** *o* **upon** tropezar con.
stump ➤ *s (of tree)* tocón *m; (limb)* muñon *m* ➤ *tr* dejar perplejo.
stun ➤ *tr* aturdir.
stunning ➤ *adj (looks)* imponente.
stunt ➤ *s (feat)* proeza ■ **publicity s.** truco publicitario.
stupefy ➤ *tr* atontar.
stupid ➤ *adj* estúpido, tonto.
stupidity ➤ *s* estupidez *f,* tontería.
sturdy ➤ *adj* robusto; *(shoes)* fuerte.
stutter ➤ *intr* tartamudear ➤ *s* tartamudeo.
sty ➤ *s (for swine)* pocilga.
style ➤ *s* estilo; *(type)* modelo, tipo ■ **in s.** *(in vogue)* de moda.
stylish ➤ *adj* a la moda.
subconscious ➤ *s* subconsciente *m.*
subdue ➤ *tr* sojuzgar, dominar.
subject ➤ *adj (to a ruler)* sometido ■ **s. to** sujeto a ➤ *s (topic)* tema *m;* GRAM. sujeto; *(of country)* súbdito/a; *(course)* asignatura ➤ *tr* someter ■ **to s. to** exponer a.
subjugate ➤ *tr* subyugar.
sublime ➤ *adj* sublime.
submarine ➤ *adj & s* submarino.

submerge ➤ tr & intr sumergir(se).
submit ➤ tr someter; (evidence, plan) presentar ➤ intr someterse.
subordinate ➤ adj & s subordinado/a ➤ tr subordinar.
subscribe ➤ intr suscribirse, abonarse (to a).
subscriber ➤ s suscriptor/a.
subscription ➤ s suscripción f, abono.
subside ➤ intr apaciguarse.
subsidy ➤ s subvención f.
subsist ➤ intr subsistir.
substance ➤ s sustancia.
substantial ➤ adj sustancial; (meal) sustancioso; (considerable) considerable; (well-to-do) adinerado.
substitute ➤ s sustituto/a ➤ tr & intr substituir.
subtitle ➤ s subtítulo ➤ tr subtitular.
subtle ➤ adj sutil.
subtract ➤ tr sustraer, restar.
subtraction ➤ s sustracción f, resta.
suburb ➤ s suburbio ■ pl afueras.
suburban ➤ adj suburbano.
subversive ➤ adj subversivo.
subway ➤ s subterráneo, metro.
succeed ➤ intr tener éxito; (to turn out well) salir bien; (to follow) suceder.
success ➤ s éxito.
successful ➤ adj de éxito, exitoso.
succession ➤ s sucesión f ■ in s. seguido.
successive ➤ adj sucesivo.
successor ➤ s sucesor/a.
such ➤ adj (of this nature) tal, semejante; (so much) tanto ■ s. and s. tal y cual • s. as (tal) como • s. as it is tal cual es ➤ adv tan ➤ pron ■ and s. y cosas por el estilo • as s. en sí • s. is life así es la vida.
suck ➤ tr chupar ➤ intr dar chupadas ➤ s chupada.
sudden ➤ adj (unforeseen) imprevisto; (abrupt) brusco; (swift) súbito, repentino ■ all of a s. de repente.
suddenly ➤ adv de repente.
suds ➤ s espuma.
sue ➤ tr DER. demandar ➤ intr entablar acción judicial.
suede o **suède** ➤ s gamuza, ante m.
suffer ➤ tr & intr sufrir ■ to s. from adolecer de.
sufficient ➤ adj bastante, suficiente.
sufficiently ➤ adv bastante.
suffix ➤ s sufijo.
suffocate ➤ tr & intr sofocarse.
suffrage ➤ s sufragio.
sugar ➤ s azúcar mf ➤ tr azucarar.
suggest ➤ tr sugerir; (to imply) insinuar.
suggestion ➤ s sugerencia.
suicide ➤ s suicidio; (person) suicida mf ■ to commit s. suicidarse.
suit ➤ s traje m; (set) conjunto; (cards) palo ➤ tr satisfacer; (to look good) quedar bien ■ to s. oneself hacer lo que uno quiere.
suitable ➤ adj conveniente; (compatible) compatible.
suitcase ➤ s maleta.
suite ➤ s (apartment) suite f; (furniture) juego; MÚS. suite.
suitor ➤ s (wooer) pretendiente m; DER. peticionario/a.
sulfur ➤ s azufre m.
sulk ➤ intr estar de malhumor.
sullen ➤ adj resentido.
sum ➤ s suma; (of money) cantidad f ➤ tr ■ to s. up sumar, resumir.
summarize ➤ tr resumir.
summary ➤ adj sumario; (fast) rápido ➤ s resumen m.
summer ➤ s verano ➤ intr veranear (at, in en).
summit ➤ s GEOG., POL. cumbre f.
summon ➤ tr convocar; (person) llamar; DER. citar.
summons ➤ s DER. citación f judicial.
sun ➤ s sol m ➤ intr asolearse.
sunbathe ➤ intr tomar el sol.
sunburn ➤ quemadura de sol.
Sunday ➤ s domingo.
sundown ➤ s ocaso.
sunflower ➤ s girasol m.
sunglasses ➤ spl lentes o gafas de sol.
sunlight ➤ s luz f del sol.
sunny ➤ adj soleado.
sunrise ➤ s amanecer m.
sunset ➤ s ocaso.
sunshine ➤ s luz f del sol.
sunstroke ➤ s insolación f.
suntan ➤ s bronceado.
super ➤ adj FAM. estupendo.
superb ➤ adj soberbio.
superficial ➤ adj superficial.
superfluous ➤ adj superfluo.
superintendent ➤ s superintendente mf.
superior ➤ adj & s superior m.
supermarket ➤ s supermercado.
supernatural ➤ adj sobrenatural.
superstition ➤ s superstición f.
superstitious ➤ adj supersticioso.
supervise ➤ tr supervisar.
supervisor ➤ s supervisor/a.
supper ➤ s cena ■ to have s. cenar.
supplement ➤ s suplemento ➤ tr suplir.
supplementary ➤ adj suplementario.
supplier ➤ s suministrador/a.
supply ➤ tr suministrar; (to satisfy) satisfacer ➤ s suministro; (stock) surtido ■ in short s. escaso ■ pl provisiones.
support ➤ tr sostener; (to bear) soportar; (a child) mantener; (with money) ayudar ■ to s. oneself ganarse la vida ➤ s apoyo; ARQ., TEC. soporte m.
supporter ➤ s TEC. soporte m; (advocate) partidario/a; (fan) hincha mf.
supportive ➤ adj sustentador.
suppose ➤ tr suponer; (to believe) creer ➤ intr imaginarse.
supposed ➤ adj supuesto.
suppository ➤ s supositorio.
suppress ➤ tr suprimir; (to prohibit) prohibir; (to repress) reprimir; (laughter) contener.
suppurate ➤ intr supurar.
supremacy ➤ s supremacía.
supreme ➤ adj supremo ■ s. court corte supremo.
surcharge ➤ s sobrecarga, recargo ➤ tr sobrecargar, recargar.
sure ➤ adj seguro; (infallible) certero; (hand) firme ■ to make s. segurarse ➤ adv seguramente; (of course) claro.
surety ➤ s seguridad f; (pledge) garantía; (person) garante mf.
surf ➤ s oleaje m ➤ intr hacer surfing ➤ tr COMPUT. navegar por (Internet).
surface ➤ s superficie f ➤ adj superficial ➤ intr salir a la superficie.
surfboard ➤ s tabla de surf.
surfing ➤ s surfing m.
surge ➤ intr (energy, enthusiasm) subir súbitamente ➤ s (onrush) arranque m; ELEC. sobretensión f.
surgeon ➤ s cirujano/a.
surgery ➤ s intervención quirúrgica; (room) quirófano; (work) cirugía.
surgical ➤ adj quirúrgico.
surname ➤ s apellido.
surpass ➤ tr sobrepasar.
surplus ➤ adj & s excedente m.
surprise ➤ tr sorprender ■ to be surprised at sorprenderse de o con ➤ s sorpresa.
surprising ➤ adj sorprendente.
surrender ➤ tr entregar; (hope) abandonar ➤ intr rendirse ➤ s rendición f.
surround ➤ tr rodear.
surroundings ➤ spl alrededores m.
survey ➤ tr inspeccionar; (land) medir ➤ intr hacer una encuesta ➤ s inspección f; (poll) encuesta; (of land) medición f.
surveyor ➤ s agrimensor/a.
survive ➤ tr & intr sobrevivir.
survivor ➤ s sobreviviente mf.
suspect ➤ tr sospechar ➤ s & adj sospechoso/a.
suspend ➤ tr & intr suspender.
suspenders ➤ spl tirantes m.
suspense ➤ s (doubt) incertidumbre f; CINEM., LIT. suspense, suspenso.
suspension ➤ s suspensión f.
suspicion ➤ s sospecha.
suspicious ➤ adj sospechoso.
sustain ➤ tr sostener.
swallow[1] ➤ tr & intr tragar.
swallow[2] ➤ s ORNIT. golondrina.
swamp ➤ s pantano ➤ tr inundar.
swan ➤ s cisne m.
swarm ➤ s enjambre ➤ intr pulular, hormiguear; (bees) enjambrar.
swat ➤ tr aplastar.
sway ➤ tr influir en, persuadir ➤ intr balancearse ➤ s influencia, dominio.
swear✧ ➤ tr & intr jurar ■ to s. at maldecir.
sweat✧ ➤ intr sudar ➤ s sudor m.
sweater ➤ s suéter m.
sweatshirt ➤ s sudadera.
sweep✧ ➤ tr & intr barrer ➤ s ■ to make a clean s. hacer tabla rasa.
sweepstakes ➤ s lotería.
sweet ➤ adj dulce ■ s. pepper pimiento morrón • s. potato batata ➤ s dulce m.
sweeten ➤ tr & intr endulzar(se).
sweetheart ➤ s enamorado/a.
swell✧ ➤ tr & intr hinchar(se); (to increase) aumentar.
swelling ➤ s MED. hinchazón f.
swerve ➤ tr & intr desviar(se) ➤ s desviación f.
swift ➤ adj veloz ➤ s ORNIT. vencejo.
swim✧ ➤ intr nadar ■ swimming pool piscina ➤ s ■ to go for o take a s. ir a nadar.
swimsuit ➤ s traje m de baño.
swindle ➤ tr timar ➤ s timo.
swine ➤ s cerdo(s).
swing✧ ➤ intr oscilar; (on a swing) columpiarse ➤ tr hacer oscilar; (on a swing) columpiar ➤ s (for children) columpio; MÚS. ritmo.
switch ➤ s ELEC. interruptor m ➤ tr (to shift) cambiar de; (to exchange) intercambiar; F.C. desviar ■ to s. off desconectar; (lights) apagar • to s. on conectar; (lights) encender ➤ intr cambiar.
sword ➤ s espada.
syllable ➤ s sílaba.
syllabus ➤ s programa m de estudios.
symbol ➤ s símbolo.
symbolic(al) ➤ adj simbólico.
symbolism ➤ s simbolismo.
symmetric(al) ➤ adj simétrico.
symmetry ➤ s simetría.
sympathetic ➤ adj compasivo.
sympathize ➤ intr compadecerse; (to understand) comprender.
sympathy ➤ s simpatía; (understanding) comprensión f; (condolence) pésame m.
symphony ➤ s MÚS. sinfonía.
symptom ➤ s MED. síntoma m.
synagogue ➤ s sinagoga.
synchronize ➤ tr sincronizar.
syndicate ➤ s sindicato.
syndrome ➤ s síndrome m.
synonym ➤ s sinónimo.
synthesis ➤ s síntesis f.
synthetic ➤ adj & s (material) sintético.
syringe ➤ s jeringa.
syrup ➤ s almíbar m.
system ➤ s sistema m; (human body) organismo; ANAT. aparato.
systematic ➤ adj sistemático.

T

tab ➤ s lengüeta; (bill) cuenta.
table ➤ s mesa; (data) tabla.
tablecloth ➤ s mantel m.
tablespoon ➤ s cuchara de sopa; (quantity) cucharada.
tablet ➤ s tableta, tablilla.
taboo ➤ s & adj tabú m.
tack ➤ s tachuela ➤ tr ■ to t. on añadir.
tackle ➤ s (gear) equipo, avíos m; MARÍT. aparejo ➤ tr atacar, abordar.
tacky ➤ adj FAM. cursi, vulgar.
tact ➤ s tacto.
tactful ➤ adj discreto.
tactic ➤ s táctica ■ tactics ssg táctica.
tag ➤ s (label) etiqueta ➤ intr ■ to t. along seguir, acompañar.
tail ➤ s cola ■ t. pipe tubo de escape ■ pl (coin) cruz, reversa.
tailor ➤ s sastre m.
tailored ➤ adj hecho a medida.
taint ➤ tr & intr manchar(se) ➤ s mácula, defecto.
take✧ ➤ tr tomar; (to a place) llevar; (to withstand) soportar; (advice) seguir; (photo) sacar ■ to t. along llevarse • to t. apart (to disassemble) desarmar • to t. away (to remove) quitar, sacar; (to subtract) restar; (to carry away) llevarse • to t. back (to return) devolver; (a statement) retractar • to t. in (to understand) comprender; (to include) incluir; (to deceive) engañar • to t. it out on desahogarse con • to t. off quitar; (clothes, hat) quitarse; (time) tomarse; (to deduct) rebajar • to t. out poner afuera; (to remove) sacar; (stain, spot) quitar • to t. up with asociarse con ➤ intr ■ to t. off (to leave) irse; (aircraft) despegar • to t. over asumir la autoridad ➤ s (receipts) ingresos; (in hunting) presa; (in fishing) pesca; CINEM. toma.
takeover ➤ s toma de poder.
talc o **talcum** ➤ s talco.
tale ➤ s cuento; (lie) mentira.
talent ➤ s talento.
talented ➤ adj talentoso.
talk ➤ tr hablar ■ to t. into persuadir a • to t. nonsense decir tonterías • to t. out of disuadir a ➤ intr hablar; (to chat) charlar • to t. back replicar ➤ s conversación f; (speech) discurso; (rumor) rumor m ■ pl negociaciones.
talkative ➤ adj hablador, locuaz.
tall ➤ adj alto ■ how t. are you? ¿cuánto mides? • six feet t. seis pies de alto.
tambourine ➤ s pandereta.
tame ➤ adj domesticado; (gentle) manso; (docile) dócil ➤ tr domesticar.
tamper ➤ intr ■ to t. with interferir en.
tampon ➤ s tapón m, tampón m.
tan ➤ tr broncear ➤ intr broncearse, tostarse ➤ adj bronceado.
tangerine ➤ s mandarina.
tangled ➤ adj enredado, embrollado.
tank ➤ s tanque m.
tanker ➤ s (ship) buque m tanque; (truck) camión m tanque.
tantalize ➤ tr tentar.
tap[1] ➤ tr golpear ligeramente; (foot, finger) dar golpecitos con ➤ intr dar golpes ligeros; (fingers) tamborilear; (feet) zapatear ➤ s golpe ligero ■ t. dance zapateo americano.
tap[2] ➤ s (faucet) grifo ■ on t. de barril.
tape ➤ s cinta; (recording) grabación f (en cinta magnética) ■ measuring t. cinta métrica • t. player, t. recorder grabadora ➤ tr (to stick) pegar con cinta adhesiva; (to record) grabar.
taper ➤ intr ■ to t. off disminuir.
tapestry ➤ s tapiz m.
tar ➤ s alquitrán m.
tardy ➤ adj tardío ■ to be t. llegar tarde.
target ➤ s blanco; (goal) meta.
tariff ➤ s tarifa.
tarpaulin o **tarp** ➤ s alquitranado.
tarragon ➤ s estragón m.
tart ➤ s pastelillo.
task ➤ s tarea ■ t. bar COMPUT. barra de tareas • t. force fuerza operante.
taste ➤ tr probar; (to sample) catar ➤ intr (food) tener sabor ■ to t. like sabor a ➤ s gusto.
tasteful ➤ adj de buen gusto.
tasty ➤ adj sabroso.
tattered ➤ adj andrajoso.
tattoo ➤ s tatuaje m ➤ tr tatuar.
tavern ➤ s taverna.
tax ➤ s impuesto ➤ tr gravar.
taxable ➤ adj gravable.
tax-free ➤ libre de impuestos.
taxi o **taxicab** ➤ s taxi m.
taxpayer ➤ s contribuyente mf.
tea ➤ s té m.
teach✧ ➤ tr enseñar; (students) dar clases a; (a subject) dar clases de ➤ intr ser maestro/a.
teacher ➤ s maestro/a, profesor/a.
teaching ➤ s enseñanza.
teacup ➤ s taza (de té).
team ➤ s equipo ➤ intr ■ to t. up with unir fuerzas con.
teammate ➤ s compañero/a de equipo.
teapot ➤ s tetera.
tear[1]✧ ➤ tr desgarrar, rasgar ■ to t. down demoler • to t. off o out arrancar • to t. down (to demolish) demoler • to t. in o to pieces despedazar • to t. up hacer pedazos ➤ intr desgarrarse, rasgarse ➤ s desgarradura, rasgadura.
tear[2] ➤ s lágrima ■ pl lágrimas, llanto • in t. llorando.
tease ➤ tr (to annoy) fastidiar; (to make fun of) tomar el pelo a.
teaspoon ➤ s cucharita de té; (quantity) cucharadita.
technical ➤ adj técnico.
technician ➤ s técnico/a.
technique ➤ s técnica.
technology ➤ s tecnología.
teddy bear ➤ s osito de juguete.
tedious ➤ adj tedio.
teen o **teenager** ➤ s joven mf, adolescente mf.
telecast ➤ tr & intr televisar ➤ s transmisión f de televisión.
telecommunications ➤ spl telecomunicaciones f.
telegram ➤ s telegrama m.
telegraph ➤ s telégrafo ➤ tr telegrafiar.
telephone ➤ s teléfono ➤ tr telefonear ➤ intr comunicarse por teléfono.
telephoto ➤ adj telefotográfico.
telescope ➤ s telescopio.
televise ➤ tr & intr televisar.
television ➤ s televisión f; (set) televisor m ■ t. screen pantalla (del televisor).
tell✧ ➤ tr decir; (story) contar; (news) comunicar; (future) adivinar ■ all told

en total • **to t. apart** distinguir.
teller ➤ *s* cajero/a.
temper ➤ *s* temperamento ▪ **to keep, lose one's t.** dominarse, enfadarse.
temperament ➤ *s* temperamento.
temperature ➤ *s* temperatura.
tempest ➤ *s* tempestad *f.*
temple[1] ➤ *s* templo; *(synagogue)* sinagoga.
temple[2] ➤ *s* ANAT. sien *f.*
temporary ➤ *adj* transitorio; *(worker)* temporero, temporario; *(position)* interino ➤ *s* temporero/a.
tempt ➤ *tr* tentar.
temptation ➤ *s* tentación *f.*
tempting ➤ *adj* tentador.
ten ➤ *s & adj* diez *m* ▪ **t. o'clock** las diez.
tenant ➤ *s* inquilino/a.
tend[1] ➤ *intr (to head)* dirigirse; *(to be likely)* tender; *(to be inclined)* propender a.
tend[2] ➤ *tr (to care for)* cuidar, atender.
tendency ➤ *s* tendencia.
tender ➤ *adj (soft)* tierno; *(delicate)* delicado; *(affectionate)* cariñoso.
tenderloin ➤ *s* lomo, filete *m.*
tenderness ➤ *s* ternura.
tennis ➤ *s* tenis *m.*
tense[1] ➤ *adj (strained)* tenso.
tense[2] ➤ *s* GRAM. tiempo.
tension ➤ *s* tensión *f.*
tent ➤ *s* tienda.
tentative ➤ *adj* experimental; *(provisional)* provisorio; *(unsure)* indeciso.
tenth ➤ *s & adj* décimo.
tepid ➤ *adj* tibio.
term ➤ *s (time period)* período, plazo; *(school year)* período académico; *(deadline)* término, fin *m* ▪ **in no uncertain terms** muy claramente • **in terms of** en cuanto a • **in the long t.** a la larga ▪ *pl* condiciones ▪ **to be on good t.** tener buenas relaciones.
terminal ➤ *adj* fatal; *(final)* final ➤ *s (bus, train)* terminal *f;* COMPUT., ELEC. terminal *m.*
terminate ➤ *tr & intr* terminar.
terrace ➤ *s* terraza; *(balcony)* balcón *m; (roof)* azotea ➤ *tr* terraplenar.
terrain ➤ *s* terreno.
terrible ➤ *adj* terrible; *(tremendous)* tremendo.
terrific ➤ *adj* tremendo, bárbaro.
terrify ➤ *tr* aterrorizar.
territory ➤ *s* territorio.
terror ➤ *s* terror *m.*
terrorism ➤ *s* terrorismo.
terrorist ➤ *s* terrorista *mf.*
terrorize ➤ *tr* aterrorizar.
test ➤ *s* examen *m,* prueba ▪ **t. tube** tubo de ensayo, probeta ➤ *tr* examinar; *(equipment)* someter a prueba.
testify ➤ *intr* declarar ➤ *tr* ▪ **to t. that** testificar que • **to t. to** testificar.
testimony ➤ *s* testimonio.
tetanus ➤ *s* tétano.
text ➤ *s* texto.
textbook ➤ *s* libro de texto.
textile ➤ *s & adj* textil *m.*
texture ➤ *s* textura.
than ➤ *conj* que ▪ **more t. half** más de la mitad • **other t.** aparte de • **rather t.** ántes que.
thank ➤ *tr* agradecer, dar las gracias a ▪ **t. you** gracias (*for* por).
thankful ➤ *adj* agradecido.
thanks ➤ *spl* gracias; *(acknowledgment)* reconocimiento; *(gratitude)* gratitud *f.*
thanksgiving ➤ *s* acción *f* de gracias.
that ➤ *adj (near)* ese; *(distant)* aquel ▪ **t. one** ése; aquél ➤ *pron* ése; aquél; *(neuter)* eso, aquello ▪ **like t.** así • **the dog t. barked** el perro que ladró ➤ *adv (so)* tan ▪ **t. high** así de alto • **t. many** tantos • **t. much** tanto ➤ *conj* que ▪ **so t.** para que.
thaw ➤ *intr* derretirse ➤ *tr* ▪ **to t. out** *(food)* descongelar ➤ *s* tiempo tibio.
the *art def* el, la, lo, las, los.
theater *o* **theatre** ➤ *s* teatro.
theft ➤ *s* robo.
their ➤ *pron* su, suyo, suya, de ellos, de ellas.
theirs ➤ *pron* (el) suyo, (la) suya, etc.
them ➤ *pron (as direct object)* los, las; *(as indirect object)* les; *(as object of preposition)* ellos, ellas.
theme ➤ *s* tema *m; (written)* ensayo.
themselves ➤ *pron (object)* se; *(subject)* mismos, mismas; *(object of preposition)* sí mismos, sí mismas ▪ **among t.** entre ellos.
then ➤ *adv (at that time, in that case)* entonces; *(afterward)* después; *(in addition)* además; *(consequently)* en consecuencia.
theology ➤ *s* teología.
theoretical ➤ *adj* teórico.
theory ➤ *s* teoría.
therapeutic ➤ *s* terapéutico.
therapist ➤ *s* terapeuta *mf.*
therapy ➤ *s* MED. terapia; PSIC. psicoterapia.
there ➤ *adv* allí, allá, ahí; *(in that matter)* en eso ➤ *pron* ▪ **t. are** hay • **t. is** hay • **t. was** había, hubo • **t. were** habían, hubieron • **t. will be** habrá.
therefore ➤ *adv* por lo tanto.
thermal ➤ *adj* termal.
thermometer ➤ *s* termómetro.
thermostat ➤ *s* termostato.
these ➤ *pl de* **this.**
they ➤ *pron* ellos, ellas ▪ **t. say** se dice.
thick ➤ *adj* grueso; *(not watery)* espeso ▪ **two meters t.** dos metros de grosor.
thicken ➤ *tr & intr* espesar(se).
thickness ➤ *s* grosor *m,* espesor *m.*
thief ➤ *s* ladrón/ona.
thigh ➤ *s* muslo.
thimble ➤ *s* dedal *m.*
thin ➤ *adj* delgado; *(sparse)* escaso; *(hair)* ralo; *(soup)* aguado; *(weak)* débil.
thing ➤ *s* cosa ▪ **for one t.** en primer lugar • **it's a good t. that** menos mal que ▪ *pl (stuff, conditions)* cosas; *(equipment)* equipo.
think✧ ➤ *tr & intr* pensar (*about* en); *(to regard, believe)* creer, parecerle a uno ▪ **I t. so** creo que sí • **to t. of** pensar; *(to recall)* recordar • **to t. over** *o* **through** pensar bien • **to t. up** inventar.
third ➤ *s* tercero; *(part)* tercio, tercera parte; MÚS., AUTO. tercera ➤ *adj* tercero.
thirst ➤ *s* sed *f.*
thirsty ➤ *adj* sediento ▪ **to be t.** tener sed.
thirteen ➤ *s & adj* trece *m.*
thirty ➤ *adj & s* treinta *m.*
this ➤ *pron* éste, ésta; *(neuter)* esto ➤ *adj* este, esta ▪ **t. one** éste, ésta ➤ *adv (so)* tan ▪ **t. long** así de largo • **t. many** tantos • **t. much** tanto.
thorn ➤ *s* espina.
thorough ➤ *adj* completo; *(detailed)* detallado, minucioso; *(total)* total.
those ➤ *pl de* **that.**
though ➤ *conj* aunque ▪ **as t.** como si • **even t.** aunque ➤ *adv* sin embargo, no obstante.
thought ➤ *s* pensamiento; *(idea)* idea; *(consideration)* consideración *f; (intention, purpose)* intención *f,* propósito ▪ **on second t.** pensándolo bien.
thoughtful ➤ *adj* atento, solícito.
thoughtless ➤ *adj (careless)* descuidado; *(inconsiderate)* falto de consideración.
thousand ➤ *s & adj* mil *m.*
thread ➤ *s* hilo; *(of a screw)* rosca ➤ *tr (needle, beads)* ensartar.
threat ➤ *s* amenaza.
threaten ➤ *tr & intr* amenazar.
three ➤ *s & adj* tres *m* ▪ **t. hundred** trescientos • **t. o'clock** las tres.
thresh ➤ *tr* trillar.
threshold ➤ *s* umbral *m.*
thrift ➤ *s* economía, ahorro.
thrill ➤ *tr* encantar, deleitar ➤ *s* emoción *f.*
thriller ➤ *s* FAM. novela *o* película de suspenso.
thrive✧ ➤ *intr* prosperar; *(to flourish)* crecer.
throat ➤ *s* garganta.
throb ➤ *intr (to beat)* latir; *(pain)* dar punzadas ➤ *s* latido; *(of pain)* punzada.
throne ➤ *s* trono.
throng ➤ *s* muchedumbre *f* ➤ *tr* atestar.
through ➤ *prep* por; *(among)* a través de; *(by the agency of)* por medio de, a través de; *(during)* durante; *(between)* entre ▪ **Monday t. Friday** de lunes a viernes ➤ *adv (from one end to another)* de un lado al otro; *(from beginning to end)* hasta el final; *(completely)* completamente ▪ **to carry something t.** llevar algo a cabo • **to fall t.** fracasar ➤ *adj (flight)* directo; *(street)* de paso libre, de vía libre.
throughout ➤ *prep* por todo, en todo; *(during every part of)* durante todo ➤ *adv* por todas partes; *(completely)* completamente; *(during the entire time)* todo el tiempo.
throw✧ ➤ *tr* tirar, arrojar; *(punches, party)* dar; *(switch)* echar ▪ **to t. away** tirar, desechar • **to t. out** *(to reject)* rechazar; *(to throw away)* tirar ➤ *intr* ▪ **to t. up** vomitar, devolver ➤ *s* lanzamiento, tiro; *(of dice)* lance *m; (coverlet)* colcha, cobertor *m; (rug)* alfombra pequeña.
throwaway ➤ *adj* desechable.
thrust✧ ➤ *tr (to push)* empujar; *(knife)* clavar; *(to put in)* meter ➤ *s* empujón *m;* FÍS. empuje *m.*
thug ➤ *s* maleante *m,* matón *m.*
thumb ➤ *s* pulgar *m* ➤ *intr* ▪ **to t. through** hojear.
thumbtack ➤ *s* chinche *f,* chincheta.
thunder ➤ *s* trueno ➤ *intr* tronar.
thunderstorm ➤ *s* tronada.
Thursday ➤ *s* jueves *m.*
thus ➤ *adv* así, de esta manera; *(therefore)* por eso ▪ **t. far** hasta ahora.
thyme ➤ *s* tomillo.
tick[1] ➤ *intr & s* (hacer) tictac *m.*
tick[2] ➤ *s* ENTOM. garrapata.
ticket ➤ *s (for travel)* billete *m,* boleto; *(for movies, theater)* entrada, boleto; *(speeding, parking)* boleta ▪ **t. office** *o* **window** taquilla ➤ *tr* vender billete a; *(a motorist)* darle una boleta a.
tickle ➤ *tr* cosquillear; *(to delight)* deleitar ➤ *s* cosquilleo.
tidbit ➤ *s* bocado.
tide ➤ *s* marea.
tidy ➤ *adj* ordenado, arreglado ➤ *tr & intr* ▪ **to t. up** ordenar.
tie ➤ *tr* atar; *(to knot)* anudar; *(to link)* ligar ▪ **to t. down** atar, sujetar • **to t. up** atar; *(traffic)* obstruir; *(boat)* amarrar ➤ *intr (contestants)* empatar ➤ *s (necktie)* corbata; *(draw)* empate *m; (bond)* lazo, vínculo.
tiger ➤ *s* tigre *m.*
tight ➤ *adj (screw, knot)* apretado; *(sealed)* hermético; *(clothes, shoes)* ajustado; *(stingy)* tacaño ➤ *adv (firmly)* bien, fuertemente; *(soundly)* profundamente.
tighten ➤ *tr* apretar; *(a cord)* tensar.
tights ➤ *spl* malla.
tile ➤ *s (of a roof)* teja; *(of a floor)* losa, baldosa; *(of a wall)* azulejo.
till[1] ➤ *tr* AGR. labrar, cultivar.
till[2] ➤ *prep* hasta (donde) ➤ *conj* hasta que.
tilt ➤ *tr & intr* inclinar(se) ➤ *s* inclinación *f.*
timber ➤ *s* árboles maderables; *(lumber)* maderamen *m; (beam)* viga.
time ➤ *s* tiempo; *(moment)* momento; *(a specified time)* hora; *(occasion)* ocasión *f; (instance)* vez *f* ▪ **all the t.** todo el tiempo; *(always)* siempre • **(at) any t.** en cualquier momento • **at all times** en todo momento • **at a t.** a la vez • **at no t.** nunca • **at times** a veces • **each** *o* **every t.** cada vez • **for the t. being** por el momento • **in due t.** en su día • **on t.** a tiempo • **t. off** tiempo libre • **t. out** DEP. interrupción temporal • **t. zone** huso horario • **to waste t.** perder el tiempo • **what t. is it?** ¿qué hora es? ➤ *tr* fijar la hora *o* el tiempo de; *(to record)* cronometrar.
timely ➤ *adv* oportuno; *(punctual)* puntual.
timer ➤ *s* reloj automático.
times ➤ *prep* multiplicado (por).
timetable ➤ *s* horario.
timid ➤ *adj* tímido.
timing ➤ *s* oportunidad *f;* DEP. coordinación *f.*
tin ➤ *s* estaño; *(container)* lata.
tinfoil *o* **tin foil** ➤ *s* papel *m* de estaño.
tingle ➤ *intr & s* (sentir) picazón *f.*
tinsel ➤ *adj & s* (de) oropel *m.*
tint ➤ *s* matiz *m* ➤ *tr* matizar.
tiny ➤ *adj* minúsculo.
tip[1] ➤ *s (end)* punta, cabo.
tip[2] ➤ *tr & intr* volcar, derribar; *(to tilt)* inclinar(se) ▪ **to t. over** volcar(se).
tip[3] ➤ *s (gratuity)* propina; *(information)* información *f; (advice)* consejo ➤ *tr* dar una propina ▪ **to t. off** dar una información.
tip-off ➤ *s* FAM. información *f,* soplo.
tiptoe ➤ *intr & adv* (andar) de puntillas.
tire[1] ➤ *tr & intr* cansar(se); *(to bore)* aburrir(se).
tire[2] ➤ *s* AUTO. llanta, neumático.
tired ➤ *adj* cansado; *(hackneyed)* trillado.
tiresome ➤ cansado, tedioso.
tissue ➤ *s* BIOL. tejido; *(for the nose)* pañuelo de papel ▪ **t. paper** papel de seda.
title ➤ *s* título ➤ *tr* titular.
titular ➤ *adj* titular; *(nominal)* nominal.
to ➤ *prep* a; *(direction)* hacia; *(as far as, until)* hasta; *(against)* contra; *(of, for)* de, para ▪ **it's ten to six** son las seis menos diez.
toad ➤ *s* sapo.
toast[1] ➤ *tr & intr* tostar(se) ➤ *s* tostada.
toast[2] ➤ *s (drink)* brindis *m.*
toaster ➤ *s* tostadora.
tobacco ➤ *s* tabaco.
today ➤ *adv & s* hoy *m.*
toddler ➤ *s* niño que empieza a andar.
toe ➤ *s* dedo del pie; *(of a shoe, sock)* puntera.
toenail ➤ *s* uña del dedo del pie.
toffee ➤ *s* caramelo.
together ➤ *adv* juntos; *(in total)* en total, todos (juntos) ▪ **to come** *o* **to get t.** juntarse, reunirse • **to go t.** *(colors, flavors)* armonizar.
toil ➤ *intr* trabajar duro, afanarse ➤ *s* trabajo, afán *m.*
toilet ➤ *s* retrete *m,* lavabo ▪ **t. paper** papel higiénico.
toiletry ➤ *s* artículo de tocador.
token ➤ *s* señal *f,* prueba; *(coin)* ficha ➤ *adj* simbólico.
tolerance ➤ *s* tolerancia.
tolerant ➤ *adj* tolerante.
tolerate ➤ *tr* tolerar; *(suffering, pain)* sufrir, aguantar.
toll ➤ *s* peaje *m; (on phone call)* tasa.
tollbooth ➤ *s* caseta de peaje.
tomato ➤ *s* tomate *m; (plant)* tomatera.
tomb ➤ *s* tumba; *(place)* sepultura.
tombstone ➤ *s* lápida.
tomorrow ➤ *s & adv* mañana ▪ **the day after t.** pasado mañana.
ton ➤ *s* tonelada ▪ *pl* FAM. montones.
tone ➤ *s* tono.
tongs ➤ *spl* tenacillas.
tongue ➤ *s* lengua.
tonic ➤ *s* tónico; MÚS., FONÉT. tónica; *(quinine water)* agua tónica.
tonight ➤ *adv & s* esta noche.
tonsil ➤ *s* amígdala.
too ➤ *adv (also)* también; *(as well as)* además; *(excessively)* demasiado; *(very)* muy ▪ **not t.** FAM. no muy, nada • **t. many** *o* **much** demasiados.
tool ➤ *s* herramienta; *(utensil)* utensilio, útil *m.*
tooth ➤ *s* diente *m.*
toothache ➤ *s* dolor *m* de muelas.
toothbrush ➤ *s* cepillo de dientes.
toothpaste ➤ *s* pasta dentífrica.
toothpick ➤ *s* mondadientes *m.*
top ➤ *s* parte *f* superior *o* de arriba; *(of the head)* coronilla; *(of a container)* borde *m; (of a mountain)* cumbre *f; (of a tree, hat)* copa; *(of a bottle, pan)* tapa ▪ **from t. to bottom** de arriba abajo • **on t.** encima • **on t. of** además de ➤ *adj* de arriba; *(topmost)* último; *(highest)* más alto; *(great)* de categoría; *(best)* mejor; *(maximum)* máximo ➤ *tr* rematar; *(to surpass)* superar ▪ **to t. it off** por si fuera poco.
topaz ➤ *s* topacio.
topic ➤ *s* tópico, tema *m.*
topography ➤ *s* topografía.
topple ➤ *tr* derribar; *(government)* volcar.
torch ➤ *s* antorcha.
torment ➤ *s* tormento ➤ *tr* atormentar; *(to pester)* molestar.
tornado ➤ *s* tornado.
torrent ➤ *s* torrente *m.*
torrid ➤ *adj* tórrido.
tortoise ➤ *s* tortuga de tierra.
torture ➤ *s* tortura ➤ *tr* torturar.
torturer ➤ *s* torturador/a.
toss ➤ *tr* tirar, lanzar; *(one's head, hair)* echar hacia atrás; *(salad)* revolver; *(coin)* echar a cara o cruz ➤ *intr (in bed)* revolverse.
total ➤ *s* total *m; (entirety)* totalidad *f* ➤ *adj* total ➤ *tr* totalizar ▪ **to t. up to** ascender a.
totalitarian ➤ *adj & s* totalitario/a.
touch ➤ *tr* tocar; *(to concern)* concernir a; *(to move)* conmover ▪ **to t. off** desencadenar, provocar • **to t. up** retocar ➤ *intr* tocarse; *(to be in contact)* estar en contacto ▪ **to t. down** AVIA. aterrizar

➤ *s* toque *m; (sense)* tacto; *(mild attack)* ataque ligero; *(dash)* pizca, poquito ■ **by t.** al tacto • **final** *o* **finishing t.** último toque • **to be out of t. with** *(people)* haber perdido el contacto con; *(things)* no estar al tanto de • **to keep in t.** mantenerse en contacto • **to lose one's t.** perder la mano.
touch-and-go ➤ *adj* arriesgado.
touched ➤ *adj* conmovido.
touching ➤ *adj* conmovedor.
touchup ➤ *s* retoque *m.*
touchy ➤ *adj (oversensitive)* susceptible, quisquilloso; *(situation)* delicado.
tough ➤ *adj* duro; *(physically hardy)* fuerte, robusto; *(harsh)* severo, áspero; *(aggressive)* agresivo; *(unyielding)* inflexible ■ **t. luck!** ¡mala suerte! ➤ *s* matón *m.*
toughen ➤ *tr & intr* endurecer(se).
tough-minded ➤ *adj* duro (de carácter).
toupee ➤ *s* peluquín *m.*
tour ➤ *s* excursión *f,* viaje *m; (visit)* visita; TEAT. gira ➤ *tr* recorrer, hacer un viaje por; TEAT. presentar en gira ➤ *intr* ir de viaje.
touring ➤ *s* turismo ➤ *adj* de turismo; *(theatrical company)* que está de gira.
tourism ➤ *s* turismo.
tourist ➤ *adj & s* (de) turista *mf.*
tournament ➤ *s* torneo.
tourniquet ➤ *s* torniquete *m.*
tousle ➤ *tr* desordenar, desarreglar.
tout ➤ *tr* recomendar.
tow ➤ *tr* remolcar ➤ *s* remolque *m* ■ **t. truck** remolcador.
toward(s) ➤ *prep* hacia.
towel ➤ *s* toalla, paño ➤ *tr & intr* secar(se) *o* frotar(se) con toalla.
tower ➤ *s* torre *f* ■ **control t.** AER. torre de control ➤ *intr* elevarse ■ **to t. over** *o* **above** dominar, destacarse sobre.
town ➤ *s (city)* ciudad *f; (village)* pueblo ■ **t. hall** ayuntamiento.
township ➤ *s* municipio.
toxic ➤ *adj* tóxico.
toxin ➤ *s* toxino.
toy ➤ *adj & s* (de) juguete *m* ➤ *intr* ■ **to t. with** jugar con; *(idea)* dar vueltas a.
trace ➤ *s* huella, rastro; *(sign)* señal *f,* indicio; *(bit)* pizca ➤ *tr (to copy)* dibujar, trazar; *(to follow a trail)* seguir.
track ➤ *s (path)* camino, senda; *(footprint)* huella; *(of a person)* pista; *(of things)* vestigio, rastro; *(railway)* vía (férrea); DEP. *(for running)* pista; *(sport)* atletismo en pista ■ **to keep t. of** seguir con atención • **to lose t. of** *(person)* perder a uno de vista; *(time)* perder la noción de ➤ *tr* seguir ■ **to t. down** localizar.
trackball ➤ COMPUT. seguibola.
tractor ➤ *s* tractor *m.*
trade ➤ *s* ocupación *f; (commerce)* comercio, negocio; *(exchange)* cambio ■ **t. union** sindicato, gremio ➤ *intr* comerciar, negociar ➤ *tr* cambiar, trocar ■ **to t. off** trocar.
trademark ➤ *s* marca registrada *o* de fábrica.
trading ➤ *s* comercio.
tradition ➤ *s* tradición *f.*
traditional ➤ *adj* tradicional.
traditionalist ➤ *s & adj* tradicionalista *mf.*
traffic ➤ *s* tráfico ■ **t. jam** embotellamiento • **t. light** luz de tráfico, semáforo ➤ *intr* traficar.
tragedy ➤ *s* tragedia.
tragic ➤ *adj* trágico.
trail ➤ *tr (to drag)* arrastrar; *(to track)* rastrear; *(to follow)* seguir ➤ *intr* arrastrarse; *(a plant)* trepar ➤ *s (trace)* huella, rastro; *(of a person)* pista; *(path)* camino, sendero.
trailer ➤ *s (vehicle)* remolque *m.*
train ➤ *s* tren *m; (of a dress)* cola; *(of thought)* hilo ➤ *tr (a person)* enseñar; *(an animal)* amaestrar ➤ *intr* prepararse; *(athlete)* entrenarse.
trained ➤ *adj* entrenado; *(physically)* preparado; *(animals)* amaestrado.
trainer ➤ *s* DEP. entrenador/a; *(of animals)* amaestrador/a.
training ➤ *s* adiestramiento; *(of animals)* amaestramiento; DEP. entrenamiento.
trait ➤ *s* rasgo.
traitor ➤ *s* traidor/a.
tram ➤ *s (cable car)* teleférico; G.B. tranvía *m.*
tramp ➤ *s* vagabundo/a.
trample ➤ *tr* pisotear.
tranquil ➤ *adj* tranquilo.
tranquilizer ➤ *s* tranquilizante *m.*
tranquil(l)ity ➤ *s* tranquilidad *f.*
transact ➤ *tr* tramitar.
transaction ➤ *s (act)* negociación *f; (deal)* transacción *f* ■ *pl* actas.
transcend ➤ *tr & intr* transcender.
transfer ➤ *tr (to convey)* trasladar; *(to shift)* transferir ➤ *intr (to move)* trasladarse; *(passenger)* transbordar ➤ *s* boleto de transbordo; *(of money)* transferencia; *(of power)* transmisión *f.*
transferal ➤ *s* transferencia.
transform ➤ *tr* transformar.
transformation ➤ *s* transformación *f.*
transformer ➤ *s* transformador *m.*
transfusion ➤ *s* MED. transfusión *f.*
transistor ➤ *s* transistor *m.*
transit ➤ *s* tránsito.
transition ➤ *s* transición *f.*
transitive ➤ *adj & s* (verbo) transitivo.
translate ➤ *tr* traducir.
translation ➤ *s* traducción *f.*
translator ➤ *s* traductor/a.
transmission ➤ *s* transmisión *f* ■ **automatic t.** AUTO. cambio automático.
transmit ➤ *tr* transmitir.
transmitter ➤ *s* transmisor *m.*
transparent ➤ *adj* transparente.
transplant ➤ *tr* trasplantar ➤ *s* trasplante *m.*
transport ➤ *tr* transportar ➤ *s* transporte *m.*
transportation ➤ *s* transportación *f.*
trap ➤ *s* trampa; *(in pipe)* sifón *m* ➤ *tr (to ensnare)* coger en una trampa; *(to catch)* atrapar.
trash ➤ *s* basura, desperdicios ■ **t. can** cubo de la basura ➤ *tr* JER. destrozar.
travel ➤ *intr* viajar; *(light, sound)* propagarse ➤ *tr* viajar por ➤ *s* viajar *m* ■ *pl* viajes.
travel(l)er ➤ *s* viajero/a ■ **t.'s check** cheque de viajero.
tray ➤ *s* bandeja.
treacherous ➤ *adj* traicionero; *(dangerous)* peligroso.
tread✧ ➤ *tr & intr* pisar ■ **t. water** pedalear en el agua ➤ *s* pisada; *(of stair)* huella; *(of tire)* banda de rodadura.
treason ➤ *s* traición *f.*
treasure ➤ *s* tesoro ➤ *tr* estimar.
treasurer ➤ *s* tesorero/a.
treasury ➤ *s* tesorería.
treat ➤ *tr* tratar; *(to invite)* convidar, invitar ➤ *s (present)* regalo; *(delight)* placer *m* ■ **it's my t.** invito yo.
treatment ➤ *s* tratamiento.
treaty ➤ *s* convenio, tratado.
tree ➤ *s* árbol *m.*
tremble ➤ *intr* temblar.
tremendous ➤ *adj* tremendo.
tremor ➤ *s* temblor *m.*
trench ➤ *s (ditch)* foso; MIL. trinchera.
trend ➤ *s* dirección *f; (fashion)* moda ➤ *intr* tender.
trendy ➤ *adj* FAM. que sigue la última moda.
trespass ➤ *intr* entrar ilegalmente (*on* en) ➤ *s* entrada ilegal ■ *pl* pecados.
trial ➤ *s (test)* ensayo; *(attempt)* tentativa; DER. proceso, juicio ■ **on t.** enjuiciado, procesado ➤ *adj* de prueba.
triangle ➤ *s* triángulo.
tribe ➤ *s* tribu *f.*
tribunal ➤ *s* tribunal *m.*
tribute ➤ *s* tributo.
trick ➤ *s* truco; *(swindle)* estafa; *(prank)* travesura; *(skill)* maña ➤ *tr* engañar, burlar.
trickle ➤ *intr* gotear ■ *s* goteo.
tricky ➤ *adj (wily)* astuto; *(situation, problem)* delicado, complicado.
tricycle ➤ *s* triciclo.
trifle ➤ *s* nadería ■ **a t.** un poquito ➤ *intr* jugar (*with* con).
trigger ➤ *s* gatillo.
trillion ➤ *s* E.U. [10^{12}] billón *m;* G.B. [10^{18}] trillón.
trim ➤ *tr (hair, nails)* recortar; *(branches)* podar.
trip ➤ *s* viaje *m* ➤ *intr (to stumble)* dar un traspié ➤ *tr (person)* hacer tropezar; *(alarm)* hacer sonar.
triple ➤ *adj & s* triple *m* ➤ *tr & intr* triplicar(se).
tripod ➤ *s* trípode *m.*
triumph ➤ *intr* triunfar ➤ *s* triunfo.
trivial ➤ *adj* insignificante, trivial.
trolley ➤ *s* tranvía *m.*
trombone ➤ *s* trombón *m.*
troop ➤ *s* grupo ■ *pl* MIL. tropas.
trophy ➤ *s* trofeo.
tropic ➤ *s* trópico ➤ *adj* tropical.
tropical ➤ *adj* tropical.
trot ➤ *s* trote *m* ➤ *intr* trotar.
trouble ➤ *s (misfortune)* desgracia; *(distress)* apuro, aprieto; *(effort)* esfuerzo ■ **to be in t.** estar en un aprieto • **to get into t.** meterse en líos • **to start t.** dar problemas • **to take the t.** to tomarse la molestia de ➤ *tr (to worry)* preocupar; *(to afflict)* afligir; *(to bother)* molestar.
troublesome ➤ *adj (worrisome)* inquietante; *(difficult)* dificultoso.
trousers ➤ *spl* pantalones *m.*
trout ➤ *s* trucha.
truce ➤ *s* tregua.
truck ➤ *s & tr* (transportar en) camión *m.*
true ➤ *adj* verdadero; *(loyal)* leal ■ **to come t.** realizarse • **t. to life** conforme a la realidad.
truly ➤ *adv* verdaderamente ■ **yours t.** suyo atentamente.
trumpet ➤ *s* trompeta.
trunk ➤ *s* tronco; *(elephant)* trompa; *(luggage)* baúl *m;* AUTO. maletero ■ *pl* **swimming t.** traje de baño.
trust ➤ *s* confianza; *(charge)* custodia; COM., FIN. trust *m,* consorcio ■ **in t.** DER. en depósito ➤ *tr* tener confianza en, fiarse de.
trustee ➤ *s* DER. fideicomisario/a; *(of a board)* síndico.
trusty ➤ *adj* de confianza.
truth ➤ *s* verdad *f.*
try ➤ *tr (to test, taste)* probar; *(to make an effort at)* tratar; DER. *(case)* someter a juicio; *(person)* procesar ■ **to t. on** próbarse • **to t. out** probar ➤ *intr* esforzarse ➤ *s* tentativa, intento.
tryout ➤ *s* prueba de aptitud; *(audition)* audición *f.*
T-shirt ➤ *s* camiseta.
tub ➤ *s (vessel)* tonel *m; (bathtub)* bañera.
tuba ➤ *s* tuba.
tube ➤ *s* tubo; FAM. *(TV)* tele *f.*
tuberculosis ➤ *s* tuberculosis *f.*
Tuesday ➤ *s* martes *m.*
tuft ➤ *s* mechón *m; (crest)* copete *m.*
tug ➤ *tr (to pull)* tirar de; *(to drag)* arrastrar ➤ *s* tirón *m.*
tugboat ➤ *s* remolcador *m.*
tuition ➤ *s* matrícula.
tulip ➤ *s* tulipán *m.*
tulle ➤ *s* tul *m.*
tumble ➤ *intr (to roll)* rodar; *(to fall)* caerse ➤ *s* tumbo, caída.
tumbleweed ➤ *s* planta rodadora.
tumbling ➤ *s* acrobacia.
tumescence ➤ *s* tumescencia.
tummy ➤ *s* FAM. barriga.
tumor ➤ *s* tumor *m.*
tumult ➤ *s* tumulto.
tumultuous ➤ *adj* tumultuoso.
tuna ➤ *s* atún *m.*
tundra ➤ *s* tundra.
tune ➤ *s* melodía ■ **in t.** afinado • **out of t.** desafinado • **to carry a t.** cantar afinado ➤ *tr* MÚS. afinar; MEC. poner a punto ■ **to t. in** RAD., TELEV. sintonizar • **to t. out** JER. no prestar atención a.
tuner ➤ *s (person)* afinador/a; RAD. sintonizador *m.*
tune-up ➤ *s* puesta a punto.
tungsten ➤ *s* tungsteno.
tunic ➤ *s* túnica.
tunnel ➤ *s* túnel *m* ➤ *tr (one's way)* cavar ➤ *intr* hacer un túnel.
turban ➤ *s* turbante *m.*
turbine ➤ *s* turbina.
turbojet ➤ *s* turborreactor *m.*
turboprop ➤ *s* turbopropulsor *m.*
turbulence ➤ *s* turbulencia.
turbulent ➤ *adj* turbulento.
tureen ➤ *s* sopera.
turf ➤ *s (sod)* césped *m;* JER. territorio.
turkey ➤ *s* pavo, guajolote *m.*
turmeric ➤ *s* cúrcuma.
turmoil ➤ *s* confusión *f.*
turn ➤ *tr (to revolve)* dar vueltas a; *(to flip)* pasar, volver; *(to rotate)* girar; *(corner)* doblar; *(stomach)* revolver; *(to direct)* dirigir ■ **to t. away** *(to send away)* negar la entrada a; *(to deflect)* rechazar; *(head)* volver; *(eyes)* desviar • **to t. back** hacer retroceder; *(clock)* retrasar • **to t. down** *(light, sound)* bajar; *(to reject)* rechazar • **to t. into** transformar en • **to t. off** *(radio, light)* apagar; *(tap, gas)* cerrar; *(electricity, water)* cortar; *(engine)* parar • **to t. on** *(radio)* poner; *(light)* encender; *(engine)* poner en marcha; *(a tap)* abrir; *(stove, fire)* encender, prender • **to t. out** *(light)* apagar • **to t. over** *(object)* invertir, volcar; *(idea)* considerar; *(to transfer)* entregar • **to t. up** *(light, sound)* subir ➤ *intr (to rotate)* girar; *(to change direction)* dar la vuelta; *(to become)* ponerse, volverse ■ **to t. around** darse vuelta • **to t. away** volver la cara *o* la espalda • **to t. back** retroceder • **to t. into** volverse • **to t. off** desviarse • **to t. out** resultar • **to t. over** *(car, truck)* volcar; *(in bed)* voltearse • **to t. up** aparecer ➤ *s* vuelta; *(rotation)* rotación *f; (change)* cambio; *(opportunity)* turno ■ **at every t.** a cada instante • **by turns** por turnos • **to take turns** turnarse.
turning ➤ *s* viraje *m* ■ **t. point** momento crucial.
turnip ➤ *s* nabo.
turnoff ➤ *s* desvío; JER. cosa *o* persona repugnante.
turnout ➤ *s (attendance)* concurrencia.
turnover ➤ *s (pastry)* empanada; *(of staff)* cambio de personal.
turnpike ➤ *s* autopista de peaje.
turpentine ➤ *s* trementina.
turquoise ➤ *adj & s* (de) turquesa.
turtle ➤ *s* tortuga.
turtleneck ➤ *s* cuello vuelto *o* alto.
tusk ➤ *s* colmillo.
tutor ➤ *s* profesor/a particular; *(in universities)* tutor/a ➤ *tr* dar clases particulares a.
tuxedo ➤ *s* smoking *m.*
TV ➤ *s* televisión *f; (set)* televisor *m.*
tweezers ➤ *spl* pinzas.
twelfth ➤ *adj & s* duodécimo.
twelve ➤ *s & adj* doce *m* ■ **t. o'clock** las doce.
twenty ➤ *adj & s* veinte *m.*
twice ➤ *adv* dos veces, el doble.
twig ➤ *s* ramita.
twilight ➤ *s* crepúsculo.
twin ➤ *adj & s* gemelo/a ■ **t. bed** cama separada *o* gemela.
twine ➤ *s* cordel *m,* bramante *m.*
twinge ➤ *s* punzada.
twinkle ➤ *intr* centellear; *(eyes)* brillar ➤ *s* centelleo.
twinkling ➤ *s* centelleo; FIG. instante *m.*
twist ➤ *tr* torcer; *(jar top)* dar vueltas a ➤ *s (of a road, river)* vuelta, recodo; *(of an ankle)* torcedura.
twister ➤ *s* ciclón *m,* tornado.
two ➤ *s & adj* dos *m* ■ **t. hundred** doscientos • **t. o'clock** las dos.
twofold ➤ *adj* doble.
two-way ➤ *adj* de doble dirección.
type ➤ *s* tipo ➤ *tr & intr* escribir a máquina.
typeface ➤ *s* tipografía.
typesetter ➤ *s* tipógrafo/a.
typewriter ➤ *s* máquina de escribir.
typhoid ➤ *adj* tifoideo ➤ *s* tifoidea.
typhus ➤ *s* tifus *m.*
typical ➤ *adj* típico.
typist ➤ *s* mecanógrafo/a.
tyranny ➤ *s* tiranía.

U

udder ➤ *s* ubre *f.*
UFO ➤ *s* ovni *m.*
ugliness ➤ *s* fealdad *f.*
ugly ➤ *adj* feo.
ulcer ➤ *s* úlcera.
ultimate ➤ *adj* último.
ultrasound ➤ *s* ultrasonido.
umbrella ➤ *s* paraguas *m.*
umpire ➤ *s* árbitro/a ➤ *tr* arbitrar.
unable ➤ *adj* incapaz.
unacceptable ➤ *adj* inaceptable.
unaccompanied ➤ *adj* solo.
unaccounted ➤ *adj* ■ **u. for** desaparecido; *(unexplained)* inexplicado.
unafraid ➤ *adj* sin temor.
unanimous ➤ *adj* unánime.
unarmed ➤ *adj* desarmado; *(defenseless)* indefenso.
unattractive ➤ *adj* poco atractivo.
unauthorized ➤ *adj* desautorizado.
unavailable ➤ *adj (not available)* no disponible; *(busy)* ocupado.
unavoidable ➤ *adj* inevitable.
unaware ➤ *adj* ignorante ■ **to be u. of** no darse cuenta de ➤ **unaware(s)** *adv* de improviso.
unbearable ➤ *adj* insoportable.
unbelievable ➤ *adj* increíble.
unbreakable ➤ *adj* irrompible.
unbutton ➤ *tr & intr* desabotonar(se).

uncalled-for ➤ adj (undeserved) inmerecido; (out of place) inapropiado.
uncanny ➤ adj inexplicable.
uncertain ➤ adj incierto; (undecided) indeciso.
uncertainty ➤ s incertidumbre f.
unchanged ➤ adj inalterado.
unclaimed ➤ adj no reclamado.
uncle ➤ s tío ■ **U. Sam** (el) tío Sam.
unclear ➤ adj confuso.
uncomfortable ➤ adj incómodo.
uncommon ➤ adj poco común, raro.
unconditional ➤ adj incondicional.
unconfirmed ➤ adj no confirmado.
unconscious ➤ adj & s inconsciente m.
unconstitutional ➤ adj inconstitucional.
uncooked ➤ adj crudo.
uncover ➤ tr destapar, revelar.
undamaged ➤ adj libre de daño.
undecided ➤ adj no resuelto.
undeniable ➤ adj innegable.
under ➤ prep (por) debajo (de); (beneath) bajo; (less than) menos de; (during) durante el reinado de ■ **u. the circumstances** dadas las circunstancias ➤ adv bajo, debajo.
underage ➤ adj menor de edad.
underarm ➤ s axila, sobaco.
undercharge ➤ tr COM. cobrar menos de lo debido.
underclothes ➤ s ropa interior.
undercover ➤ adj clandestino.
underdone ➤ adj poco hecho.
underestimate ➤ tr subestimar ➤ s subestimación f.
undergo ➤ tr (to experience) experimentar; (to endure) sufrir.
undergraduate ➤ s & adj (de o para) estudiante mf universitario no graduado.
underground ➤ adj subterráneo; (secret) clandestino ➤ adv bajo tierra.
underline ➤ tr subrayar ➤ s raya.
underneath ➤ adv (por) debajo; (on the lower part) en la parte inferior ➤ prep bajo, debajo de ➤ s parte f inferior.
underpants ➤ spl calzoncillos.
underpass ➤ s paso por debajo.
underscore ➤ tr subrayar.
undershirt ➤ s camiseta.
understand ➤ tr & intr entender, comprender.
understandable ➤ adj comprensible.
understanding ➤ s comprensión f; (agreement) acuerdo ➤ adj comprensivo.
understood ➤ adj entendido; (implied) sobreentendido.
undertake ➤ tr (task) emprender; (duty) encargarse de.
undertaker ➤ s agente mf funerario.
underwater ➤ adj subacuático.
underwear ➤ s ropa interior.
undo ➤ tr anular; (to untie) desatar; (to open) desenvolver; (to ruin) arruinar.
undress ➤ tr & intr desvestir(se) ➤ s desnudez f.
uneasy ➤ adj inquieto.
uneducated ➤ adj inculto.
unemployed ➤ adj desempleado.
unemployment ➤ s desempleo.
unequal ➤ adj desigual.
uneven ➤ adj desigual.
uneventful ➤ adj sin novedad.
unexpected ➤ adj inesperado.
unfair ➤ adj injusto.
unfaithful ➤ adj infiel; (adulterous) adúltero; (inaccurate) inexacto.
unfamiliar ➤ adj desconocido ■ **u. with** no familiarizado con.
unfashionable ➤ adj fuera de moda.
unfasten ➤ tr & intr desatar(se).
unfavorable ➤ adj desfavorable; (negative) negativo.
unfinished ➤ adj incompleto.
unfit ➤ adj incapaz (for, to de); (unsuitable) inadecuado; (unqualified) incompetente.
unfold ➤ tr & intr desdoblar(se); (plot) desarrollar(se).
unforgettable ➤ adj inolvidable.
unforgivable ➤ adj imperdonable.
unformatted ➤ adj sin formatear.
unfortunate ➤ adj desafortunado ➤ s desgraciado.
unfriendly ➤ adj hostil.
unfurl ➤ tr & intr desplegar(se).
unfurnished ➤ adj desamueblado.
ungrateful ➤ adj desagradecido.
unhappiness ➤ s desgracia.
unhappy ➤ adj infeliz; (unlucky) desafortunado.
unhealthy ➤ adj enfermizo; (unwholesome) insalubre.
unhook ➤ tr desenganchar.
uniform ➤ adj & s uniforme m.
unify ➤ tr & intr unificar(se).
unilateral ➤ adj unilateral.
unimportant ➤ adj poco importante.
uninformed ➤ adj mal informado.
uninhabited ➤ adj inhabitado.
uninterrupted ➤ adj ininterrumpido.
union ➤ s unión f; (labor) gremio, sindicato.
unique ➤ adj único; (peerless) sin igual.
unit ➤ s unidad f; (part) parte f; (device) aparato.
unite ➤ tr & intr unir(se).
unity ➤ s unidad f.
universal ➤ adj universal.
universe ➤ s universo.
university ➤ s universidad f.
unjust ➤ adj injusto.
unkind ➤ adj poco amable.
unknown ➤ adj desconocido.
unlawful ➤ adj ilegal.
unleaded ➤ adj sin plomo.
unless ➤ conj a menos que.
unlike ➤ prep diferente de; (not typical of) no característico de.
unlikely ➤ adj improbable.
unload ➤ tr & intr descargar.
unlock ➤ tr & intr abrir(se).
unlucky ➤ adj desgraciado ■ **to be u.** tener mala suerte.
unmarried ➤ adj soltero.
unnecessary ➤ adj innecesario.
unnoticed ➤ adj inadvertido.
unoccupied ➤ adj (vacant) desocupado; (idle) desempleado.
unofficial ➤ adj extraoficial.
unpack ➤ tr desempacar; (to unload) descargar ➤ intr deshacer las maletas.
unpaid ➤ adj no remunerado.
unpleasant ➤ adj desagradable.
unplug ➤ tr destapar; ELEC. desenchufar.
unpopular ➤ adj impopular.
unpredictable ➤ adj que no se puede predecir o pronosticar.
unprepared ➤ adj desprevenido.
unprejudiced ➤ adj imparcial.
unqualified ➤ adj incompetente.
unreasonable ➤ adj irrazonable.
unrelated ➤ adj inconexo.
unreliable ➤ adj que no es de fiar.
unrest ➤ s desasosiego.
unroll ➤ tr & intr desenrollar(se).
unscrew ➤ tr destornillar; (to loosen) desenroscar.
unselfish ➤ adj generoso.
unsettled ➤ adj inestable; (not resolved) pendiente.
unskilled ➤ adj inexperto, sin entrenamiento; (work) no especializado.
unsolved ➤ adj sin resolver.
unsteady ➤ adj inestable; (hands) tembloroso.
unsuccessful ➤ adj fracasado; (futile) infructuoso ■ **to be u.** no tener éxito.
unsuitable ➤ adj inadecuado; (inconvenient) inconveniente; (unbecoming) inapropiado.
untangle ➤ tr desenredar.
untidy ➤ adj desordenado.
untie ➤ tr & intr desatar(se).
until ➤ prep & conj hasta (que).
untimely ➤ adj inoportuno.
untrue ➤ adj falso; (inaccurate) inexacto.
unused ➤ adj sin usar; (new) nuevo ■ **u. to** no acostumbrado a.
unusual ➤ adj fuera de lo común; (exceptional) extraordinario.
unwell ➤ adj enfermo, indispuesto.
unwilling ➤ adj no dispuesto.
unworthy ➤ adj despreciable ■ **u. of** no digno de.
unwrap ➤ tr desenvolver.
unzip ➤ tr bajar la cremallera de.
up ➤ adv hacia arriba, en lo alto ■ **close up** cerca • **from ten dollars up** de diez dólares para arriba • **high up** muy arriba • **to come o go up** to acercarse a • **to feel up to** sentirse capaz de • **to get up** levantarse • **up against** junto a • **up to** hasta • **up to date** al día ➤ adj ■ **to be up** haberse levantado (de la cama) • **to be up against** tener que hacer frente a • **to be up for** (office) ser candidato a; (to feel like) tener ganas de • **to be up on** estar bien enterado sobre • **to be up to something** estar tramando algo • **up in arms** furioso ➤ prep arriba ➤ s ■ **ups and downs** altibajos ➤ tr (to increase) aumentar.
upbeat ➤ adj FAM. optimista.
upbringing ➤ s crianza.
upgrade ➤ tr mejorar la calidad de; COMPUT. actualizar ➤ intr hacer una actualización ➤ s cuesta; COMPUT. actualización f, upgrade m.
uphill ➤ adj ascendente; (difficult) arduo ➤ s cuesta ➤ adv cuesta arriba.
upholster ➤ tr tapizar.
upload ➤ tr COMPUT. subir, cargar.
upon ➤ prep sobre, por.
upper ➤ adj superior ■ **u. case** mayúsculas.
upright ➤ adj vertical; (honorable) recto ➤ adv verticalmente.
uproar ➤ s alboroto.
upset ➤ tr (to tip over) volcar; (to throw into disorder) desordenar; (physically, mentally) perturbar; (the stomach) caer mal a; (an opponent) vencer inesperadamente ➤ s vuelco; (trouble) molestia; (defeat) derrota inesperada ➤ adj (disordered) desordenado; (worried) preocupado.
upside-down ➤ adv al revés ■ **to turn u.** volcar(se); FIG. trastornar(se).
upstairs ➤ adv arriba; (on upper floor) en el piso superior ➤ s piso de arriba.
upswing ➤ s alza.
up-to-date ➤ adj al día.
upward ➤ adj ascendente ➤ adv hacia o para arriba.
urge ➤ tr incitar; (to exhort) exhortar; (to advocate) propugnar ➤ s impulso; (desire) deseo.
urgency ➤ s urgencia.
urgent ➤ adj urgente.
Uruguayan ➤ adj & s uruguayo/a.
us ➤ pron ■ **she took us downtown** nos llevó al centro • **to us** a nosotros.
use ➤ tr usar, emplear ■ **to be used as,** for servir de, para • **to u. up** agotar ➤ intr ■ **I used to go. . .** yo solía ir. . . ■ **to get used to** acostumbrarse a ➤ s uso; (usefulness) utilidad f.
used ➤ adj usado.
useful ➤ adj útil.
usefulness ➤ s utilidad f.
useless ➤ adj ineficaz; (futile) inútil.
user ➤ s usuario/a; (addict) adicto/a.
username ➤ s nombre m de usuario/a.
usher ➤ s acomodador/a.
usual ➤ adj usual; (customary) acostumbrado ■ **as u.** como de costumbre.
usually ➤ adv usualmente, por lo común.
utensil ➤ s utensilio.
utility ➤ s utilidad f.
utilize ➤ tr utilizar.
utmost ➤ adj sumo ➤ s máximo ■ **to do one's u.** hacer todo lo posible.
utter[1] ➤ tr decir, pronunciar.
utter[2] ➤ adj total, absoluto.
U-turn ➤ s AUTO. media vuelta.

V

vacancy ➤ s vacío; (unfilled job) vacante f; (in a hotel) habitación f libre.
vacant ➤ adj vacío; (seat, room) libre.
vacation ➤ s vacaciones f ➤ intr ir de vacaciones.
vaccinate ➤ tr & intr vacunar.
vaccination ➤ s vacunación f.
vacuum ➤ s vacío ■ **v. cleaner** aspiradora ➤ tr & intr pasar la aspiradora (por).
vague ➤ adj vago; (shape) borroso.
vain ➤ adj vano, inútil; (conceited) vanidoso.
valid ➤ adj válido.
validity ➤ s validez f.
valley ➤ s valle m.
valuable ➤ adj valioso ➤ **valuables** spl objetos de valor.
value ➤ s valor m; (importance) importancia ➤ tr estimar, valorar.
valve ➤ s válvula.
van ➤ s (truck) camioneta, furgoneta.
vandalize ➤ tr destrozar, destruir.
vanilla ➤ s vainilla.
vanish ➤ intr desaparecer.
vanity ➤ s vanidad.
vanquish ➤ tr derrotar, vencer.
vapor ➤ s vapor.
variety ➤ s variedad f; (assortment) surtido.
various ➤ adj (several) varios; (different) diferente.
varnish ➤ s barniz m ➤ tr barnizar.
vary ➤ tr variar ➤ intr variar, cambiar; (to differ) diferir; (to deviate) desviarse.
vase ➤ s jarrón m, florero.
vast ➤ adj vasto, inmenso.
vault ➤ s bóveda.
VCR ➤ s grabadora de video.
veal ➤ s (carne f de) ternera.
vegetable ➤ s verdura, legumbre ➤ adj vegetal.
vegetarian ➤ adj & s vegetariano/a.
vegetation ➤ s vegetación f.
vehicle ➤ s vehículo.
veil ➤ s & tr (cubrir con un) velo.
vein ➤ s vena.
velvet ➤ s terciopelo.
Venetian blind ➤ s persiana veneciana.
vengeance ➤ s venganza.
Venezuelan ➤ adj & s venezolano/a.
venison ➤ s (carne f de) venado.
vent ➤ s respiradero; (hole) abertura.
ventilation ➤ s ventilación f.
verb ➤ s verbo.
verdict ➤ s veredicto; FIG. opinión f.
verge ➤ s borde m.
verify ➤ tr verificar.
vermouth ➤ s vermut m.
verse ➤ s verso; (stanza) estrofa; (of a song) cuplé m; BIBL. versículo.
version ➤ s versión f.
versus ➤ prep contra.
vertical ➤ adj & s vertical f.
very ➤ adv muy ■ **at the v. least** como mínimo • **not v.** poco • **the v. best** el o lo mejor • **v. much (so)** muchísimo.
vessel ➤ s vaso; MARÍT. nave.
vest ➤ s chaleco.
vestry ➤ s sacristía.
veteran ➤ adj & s veterano/a.
veterinarian ➤ s veterinario/a.
vex ➤ tr fastidiar, molestar.
via ➤ prep vía ■ **v. air mail** por vía aérea.
vibrate ➤ tr & intr vibrar.
vibration ➤ s vibración f.
vice[1] ➤ s vicio.
vice[2] ➤ s ■ **v. president** vice presidente ➤ prep ■ **v. versa** viceversa.
vicinity ➤ s vecindad f, proximidad f.
vicious ➤ adj vicioso, malicioso; (attack) violento, fuerte; (animal) salvaje.
victim ➤ s víctima.
victory ➤ s victoria, triunfo.
video ➤ adj & s video o vídeo.
videocassette ➤ s videocasete m.
videodisc/disk ➤ s videodisco.
video game ➤ s videojuego.
videotape ➤ s & tr (grabar en) videocinta.
view ➤ s (sight, vista) vista; (opinion) opinión f; (approach) enfoque m ➤ tr ver, mirar.
viewer ➤ s espectador/a; (television viewer) televidente mf.
viewpoint ➤ s punto de vista.
vigor ➤ s vigor m.
vigorous ➤ adj vigoroso, fuerte.
vile ➤ adj vil, odioso.
villa ➤ s villa, quinta.
village ➤ s aldea; (town) pueblo.
villager ➤ s aldeano/a.
villain ➤ s villano/a.
vine ➤ s parra, vid.
vinegar ➤ s vinagre m.
vineyard ➤ s viñedo, viña.
vinyl ➤ s vinilo.
violate ➤ tr violar.
violation ➤ s violación f.
violence ➤ s violencia.
violent ➤ adj violento.
violet ➤ s violeta.
violin ➤ s violín m.
VIP ➤ s FAM. personalidad f (importante).
virgin ➤ s & adj virgen mf.
virtual ➤ adj virtual.
virtue ➤ s virtud f.
virtuous ➤ adj virtuoso.
virus ➤ s virus m.
visa ➤ s visa, visado.
visibility ➤ s visibilidad f.
visible ➤ adj visible.
vision ➤ s vista, visión f; (foresight) clarividencia, previsión f; (mental image) visión, fantasía.
visit ➤ tr visitar ➤ intr hacer una visita, ir de visita ➤ s visita.
visitor ➤ s visitante mf, visita.
vitamin ➤ s vitamina.
vivid ➤ adj vivo.
vocabulary ➤ s vocabulario.
vocalist ➤ s vocalista mf.
vocational ➤ adj vocacional.
vogue ➤ s moda, boga ■ **in v.** de moda.

voice ➤ *s* voz *f* ■ **at the top of ones' v.** a voz en cuello • **v. mail** correo de voz.
void ➤ *adj* vacío; DER. nulo, inválido ➤ *tr* invalidar ➤ *s* vacío.
volcano ➤ *s* volcán *m.*
volume ➤ *s* volumen *m.*
voluntary ➤ *adj* voluntario.
volunteer ➤ *s & adj* voluntario/a.
vomit ➤ *tr & intr* vomitar ➤ *s* vómito.
vote ➤ *s* voto; *(act, result)* votación *f* ➤ *intr & tr* votar.
voter ➤ *s* votante *mf*, elector/a.
voting ➤ *s* votación *f* ➤ *adj* votante; *(campaign)* electoral.
vouch ➤ *intr* ■ **to v. for** garantizar, responder por.
voucher ➤ *s* comprobante *m*, vale *m.*
vow ➤ *s* promesa; RELIG. voto ➤ *tr* prometer, jurar.
vowel ➤ *s* vocal *f.*
voyage ➤ *s* viaje *m* ➤ *intr* viajar.
vulgar ➤ *adj* vulgar; *(rude)* grosero; *(taste)* cursi.

W

wade ➤ *intr* caminar (por el agua) ■ **to w. across** vadear.
wafer ➤ *s* oblea; CUL. galleta, barquillo.
wag ➤ *tr & intr* menear(se), sacudir(se) ➤ *s* meneo, sacudida.
wage ➤ *s* pago, sueldo ■ *pl (pay)* salario.
wagon ➤ *s* vagón *m; (station wagon)* furgoneta.
waist ➤ *s* cintura; *(of garment)* talle *m.*
wait ➤ *intr* esperar ■ **to w. up** esperar sin acostarse ➤ *s* espera.
waiter ➤ *s* camarero.
waiting room ➤ *s* sala de espera.
waitress ➤ *s* camarera.
wake✧ ➤ *intr & tr* despertar(se) ➤ *s* velatorio.
walk ➤ *intr* caminar, andar; *(to go on foot)* ir a pie; *(to stroll)* pasear ➤ *tr* caminar por; *(a distance)* caminar, andar ➤ *s* paseo ■ **to go for** *o* **to take a w.** dar un paseo.
walk-in ➤ *adj (services)* que no requiere cita previa.
wall ➤ *s* pared *f; (around a house)* muro; *(of city)* muralla.
wallet ➤ *s* billetera, cartera.
wallpaper ➤ *s* papel *m* de empapelar ➤ *tr & intr* empapelar.
walnut ➤ *s* nuez *f; (tree)* nogal *m.*
walrus ➤ *s* morsa.
waltz ➤ *s & intr* (bailar el) vals *m.*
wander ➤ *intr* vagar.
wane ➤ *intr* disminuir; *(moon)* menguar.
want ➤ *tr* querer; *(to desire)* desear; *(to need)* necesitar.
war ➤ *s & adj* (de) guerra.
ward ➤ *s* distrito; *(of hospital)* sala; *(minor)* pupilo/a ➤ *tr* ■ **to w. off** prevenir.
wardrobe ➤ *s* armario; *(garments)* vestuario.
wares ➤ *spl* mercancías.
warehouse ➤ *s* almacén *m.*
warm ➤ *adj* tibio, caliente; *(weather)* cálido, caluroso; *(clothing)* que mantiene abrigado ➤ *tr* calentar ■ **to w. up** *(food)* recalentar; DEP. calentarse.
warmth ➤ *s* calor *m;* FIG. afecto.
warm-up ➤ *s* DEP. calentamiento.
warn ➤ *tr & intr* advertir.
warning ➤ *s* advertencia; *(signal)* señal *f; (advice)* aviso.
warrant ➤ *s* autorización *f*, orden *f* judicial ➤ *tr* justificar.
warranty ➤ *s* garantía.
warrior ➤ *s* guerrero/a.
was ➤ *vea* **be** *en tabla de verbos.*
wash ➤ *tr* lavar ➤ *intr* lavarse; *(clothes)* lavar ropa ■ **to w. up** lavarse; *(the dishes)* lavar los platos ➤ *s* lavado; *(clothes)* ropa para lavar.
washable ➤ *adj* lavable.
washbasin ➤ *s* lavabo.
washing machine ➤ *s* lavadora.
washroom ➤ *s* baño.
wasp ➤ *s* avispa.
waste ➤ *tr (money)* despilfarrar; *(time)* perder; *(talent)* desperdiciar ➤ *s* despilfarro; *(wastage)* desperdicios; *(of time, energy)* pérdida; *(garbage)* basura ■ **to go to w.** desperdiciarse.
wastebasket ➤ *s* cesto de papeles.
watch ➤ *intr* mirar ➤ *tr* mirar; *(to pay attention to)* fijarse en; *(to guard)* vigilar; *(to take care of)* cuidar ➤ *s* reloj *m; (act)* vigilia, vela.
water ➤ *s* agua ➤ *tr (a garden)* regar.
watercolor ➤ *adj & s* (de) acuarela.
waterfall ➤ *s* catarata, cascada.
watering can ➤ *s* regadera.
watermelon ➤ *s* sandía.
waterproof ➤ *adj* impermeable.
watt ➤ *s* vatio, watt *m.*
wave ➤ *intr & tr* agitar(se) ■ **to w. goodbye** decir adiós con la mano ➤ *s* ola; *(surface, hair)* ondulación *f.*
wavelength ➤ *s* longitud *f* de onda.
wavy ➤ *adj* ondulante, onduloso; *(curly)* ondulado.
wax ➤ *s* cera ➤ *tr* encerar.
way ➤ *s* camino; *(direction)* dirección *f; (method)* manera, modo ■ **all the w.** hasta el final; *(completely)* en todo • **by the w.** a propósito • **by w. of** vía • **in a w.** en cierto modo • **in every w.** en todos los aspectos • **(in) no w.** de ninguna manera • **on the w.** en camino • **right of w.** derecho de paso • **this, that w.** por aquí, allí; *(manner)* así • **which w?** ¿por dónde?
we ➤ *pron* nosotros, nosotras.
weak ➤ *adj* débil; *(fragile)* frágil; *(unconvincing)* poco convincente.
weaken ➤ *tr & intr* debilitar(se).
weakness ➤ *s* debilidad *f.*
wealth ➤ *s (riches)* riqueza.
wealthy ➤ *adj* rico.
weapon ➤ *s* arma.
wear✧ ➤ *tr* llevar; *(to damage)* deteriorar; *(to exhaust)* agotar ■ **to w. off** pasar • **to w. out** gastar(se) ➤ *s* uso; *(clothing)* ropa; *(damage)* desgaste *m.*
weary ➤ *adj* fatigado.
weasel ➤ *s* ZOOL. comadreja.
weather ➤ *s* tiempo.
weave✧ ➤ *tr & intr* tejer; *(to interlace)* entrelazar(se) ➤ *s* tejido.
web ➤ *s* telaraña; *(net)* red ■ **W. web** *m.*
webpage ➤ *s* página web.
website ➤ *s* sitio web, website *m.*
wedding ➤ *s* boda.
wedge ➤ *s* cuña; *(slice)* trozo; *(for securing)* calce *m* ➤ *tr* calzar.
Wednesday ➤ *s* miércoles *m.*
weed ➤ *s* mala hierba.
week ➤ *s* semana.
weekday ➤ *s* día *m* de trabajo.
weekend ➤ *s* fin *m* de semana.
weekly ➤ *adj & adv* semanal(mente) ➤ *s* semanario.
weep✧ ➤ *intr* llorar.
weigh ➤ *tr & intr* pesar.
weight ➤ *s* peso ■ **to gain** *o* **or put on w.** engordar • **to lose w.** adelgazar.
weird ➤ *adj* raro, extraño.
welcome ➤ *adj* bienvenido ■ **you're w.!** ¡no hay de qué!, ¡de nada! ➤ *tr* dar la bienvenida a; *(to accept)* aceptar con beneplácito ➤ *interj* ¡bienvenido!
weld ➤ *tr* soldar.
welfare ➤ *s* bienestar *m; (benefits)* asistencia social.
well[1] ➤ *s* pozo.
well[2] ➤ *adv* bien ■ **as w.** también • **as w. as** además de; *(just as)* así como • **that is just as w.** es mejor así • **to do w.** prosperar ➤ *adj* bien ■ **to get w.** mejorar ➤ *interj* ¡bueno!
well-behaved ➤ *adj* bien educado.
well-being ➤ *s* bienestar *m.*
well-done ➤ *adj (food)* bien cocido.
well-known ➤ *adj* bien conocido.
well-mannered ➤ *adj* educado.
well-to-do ➤ *adj* próspero.
went ➤ *vea* **go** *en tabla de verbos.*
were ➤ *vea* **be** *en tabla de verbos.*
west ➤ *s* oeste *m*, occidente *m* ➤ *adj* del oeste, occidental ➤ *adv* al oeste, hacia el oeste.
western ➤ *adj* occidental, del oeste ➤ *s* película del oeste.
westerner ➤ *s* habitante *mf* del oeste.
westward ➤ *adv* hacia el oeste.
wet✧ ➤ *adj* mojado; *(rainy)* lluvioso; *(paint)* fresco ■ **to get w.** mojarse • **soaking w.** empapado ➤ *tr* mojar.
whale ➤ *s* ZOOL. ballena.
wharf ➤ *s* muelle *m.*
what ➤ *pron* qué; *(which)* cuál ■ **w?** ¿cómo? • **w. for?** ¿para qué? • **w. is that?** ¿qué es eso? • **w. I've learned** lo que he aprendido ➤ *adj* qué; *(which)* cuál ■ **w. music do you like?** ¿qué música te gusta? ➤ *interj* ¡cómo! ■ **w. a pity!** ¡qué lástima!
whatever ➤ *pron* ■ **do w. you want** haz lo que quieras • **w. happens** pase lo que pase ➤ *adj (any)* cualquiera que; *(of any kind at all)* de ninguna clase.
wheat ➤ *s* trigo.
wheel ➤ *s* rueda; *(steering)* volante *m.*
wheelbarrow ➤ *s* carretilla.
when ➤ *adv* cuándo ■ **w. will we get there?** ¿a qué hora vamos a llegar? ➤ *conj* cuando; *(as soon as)* al, en cuanto; *(if)* si ➤ *pron* cuándo.
whenever ➤ *adv & conj* cuando quiera (que); *(when)* cuando; *(every time that)* siempre que.
where ➤ *adv* dónde; *(from where)* de dónde; *(to where)* adónde ■ **w. is . . .?** ¿dónde está . . .? ➤ *conj* donde, en dónde; *(to where)* a donde.
whereas ➤ *conj (since)* visto que; *(while)* mientras (que).
wherever ➤ *adv & conj* dondequiera que.
whether ➤ *conj (if)* si ■ **w. he wins or loses** sea que él gane o pierda.
which ➤ *pron* ■ **my house, w. is small** mi casa, la cual es pequeña • **w. of these . . .?** ¿cuál de éstos . . .? • **w. of you?** ¿quién de ustedes? ➤ *adj* • **for w. reason** por cuya razón • **w. color do you like?** ¿qué color te gusta? • **w. one?** ¿cuál? • **w. way?** ¿por dónde?
whichever ➤ *pron* cualquiera ➤ *adj* cualquier (que sea).
while ➤ *s* rato, tiempo ■ **once in a w.** de vez en cuando • **to be worth (one's) w.** valer la pena ➤ *conj* mientras (que); *(although)* aunque.
whim ➤ *s* capricho, antojo.
whine ➤ *intr* gimotear; *(to complain)* quejarse; *(bullet)* silbar ➤ *s* gimoteo; *(complaint)* quejido; *(bullet)* silbido.
whip ➤ *tr* azotar; *(cream, eggs)* batir ➤ *s* azote *m*, látigo.
whipped cream ➤ *s* nata batida.
whir ➤ *intr* zumbar ➤ *s* zumbido.
whirl ➤ *intr* dar vueltas ➤ *s* giro.
whirlwind ➤ *s* torbellino.
whisk ➤ *tr* CUL. batir ➤ *intr* moverse rápidamente ➤ *s* CUL. batidor *m.*
whiskey ➤ *s* whisky *m.*
whisper ➤ *s* susurro ➤ *intr* susurrar.
whistle ➤ *intr* silbar; *(with a device)* pitar ➤ *tr* silbar ➤ *s* pito, silbato; *(act, sound)* silbido, pitido.
white ➤ *s* blanco; *(of an egg)* clara ➤ *adj* blanco.
who ➤ *pron* quién, quien ■ **it was my sister w. called** fue mi hermana quien llamó • **my sister, w. is sick** mi hermana, que está enferma • **the one(s) w.** el (los) que • **w. knows?** ¿quién sabe?
whoever ➤ *pron* quienquiera que; *(the one who)* el que, quien.
whole ➤ *adj* entero, todo; *(total)* total; *(healthy)* sano; *(undamaged)* intacto ■ **a w. lot of** muchísimo ➤ *s* todo, totalidad *f; (complete entity)* suma ■ **as a w.** en conjunto • **on the w.** en general.
wholesale ➤ *adj & adv* al por mayor.
wholesome ➤ *adj* sano.
whole-wheat ➤ *adj* de trigo entero.
whom ➤ *pron* ■ **from w. . . .?** ¿de quién . . .? • **the man with w. . . .** el hombre con quien . . . .
whose ➤ *pron & adj* ■ **the girl w. shirt is red** la chica cuya camisa es roja • **w. shirt is this?** ¿de quién es esta camisa?
why ➤ *adv* por qué, para qué ■ **w. not?** ¿por qué no? ➤ *conj* por (lo) que.
wick ➤ *s* mecha.
wicked ➤ *adj* malvado; *(mischievous)* travieso.
wicker ➤ *s* mimbre *m.*
wide ➤ *adj* ancho ■ **two feet w.** dos pies de ancho ➤ *adv* ■ **w. apart** muy separados • **w. open** de par en par.
widely ➤ *adv (very)* muy; *(much)* mucho; *(extensively)* extensamente.
widen ➤ *tr & intr* ensanchar(se).
widespread ➤ *adj* extendido; *(prevalent)* general.
widow ➤ *s* viuda.
widower ➤ *s* viudo.
width ➤ *s* anchura, ancho.
wife ➤ *s* esposa, mujer *f.*
wig ➤ *s* peluca.
wild ➤ *adj* salvaje; *(plant)* silvestre; *(crazy)* loco, extraviado; *(frenzied)* frenético; *(guess)* al azar ➤ *adv* alocadamente ➤ *s* ■ **in the w.** en estado natural • **the w.** naturaleza.
wilderness ➤ *s* región *f* sin cultivar.
wildflower ➤ *s* flor *f* silvestre.
wildlife ➤ *s* fauna.
will[1] ➤ *s* voluntad *f;* DER. testamento ➤ *tr* querer; *(to order)* ordenar.
will[2] ➤ *aux* ■ **they w. come** vendrán • **you w. regret this** lo vas a lamentar • **w. you help me?** ¿quieres ayudarme?
willful ➤ *adj* obstinado.
willing ➤ *adj* de buena voluntad.
willow ➤ *s* sauce *m.*
willpower ➤ *s* fuerza de voluntad.
win✧ ➤ *intr & tr* ganar ➤ *s* victoria, triunfo.
wind[1] ➤ *s* viento; *(air)* aire *m* ■ *pl* MÚS. instrumentos de viento.
wind[2]✧ ➤ *tr* envolver; *(to entwine)* enrollar; *(a watch)* dar cuerda a ➤ *intr (road)* serpentear; *(rope)* enrollarse.
windmill ➤ *s* molino de viento.
window ➤ *s* ventana; *(small)* ventanilla; *(of a shop)* escaparate *m.*
windshield ➤ *s* parabrisas *m* ■ **w. wiper** limpiaparabrisas.
windy ➤ *adj* ventoso.
wine ➤ *s* vino.
wineglass ➤ *s* copa para vino.
wing ➤ *s* ala ■ *pl* TEAT. bastidores.
wink ➤ *intr* guiñar ➤ *s* guiño.
winner ➤ *s* ganador/a.
winter ➤ *s* invierno.
wipe ➤ *tr* limpiar; *(to dry)* secar ■ **to w. off** quitar • **to w. out** destruir; *(a debt)* cancelar.
wire ➤ *s* alambre *m;* ELEC. cable *m; (telegram)* telegrama.
wireless ➤ *adj* inalámbrico.
wiring ➤ *s* instalación eléctrica.
wisdom ➤ *s* sabiduría.
wise ➤ *adj* sabio; *(judicious)* juicioso; *(sensible)* sensato.
wish ➤ *s* deseo ➤ *tr* querer, desear; *(to like to)* gustar; *(to bid)* dar.
wit ➤ *s* inteligencia; *(cleverness)* ingenio ■ *pl* juicio.
witch ➤ *s* bruja.
with ➤ *prep* con ■ **to tremble w. fear** temblar de miedo • **w. me** conmigo • **w. you** contigo, con usted(es).
withdraw ➤ *tr* sacar, quitar; *(to retract)* retractar ➤ *intr (to retreat)* retraerse; *(to draw away)* apartarse.
withdrawn ➤ *adj* remoto; *(shy)* tímido.
wither ➤ *intr* marchitarse.
withhold ➤ *tr* retener, contener.
within ➤ *adv* dentro; *(indoors)* adentro; *(inwardly)* internamente ➤ *prep* dentro de; *(distance)* a menos de; *(time)* antes de; *(not beyond)* dentro de los límites de ➤ *s* adentro.
without ➤ *adv* fuera ➤ *prep* sin; *(on the outside of)* (a)fuera de ■ **it goes w. saying** se sobreentiende • **to do w.** pasar(se) sin.
withstand ➤ *tr* resistir a.
witness ➤ *s* testigo/a ➤ *tr & intr* atestiguar.
witty ➤ *adj* ingenioso, gracioso.
wizard ➤ *s* hechicero.
wobbly ➤ *adj* tembloroso.
wolf ➤ *s* lobo ➤ *tr* ■ **to w. down** comer vorazmente.
woman ➤ *s* mujer *f* ■ **women** mujeres.
wonder ➤ *s* maravilla; *(astonishment)* asombro ➤ *intr (to ponder)* pensar; *(to be doubtful)* dudar ➤ *tr* preguntarse.
wonderful ➤ *adj* maravilloso.
wood ➤ *s* madera; *(firewood)* leña ■ *pl* bosque.
wooden ➤ *adj* de madera.
wool ➤ *s* lana.
woolen ➤ *adj* de lana.
word ➤ *s* palabra ■ **in other words** mejor dicho • **take my w. for it** se lo aseguro • **to keep one's w.** cumplir la palabra • **w. processing** procesamiento de texto • **w. processor** procesador de texto ■ *pl* MÚS. letra.
work ➤ *s* trabajo; *(job)* empleo; *(result)* obra ■ **the works** JER. todo, de todo • **w. force** mano de obra ➤ *intr* trabajar; *(to operate)* funcionar ➤ *tr (machine)* manejar; *(miracle)* hacer; *(slave)* hacer trabajar ■ **to w. out** solucionar.
worker ➤ *s* trabajador/a.
workout ➤ *s* ejercicio.
workshop ➤ *s* taller *m.*
workstation ➤ *s* consola, estación *f* de trabajo.
world ➤ *s* mundo.
worldly ➤ *adj* secular; *(worldly-wise)* sofisticado.
worldwide ➤ *adj* mundial.
World Wide Web ➤ *s* Red *f.*
worm ➤ *s* gusano.
worn-out ➤ *adj (used)* gastado; *(exhausted)* agotado.
worry ➤ *intr & tr* preocupar(se) ➤ *s*

preocupación f.
worse ➤ adj peor ■ to get w. empeorar ➤ adv peor; (more severely) más.
worsen ➤ tr & intr empeorar(se).
worship ➤ s adoración f; devoción f ➤ tr & intr venerar.
worst ➤ adj & adv peor ➤ s ■ at w. o if w. comes to w. en el peor de los casos.
worth ➤ s valor m; (wealth) fortuna; (merit) mérito ➤ adj que vale ■ to be w. valer; (to be the equivalent of) valer por • to be w. it valer la pena.
worthless ➤ adj sin valor.
worthy ➤ adj meritorio.
would ➤ vea will en tabla de verbos.
wound ➤ s herida ➤ tr & intr herir.
woven ➤ adj tejido.
wrap◊ ➤ tr envolver ■ to be wrapped up in estar absorto en • to w. up (to end) cerrar; (to summarize) resumir ➤ intr enrollarse ➤ s (cloak) manto ■ to keep under wraps mantener en secreto.
wrapper ➤ s envoltura.
wrap-up ➤ s resumen m.
wrath ➤ s ira.
wreath ➤ s guirnalda.
wreck ➤ s destrucción f; (crash) choque m; (shipwreck) naufragio; (collision remains) destrozos ➤ tr destrozar, arruinar.
wrench ➤ s MEC. llave f ➤ tr torcer.
wrestle ➤ intr & tr luchar (con o contra).
wrestling ➤ s lucha.
wretched ➤ adj desgraciado, miserable.
wring◊ ➤ tr escurrir.
wrinkle ➤ s arruga ➤ tr arrugar, fruncir.
wrist ➤ s muñeca ■ w. watch reloj de pulsera.
write◊ ➤ tr & intr escribir.

writer ➤ s escritor/a.
writing ➤ s escritura f; (handwriting) letra; (work) escrito ■ in w. por escrito.
wrong ➤ adj malo; (unfair) injusto; (incorrect) erróneo; (mistaken) equivocado ■ to be w. hacer mal; (to be mistaken) equivocarse; (to be amiss) andar mal ➤ adv mal ■ to do, get w. hacer, tener mal • to go w. (to act mistakenly) fallar; (to go amiss) salir mal ➤ s mal m; (unjust act) injusticia; (bad deed) maldad f; (fault) error m ■ to be in the w. no tener razón ➤ tr ser injusto con.
wrought ➤ adj ■ w. iron hierro forjado.

X

X-mas ➤ s FAM. Navidad f.
X-rated ➤ adj no apto para menores de 18 años.
x-ray o **X-ray** ➤ s radiografía; FÍS. rayo X ➤ tr radiografiar.
xylophone ➤ s xilófono.

Y

yacht ➤ s yate m.
yak ➤ s ZOOL. yac m.
yam ➤ s ñame f; (sweet potato) batata.
Yankee ➤ adj & s yanqui mf.
yard[1] ➤ s (measure) yarda.
yard[2] ➤ s jardín m.
yarn ➤ s hilo.
yawn ➤ intr bostezar ➤ s bostezo.
year ➤ s año ■ school y. año escolar ■ pl (age) edad.
yearly ➤ adj anual.
yearn ➤ intr añorar.
yearning ➤ s anhelo, añoranza.
yeast ➤ s levadura.
yell ➤ tr & intr gritar ➤ s grito.
yellow ➤ s & adj amarillo.

yes ➤ adv sí.
yesterday ➤ adv ayer ➤ s (el día de) ayer m ■ the day before y. anteayer.
yet ➤ adv todavía, aún; (thus far) ya; (still more) aún más; (eventually) probablemente ■ as (of) y. hasta ahora • not y. todavía no ➤ conj (nevertheless) sin embargo; (but) pero.
yield ➤ tr dar, producir ➤ intr rendirse; (in traffic) ceder el paso ■ to y. to ceder a ➤ s rendimiento.
yoga ➤ s yoga m.
yogurt ➤ s yogur m.
yolk ➤ s yema.
you ➤ pron [sujeto] (familiar) tú, vosotros, vosotras; (formal) usted, ustedes; [complemento] (familiar, direct and indirect) te, os; (formal, direct) lo, la, los, las; (formal, indirect) le, les, se; [después de preposición] (familiar) ti, vosotros, vosotras; (formal) usted, ustedes ■ if I were y. yo que tú • with y. contigo, con usted(es).
young ➤ adj joven ➤ s pl jóvenes mf; (offspring) cría (de animal).
youngster ➤ s jovencito/a.
your ➤ adj (familiar, sg.) tu(s); (formal, sg.) su(s), de usted; (familiar, pl.) vuestro(s), vuestra(s); (formal, pl.) su(s), de ustedes.
yours ➤ pron (familiar, sg.) (el) tuyo, (la) tuya; (formal, sg.) (el o la) de usted, el suyo, la suya; (familiar, pl.) (el) vuestro, (la) vuestra; (formal, pl.) (el o la) de ustedes, (el) suyo, (la) suya.
yourself ➤ pron (familiar) tú (mismo, misma); (formal) usted (mismo, misma).
yourselves ➤ pron (familiar) vosotros (mismos), vosotras (mismas); (formal) ustedes (mismos, mismas).
youth ➤ s juventud f; (young person)

joven mf.
youthful ➤ adj joven, juvenil.
yo-yo ➤ s yoyó.

Z

zany ➤ adj estrafalario.
zeal ➤ s celo, ahínco.
zealotry ➤ s fanatismo.
zealous ➤ adj fervoroso.
zebra ➤ s cebra.
zenith ➤ s cenit m.
zephyr ➤ s brisa.
zero ➤ s cero; (nothing) nada ➤ adj nulo ➤ tr & intr ■ to z. in on apuntar hacia.
zest ➤ s gusto, sabor m; (enjoyment) brío.
zigzag ➤ s & adj (en) zigzag m ➤ adv zigzagueando ➤ intr ir zigzagueando.
zillion ➤ s FAM. número astronómico.
zinc ➤ s cinc m.
zip ➤ s vigor m ➤ intr zumbar ■ to z. by pasar como una bala • to z. up subir o cerrar la cremallera.
zip code ➤ s código postal.
zipper ➤ s cremallera.
zodiac ➤ s zodíaco.
zonal ➤ adj zonal.
zone ➤ s zona ➤ tr dividir en zonas.
zoning ➤ s restricciones f para edificar en un barrio urbano.
zoo ➤ s zoo.
zoologist ➤ s zoólogo/a.
zoology ➤ s zoología.
zoom ➤ intr (to buzz) zumbar; (to go fast) ir zumbando; FOTOG. (in) acercarse; (out) alejarse ➤ s (sound) zumbido; AVIA. subida vertical.
zucchini ➤ s zapallito italiano.

ABCDEFGHI-HESS-065432 1

NUMBERS/ NÚMEROS

	Cardinal Numbers	Números Cardinales	Ordinal Numbers	Números Ordinales
1	one	uno	first	primero
2	two	dos	second	segundo
3	three	tres	third	tercero
4	four	cuatro	fourth	cuarto
5	five	cinco	fifth	quinto
6	six	seis	sixth	sexto
7	seven	siete	seventh	séptimo
8	eight	ocho	eighth	octavo
9	nine	nueve	ninth	noveno; nono
10	ten	diez	tenth	décimo
11	eleven	once	eleventh	undécimo
12	twelve	doce	twelfth	duodécimo
13	thirteen	trece	thirteenth	decimotercero
14	fourteen	catorce	fourteenth	decimocuarto
15	fifteen	quince	fifteenth	decimoquinto
16	sixteen	dieciséis	sixteenth	decimosexto
17	seventeen	diecisiete	seventeenth	decimoséptimo
18	eighteen	dieciocho	eighteenth	decimoctavo
19	nineteen	diecinueve	nineteenth	decimonoveno; decimonono
20	twenty	veinte	twentieth	vigésimo
21	twenty-one	veintiuno	twenty-first	vigésimo primero
30	thirty	treinta	thirtieth	trigésimo
40	forty	cuarenta	fortieth	cuadragésimo
50	fifty	cincuenta	fiftieth	quincuagésimo
60	sixty	sesenta	sixtieth	sexagésimo
70	seventy	setenta	seventieth	septuagésimo
80	eighty	ochenta	eightieth	octogésimo
90	ninety	noventa	ninetieth	nonagésimo
100	one hundred	cien	(one) hundredth	centésimo
101	one hundred and one	ciento uno	(one) hundred and first	centésimo primero
200	two hundred	doscientos	two-hundredth	ducentésimo
300	three hundred	trescientos	three-hundredth	tricentésimo
400	four hundred	cuatrocientos	four-hundredth	cuadringentésimo
500	five hundred	quinientos	five-hundredth	quingentésimo
600	six hundred	seiscientos	six-hundredth	sexagésimo
700	seven hundred	setecientos	seven-hundredth	septingentésimo
800	eight hundred	ochocientos	eight-hundredth	octingentésimo
900	nine hundred	novecientos	nine-hundredth	noningentésimo
1000	one thousand	mil	(one) thousandth	milésimo
100,000	one hundred thousand	cien mil	(one) hundred thousandth	cienmilésimo
1,000,000	one million	un millón	(one) millionth	millonésimo